WA 1165798 7

PLEASE CHECK FOR
DISK IN BACK OF BOOK

De

Pr

Pr

**UNIVERSITY OF GLAMORGAN
LEARNING RESOURCES CENTRE**

Pontypridd, Mid Glamorgan, CF37 1DL
Telephone: Pontypridd (01443) 482626

Books are to be returned on or before the last date below

- 1 OCT 1999

1 0 MAY 2000

2 0 MAR 2001

2 3 SEP 2006

D1464985

Please remove the
cassette/disk from this
book when using the
self service machine

Delphi™ Programming Problem Solver

Neil Rubenking

IDG Books Worldwide, Inc.

Foster City, CA • Chicago, IL • Indianapolis, IN • Braintree, MA • Southlake, TX

Delphi ™ Programming Problem Solver

Published by
IDG Books Worldwide, Inc.
An International Data Group Company
919 E. Hillsdale Blvd.
Suite 400
Foster City, CA 94404

Text and art copyright © 1996 by IDG Books Worldwide, Inc. All rights reserved. No part of this book, including interior design, cover design, and icons, may be reproduced or transmitted in any form, by any means (electronic, photocopying, recording, or otherwise) without the prior written permission of the publisher.

Library of Congress Catalog Card No.: 96-75400

ISBN: 1-56884-795-5

Printed in the United States of America

10 9 8 7 6 5 4 3 2 1
1O/RR/QU/ZW/BR

Distributed in the United States by IDG Books Worldwide, Inc.

Distributed by Macmillan Canada for Canada; by Computer and Technical Books for the Caribbean Basin; by Contemporanea de Ediciones for Venezuela; by Distribuidora Cuspide for Argentina; by CITEC for Brazil; by Ediciones ZETA S.C.R. Ltda. for Peru; by Editorial Limusa SA for Mexico; by Transworld Publishers Limited in the United Kingdom and Europe; by Al-Maiman Publishers & Distributors for Saudi Arabia; by Simron Pty. Ltd. for South Africa; by IDG Communications (HK) Ltd. for Hong Kong; by Toppan Company Ltd. for Japan; by Addison Wesley Publishing Company for Korea; by Longman Singapore Publishers Ltd. for Singapore, Malaysia, Thailand, and Indonesia; by Unalis Corporation for Taiwan; by WS Computer Publishing Company, Inc. for the Philippines; by WoodsLane Pty. Ltd. for Australia; by WoodsLane Enterprises Ltd. for New Zealand.

For general information on IDG Books Worldwide's books in the U.S., please call our Consumer Customer Service department at 800-762-2974. For reseller information, including discounts and premium sales, please call our Reseller Customer Service department at 800-434-3422.

For information on where to purchase IDG Books Worldwide's books outside the U.S., contact IDG Books Worldwide at 415-655-3021 or fax 415-655-3295.

For information on translations, contact Marc Jeffrey Mikulich, Director, Foreign & Subsidiary Rights, at IDG Books Worldwide, 415-655-3018 or fax 415-655-3295.

For sales inquiries and special prices for bulk quantities, write to the address above or call IDG Books Worldwide at 415-655-3200.

For information on using IDG Books Worldwide's books in the classroom, or ordering examination copies, contact the Education Office at 800-434-2086 or fax 817-251-8174.

For authorization to photocopy items for corporate, personal, or educational use, please contact Copyright Clearance Center, 222 Rosewood Drive, Danvers, MA 01923, or fax 508-750-4470.

Limit of Liability/Disclaimer of Warranty: Author and Publisher have used their best efforts in preparing this book. IDG Books Worldwide, Inc., and Author make no representation or warranties with respect to the accuracy or completeness of the contents of this book and specifically disclaim any implied warranties of merchantability or fitness for any particular purpose and shall in no event be liable for any loss of profit or any other commercial damage, including but not limited to special, incidental, consequential, or other damages.

Trademarks: Delphi is a trademark of Borland International, Incorporated. All brand names and product names used in this book are trademarks, registered trademarks, or trade names of their respective holders. IDG Books Worldwide is not associated with any product or vendor mentioned in this book.

is a trademark under exclusive license to IDG Books Worldwide, Inc., from International Data Group, Inc.

Learning Resources
Centre

1165 7957

ABOUT IDG BOOKS WORLDWIDE

Welcome to the world of IDG Books Worldwide.

IDG Books Worldwide, Inc., is a subsidiary of International Data Group, the world's largest publisher of computer-related information and the leading global provider of information services on information technology. IDG was founded more than 25 years ago and now employs more than 7,700 people worldwide. IDG publishes more than 250 computer publications in 67 countries (see listing below). More than 70 million people read one or more IDG publications each month.

Launched in 1990, IDG Books Worldwide is today the #1 publisher of best-selling computer books in the United States. We are proud to have received 8 awards from the Computer Press Association in recognition of editorial excellence and three from Computer Currents' First Annual Readers' Choice Awards, and our best-selling ...*For Dummies*® series has more than 19 million copies in print with translations in 28 languages. IDG Books Worldwide, through a joint venture with IDG's Hi-Tech Beijing, became the first U.S. publisher to publish a computer book in the People's Republic of China. In record time, IDG Books Worldwide has become the first choice for millions of readers around the world who want to learn how to better manage their businesses.

Our mission is simple: Every one of our books is designed to bring extra value and skill-building instructions to the reader. Our books are written by experts who understand and care about our readers. The knowledge base of our editorial staff comes from years of experience in publishing, education, and journalism — experience which we use to produce books for the '90s. In short, we care about books, so we attract the best people. We devote special attention to details such as audience, interior design, use of icons, and illustrations. And because we use an efficient process of authoring, editing, and desktop publishing our books electronically, we can spend more time ensuring superior content and spend less time on the technicalities of making books.

You can count on our commitment to deliver high-quality books at competitive prices on topics you want to read about. At IDG Books Worldwide, we continue in the IDG tradition of delivering quality for more than 25 years. You'll find no better book on a subject than one from IDG Books Worldwide.

John Kilcullen
President and CEO
IDG Books Worldwide, Inc.

IDG Books Worldwide, Inc., is a subsidiary of International Data Group, the world's largest publisher of computer-related information and the leading global provider of information services on information technology. International Data Group publishes over 250 computer publications in 67 countries. Seventy million people read one or more International Data Group publications each month. International Data Group's publications include: **ARGENTINA:** Computerworld Argentina, GamePro, Infoworld, PC World Argentina; **AUSTRALIA:** Australian Macworld, Client/Server Journal, Computer Living, Computerworld, Digital News, Network World, PC World, Publishing Essentials, Reseller; **AUSTRIA:** Computerwelt, PC TEST; **BELARUS:** PC World Belarus; **BELGIUM:** Data News; **BRAZIL:** Annuário de Informática, Computerworld Brazil, Connections, Super Game Power, Macworld, PC World Brazil, Publish Brazil, SUPERGAME; **BULGARIA:** Computerworld Bulgaria, Networkworld/Bulgaria, PC & MacWorld Bulgaria; **CANADA:** CIO Canada, ComputerWorld Canada, InfoCanada, Network World Canada, Reseller World; **CHILE:** Computerworld Chile, GamePro, PC World Chile; **COLUMBIA:** Computerworld Colombia, GamePro, PC World Colombia; **COSTA RICA:** PC World Costa Rica/Nicaragua; **THE CZECH AND SLOVAK REPUBLICS:** Computerworld Czechoslovakia, Elektronika Czechoslovakia, PC World Czechoslovakia; **DENMARK:** Communications World, Computerworld Danmark, Macworld Danmark, PC World Danmark, PC World Danmark Supplements, TECH World; **DOMINICAN REPUBLIC:** PC World Republica Dominicana; **ECUADOR:** PC World Ecuador, GamePro; **EGYPT:** Computerworld Middle East, PC World Middle East; **EL SALVADOR:** PC World Centro America; **FINLAND:** MikroPC, Tietoverkko, Tietoviikko; **FRANCE:** Distribuetique, Golden, Info PC, Le Guide du Monde Informatique, Le Monde Informatique, Reseaux & Telecoms; **GERMANY:** Computer Business, Computerwoche, Computerwoche Extra, Computerwoche Focus, Electronic Entertainment, GamePro, I/M Information Management, Macwelt, PC Welt; **GREECE:** GamePro, Macworld & Publish; **GUATEMALA:** PC World Centro America; **HONDURAS:** PC World Centro America; **HONG KONG:** Computerworld Hong Kong, PCWorld Hong Kong, Publish in Asia; **HUNGARY:** ABCD CD-ROM, Computerworld Szamitastechnika, PC & Mac World Hungary, PC-X Magazine; **INDIA:** Computerworld India, PC World India, Publish in Asia; **INDONESIA:** InfoKomputer PC World, Komputek Computerworld, Publish in Asia; **IRELAND:** ComputerScope, PC Live!; **ISRAEL:** PC World 32 BIT, People & Computers; **ITALY:** Computerworld Italia, Computerworld Italia Special Editions, Lotus Italia, Macworld Italia, Networking Italia, PC Shopping, PC World Italia, PC World/Walt Disney; **JAPAN:** Macworld Japan, Nikkei Personal Computing, SunWorld Japan, Windows World Japan; **KENYA:** East African Computer News; **KOREA:** Hi-Tech Information/Computerworld, Macworld Korea, PC World Korea; **MACEDONIA:** PC World Macedonia; **MALAYSIA:** Computerworld Malaysia, PC World Malaysia, Publish in Asia; **MEXICO:** Computerworld Mexico, GamePro, Macworld, PC World Mexico; **MYANMAR:** PC World Myanmar; **NETHERLANDS:** Computable, Computer! Totaal, LAN Magazine, Macworld, Net Magazine; **NEW ZEALAND:** Computer Buyer, Computerworld New Zealand, MTB, Network World, PC World New Zealand; **NICARAGUA:** PC World Costa Rica/Nicaragua; **NIGERIA:** PC World Africa; **NORWAY:** Computerworld Norge, Computerworld Privat, CW Rapport Klient/Tjener, CW Rapport Nettverk & Telecom, CW Rapport Offentlig Sektor, IDG's KURSGUIDE, Macworld Norge, Multimedia World, PC World Ekspress, PC World Nettverk, PC World Norge, PC World's Produktguide, Windows Spesial; **PAKISTAN:** Computerworld Pakistan, PC World Pakistan; **PANAMA:** GamePro, PC World Panama; **PARAGUAY:** PC World Paraguay; **P. R. OF CHINA:** China Computerworld, China Infoworld, Computer & Communication, Electronic Product World, Electronics Today, Game Camp, PC World China, Popular Computer Week, Software World, Telecom Product World; **PERU:** Computerworld Peru, GamePro, PC World Profesional Peru, PC World Peru; **POLAND:** Computerworld Poland, Computerworld Special Report, Macworld, Networld, PC World Komputer; **PHILIPPINES:** Computerworld Philippines, PC Digest, Publish in Asia; **PORTUGAL:** Cerebro/PC World, Correio Informático/Computerworld, Mac•In/PC•In Portugal; **PUERTO RICO:** PC World Puerto Rico; **ROMANIA:** Computerworld Romania, PC World Romania, Telecom Romania; **RUSSIA:** Computerworld Rossiya, Network World Russia, PC World Russia; **SINGAPORE:** Computerworld Singapore, PC World Singapore, Publish in Asia; **SLOVENIA:** MONITOR; **SOUTH AFRICA:** Computing S.A., Network World S.A., Software World; **SPAIN:** Computerworld España, COMUNICACIONES WORLD, Dealer World, Macworld España, PC World España; **SWEDEN:** CAP&Design, Computer Sweden, Corporate Computing, MacWorld, Maxi Data, MikroDatorn, Nätverk & Kommunikation, PC/Aktiv, PC World, Windows World; **SWITZERLAND:** Computerworld Schweiz, Macworld Schweiz, PCtip; **TAIWAN:** Computerworld Taiwan, Macworld Taiwan, PC World Taiwan, Publish Taiwan, Windows World; **THAILAND:** Thai Computerworld, Publish in Asia; **TURKEY:** Computerworld Monitör, MACWORLD Turkiye, PC World Turkiye; **UKRAINE:** Computerworld Kiev, Computers & Software Magazine, PC World Ukraine; **UNITED KINGDOM:** Acorn User, Amiga Action, Amiga Computing, Amiga, Appletalk, CD Powerplay, CD-ROM Now, Computing, Connexion, GamePro, Lotus Magazine, Macaction, Macworld, Open Computing, Parents and Computers, PC Home, PC Works, The WEB; **UNITED STATES:** Cable in the Classroom, CD Review, CIO Magazine, Computerworld, Computerworld Client/Server Journal, Digital Video Magazine, DOS World, Electronic, InfoWorld, I-Way, Macworld, Maximize, MULTIMEDIA WORLD, Network World, PC World, PUBLISH, SWATPro Magazine, Video Event, WebMaster; **URUGUAY:** PC World Uruguay; **VENEZUELA:** Computerworld Venezuela, GamePro, PC World Venezuela; and **VIETNAM:** PC World Vietnam   10/17/95

Credits

Group Publisher
Brenda McLaughlin

Publisher
Christopher J. Williams

Publishing Director
John Osborn

Senior Acquisitions Manager
Amorette Pedersen

Managing Editor
Kim Field

Editorial Director
Anne Marie Walker

Creative Services
Julia Stasio

Project Editor
Jim Markham

Editorial Assistant
Tracy J. Brown

Manuscript Editor
Linda D. Greenwood

Technical Editor
Danny Thorpe

Composition and Layout
Ronnie K. Bucci
Dusty Parsons
Andrew Stachiewicz

Proofreader
Deb Kaufmann

Indexer
Liz Cunningham

Book Design
Greg Johnson, Art Directions

Author Bio

Neil Rubenking has been fascinated with Delphi and its precursor Turbo Pascal from the beginning. In 1986, *PC Magazine* enlisted him to handle the torrent of Turbo Pascal tips submitted by readers. By 1990, he had become *PC Magazine's* Technical Editor, and a coast-to-coast telecommuter. His "User to User" column showcases tips from *PC Magazine* readers on using DOS, Windows, and Windows 95. Between editing articles and writing PC Magazine utilities in Pascal, Visual Basic, and Delphi, Neil has found time to write six books on programming, including *PC Magazine Turbo Pascal for Windows Techniques and Utilities* and the popular *Delphi Programming for Dummies.*

Acknowledgments

Writing this book *during* the development of Delphi 2.0 put a strain both on me and on the Delphi development team members who fielded my numerous questions. A round of applause for them, please! I'm especially grateful to team member Danny Thorpe for managing to perform a thorough technical review during the final weeks of the Delphi 2.0 beta test. Danny's sage advice greatly enhanced many of the example programs

Thanks, too, to everyone who bought *Delphi Programming for Dummies*, learned to program in Delphi, and then demanded something more advanced. And special thanks to those of you who posted tough questions on Borland's DELPHI forum on CompuServe. Keep those questions coming!

(The publisher would also like to give special thanks to Patrick McGovern, without whom this book would not have been possible.)

Dedication

For Janet, Katherine, Sophie, and John

CONTENTS

Introduction **1**

Part I   Forms **7**

Chapter 1   Form Basics **9**

Unusual Window Styles **9**
Eliminating a form's caption but leaving the border 9
Getting the "tiny title bar" effect 12
Painting on Forms **17**
Painting a form's background with a pattern 17
Taking over drawing a form's caption 23
Putting a button on a form's title bar 27
Taking over drawing a form's frame 30
Transforming Forms **32**
Using a form as a component on another form 33
Adding a menu to a dialog form 35

Chapter 2   Multipage Forms and More **39**

Managing Forms **39**
Creating modal forms only as needed 39
Managing multiple form instances without MDI 43
Creating a base form type and deriving descendants,
    even in Delphi 1.0 47
Reducing resource consumption by multipage forms 48
Form Miscellany **56**

Controlling the sizing of a form 57

Modifying a form generated by MessageDlg 61

Using the nifty Windows 95 question-mark help icon 65

Simulating the question-mark help icon in Windows 3.1 67

Revealing a hidden form when the mouse is at the edge of the screen ... 71

Chapter 3   Multiple Document Interface Forms **79**

  MDI Size and Position **79**

Controlling the initial size and placement of MDI windows 79

Avoiding the initial flash of a maximized MDI child 81

Hiding and showing MDI child windows 84

  MDI Communication **87**

Allowing MDI child and main forms to reference each other 87

Permitting just one of an MDI child type 89

Putting the window list on a merged menu 93

Creating specialized menus for child forms 94

  MDI Appearance **98**

Creating an MDI form with no menu 98

Exempting a child window from Tile and Cascade 99

Giving an MDI main form background wallpaper 103

Adding a Windows 95 help button to an MDI child form 108

Part II   Components **113**

  Chapter 4   Components in General **115**

    Component Arrays **115**

Creating a component array 115

Really creating a component array 116

Creating an array of components at runtime 119

    Component Lists **121**

Processing all components of one type 121

Creating a component array whose size isn't known until runtime 126

    Component Miscellany **129**

I've lost a component—help! 129

Supplying status-bar hints and flyover help 130

Distinguishing different types of components

in a shared event handler 134

  Chapter 5   Menus **137**

    Pop-Up Menus **137**

Making a pop-up menu see through components 137

Defining accelerator resources for hotkeys 139

Creating submenu items at runtime 142
Help Menus **142**
Forcing the "Help" menu to the right-hand side of the menu bar 142
Implementing standard Help menu items 144
Menu Appearance **147**
Using bitmap menu items 147
Changing the menu check mark 150
Creating owner-draw menu items 156
Menu Nuts and Bolts **160**
How to change properties of a merged menu 160
Creating a menu structure at runtime 163
Determining whether a menu item
sharing an event handler is a top-level item 163

Chapter 6   Edit Controls **167**
Memo Rows and Columns **167**
Reporting a memo's current row and column 167
Setting up a memo box with full row and column support 172
Manipulating Text **176**
Sorting the lines in a memo 177
Right-aligning an edit box 180
Adding a simple Undo command to a memo 182
Inserting characters in the current edit control,
no matter what kind it is 184
Cutting and copying from an active edit or memo 188
Event Handler Errors **191**
Getting stack overflow in OnChange 192
Edit box's text coming out backward 192
Rich Edit Riches **193**
Getting beyond the 32K limit 193
Using multiple fonts and styles 194
Using the Rich Edit component in an editor 194

Part III   More Components **209**
Chapter 7   List and Combo Boxes **211**
Owner-Draw List Boxes **211**
Varying text colors and styles 212
Varying fonts and font sizes 215
Displaying bitmaps in a list box 218
Owner-draw variable list box does not
recognize changes in item height 222

Enhancing the List Box Object **225**
Items are wider than the list box 225
Using tabs in list box items 228
Dragging and Lists **233**
Letting the user reorder items by dragging 233
Dragging multiple items from a list box 236
List Box Miscellany **239**
Sorting a list box my way 239
Creating a multiselect combo box 245
Creating a list box with incremental search 248
Taking control of list box scrolling 250

Chapter 8   Grid Components **257**
Cell Drawing and Alignment **257**
Displaying a huge number of cells 258
Right-justifying or centering text in a grid cell 260
Decimal-aligning numbers in a grid 262
Cell Selection **265**
Row select doesn't work right 266
Disjointing selection of grid cells 266
Copying a selection to the clipboard 269
Responding when a new cell is selected 272
Grid Colors **275**
Grids show selection even when they don't have the focus 276
Fully controlling grid color 279
Grid Miscellany **281**
Deleting or inserting rows and columns 281
Controlling paging in a grid 285
Putting other components in cells 290

Chapter 9   Graphical Components **295**
An Angle on Text **295**
Drawing text at different angles 295
Creating vertical and angled labels 298
Dragging Graphics **306**
Dragging and dropping components at runtime 306
"Rubber-band" drawing of a rectangle 310
Creating a splitter bar 312
Bitmaps and Metafiles **316**
Creating a metafile 316
Creating an enhanced metafile 320
Dragging a sprite 323

Simulating VB PicClip control 326
Creating a gradient fill background 329

Chapter 10   Various Components **335**
Button Components **335**
Using a bitmap resource as a button glyph 335
Using an icon as a button glyph 339
Building a button with a multiline caption 341
Making a button repeat when held down 346
Deselecting all of a radio group or set of radio buttons 350
Odds and Ends **353**
Controlling common dialog position 354
Converting an .ICO file to .BMP 357
Panels shift position at runtime! 358
Creating a simple splitter bar 362
Alignment property for labels doesn't work! 366
Need a Delay procedure! 366

Chapter 11   Database Programming **369**
Grid Appearance **369**
Centered fields look ugly! 369
Using the grid column editor in Delphi 2.0 372
Highlighting a row based on field value 376
Problems moving and resizing columns at design time 379
Updating Edit Controls **380**
Updating a memo field 380
Modifying data-aware edit text 383
More Grid Goodies **386**
Showing memo and graphic fields in a grid 387
Duplicating Paradox multirecord objects 394
Sharing Tables **398**
Two forms accessing the same table (16-bit) 398
Two forms accessing the same table (32-bit) 401

Part IV   Inside Delphi **405**

Chapter 12   The Object Pascal Language **407**
Variable Size Arrays **407**
Arrays with fixed size determined at runtime 407
Arrays whose size will vary at runtime 408
Storing objects in a list 411

Date and Time **416**

Understanding TDateTime 416

Formatting elapsed time 419

Performing date math 419

Function Arguments **422**

Using a variable number of parameters 422

Passing a partial array as an open array 423

Using variable types of parameters 430

Language Miscellany **434**

"Call to RegisterClass is missing" 434

Can't create a Delphi object variable! 434

Raising numbers to a specified power 435

Getting a DOS environment variable 436

Pixels change color unexpectedly 438

Padding or chopping a string to a given length 441

Can't read files written by older programs 441

Chapter 13   The Application Object **447**

Activity When Minimized **447**

Detecting Windows 95 447

Keeping a program always iconic 448

Changing an icon while running 449

Painting on an icon 451

Drawing attention to an icon 455

Control Application Loading **458**

Displaying a "splash screen" 459

Loading only one instance 461

Choosing a main form at runtime 463

Application and Form as Partners **464**

Adding an always-on-top command to the system menu 464

Accepting files dragged from File Manager or Explorer 467

Application Miscellany **470**

Tracking which component the mouse is over 470

"Run minimized" is ignored 472

Supplying context-sensitive help for text 474

Program is unresponsive when in a loop 476

Part V Windows Programming **481**

Chapter 14   Windows API Functions **483**

Callbacks **483**
Listing windows and children 484
Getting detailed font info 487
Using a method as a callback 493
Playing Sounds **495**
Playing a .WAV file without the media player component 495
Playing sounds from memory 499
Tasks **501**
Watching the clipboard's contents 501
Executing another program and waiting for it to end 505
Executing and controlling other programs 505
Getting a list of active tasks 512
Getting a list of active processes 514

Chapter 15   Windows Messages and Resources **523**

Resource Basics **523**
Understanding resource error message on program load 524
Avoiding resource disappearance 524
Creating a resource file 525
Using Resources **526**
Storing bitmaps as resources 526
Creating and using a special cursor 529
Supporting multiple languages 531
Embedding .WAV files in a program 535
Using Windows Messages **538**
Responding to an undocumented message 538
Sending an undocumented message 541
Communicating between programs 545
Controlling the screen saver 548

Chapter 16   Dynamic Link Libraries **551**

DLL Basics **551**
Writing and using a DLL 551
Putting a form inside a DLL 555

DLL Calling Variations **560**

Calling DLLs from Visual Basic 560

Calling DLLs from a macro language 563

Loading a DLL at runtime 565

Creating a language-flexible program 566

DLL Difficulties **572**

DLL changes don't take effect 572

Avoiding DLL trouble 573

End-User License Agreement **575**

Index **483**

Introduction

*D*elphi makes Windows programming absurdly easy, as long as you're satisfied with the default behavior of Delphi's forms and components. Because Delphi programming is generally so smooth, running into a problem can be a rude awakening. Delphi's menu component is easy to use, but it does not support owner-draw menu items, for example. The bitmap button component allows colored text, but not multiline text. Enhancing a program with a feature that's not intrinsically supported in Delphi can mean anything from writing an event handler to writing a brand-new component, and can require a surprising amount of low-level Windows programming expertise.

That's where this book comes in. It's a collection of solutions for questions posed by Delphi programmers and problems encountered in real situations. It is by no means an exhaustive reference on Delphi programming; the Delphi manuals serve that purpose. When you hit a roadblock, when the manuals do not help, when it seems you need to go beyond the ordinary borders of Delphi programming—that's when you'll want to turn to this book. Most of the solutions contained herein apply equally to Delphi 1.0 and Delphi 2.0. Those that are specific to 16-bit or 32-bit programming will be clearly marked within the text.

Who Should Read This Book

This book is meant as a resource for every Delphi programmer, from beginner to expert. Some of its solutions draw on lesser known features of Delphi, some require creation of new components, and others go straight to the Windows Application Programming Interface (API). No matter how new you are to Delphi programming, you can run and study the example programs. And no matter how expert you are, there are always new techniques to be learned.

How This Book Is Organized

The 16 chapters of problems and solutions are grouped into the following five parts:

- ◆ Part I: Forms
- ◆ Part II: Components
- ◆ Part III: More Components
- ◆ Part IV: Inside Delphi
- ◆ Part V: Windows Programming

However, the categories necessarily overlap. Forms *are* components, components don't exist without forms, all Delphi programming uses the Object Pascal language, and Delphi programming *is* Windows programming. You'll get the most benefit if you read through the entire book and familiarize yourself with its contents. Then, when you run into a problem, you'll have an idea where to look.

Naturally, you won't have encountered all or even most of the problems, or you won't have recognized them as having a possible solution. You may not have realized that it's possible to control the drawing of your program's title bar, or to activate another program's menu commands. You're bound to get new ideas for your own programs by reading through *all* the solutions.

The Program Listings

All but the simplest solutions are demonstrated with an example program; most are illustrated with a screen shot. The complete source code for all the example programs is contained on the diskette bound into this book. Each printed listing begins with a caption containing the program's name, which is the main source code filename with its .DPR extension removed. The listing includes the complete code for the .PAS source file corresponding to each form, a stripped-down list of components and properties for the form, and, where necessary, the main .DPR project file. Ancillary files, such as resource scripts, may be included as well. The listing for a simple project might look like this:

PROJECT1

UNIT1.DEX

```
object Form1: TForm1
  Caption = 'Example Form'
  Position = poDefault
  Scaled = False
end
```

FILE UNIT1.PAS

```
unit Unit1;

interface

uses SysUtils, WinTypes, WinProcs, Messages, Classes, Graphics,
  Controls, Forms, Dialogs;

type
  TForm1 = class(TForm)
    procedure FormClick(Sender: TObject);
  end;

var Form1: TForm1;

implementation

{$R *.DFM}

procedure TForm1.FormClick(Sender: TObject);
begin
  MessageBeep(0);
end;

end.
```

Every Delphi form is described by a binary file with the extension .DFM. You can load a .DFM file into Delphi's Code Editor and view the form's components and properties as text. The .DEX file included with each listing is an *extract* of the .DFM file. It omits all nonessential properties, including size and position. In the preceding example, I changed the caption from its default of 'Form1', set the Position property to poDefault, and Scaled to False, so those three properties appear in the .DEX file.

You *could* use Delphi's CONVERT program to turn a .DEX file into an actual Delphi form, although all the components would appear at their default size, stacked in the top left corner. However, the actual purpose of the .DEX file is to let you refer to important component properties without drowning in a welter of detail.

In the .PAS program listings, Delphi-generated code appears in regular text whereas programmer-generated code appears in **boldface text**. Delphi generated the framework for the OnClick event handler in the example, but I added the call to MessageBeep. Hence the latter is displayed in boldface.

To load and run one of the sample programs, first copy its files from the diskette to a directory of your choice. By default, Delphi will store the compiled .EXE and temporary files in the same directory as the source code. That step will not succeed if the source code is on a diskette with limited free space.

What about cutting out sections of code to use in your own programs? Go ahead— that's what it's for. The example programs are kept deliberately simple, so nobody will be tempted to sell the compiled .EXEs as stand-alone utility programs. The one thing you can't do, naturally, is claim the example programs as your own work and sell them as such.

Other Listings

A few of the code listings define a component object or property editor object rather than a program. These will be introduced by a listing caption giving the *internal* name of the object; for example, TListBoxHorz or TAboutBoxProperty. The source code listing for the object will follow, together with any supporting files.

To install a component, copy its source code from the diskette to a directory on your hard disk, together with all supporting files. These will include 16-bit and 32-bit resource files with the same filename as the component's main source code file and the extension .R16 and .R32. You'll want to put all the components from this book in the same directory, as the length of Delphi's component directory list is limited. Once the files are in place, choose Install Components . . . from the Options menu in Delphi 1.0, or choose Install . . . from the Component menu in Delphi 2.0.

Delphi Versions, Windows Versions

All the example programs in this book either work with both Delphi 1.0 and Delphi 2.0, or include conditional compilation code to prevent them from running under the wrong version. For example:

```
{$IFNDEF Win32}
HALT! This program requires Delphi 2.0!
{$ENDIF}
```

Where necessary, conditional compilation has been used to adapt the program for use under both Delphi versions.

Conditional compilation is not available at the component level—you cannot place a component in the Form Designer that will be a TMemo in Delphi 1.0 but morph into a TRichEdit in Delphi 2.0. A few of the example programs use conditional compilation to *replace* a component on the form at runtime with a more advanced component when compiled under Delphi 2.0.

All the example programs have been tested using the following combinations of Delphi version and Windows platform:

Delphi 1.0 (16-bit), Windows for Workgroups 3.11
Delphi 1.0 (16-bit), Windows 95
Delphi 2.0 (32-bit), Windows 95
Delphi 2.0 (32-bit), Windows NT 3.51

Where necessary, the example programs include code specific to individual Windows platforms. For example, the DrawIcon program in Chapter 13, "The Application Object," responds to WM_PAINT messages to draw on the icon in Windows 3.x and Windows NT. In Windows 95, however, minimized programs do not receive WM_PAINT messages, so the program creates a new icon on the fly as needed.

Further Questions

Obviously, this book can't answer every possible question about Delphi. You're welcome to e-mail me about Delphi problems you run into that are not covered here. I can't promise a response to *every* message, but at least your question may spark a solution for a future volume. The best place to get an answer is in the Delphi forum on CompuServe (GO DELPHI). If you don't have CompuServe forum access, you can contact me at one of these e-mail addresses:

MCI mail: 326-3042
CompuServe: 72241,50
Internet: nrubenki@zd.com

FORMS

Window is the name for that ubiquitous rectangular screen area in which a program communicates with the user, and from which Microsoft Windows gets its name. Confusingly, in programmer-speak, just about every on-screen object in a Windows program is itself a window. Buttons, check boxes, list boxes, and memo boxes are all windows by virtue of having a window handle and processing messages from Windows.

The form in Delphi offers no such confusion—it matches the original idea of a window as a rectangular area on the screen. Every Delphi program that has an on-screen presence relies on a descendant of the TForm object, and you design a program's interface by placing components on the form. It's simple to create a form by setting properties . . . simple; that is, until you try something unusual like creating a bordered form with no caption, or adding the Windows 95 help button to the title bar. This section will explore questions that come up when you move beyond simple form properties.

CHAPTER 1

Form Basics

*A*lmost every Delphi program is based around one or more forms—the form is the face *presented by the program to the user. In Delphi, user interface design consists of placing and arranging components on a form, and programming mostly involves attaching event handlers to those components. Delphi gives a certain amount of control over a form's behavior and appearance through its properties. However, there are many possibilities in Windows that aren't directly enabled by form properties. This chapter will explore the frontier just beyond what's ordinarily possible.*

Unusual Window Styles

The BorderStyle property lets you define your form's border as resizeable, fixed-size single, dialog-box style, or no border at all. In Delphi 2.0, BorderStyle also lets you identify a form as a Windows 95 tool window, fixed-size or resizeable. Internally, each BorderStyle corresponds to a particular set of windows style bits (constants with names like WS_POPUP and WS_CHILD). However, many more effects are possible if you take control of the window style yourself.

 Eliminating a form's caption but leaving the border

16 32

The only way to eliminate a form's caption bar using Delphi properties is to set the BorderStyle to bsNone. However, this completely eliminates the border, leaving a rather odd-looking window.

Fortunately, the window-creation process is exposed for your meddling in TForm's CreateParams virtual method. By overriding CreateParams and changing the Style field of the Params argument, you can set any combination of window style bits that you desire. Specifically, by including the WS_POPUP bit in the style and masking out the WS_DLGFRAME bit, you eliminate the caption. If the BorderStyle was bsSizeable, it will still have a resizeable border; if it was bsSingle or bsDialog, the border will not resize. Figure 1-1 shows what such a program looks like.

FIGURE 1-1: This form, with a sizeable border but no title bar, doesn't match any of the Delphi form styles. It's shown running under Windows 3.1 because the sizeable border is more visible.

SIZFRAM

SIZFRAMU.DEX

```
object Form1: TForm1
  Scaled = False
  object Label1: TLabel
    Caption = 'I'
    Color = clRed
    Font.Color = clWhite
    Font.Height = -32
    Font.Name = 'Wingdings'
    ParentColor = False
    ParentFont = False
  end
  object BitBtn1: TBitBtn
    Kind = bkClose
  end
end
```

SIZFRAMU.PAS

```
unit Sizframu;

interface

uses SysUtils, WinTypes, WinProcs, Messages, Classes, Graphics,
  Controls, Forms, Dialogs, StdCtrls, Buttons;
```

```
type
  TForm1 = class(TForm)
    BitBtn1: TBitBtn;
    Label1: TLabel;
  private
    procedure CreateParams(VAR Params: TCreateParams);
      override;
    procedure WM_NcHitTest(VAR Msg: TWMNcHitTest);
      message WM_NCHITTEST;
  end;

var Form1: TForm1;

implementation
{$R *.DFM}

procedure TForm1.CreateParams(VAR Params: TCreateParams);
begin
  Inherited CreateParams(Params);
  WITH Params DO
    Style := (Style OR WS_POPUP) AND (NOT WS_DLGFRAME);
  end;

procedure TForm1.WM_NcHitTest(VAR Msg: TWMNcHitTest);
begin
  Inherited;
  WITH Msg DO
    IF PtInRect(Label1.BoundsRect,
      {Point(XPos,YPos) is used rather than just Msg.Pos to
       handle TPoint/TSmallPoint difference in Delphi32}
      ScreenToClient(Point(XPos,YPos))) THEN
        Result := HTCAPTION;
  end;
end.
```

Taking control of the form's windows style bits is as simple as overriding the CreateParams method. As usual for overriding methods, the new CreateParams calls the inherited method first. It then includes the WS_POPUP bit by ORing it with the style and masks out the WS_DLGFRAME bit by ANDing its inverse with the style. That's what it takes to eliminate the caption.

Normally, to move a window you drag the title bar, and to close it you double-click the system menu box. When the title bar is absent, the program needs to provide a way to move and close its window. In this case, the Close button shuts the program down, and the white-on-red hand glyph provides a handle for moving the window around.

The hand glyph is just a colorful TLabel with its font set to WingDings. The program convinces Windows that this label is a caption bar by responding to the WM_NCHITTEST message. As always, it calls the inherited message handler first. Then, if the mouse cursor is over the label, it changes the return value to HTCAPTION.

You'll find all the WS_Xxx style bit constants listed in the online help. Go ahead and experiment with different combinations, but do save your experimental programs before running them. There are some combinations of styles that just don't work!

Getting the "tiny title bar" effect

Many modern programs use a special kind of title bar on floating toolbars or similar windows. The Toolbox window in Visual Basic is an example. In such a window, the title bar is about half the usual height, and the system menu box is correspondingly narrower. Figure 1-2 shows two versions of a tiny title bar window.

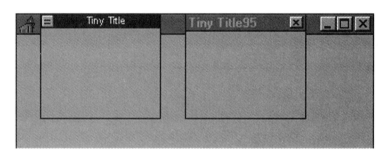

FIGURE 1-2: In Windows 95, a style bit turns a window into a tiny title window; you can also build this kind of window without help from Win95.

TINYT

TINYTMU.DEX

```
object Form1: TForm1
  BorderStyle = bsSingle
  Caption = ' '
  Position = poDefault
  Scaled = False
  OnCreate = FormCreate
end
```

TINYTMU.PAS

```
unit Tinytmu;

interface

uses SysUtils, WinTypes, WinProcs, Messages, Classes, Graphics,
  Controls, Forms, Dialogs, StdCtrls;

type
  TForm1 = class(TForm)
    procedure FormCreate(Sender: TObject);
  end;

var Form1: TForm1;

implementation
USES TinyTTu, TinyT95u;
{$R *.DFM}

procedure TForm1.FormCreate(Sender: TObject);
begin
  Form2 := TForm2.Create(Application);
  Form2.Top := Top;
  Form2.Left := Left + 24;
  IF Swap(LoWord(GetVersion)) >= $35F THEN
    BEGIN
      Form3 := TForm3.Create(Application);
      Form3.Top := Top;
      Form3.Left := Form2.Left + Form2.Width + 24;
    END;
end;

end.
```

TINYT95U.DEX

```
object Form3: TForm3
  BorderIcons = [biSystemMenu]
  BorderStyle = bsSingle
  Caption = 'Tiny Title95'
  FormStyle = fsStayOnTop
  Position = poDefault
  Scaled = False
  Visible = True
end
```

TINYT95U.PAS

```
unit tinyt95u;

interface

uses SysUtils, Wintypes, WinProcs, Messages, Classes, Graphics,
  Controls, Forms, Dialogs;

type
  TForm3 = class(TForm)
  private
    procedure CreateParams(VAR Params: TCreateParams);
      override;
  end;

var Form3: TForm3;

implementation

{$R *.DFM}

{$IFNDEF Win32}
CONST WS_EX_TOOLWINDOW = $80;
{$ENDIF}

procedure TForm3.CreateParams(VAR Params: TCreateParams);
begin
  Inherited CreateParams(Params);
  WITH Params DO
    ExStyle := (ExStyle OR WS_EX_TOOLWINDOW);
end;

end.
```

TINYTTU.DEX

```
object Form2: TForm2
  BorderIcons = [biSystemMenu]
  BorderStyle = bsSingle
  Caption = 'Tiny Title'
  FormStyle = fsStayOnTop
  Position = poDefault
  Scaled = False
  Visible = True
  OnCreate = FormCreate
  object Shape1: TShape
    Brush.Color = clInactiveCaption
  end
  object Label1: TLabel
    Alignment = taCenter
    AutoSize = False
    Caption = 'Tiny Title'
    Color = clInactiveCaption
    Font.Color = clInactiveCaptionText
```

```
      Font.Height = -9
      ParentColor = False
      ParentFont = False
      Transparent = True
    end
    object SpeedButton1: TSpeedButton
      Caption = '='
    end
end
```

TINYTTU.PAS

```
unit Tinyttu;

interface

uses SysUtils, WinTypes, WinProcs, Messages, Classes, Graphics,
  Controls, Forms, Dialogs, Buttons, StdCtrls, ExtCtrls;

type
  TForm2 = class(TForm)
    SpeedButton1: TSpeedButton;
    Label1: TLabel;
    Shape1: TShape;
    procedure FormCreate(Sender: TObject);
  private
    procedure CreateParams(VAR Params: TCreateParams);
      override;
    procedure WMNcHitTest(VAR Msg: TWMNCHitTest);
      message WM_NCHITTEST;
    procedure WMNCActivate(VAR Msg: TWMNCActivate);
      message WM_NCACTIVATE;
    procedure WMSetText(VAR Msg: TWMSetText);
      message WM_SETTEXT;
  end;

var Form2: TForm2;

implementation

{$R *.DFM}
procedure TForm2.FormCreate(Sender: TObject);
VAR
  H : hMenu;
  N : Integer;
begin
  H := GetSystemMenu(Handle, False);
  FOR N := GetMenuItemCount(H)-1 DOWNTO 0 DO
    CASE GetMenuItemID(H, N) OF
      SC_MOVE,
      SC_CLOSE : ; {leave these two in place}
      ELSE RemoveMenu(H, N, MF_BYPOSITION);
    END;
end;
```

```
procedure TForm2.CreateParams(VAR Params: TCreateParams);
begin
  Inherited CreateParams(Params);
  WITH Params DO
    Style := (Style OR WS_POPUP) AND (NOT WS_DLGFRAME);
end;

procedure TForm2.WMNcHitTest(VAR Msg: TWMNCHitTest);
VAR CurPt : TPoint;
begin
  Inherited;
  CurPt := Point(Msg.XPos-Left, Msg.YPos-Top);
  IF PtInRect(Shape1.BoundsRect, CurPt) THEN
    Msg.Result := htCaption
  ELSE IF PtInRect(SpeedButton1.BoundsRect, CurPt) THEN
    Msg.Result := htSysMenu;
end;

procedure TForm2.WMNCActivate(VAR Msg: TWMNCActivate);
CONST
  BG : ARRAY[Boolean] OF TColor =
    (clInActiveCaption, clActiveCaption);
  FG : ARRAY[Boolean] OF TColor =
    (clInactiveCaptionText, clCaptionText);
begin
  Inherited;
  Shape1.Brush.Color := BG[Msg.Active];
  Label1.Font.Color  := FG[Msg.Active];
end;

procedure TForm2.WMSetText(VAR Msg: TWMSetText);
begin
  Inherited;
  Label1.Caption := Caption;
end;
end.
```

When this project's main form is created, it in turn creates an instance of TForm2, positioning it so the top edges are aligned. If the program is executing under Windows 95, the main form also creates an instance of TForm3 and again aligns the top edges.

Under Windows 95, you can create a tiny title bar window simply by including the WS_EX_TOOLWINDOW bit in the extended style (the ExStyle field of the Params argument to CreateParams). A conditional compilation directive defines this constant if Delphi 1.0 is being used.

Building a tiny title bar form that will also work in Windows 3.1 or Windows NT takes a bit more work, but the result is more flexible. The general-purpose tiny title bar form has a single border and overrides the CreateParams method to suppress its title bar entirely. Within its border, it contains a speed button that represents the system menu box and a shape/label combination that stands in for the title bar.

The WM_NCHITTEST response method enables the speed button and shape components to masquerade as nonclient areas of the form. If the mouse cursor is within the TShape, the WM_NCHITTEST response method returns HTCAPTION; if it is within the speed button, it returns HTSYSMENU. That's all it takes! A WM_NCACTIVATE response method handles changing the color of the TShape and TLabel when the form becomes active or inactive, and a WM_SETTEXT response method automatically changes the label's caption when the main form's caption is changed.

The OnCreate event handler for the form is optional. It walks through the form's system menu and deletes everything except the Move and the Close commands. Delphi does this automatically for forms with the bsDialog style.

When your project needs a floating toolbar or other tiny title bar window, you can use one of the two techniques shown here to get it.

Painting on Forms

Most of the time, Delphi and Windows between them take care of painting all portions of your forms. The frame, the title bar, the icons on the title bar, and the client area are all displayed without any work on your part. However, you can make your programs stand out by taking over the painting of one or more of these areas.

 Painting a form's background with a pattern

To some extent, your form's client area is a miniature of the Windows desktop. You can use Control Panel to select a background color for the desktop, and you can set the form's Color property. You can put a wallpaper image on the desktop, and you can place a TImage component with Align set to alClient on the form. The desktop offers one more feature called Pattern. How can you get a pattern for a Delphi form's background?

A Delphi form has a property called Brush which is *not* the same as the Brush property of its Canvas. The latter is used in OnPaint event handlers to control the colors used in the code you write to paint on the form. The former is automatically used by Windows to paint your form's background. You can set one of the hatched brush styles, or set the brush's handle to an 8×8 pixel bitmap. Figure 1-3 shows four possibilities.

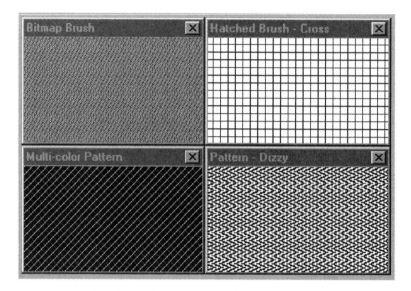

FIGURE 1-3: These four wildly different backgrounds were created by manipulating the form's Brush property.

TEXTURE

TEXTUR1U.DEX

```
object Form1: TForm1
  BorderIcons = [biSystemMenu, biMinimize]
  BorderStyle = bsSingle
  Caption = 'Textured Background Demo'
  Position = poDefault
  Scaled = False
  OnCreate = FormCreate
  object Button2: TButton
    Caption = '&Multi-color'
    OnClick = Button2Click
  end
  object Button1: TButton
    Caption = '&Bitmap'
    OnClick = Button1Click
  end
  object Button3: TButton
    Caption = '&Pattern'
    OnClick = Button3Click
  end
  object ListBox1: TListBox
    OnDblClick = Button3Click
  end
  object Button4: TButton
```

```
      Caption = '&Hatched'
      OnClick = Button4Click
    end
    object ListBox2: TListBox
    end
end
```

TEXTUR1U.PAS

```
unit textur1u;

interface

uses SysUtils, WinTypes, WinProcs, Messages, Classes, Graphics,
  Controls, Forms, Dialogs, StdCtrls;

type
  TForm1 = class(TForm)
    Button2: TButton;
    Button1: TButton;
    Button3: TButton;
    ListBox1: TListBox;
    Button4: TButton;
    ListBox2: TListBox;
    procedure Button3Click(Sender: TObject);
    procedure FormCreate(Sender: TObject);
    procedure Button1Click(Sender: TObject);
    procedure Button4Click(Sender: TObject);
    procedure Button2Click(Sender: TObject);
  end;

var Form1: TForm1;

implementation
Uses textur2u, IniFiles;

{$R *.DFM}

procedure TForm1.FormCreate(Sender: TObject);
begin
  WITH TIniFile.Create('CONTROL.INI') DO
    try
      ReadSection('Patterns', ListBox1.Items);
      WITH ListBox1.Items DO Delete(IndexOf('(None)'));
    finally
      Free;
    end;
  ListBox2.Items.SetText('Horizontal'#13'Vertical'#13'FDiagonal'+
    #13'BDiagonal'#13'Cross'#13'DiagCross');
  ListBox1.ItemIndex := 0;
  ListBox2.ItemIndex := 0;
end;

procedure TForm1.Button1Click(Sender: TObject);
begin
```

```
      WITH TForm2.Create(Application) DO
        BEGIN
          SetTexture(0, '');
          Caption := 'Bitmap Brush';
          Show;
        END;
  end;

  procedure TForm1.Button2Click(Sender: TObject);
  begin
    WITH TForm2.Create(Application) DO
      BEGIN
        SetTexture(1, '');
        Caption := 'Multi-color Pattern';
        Show;
      END;
  end;

  procedure TForm1.Button3Click(Sender: TObject);
  begin
    WITH TIniFile.Create('CONTROL.INI') DO
      try
        WITH TForm2.Create(Application) DO
          BEGIN
            WITH ListBox1 DO
              BEGIN
                SetTexture(8, ReadString('Patterns',
                  Items[ItemIndex], ''));
                Caption := 'Pattern - ' + Items[ItemIndex];
              END;
            Show;
          END;
      finally
        Free;
      end;
  end;

  procedure TForm1.Button4Click(Sender: TObject);
  begin
    WITH TForm2.Create(Application) DO
      BEGIN
        WITH ListBox2 DO
          BEGIN
            SetTexture(ItemIndex+2, '');
            Caption := 'Hatched Brush - ' + Items[ItemIndex];
          END;
        Show;
      END;
  end;

  end.
```

TEXTUR2U.DEX

```
object Form2: TForm2
  BorderIcons = [biSystemMenu]
  BorderStyle = bsDialog
  Position = poDefault
  Scaled = False
  OnCreate = FormCreate
end
```

TEXTUR2U.PAS

```pascal
unit textur2u;

interface

uses SysUtils, WinTypes, WinProcs, Messages, Classes, Graphics,
  Controls, Forms, Dialogs, StdCtrls, Buttons;

type
  TForm2 = class(TForm)
    procedure FormCreate(Sender: TObject);
  public
    procedure SetTexture(Tex: Word; const S: String);
  end;

var Form2: TForm2;

implementation

{$R *.DFM}
{$IFDEF Win32}
{$R BACKBR32.RES}
{$ELSE}
{$R BACKBRSH.RES}
{$ENDIF}

procedure TForm2.SetTexture(Tex: Word; const S: String);
VAR
  Ro, Co, N : Integer;
  Stream    : TStream;
  Patt      : ARRAY[0..7] OF Integer;
begin
  CASE Tex OF
    0 : Brush.Bitmap.Handle:=LoadBitmap(hInstance, 'BACKBRSH');
    1 : FOR Ro := 0 TO 7 DO
          FOR Co := 0 TO 7 DO
            IF (Co+Ro) MOD 8=0 THEN
              Brush.Bitmap.Canvas.Pixels[Co,Ro] := clYellow
            ELSE IF (Co+7-Ro) MOD 8=0 THEN
              Brush.Bitmap.Canvas.Pixels[Co,Ro] := clRed
            ELSE   Brush.Bitmap.Canvas.Pixels[Co,Ro] := clBlack;
    2..7 : BEGIN
      Brush.Color := clBlue;
```

```
        Brush.Style := TBrushStyle(Tex);
      END;
    8 : BEGIN
      Stream := TMemoryStream.Create;
      try
        Stream.WriteBuffer(s[1], length(s));
        Stream.Position := 0;
        N := 0;
        WITH TParser.Create(Stream) DO
          try
            WHILE Token <> toEOF DO
              BEGIN
                CheckToken(toInteger);
                Patt[N] := TokenInt;
                N := N+1;
                NextToken;
              END;
          finally
            Free;
          end;
      finally
        Stream.Free;
      end;
      FOR Ro := 0 TO 7 DO
        FOR Co := 0 TO 7 DO
          IF Patt[Ro] AND (1 SHL Co)=0 THEN
            Brush.Bitmap.Canvas.Pixels[Co,Ro] := clWhite
          ELSE Brush.Bitmap.Canvas.Pixels[Co,Ro] := clBlack;
    END;
  END;
end;
procedure TForm2.FormCreate(Sender: TObject);
begin
  Brush.Bitmap := TBitmap.Create;
  Brush.Bitmap.Width  := 8;
  Brush.Bitmap.Height := 8;
  Left := Random(Screen.Width - Width);
  Top := Random(Screen.Height - Height);
end;
procedure TForm2.FormDestroy(Sender: TObject);
begin
  Brush.Bitmap.Free;
end;

end.
```

The main form starts out by reading the key names from the Patterns section from
CONTROL.INI into a list box, using the ReadSection method of the TIniFile object.

It then loads a second list box with the names of the available hatched brushes and selects the first item in each list box.

Each of the four buttons creates an instance of the secondary form, calls its SetTexture method, sets its caption, and then shows it. The background brush for the form is created in its OnCreate event handler; SetTexture initializes the brush.

For a bitmap-based background, SetTexture loads the brush with a bitmap stored in a resource. Note that the resource exists in both 16-bit and 32-bit forms. The multicolor pattern brush is created by setting the pixels in the brush's bitmap to red, yellow, or black according to a simple formula. And, for a hatched brush, SetTexture sets the brush's Style property to the constant corresponding to the desired style.

Converting a Windows pattern into a bitmap is more challenging. The pattern is stored in CONTROL.INI as a series of eight numeric strings separated by spaces. Parsing this string into eight integers would be tedious without help from Delphi's virtually undocumented TParser object. TParser takes a stream of text and breaks it down into tokens, such as words or numbers. SetTexture loads the string into a memory stream, then parses it into eight integers with the help of a TParser. The 0 and 1 bits of the eight integers represent the white and black pixels in the pattern.

The demo program can use any pattern available to Windows. Of course, you can design your own patterns as well. Users are likely to remember a form whose background is like one of those shown in Figure 1-3!

Taking over drawing a form's caption

16 32

Form design in Delphi is restricted to the client area of the form—the area inside the frame. Windows draws the title bar using the appropriate system colors. If you could draw the title bar yourself, your program would stand out on the desktop.

The title bar is part of the nonclient area of a window, and it gets painted in response to the WM_NCPAINT (NC for nonclient) message. In addition, the WM_NCACTIVATE message signals the need to repaint in a different color because the window became active or inactive. Changing the caption text also requires a repaint. Figure 1-4 shows two instances of a program whose title bar stands out. Normally, titles are centered in Windows 3.1 and left-aligned in Windows 95. This window reverses the standard; it has a left-aligned title in Windows 3.1 and a centered title in Windows 95. In addition, the Times New Roman font used for the title is bold when the window is active, italic when it's inactive.

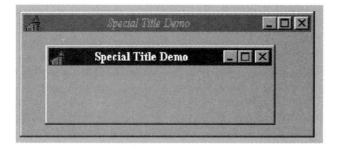

FIGURE 1-4: This program draws its own caption and thus can control its font and its placement within the title bar.

MYTITLE

MYTITLEU.DEX

```
object Form1: TForm1
  Caption = 'Special Title Demo'
  Position = poDefault
  Scaled = False
end
```

MYTITLEU.PAS

```
unit Mytitleu;

interface

uses SysUtils, WinTypes, WinProcs, Messages, Classes, Graphics,
  Controls, Forms, Dialogs, StdCtrls;

type
  TForm1 = class(TForm)
  private
    procedure DrawTitle(IsActive: Boolean ;const S : String);
    procedure WMNCPaint(VAR Msg: TWMNCPaint);
      message WM_NCPAINT;
    procedure WMNCActivate(VAR Msg: TWMNCActivate);
      message WM_NCACTIVATE;
    procedure WMSetText(VAR Msg: TWMSetText);
      message WM_SETTEXT;
  end;

var Form1: TForm1;
{$R *.DFM}

implementation

procedure TForm1.DrawTitle(IsActive: Boolean ;const S : String);
```

```
VAR
  TopOfs : Word;
  R      : TRect;
  XF,            {frame width}
  YF,            {frame height}
  XS,            {caption bar button width}
  YS : Integer;  {caption bar button height}
CONST
  BG : ARRAY[Boolean] OF TColor = (clInActiveCaption,
    clActiveCaption);
  FG : ARRAY[Bool] OF TColor = (clInactiveCaptionText,
    clCaptionText);
  FS : ARRAY[Bool] OF TFontStyles = ([fsItalic], [fsBold]);
begin
  XF := GetSystemMetrics(SM_CXFRAME);
  YF := GetSystemMetrics(SM_CYFRAME);
  XS := GetSystemMetrics(SM_CXSIZE);
  YS := GetSystemMetrics(SM_CYSIZE);
  WITH Canvas DO
    try
      Handle := GetWindowDC(Self.Handle);
      {set R to the title portion of caption bar}
      R := Bounds(XF, YF, ClientWidth, YS);
      IF biSystemMenu IN BorderIcons THEN R.Left := R.Left+XS+1;
      IF biMinimize IN BorderIcons THEN R.Right := R.Right-XS-1;
      IF biMaximize IN BorderIcons THEN R.Right := R.Right-XS-1;
      IF Swap(LoWord(GetVersion)) >= $35F THEN
        R.Right := R.Right-XS-1;
      {select colors and font for caption}
      Brush.Color := BG[IsActive];
      Font.Color  := FG[IsActive];
      Font.Style  := FS[IsActive];
      Font.Name   := 'Times New Roman';
      TopOfs := TextHeight(S);
      IF TopOfs > YS THEN TopOfs := 0
      ELSE TopOfs := (YS-TopOfs) DIV 2;
      IF Swap(LoWord(GetVersion)) >= $35F THEN {if Win95}
        BEGIN
          {write caption (centered, like Win3.1)}
          SetTextAlign(Handle, TA_CENTER);
          TextRect(R, (R.Right+R.Left) DIV 2, R.Top+TopOfs, S);
        END
      ELSE
        {write caption (left aligned, like Win95)}
        TextRect(R, R.Left+2, R.Top+TopOfs, S);
    finally
      ReleaseDC(Self.Handle, Handle);
      Handle := 0;
    end;
end;

procedure TForm1.WMNCPaint(VAR Msg: TWMNCPaint);
begin
```

```
  Inherited;
  DrawTitle(Active, Caption);
end;

procedure TForm1.WMNCActivate(VAR Msg: TWMNCActivate);
begin
  Inherited;
  DrawTitle(Msg.Active, Caption);
end;

procedure TForm1.WMSetText(VAR Msg: TWMSetText);
begin
  Inherited;
  DrawTitle(Active, Caption);
end;

end.
```

When this form receives a WM_NCPAINT message, it calls the inherited message handler to draw the frame, then calls its private method DrawTitle to overwrite the caption area with a special caption. It also calls DrawTitle when the form's activation state changes and when the caption text changes.

So as not to be *too* different from other windows, it uses the system colors for the active and inactive text and background. The DrawTitle routine begins by calling GetSystemMetrics to get the X and Y dimensions of both the window frame and the buttons on the caption bar. These dimensions are calculated each time the title needs to be painted, because the user can change the frame width using Control Panel's Desktop applet.

The form's Canvas property encapsulates the most useful drawing functions in a Delphi object, but it normally limits drawing to the form's client area. DrawTitle sets the Handle property of the form's Canvas to the device context returned by the Application Program Interface (API) function GetWindowDC. This device context includes the entire window, frame and all. DrawTitle calculates the dimensions of the title rectangle and sets up the color and font to represent the active/inactive state of the window. Then it uses the TextRect method of TCanvas to write the title. This method clips the text to the specified rectangle and, by default, draws it left-aligned. If the program is running under Windows 95, DrawTitle draws the title centered.

When the function has finished, it releases the device context and sets the form's Canvas's Handle property to 0. Next time the handle is needed, the Canvas will recreate it.

This method of drawing the title has one added advantage. Although the Caption property of a Delphi form is a 255-character string, Windows 3.1 limits captions to 79 characters. A title bar drawn under program control can accommodate longer captions.

In your own programs you can draw the title bar just about any way you want—make it rainbow-colored, perhaps, or draw a graphic on it. However, you want to be careful not to upset the user. There's a fine line between making your program *distinctive* and making it *weird!* Note, too, that Microsoft officially frowns on all nonclient painting. A program that paints the title bar correctly for Windows 3.1 won't look right under Windows 95. The example programs shown here adapt to Windows 3.1, Windows 95, and Windows NT. However, there's no guarantee that they'll work with the *next* major revision of Windows.

Putting a button on a form's title bar

16 32

You can't place a Delphi component on the title bar, so there's literally no way to put a button there. However, Windows does give you an opportunity to participate in the process of drawing the title bar. It sends WM_NCPAINT messages when the nonclient area of the window needs to be painted, and WM_NCACTIVATE messages when the title bar needs to be redrawn because the window became active or inactive. A program that draws on the title bar must do so in response to these two messages, as well as to WM_SETTEXT (which changes the caption). Figure 1-5 is a program that puts a triangle-marked button on the title bar. Of course, it's essential for such a program to recognize which Windows platform it's running under, and place the button appropriately. And there's no guarantee that the placement will still be correct under the next major revision of Windows.

FIGURE 1-5: In Windows 95, this program places a new button to the left of the cluster in the top right corner; in Windows 3.1, the new button goes just to the right of the system menu box.

TITLBTN

TITLBTNU.DEX

```
object Form1: TForm1
  Caption = 'Title Bar Button'
  Position = poDefault
  Scaled = False
  OnResize = FormResize
end
```

TITLBTNU.PAS

```
unit Titlbtnu;

interface

uses SysUtils, WinTypes, WinProcs, Messages, Classes, Graphics,
  Controls, Forms, Dialogs;

type
  TForm1 = class(TForm)
    procedure FormResize(Sender: TObject);
  private
    NewButton : TRect;
    procedure DrawNewButton;
    procedure WMNCPaint(VAR Msg: TWMNCPaint);
      message WM_NCPAINT;
    procedure WMNCActivate(VAR Msg: TWMNCActivate);
      message WM_NCACTIVATE;
    procedure WMSetText(VAR Msg: TWMSetText);
      message WM_SETTEXT;
    procedure WMNCHitTest(VAR Msg: TWMNCHitTest);
      message WM_NCHITTEST;
    procedure WMNCLButtonDown(VAR Msg: TWMNCLButtonDown);
      message WM_NCLBUTTONDOWN;
  end;

var Form1: TForm1;
{$R *.DFM}

implementation
USES Buttons; {for DrawButtonFace}
const htNewBtn = htSizeLast+1;

procedure TForm1.DrawNewButton;
VAR
  XF, YF, XS, YS : Integer;
begin
  XF := GetSystemMetrics(SM_CXFRAME);
  YF := GetSystemMetrics(SM_CYFRAME);
  XS := GetSystemMetrics(SM_CXSIZE);
  YS := GetSystemMetrics(SM_CYSIZE);
  IF Swap(LoWord(GetVersion)) >= $35F THEN
    NewButton := Bounds(Width-XF-4*XS+2, YF+2, XS-2, YS-3)
  ELSE
    NewButton := Bounds(XF+XS+1, YF-1, XS+2, YS+2);
  Canvas.Handle := GetWindowDC(Self.Handle);
  try
    DrawButtonFace(Canvas, NewButton, 1,
      bsAutoDetect, False, False, False);
    Canvas.Pen.Color := clRed;
    Canvas.Brush.Color := clYellow;
    WITH NewButton DO
      Canvas.Polygon([Point(Left+2, Bottom-4),
        Point((Left+Right)DIV 2-1, Top+3),
```

```
              Point(Right-4, Bottom-4)]);
    finally
      ReleaseDC(Self.Handle, Canvas.Handle);
      Canvas.Handle := 0;
    end;
  end;

procedure TForm1.WMNCPaint(VAR Msg: TWMNCPaint);
begin
  Inherited;
  DrawNewButton;
end;

procedure TForm1.WMNCActivate(VAR Msg: TWMNCActivate);
begin
  Inherited;
  DrawNewButton;
end;

procedure TForm1.WMSetText(VAR Msg: TWMSetText);
begin
  Inherited;
  DrawNewButton;
end;

procedure TForm1.WMNCHitTest(VAR Msg: TWMNCHitTest);
begin
  Inherited;
  WITH Msg DO
    IF PtInRect(NewButton, Point(XPos-Left, YPos-Top)) THEN
      Result := htNewBtn;
end;

procedure TForm1.WMNCLButtonDown(VAR Msg: TWMNCLButtonDown);
begin
  Inherited;
  IF Msg.HitTest=htNewBtn THEN
    ShowMessage('You pressed the new button');
end;

procedure TForm1.FormResize(Sender: TObject);
begin
  {Force the button to re-position}
  Perform(WM_NCACTIVATE, Word(Active), 0);
end;
end.
```

As with the previous solution, this program has to draw the modified title bar in response to the WM_NCPAINT, WM_NCACTIVATE, or WM_SETTEXT messages. The default drawing of the caption will overwrite the button, so it needs to be redrawn on those three occasions. The DrawNewButton method makes use of the handy function DrawButtonFace, found in Delphi's Buttons unit. This function draws a standard button face, pushed in or not, focused or not, depending on the parameters you pass it. For simplicity, the DrawNewButton just draws a triangle on the new button using the Canvas object's Polygon method.

The title bar also needs to be redrawn when the window is resized, especially in Windows 95, where the button's position is relative to the right-hand side of the form. The form's OnResize event handler sends the form a WM_NCACTIVATE message, which forces a redraw of the title bar.

A handler for the WM_NCHITTEST message returns a new value, htNewBtn, if the mouse cursor is within the new button. This prevents the confusion that would ensue if the user could drag the window around using the new button. It also causes the WM_NCLBUTTONDOWN message to pass the htNewBtn constant when the mouse is clicked on the new button. This example program just displays a message when the new button is clicked; in a real implementation, it would activate some feature of the program.

Taking over drawing a form's frame

16 32

One of the good things about Windows is that all programs are created equal. They all have the same shape (rectangular) and the same kind of border, title bar, and so on. That means a window whose frame is different from the usual will really stand out, as Figure 1-6 shows.

FIGURE 1-6: This black-and-yellow framed window will certainly get the user's attention!

ODDFRAME

ODDFRAMU.DEX

```
object Form1: TForm1
  Caption = 'Odd Frame Window'
  Position = poDefault
  Scaled = False
  Visible = True
  OnResize = FormResize
end
```

ODDFRAMU.PAS

```pascal
unit oddframu;

interface

uses SysUtils, WinTypes, WinProcs, Messages, Classes, Graphics,
  Controls, Forms, Dialogs, StdCtrls, ExtCtrls;

type
  TForm1 = class(TForm)
    procedure FormResize(Sender: TObject);
  private
    procedure DrawOddFrame;
    procedure WMNCPaint(VAR Msg: TWMNCPaint);
      message WM_NCPAINT;
    procedure WMNCActivate(VAR Msg: TWMNCActivate);
      message WM_NCActivate;
  end;

var Form1: TForm1;
{$R *.DFM}

implementation

procedure TForm1.DrawOddFrame;
VAR
  R      : TRect;
  YF, N : Integer;
begin
  YF := GetSystemMetrics(SM_CYFRAME);
  Canvas.Handle := GetWindowDC(Self.Handle);
  WITH Canvas DO
    try
      R := Bounds(0, 0, Width, Height);
      Pen.Color := clYellow;
      Brush.Style := bsClear;
      N := 0;
      REPEAT
        Pen.Style := psSolid;
        WITH R DO Rectangle(Left, Top, Right, Bottom);
        WITH Pen DO
          IF Color = clYellow THEN Color := clBlack
          ELSE Color := clYellow;
        Pen.Style := psDot;
        WITH R DO Rectangle(Left, Top, Right, Bottom);
        InflateRect(R, -1, -1);
        Inc(N);
      UNTIL N >= YF;
    finally
      ReleaseDC(Self.Handle, Handle);
      Handle := 0;
    end;
end;
```

```
procedure TForm1.WMNCActivate(VAR Msg: TWMNCActivate);
begin
  Inherited;
  DrawOddFrame;
end;
procedure TForm1.WMNCPaint(VAR Msg: TWMNCPaint);
begin
  Inherited;
  DrawOddFrame;
end;
procedure TForm1.FormResize(Sender: TObject);
begin
  DrawOddFrame;
  {Force redraw of caption area}
  Perform(WM_NCACTIVATE, Word(Active), 0);
end;

end.
```

The frame needs to be redrawn when the window is resized and when a WM_NCPAINT or WM_NCACTIVATE message is received. As in the MYTITLE example, the program sets the handle of the form's canvas to the device context returned by GetWindowDC. The odd frame shown in the figure is created by repeatedly drawing a solid rectangle and then a dotted rectangle, alternating yellow on black with black on yellow, and shrinking the rectangle by one pixel on each repetition.

That's probably enough about making your programs stand out by drawing them counter to the standard Windows style. It's definitely a double-edged sword; if the program is too different, the users will reject it. And there's always the risk that such a program will need to be rewritten to account for changes to the default nonclient painting behavior the next time Microsoft updates Windows.

Transforming Forms

A form is a form is a form . . . or is it? What if a form is a component on another form? What if a dialog box is a form with a menu? Sometimes treating a form as something it isn't yields good results; sometimes not.

Using a form as a component on another form

16 32

The MDI system is a well-defined way to enclose one or many child forms in a parent form, but it comes with a fair amount of baggage. If you want to create a child form that stays within the main form, say, for a floating toolbar, it may not be worthwhile to drag in the entire Multiple Document Interface (MDI) system. Again, the key lies in the CreateParams method. As Figure 1-7 shows, by overriding this method, you can make Windows create your form as a child window of the main form.

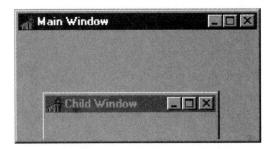

FIGURE 1-7: In this program, the secondary window belongs to the main window and cannot be moved outside of it.

CHILDWIN

CHILDMU.DEX

```
object Form1: TForm1
  Caption = 'Main Window'
  Position = poDefault
  Scaled = False
end
```

CHILDMU.PAS

```
unit Childmu;

interface

uses SysUtils, WinTypes, WinProcs, Messages, Classes, Graphics,
  Controls, Forms, Dialogs;
```

```
type
  TForm1 = class(TForm)

  end;
var Form1: TForm1;
implementation
{$R *.DFM}
end.
```

CHILDCU.DEX

```
object Form2: TForm2
  Caption = 'Child Window'
  Position = poDefault
  Scaled = False
  Visible = True
  OnClose = FormClose
end
```

CHILDCU.PAS

```
unit Childcu;
interface
uses SysUtils, WinTypes, WinProcs, Messages, Classes, Graphics,
  Controls, Forms, Dialogs;
type
  TForm2 = class(TForm)
    procedure FormClose(Sender: TObject; var Action:
      TCloseAction);
  private
    procedure CreateParams(VAR Params: TCreateParams);
      override;
  end;
var Form2: TForm2;
implementation
{$R *.DFM}
procedure TForm2.CreateParams(VAR Params: TCreateParams);
begin
  Inherited CreateParams(Params);
  WITH Params DO
    BEGIN
      WndParent := Application.MainForm.Handle;
      Style := (Style OR WS_CHILD) AND NOT (WS_POPUP);
      Width := 180;
      Height := 60;
```

```
    END;
  Parent := Application.MainForm;
end;
procedure TForm2.FormClose(Sender: TObject; var Action:
  TCloseAction);
begin
  Action := caMinimize;
end;

end.
```

It's necessary to let both Windows and Delphi know about the parent-child relationship. Windows gets the message when you set Params.WndParent to the main form's handle. Delphi understands the same thing when you set the form's Parent property to the main form. It's a relatively painless operation. Chances are you won't want to destroy this child window, so its OnClose handler sets the close action to caMinimize. Now, like any other component that's a child of the main form, it gets clipped at the form's boundaries. Naturally, it minimizes within the main form as well.

Adding a menu to a dialog form

16 32

By definition, a Windows dialog box does not have a menu. However, Windows 3.1 doesn't back up that definition with any muscle. Wouldn't it be convenient to add a menu to forms that are really dialog boxes? This time the answer is no! For starters, Delphi doesn't permit it; if you set the form's BorderStyle to bsDialog, you won't see a menu. Although you *can* use CreateParams to convert a form with a menu into a dialog box, Figure 1-8 shows why you shouldn't, at least not under Windows 3.1.

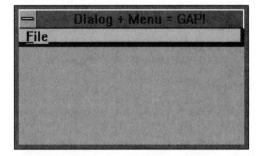

FIGURE 1-8: If you force a dialog box to have a menu in Windows 3.1, you'll get an ugly gap between the menu and the form's client area.

DLGMENU

DLGMENUU.DEX

```
object Form1: TForm1
  BorderIcons = [biSystemMenu]
  Caption = 'Dialog + Menu = GAP!'
  Menu = MainMenu1
  Position = poDefaultPosOnly
  Scaled = False
  Visible = True
  OnCreate = FormCreate
  object MainMenu1: TMainMenu
    object File1: TMenuItem
      Caption = '&File'
    end
  end
end
```

DLGMENUU.PAS

```
unit Dlgmenuu;

interface

uses SysUtils, WinTypes, WinProcs, Messages, Classes, Graphics,
  Controls, Forms, Dialogs, Menus;

type
  TForm1 = class(TForm)
    MainMenu1: TMainMenu;
    File1: TMenuItem;
    procedure FormCreate(Sender: TObject);
  private
    procedure CreateParams(VAR Params: TCreateParams);
      override;
  end;

var Form1: TForm1;

implementation
{$R *.DFM}
procedure TForm1.CreateParams(VAR Params: TCreateParams);
begin
  Inherited CreateParams(Params);
  WITH Params DO
    BEGIN
      ExStyle := ExStyle OR WS_EX_DLGMODALFRAME;
      Style := Style AND NOT (WS_THICKFRAME OR WS_GROUP OR
        WS_TABSTOP);
    END;
end;
```

```
procedure TForm1.FormCreate(Sender: TObject);
begin
  {$IFDEF Win32}
  Caption := 'No problem in Win32';
  {$ELSE}
  IF Swap(LoWord(GetVersion)) >= $35F THEN
    Caption := 'No problem in Win95';
  {$ENDIF}
end;

end.
```

As you'll see if you run this program under Windows 3.1, the default window-drawing code can't handle the combination of a dialog-box style and a menu. Some internal calculation assumes that the window is *not* a dialog box. The result is an ugly gap below the menu.

Programs that only run under Windows 95 or Windows NT can get away with shoehorning a menu onto a dialog box. Whatever the problem was in Windows 3.1, it's fixed in both of the more advanced platforms.

CHAPTER 2

Multipage Forms and More

T *his chapter will continue to explore forms and their variations—the topic is almost inexhaustible. You'll learn how to save resources in multipage forms by creating and destroying the pages as needed, how to reveal a hidden form based on the mouse's position on the desktop, and how to add a Windows 95-style help button even under Windows 3.1.*

Managing Forms

By default, Delphi-generated code creates all of a program's forms at startup, hiding the ones that are not initially visible. That's handy if you are a beginner, because it eliminates problems that can occur if you forget to initialize a form. However, taking charge of form creation reduces both your program's start-up time and its impact on system resources.

 Creating modal forms only as needed

16 32

Many projects consist of one main form and a handful of secondary dialog-box forms. The secondary forms are used only to get information from the user. There's no real need for them when they're not in use, because they *do* tie up memory and system resources.

In most cases, dialog-box forms can and should be created and destroyed with each use. The program that follows shows how to do this. What the program *can't* show directly is that you must go into the Project Options dialog, select the Forms page, and move the dialog-box form from the Auto-Create list to the Available list (Figure 2-1).

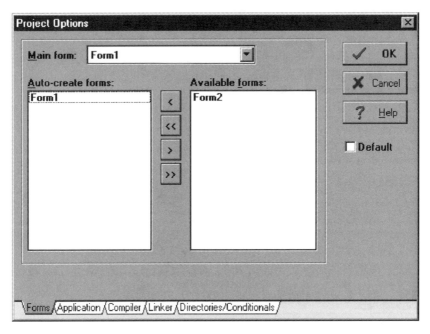

FIGURE 2-1: By moving a form from the Auto-Create list to the Available list, you make your program responsible for creating and destroying it.

MODALD

MODALD1U.DEX

```
object Form1: TForm1
  Caption = 'Create-On-Demand Dialog'
  Position = poDefault
  Scaled = False
  object Edit1: TEdit
    MaxLength = 40
  end
  object Button1: TButton
    Caption = 'Change-Case Dialog'
    Default = True
    OnClick = Button1Click
  end
end
```

MODALD1U.PAS

```
unit Modald1u;

interface

uses SysUtils, WinTypes, WinProcs, Messages, Classes, Graphics,
  Controls, Forms, Dialogs, StdCtrls;

type
  TForm1 = class(TForm)
    Edit1: TEdit;
    Button1: TButton;
    procedure Button1Click(Sender: TObject);
  end;

var Form1: TForm1;

implementation
USES ModalD2u;
{$R *.DFM}

procedure TForm1.Button1Click(Sender: TObject);
begin
  WITH TForm2.Create(Application) DO
    try
      {load modal dialog with data}
      Label1.Caption := Edit1.Text;
      IF ShowModal = mrOK THEN
        {retrieve modified data}
        Edit1.Text := Label1.Caption;
    finally
      Free;
    end;
end;

end.
```

MODALD2U.DEX

```
object Form2: TForm2
  BorderStyle = bsDialog
  Caption = 'Change Case'
  Position = poDefault
  Scaled = False
  object Label1: TLabel
    Caption = 'Label1'
  end
  object RadioGroup1: TRadioGroup
    Caption = 'Case'
    Columns = 3
    Items.Strings = (
      '&UPPER CASE'
      '&lower case'
      '&Title Case')
```

```
    OnClick = RadioGroup1Click
  end
  object BitBtn1: TBitBtn
    Kind = bkOK
  end
  object BitBtn2: TBitBtn
    Kind = bkCancel
  end
end
```

MODALD2U.PAS

```
unit Modald2u;

interface

uses SysUtils, WinTypes, WinProcs, Messages, Classes, Graphics,
  Controls, Forms, Dialogs, StdCtrls, Buttons, ExtCtrls;

type
  TForm2 = class(TForm)
    Label1: TLabel;
    RadioGroup1: TRadioGroup;
    BitBtn1: TBitBtn;
    BitBtn2: TBitBtn;
    procedure RadioGroup1Click(Sender: TObject);
  end;

var Form2: TForm2;

implementation

{$R *.DFM}

procedure TForm2.RadioGroup1Click(Sender: TObject);
VAR
  N : Integer;
  S : String;
begin
  WITH Sender AS TRadioGroup DO
    CASE ItemIndex OF
      0 : Label1.Caption := AnsiUpperCase(Label1.Caption);
      1 : Label1.Caption := AnsiLowerCase(Label1.Caption);
      2 : BEGIN
        S := lowerCase(Label1.Caption);
        IF IsCharAlpha(S[1]) THEN
          AnsiUpperBuff(@S[1],1);
        FOR N := 2 TO Length(S) DO
          IF NOT IsCharAlpha(S[N-1]) THEN
            IF IsCharAlpha(S[N]) THEN
              AnsiUpperBuff(@S[N],1);
        Label1.Caption := S;
      END;
```

```
      END;
  end;

  end.
```

Study the Button1Click event handler in the main form's unit—it demonstrates the correct way to create and to use a modal dialog-box form:

- ◆ Create the dialog
- ◆ Start a try..finally block
- ◆ Load the dialog with data
- ◆ Call the dialog's ShowModal method
- ◆ If ShowModal returns mrOK, retrieve data from the dialog
- ◆ In the finally part of the try..finally block, free the dialog you created

Once you are accustomed to this style of coding, it becomes second nature. Do note that this advice is valid *only* for modal forms! Because the ShowModal method does not return until the user closes the form, it is safe to free the form after ShowModal. If you use Show for a nonmodal form, the secondary form must free itself upon being closed. That's easily accomplished by putting the line

```
  Action := caFree;
```

in its OnClose event handler.

Managing multiple form instances without MDI

16 32

When an application's main form's FormStyle is fsMDIForm, its MDIChildCount property holds the number of existing MDI child forms, and the MDIChildren array property gives access to all of them. That makes it easy to accomplish something like globally changing the base font for all forms. Wouldn't it be convenient if you could do the same kind of thing in a non-MDI program?

You can, of course, refer directly to the Delphi-generated form variables (named by default Form1, Form2, Form3 and so on). However, it's possible for your program to create valid instances of those form types without any reference to the specific variable. Fortunately, you can access all forms in a project through the Screen object.

Screen.FormCount is the number of active forms in the program, and Screen.Forms is an array that gives access to all of them. Figure 2-2 is an example of what is possible when you take charge of Screen.Forms.

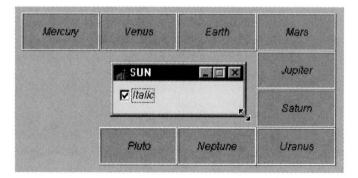

FIGURE 2-2: In this fanciful program, nine secondary windows are maintained at a steady "orbit" as the main program is moved or resized.

MANAGE

MANAGE1U.DEX

```
object Form1: TForm1
  BorderIcons = [biSystemMenu, biMinimize]
  Caption = 'SUN'
  Color = clYellow
  Scaled = False
  OnCreate = FormCreate
  object Button1: TButton
    Caption = '&Orbit'
    OnClick = Button1Click
  end
  object CheckBox1: TCheckBox
    Caption = 'Italic'
    OnClick = CheckBox1Click
  end
end
```

MANAGE1U.PAS

```
unit Manage1u;

interface

uses SysUtils, WinTypes, WinProcs, Messages, Classes, Graphics,
  Controls, Forms, Dialogs, StdCtrls, Manage2u;

type
  TForm1 = class(TForm)
    CheckBox1: TCheckBox;
```

```
    procedure FormCreate(Sender: TObject);
    procedure CheckBox1Click(Sender: TObject);
    procedure FormResize(Sender: TObject);
  private
    Planets: ARRAY[0..8] OF TForm2;
    procedure WMMove(VAR Msg: TWMMove); message WM_MOVE;
  end;

var Form1: TForm1;

implementation

{$R *.DFM}

procedure TForm1.FormCreate(Sender: TObject);
VAR N : Integer;
begin
  FOR N := 0 TO 8 DO Planets[N] := TForm2.Create(Application);
  WITH Planets[0] DO P.Caption := 'Mercury';
  WITH Planets[1] DO P.Caption := 'Venus';
  WITH Planets[2] DO P.Caption := 'Earth';
  WITH Planets[3] DO P.Caption := 'Mars';
  WITH Planets[4] DO P.Caption := 'Jupiter';
  WITH Planets[5] DO P.Caption := 'Saturn';
  WITH Planets[6] DO P.Caption := 'Uranus';
  WITH Planets[7] DO P.Caption := 'Neptune';
  WITH Planets[8] DO P.Caption := 'Pluto';
  FormResize(Self);
end;

procedure TForm1.FormResize(Sender: TObject);
VAR
  OrbitRect        : TRect;
  X, Y, dX, dY, N : Integer;
begin
  OrbitRect := BoundsRect;
  InflateRect(OrbitRect, 12, 12);
  X  := 0; Y  := 0;
  dX := 1; dY := 0;
  FOR N := 0 TO 8 DO
    WITH Planets[N] DO
      BEGIN
        IF X = 0 THEN
          BEGIN
            X := OrbitRect.Left-Width;
            Y := OrbitRect.Top-Height;
          END
        ELSE
          BEGIN
            X := X + dX * Width;
            Y := Y + dY * Height;
          END;
        SetBounds(X, Y, Width, Height);
        BringToFront;
        CASE dX OF
```

```
          1  : IF BoundsRect.Right>OrbitRect.Right THEN
                  BEGIN
                    dX := 0;
                    dY := 1;
                    X  := OrbitRect.Right;
                  END;
          0  : IF (dY > 0) AND (BoundsRect.Bottom >
                  OrbitRect.Bottom) THEN
                  BEGIN
                    dX := -1;
                    dY := 0;
                    Y  := OrbitRect.Bottom;
                  END;
         -1 : IF Left < OrbitRect.Left THEN
                  BEGIN
                    dX := 0;
                    dY := -1;
                    X  := OrbitRect.Left-Width;
                  END;
      END;
    END;
end;
procedure TForm1.CheckBox1Click(Sender: TObject);
VAR N : Integer;
begin
  FOR N := 0 TO Screen.FormCount-1 DO
    IF Screen.Forms[N] IS TForm2 THEN
      WITH Screen.Forms[N].Font DO
        IF (Sender AS TCheckBox).Checked THEN
          Style := Style + [fsItalic]
        ELSE Style := Style - [fsItalic];
end;
procedure TForm1.WMMove(VAR Msg: TWMMove);
begin
  Inherited;
  FormResize(Self);
end;

end.
```

MANAGE2U.DEX

```
object Form2: TForm2
  BorderIcons = []
  BorderStyle = bsNone
  Position = poDefault
  Scaled = False
  Visible = True
  object P: TPanel
    Align = alClient
    BevelInner = bvLowered
  end
end
```

The Pascal source for the secondary form is omitted here because it contains nothing but Delphi-created code. Upon creation, the main form creates nine instances of TForm2, assigning them to the nine elements of the private data field Planets. We'll come back to this array shortly.

When the user clicks the Italic check box, the program steps through the Screen object's Forms list, checking whether each of its elements is of type TForm2. If so, it sets that form's base font to include or exclude the fsItalic constant, depending on whether the check box is checked or empty.

The problem with the Screen object's Forms array is that the order of its elements is constantly in flux. Each time a particular form is activated, it moves to the front of the list, which is all right when all you're doing is changing the font for each secondary form. However, if you are using the same technique to place the secondary forms in "orbit" around the main form, their order repeatedly changes.

The Planets array created in the form's OnCreate event handler serves to allow in-order processing of the nine secondary windows. When the OnResize event handler is triggered, it calculates new positions for each of the secondary windows, starting to the left and above the main window and moving clockwise. This event is called directly from the OnCreate event handler, to set the initial placement of the secondary windows. It's also called from the WM_MOVE message response method, to ensure that the secondary windows move whenever the main window moves.

Any time you need to locate all forms of a given type, step through the Screen.Forms array, as the CheckBox1Click method does. If the processing order for the secondary forms is important, the program will have to create its own array, similar to the Planets array in the example program.

Creating a base form type and deriving descendants, even in Delphi 1.0

16 32

Delphi is an Object Oriented Programming (OOP) language that eases the process of creating new components by extending existing components. What a surprise, then, to find that you can't do the same for forms unless you're running Delphi 2.0! Delphi 2.0 has visual form inheritance; you can easily create TForm descendants and build new forms that inherit from them. Delphi 1.0 merely lets you create form templates, which are not true descendant objects. Once you create a new form based on a template, the connection is broken—improvements in the template will not be reflected in the form. And you simply can't use an object other than TForm as the basis for a new form in the Delphi 1.0 form designer.

If you're willing to stick with defining data fields and writing methods, you definitely *can* make use of TForm descendants in Delphi 1.0. Rather than create a specific example of this technique, we'll make use of it in answering the next question. The important point to remember is that *only* user-defined data fields and methods will be correctly passed along to the descendant forms. Components placed on the ancestor won't appear in the descendant, properties won't carry over, and event handlers will be stepped on if the descendant defines the same event handler. Virtual methods of TForm are fair game, as are data fields and methods you invent yourself. Again, this is a limitation of Delphi 1.0; Delphi 2.0 has visual inheritance.

 ## Reducing resource consumption by multipage forms

16 32

The TNotebook and TTabbedNotebook components (plus TPageControl in Delphi 2.0) let you put an amazing number of components on a single form by "layering" the form into multiple pages. However, when the form is active, *all* those components use memory and system resources. If you're not careful, your program could consume a substantial percentage of free system resources, especially in Windows 3.1.

The components on each page of a TNotebook aren't completely initialized until the first time that page is displayed. As a general rule, Delphi programs do not allocate system resources until they're needed. From that point on, though, the component continues to take up memory and resources.

One possible solution would be to create all the components on each page at the time the user flips to that page, and destroy them when another page becomes current. However, that would completely undermine Delphi's advantage of *visual* user interface design. A better solution is to create a separate form for each page and force the active one to be a child window of the main form. When the user clicks on a tab, the current page form is destroyed and an instance of the new form is created. Of course, the main form has to store any data specific to each page before destroying it, and load that data upon returning to the page. The program shown in Figure 2-3 has three different page form types, two of which are repeated, for a total of five pages.

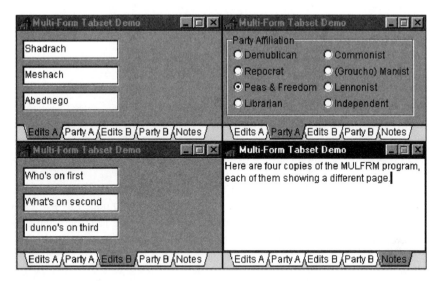

FIGURE 2-3: Each page of this multipage form is a separate form, created and destroyed as needed; four separate instances of the program are shown here.

PGFORM.PAS

```pascal
unit Pgform;

interface

uses SysUtils, WinTypes, WinProcs, Messages, Classes, Graphics,
  Controls, Forms, Dialogs, StdCtrls;

type
  TChildData = RECORD
    cdSize: Word;
    cdStorage: Pointer;
  END;

  TPageForm = class(TForm)
  private
    PROCEDURE CreateParams(VAR Params: TCreateParams);
      override;
  public
    PROCEDURE StoreData(VAR TC: TChildData); virtual; abstract;
    PROCEDURE LoadData(VAR TC: TChildData);  virtual; abstract;
  end;

implementation

PROCEDURE TPageForm.CreateParams(VAR Params: TCreateParams);
```

```
BEGIN
  Inherited  CreateParams(Params);
  WITH Params DO
    BEGIN
      WndParent := Application.MainForm.Handle;
      Style := WS_CHILD OR WS_CLIPSIBLINGS OR WS_CLIPCHILDREN;
      Align := alClient;
    END;
END;

end.
```

Every form you design to represent a page will need a CreateParams method to make it into a borderless child window of the main form. Each page form will also need a method to store its important data in the main form and to reload that data. The preceding source file defines a TForm descendant that incorporates these requirements.

Note that the entire unit is shown in boldface; that means you type the whole thing. There's no associated .DFM file, and no Delphi-created variable of this type. Each form in a page-form project will include this form in its uses clause.

MULFRM

MULFRM4U.DEX

```
object Form4: TForm4
  ActiveControl = Memo1
  Position = poDefault
  Scaled = False
  object Memo1: TMemo
    Align = alClient
  end
end
```

MULFRM4U.PAS

```
unit Mulfrm4u;

interface

uses SysUtils, WinTypes, WinProcs, Messages, Classes, Graphics,
  Controls, Forms, Dialogs, PgForm, StdCtrls, ExtCtrls;

type
  TForm4 = class(TPageForm)
    Memo1: TMemo;
  public
    PROCEDURE StoreData(VAR TC: TChildData); override;
    PROCEDURE LoadData(VAR TC: TChildData);  override;
  end;
```

```
var Form4: TForm4;

implementation

{$R *.DFM}
PROCEDURE TForm4.StoreData(VAR TC: TChildData);
BEGIN
  TC.cdSize := Memo1.GetTextLen+1;
  GetMem(TC.cdStorage, TC.cdSize);
  Memo1.GetTextBuf(PChar(TC.cdStorage), TC.cdSize);
END;

PROCEDURE TForm4.LoadData(VAR TC: TChildData);
BEGIN
  IF TC.cdStorage=NIL THEN
    Memo1.Text := 'Notes go here'
  ELSE
    BEGIN
      Memo1.SetTextBuf(TC.cdStorage);
      FreeMem(TC.cdStorage, TC.cdSize);
      TC.cdStorage := NIL;
    END;
END;

end.
```

MULFRM3U.DEX

```
object Form3: TForm3
  ActiveControl = RadioGroup1
  Position = poDefault
  Scaled = False
  object RadioGroup1: TRadioGroup
    Caption = 'Party Affiliation'
    Columns = 2
    Items.Strings = (
      'Demublican'
      'Repocrat'
      'Peas && Freedom'
      'Librarian'
      'Commonist'
      '(Groucho) Marxist'
      'Lennonist'
      'Independent')
  end
end
```

MULFRM3U.PAS

```
unit Mulfrm3u;

interface
```

```
uses SysUtils, WinTypes, WinProcs, Messages, Classes, Graphics,
  Controls, Forms, Dialogs, StdCtrls, ExtCtrls, PgForm;

type
  TForm3 = class(TPageForm)
    RadioGroup1: TRadioGroup;

  public
    PROCEDURE StoreData(VAR TC: TChildData); override;
    PROCEDURE LoadData(VAR TC: TChildData);  override;
  end;

var Form3: TForm3;

implementation

{$R *.DFM}
PROCEDURE TForm3.StoreData(VAR TC: TChildData);
BEGIN
  LongInt(TC.cdStorage) := RadioGroup1.ItemIndex +1;
END;

PROCEDURE TForm3.LoadData(VAR TC: TChildData);
BEGIN
  RadioGroup1.ItemIndex := LongInt(TC.cdStorage)-1;
END;

end.
```

MULFRM2U.DEX

```
object Form2: TForm2
  ActiveControl = Edit1
  Position = poDefault
  Scaled = False
  object Edit1: TEdit
  end
  object Edit2: TEdit
  end
  object Edit3: TEdit
  end
end
```

MULFRM2U.PAS

```
unit Mulfrm2u;

interface

uses SysUtils, WinTypes, WinProcs, Messages, Classes, Graphics,
  Controls, Forms, Dialogs, StdCtrls, PgForm;
```

```
type
  TForm2 = class(TPageForm)
    Edit1: TEdit;
    Edit2: TEdit;
    Edit3: TEdit;
  public
    PROCEDURE StoreData(VAR TC: TChildData); override;
    PROCEDURE LoadData(VAR TC: TChildData);  override;
  end;

var Form2: TForm2;

implementation

{$R *.DFM}
PROCEDURE TForm2.StoreData(VAR TC: TChildData);
VAR PC : PChar;
BEGIN
  TC.cdSize := Edit1.GetTextLen +
             Edit2.GetTextLen +
             Edit3.GetTextLen + 4;
  GetMem(TC.cdStorage, TC.cdSize);
  PC := TC.cdStorage;
  Edit1.GetTextBuf(PC, TC.cdSize);
  PC := StrEnd(PC) + 1;
  Edit2.GetTextBuf(PC, TC.cdSize);
  PC := StrEnd(PC) + 1;
  Edit3.GetTextBuf(PC, TC.cdSize);
END;

PROCEDURE TForm2.LoadData(VAR TC: TChildData);
VAR PC : PChar;
BEGIN
  IF TC.cdStorage=NIL THEN
    BEGIN
      Edit1.Text := 'Curly';
      Edit2.Text := 'Larry';
      Edit3.Text := 'Moe';
    END
  ELSE
    BEGIN
      PC := TC.cdStorage;
      Edit1.Text := StrPas(PC);
      PC := StrEnd(PC) + 1;
      Edit2.Text := StrPas(PC);
      PC := StrEnd(PC) + 1;
      Edit3.Text := StrPas(PC);
      FreeMem(TC.cdStorage, TC.cdSize);
      TC.cdStorage := NIL;
    END;
END;

end.
```

MULFRM1U.DEX

```
object Form1: TForm1
  Caption = 'Multi-Form Tabset Demo'
  Position = poDefault
  Scaled = False
  OnActivate = FormActivate
  object TabSet1: TTabSet
    Align = alBottom
    Tabs.Strings = (
      'Edits A'
      'Party A'
      'Edits B'
      'Party B'
      'Notes')
    TabIndex = 0
    OnChange = TabSet1Change
  end
end
```

MULFRM1U.PAS

```
unit Mulfrm1u;

interface

uses SysUtils, WinTypes, WinProcs, Messages, Classes, Graphics,
  Controls, Forms, Dialogs, Tabs, PgForm;

type
  TForm1 = class(TForm)
    TabSet1: TTabSet;
    procedure FormActivate(Sender: TObject);
    procedure TabSet1Change(Sender: TObject; NewTab: Integer;
      var AllowChange: Boolean);
  private
    Child : TPageForm;
    ChildData: ARRAY[0..4] OF TChildData;
  end;

var Form1: TForm1;

implementation
USES MulFrm2u, MulFrm3u, MulFrm4u;
{$R *.DFM}

procedure TForm1.FormActivate(Sender: TObject);
begin
  FillChar(ChildData, SizeOf(ChildData), 0);
  Child := TForm2.Create(Application);
  Child.Parent := Self;
  Child.LoadData(ChildData[0]);
  Child.Show;
```

```
    ActiveControl := Child.ActiveControl;
  end;
procedure TForm1.TabSet1Change(Sender: TObject; NewTab: Integer;
  var AllowChange: Boolean);
begin
  LockWindowUpdate(Handle);
  WITH Sender AS TTabSet DO
    Child.StoreData(ChildData[TabIndex]);
  Child.Free;
  CASE NewTab OF
    0, 2 : Child := TForm2.Create(Application);
    1, 3 : Child := TForm3.Create(Application);
    4    : Child := TForm4.Create(Application);
  END;
  Child.Parent := Self;
  Child.LoadData(ChildData[NewTab]);
  LockWindowUpdate(0);
  Child.Show;
  ActiveControl := Child.ActiveControl;
end;

end.
```

Delphi will only create direct TForm descendants, but once a form is created, you can *change* its ancestry quite easily. Just add PgForm to the uses clause at the start of the program, and change TForm to TPageForm in the first line of the form object definition.

You'll also have to define public StoreData and LoadData methods specific to each form. If the form has no data that needs to be saved, you still must indicate that fact by providing do-nothing methods. The methods of TPageForm are defined as *abstract*, which means they must never be directly called. Finally, you must be sure to move all the page forms from the Auto-Create list to the Available list in the Forms page of the Project Options dialog box.

In the example program, the TForm4 form only contains a memo box. To store its data, it calls the memo box's GetTextLen method to determine the required storage, then it copies the data using its GetTextBuf method. Note that here and in each secondary form the data is stored in a variable that belongs to the main form. The LoadData method loads the memo box's text from the passed storage pointer, inserting a default string if the pointer is NIL. Of course, if this program were meant for Delphi 2.0 and only Delphi 2.0, it could refer directly to the memo's Text property, without resorting to GetTextBuf. However, as written, it is compatible with both versions of Delphi.

The stored data for TForm3 is simply a single integer that defines which radio button is selected. There's no need to deal with allocating and deallocating storage. The

StoreData method assigns the current item plus one to the storage pointer, and the LoadData method sets the current item to the numeric value of the pointer minus one. When it's first loaded, the form receives a NIL pointer. The numeric equivalent is zero, so the initial ItemIndex will be −1, meaning no item has been selected.

TForm2 is a more typical dialog-style form with several edit boxes. To store the data, it allocates enough space to hold the text of all three edit boxes, then concatenates that text within the allocated space. To load the data, it simply extracts the three strings. Here again the LoadData method defines special default behavior if the data pointer passed to it is NIL.

Finally, we get to the main form of the project, which has no components except a tab set across the bottom. In its OnCreate event handler, it initializes the child data field to be an instance of TForm2, calls the child form's LoadData method, displays it, and sets the main form's active control to be the child form's active control.

When the user clicks on a new tab, the main form stores the current child form's data and frees the form. Then, depending on which tab was clicked, it initializes the child data field to a new form. It calls the LoadData method for the new child, displays it, and sets the active control as before.

If you decide to *convert* an existing multipage form to this style, here's a tip for moving the components from each page. Hold down Ctrl while you drag a box around all the components on one page—that will select them without reference to the underlying page. Now, cut them from the notebook and paste them into a new form. Transmogrify the new form into a TPageForm descendant as described above, add LoadData and StoreData methods, and you're finished.

Creating a multipage form program in this way is definitely more work than just using one of Delphi's notebook-type components. However, a program created in this way will have substantially less impact on free system resources. If your programs need to run under Windows 3.1, that can be a very serious consideration.

Form Miscellany

This section is a catch-all for useful and unusual techniques involving forms. You'll learn, among other things, how to add the question-mark help button to the caption bar of 32-bit programs, and how to simulate it for 16-bit programs.

Controlling the sizing of a form

16 32

Delphi 1.0 offers four border styles for forms; one can be resized freely, the other three have fixed size at run time. Delphi 2.0 adds two more border styles, one resizeable and one fixed. Sometimes, though, you might want to let the user resize a form, but only within a certain range.

Windows provides the solution to this one with the WM_GETMINMAXINFO message. Before an on-screen window is resized, Windows sends this message to it, passing a pointer to a structure containing four pairs of coordinates that define:

1. The size of the maximized window

2. The position of the maximized window

3. The largest size for a nonmaximized window

4. The smallest size for a nonmaximized window

Windows fills these coordinates with default values, but your program can respond to this message and *change* those values. The program shown in Figure 2-4 demonstrates a few of the many possibilities.

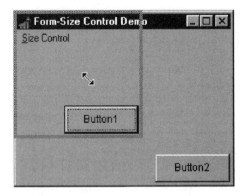

FIGURE 2-4: By responding to WM_GETMINMAXINFO, this form limits resizing to the range from the bottom corner of Button1 to the bottom corner of Button2.

SIZCTRL

SIZCTRLU.DEX

```
object Form1: TForm1
  AutoScroll = False
  Caption = 'Form-Size Control Demo'
  Menu = MainMenu1
  OnCreate = FormCreate
  object Button1: TButton
    Caption = 'Button1'
  end
  object Button2: TButton
    Caption = 'Button2'
  end
  object MainMenu1: TMainMenu
    object SizeControl1: TMenuItem
      Caption = '&Size Control'
      object none1: TMenuItem
        Caption = '&None'
        Checked = True
        OnClick = AllMenuClick
      end
      object S1: TMenuItem
        Tag = 1
        Caption = 'Show &All Controls'
        OnClick = AllMenuClick
      end
      object LimitedRange1: TMenuItem
        Tag = 2
        Caption = 'Limited &Range'
        OnClick = AllMenuClick
      end
      object ScreenTop1: TMenuItem
        Tag = 3
        Caption = 'Screen &Top Maximize'
        OnClick = AllMenuClick
      end
    end
  end
end
```

SIZCTRLU.PAS

```
unit Sizctrlu;

interface

uses SysUtils, WinTypes, WinProcs, Messages, Classes, Graphics,
  Controls, Forms, Dialogs, Menus, StdCtrls;
```

```
type
  TForm1 = class(TForm)
    MainMenu1: TMainMenu;
    SizeControl1: TMenuItem;
    Button1: TButton;
    none1: TMenuItem;
    S1: TMenuItem;
    LimitedRange1: TMenuItem;
    ScreenTop1: TMenuItem;
    Button2: TButton;
    procedure FormCreate(Sender: TObject);
    procedure AllMenuClick(Sender: TObject);
  private
    MaxPt : TPoint;
    Sz    : Integer;
    procedure WmGetMinMaxInfo(VAR Msg: TWmGetMinMaxInfo);
      message WM_GETMINMAXINFO;
  end;

var Form1: TForm1;

implementation

{$R *.DFM}

procedure TForm1.FormCreate(Sender: TObject);
VAR
  N    : Word;
  NuPt : TPoint;
begin
  MaxPt := Point(0,0);
  FOR N := 0 TO ControlCount-1 DO
    WITH Controls[N].BoundsRect DO
      BEGIN
        NuPt := Point(Right + 1 + Width - ClientWidth,
          Bottom + 1 + Height - ClientHeight);
        IF NuPt.X > MaxPt.X THEN MaxPt.X := NuPt.X;
        IF NuPt.Y > MaxPt.Y THEN MaxPt.Y := NuPt.Y;
      END;
end;

procedure TForm1.WmGetMinMaxInfo(VAR Msg: TWmGetMinMaxInfo);
BEGIN
  WITH Msg.MinMaxInfo^ DO
    CASE Sz OF
      1 : PtMinTrackSize := MaxPt;
      2 : WITH Button1.BoundsRect DO
            BEGIN
              PtMinTrackSize.X := Right + 1 + Width - ClientWidth;
              PtMinTrackSize.Y := Bottom + Height - ClientHeight+1;
              PtMaxTrackSize := MaxPt;
            END;
      3 : BEGIN
            PtMaxSize.Y := Self.Height - Self.ClientHeight;
            PtMaxTrackSize.Y := PtMaxSize.Y;
```

```
          END;
      END;
  END;
  procedure TForm1.AllMenuClick(Sender: TObject);
  VAR N : Integer;
  begin
    WITH SizeControl1 DO
      FOR N := 0 TO Count-1 DO
        Items[N].Checked := Items[N] = Sender;
    WITH Sender AS TMenuItem DO Sz := Tag;
    SetBounds(Left+1, Top, Width, Height);
    SetBounds(Left-1, Top, Width, Height);
  end;

  end.
```

The form's OnCreate event handler sets the private data field MaxPt to the bottom right corner of a rectangle that encloses all components on the form. To do so, it steps through the Controls array property which lists all components that have the form as their parent (as opposed to having another component as their parent). For each such component, it adjusts the X or Y value of MaxPt as necessary.

Each of the four menu choices has a different Tag property, from 0 to 3, and all four are connected to the same OnClick event handler. This handler sets the Checked property of the selected menu item to True and sets the other three to False. It sets the private data field Sz to the selected item's Tag. Finally, it tweaks the form's size to force a WM_GETMINMAXINFO call using the newly selected mode.

The WM_GETMINMAXINFO message handler modifies the MinMaxInfo structure passed to it in order to control the form's sizing. If the user selected Show All Controls, it sets the PtMinTrackSize field to MaxPt, calculated earlier. If Limit Size was chosen, it sets PtMaxTrackSize to MaxPt and PtMinTrackSize to the bottom right corner of Button1, thus limiting resizing to the range between the corners of the two buttons. And, if Screen Top Maximize was the choice, it sets the Y (height) value of both PtMaxSize and PtMaxTrackSize so that only the menu shows. When the form is maximized, it hugs the top edge of the screen just as Delphi does.

By setting various elements of the data structure passed with the WM_GETMIN-MAXINFO message, you can fine-tune the sizing of your forms. There's no need to settle for the all-or-nothing sizing you get by setting BorderStyle.

Modifying a form generated by MessageDlg

16 32

The handy MessageDlg function displays the string passed to it in a standard form, with an icon indicating the message type, and with one or more buttons. However, the caption is always Warning, Error, Information, or Confirm, and the font and color are always the same.

For a more distinctive message dialog, you could rewrite MessageDlg from scratch. However, with a small amount of chicanery, you can take advantage of the existing MessageDlg code and still control the appearance of the window, as Figure 2-5 shows.

FIGURE 2-5: Moments after its creation, this MessageDlg was modified by an OnTimer event handler in the program that created it.

MODMSGD

MODMSGDU.DEX

```
object Form1: TForm1
  BorderIcons = [biSystemMenu, biMinimize]
  BorderStyle = bsSingle
  Caption = 'MessageDlg Modification'
  object TLabel
    Caption = '&Caption:'
    FocusControl = Edit1
  end
  object Label1: TLabel
    AutoSize = False
```

```
          Caption = 'Sample'
          Color = clYellow
          Font.Color = clBlue
          ParentColor = False
          ParentFont = False
        end
        object TLabel
          Caption = 'Co&lor:'
          FocusControl = ColorGrid1
        end
        object Bevel1: TBevel
          Align = alTop
          Shape = bsBottomLine
        end
        object Button2: TButton
          Caption = '&Modified MessageDlg'
          OnClick = Button2Click
        end
        object Button1: TButton
          Caption = '&Ordinary MessageDlg'
          OnClick = Button1Click
        end
        object Edit1: TEdit
          Text = 'Red Alert!'
        end
        object ColorGrid1: TColorGrid
          ForegroundIndex = 4
          BackgroundIndex = 11
          OnChange = ColorGrid1Change
        end
        object Button3: TButton
          Caption = '&Font...'
          OnClick = Button3Click
        end
        object FontDialog1: TFontDialog
          MinFontSize = 8
          MaxFontSize = 36
          Options = [fdForceFontExist, fdLimitSize]
        end
        object Timer1: TTimer
          Enabled = False
          Interval = 50
          OnTimer = Timer1Timer
        end
      end
    end
```

MODMSGDU.PAS

```
unit Modmsgdu;

interface
```

```
uses SysUtils, WinTypes, WinProcs, Messages, Classes, Graphics,
  Controls, Forms, Dialogs, ExtCtrls, ColorGrd, StdCtrls;
type
  TForm1 = class(TForm)
    Button2: TButton;
    Button1: TButton;
    Edit1: TEdit;
    ColorGrid1: TColorGrid;
    Label1: TLabel;
    Button3: TButton;
    FontDialog1: TFontDialog;
    Bevel1: TBevel;
    Timer1: TTimer;
    procedure Timer1Timer(Sender: TObject);
    procedure Button1Click(Sender: TObject);
    procedure ColorGrid1Change(Sender: TObject);
    procedure Button3Click(Sender: TObject);
    procedure Button2Click(Sender: TObject);
  end;

var Form1: TForm1;

implementation

{$R *.DFM}
procedure TForm1.ColorGrid1Change(Sender: TObject);
begin
  Label1.Color := (Sender AS TColorGrid).BackgroundColor;
  Label1.Font.Color := (Sender AS TColorGrid).ForegroundColor;
end;

procedure TForm1.Button1Click(Sender: TObject);
begin
  MessageDlg('This is not a very important message', mtInformation,
    [mbOk, mbCancel], 0);
end;

procedure TForm1.Button2Click(Sender: TObject);
begin
  Timer1.Enabled := True;
  MessageDlg('This is a very important message, too important for'+
    ' an ordinary MessageDlg', mtInformation, [mbOk, mbCancel], 0);
end;

procedure TForm1.Button3Click(Sender: TObject);
begin
  FontDialog1.Font := Label1.Font;
  IF FontDialog1.Execute THEN
    Label1.Font := FontDialog1.Font;
end;

procedure TForm1.Timer1Timer(Sender: TObject);
VAR
  TheMessageDlg : TForm;
  N             : Integer;
  TheLabel      : TLabel;
```

```
       R1, R2        : TRect;
       Buff          : ARRAY[0..255] OF Char;
begin
   TheMessageDlg := NIL;
   {message dialog will be the only plain TForm}
   FOR N := 0 TO Screen.FormCount-1 DO
     IF Screen.Forms[N].ClassName = 'TForm' THEN
       BEGIN
         TheMessageDlg := Screen.Forms[N];
         Break;
       END;
   IF TheMessageDlg = NIL THEN Exit;
   (Sender AS TTimer).Enabled := False;
   WITH TheMessageDlg DO
     BEGIN
       {Set the caption of our choice}
       Caption  := Edit1.Text;
       TheLabel := NIL;
       {Locate the message label, ensure button fonts unchanged}
       FOR N := 0 TO ControlCount-1 DO
         IF Controls[N] IS TLabel THEN
           TheLabel := TLabel(Controls[N])
         ELSE IF Controls[N].InheritsFrom(TButton) THEN
           WITH TButton(Controls[N]) DO
             ParentFont := FALSE;
       IF TheLabel = NIL THEN Exit;
       {Get current text rectangle, considering word-wrap}
       R1 := Rect(0,0,Width-10-TheLabel.Left, 0);
       DrawText(Canvas.Handle, StrPCopy(Buff, TheLabel.Caption), -1,
         R1, DT_CALCRECT OR DT_WORDBREAK);
       {Set the new font and color}
       Color := Label1.Color;
       Font  := Label1.Font;
       Tag := 0;
       {Get the new text rectangle}
       R2 := Rect(0, 0, Width - 10 - TheLabel.Left, 0);
       DrawText(Canvas.Handle, StrPCopy(Buff, TheLabel.Caption), -1,
         R2, DT_CALCRECT OR DT_WORDBREAK);
       {Expand the window and move the buttons}
       Height := Height + R2.Bottom - R1.Bottom;
       FOR N := 0 TO ControlCount-1 DO
         IF Controls[N].InheritsFrom(TButton) THEN
           WITH Controls[N] AS TButton DO
             Top := Top + R2.Bottom - R1.Bottom;
     END;
end;
end.
```

This example program is a test bed for modifying message dialogs—it allows you to choose the foreground color, the background color, the font, and the title for the dialog. A standard font common dialog provides a choice of fonts. The actual modifications take place in the Timer1Timer method; to create a modified message dialog, simply enable the timer just before calling the MessageDlg function.

The OnTimer event handler method starts by seeking the MessageDlg form in the Screen.Forms array. Every form created in the Delphi form designer is a descendant of TForm, but the message dialog is a pure, unadorned TForm. If the form isn't found, the method simply exits and tries again on its next activation. When it *does* find the form, it disables the timer and continues.

After setting the message dialog's caption to the desired text, the event handler seeks the label that holds the message. It also sets the ParentFont property of any buttons to False, so changes to the dialog's font will not affect the buttons.

Now we use a nifty feature of the Windows API function DrawText. When called with flags DT_CALCRECT and DT_WORDBREAK, DrawText draws nothing, but calculates the size of the rectangle needed to hold the word-wrapped text. The OnTimer event handler performs this calculation before and after changing the message dialog's font. It changes the window height by the difference, and moves the buttons as well.

Whew! That was quite a bit of work just to change the appearance of a MessageDlg. However, if you look at the VCL source code file DIALOGS.PAS, you'll see that duplicating MessageDlg would also be quite a bit of work.

Using the nifty Windows 95 question-mark help icon

32

You may have noticed that many Windows 95 windows have a new button on the title bar. It's a little question mark, and when you press the button, the cursor changes to an arrow with a question mark. Click on a control in the window and a panel with help about that control appears. How can you add this functionality to your Delphi forms?

Delphi 2.0 makes adding and supporting the help button incredibly simple. Double-click the form's BorderStyle property, set biHelp to True, and set biMaximize and biMinimize to False. Now, under both Windows 95 and Windows NT, the form will sport a help button icon. Naturally, you must supply a help file containing short topics for each control you want handled in this way. Figure 2-6 shows what the help panel looks like.

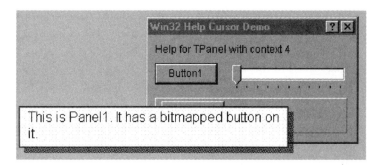

FIGURE 2-6: Click on the Windows 95 title bar help button and click on a component; if help is defined for that component, you'll see it in a panel.

HELPBTN

HELPBTNU.DEX

```
object Form1: TForm1
  BorderIcons = [biSystemMenu, biHelp]
  Caption = 'Win32 Help Cursor Demo'
  Position = poDefault
  Scaled = False
  object Button1: TButton
    HelpContext = 1
    Caption = 'Button1'
  end
  object TrackBar1: TTrackBar
    HelpContext = 2
    Orientation = trHorizontal
  end
  object Panel1: TPanel
    HelpContext = 4
    Caption = 'Panel1'
    object BitBtn1: TBitBtn
      HelpContext = 3
      Kind = bkYes
    end
  end
end
```

HELPBTNU.PAS

```
unit helpbtnu;
{$IFNDEF Win32}
Halt! 32-bit Delphi required. For 16-bit Delphi, use HELPCUR.DPR.
{$ENDIF}
interface
```

```
uses SysUtils, Windows, Messages, Classes, Graphics, Controls,
  Forms, Dialogs, StdCtrls, Buttons, ExtCtrls, ComCtrls;
type
  TForm1 = class(TForm)
    Button1: TButton;
    TrackBar1: TTrackBar;
    Panel1: TPanel;
    BitBtn1: TBitBtn;
  end;
var Form1: TForm1;
implementation
{$R *.DFM}
end.
```

When the user clicks the help cursor on a control, a panel window appears displaying the help page corresponding to the control's HelpContext property.

Any time you write a dialog-type window for use solely in 32-bit Windows, consider including this help button functionality.

Simulating the question-mark help icon in Windows 3.1

 16

You can only use the built-in support for the Windows 95-style help button in a 32-bit program. Once you get accustomed to it, though, you may regret its absence in your 16-bit programs. Fortunately, you can simulate the help button quite nicely in 16-bit Delphi, as Figure 2-7 shows.

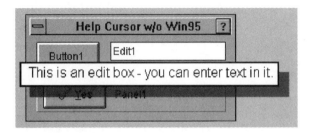

FIGURE 2-7: The help button on this 16-bit program functions just like the Windows 95 help button.

HELPCUR

HELPCURU.DEX

```
object Form1: TForm1
  BorderStyle = bsDialog
  Caption = 'Help Cursor w/o Win95'
  Ctl3D = False
  Color = clBtnFace
  Position = poDefault
  Scaled = False
  OnCreate = FormCreate
  OnMouseUp = FormMouseUp
  object Button1: TButton
    HelpContext = 1
    Caption = 'Button1'
  end
  object Panel1: TPanel
    HelpContext = 4
    Caption = 'Panel1'
    object BitBtn1: TBitBtn
      HelpContext = 3
      Kind = bkYes
    end
  end
  object Edit1: TEdit
    HelpContext = 5
    Text = 'Edit1'
  end
end
```

HELPCURU.PAS

```
unit Helpcuru;

interface

uses SysUtils, WinTypes, WinProcs, Messages, Classes, Graphics,
  Controls, Forms, Dialogs, Buttons, ExtCtrls, StdCtrls;

type
  TForm1 = class(TForm)
    Button1: TButton;
    Panel1: TPanel;
    BitBtn1: TBitBtn;
    Edit1: TEdit;
    procedure FormMouseUp(Sender: TObject; Button: TMouseButton;
      Shift: TShiftState; X, Y: Integer);
    procedure FormCreate(Sender: TObject);
  private
    NewButton : TRect;
    procedure DrawNewButton;
```

```
      procedure WMNCPaint(VAR Msg: TWMNCPaint);
        message WM_NCPAINT;
      procedure WMNCActivate(VAR Msg: TWMNCActivate);
        message WM_NCACTIVATE;
      procedure WMSetText(VAR Msg: TWMSetText);
        message WM_SETTEXT;
      procedure WMNCHitTest(VAR Msg: TWMNCHitTest);
        message WM_NCHITTEST;
      procedure WMNCLButtonUp(VAR Msg: TWMNCLButtonUp);
        message WM_NCLBUTTONUP;
  end;

var Form1: TForm1;

implementation
const
  HTHLPBTN = htSizeLast+1;
  SM_CXSMSIZE = 52;
  SM_CYSMSIZE = 53;

{$IFDEF Win32}
{$R HELPAR32.RES}
{$ELSE}
{$R HELPAR16.RES}
{$ENDIF}

{$R *.DFM}
procedure TForm1.FormCreate(Sender: TObject);
begin
  Screen.Cursors[1] := LoadCursor(hInstance, 'HELPARROW');
end;

procedure TForm1.FormMouseUp(Sender: TObject; Button:
  TMouseButton; Shift: TShiftState; X, Y: Integer);
VAR HelpControl : TControl;
begin
  IF Screen.Cursor = 1 THEN
    BEGIN
      HelpControl := FindDragTarget(ClientToScreen(
        Point(X,Y)), True);
      Screen.Cursor := crDefault;
      ReleaseCapture;
      IF HelpControl <> NIL THEN
        IF HelpControl IS TWinControl THEN
          IF TWinControl(HelpControl).HelpContext > 0 THEN
            Application.HelpCommand(HELP_CONTEXTPOPUP,
              TWinControl(HelpControl).HelpContext);
    END;
end;

procedure TForm1.DrawNewButton;
VAR
  R   : TRect;
  Vert: Integer;
begin
  IF Swap(LoWord(GetVersion)) >= $35F THEN
```

```
      NewButton := Bounds(Width - GetSystemMetrics(SM_CXDLGFRAME) -
        2*GetSystemMetrics(SM_CXSMSIZE) - 6,
        GetSystemMetrics(SM_CYDLGFRAME) + 2,
        GetSystemMetrics(SM_CXSMSIZE),
        GetSystemMetrics(SM_CYSMSIZE))
    ELSE
      NewButton := Bounds(Width - GetSystemMetrics(SM_CXDLGFRAME) -
        GetSystemMetrics(SM_CXSIZE) - 2,
        GetSystemMetrics(SM_CYDLGFRAME) + 1,
        GetSystemMetrics(SM_CXSIZE),
        GetSystemMetrics(SM_CYSIZE));
    Canvas.Handle := GetWindowDC(Self.Handle);
    WITH Canvas DO
      try
        Font.Name := 'Arial';
        Font.Size := 9;
        Font.Style := [fsBold];
        SetTextAlign(Handle, TA_CENTER);
        R := DrawButtonFace(Canvas, NewButton, 1, bsAutoDetect,
          False, False, False);
        InflateRect(R, -1, -1);
        IF Swap(LoWord(GetVersion)) >= $35F THEN Vert := 4
        ELSE Vert := 7;
        TextRect(R, (R.Right+R.Left) DIV 2, Vert, '?');
      finally
        ReleaseDC(Self.Handle, Handle);
        Handle := 0;
      end;
end;

procedure TForm1.WMNCPaint(VAR Msg: TWMNCPaint);
BEGIN
  Inherited;
  DrawNewButton;
END;

procedure TForm1.WMNCActivate(VAR Msg: TWMNCActivate);
BEGIN
  Inherited;
  DrawNewButton;
END;

procedure TForm1.WMSetText(VAR Msg: TWMSetText);
BEGIN
  Inherited;
  DrawNewButton;
END;

procedure TForm1.WMNCHitTest(VAR Msg: TWMNCHitTest);
BEGIN
  Inherited;
  WITH Msg DO
    IF PtInRect(NewButton, Point(XPos-Left, YPos-Top)) THEN
      Result := htHlpBtn;
END;
```

```
procedure TForm1.WMNCLButtonUp(VAR Msg: TWMNCLButtonUp);
begin
  Inherited;
  IF Msg.HitTest=htHlpBtn THEN
    IF Screen.Cursor = crDefault THEN
      BEGIN
        Screen.Cursor := 1;
        SetCapture(Handle);
      END;
end;
end.
```

As you can see, there's a lot more work involved when the operating system isn't managing the help cursor. First, the program has to place a button on the form's title bar—you learned how to do that in Chapter 1, "Form Basics." It responds to the WM_NCHITTEST message by setting the result to a particular value when the mouse cursor is over the help button. And, when the user clicks on the help button, it sets the system cursor to a user-defined cursor that resembles the Windows 95 help cursor. Finally, it calls the Windows API function SetCapture to send all mouse events to the form until further notice.

The form's OnMouseUp event handler checks whether the special cursor is active. If so, it calls the FindDragTarget function to access the component that's under the cursor. It restores the cursor and releases the mouse. Then, if the cursor was over a valid component that has a nonzero HelpContext, it displays the help for that component in a context-based, pop-up window.

This help-button simulation is somewhat awkward, and doesn't support every feature of the help button built into Windows 95 and Windows NT. Use the native operating system help button in 32-bit programs; only use the simulation when compiling for 16-bit Windows.

Revealing a hidden form when the mouse is at the edge of the screen

16 32

A Delphi form can respond to mouse events that occur within its boundaries. A 16-bit program can also call SetCapture to trap all mouse events anywhere on the screen, but this prevents other windows from getting mouse events. (32-bit programs can only capture mouse events for windows within the same process.) How can a hidden window automatically reveal itself when the mouse moves, for example, to the top of the screen?

In order to get notification of all mouse events, a program needs to establish a hook function for the WH_MOUSE hook. This is a highly nonvisual, non-OOP process—it happens via API function calls, and the hook callback function must reside in a Dynamic Link Library (DLL). Here's a sample DLL that sends the window that invoked it a special message whenever the mouse comes near the edge of the screen.

MOUSHOOK

MOUSHOOK.DPR

```
Library Moushook;

USES WinTypes, WinProcs;

{$I DLLSHARE.INC}

VAR PSH : PSharedData;

function MouseProc(Code: Integer; wParam: Cardinal; lParam:
  LongInt) : LongInt; Export; {$IFDEF Win32}StdCall;{$ENDIF}
VAR
  hMap    : THandle;
  TB, LR : Integer;
BEGIN
  Result := 0;
  {$IFDEF Win32}
  hMap := OpenFileMapping(FILE_MAP_ALL_ACCESS, False, MapName);
  IF hMap = 0 THEN Exit;
  PSH := MapViewOfFile(hMap, FILE_MAP_ALL_ACCESS, 0, 0, 0);
  IF PSH = NIL THEN
    BEGIN
      CloseHandle(hMap);
      Exit;
    END;
  {$ELSE}
  IF PSH = NIL THEN Exit;
  {$ENDIF}
  IF Code >= 0 THEN
    WITH PMouseHookStruct(lParam)^, Pt DO
      BEGIN
        IF X < PSH^.Threshold THEN
          LR := 1      {left}
        ELSE IF X > PSH^.SWid - PSH^.Threshold THEN
          LR := 2      {right}
        ELSE LR := 0;  {neither}
        IF Y < PSH^.Threshold THEN
          TB := 3      {top}
        ELSE IF Y > PSH^.SHig - PSH^.Threshold THEN
          TB := 6      {bottom}
        ELSE TB := 0;  {neither}
        {TB+LR+9 = htLeft thru htBottomRight}
        IF TB+LR > 0 THEN
          SendMessage(PSH^.HWnd, PSH^.EdgeMessage, TB+LR+9, 0);
      END;
```

```
    IF PSH^.OldH <> 0 THEN
      Result := CallNextHookEx(PSH^.OldH, code, wParam, lParam);
    {$IFDEF Win32}
    UnMapViewOfFile(PSH);
    CloseHandle(hMap);
    {$ENDIF}
END;

Function HookMouse(P : PSharedData) : HHook; Export;
BEGIN
  PSH := P; {pointless but harmless in Win32}
  Result := SetWindowsHookEx(WH_MOUSE,
    {$IFDEF Win32}@{$ENDIF}MouseProc, hInstance, 0);
end;

PROCEDURE UnHookMouse(OldH : HHook); Export;
BEGIN
  UnHookWindowsHookEx(OldH);
END;

EXPORTS
  HookMouse      INDEX 1,
  UnHookMouse    INDEX 2;

begin
end.
```

DLLSHARE.INC

```
TYPE

  TSharedData = RECORD
    HWnd        : Integer;
    EdgeMessage : Cardinal;
    OldH        : HHook;
    Threshold   : Integer;
    SWid, SHig  : Integer;
  END;
  PSharedData = ^TSharedData;

CONST MapName = 'NJRMouseHookSharedData';
```

The DLL needs to store the window handle of the calling program, and that presents a real problem. In 32-bit Windows, global variables in a DLL are not shared when different processes invoke the DLL. And, in effect, any running process "invokes" this DLL when the mouse hook callback is activated. In short, the DLL cannot rely on global variables.

The solution involves using a *memory-mapped file* created by the program that invokes the DLL. A memory-mapped file is effectively a shared area of memory—a program that opens the memory-mapped file ends up with a pointer that can be used to access the data in the memory-mapped file. In this example, the include file

DLLSHARE.INC defines a data type for the shared data and a constant name for the memory-mapped file. When the DLL is compiled under 32-bit Delphi, the mouse hook procedure opens the memory-mapped file and uses the resulting pointer any time it needs access to "global" variables. If 16-bit Delphi is used, the same pointer variable is simply initialized to point to a shared data area in the calling program.

With the intricacies of 32-bit Windows hooks out of the way, the DLL is quite simple. The mouse hook procedure is called on any mouse event, system-wide. If the mouse is within a specific number of pixels from one of the screen edges or corners, the hook procedure sends back a message that encodes which edge or corner the mouse approached. Figure 2-8 shows a program that makes use of this DLL.

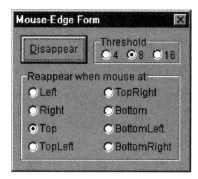

FIGURE 2-8: Select an edge or corner of the screen and press the button; the form is invisible until the mouse cursor comes close to the selected edge or corner.

EDGE

EDGEU.DEX

```
object Form1: TForm1
  BorderIcons = [biSystemMenu]
  BorderStyle = bsDialog
  Caption = 'Mouse-Edge Form'
  Position = poDefault
  Scaled = False
  OnCreate = FormCreate
  OnDestroy = FormDestroy
  object RadioGroup1: TRadioGroup
    Caption = 'Reappear when mouse at:'
    Columns = 2
    ItemIndex = 2
    Items.Strings = (
      'Left'
```

```
              'Right'
              'Top'
              'TopLeft'
              'TopRight'
              'Bottom'
              'BottomLeft'
              'BottomRight')
        end
        object Button1: TButton
          Caption = '&Disappear'
          Default = True
          OnClick = Button1Click
        end
        object RadioGroup2: TRadioGroup
          Caption = 'Threshold'
          Columns = 3
          ItemIndex = 1
          Items.Strings = (
            '4'
            '8'
            '16')
          OnClick = RadioGroup2Click
        end
      end
```

EDGEU.PAS

```
      unit Edgeu;

      interface

      uses SysUtils, WinTypes, WinProcs, Messages, Classes, Graphics,
        Controls, Forms, Dialogs, StdCtrls, ExtCtrls;

      {$I DLLSHARE.INC}

      type
        HookMouseType = function(P: PSharedData) : HHook;
        UnHookMouseType = PROCEDURE (OldH : HHook);
      type
        TForm1 = class(TForm)
          RadioGroup1: TRadioGroup;
          Button1: TButton;
          RadioGroup2: TRadioGroup;
          procedure FormCreate(Sender: TObject);
          procedure Button1Click(Sender: TObject);
          procedure FormDestroy(Sender: TObject);
          procedure RadioGroup2Click(Sender: TObject);
        private
          PSH         : PSharedData;
          hMap        : THandle;
          DllHandle   : THandle;
          HookMouse   : HookMouseType;
```

```
        UnHookMouse : UnHookMouseType;
        Installed   : Boolean;
        procedure DefaultHandler(VAR Message); override;
      end;

var Form1: TForm1;

implementation
{$R *.DFM}

procedure TForm1.DefaultHandler(VAR Message);
begin
  Inherited DefaultHandler(Message);
  IF PSH = NIL THEN Exit;
  IF Visible THEN Exit;
  WITH TMessage(Message) DO
    BEGIN
      IF Msg <> PSH^.EdgeMessage THEN Exit;
      IF wParam <> RadioGroup1.ItemIndex+10 THEN Exit;
      CASE wParam OF
        htLeft, htTopLeft, htBottomLeft :
          Left := PSH^.Threshold;
        htRight, htTopRight, htBottomRight :
          Left := PSH^.SWid - Width - PSH^.Threshold;
      END;
      CASE wParam OF
        htTop, htTopLeft, htTopRight :
          Top := PSH^.Threshold;
        htBottom, htBottomLeft, htBottomRight :
          Top := PSH^.SHig - Height - PSH^.Threshold;
      END;
      Visible := True;
      UnHookMouse(PSH^.OldH);
    END;
end;

procedure TForm1.FormCreate(Sender: TObject);
begin
  {$IFDEF Win32}
  hMap := CreateFileMapping($FFFFFFFF, NIL, PAGE_READWRITE, 0,
    SizeOf(TSharedData), MapName);
  IF hMap = 0 THEN Exit;
  PSH := MapViewOfFile(hMap, FILE_MAP_ALL_ACCESS, 0, 0, 0);
  IF PSH = NIL THEN Exit;
  {$ELSE}
  New(PSH);
  {$ENDIF}
  DllHandle := LoadLibrary('MOUSHOOK.DLL');
  IF DllHandle <= HINSTANCE_ERROR THEN Exit;
  @HookMouse := GetProcAddress(DllHandle, 'HookMouse');
  IF @HookMouse = NIL THEN Exit;
  @UnHookMouse := GetProcAddress(DllHandle, 'UnHookMouse');
  IF @UnHookMouse = NIL THEN Exit;
  WITH PSH^ DO
    BEGIN
```

```
        HWnd          := Handle;
        EdgeMessage   := RegisterWindowMessage('EdgeMessage');
        Threshold     := 8;
        SWid          := Screen.Width;
        SHig          := Screen.Height;
      END;
    Installed := True;
  end;
  procedure TForm1.Button1Click(Sender: TObject);
  begin
    IF Installed THEN
      BEGIN
        PSH^.OldH := HookMouse(PSH);
        Visible := False;
      END
    ELSE ShowMessage('Mouse hook was not successfully installed');
  end;
  procedure TForm1.FormDestroy(Sender: TObject);
  begin
    IF DllHandle > HINSTANCE_ERROR THEN FreeLibrary(DllHandle);
    {$IFDEF Win32}
    IF PSH <> NIL THEN UnMapViewOfFile(PSH);
    IF hMap <> 0 THEN CloseHandle(hMap);
    {$ENDIF}
    PSH := NIL;
  end;
  procedure TForm1.RadioGroup2Click(Sender: TObject);
  begin
    WITH Sender AS TRadioGroup DO
      PSH^.Threshold := StrToIntDef(Items[ItemIndex], 8);
  end;
  end.
```

The OnCreate event handler for this form either opens a memory-mapped file and maps it to the pointer PSH (in 32-bit Delphi) or simply allocates memory for PSH (in 16-bit Delphi). It then dynamically loads the HookMouse and UnHookMouse functions in the DLL—dynamic loading is necessary because the shared memory area must be created before the DLL loads. It initializes the shared data area, using RegisterWindowsMessage to get a unique message code for the DLL to use, and sets the activation threshold to 8 pixels.

When the user presses the Disappear button, it activates the mouse hook, sets the form's Visible property to False, and waits for the special message. A registered Windows message doesn't have a fixed value, so trapping it requires overriding DefaultHandler. When the DefaultHandler method detects an EdgeMessage message, it checks whether the edge code in the wParam matches the selected radio button. If so, it moves the form near the edge, makes it visible again, and deactivates the mouse hook.

System-wide hook procedures let your programs hook into Windows at a very low level. However, they also have the potential to slow down the entire system. Certainly, a program that installs a system-wide hook should leave it active only when necessary. Of course, if the hook DLL needs to be compiled with 32-bit Delphi, you'll have to deal with the absence of shared global variables by creating a memory-mapped file.

3

Multiple Document Interface Forms

*M*icrosoft's programming style guides now recommend against using the Multiple
Document Interface (MDI) style for applications, but MDI just will not die. MDI
programs conveniently provide views of multiple data sets or different views of the same
data set by using child windows that bear the same relationship to the main window as the
main window has to the Windows desktop. In this chapter, you'll learn how to exempt MDI
child windows from the Tile and Cascade operations, how to control the initial size of MDI
child windows, and how to wallpaper the MDI main window's background.

MDI Size and Position

MDI forms do not behave precisely the same as non-MDI forms, and sometimes the
difference can be significant. For example, an MDI child form with WindowState set to
wsMaximized will first appear at normal size and then maximize, producing an annoying
flash. And you cannot hide an MDI form by setting its Visible property to False. For
good-looking MDI applications, you'll want to take full control of form size and position.

*Controlling the initial size and placement
of MDI windows*

16 32

When the Position property for a TForm is set to poDesigned, the form should
appear with precisely the size and position it had at the time you created it.

However, when the form is an MDI child form, Windows takes over its initial size and position. Setting the size and position in the OnCreate event handler doesn't work either.

To set the size and location of an MDI child window successfully, you can override the CreateParams method. The X, Y, Width, and Height values you set in this method will take effect whether or not the form is an MDI form. This is a valuable enough feature that we'll create a TForm-descendant type to encapsulate it.

INITFORM.PAS

```
unit InitForm;

interface

uses SysUtils, WinTypes, WinProcs, Messages, Classes, Graphics,
  Controls, Forms, Dialogs;

type
  TInitSPForm = class(TForm)
  private
    IniName: String;
    procedure CreateParams(VAR Params: TCreateParams);
      override;
    destructor Destroy; override;
  end;

var InitSPForm: TInitSPForm;

implementation
uses IniFiles;

procedure TInitSPForm.CreateParams(VAR Params: TCreateParams);
BEGIN
  Inherited CreateParams(Params);
  IniName := ChangeFileExt(Application.ExeName, '.INI');
  WITH Params DO
    WITH TIniFile.Create(IniName) DO
      try
        X := ReadInteger(Self.ClassName, 'Left', Self.Left);
        Y := ReadInteger(Self.ClassName, 'Top', Self.Top);
        Width := ReadInteger(Self.ClassName, 'Width', Self.Width);
        Height := ReadInteger(Self.ClassName,'Height',Self.Height);
      finally
        Free;
      end;
END;

destructor TInitSPForm.Destroy;
begin
  WindowState := wsNormal;
  WITH TIniFile.Create(IniName) DO
    try
      WriteInteger(Self.ClassName, 'Left', Left);
```

```
      WriteInteger(Self.ClassName, 'Top', Top);
      WriteInteger(Self.ClassName, 'Width', Width);
      WriteInteger(Self.ClassName, 'Height', Height);
    finally
      Free;
    end;
  Inherited Destroy;
end;

end.
```

The form type defined in this unit serves as ancestor for any form that needs to save its size and position in an .INI file. To apply this functionality to an existing form, add InitForm to the uses clause, then find the initial declaration of the form type and change class(TForm) to class(TInitSPForm). That's it! The first time such a form is created, it will appear with the size and position it had at design time. Thereafter, it will use the size and position it had when it was previously closed. Since the initial position of an MDI child form is relative to its parent, you should design the MDI child form as if the desktop were its parent.

The code that loads and saves size and position information uses an .INI file in your program's own directory to do so. It gets the .INI file name by taking the application's executable name and changing the extension to .INI. The section heading for each form is named with that form's ClassName. If your program needs to control the initial position of multiple forms of the same type, you'll need to modify the code to distinguish the different forms.

The program INITSIZ.DPR demonstrates this technique, but it's so simple there's no need to list it here. Again, you can make any form store its size and position in an .INI file simply by editing its source code to add InitForm to the uses clause and make it a descendant of TInitSPForm, rather than TForm. This applies to MDI main forms, MDI child forms, and non-MDI forms.

Avoiding the initial flash of maximized MDI child

16 32

An MDI child form whose WindowState property is wsMaximized will first appear in a nonmaximized state and then will visibly maximize itself. Under Windows 95, it looks even worse; instead of flashing straight to the maximized state, the window visibly zooms from normal to maximized.

The Windows API function LockWindowUpdate comes to the rescue here. Pass a window's handle to LockWindowUpdate and Windows stops updating that window.

Pass 0 to LockWindowUpdate and the previously locked window returns to normal. The program that follows demonstrates both the problem and its solution.

MAXMDI

MAXMDI1U.DEX

```
object Form1: TForm1
  Caption = 'Initially Maximized MDI Child Demo'
  FormStyle = fsMDIForm
  Menu = MainMenu1
  Position = poDefault
  Scaled = False
  object MainMenu1: TMainMenu
    object File1: TMenuItem
      Caption = 'File'
      object CreateMaxChild1: TMenuItem
        Caption = '&Create MaxChild'
        OnClick = CreateMaxChild1Click
      end
      object CreateMaxwoFlash1: TMenuItem
        Caption = 'Create Max w/o &Flash'
        OnClick = CreateMaxwoFlash1Click
      end
    end
  end
end
```

MAXMDI1U.PAS

```
unit Maxmdi1u;

interface

uses SysUtils, WinTypes, WinProcs, Messages, Classes, Graphics,
  Controls, Forms, Dialogs, Menus;

type
  TForm1 = class(TForm)
    MainMenu1: TMainMenu;
    File1: TMenuItem;
    CreateMaxChild1: TMenuItem;
    CreateMaxwoFlash1: TMenuItem;
    procedure CreateMaxChild1Click(Sender: TObject);
    procedure CreateMaxwoFlash1Click(Sender: TObject);
  end;

var Form1: TForm1;

implementation
Uses MaxMdi2u;
{$R *.DFM}

procedure TForm1.CreateMaxChild1Click(Sender: TObject);
begin
```

```
    TForm2.Create(Application);
end;
procedure TForm1.CreateMaxwoFlash1Click(Sender: TObject);
begin
  LockWindowUpdate(Handle);
  TForm2.Create(Application);
  LockWindowUpdate(0);
end;

end.
```

MAXMDI2U.DEX

```
object Form2: TForm2
  FormStyle = fsMDIChild
  Position = poDefault
  Scaled = False
  Visible = True
  WindowState = wsMaximized
  OnClose = FormClose
end
```

MAXMDI2U.PAS

```
unit Maxmdi2u;

interface

uses SysUtils, WinTypes, WinProcs, Messages, Classes, Graphics,
  Controls, Forms, Dialogs;

type
  TForm2 = class(TForm)
    procedure FormClose(Sender: TObject; var Action: TCloseAction);
  end;

var Form2: TForm2;

implementation

{$R *.DFM}

procedure TForm2.FormClose(Sender: TObject; var Action:
  TCloseAction);
begin
  Action := caFree;
end;

end.
```

Yes, it really is that simple! Keep the LockWindowUpdate function in mind any time your programs have display problems. If the problems are caused by displaying the steps of an unfinished process, LockWindowUpdate may be able to smooth the transition.

Hiding and showing MDI child windows

16

The default behavior for non-MDI Delphi forms is that they're created when the program starts and remain in existence until it ends. All except the main form are created with Visible set to False, and the program controls their availability by making them visible and invisible. However, you cannot set Visible to False for an MDI child form; Delphi won't let you.

As it turns out, there's good reason for this prohibition. In 16-bit Windows, the MDI system has some internal problems that surface when MDI child windows are hidden, according to Delphi architect Chuck Jazdzewski. However, it *is* possible to hide and show MDI child windows, and the problems Chuck notes are not guaranteed to afflict your program. If you're bold, here's the way.

MDIHIDE

MDIHIDU1.DEX

```
object Form1: TForm1
  Caption = 'Hiding an MDI Child Window'
  FormStyle = fsMDIForm
  Menu = MainMenu1
  Position = poDefault
  Scaled = False
  OnCreate = FormCreate
  object Panel1: TPanel
    Align = alBottom
    BevelInner = bvLowered
    object Button1: TButton
      Caption = '&Hide'
      OnClick = Button1Click
    end
    object Button2: TButton
      Caption = 'Show (&Right)'
      OnClick = Button2Click
    end
    object Button3: TButton
      Caption = 'Show (&Wrong)'
      OnClick = Button3Click
    end
  end
  object MainMenu1: TMainMenu
    object File1: TMenuItem
      Caption = '&File'
    end
  end
end
```

MDIHIDU1.PAS

```
unit Mdihidu1;

interface

uses SysUtils, WinTypes, WinProcs, Messages, Classes, Graphics,
  Controls, Forms, Dialogs, StdCtrls, ExtCtrls, Menus;

type
  TForm1 = class(TForm)
    MainMenu1: TMainMenu;
    File1: TMenuItem;
    Panel1: TPanel;
    Button1: TButton;
    Button2: TButton;
    Button3: TButton;
    procedure Button2Click(Sender: TObject);
    procedure Button1Click(Sender: TObject);
    procedure Button3Click(Sender: TObject);
    procedure FormCreate(Sender: TObject);
  end;

var Form1: TForm1;

implementation
USES MdiHidu2;
{$R *.DFM}

procedure TForm1.Button1Click(Sender: TObject);
begin
  IF Form2.WindowState = wsMaximized THEN
    Form2.WindowState := wsNormal;
  ShowWindow(Form2.Handle,SW_Hide);
end;

procedure TForm1.Button2Click(Sender: TObject);
begin
  SetWindowPos(Form2.Handle,HWND_TOP,0,0,0,0,
    SWP_NoMove or SWP_NoSize or SWP_ShowWindow);
  WinProcs.SetFocus(Form2.Handle);
end;

procedure TForm1.Button3Click(Sender: TObject);
begin
  ShowWindow(Form2.Handle, SW_SHOW);
end;

procedure TForm1.FormCreate(Sender: TObject);
begin
  {$IFDEF Win32}
  ShowMessage('This problem does not occur in Win32');
  {$ENDIF}
end;

end.
```

MDIHIDU2.DEX

```
object Form2: TForm2
  FormStyle = fsMDIChild
  Position = poDefault
  Scaled = False
  Visible = True
  object TabbedNotebook1: TTabbedNotebook
    Align = alClient
    object TTabPage
      Caption = 'Default'
    end
    object TTabPage
      Caption = 'Two'
    end
    object TTabPage
      Caption = 'Three'
    end
  end
end
```

MDIHIDU2.PAS

```
unit Mdihidu2;

interface

uses SysUtils, WinTypes, WinProcs, Messages, Classes, Graphics,
  Controls, Forms, Dialogs, TabNotBk;

type
  TForm2 = class(TForm)
    TabbedNotebook1: TTabbedNotebook;
  end;

var Form2: TForm2;

implementation

{$R *.DFM}

end.
```

Hide an MDI child window by calling the Windows API function ShowWindow, passing the constant SW_HIDE. However, if you try to make it visible again the same way, you may be disappointed. The tabbed notebook on the secondary window serves to show just what's wrong with the wrong way. When ShowWindow is called from an event handler belonging to a component on the main form, the child window does not gain the focus correctly. The tabbed notebook is unresponsive and mouse clicks are ignored.

Oddly enough, the correct way to bring the hidden window back to life is via a call to SetWindowPos. (This method was discovered by CompuServe Delphi forum member

Uli Zindler, who analyzed the technique used by Microsoft Access.) SetWindowPos has a number of different functions including setting a window's size, its position, and its place in the window stack (Z order). It also includes flags to cancel any of the functions you don't want. In this case, cancel all three and add the SWP_SHOWWINDOW flag. A call to SetFocus (the API function, not the method) gets the window correctly hooked up again.

MDI Communication

Occasionally, an MDI application will be so self-contained that its main form and child forms don't need to communicate with each other. In such a program, all forms would be auto-created, and no child form would ever be destroyed. However, if the main form needs the ability to create child forms, it must have access to the child form units. In many cases, a still greater degree of intimacy is required.

Allowing MDI child and main forms to reference each other

16 32

MDI main forms and child forms are all part of the same application, but they *are* separate. There are several different ways to give the main form access to the child forms and vice versa, such as the following:

◆ Using each other

◆ Maintaining anonymity

◆ Putting it on the menu

◆ Getting a window list

Using Each Other. If the main form needs access to components on a child form, or if the main form needs the ability to *create* child forms, it needs to include the child form's unit in its implementation uses clause. This is a second uses clause that comes at the start of the unit's implementation section.

The MaxMDI example program in the previous section "Avoiding the initial flash of maximized MDI child" is an example of this technique in action. Because the main program has MaxMdi2U in its implementation uses clause, it's able to create a new instance of TForm2. Omit that unit from the uses clause, and the references to TForm2 will trigger "Unknown Identifier" compiler errors.

When the child needs to access specific components of the main form, the implementation uses clause again supplies the solution. Add the main form's unit to the child form's implementation uses clause.

Why this emphasis on the implementation uses clause as opposed to the interface uses clause? If the main form uses the child form and the child form uses the main form, this can produce what's called a circular reference. When Delphi compiles a unit, it first compiles all files in the interface uses clause. If one of the units in the interface uses clause references the unit that's being compiled in *its* interface uses clause, each unit must be compiled before the other can be compiled—an impossibility. Using the implementation uses clause avoids the circular reference problem.

Maintaining Anonymity. Sometimes a child form needs access to the standard TForm properties or methods of the main form. For example, it might be desirable to call the Tile or Cascade methods of the main form. In that case, a reference to Application.MainForm will do the job. The example program for the "Creating specialized menus for child forms section later in this chapter exemplifies this technique.

If the main form needs access to the active MDI child, again sticking to the properties and methods present in TForm, it can refer to its own ActiveMDIChild property. Always check first to ensure this property is not NIL, as sometimes there may be no MDI children.

To flip through a list of all the MDI children, look at the MDIChildren array property. The number of children is held in MDIChildCount property. The example program for the "Permitting just one of an MDI child type" section later in this chapter uses this technique to determine whether a particular MDI child type is present.

Putting It on the Menu. MDI child forms can have their own menus that replace or merge with the main form's menu when the child form is active. No programming is needed to accomplish this feat. The AutoMerge property of a child form's menu is true by default. All you need to do is set the GroupIndex properties of the top-level menu items in both the main and the child forms to control merging.

From left to right, the GroupIndex values must not decrease. A top-level menu item can have any GroupIndex equal to or greater than the item to its left. Top-level items with the same GroupIndex form a group (of course!). When a child menu merges with the main menu, each of its groups replaces any existing group in the main menu that has the same GroupIndex. If no group exists with the same index, the child menu's group is inserted in numeric order. You'll see this technique in action later in the chapter, in the "Putting the window list on a merged menu" section.

Getting a Window List. Many MDI programs attach a list of open child windows to the bottom of one of their menus, typically the Window menu. Clicking a window's name on this menu activates it. To do this in Delphi, set the main form's WindowMenu property to the name of the desired top-level menu item. That's all! Up to nine windows will appear in the list; if there are more, they'll automatically be displayed in a dialog box invoked by a More Windows . . . menu item that appears at the bottom of the list. The program example in the "Exempting a child window from tile and cascade" section uses a WindowMenu.

Permitting just one of an MDI child type

| 16 | 32 |

Many MDI programs manage numerous child windows that are all of the same type; Program Manager is perhaps the most famous example. However, there's no requirement that all MDI child windows be the same type. You might want to implement a floating toolbar as an MDI child window, for example. It could be present or absent at the user's request, but you'd never want more than one of them.

It turns out that you can embed the necessary functionality right in the child window. Figure 3-1 shows an example. Choose Multi from the File menu and another instance of TForm3 is created. What happens when you choose Lone depends on whether an instance of TForm2 already exists. If so, it's brought to the front and, if necessary, restored from a minimized state. If not, an instance of TForm2 is created.

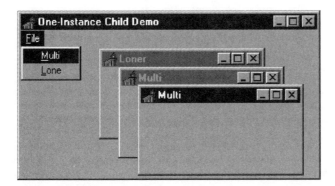

FIGURE 3-1: Selecting Lone from the menu will activate the child window of type TForm2 if one is present, or create one if it is not present.

LONE

LONE1U.DEX

```
object Form1: TForm1
  Caption = 'One-Instance Child Demo'
  FormStyle = fsMDIForm
  Menu = MainMenu1
  Position = poDefault
  Scaled = False
  Visible = True
  object MainMenu1: TMainMenu
    object File1: TMenuItem
      Caption = '&File'
      object Multi1: TMenuItem
        Caption = '&Multi'
        OnClick = Multi1Click
      end
      object Lone1: TMenuItem
        Caption = '&Lone'
        OnClick = Lone1Click
      end
    end
  end
end
```

LONE1U.PAS

```
unit Lone1u;

interface

uses SysUtils, WinTypes, WinProcs, Messages, Classes, Graphics,
  Controls, Forms, Dialogs, Menus;

type
  TForm1 = class(TForm)
    MainMenu1: TMainMenu;
    File1: TMenuItem;
    Lone1: TMenuItem;
    Multi1: TMenuItem;
    procedure Multi1Click(Sender: TObject);
    procedure Lone1Click(Sender: TObject);
  end;

var Form1: TForm1;

implementation
USES Lone2u, Lone3u;
{$R *.DFM}

procedure TForm1.Multi1Click(Sender: TObject);
begin
  TForm3.Create(Application);
end;
```

```
procedure TForm1.Lone1Click(Sender: TObject);
begin
  TForm2.GetLoner;
end;

end.
```

LONE2U.DEX

```
object Form2: TForm2
  Caption = 'Loner'
  FormStyle = fsMDIChild
  Position = poDefault
  Scaled = False
  Visible = True
  OnClose = FormClose
end
```

LONE2U.PAS

```
unit Lone2u;

interface

uses SysUtils, WinTypes, WinProcs, Messages, Classes, Graphics,
  Controls, Forms, Dialogs;

type
  TForm2 = class(TForm)
    procedure FormClose(Sender: TObject; var Action: TCloseAction);
  public
    class procedure GetLoner;
  end;

var Form2: TForm2;

implementation

{$R *.DFM}

class procedure TForm2.GetLoner;
VAR
  F : TForm2;
  N : Integer;
BEGIN
  F := NIL;
  WITH Application.MainForm DO
    FOR N := 0 TO MDIChildCount-1 DO
      IF MdiChildren[N] IS TForm2 THEN
        F := MdiChildren[N] AS TForm2;
  IF F = NIL THEN
    TForm2.Create(Application)
  ELSE
    WITH F DO
      BEGIN
```

```
                 IF WindowState = wsMinimized THEN WindowState := wsNormal;
                 BringToFront;
             END;
    END;

procedure TForm2.FormClose(Sender: TObject; var Action:
  TCloseAction);
begin
  Action := caFree;
end;

end.
```

LONE3U.DEX

```
object Form3: TForm3
  Caption = 'Multi'
  FormStyle = fsMDIChild
  Position = poDefault
  Scaled = False
  Visible = True
  OnClose = FormClose
end
```

LONE3U.PAS

```
unit Lone3u;

interface

uses SysUtils, WinTypes, WinProcs, Messages, Classes, Graphics,
  Controls, Forms, Dialogs;

type
  TForm3 = class(TForm)
    procedure FormClose(Sender: TObject; var Action: TCloseAction);
  end;

var Form3: TForm3;

implementation

{$R *.DFM}

procedure TForm3.FormClose(Sender: TObject; var Action:
  TCloseAction);
begin
  Action := caFree;
end;

end.
```

GetLoner is a *class method* of TForm2—it does not belong to any one instance, but to the class as a whole. That means you can call it without necessarily creating an instance of TForm2.

GetLoner flips through the main form's MDIChildren array looking for a child whose type is TForm2. If none is found, it creates one. If an instance of TForm2 is found, the method brings it to the front and, if it was minimized, restores it.

Note well the technique used in the GetLoner method to find an instance of TForm2. You can use this technique any time you need to determine whether an MDI child of a particular type exists, or whenever you need to perform some action on all MDI children of a given type.

Putting the window list on a merged menu

16 32

By setting the WindowMenu property of the main MDI form to a top-level menu item, you automatically get a child form list appended to that menu. Up to nine child form names appear; if there's overflow, a More Windows . . . menu item shows all of them. Click on a name to activate that form. However, this only works for a menu item belonging to the main form. How can you append the window list to a menu that only appears when one or more child forms are active?

Well, you cannot do it by setting the main form's WindowMenu to a menu item on the child window. What you *can* do, though, is emulate the VCL code that does the job for TForm. In the OnClick event handler for the top-level menu item that should contain the window list, you'll send a message that causes Windows to append the list to that menu item.

Internally, MDI child forms are managed by an invisible window that occupies the client area of the main MDI form. The ClientHandle property holds the window handle of the client window—this window has no Delphi object associated with it. To set the location of the window list, the program sends the WM_SETMDIMENU message to the client window's handle. Note that conditional compilation is required because the parameters for this message change in 32-bit Windows. In 32-bit Windows, the wParam is the handle of the main menu and the lParam is the handle of the submenu that is to receive the list. In 16-bit Windows, the wParam is 0 and the lParam contains the main menu handle in its low word and the submenu handle in its high word. See the next section's program for an example.

Creating specialized menus for child forms

16 32

Some menu commands, such as Tile and Cascade, are pointless when no child window is open. Others are specific to one type of child window and should not appear unless the active child form is that type. Delphi has built-in handling for child-specific menus. When the AutoMerge property is True (as it is by default for MDI child windows), the active child window's menu items will be merged into the main menu according to their GroupIndex.

Each top-level menu item must have a GroupIndex equal to or greater than that of the item to its left. Items with the *same* GroupIndex form a group, naturally. When the child menu is merged into the main menu, each of its groups replaces any existing group with the same index. If no matching group exists, the child menu's group gets inserted in numeric order. Figure 3-2 shows an example.

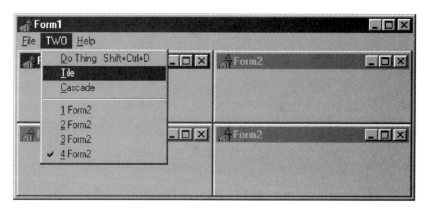

FIGURE 3-2: Having Tile and Cascade menu choices appear only when child windows are present is easy; getting the window list attached to a menu belonging to the child window is not!

MERGE

MERGE1U.DEX

```
object Form1: TForm1
  FormStyle = fsMDIForm
  Menu = MainMenu1
  Position = poDefault
  Scaled = False
  Visible = True
  WindowMenu = ONE1
```

```
object MainMenu1: TMainMenu
  object File1: TMenuItem
    Caption = '&File'
    object NewForm21: TMenuItem
      Caption = 'New Form&2'
      OnClick = NewForm21Click
    end
  end
  object ONE1: TMenuItem
    Caption = 'ONE'
    GroupIndex = 1
    object DoThing1: TMenuItem
      Caption = '&Do Thing'
      OnClick = DoThing1Click
      ShortCutText = 'Shift+Ctrl+D'
    end
  end
  object Help1: TMenuItem
    Caption = '&Help'
    GroupIndex = 2
  end
end
end
```

MERGE1U.PAS

```
unit Merge1u;

interface

uses SysUtils, WinTypes, WinProcs, Messages, Classes, Graphics,
  Controls, Forms, Dialogs, Menus;

type
  TForm1 = class(TForm)
    MainMenu1: TMainMenu;
    File1: TMenuItem;
    Help1: TMenuItem;
    NewForm21: TMenuItem;
    ONE1: TMenuItem;
    DoThing1: TMenuItem;
    procedure NewForm21Click(Sender: TObject);
    procedure DoThing1Click(Sender: TObject);
  end;

var Form1: TForm1;

implementation
USES Merge2u;
{$R *.DFM}

procedure TForm1.NewForm21Click(Sender: TObject);
begin
  TForm2.Create(Application);
end;
```

```
procedure TForm1.DoThing1Click(Sender: TObject);
begin
  IF Caption = 'Form1' THEN
    Caption := 'Changed Form1'
  ELSE Caption := 'Form1';
end;

end.
```

MERGE2U.DEX

```
object Form2: TForm2
  FormStyle = fsMDIChild
  Menu = MainMenu1
  Position = poDefault
  Scaled = False
  Visible = True
  OnClose = FormClose
  object MainMenu1: TMainMenu
    object TWO1: TMenuItem
      Caption = 'TWO'
      GroupIndex = 1
      OnClick = TWO1Click
      object DoThing1: TMenuItem
        Caption = '&Do Thing'
        OnClick = DoThing1Click
        ShortCutText = 'Shift+Ctrl+D'
      end
      object Tile1: TMenuItem
        Caption = '&Tile'
        OnClick = Tile1Click
      end
      object Cascade1: TMenuItem
        Caption = '&Cascade'
        OnClick = Cascade1Click
      end
    end
  end
end
```

MERGE2U.PAS

```
unit Merge2u;

interface

uses SysUtils, WinTypes, WinProcs, Messages, Classes, Graphics,
  Controls, Forms, Dialogs, Menus;

type
  TForm2 = class(TForm)
    MainMenu1: TMainMenu;
    TWO1: TMenuItem;
```

```
      DoThing1: TMenuItem;
      Tile1: TMenuItem;
      Cascade1: TMenuItem;
      procedure FormClose(Sender: TObject; var Action: TCloseAction);
      procedure DoThing1Click(Sender: TObject);
      procedure Tile1Click(Sender: TObject);
      procedure Cascade1Click(Sender: TObject);
      procedure TWO1Click(Sender: TObject);
    end;

var Form2: TForm2;

implementation

{$R *.DFM}

procedure TForm2.FormClose(Sender: TObject; var Action:
  TCloseAction);
begin
  Action := caFree;
end;

procedure TForm2.DoThing1Click(Sender: TObject);
begin
  IF Caption = 'Form2' THEN
    Caption := 'Changed Form2'
  ELSE Caption := 'Form2';
end;

procedure TForm2.Tile1Click(Sender: TObject);
begin
  Application.MainForm.Tile;
end;

procedure TForm2.Cascade1Click(Sender: TObject);
begin
  Application.MainForm.Cascade;
end;

procedure TForm2.TWO1Click(Sender: TObject);
begin
  WITH Application.MainForm DO
    {$IFDEF Win32} {WM_MDISETMENU msg parameters change in Win32}
    SendMessage(ClientHandle,WM_MDISETMENU, Menu.Handle,
      (Sender AS TMenuItem).Handle);
    {$ELSE}
    SendMessage(ClientHandle,WM_MDISETMENU,0,LongInt(Menu.Handle)
      OR LongInt((Sender AS TMenuItem).Handle) SHL 16);
    {$ENDIF}
end;
end.
```

The three top-level menu items in the main form (File, ONE, and Help) have their GroupIndex properties set to 0, 1, and 2, respectively. The top-level menu item TWO in the secondary form has a GroupIndex of 1. When a child form is created, the TWO menu replaces ONE in the main menu. When the last child form is destroyed, ONE reappears. Both menu items have a submenu item named Do Thing with shortcut key Shift+Ctrl+D. Selecting this menu choice or pressing the key calls the event handling code in the active form, whether it's the main form or a child.

As described in the preceding section, the OnClick handler for the TWO menu item appends the window list to the drop-down menu just before it appears. As for tiling and cascading child windows, the child form simply calls the Tile and Cascade methods of Application.MainForm. Any time your program needs to access the main form strictly for methods and properties present in TForm, it can go directly through Application.MainForm. And, if you need to attach the window list to a menu that's not available in the main form at design time, remember the WM_SETMDIMENU message.

MDI Appearance

The MDI application style is well defined, but there are areas for customization, at least as far as appearance goes. It's important to know what you can change, and also what you cannot change.

 Creating an MDI form with no menu

| 16 | 32 |

The MDI style can be convenient for showing different sets of data, or different views of the same data set. A toolbar with buttons can supplement the menu nicely. If the program is simple enough, can you just dispense with the menu?

This time the answer is _NO_. An MDI form without a menu is fatally flawed. To see why, consider what happens when you maximize an MDI child window. The child form's system menu box and restore button append themselves to the main form's menu, one at the left and one at the right.

What happens if there is no menu? The child form maximizes to take up all the space within the main form, but its system menu box and restore button simply disappear. The only indication that a maximized child window exists is the main form's caption, which will be something like Main Form - [Child Form]. That _is_ awkward! Don't pick a fight with Windows—always give your MDI forms a main menu. You'll note that all the examples in this chapter have at least one menu item, even if it's not functional.

Exempting a child window from Tile and Cascade

16 32

It's possible to create MDI child windows that don't have a resizeable border; for example, as floating toolbars. However, these windows interact oddly with the MDI functions Tile and Cascade. Tile tries to make all the windows the same size; the fixed-size window will either have a gap around it or overlap others.

Exempting one window from Tile and Cascade involves the tricky step of hiding an MDI child window. As noted in the previous "Hiding and showing MDI child windows" section, Delphi does not let you set an MDI child form's Visible property to False because of certain problems deep inside the Windows MDI system. Figure 3-3 shows a program in which a small, fixed-size window is exempt from the Tile and Cascade operations.

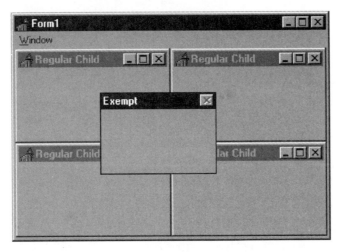

FIGURE 3-3: A fixed-size window does not tile well; this one simply opts out of the tiling process.

EXEMPT

EXEMPT1U.DEX

```
object Form1: TForm1
  FormStyle = fsMDIForm
  Menu = MainMenu1
  Position = poDefault
  Scaled = False
  Visible = True
  WindowMenu = Window1
  object MainMenu1: TMainMenu
```

```
      object Window1: TMenuItem
        Caption = '&Window'
        object New1: TMenuItem
          Caption = '&New'
          OnClick = New1Click
          ShortCutText = 'Shift+Ctrl+N'
        end
        object Cascade1: TMenuItem
          Caption = '&Cascade'
          OnClick = Cascade1Click
          ShortCutText = 'Shift+Ctrl+C'
        end
        object Tile1: TMenuItem
          Caption = '&Tile'
          OnClick = Tile1Click
          ShortCutText = 'Shift+Ctrl+T'
        end
      end
    end
end
```

EXEMPT1U.PAS

```
unit Exempt1u;

interface

uses SysUtils, WinTypes, WinProcs, Messages, Classes, Graphics,
  Controls, Forms, Dialogs, Menus;

type
  TForm1 = class(TForm)
    MainMenu1: TMainMenu;
    Window1: TMenuItem;
    Tile1: TMenuItem;
    Cascade1: TMenuItem;
    New1: TMenuItem;
    procedure New1Click(Sender: TObject);
    procedure Tile1Click(Sender: TObject);
    procedure Cascade1Click(Sender: TObject);
  end;

var Form1: TForm1;

implementation
USES Exempt2u, Exempt3u;
{$R *.DFM}

procedure TForm1.New1Click(Sender: TObject);
begin
  TForm3.Create(Application);
end;

procedure TForm1.Tile1Click(Sender: TObject);
begin
```

```
  LockWindowUpdate(Handle);
  ShowWindow(Form2.Handle, SW_HIDE);
  Tile;
  SetWindowPos(Form2.Handle, 0,0,0,0,0, SWP_NOSIZE OR
    SWP_NOMOVE OR SWP_NOZORDER OR SWP_SHOWWINDOW);
  WinProcs.SetFocus(Form2.Handle);
  LockWindowUpdate(0);
end;

procedure TForm1.Cascade1Click(Sender: TObject);
begin
  LockWindowUpdate(Handle);
  ShowWindow(Form2.Handle, SW_HIDE);
  Cascade;
  SetWindowPos(Form2.Handle, 0,0,0,0,0, SWP_NOSIZE OR
    SWP_NOMOVE OR SWP_NOZORDER OR SWP_SHOWWINDOW);
  WinProcs.SetFocus(Form2.Handle);
  LockWindowUpdate(0);
end;

end.
```

EXEMPT2U.DEX

```
object Form2: TForm2
  BorderIcons = []
  BorderStyle = bsSingle
  Caption = 'Exempt'
  FormStyle = fsMDIChild
  Position = poDefault
  Scaled = False
  Visible = True
end
```

EXEMPT2U.PAS

```
unit Exempt2u;

interface

uses SysUtils, WinTypes, WinProcs, Messages, Classes, Graphics,
  Controls, Forms, Dialogs;

type
  TForm2 = class(TForm)
  end;

var Form2: TForm2;

implementation

{$R *.DFM}

end.
```

EXEMPT3U.DEX

```
object Form3: TForm3
  Caption = 'Regular Child'
  FormStyle = fsMDIChild
  Position = poDefault
  Scaled = False
  Visible = True
  OnClose = FormClose
end
```

EXEMPT3U.PAS

```
unit Exempt3u;

interface

uses SysUtils, WinTypes, WinProcs, Messages, Classes, Graphics,
  Controls, Forms, Dialogs;

type
  TForm3 = class(TForm)
    procedure FormClose(Sender: TObject; var Action: TCloseAction);
  end;

var Form3: TForm3;

implementation

{$R *.DFM}

procedure TForm3.FormClose(Sender: TObject; var Action:
  TCloseAction);
begin
  Action := caFree;
end;

end.
```

There are two important techniques here. The event handlers that Tile and Cascade child windows are identical except for the method of Application.MainForm called out in the middle. To start, each calls the Windows API function LockWindowUpdate to prevent the main window from being updated, then hides the exempt form. After calling the Tile or Cascade method, each event handler unhides the exempt form and calls LockWindowUpdate again to permit updating the main window.

Since Delphi does not permit setting Visible to False for an MDI child form, the program calls on the Windows API to hide the exempt form. Then, based on observation of MDI programs that successfully hide and show MDI children, it uses SetWindowPos to redisplay the hidden child, and calls the API function SetFocus to get it back into action. Of course, this has the effect of making the exempt form active after each tile or cascade operation. If it didn't, the tiny exempt form would almost certainly disappear beneath the larger regular child windows.

Giving an MDI main form background wallpaper

16 32

An MDI program is a lot like a miniature Windows desktop. Other windows live entirely within it, never leaving its boundaries. Wouldn't it be impressive if an MDI main form could have *wallpaper*, just like the desktop?

This task is surprisingly tough, but it can be handled, as Figure 3-4 shows. Delphi cannot associate a component with the MDI client window because Windows does not allow it to be superclassed. Thus, the solution relies almost completely on the Windows API.

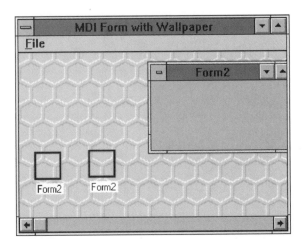

FIGURE 3-4: This MDI form paints its client area with a bitmap; the child form's icon is mostly transparent, to show that the background displays fine behind an icon.

WALLP

WALLPMU.DEX

```
object Form1: TForm1
  Caption = 'MDI Form with Wallpaper'
  FormStyle = fsMDIForm
  Menu = MainMenu1
  Position = poDefault
```

```
              Scaled = False
              Visible = True
              OnActivate = FormActivate
              object Image1: TImage
              end
              object MainMenu1: TMainMenu
                object File1: TMenuItem
                  Caption = '&File'
                  object NewForm21: TMenuItem
                    Caption = '&New Form2'
                    OnClick = NewForm21Click
                  end
                end
              end
            end
```

WALLPMU.PAS

```
unit wallpmu;

interface

uses SysUtils, WinTypes, WinProcs, Messages, Classes, Graphics,
  Controls, Forms, Dialogs, ExtCtrls, Menus;

type
  TForm1 = class(TForm)
    MainMenu1: TMainMenu;
    File1: TMenuItem;
    Image1: TImage;
    NewForm21: TMenuItem;
    procedure FormActivate(Sender: TObject);
    procedure NewForm21Click(Sender: TObject);
  private
    bmW, bmH : Integer;
    FPrevClientProc : TFarProc;
  public
    PROCEDURE PaintUnderIcon(F: TForm; D: hDC);
  end;

var Form1: TForm1;

implementation
USES wallpcu;
{$R *.DFM}

FUNCTION ClientWndProc(H: HWnd; Msg: Cardinal; wParam: Cardinal;
  lParam: LongInt) : LongInt; FAR; {$IFDEF Win32} StdCall; {$ENDIF}
VAR Ro, Co : Integer;
begin
  WITH Form1 DO
    case Msg of
      WM_ERASEBKGND: begin
        FOR Ro := 0 TO ClientHeight DIV bmH DO
          FOR Co := 0 TO ClientWIDTH DIV bmW DO
            BitBlt(wParam, Co*bmW, Ro*bmH, bmW, bmH,
```

```
                     Image1.Picture.Bitmap.Canvas.Handle, 0, 0, SRCCOPY);
          Result := 1;
        end;
      WM_VSCROLL, WM_HSCROLL : begin
        Result := CallWindowProc(FPrevClientProc,
          ClientHandle, Msg, wParam, lParam);
        InvalidateRect(ClientHandle, NIL, True);
      end;
      else
        Result := CallWindowProc(FPrevClientProc,
          Form1.ClientHandle, Msg, wParam, lParam);
    end;
end;

procedure TForm1.FormActivate(Sender: TObject);
begin
  bmW := Image1.Picture.Width;
  bmH := Image1.Picture.Height;
  {DO NOT attempt subclass in OnCreate; fails in Delphi32}
  FPrevClientProc := Pointer(SetWindowLong(ClientHandle,
    GWL_WNDPROC, LongInt(@ClientWndProc)));
end;

PROCEDURE TForm1.PaintUnderIcon(F: TForm; D: hDC);
VAR
  DestR, WndR : TRect;
  Ro, Co,
  xOfs, yOfs,
  xNum, yNum  : Integer;
BEGIN
  {calculate number of tilings to fill D}
  GetClipBox(D, DestR);
  WITH DestR DO
    BEGIN
      xNum := Succ((Right-Left) DIV bmW);
      yNum := Succ((Bottom-Top) DIV bmW);
    END;
  {calculate offset of image in D}
  GetWindowRect(F.Handle, WndR);
  WITH ScreenToClient(WndR.TopLeft) DO
    BEGIN
      xOfs := X MOD bmW;
      yOfs := Y MOD bmH;
    END;
  FOR Ro := 0 TO xNum DO
    FOR Co := 0 TO yNum DO
      BitBlt(D, Co*bmW-xOfs, Ro*bmH-Yofs, bmW, bmH,
        Image1.Picture.Bitmap.Canvas.Handle, 0, 0, SRCCOPY);
END;

procedure TForm1.NewForm21Click(Sender: TObject);
begin
  TForm2.Create(Application);
end;

end.
```

WALLPCU.DEX

```
object Form2: TForm2
  FormStyle = fsMDIChild
  Position = poDefault
  Scaled = False
  Visible = True
end
```

WALLPCU.PAS

```
unit wallpcu;

interface

uses SysUtils, WinTypes, WinProcs, Messages, Classes, Graphics,
  Controls, Forms, Dialogs;

type
  TForm2 = class(TForm)
  private
    procedure WMIconEraseBkgnd(VAR Message: TWMIconEraseBkgnd);
      message WM_ICONERASEBKGND;

  end;

var Form2: TForm2;

implementation
{$R *.DFM}
USES WallPMu;

procedure TForm2.WMIconEraseBkgnd(VAR Message: TWMIconEraseBkgnd);
BEGIN
  Inherited;
  TForm1(Application.Mainform).PaintUnderIcon(Self, Message.DC);
  Message.Result := 0;
END;

end.
```

The essential point to learn here is that the client area of an MDI form does *not* belong to the form. Rather, it belongs to a separate window called the MDI client window. This window, whose handle is stored in the main form's ClientHandle property, manages the child windows and owns the client area. To paint the client area, a program must respond to WM_ERASEBKGND messages sent to the client window.

The catch is, there is no Delphi form or component corresponding to the client window. All you have is its handle. That leaves just one solution for responding to messages: you must *subclass* the client window. That means you will give it a new window procedure, handling certain messages and passing the rest to the old window procedure. In the bad old days, before visual development environments, *every* Windows program had to deal with messages in this way. Consider yourself lucky!

The header for the new window procedure requires the StdCall keyword in Delphi32, but the body of the procedure is the same. When WM_ERASEBKGND is received, the window procedure repeatedly paints the image contained in component Image1 to fill the client area. If the window scrolls horizontally or vertically, the window procedure forces a complete repaint. Without this step, scrolling the window produces regions in which the background bitmaps do not line up properly.

That *almost* does the job, but there's one more thing. In Windows 3.1, the background of a minimized child window must be painted in response to the WM_ICONERASEBKGND message sent to the child. This message carries with it a device context to be used for painting. The child form responds to WM_ICONERASEBKGND by calling the main form's public PaintUnderIcon method and passing that device context.

PaintUnderIcon tiles the rectangular area under the icon in almost the same way the program tiles the whole form. The difference is that it has to calculate an initial offset, so the under-icon tiling lines up perfectly with the rest of the background. In Windows 95, minimized MDI child windows appear as small rectangles, not as icons, so this step is not truly necessary in a Win95-specific program. Figure 3-5 shows what a wallpapered MDI form looks like in Windows 95.

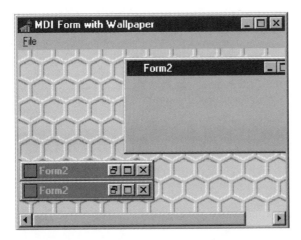

FIGURE 3-5: Here's what an MDI form with a bitmap background looks like in Windows 95; note that the minimized child windows do not appear as icons.

Adding a Windows 95 help button to an MDI child form

32

The preceding chapter demonstrated how to implement the Windows 95 help button, but the BorderIcons.biHelp property doesn't add the help button to an MDI child window. A different approach is required, one that was discovered by Brian Foley of TurboPower Software. See Figure 3-6.

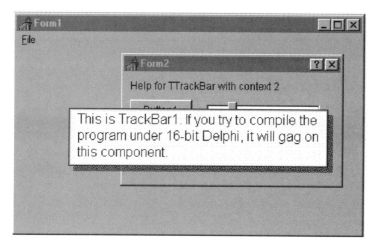

FIGURE 3-6: It takes some finagling, but you can apply the Windows 95 help button to MDI child windows, too.

MDIHLP

MDIHLP1U.DEX

```
object Form1: TForm1
  FormStyle = fsMDIForm
  Menu = MainMenu1
  Position = poDefault
  Scaled = False
  Visible = True
  object MainMenu1: TMainMenu
    object File1: TMenuItem
      Caption = '&File'
    end
  end
end
```

MDIHLP1U.PAS

```
unit mdihlp1u;

{$IFNDEF Win32}
HALT! This is a Delphi32 program only
{$ENDIF}

interface

uses SysUtils, Windows, Messages, Classes, Graphics, Controls,
  Forms, Dialogs, Menus;

type
  TForm1 = class(TForm)
    MainMenu1: TMainMenu;
    File1: TMenuItem;
  end;

var Form1: TForm1;

implementation

{$R *.DFM}

end.
```

MDIHLP2U.DEX

```
object Form2: TForm2
  FormStyle = fsMDIChild
  Position = poDefault
  Scaled = False
  Visible = True
  object Label1: TLabel
  end
  object Button1: TButton
    HelpContext = 1
    Caption = 'Button1'
  end
  object TrackBar1: TTrackBar
    HelpContext = 2
    Orientation = trHorizontal
  end
  object Panel1: TPanel
    HelpContext = 4
    Caption = 'Panel1'
    object BitBtn1: TBitBtn
      HelpContext = 3
      Caption = 'BitBtn1'
      Kind = bkYes
    end
  end
end
```

MDIHLP2U.PAS

```pascal
unit mdihlp2u;

interface

uses SysUtils, Windows, Messages, Classes, Graphics, Controls,
  Forms, Dialogs, Buttons, ExtCtrls, ComCtrls, StdCtrls;

type
  TWMHelp = record
    Msg      : Cardinal;
    Unused   : LongInt;
    HelpInfo : PHelpInfo;
    Result   : LongBool;
  END;
  TForm2 = class(TForm)
    Button1: TButton;
    TrackBar1: TTrackBar;
    Panel1: TPanel;
    BitBtn1: TBitBtn;
    Label1: TLabel;
  private
    procedure CreateWindowHandle(const Params: TCreateParams);
      override;
    procedure DestroyWindowHandle; override;
    procedure WMHelp(VAR Msg: TWMHelp); message WM_HELP;
  end;

var Form2: TForm2;

implementation

{$R *.DFM}
procedure TForm2.CreateWindowHandle(const Params: TCreateParams);
VAR OVI: TOsVersionInfo;
begin
  OVI.dwOsVersionInfoSize := SizeOf(TOsVersionInfo);
  GetVersionEx(OVI);
  IF OVI.dwPlatformID <> VER_PLATFORM_WIN32_WINDOWS THEN
    BEGIN
      Inherited CreateWindowHandle(Params);
      ShowMessage('Feature only available under Windows 95');
      PostQuitMessage(Application.MainForm.Handle);
    END
  ELSE
    WITH Params DO
      WindowHandle:= CreateWindowEx(ExStyle OR WS_EX_CONTEXTHELP OR
        WS_EX_MDICHILD, WinClassName, Caption, Style AND NOT
        (WS_MAXIMIZEBOX OR WS_MINIMIZEBOX), X, Y, Width, Height,
        Application.MainForm.ClientHandle, 0, HInstance, Param);
end;

procedure TForm2.DestroyWindowHandle;
begin
  WITH Application.MainForm DO
    SendMessage(ClientHandle, WM_MDIDESTROY, Handle, 0);
end;
```

```
procedure TForm2.WMHelp(VAR Msg: TWMHelp);
TYPE
  THelpIds = record
    thID, thContext: Integer;
  END;
VAR
  aMenuHelpIDs : ARRAY[0..1] OF THelpIds;
  TC           : TWinControl;
  N            : Word;
BEGIN
  Msg.Result := False;
  IF Msg.HelpInfo^.iContextType=HELPINFO_WINDOW THEN
    BEGIN
      TC := FindControl(Msg.HelpInfo^.hItemHandle);
      IF TC <> NIL THEN
        BEGIN
          FillChar(aMenuHelpIds, SizeOf(aMenuHelpIds), 0);
          aMenuHelpIDs[0].thID := Msg.HelpInfo^.iCtrlID;
          aMenuHelpIDs[0].thContext := TC.HelpContext;
          Label1.Caption := Format('Help for %s with context %d',
            [TC.ClassName, TC.HelpContext]);
          Msg.Result := WinHelp(Msg.HelpInfo^.hItemHandle,
            PChar(Application.HelpFile), HELP_WM_HELP,
            LongInt(@aMenuHelpIDs));
        END;
    END;
END;
end.
```

The reason you cannot simply override CreateParams is that the WS_EX_CONTEXT-HELP style is not valid in a window created by sending a WM_MDICREATE message to the client window (the standard way of creating an MDI child window). However, Windows 95 giveth with one hand what it taketh away with the other. In Windows 95, it's possible to create an MDI child window using the usual CreateWindow call by including the new style bit WS_EX_MDICHILD.

The child window in this case overrides the CreateWindowHandle and DestroyWindowHandle methods to force the creation of an MDI child window having the help button on its title bar. Just as with the BorderIcons.biHelp property, the window must not have either a maximize or a minimize button. When the user presses the help button and then clicks on a control, the form receives a WM_HELP message. The WM_HELP message response method takes this message and builds the correct parameters for a call to WinHelp using the HELP_WM_HELP command. In a non-MDI form with BorderIcons.biHelp set to True, Delphi handles this processing automatically.

This technique is specific to Windows 95; it will not work under Windows NT. The CreateWindowHandle method checks the platform using the GetVersionEx API function. If the result is anything but VER_PLATFORM_WIN32_WINDOWS (which indicates Windows 95), it displays a warning and ends the program.

COMPONENTS

Components are the basic building blocks of a Delphi program. Designing a user interface can be as simple as dragging components onto a form and setting their properties appropriately. If the form is the face your program presents to the world, components are the eyes, the mouth, and other features. The metaphor is almost literal, since components can "speak" to the user by presenting data, and "listen" by accepting input.

Because components are so important, this book devotes nearly half of its chapters to them. Chapters in Part II will cover topics related to components in general, and to three essential components: the menu, the edit box, and the list box. It's surprising how many variations you can accomplish with these simple components.

Delphi components are written in Delphi, and extending existing components can be quite simple. Several solutions in these chapters will involve the creation of descendant components that add new functionality or modify existing behavior. You'll create and install new components in the component palette, and also learn how to create derived components *without* installing them.

CHAPTER 4

Components in General

*E*very individual component has its own purpose and its own special techniques. Several of the following chapters discuss specific components. This chapter covers component arrays, shared event handlers, flyover help, and other topics not linked to specific components.

Component Arrays

Visual Basic (VB) programmers moving to Delphi are often desperate to find the equivalent of VB component arrays. In truth, because multiple Delphi components—even components of different types—can share event handlers, many of the reasons for using component arrays in VB do not apply to Delphi. However, if you truly need a component array, you can create one.

 Creating a component array

`16` `32`

The first step is to consider *why* you want a component array. In Visual Basic, the only way multiple controls can share the same event handler is if they are members of an array.

In Delphi, components can share an event handler without being members of an array. Simply select all the components that are to share the same event handler, flip to the Object Inspector's events page, click on the desired event, and select an event handler.

VB controls that share an event handler must all be the same type, whereas Delphi has no such limitation. As long as all the components respond to a given event with the same type of event handler, you can attach them to the same handler. If you select a group of components of various types and the event you want them to share does not appear in the Object Inspector, that's a clue that one or more of the components cannot share. Either it does not respond to the event, or it responds using a different type of event handler.

In Delphi, you can even connect different events to the same handler, as long as the handler type is compatible. Compatible in this case means that the two event handlers are defined as taking the same set of parameters. For example, OnClick and OnDblClick both take a simple event handler whose one parameter is Sender (a pointer to the component that triggered the event). You can, for example, connect a button's OnClick event and a list box's OnDblClick event to a handler that processes the selected items in the list.

Really creating a component array

16 32

The preceding section attempted to discourage you from creating an array when it's not necessary. One good reason to want an array is for processing all the array elements in a loop. In that case, an array will indeed be helpful, and not difficult to create. The program in Figure 4-1 sets up an array whose elements refer to six buttons already present on the form.

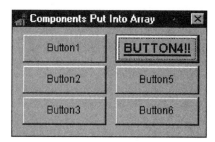

FIGURE 4-1: These six buttons share an event handler that sets all six to a plain font, then sets the one that was pressed to something that stands out a bit.

CARRAY

CARRAYU.DEX

```
object Form1: TForm1
  BorderIcons = [biSystemMenu]
  BorderStyle = bsSingle
```

```
     Caption = 'Components Put Into Array'
     Position = poDefault
     Scaled = False
     OnCreate = FormCreate
     object Button1: TButton
       Caption = 'Button1'
       OnClick = Button1Click
     end
     object Button2: TButton
       Caption = 'Button2'
       OnClick = Button1Click
     end
     object Button3: TButton
       Caption = 'Button3'
       OnClick = Button1Click
     end
     object Button4: TButton
       Caption = 'Button4'
       OnClick = Button1Click
     end
     object Button5: TButton
       Caption = 'Button5'
       OnClick = Button1Click
     end
     object Button6: TButton
       Caption = 'Button6'
       OnClick = Button1Click
     end
   end
```

CARRAYU.PAS

```
unit Carrayu;

interface

uses SysUtils, WinTypes, WinProcs, Messages, Classes, Graphics,
  Controls, Forms, Dialogs, StdCtrls;

type
  TForm1 = class(TForm)
    Button1: TButton;
    Button2: TButton;
    Button3: TButton;
    Button4: TButton;
    Button5: TButton;
    Button6: TButton;
    procedure FormCreate(Sender: TObject);
    procedure Button1Click(Sender: TObject);
  private
    Buttons: ARRAY[1..6] OF TButton;
  end;
```

```
var Form1: TForm1;

implementation

{$R *.DFM}

procedure TForm1.FormCreate(Sender: TObject);
VAR N : Word;
begin
  FOR N := 1 TO 6 DO
    Buttons[N] := FindComponent('Button' + IntToStr(N))
      AS TButton;
end;

procedure TForm1.Button1Click(Sender: TObject);
{All six buttons are connected to this handler}
VAR N : Word;
begin
  FOR N := 1 TO 6 DO
    BEGIN
      Buttons[N].Caption := 'Button'+IntToStr(N);
      Buttons[N].Font.Style := [];
      Buttons[N].Font.Size := 9;
    END;
  WITH Sender AS TButton DO
    BEGIN
      Caption := UpperCase(Caption) + '!!';
      Font.Style := [fsBold, fsUnderline];
      Font.Size := 11;
    END;
end;

end.
```

The array Buttons is declared in the private section of the form's object definition. Each element is just a pointer, so the Buttons array only uses 24 bytes of storage. In the form's OnCreate event handler, a simple loop calls the useful method FindComponent to search for components named Button1 through Button6 and assigns the array's elements to point to them. FindComponent is defined as returning a generic TComponent, so it's almost always necessary to typecast the value it returns to the desired type.

All six buttons connect to the same OnClick event handler. This event handler steps through the array and restores each button's original name and font. Then it takes the particular button that was pressed, gives it a large, bold, underlined font, and appends a pair of exclamation points to its caption. Any time you need to process a whole group of components in the same way, you can use a component array like this.

Creating an array of components at runtime

16 32

Sometimes it's not enough to shoehorn existing components into an array. Sometimes you need to create the array of components at runtime. That's easily done; Figure 4-2 shows an example.

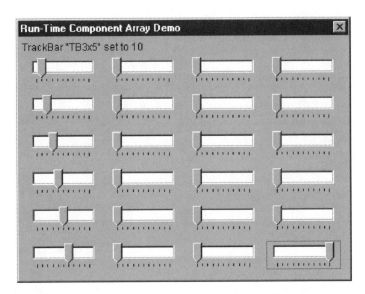

FIGURE 4-2: The 24 trackbars were created in this form's OnCreate event handler (compile the program for 16-bit Delphi and it displays 24 buttons).

COMPARR

COMPARRU.DEX

```
object Form1: TForm1
  BorderIcons = [biSystemMenu, biMinimize]
  BorderStyle = bsDialog
  Caption = 'Run-Time Component Array Demo'
  Position = poDefault
  Scaled = False
  OnCreate = FormCreate
  object Label1: TLabel
  end
end
```

COMPARRU.PAS

```
unit comparru;

interface

uses SysUtils, WinTypes, WinProcs, Messages, Classes, Graphics,
  Controls, Forms, StdCtrls {$IFDEF Win32}, ComCtrls{$ENDIF};

type
  TForm1 = class(TForm)
    Label1: TLabel;
    procedure FormCreate(Sender: TObject);
    procedure Button1Click(Sender: TObject);
    procedure TrackBar1Change(Sender: TObject);
  private
    CompArray: ARRAY[0..3, 0..5] OF
      {$IFDEF Win32}TTrackBar{$ELSE}TButton{$ENDIF};
  end;

var Form1: TForm1;

implementation

{$R *.DFM}

procedure TForm1.FormCreate(Sender: TObject);
VAR Co, Ro : Integer;
begin
  FOR Co := 0 TO 3 DO
    FOR Ro := 0 TO 5 DO
      BEGIN
        CompArray[Co,Ro] := {$IFDEF Win32}TTrackBar{$ELSE}TButton
          {$ENDIF}.Create(Self);
        WITH CompArray[Co,Ro] DO
          BEGIN
            Parent := Self;
            BoundsRect := Rect(8 + (95*Co), 22 + (43*Ro),
              97 + (95*Co), 55 + (43*Ro));
            {$IFDEF Win32}
            Name := Format('TB%dx%d',[Co,Ro]);
            OnChange := TrackBar1Change;
            {$ELSE}
            Caption := Format('(%dx%d)',[Co,Ro]);
            OnClick := Button1Click;
            {$ENDIF}
          END;
      END;
end;

procedure TForm1.Button1Click(Sender: TObject);
begin
  Label1.Caption := Format('Button "%s" was pressed',
    [(Sender AS TButton).Caption]);
end;

procedure TForm1.TrackBar1Change(Sender: TObject);
```

```
begin
  {$IFDEF Win32}
  WITH Sender AS TTrackBar DO
    Label1.Caption := Format('TrackBar "%s" set to %d',
      [Name, Position]);
  {$ENDIF}
end;

end.
```

The most important line in this whole program is the one that says "Parent := Self;". The Create constructor of a TComponent descendant sets the *owner* property of the component to the value passed to it, usually Self, referring to the form. When the owner is destroyed, it takes along all the components it owns. But the parent property may be the form or it may be some other container object like a group box or a notebook page. The component will not be visible until its parent property is assigned.

Notice that each component also has an event handler assigned. The easiest way to create event handlers for components that you'll be creating at runtime is to drop a temporary component of that type on the form, create the handler as if for that component, and then delete it. This will have the added advantage of putting any necessary units in the program's uses clause.

As you can see from this program, component arrays do not have to be one-dimensional. You can set up the array with any number of dimensions that are convenient, as long as you create the elements correctly.

Component Lists

If the number of components needed could vary widely or change during the course of the program, an array may not be the best structure. Delphi's TList object is adept at handling lists of objects that vary in size, while making them as easily accessible as an ordinary array. In fact, there are a couple of interesting component lists already built into Delphi's objects!

Processing all components of one type

16 32

Suppose your program allows the user to choose a font for buttons—how do you change the font of every button? Or perhaps you need to clear all edit boxes at once.

If such a process is frequently executed, or if a certain order must be maintained, use an array. But a general sweep through all of a form's components can be accomplished using the form's ComponentCount property and Components array property. Internally, the elements of this array property are stored in a TList, but Delphi lets you access them in convenient array form.

If you need to distinguish between components whose parent is the form itself and those whose parent is a container of some type, the ControlCount property and Controls array will serve. Here again the elements of the Controls array property are stored internally in a TList. Figure 4-3 shows a program that exercises both arrays.

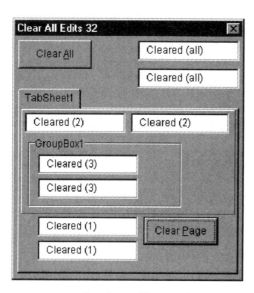

FIGURE 4-3: The Clear All button clears every TEdit and descendant found in the Components array; the Clear Page button clears only those whose parent is the tabsheet page (in 16-bit Delphi, a tabbed notebook is used).

ALLEDIT

ALLEDITU.DEX

```
object Form1: TForm1
  BorderIcons = [biSystemMenu]
  BorderStyle = bsDialog
  Caption = 'Clear All Edits'
  Position = poDefault
  Scaled = False
  OnCreate = FormCreate
  object Edit1: TEdit
```

```
      Text = 'Edit1'
    end
  object TabbedNotebook1: TTabbedNotebook
    object TTabPage
      Caption = 'Default'
      object Panel1: TPanel
        Align = alTop
        object TEdit
        end
        object TEdit
        end
        object GroupBox1: TGroupBox
          Caption = 'GroupBox1'
          object TEdit
          end
          object TEdit
          end
        end
      end
      object TEdit
      end
      object TEdit
      end
      object Button2: TButton
        Caption = 'Clear &Page'
        OnClick = Button2Click
      end
    end
  end
  object TEdit
  end
  object Button1: TButton
    Caption = 'Clear &All'
    OnClick = Button1Click
  end
end
```

ALLEDITU.PAS

```
unit Alleditu;

interface

uses SysUtils, WinTypes, WinProcs, Messages, Classes, Graphics,
  Controls, Forms, Dialogs, StdCtrls, ExtCtrls, TabNotBk
  {$IFDEF Win32}, ComCtrls{$ENDIF};

type
  TForm1 = class(TForm)
    Edit1: TEdit;
    TabbedNotebook1: TTabbedNotebook;
    Panel1: TPanel;
    Button1: TButton;
```

```
      Button2: TButton;
      GroupBox1: TGroupBox;
      procedure Button1Click(Sender: TObject);
      procedure Button2Click(Sender: TObject);
      procedure FormCreate(Sender: TObject);
    private
      {$IFDEF Win32}
      PageControl1 : TPageControl;
      {$ENDIF}
    end;

var Form1: TForm1;

implementation

{$R *.DFM}

procedure TForm1.Button1Click(Sender: TObject);
VAR N : Word;
begin
  FOR N := 0 TO ComponentCount-1 DO
    IF Components[N] IS TEdit THEN
      TEdit(Components[N]).Text := 'Cleared (all)';
end;

procedure TForm1.Button2Click(Sender: TObject);
  procedure ClearContainer(TC: TControl; Lev: Word);
  VAR N : Word;
  BEGIN
    IF TC IS TWinControl THEN
      WITH TWinControl(TC) DO
        IF ControlCount > 0 THEN
          FOR N := 0 TO ControlCount-1 DO
            ClearContainer(Controls[N], Lev+1);
    IF TC IS TEdit THEN
      TEdit(TC).Text := Format('Cleared (%d)', [Lev]);
  END;
begin
  {$IFDEF Win32}
  ClearContainer(PageControl1.ActivePage, 0)
  {$ELSE}
  ClearContainer(TabbedNotebook1.Pages.Objects[0]
    AS TTabPage, 0);
  {$ENDIF}
end;

procedure TForm1.FormCreate(Sender: TObject);
{$IFNDEF Win32}
begin
{$ELSE}
VAR N : Word;
begin
  {create a page control and move the components to it}
  PageControl1 := TPageControl.Create(Self);
  WITH PageControl1 DO
```

```
        BEGIN
          Parent := Self;
          BoundsRect := TabbedNotebook1.BoundsRect;
          WITH TTabSheet.Create(PageControl1) DO
            BEGIN
              PageControl := PageControl1;
              Caption := 'TabSheet1'
            END;
        END;
      WITH TabbedNotebook1.Pages.Objects[0] AS TTabPage DO
        FOR N := ControlCount-1 DOWNTO 0 DO
          Controls[N].Parent := PageControl1.ActivePage;
      TabbedNotebook1.Free;
      Caption := 'Clear All Edits 32';
      {$ENDIF}
    end;

  end.
```

The Button1Click method steps through the form's Components array, checking all indices from 0 to ComponentCount -1. For each component in the array, it checks whether that component is a TEdit. If so, it sets the component's text property to "Cleared (all)". Remember that the IS operator in this case returns True if the component is a TEdit or any descendant of TEdit, including TMemo and TRichEdit.

Note that once the event handler has determined that the component really is a TEdit, it makes a simple typecast rather than using the AS operator. AS raises an exception if the typecast is invalid, but we already know from the IS test that this typecast is valid. There's no point in spending CPU time testing the validity of the typecast twice.

Clearing all the components on the notebook page is a bit more troublesome. The Controls array is a property of every TWinControl; it will be non-empty for a component that contains other components. The example form has a tabbed notebook with a panel on its first page and a group box on the panel. The notebook page, the panel, and the group box each are parent to two TEdits. To find all TEdits on the page, process not only the two directly on the page but the two on the panel, and the two in the group box on the panel.

The ClearContainer procedure can serve as a model for any routine that must act on all components contained in a particular component or in a container. Initially, the tabbed notebook's first and only page is passed to ClearContainer. It processes each component in the page's Controls list in two ways. If the component is a container, ClearContainer calls itself recursively to clear the component's contents. If the component is a TEdit, its text is set to "Cleared" followed by the depth of the component.

If this program is compiled under Delphi32, it takes advantage of the new Windows 95 common controls by substituting PageControl and TabSheet components for the tabbed notebook. The tabbed notebook is still available in Delphi 2.0, of course, but it doesn't quite give the Windows 95 look. Of course, a program designed only for Delphi 2.0 could simply use the Windows 95 controls from the start—the substitution is required because this program can also be compiled under Delphi 1.0. The OnCreate handler first creates the new container components to match the size of the tabbed notebook. It then transfers all components from the tabbed notebook's first page to the PageControl's first TabSheet. Then it discards the tabbed notebook.

Any time you need to locate all components of a certain type, use the Components array. And, if you must restrict your search to components whose parent is a particular container (including the form), use the container's Controls array.

Creating a component array whose size isn't known until runtime

16 32

As previously noted, Delphi's visual components have the array properties Components and Controls. The number of items in these arrays is ComponentCount and ControlCount. In general, ComponentCount will be 0 for any component except the form itself, and ControlCount will be 0 except for certain components that serve as containers, such as TPanel and TGroupBox. Suppose, however, you want to create your own list of components, completely under your program's control.

Figure 4-4 shows a program that handily makes use of a component list. The scroll box at the left contains a bitmapped button corresponding to each drive in a hidden drive combo box. The buttons are contained in a TList, and pressing one of them switches the directory list box to that drive.

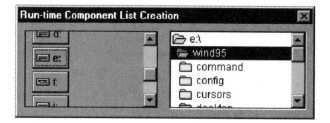

FIGURE 4-4: The glyphs on the bitmapped buttons in this program were copied from a hidden directory combo box.

CLIST

CLISTU.DEX

```
object Form1: TForm1
  BorderStyle = bsDialog
  Caption = 'Run-time Component List Creation'
  Position = poDefault
  Scaled = False
  OnCreate = FormCreate
  object ScrollBox1: TScrollBox
  end
  object DirectoryListBox1: TDirectoryListBox
  end
  object DriveComboBox1: TDriveComboBox
    Visible = False
  end
end
```

CLISTU.PAS

```
unit Clistu;

interface

uses SysUtils, WinTypes, WinProcs, Messages, Classes, Graphics,
  Controls, Forms, Dialogs, StdCtrls, FileCtrl;

type
  TForm1 = class(TForm)
    DriveComboBox1: TDriveComboBox;
    ScrollBox1: TScrollBox;
    DirectoryListBox1: TDirectoryListBox;
    procedure FormCreate(Sender: TObject);
    procedure BitBtn1Click(Sender: TObject);
  private
    BtnList : TList;
  end;

var Form1: TForm1;

implementation
USES Buttons; {for TBitBtn}
{$R *.DFM}

procedure TForm1.FormCreate(Sender: TObject);
VAR N : Word;
begin
  BtnList := TList.Create;
  WITH DriveComboBox1 DO
    FOR N := 0 TO Items.Count-1 DO
      BEGIN
        BtnList.Add(TBitBtn.Create(Self));
        WITH TBitBtn(BtnList[N]) DO
```

```
          BEGIN
            Parent := ScrollBox1;
            BoundsRect := Rect(8, 8+N*28, 53, 33+N*28);
            OnClick := BitBtn1Click;
            WITH DriveComboBox1.Items DO
              Glyph := Objects[N] AS TBitmap;
            Caption := Copy(DriveComboBox1.Items[N], 1, 2);
            Margin  := 4;
          END;
      END;
    ActiveControl := TBitBtn(BtnList[DriveComboBox1.ItemIndex]);
  end;

  procedure TForm1.BitBtn1Click(Sender: TObject);
  VAR OldMode : Word;
  begin
    OldMode := SetErrorMode(SEM_FAILCRITICALERRORS);
    Screen.Cursor := crHourglass;
    try
      try
        WITH Sender AS TBitBtn DO
          DirectoryListBox1.Drive := Caption[1];
      except
        ON EInOutError DO
          MessageBeep(MB_ICONSTOP);
      end;
    finally
      SetErrorMode(OldMode);
      Screen.Cursor := crDefault;
    end;
  end;
end.
```

The form's OnCreate event handler creates one bitmapped button for each drive in the nonvisible drive combo box. The button's owner is the form, but its parent is the scroll box. Each button has the drive letter as its caption and the bitmap used in the drive combo box as its glyph—stealing those bitmaps from the drive combo box is simple.

Pressing any of the drive buttons switches the directory list box to display that drive. However, there's a potential problem if the drive is not ready. By passing the constant SEM_FAILCRITICALERRORS to the Windows API function SetErrorMode, the program tells Windows that it will take responsibility for handling errors. Within the OnClick event handler, a try . . . except block causes the program to beep if it fails to switch to the new drive, and a try . . . finally block ensures that the cursor and the error mode will be restored to their previous values.

When you need to create a list of components and cannot know the number until runtime, the scroll box component is very handy. Give the scroll box as much space as you can spare and simply define the listed components with the scroll box as their parent. The scrolling portion of the box grows as necessary to accommodate the added components.

Component Miscellany

Components are the heart of Delphi programming, so they generate plenty of questions. As previously noted, the next several chapters will cover solutions related to specific components. The remainder of this chapter covers various topics not specific to any individual component type.

 I've lost a component—help!

16 32

You know ListBox7 is around somewhere, because your program refers to it by name. You can't see it anywhere so it must be positioned somewhere off the form or hidden behind another component. How can you get it back?

If the component has a visual representation at runtime, finding a little lost component is child's play. Find the component in the Object Inspector's pull-down list, set the Left and Top properties to 0, and the component will move to the top left corner of the form. If you still don't see it, click on the form's title bar and then select Bring to Front from the Edit menu. Move the component back to its normal niche and all will be well.

If the errant component is a nonvisual one such as a menu or a common dialog, you're in a bit of a bind, because the location properties for these components aren't accessible in the Object Inspector. But you can still bring them back into view at design time.

First, maximize the form. Chances are good your nonvisual components are now visible. If so, drag them to a location that's visible at the form's normal size and then restore the form to that size. Simple!

It's possible that the component will not show up even when the form is maximized. This could happen, for example, if you changed the screen resolution on your development machine. In that case, follow these four steps precisely:

1. Save your project
2. Click on the Object Inspector, and select the lost component in the list at the top

3. Click on the *title bar* of the form

4. Press Ctrl+X, then Ctrl+V

When you cut and paste a nonvisual component, Delphi places it at the top left corner of the form. Now it's in view again. One warning; if the component appears in other component property lists, it will be removed when it's cut and you'll have to restore it by hand. This is most likely to happen with a pop-up menu.

You may prefer this different technique for rescuing a strayed nonvisual component, as it doesn't risk cutting any connections to other components. Load the form's .DFM file into Delphi's code editor so you can edit it in text form. Find the nonvisual component in the listing and set its Left and Top properties to zero. When you close the text representation of the form and reopen the form designer, the component will be back in view.

Supplying status-bar hints and flyover help

16 32

Delphi supports all kinds of help for the user, from context-sensitive help file access to real-time "flyover" hints and status-bar hints. A component's help context is stored in its HelpContext property, but both flyover help and status-bar hints use the Hint property. How can you distinguish the two?

As the program in Figure 4-5 shows, it is possible to use both types of help in one program. It makes sense to have a short hint in the flyover help box and a longer hint on the status bar.

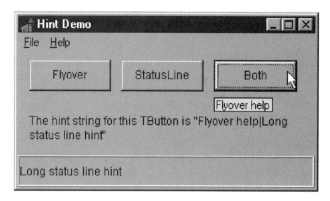

FIGURE 4-5: By manipulating the hint property, you can give components flyover help, status-bar hints, or both.

HINTS

HINTSU.DEX

```
object Form1: TForm1
  BorderIcons = [biSystemMenu, biMinimize]
  BorderStyle = bsSingle
  Caption = 'Hint Demo'
  Menu = MainMenu1
  Position = poDefault
  Scaled = False
  ShowHint = True
  OnCreate = FormCreate
  object Label1: TLabel
    AutoSize = False
    Caption = 'Click things!'
    WordWrap = True
  end
  object Panel1: TPanel
    Align = alBottom
    Alignment = taLeftJustify
    BevelInner = bvLowered
  end
  object Button1: TButton
    Hint = 'Flyover help only|'
    Caption = 'Flyover'
    OnClick = Button1Click
  end
  object Button2: TButton
    Hint = '|Long status line hint only'
    Caption = 'StatusLine'
    OnClick = Button1Click
  end
  object Button3: TButton
    Hint = 'Flyover help|Long status line hint'
    Caption = 'Both'
    OnClick = Button1Click
  end
  object MainMenu1: TMainMenu
    object File1: TMenuItem
      Caption = '&File'
      Hint = 'Hint for File menu'
      object New1: TMenuItem
        Caption = '&New'
        OnClick = Button1Click
      end
      object Exit1: TMenuItem
        Caption = 'E&xit'
        Hint = 'Choosing this item will exit the program'
        OnClick = Exit1Click
      end
    end
```

```
      object Help1: TMenuItem
        Caption = '&Help'
        Hint = 'Hint for Help Menu'
        object Contents1: TMenuItem
          Caption = '&Contents'
          OnClick = Button1Click
        end
        object About1: TMenuItem
          Caption = '&About'
          Hint = 'This menu item WOULD bring up the About box.'
          OnClick = Button1Click
        end
      end
    end
end
```

HINTSU.PAS

```
unit Hintsu;

interface

uses SysUtils, WinTypes, WinProcs, Messages, Classes, Graphics,
  Controls, Forms, Menus, StdCtrls, ExtCtrls;

type
  TForm1 = class(TForm)
    Panel1: TPanel;
    Button1: TButton;
    Button2: TButton;
    Button3: TButton;
    Label1: TLabel;
    MainMenu1: TMainMenu;
    File1: TMenuItem;
    Exit1: TMenuItem;
    Help1: TMenuItem;
    About1: TMenuItem;
    New1: TMenuItem;
    Contents1: TMenuItem;
    procedure FormCreate(Sender: TObject);
    procedure Exit1Click(Sender: TObject);
    procedure Button1Click(Sender: TObject);
  private
    procedure AppOnHint(Sender: TObject);
  end;

var Form1: TForm1;

implementation

{$R *.DFM}

procedure TForm1.AppOnHint(Sender: TObject);
BEGIN
  Panel1.Caption := Application.Hint;
END;
```

```
procedure TForm1.FormCreate(Sender: TObject);
VAR N : Word;
begin
  Application.OnHint := AppOnHint;
  FOR N := 0 TO ComponentCount-1 DO
    IF Components[N] IS TControl THEN
      WITH TControl(Components[N]) DO
        BEGIN
          IF Hint = '' THEN
            Hint := Name + ' hint|Generic hint for the '+
              ClassName+' named '+Name;
        END
    ELSE IF Components[N] IS TMenuItem THEN
      WITH TMenuItem(Components[N]) DO
        IF Hint = '' THEN
          Hint := 'Generic hint for the TMenuItem named '
            + Name;
end;

procedure TForm1.Exit1Click(Sender: TObject);
begin
  Close;
end;


procedure TForm1.Button1Click(Sender: TObject);
VAR TheHint: String;
begin
  TheHint := '';
  IF Sender IS TMenuItem THEN
    TheHint := TMenuItem(Sender).Hint
  ELSE IF Sender IS TControl THEN
    TheHint := TControl(Sender).Hint;
  IF TheHint <> '' THEN
    Label1.Caption := Format('The hint string for '+
        'this %s is "%s"', [Sender.ClassName, TheHint]);
end;


end.
```

Adding flyover help is simply a matter of setting the form's ShowHint property to True and assigning Hint property strings to the components. If an upright bar character (|) is present in the hint string, only the portion before the bar will be used in flyover help.

Status-bar help is just as easy to implement, although not as automated. The AppOnHint method is much like any other event handler, but you must type the whole event handler, declare it in the form's private section, and set Application.OnHint to point to it in the form's OnCreate event handler. Within the handler, the usual behavior is to set a bottom-aligned panel's caption to the current hint string. If an upright bar character (|) is present in the hint string, only the portion *after* the bar will be used as the status-bar help line.

This particular program also sets up a generic hint string for any component that does not have one. It steps through the Components array and checks each element to see if it's a TControl or a descendant. If it is, and its hint string is empty, a hint containing the control type and the name is generated. If this element is not a TControl, the code checks whether it's a TMenuItem with no hint and, if so, generates an appropriate hint string.

Distinguishing different types of components in a shared event handler

16 32

It's all very well to say that many different types of components can share the same event handler, but you'll often need to refer to component properties within the handler.

If the properties you want to reference are common to all the component types that share the event handler, you *may* be able to get access by typecasting the Sender parameter to a common ancestor of all the component types. However, the shared ancestor frequently will have the desired property in its Protected section, making it unavailable for use. The program shown in Figure 4-6 demonstrates what you can do about that.

FIGURE 4-6: All the components in this form share one OnClick event handler.

SHAREV

SHAREVU.DEX

```
object Form1: TForm1
  BorderIcons = [biSystemMenu, biMinimize]
  BorderStyle = bsDialog
  Caption = 'Shared Event Handler'
  Position = poDefault
  Scaled = False
  object Label1: TLabel
    Caption = 'Label1'
    OnClick = Label1Click
  end
  object Edit1: TEdit
    Text = 'Edit1'
    OnClick = Label1Click
  end
  object Memo1: TMemo
    OnClick = Label1Click
  end
  object Button1: TButton
    Caption = 'Button1'
    OnClick = Label1Click
  end
  object RadioButton1: TRadioButton
    Caption = 'RadioButton1'
    OnClick = Label1Click
  end
  object CheckBox1: TCheckBox
    Caption = 'CheckBox1'
    OnClick = Label1Click
  end
  object BitBtn1: TBitBtn
    OnClick = Label1Click
    Kind = bkYes
  end
end
```

SHAREVU.PAS

```
unit Sharevu;

interface

uses SysUtils, WinTypes, WinProcs, Messages, Classes, Graphics,
  Controls, Forms, Dialogs, StdCtrls, Buttons;

type
  TForm1 = class(TForm)
    Label1: TLabel;
    Edit1: TEdit;
```

```
      Memo1: TMemo;
      Button1: TButton;
      RadioButton1: TRadioButton;
      CheckBox1: TCheckBox;
      BitBtn1: TBitBtn;
      procedure Label1Click(Sender: TObject);
    end;

var Form1: TForm1;

implementation

{$R *.DFM}

procedure TForm1.Label1Click(Sender: TObject);
begin
  IF Sender IS TLabel THEN
    TLabel(Sender).Caption := 'Clicked Label'
  ELSE IF Sender IS TCustomEdit THEN
    TCustomEdit(Sender).Text := 'Clicked Edit'
  ELSE IF Sender IS TButtonControl THEN
    TButton(Sender).Caption := 'Clicked Button';
end;

end.
```

Both the edit box and the memo box have a Text property defined in their common ancestor TCustomEdit. If the component that triggered the OnClick event is a descendant of TCustomEdit, the event handler typecasts the sender to TCustomEdit and sets its text. The label component has no useful common ancestors with the other components on the form, so it's treated separately. If the OnClick event handler is triggered by a label, it typecasts the sender to TLabel and sets its caption.

Both buttons, the check box and the radio button have a Caption property, and their common ancestor TButtonControl also has a Caption property. However, this property is protected in TButtonControl, so the event handler typecasts a sender of these types to TButton to set its caption.

Strictly speaking, you can only typecast an object to its actual type or to a direct ancestor of that type. TButton is not an ancestor of TRadioButton or of TCheckBox. What legitimizes this typecast is that it refers only to a property (Caption) belonging to the common ancestor. This technique of typecasting to a "cousin" class can be useful, but you must be extremely careful to refer only to properties and methods that exist in a common ancestor of the declared object type and the actual object type.

CHAPTER 5

Menus

*D*elphi provides components for displaying both standard, across-the-top menus and Windows 95-style, pop-up menus (whether or not you're using Windows 95). This chapter demonstrates how to simulate "accelerator" resources using a hidden menu, how to create a menu at runtime, and how to use features such as owner-draw menu items that are not implemented in the Delphi menu components.

Pop-Up Menus

In Windows 95, just about anything on the screen responds to a right-click by displaying a pop-up menu. When you program with Delphi, your programs can have those menus whether or not they're running under Windows 95. And, as it turns out, there are some unexpected side benefits to using pop-up menus.

 Making a pop-up menu see through components

16 32

To make a pop-up menu appear on a right-click of the form, set the menu's AutoPop property to True and set the form's PopupMenu property to the name of the menu. However, you may be surprised to find that right-clicking any component on the form also brings up the pop-up menu, and the menu's PopupComponent run-time property indicates that it popped up over the form. It's as if the components are transparent to the right-click.

There are two ways to handle this problem. You may want a pop-up menu to only appear when the form itself is right-clicked. In that case, create a second pop-up menu with no menu items, select all the components on the form, and set their PopupMenu property to this empty menu. Alternatively, you may want the main pop-up menu to appear, but have it "know" that it's over a component rather than over the form. In that case, select all the components and set their PopupMenu property to the main pop-up menu. This program demonstrates three possibilities: the form's pop-up menu is suppressed for one button, is not suppressed for another, and is shared by a third.

NOPOP

NOPOPU.DEX

```
object Form1: TForm1
  PopupMenu = PopupMenu1
  Position = poDefault
  Scaled = False
  object Label1: TLabel
  end
  object Button1: TButton
    Caption = 'Popup Suppressed'
    PopupMenu = PopupMenu2
  end
  object Button2: TButton
    Caption = 'Popup Not Suppressed'
  end
  object Button3: TButton
    Caption = 'Popup Shared'
    PopupMenu = PopupMenu1
  end
  object PopupMenu1: TPopupMenu
    OnPopup = PopupMenu1Popup
    object Foo1: TMenuItem
      Caption = '&Foo'
    end
    object Bar1: TMenuItem
      Caption = '&Bar'
    end
  end
  object PopupMenu2: TPopupMenu
  end
end
```

NOPOPU.PAS

```
unit Nopopu;

interface

uses SysUtils, WinTypes, WinProcs, Messages, Classes, Graphics,
  Controls, Forms, Menus, StdCtrls;

type
```

```
    TForm1 = class(TForm)
      PopupMenu1: TPopupMenu;
      Foo1: TMenuItem;
      Bar1: TMenuItem;
      Button1: TButton;
      Button2: TButton;
      PopupMenu2: TPopupMenu;
      Label1: TLabel;
      Button3: TButton;
      procedure PopupMenu1Popup(Sender: TObject);
    end;

  var Form1: TForm1;

  implementation

  {$R *.DFM}

  procedure TForm1.PopupMenu1Popup(Sender: TObject);
  begin
    WITH Sender AS TPopupMenu DO
      Label1.Caption :='Popped up over a '+
        PopupComponent.ClassName;
  end;

  end.
```

The OnPopup event handler for the main pop-up menu component simply sets the caption of a label to the class name of the component over which it popped up, to demonstrate that this information is available. You can write the OnPopup handler to enable or disable items in the menu based on what kind of component was clicked.

Defining accelerator resources for hotkeys

16 32

If you've done any Windows programming before learning Delphi, you may have used a type of resource called ACCELERATOR. An accelerator resource translates a particular keystroke into a WM_COMMAND message for your program. The old-fashioned way of establishing shortcut keys for menu items had been to define an accelerator with the same command ID as the menu item. Delphi handles menu shortcuts *for* you, but if you attempt to load an accelerator resource for nonmenu-related shortcut keys, you'll find it does not work.

As it turns out, you can use Delphi's menu shortcuts in exactly the same way as old-fashioned accelerator resources, except without the bother of using a resource compiler. Create a pop-up menu with AutoPop set to False, set the form's PopupMenu to point to it, and create a menu item for each "accelerator," setting its Shortcut property to the desired key combination. Or, if you prefer, create a top-level item in the main menu to hold the shortcuts, and set its Visible property to False. Either way, you control the action of each key by setting the OnClick property of its corresponding event handler. Here's a program that demonstrates both techniques and, as a bonus, shows how to create menu items at runtime.

ACCEL

ACCELU.DEX

```
object Form1: TForm1
  Caption = 'Simulated Accelerators Demo'
  Menu = MainMenu1
  PopupMenu = PopupMenu1
  Position = poDefault
  Scaled = False
  OnCreate = FormCreate
  object Label1: TLabel
    Caption = 'Press Ctrl+F1 thru Ctrl+F12'
  end
  object Label2: TLabel
    Caption = 'or Shift+Ctrl+A thru Shift+Ctrl+Z'
  end
  object Label3: TLabel
    Caption = 'You pressed...'
  end
  object PopupMenu1: TPopupMenu
    AutoPopup = False
  end
  object MainMenu1: TMainMenu
    object File1: TMenuItem
      Caption = '&File'
    end
    object Invisible1: TMenuItem
      Caption = 'Invisible'
      Visible = False
    end
    object Help1: TMenuItem
      Caption = '&Help'
    end
  end
end
```

ACCELU.PAS

```
unit Accelu;

interface

uses SysUtils, WinTypes, WinProcs, Messages, Classes, Graphics,
  Controls, Forms, Menus, StdCtrls;
```

```
type
  TForm1 = class(TForm)
    Label1: TLabel;
    PopupMenu1: TPopupMenu;
    MainMenu1: TMainMenu;
    File1: TMenuItem;
    Invisible1: TMenuItem;
    Help1: TMenuItem;
    Label2: TLabel;
    Label3: TLabel;
    procedure AllClick(Sender: TObject);
    procedure FormCreate(Sender: TObject);
  end;

var Form1: TForm1;

implementation

{$R *.DFM}

procedure TForm1.AllClick(Sender: TObject);
begin
  WITH Sender AS TMenuItem DO
    Label3.Caption := 'You pressed '+ShortCutToText(ShortCut);
end;

procedure TForm1.FormCreate(Sender: TObject);
VAR N : Integer;
begin
  WITH PopupMenu1 DO
    FOR N := 1 TO 12 DO
      Items.Add(NewItem('', ShortCut(VK_F1+N-1, [ssCtrl]),
        False, True, AllClick, 0, ''));
  WITH Invisible1 DO
    FOR N := 0 TO 25 DO
      Add(NewItem('', Menus.ShortCut(Ord('A')+N,
        [ssCtrl,ssShift]), False, True, AllClick, 0, ''));
end;

end.
```

Of course, both menus could have been built in the Menu Designer, but, in this case, it was substantially easier to create them at runtime using the NewItem function. This function is not a method of any Delphi object; it's just a simple function residing in the Menus unit that returns a TMenuItem initialized to match its parameters.

NewItem sets all the important properties of the TMenuItem it creates, including the keyboard shortcut. The function named ShortCut takes a virtual key code and a shift state set and returns the corresponding shortcut code. However, this name collision between the ShortCut property and the ShortCut function sometimes causes problems. The WITH PopupMenu1 compound statement works, because TPopupMenu does not have a Shortcut method. But, in the WITH Invisible1 compound statement, it's necessary to qualify the function call as Menus.ShortCut, to reference the ShortCut function in the Menus unit rather than the Shortcut property of the menu item.

Whether the menu items are created at design time or at runtime, you can use this technique whenever you need the equivalent of ACCELERATOR resources.

Creating submenu items at runtime

16 32

For an example of run-time menu item creation, refer to the preceding program. In this program, the form's OnCreate event handler adds a series of items to a pop-up menu, and adds another series of items to a top-level menu item. In both cases, the NewItem function is used to create the items. There's also a NewSubMenu function for creating a submenu, plus NewMenu and NewPopupMenu for creating the whole menu object from scratch. NewLine rounds out the set; it creates a separator. Later in this chapter, we'll create a whole submenu tree using these functions.

Help Menus

In a menu popularity contest, the Help menu would surely win. It's the first thing to which troubled users turn—heaven forbid they read the manual! Make sure your programs have a Help menu, and make sure it contains all the right items.

Forcing the "Help" menu to the right-hand side of the menu bar

16 32

You rarely see this style at present, but prior to Windows 3.1 it was quite common. Items on the menu bar would start from the left, as always, but the Help menu, the last item, would be aligned with the right edge of the menu bar. How did they do that?

This type of menu, illustrated in Figure 5-1, is not recommended in Windows 3.1 or NT, and is not *possible* in Windows 95. However, when possible, it's simple. Just prefix the help menu's caption with a backspace character, ASCII #8. This must be done at runtime; you cannot insert the needed backspace within the menu designer.

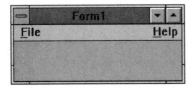

FIGURE 5-1: This Macintosh-like menu, with the Help item at the far right, can easily be created in Delphi, as long as the program does not run under Windows 95.

RITEHELP

RITEHLPU.DEX

```
object Form1: TForm1
  Menu = MainMenu1
  Position = poDefault
  Scaled = False
  OnCreate = FormCreate
  object MainMenu1: TMainMenu
    object File1: TMenuItem
      Caption = '&File'
    end
    object Help1: TMenuItem
      Caption = '&Help'
    end
  end
end
```

RITEHLPU.PAS

```
unit Ritehlpu;

interface

uses SysUtils, WinTypes, WinProcs, Messages, Classes, Graphics,
  Controls, Forms, Dialogs, Menus;

type
  TForm1 = class(TForm)
    MainMenu1: TMainMenu;
    File1: TMenuItem;
    Help1: TMenuItem;
    procedure FormCreate(Sender: TObject);
  end;

var Form1: TForm1;

implementation

{$R *.DFM}
```

```
procedure TForm1.FormCreate(Sender: TObject);
begin
  IF Swap(LoWord(GetVersion)) >= $35F THEN
    ShowMessage('This technique does not work in Windows95');
  Help1.Caption := #8+Help1.Caption;
end;

end.
```

When a 16-bit program needs to detect whether it's running Windows 95, the test to use is the one shown here. The low word of the value returned by GetVersion is the Windows version in byte-reversed format. The Swap function swaps the high and low bytes, putting the major version in the high byte. The hex number 5F is 95 in decimal; the value $35F corresponds to 3.95, which is the value returned by GetVersion to a 16-bit program. A 32-bit program making the same function call would get $400, but that's still greater than or equal to $35F.

Implementing standard Help menu items

16 32

Delphi programs easily implement context-sensitive help. Just set the application's help file in the Project Options dialog, or set Application.HelpFile in the program's code. Pressing F1 will bring up the help topic associated with the HelpContext of the active control. However, most Windows programs with help systems implement four particular items under the Help menu.

The standard help items have specific names and functions, as shown in Figure 5-2. You can add the items to a menu in the Menu Designer by inserting the Help Menu template.

FIGURE 5-2: When your program includes a help system, always add a help menu with these four standard items.

STDHLP

STDHLPU.DEX

```
object Form1: TForm1
  Menu = MainMenu1
  Position = poDefault
  Scaled = False
  OnCreate = FormCreate
  object MainMenu1: TMainMenu
    object File1: TMenuItem
      Caption = '&File'
    end
    object Help1: TMenuItem
      Caption = '&Help'
      object Contents1: TMenuItem
        Caption = '&Contents'
        OnClick = Contents1Click
      end
      object SearchforHelpOn1: TMenuItem
        Caption = '&Search for Help On...'
        OnClick = SearchforHelpOn1Click
      end
      object HowtoUseHelp1: TMenuItem
        Caption = '&How to Use Help'
        OnClick = HowtoUseHelp1Click
      end
      object N1: TMenuItem
        Caption = '-'
      end
      object AboutProgram1: TMenuItem
        Caption = 'About Program...'
        OnClick = AboutProgram1Click
      end
    end
  end
end
```

STDHLPU.PAS

```
unit Stdhlpu;

interface

uses SysUtils, WinTypes, WinProcs, Messages, Classes, Graphics,
  Controls, Forms, Dialogs, Menus;

type
  TForm1 = class(TForm)
    MainMenu1: TMainMenu;
    File1: TMenuItem;
```

```
        Help1: TMenuItem;
        Contents1: TMenuItem;
        SearchforHelpOn1: TMenuItem;
        HowtoUseHelp1: TMenuItem;
        N1: TMenuItem;
        AboutProgram1: TMenuItem;
        procedure FormCreate(Sender: TObject);
        procedure Contents1Click(Sender: TObject);
        procedure SearchforHelpOn1Click(Sender: TObject);
        procedure HowtoUseHelp1Click(Sender: TObject);
        procedure AboutProgram1Click(Sender: TObject);
    end;

var Form1: TForm1;

implementation

{$R *.DFM}

procedure TForm1.FormCreate(Sender: TObject);
begin
    Application.HelpFile := 'DELPHI.HLP';
end;

procedure TForm1.Contents1Click(Sender: TObject);
begin
    Application.HelpCommand(HELP_CONTENTS, 0);
end;

procedure TForm1.SearchforHelpOn1Click(Sender: TObject);
begin
    Application.HelpCommand(HELP_PARTIALKEY, 0);
end;

procedure TForm1.HowtoUseHelp1Click(Sender: TObject);
begin
    Application.HelpCommand(HELP_HELPONHELP, 0);
end;

procedure TForm1.AboutProgram1Click(Sender: TObject);
begin
    MessageDlg('<program name> Copyright © 1996 by Yours Truly',
        mtInformation, [mbOK], 0);
end;

end.
```

This example program uses Delphi's own help file; you may need to add a pathname to the line in the FormCreate method. Three of the four menu commands call the Application object's HelpCommand method, passing a constant that indicates what help function is wanted. The fourth uses MessageDlg to display a very simple About box. In your own programs, you'll probably want to use a separate form for the About box, one that gives more information about your program.

Menu Appearance

Windows menus tend to have a very uniform appearance. They use a standard font, and their background color, their text color, and their highlight color are controlled by Control Panel settings. However, Windows permits more freedom of expression to menu items than the Delphi menu components expose. Menu items can be bitmaps, they can use different glyphs to show the checked and unchecked state, and they can even be drawn by the form that owns them.

 ## Using bitmap menu items

Delphi's menu components make it easy to control *some* properties of menu items. You can create a shortcut, enable or disable a menu item, and check or uncheck it with ease. However, there is no built-in access to the Windows feature that allows menu items to be bitmaps rather than strings. Worse yet, if you manage to jam a bitmap into a menu item, it may unexpectedly disappear, because Delphi destroys and rebuilds menus on the fly.

The Windows API function ModifyMenu can turn an ordinary menu item into one that displays a bitmap. The program in Figure 5-3 builds bitmaps illustrating the hatched brush styles described by its six submenu items; clicking one of the items checks it and changes the form's background brush to the corresponding hatch style.

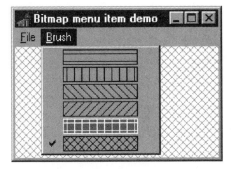

FIGURE 5-3: Bitmap menu items can sometimes be clearer than text descriptions, as this figure shows.

BITMENU

BITMENUU.DEX

```
object Form1: TForm1
  Caption = 'Bitmap menu item demo'
  Menu = MainMenu1
  Position = poDefault
  Scaled = False
  OnCreate = FormCreate
  object MainMenu1: TMainMenu
    object File1: TMenuItem
      Caption = '&File'
    end
    object Brush1: TMenuItem
      Caption = '&Brush'
      object Horizontal1: TMenuItem
        Tag = 2
        Caption = 'Horizontal'
        OnClick = BrushStyleClick
      end
      object Vertical1: TMenuItem
        Tag = 3
        Caption = 'Vertical'
        OnClick = BrushStyleClick
      end
      object FDiagonal1: TMenuItem
        Tag = 4
        Caption = 'FDiagonal'
        OnClick = BrushStyleClick
      end
      object BDiagonal1: TMenuItem
        Tag = 5
        Caption = 'BDiagonal'
        OnClick = BrushStyleClick
      end
      object Cross1: TMenuItem
        Tag = 6
        Caption = 'Cross'
        OnClick = BrushStyleClick
      end
      object DiagCross1: TMenuItem
        Tag = 7
        Caption = 'DiagCross'
        OnClick = BrushStyleClick
      end
    end
  end
end
```

BITMENUU.PAS

```pascal
unit bitmenuu;

interface

uses SysUtils, WinTypes, WinProcs, Messages, Classes, Graphics,
  Controls, Forms, Dialogs, ExtCtrls, Menus;

type
  TForm1 = class(TForm)
    MainMenu1: TMainMenu;
    File1: TMenuItem;
    Brush1: TMenuItem;
    Horizontal1: TMenuItem;
    Vertical1: TMenuItem;
    FDiagonal1: TMenuItem;
    BDiagonal1: TMenuItem;
    Cross1: TMenuItem;
    DiagCross1: TMenuItem;
    procedure FormCreate(Sender: TObject);
    procedure BrushStyleClick(Sender: TObject);
  private
    Bitmaps : ARRAY[0..5] OF TBitmap;
  end;

var Form1: TForm1;

implementation

{$R *.DFM}

procedure TForm1.FormCreate(Sender: TObject);
VAR N : Integer;
begin
  WITH Brush1 DO
    FOR N := 0 TO 5 DO
      BEGIN
        Bitmaps[N] := TBitmap.Create;
        WITH Bitmaps[N], Canvas DO
          BEGIN
            Width := 80;
            Height := 16;
            Brush.Color := clMenu;
            Rectangle(0,0,80,16);
            Brush.Color := clMenuText;
            Brush.Style := TBrushStyle(N+2);
            Rectangle(0,0,80,16);
          END;
        ModifyMenu(Handle, N, MF_BYPOSITION OR MF_BITMAP,
          GetMenuItemID(Handle, N), PChar(Bitmaps[N].Handle));
      END;
end;
```

```
procedure TForm1.BrushStyleClick(Sender: TObject);
VAR N : Integer;
begin
  WITH Brush1 DO
    FOR N := 0 TO Count-1 DO
      {$IFDEF Win32}
      Items[N].Checked := Items[N]=Sender;
      {$ELSE}
      IF Items[N] = Sender THEN
        CheckMenuItem(Handle, N, MF_BYPOSITION OR MF_CHECKED)
      ELSE
        CheckMenuItem(Handle, N, MF_BYPOSITION OR MF_UNCHECKED);
      {$ENDIF}
    WITH Sender AS TMenuItem DO Brush.Style := TBrushStyle(Tag);
    Refresh;
end;

end.
```

The form's OnCreate event handler builds five bitmaps showing the five hatched brush styles and uses ModifyMenu to assign one of them to each of the five choices under the Brush menu. That's enough to create bitmap menu items, but keeping them in place requires a bit more work if you're using 16-bit Delphi. Changing a simple property like Checked or Enabled will eliminate the bitmap, because the TMenuItem object internally calls a Windows API function that sets *all* of the menu item's properties to change any of them, and it disregards the possibility that the item might have an associated bitmap.

The OnClick event handler for this program's bitmap menu items avoids the problem by calling the Windows API function CheckMenuItem instead of setting the Checked property. It then sets the form's Brush property to the corresponding hatched brush and calls the Refresh method to redraw the form with its new background. If your menu bitmaps unexpectedly disappear under 16-bit Delphi, look for code that directly sets menu item properties. Then replace that code with an equivalent Windows API function call.

Changing the menu check mark

16 32

It's simple to set a menu item's Checked property to indicate the presence or the absence of a feature. This kind of menu item operates like a check box. However, the Checked property can also be used to make several menu items act like radio buttons; only one of them will be checked at a time. The user can be confused by these two different kinds of check marks. Delphi 2.0 automates creation of menu items that act like radio buttons, but in Delphi 1.0 some coding is necessary. However, this hand-coding also provides more flexibility, as Figure 5-4 shows.

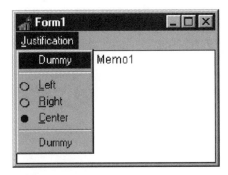

FIGURE 5-4: In this program, special bitmaps are provided to show the checked state (black circle) and the unchecked state (open circle) of mutually exclusive menu items.

RADMENU

RADMENUU.DEX

```
object Form1: TForm1
  Menu = MainMenu1
  Position = poDefault
  Scaled = False
  OnCreate = FormCreate
  object Memo1: TMemo
    Align = alClient
  end
  object MainMenu1: TMainMenu
    object Justification1: TMenuItem
      Caption = '&Justification'
      object Dummy1: TMenuItem
        Caption = 'Dummy'
      end
      object N1: TMenuItem
        Caption = '-'
      end
      object Left1: TMenuItem
        Caption = '&Left'
        OnClick = JustClick
      end
      object Right1: TMenuItem
        Tag = 1
        Caption = '&Right'
        OnClick = JustClick
```

```
          end
          object Center1: TMenuItem
            Tag = 2
            Caption = '&Center'
            OnClick = JustClick
          end
          object N2: TMenuItem
            Caption = '-'
          end
          object Dummy2: TMenuItem
            Caption = 'Dummy'
          end
        end
      end
  end
```

RADMENUU.PAS

```
unit radmenuu;

interface

uses SysUtils, WinTypes, WinProcs, Messages, Classes, Graphics,
  Controls, Forms, Dialogs, Menus, StdCtrls, ExtCtrls;

type
  TForm1 = class(TForm)
    MainMenu1: TMainMenu;
    Justification1: TMenuItem;
    Left1: TMenuItem;
    Right1: TMenuItem;
    Center1: TMenuItem;
    Memo1: TMemo;
    Dummy1: TMenuItem;
    N1: TMenuItem;
    N2: TMenuItem;
    Dummy2: TMenuItem;
    procedure FormCreate(Sender: TObject);
    procedure JustClick(Sender: TObject);
  private
    bmCheck, bmUncheck: TBitmap;
  end;

var Form1: TForm1;

implementation

{$R *.DFM}
FUNCTION MakeCheckBmp(C: Char): TBitmap;
VAR
  L : LongInt;
  R : TRect;
BEGIN
  L := GetMenuCheckMarkDimensions;
```

```
      Result := TBitmap.Create;
      WITH Result DO
        BEGIN
          Width  := LoWord(L);
          Height := HiWord(L);
          Canvas.FillRect(Rect(0, 0, Width, Height));
          Canvas.Font.Name := 'WingDings';
          Canvas.Font.Size := 10;
          R := Rect(0, 0, Width, Height);
          DrawText(Canvas.Handle, @C, 1, R, DT_CENTER OR DT_VCENTER);
        END;
  END;
  procedure TForm1.FormCreate(Sender: TObject);
  VAR N : Integer;
  begin
    bmCheck   := MakeCheckBmp('l'); {try 'n'}
    bmUncheck := MakeCheckBmp('m'); {try 'o'}
    Justification1.Items[2].Checked := True;
    FOR N := 2 TO 4 DO
      SetMenuItemBitmaps(Justification1.Handle, N, MF_BYPOSITION,
        bmUncheck.Handle, bmCheck.Handle);
  end;
  procedure TForm1.JustClick(Sender: TObject);
  VAR N : Integer;
  begin
    Memo1.Alignment := TAlignment((Sender AS TMenuItem).Tag);
    {don't set Checked property, else lose bitmaps in 16-bit}
    WITH Justification1 DO
      FOR N := 2 TO 4 DO
        IF Items[N] = Sender THEN
          CheckMenuItem(Handle, N, MF_BYPOSITION OR MF_CHECKED)
        ELSE CheckMenuItem(Handle,N,MF_BYPOSITION OR MF_UNCHECKED);
  end;

  end.
```

In order to get the radio-button style check marks in Delphi 1.0, the program needs to create bitmaps for the checked and unchecked states. (Replace bmUncheck.Handle with 0 in the code to more closely emulate the Windows 95 behavior.) The GetMenuCheckMarkDimensions API function returns the dimensions to use, and the program creates two bitmaps of those dimensions. It uses the DrawText API function to draw a character from the WingDings font on each bitmap ('l' in WingDings is a filled circle, 'm' is an open circle)—DrawText supports centering text both horizontally and vertically.

Once the bitmaps have been created, they're installed using a call to SetMenuItemBitmaps for each menu item involved. As in the bitmap menu item example, however, there's a small problem. Making a seemingly innocent change to properties of the menu item component in 16-bit Delphi will eliminate the changed bitmaps. Here again use CheckMenuItem in the OnClick handler for the menu items to check or uncheck the items without losing the check mark bitmaps.

In Delphi 2.0, the TMenuItem component's new RadioItem property controls the creation of radio button groups that function like a set of radio buttons. Set the GroupIndex property for each of the items to the same nonzero value, and set the RadioItem property to True. That's all you need to do. When the Checked property of one of the items is set to True, all the others automatically become False. And, if you're running under Windows 95 (or under Windows NT with the Windows 95 shell), the filled-circle check mark appears automatically. Here is what the example program looks like when rewritten to take advantage of Delphi 2.0.

RADMN32

RADMN32U.DEX

```
object Form1: TForm1
  Menu = MainMenu1
  Position = poDefault
  Scaled = False
  object Memo1: TMemo
    Align = alClient
  end
  object MainMenu1: TMainMenu
    object Justification1: TMenuItem
      Caption = '&Justification'
      object Dummy1: TMenuItem
        Caption = 'Dummy'
      end
      object N1: TMenuItem
        Caption = '-'
      end
      object Left1: TMenuItem
        Caption = '&Left'
        Checked = True
        GroupIndex = 1
        RadioItem = True
        OnClick = JustClick
      end
      object Right1: TMenuItem
        Tag = 1
        Caption = '&Right'
        GroupIndex = 1
        RadioItem = True
        OnClick = JustClick
      end
      object Center1: TMenuItem
        Tag = 2
        Caption = '&Center'
```

```
        GroupIndex = 1
        RadioItem = True
        OnClick = JustClick
      end
      object N2: TMenuItem
        Caption = '-'
        GroupIndex = 1
      end
      object Dummy2: TMenuItem
        Caption = 'Dummy'
        GroupIndex = 2
      end
    end
  end
end
```

RADMN32U.PAS

```
unit radmn32u;

interface

uses SysUtils, WinTypes, WinProcs, Messages, Classes, Graphics,
  Controls, Forms, Dialogs, Menus, StdCtrls, ExtCtrls;

type
  TForm1 = class(TForm)
    MainMenu1: TMainMenu;
    Justification1: TMenuItem;
    Left1: TMenuItem;
    Right1: TMenuItem;
    Center1: TMenuItem;
    Memo1: TMemo;
    Dummy1: TMenuItem;
    N1: TMenuItem;
    N2: TMenuItem;
    Dummy2: TMenuItem;
    procedure JustClick(Sender: TObject);
  end;

var Form1: TForm1;

implementation

{$R *.DFM}

procedure TForm1.JustClick(Sender: TObject);
begin
  (Sender AS TMenuItem).Checked := True;
  Memo1.Alignment := TAlignment((Sender AS TMenuItem).Tag);
end;

end.
```

As you can see, the Delphi 2.0 version requires next to no code.

Creating owner-draw menu items

16 32

Bitmap menu items are nice, but creating all those bitmaps uses a lot of resources, especially if the menu has a lot of items. It can also be tough if the exact bitmaps to use are not known at design time. Making the menu owner-draw is one way to take over the process while using fewer resources. How can you do this in Delphi?

The effort involved is little more than that of creating bitmap menu items. Your program must respond to the WM_MEASUREITEM and WM_DRAWITEM messages to tell Windows the size of each item and to do the actual drawing. This can be useful indeed, as the program in Figure 5-5 shows.

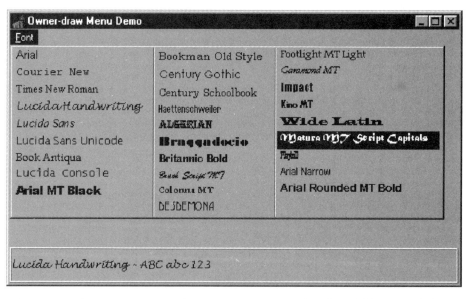

FIGURE 5-5: This menu was created at runtime to contain a list of available nonsymbol TrueType fonts; each owner-draw menu item displays in the appropriate font.

ODMENU

ODMENUU.DEX

```
object Form1: TForm1
  Caption = 'Owner-draw Menu Demo'
  Menu = MainMenu1
  Position = poDefault
```

```
    Scaled = False
    OnCreate = FormCreate
    object Panel1: TPanel
      Align = alBottom
      Alignment = taLeftJustify
      BevelInner = bvLowered
      Caption = ' Sample ABC abc 123'
    end
    object MainMenu1: TMainMenu
      object Font1: TMenuItem
        Caption = '&Font'
      end
    end
end
```

ODMENUU.PAS

```
unit Odmenuu;

interface

uses SysUtils, WinTypes, WinProcs, Messages, Classes, Graphics,
  Controls, Forms, Dialogs, Menus, StdCtrls, ExtCtrls;

type
  TForm1 = class(TForm)
    MainMenu1: TMainMenu;
    Font1: TMenuItem;
    Panel1: TPanel;
    procedure FormCreate(Sender: TObject);
    procedure FontClick(Sender: TObject);
  private
    procedure WMMeasureItem(VAR Msg: TWMMeasureItem);
      message WM_MEASUREITEM;
    procedure WMDrawItem(VAR Msg: TWMDrawItem);
      message WM_DRAWITEM;
  end;

var Form1: TForm1;

implementation

{$R *.DFM}

procedure TForm1.FormCreate(Sender: TObject);
VAR N : Integer;
  FUNCTION IsTrueTypeText(const fName: String): Boolean;
  VAR
    TTM      : TTextMetric;
    WasName : String;
  begin
    WasName := Font.Name;
    Font.Name := fName;
    GetTextMetrics(Canvas.Handle, TTM);
    Font.Name := WasName;
```

```
            Result := (TTM.tmPitchAndFamily AND TMPF_TRUETYPE > 0) AND
                (TTM.tmCharSet <> SYMBOL_CHARSET);
        end;
begin
    FOR N := 0 TO Screen.Fonts.Count-1 DO
        IF IsTrueTypeText(Screen.Fonts[N]) THEN
            Font1.Add(NewItem(Screen.Fonts[N], 0, False, True,
                FontClick, 0, ''));
    WITH Font1 DO
        FOR N := 0 TO Count-1 DO
            BEGIN
                IF (N+1) MOD 10 = 0 THEN
                    ModifyMenu(Handle, N, MF_BYPOSITION OR MF_OWNERDRAW
                        OR MF_MENUBARBREAK, GetMenuItemID(Handle, N),
                        Pointer(Items[N]))
                ELSE
                    ModifyMenu(Handle, N, MF_BYPOSITION OR MF_OWNERDRAW,
                        GetMenuItemID(Handle, N),
                        Pointer(Items[N]));
            END;
end;
procedure TForm1.WMMeasureItem(VAR Msg: TWMMeasureItem);
BEGIN
    Inherited;
    WITH Msg. MeasureItemStruct^ DO
        IF CtlType = ODT_MENU THEN
            WITH TMenuItem(Pointer(ItemData)) DO
                begin
                    Canvas.Font.Name := Caption;
                    Canvas.Font.Size := 10;
                    ItemWidth  := Canvas.TextWidth(Caption)+8;
                    ItemHeight := Canvas.TextHeight(Caption)+4;
                    Result := 1;
                end;
END;
procedure TForm1.WMDrawItem(VAR Msg: TWMDrawItem);
BEGIN
    Inherited;
    WITH Msg. DrawItemStruct^ DO
        IF CtlType = ODT_MENU THEN
            WITH TMenuItem(Pointer(ItemData)) DO
                begin
                    Canvas.Handle := hDC;
                    IF (ODA_Select AND ItemAction <> 0) AND
                        (ODS_Selected AND ItemState <> 0) THEN
                        BEGIN
                            Canvas.Brush.Color := clHighlight;
                            Canvas.Font.Color  := clHighlightText;
                        END
                    ELSE
                        BEGIN
```

```
              Canvas.Brush.Color := clMenu;
              Canvas.Font.Color  := clMenuText;
            END;
          Canvas.Font.Name := Caption;
          Canvas.Font.Size := 10;
          rcItem.Right := rcItem.Right-3;
          Canvas.TextRect(rcItem, rcItem.Left+4, rcItem.Top,
            Caption);
          Canvas.Handle := 0;
          Result := 1;
        end;
  END;
procedure TForm1.FontClick(Sender: TObject);
begin
  Panel1.Font.Name := (Sender AS TMenuItem).Caption;
  Panel1.Caption := (Sender AS TMenuItem).Caption+' - ABC abc 123';
end;
end.
```

The form's OnCreate method flips through the list of fonts provided by the Screen object's Fonts property. For each, it calls the nested IsTrueTypeText function, which returns True only if the passed string is the name of a TrueType font that's not a symbol font. (You may want to save IsTrueTypeText for your own uses!) It peruses the list of items and calls ModifyMenu to turn each into an owner-draw menu item. It passes the corresponding TMenuItem object in the 32-bit, user-defined, ItemData parameter; Windows will pass back this value with the owner-draw messages it sends. Every tenth item gets the MB_MENUBARBREAK style as well, so the menu will start a new column after every ten items.

Note that, under Windows 95, menus using the MB_MENUBREAK and MB_MENUBARBREAK do not display shortcuts correctly. This is a limitation of Windows 95, not of Delphi. This program's menu doesn't include shortcuts, so it doesn't run into trouble.

The program responds to the WM_MEASUREITEM message by returning the width and height of the item's caption, measured when using the font described by that caption. Remember, the 32-bit ItemData that was set using ModifyMenu holds a pointer to the Delphi menu item object; that's how this method gets access to the caption. WM_MEASUREITEM is called once for each item.

Actually drawing the items is handled in the WM_DRAWITEM response method. This is slightly more complicated than WM_MEASUREITEM, because it has to take into account the different states indicated by the ItemAction and ItemState fields of the passed data structure. This simple example draws each item as selected or as not selected; it ignores the possibility that an item might be checked or grayed.

As you can see, an owner-draw menu item has even more flexibility than a bitmap menu item, because its height can vary. Here again, though, if you're using 16-bit Delphi, you'll have to avoid setting menu item properties like Checked and Enabled by calling Windows API functions, such as CheckMenuItem and EnableMenuItem, instead.

Menu Nuts and Bolts

For most programs, Delphi's support of Windows menus is more than sufficient. However, some features of the Windows menu system are not implemented in the corresponding Delphi objects. It can also be necessary to dig below the surface of the features that *are* present to get the desired behavior. Here are a few examples.

 How to change properties of a merged menu

16 32

Delphi handles specialized menus for MDI child windows with amazing ease, as demonstrated in Chapter 3, "MDI Forms." However, if you try to change the state of a merged menu item (for example, to disable or to check it), you'll find it does not work.

There's an old story where the patient says, "Doc, it hurts when I do this!", and the doctor says, "So, don't *do* that!". If changing properties doesn't work when the menu is merged, do it when the menu is *not* merged, as shown in the program that follows.

MODMERGE

MODMER1U.DEX

```
object Form1: TForm1
  FormStyle = fsMDIForm
  Menu = MainMenu1
  Position = poDefault
  Scaled = False
  Visible = True
  object MainMenu1: TMainMenu
    object File1: TMenuItem
      Caption = '&File'
      object NewForm21: TMenuItem
        Caption = '&New Form2'
        OnClick = NewForm21Click
        ShortCutText = 'Ctrl+N'
      end
    end
  end
end
```

MODMER1U.PAS

```
unit modmer1u;

interface

uses SysUtils, WinTypes, WinProcs, Messages, Classes, Graphics,
  Controls, Forms, Dialogs, Menus;

type
  TForm1 = class(TForm)
    MainMenu1: TMainMenu;
    File1: TMenuItem;
    NewForm21: TMenuItem;
    procedure NewForm21Click(Sender: TObject);
  end;

var Form1: TForm1;

implementation
USES ModMer2u;
{$R *.DFM}

procedure TForm1.NewForm21Click(Sender: TObject);
begin
  TForm2.Create(Application);
end;

end.
```

MODMER2U.DEX

```
object Form2: TForm2
  FormStyle = fsMDIChild
  Menu = MainMenu1
  Position = poDefault
  Scaled = False
  Visible = True
  object Button1: TButton
    Caption = 'Enable/Disable Menu Item (&Wrong)'
    OnClick = Button1Click
  end
  object Button2: TButton
    Caption = 'Enable/Disable Menu Item (&Better)'
    OnClick = Button2Click
  end
  object Button3: TButton
    Caption = 'Enable/Disable Menu Item (&Right)'
    OnClick = Button3Click
  end
  object MainMenu1: TMainMenu
    object Toggle1: TMenuItem
      Caption = '&Enable/Disable'
      GroupIndex = 1
    end
  end
end
```

MODMER2U.PAS

```
unit modmer2u;

interface

uses SysUtils, WinTypes, WinProcs, Messages, Classes, Graphics,
  Controls, Forms, Dialogs, StdCtrls, Menus;

type
  TForm2 = class(TForm)
    MainMenu1: TMainMenu;
    Button1: TButton;
    Toggle1: TMenuItem;
    Button2: TButton;
    Button3: TButton;
    procedure Button1Click(Sender: TObject);
    procedure Button2Click(Sender: TObject);
    procedure Button3Click(Sender: TObject);
  end;

var Form2: TForm2;

implementation

{$R *.DFM}

procedure TForm2.Button1Click(Sender: TObject);
begin
  Toggle1.Enabled := NOT Toggle1.Enabled;
end;

procedure TForm2.Button2Click(Sender: TObject);
begin
  Application.Mainform.Menu.Unmerge(MainMenu1);
  Toggle1.Enabled := NOT Toggle1.Enabled;
  Application.Mainform.Menu.Merge(MainMenu1);
end;

procedure TForm2.Button3Click(Sender: TObject);
VAR
  N : Integer;
  NewValue : Boolean;
begin
  NewValue := NOT Toggle1.Enabled;
  WITH Application.MainForm DO
    BEGIN
      Menu.Unmerge(MainMenu1);
      FOR N := 0 TO MDIChildCount-1 DO
        IF MDIChildren[N] IS TForm2 THEN
          WITH TForm2(MDIChildren[N]) DO
            Toggle1.Enabled := NewValue;
      Menu.Merge(MainMenu1);
    END;
end;

end.
```

The main MDI form does nothing but permit creation of one or more child forms. Run the program, create a child form, and press the first button. The code for this button appears to toggle the enabled state of the merged menu item, but clearly nothing happens. Try the second button. This button works, because its OnClick handler calls the main menu's UnMerge method before toggling the enabled state, and then calls its Merge method.

The limitations of the second method will be clear when you create more than one child form. Because the merged menu belongs to the active child form, each form maintains the enabled state of that menu item individually. To control the enabled state across all child forms, use code like the OnClick handler for the third button. This method uses the UnMerge and Merge methods of the main form, but it also steps through the MDIChildren array and sets the enabled state of the item in question for *every* form of type TForm2.

There may be programs that need to maintain separate menu item state information for different child forms. In that case, the second button's method will be correct. For program-wide control, though, the third button's method is necessary.

Creating a menu structure at runtime

16 32

Delphi's Menu Designer lets you create a complete and complex menu structure at design time. However, that's not always what you want. Perhaps the menu in question cannot be created until runtime, or perhaps it contains a tediously large number of similar items. Wouldn't it be great to create it at runtime?

As the ACCEL program earlier in this chapter showed, it's easy enough to create menu items and add them to an existing pop-up menu or menu item. There are also a couple of different ways to create an entire menu structure at runtime. The next solution will show examples.

Determining whether a menu item sharing an event handler is a top-level item

16 32

This is perhaps an odd question, but I've been asked more than once how to determine the "level" of an arbitrary menu item. How deep is it in a nested menu structure? If you're creating the menu at design time, it might seem that you don't need to ask. However, a runtime-created menu might well have a need to know.

The program in Figure 5-6 populates an existing top-level menu item, and then creates another complete branch of the menu tree using a different method. All the menu items are hooked to the same event handler; this handler reports the nesting depth and name of the item that triggered it.

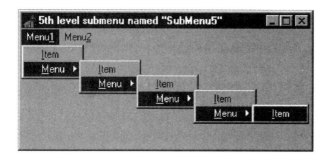

FIGURE 5-6: Don't use this menu as an example of good style! It exists simply to demonstrate run-time menu creation along with determining the level of a menu item.

ISTOPMN

ISTOPMNU.DEX

```
object Form1: TForm1
  Menu = MainMenu1
  Position = poDefault
  Scaled = False
  OnCreate = FormCreate
  object MainMenu1: TMainMenu
    object SubMenu1: TMenuItem
      Caption = 'Menu&1'
      OnClick = AClick
    end
  end
end
```

ISTOPMNU.PAS

```
unit Istopmnu;

interface

uses SysUtils, WinTypes, WinProcs, Messages, Classes, Graphics,
  Controls, Forms, Dialogs, StdCtrls, Menus;
```

```
type
  TForm1 = class(TForm)
    MainMenu1: TMainMenu;
    SubMenu1: TMenuItem;
    procedure AClick(Sender: TObject);
    procedure FormCreate(Sender: TObject);
  end;

var Form1: TForm1;

implementation

{$R *.DFM}

procedure TForm1.AClick(Sender: TObject);
VAR
  TM : TMenuItem;
  Lev : Word;
begin
  MessageBeep(0);
  TM := Sender AS TMenuItem;
  IF TM.Count > 0 THEN
    Caption := Format('submenu named "%s"', [TM.Name])
  ELSE Caption := Format('menu item named "%s"', [TM.Name]);
  Lev := 0;
  WHILE (TM.Parent <> NIL) AND (TM.Parent IS TMenuItem) DO
    BEGIN
      TM := TM.Parent;
      Inc(Lev);
    END;
  CASE Lev OF
    1 : Caption := 'Top level ' + Caption;
    2 : Caption := '2nd level ' + Caption;
    3 : Caption := '3rd level ' + Caption;
    ELSE Caption := Format('%dth level %s', [Lev, Caption]);
  END;
end;

procedure TForm1.FormCreate(Sender: TObject);
VAR
  TM : TMenuItem;
  N  : Integer;
begin
  TM := SubMenu1;
  TM.Add(NewItem('&Item', 0, False, True, AClick, 0, 'MenuItem2'));
  FOR N := 2 TO 5 DO
    BEGIN
      TM.Add(TMenuItem.Create(nil));
      TM := TM.Items[TM.Count-1];
      TM.Caption := '&Menu';
      TM.Name := 'SubMenu' + IntToStr(N);
      TM.OnClick := AClick;
      TM.Add(NewItem('&Item', 0, False, True, AClick, 0,
        'MenuItem'+IntToStr(N+1)));
    END;
```

```
MainMenu1.Items.Add(NewSubMenu('Menu&2', 0, 'SM1',
  [NewItem('&Item', 0, False, True, AClick, 0, 'MI2'),
   NewSubMenu('&Menu', 0, 'SM2',
     [NewItem('&Item', 0, False, True, AClick, 0, 'MI3'),
      NewSubMenu('&Menu', 0, 'SM3',
        [NewItem('&Item', 0, False, True, AClick, 0, 'MI4'),
         NewSubMenu('&Menu', 0, 'SM4',
           [NewItem('&Item', 0, False, True, AClick, 0, 'MI5'),
            NewSubMenu('&Menu', 0, 'SM5',
              [NewItem('&Item', 0, False, True, AClick, 0, 'MI6')
              ])
           ])
        ])
     ])
  ]));
TM := MainMenu1.Items[1];
WHILE TRUE DO
  BEGIN
    TM.OnClick := AClick;
    IF TM.Count < 2 THEN Break;
    TM := TM.Items[1];
  END;
end;

end.
```

The OnCreate event handler first builds a submenu tree below the existing top-level menu item SubMenu1. It uses a local variable TM of type TMenuItem to work its way down the tree. At each level, it creates a menu item and a submenu under TM, and then sets TM to point to the submenu. The result is the absurdly deep nested menu shown in the preceding figure.

If you've been programming in Pascal long enough to remember Borland's Turbo Vision, the second half of the OnCreate event handler will look familiar. Yes, you can create an entire menu tree in one horrendously nested statement. The final parameter of the NewSubMenu function is an array of menu items, possibly including submenus. To retain one's sanity when writing code like this, it's extremely important to keep things orderly. In the example program, the opening and closing square brackets [] that enclose each submenu's items are lined up in the same column; that really helps!

NewSubMenu does not have any provision for adding an OnClick event handler; therefore, it's necessary to "walk" the tree setting the OnClick property for every submenu after creating the second menu branch.

It's certainly simpler to create a menu in the menu designer. And, when each menu item has its own OnClick event handler, it hardly makes sense to create the items in this way. However, you will find times when run-time creation makes sense—remember this program!

CHAPTER 6

Edit Controls

*W*hen it comes to entering text, the memo box and the edit box components rule. The Windows NotePad accessory is little more than a memo box with a menu! In this chapter, you'll learn how to go from row and column coordinates to the actual character index in the memo and back, how to add an Undo feature to a memo's editing, and how to right-align edit boxes. You'll actually build a new component, a descendant of the memo box with new Row and Column properties! And we'll bring the new Windows 95 Rich Edit component into as many examples as possible.

Memo Rows and Columns

Most text editors report the cursor position in rows and in columns. However, the memo box component does not have row or column properties. It's not even obvious that the SelStart property, defined as the start of the selected region, indicates the cursor position even when no text is selected. Questions about rows and columns in memo boxes come up frequently.

 Reporting a memo's current row and column

16 32

The cursor position in a TMemo, TEdit, or TRichEdit is exposed as the SelStart property. SelStart is the number of characters from the very beginning of the component's text. But SelStart alone isn't much help if you want to, for example, position the cursor on the 10th character of the 100th line.

It turns out that all three of these components respond to Windows messages that make it possible to calculate the current row and column. Figure 6-1 shows a simple program that displays the current row and column in a TRichEdit. The source code consists of two separate programs, COORD95 for 16-bit and COORD5 for 32-bit Delphi.

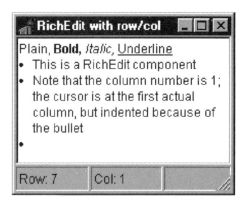

FIGURE 6-1: This program updates the row and column panels in the status bar on the rich edit box's OnSelectionChange event. Its 16-bit equivalent updates a simple panel at each keypress or mouse-click on a memo box.

COORD95

COORD95U.DEX

```
object Form2: TForm2
  Caption = 'RichEdit with row/col'
  Position = poDefault
  Scaled = False
  OnCreate = FormCreate
  object RichEdit1: TRichEdit
    Align = alClient
    OnSelectionChange = RichEdit1SelectionChange
  end
  object StatusBar1: TStatusBar
    Panels = <
      item
        Width = 72
      end
      item
        Width = 72
      end
      item
        Width = 50
```

```
      end>
    SimplePanel = False
  end
end
```

COORD95U.PAS

```
unit coord95u;
{$IFNDEF Win32}
HALT! This program requires 32-bit Delphi.
Use COORDS.DPR instead
{$ENDIF}
interface

uses SysUtils, Windows, Messages, Classes, Graphics, Controls, Forms,
  Dialogs, StdCtrls, ComCtrls, ExtCtrls, RichEdit;

type
  TForm1 = class(TForm)
    RichEdit1: TRichEdit;
    StatusBar1: TStatusBar;
    procedure FormCreate(Sender: TObject);
    procedure RichEdit1SelectionChange(Sender: TObject);
  end;

var Form1: TForm1;

implementation

{$R *.DFM}

procedure TForm1.FormCreate(Sender: TObject);
begin
  WITH RichEdit1 DO
    BEGIN
      Lines.Add('Plain, ');
      SelAttributes.Style := [fsBold];
      Lines.Add('Bold, ');
      SelAttributes.Style := [fsItalic];
      Lines.Add('Italic, ');
      SelAttributes.Style := [fsUnderline];
      Lines.Add('Underline');
      SelAttributes.Style := [];
      SelStart := Length(Text);
      Paragraph.Numbering := TNumberingStyle(PFN_BULLET);
      RichEdit1SelectionChange(RichEdit1);
    END;
  end;

procedure TForm1.RichEdit1SelectionChange(Sender: TObject);
VAR Ro, Co : Integer;
```

```
begin
  WITH Sender AS TCustomEdit DO
    BEGIN
      Ro := Perform(EM_LINEFROMCHAR, SelStart, 0);
      Co := SelStart - Perform(EM_LINEINDEX, Ro, 0);
      StatusBar1.Panels[0].Text := Format('Row: %d', [Ro+1]);
      StatusBar1.Panels[1].Text := Format('Col: %d', [Co+1]);
    END;
end;

end.
```

COORDS

COORDSU.DEX

```
object Form1: TForm1
  Caption = 'Memo box with row/col'
  Position = poDefault
  Scaled = False
  OnCreate = FormCreate
  object Panel1: TPanel
    Align = alBottom
    Alignment = taLeftJustify
    BevelInner = bvLowered
  end
  object Memo1: TMemo
    Align = alClient
    OnClick = Memo1Click
    OnKeyUp = Memo1KeyUp
  end
end
```

COORDSU.PAS

```
unit Coordsu;
{$IFDEF Win32}
HALT! Use COORD95.DPR instead, as it makes use
of 32-bit-specific components
{$ENDIF}
interface

uses SysUtils, WinTypes, WinProcs, Messages, Classes, Graphics,
  Controls, Forms, Dialogs, StdCtrls, ExtCtrls;

type
  TForm1 = class(TForm)
```

```
      Panel1: TPanel;
      Memo1: TMemo;
      procedure Memo1Click(Sender: TObject);
      procedure Memo1KeyUp(Sender: TObject; var Key: Word;
        Shift: TShiftState);
      procedure FormCreate(Sender: TObject);
    end;

var Form1: TForm1;

implementation

{$R *.DFM}

procedure TForm1.FormCreate(Sender: TObject);
begin
  Memo1Click(Memo1);
end;

procedure TForm1.Memo1Click(Sender: TObject);
VAR Ro, Co : Integer;
begin
  WITH Sender AS TCustomEdit DO
    BEGIN
      Ro := Perform(EM_LINEFROMCHAR, SelStart, 0);
      Co := SelStart - Perform(EM_LINEINDEX, Ro, 0);
      Panel1.Caption := Format('Row: %d   Col: %d', [Ro+1, Co+1]);
    END;
end;

procedure TForm1.Memo1KeyUp(Sender: TObject; var Key: Word;
  Shift: TShiftState);
begin
  Memo1Click(Sender);
end;

end.
```

The RichEdit1SelectionChange event handler in the 32-bit program and the Memo1Click handler in the 16-bit program are almost identical. Both get the current row using the EM_LINEFROMCHAR message, and both get the current column by subtracting the start of the row (retrieved using EM_LINEINDEX) from SelStart. The only difference is that the 32-bit version displays row and column using a status bar component and the 16-bit version uses a simple panel. Note that both components descend from TCustomEdit.

Of course, a Rich Edit component needs more support than this sample program gives—there's no way to change the font, for example. Later in this chapter, we'll devise a program to exercise the abilities of the Rich Edit component.

Setting up a memo box with full row and column support

16 32

Sending messages to a memo box is a quick and dirty way to find out the row and column position, but if you use this feature a lot, you'll want to make it *part* of the memo box. Here's a memo box descendant with Row, Col, and Posn properties (Posn is a LongInt with Row in its high word and Col in its low word), and an OnPosChanged event that's triggered when the cursor position is changed.

COMPONENT TRCMEMO

C_RCMEMO.PAS

```
unit C_rcmemo;

interface

uses SysUtils, WinTypes, WinProcs, Messages, Classes, Graphics,
  Controls, Forms, Dialogs, p_about, StdCtrls;

type
  TRCMemo = class(TMemo)
  protected
    fAbout: TAbout;
    fOnPosChange : TNotifyEvent;
    function GetRow : Integer;
    procedure SetRow(value : Integer);
    function GetCol : Integer;
    procedure SetCol(value : Integer);
    function GetPosn : LongInt;
    procedure SetPosn(value : LongInt);
    procedure MouseUp(Button: TMouseButton; Shift: TShiftState;
      X, Y: Integer); override;
    procedure KeyUp(var Key: Word; Shift: TShiftState);
      override;
    procedure PosChange; dynamic;
  public
    procedure CreateParams(var Params: TCreateParams);
      override;
  published
    property AboutVersion: TAbout Read fAbout Write fAbout;
    property Row : Integer Read GetRow Write SetRow default 0;
    property Col : Integer Read GetCol Write SetCol default 0;
    property Posn : LongInt Read GetPosn Write SetPosn default 0;
    property OnPosChange: TNotifyEvent Read FOnPosChange
      Write FOnPosChange;
  end;

procedure Register;
```

```
implementation
{$IFDEF Win32}
{$R *.R32}
{$ELSE}
{$R *.R16}
{$ENDIF}
procedure TRCMemo.CreateParams(var Params: TCreateParams);
BEGIN
  Inherited CreateParams(Params);
  fAbout := 0.99;
END;

function TRCMemo.GetRow : Integer;
begin
  Result := Perform(EM_LINEFROMCHAR, $FFFF, 0);
end;

function TRCMemo.GetCol : Integer;
begin
  Result := SelStart - Perform(EM_LINEINDEX, GetRow, 0);
end;

procedure TRCMemo.SetRow(value : Integer);
VAR vCol : LongInt;
begin
  vCol := GetCol;
  SelStart := Perform(EM_LINEINDEX, Value, 0);
  SetCol(vCol);
  {No call to PosChange; it's in SetCol}
end;

procedure TRCMemo.PosChange;
begin
  IF Assigned(FOnPosChange) THEN FOnPosChange(Self);
end;

procedure TRCMemo.SetCol(value : Integer);
VAR vCol : LongInt;
begin
  vCol := Perform(EM_LINELENGTH, Perform(EM_LINEINDEX,
    GetRow, 0),0);
  IF vCol > Value THEN vCol := Value;
  SelStart := Perform(EM_LINEINDEX, GetRow, 0) + vCol;
 PosChange;
end;

function TRCMemo.GetPosn : LongInt;
Var ro, co : Integer;
begin
  ro := GetRow;
  co := SelStart - Perform(EM_LINEINDEX, ro, 0);
  Result := MakeLong(co,ro);
end;

procedure TRCMemo.SetPosn(value : LongInt);
begin
```

```
        SelStart := Perform(EM_LINEINDEX, HiWord(Value), 0) +
          LoWord(Value);
        PosChange;
      end;
      procedure TRCMemo.MouseUp(Button: TMouseButton; Shift:
        TShiftState; X, Y: Integer);
      BEGIN
        Inherited MouseUp(Button, Shift, X, Y);
        PosChange;
      END;
      procedure TRCMemo.KeyUp(var Key: Word; Shift: TShiftState);
      BEGIN
        Inherited KeyUp(Key, Shift);
        PosChange;
      END;
      procedure Register;
      begin
        RegisterComponents('NJR', [TRCMemo]);
      end;
      end.
```

The RCMemo component incorporates the Windows messages needed to get or set the row or the column position. It deals with the problem of positioning the cursor on the correct column after the row changes to a shorter line. And it triggers a newly defined event OnPosChange when the position changes, due either to user manipulation or direct change by a program.

Note that in order to hook the click and mouse-up events, this component did *not* set the OnKeyUp and OnMouseUp properties. These properties could be overridden by the program that uses the component, in which case it wouldn't work. Rather, RCMemo overrides the KeyUp and MouseUp methods of TMemo. In general, the components you design should never set OnXxx properties themselves, but always find the non-event handler method that *calls* the desired event handler and override that.

The Delphi Component Writer's Guide recommends placing the bitmap resource that will represent a component on the palette in a resource file with the extension .DCR. However, this presents problems when the component must be compiled for both 16-bit and 32-bit Delphi. The RCMemo component and every component defined in this book use a different technique. The palette bitmap is compiled into separate 16-bit and 32-bit resource files, with extensions .R16 and .R32, and a conditional compilation directive immediately after the implementation line includes the appropriate resource.

For an example of the RCMemo component in action, see the next section, "Sorting the lines in a memo."

CREATING A PROPERTY EDITOR

The RCMemo component's About property is a special type of property defined in the file P_ABOUT.PAS. As Figure 6-2 shows, it incorporates a version number and a simple copyright notice into the component.

FIGURE 6-2: The About property uses a user-defined property editor to display a copyright notice for the component.

PROPERTY EDITOR TABOUTBOXPROPERTY

P_ABOUT.PAS

```
unit p_about;

interface
USES SysUtils, WinTypes, WinProcs, Messages, Classes,
  Dialogs, DsgnIntF;
type
  TAbout = Double;
  TAboutBoxProperty = Class(TFloatProperty)
    function GetAttributes: TPropertyAttributes; override;
    procedure Edit; override;
    function GetName : String; override;
    function GetValue : String; override;
  end;

procedure Register;

implementation
function TAboutBoxProperty.GetAttributes: TPropertyAttributes;
BEGIN
  Result := [paDialog, paReadOnly];
END;
```

```
procedure TAboutBoxProperty.Edit;
BEGIN
  ShowMessage(Format('%s component, version %f, '+
    #13#10'Copyright © 1996 by Neil J. Rubenking',
    [GetComponent(0).ClassName, GetFloatValue]));
END;

function TAboutBoxProperty.GetValue : String;
BEGIN
  Result := FormatFloat('"v. "#0.00', GetFloatValue);
END;

function TAboutBoxProperty.GetName : String;
BEGIN
  GetName := 'About';
END;

procedure Register;
begin
  RegisterPropertyEditor(TypeInfo(TAbout), NIL, '',
    TAboutBoxProperty);
end;

end.
```

The P_ABOUT unit defines a special data type TAbout. TAbout is defined as a Double, but, by creating a new data type, the unit can assign a property editor specific to properties of that type. The GetAttributes method indicates that the property editor will be a dialog box, and that the property itself is read-only. The Edit method displays a simple dialog box with the name and version number of the component and a copyright notice (change this to use your own name, of course!). Delphi calls the GetValue method to retrieve the string for displaying the value in the Object Inspector. The call to RegisterPropertyEditor in the Register procedure indicates that this property editor should be used for all properties of type TAbout, regardless of the component that contains them.

Not every property editor will be as simple as this one, of course, but you can use it as a jumping off point. Other components defined later in this book will use the property editor defined here.

Manipulating Text

The basic cut, copy, and paste keystrokes are built into the various edit components. Unless they're actively disabled by a particular program, they always work. To add features beyond simple cut and paste, or to otherwise manipulate the text in an edit component, you'll need to write a bit of code.

Sorting the lines in a memo

16 32

Many word processing programs allow you to sort the lines in a document or to sort the selected lines. This is certainly a convenient feature, so we'll implement it in Delphi. In Figure 6-3, the selected text in the example program's Memo box has just been sorted.

FIGURE 6-3: The program depicted here will sort all the lines in a memo, or just the selected lines.

SORTMEM

SORTMEMU.DEX

```
object Form1: TForm1
  BorderIcons = [biSystemMenu]
  BorderStyle = bsDialog
  Caption = 'Sort Memo's Contents'
  Position = poDefault
  Scaled = False
  OnCreate = FormCreate
  object Panel1: TPanel
    Align = alTop
    BevelInner = bvLowered
    object Button1: TButton
      Caption = '&Sort'
      OnClick = Button1Click
    end
  end
end
```

```
      object RCMemo1: TRCMemo
        Align = alClient
        HideSelection = False
        ScrollBars = ssVertical
        WordWrap = False
        AboutVersion = 0.99
      end
  end
```

SORTMEMU.PAS

```
unit Sortmemu;

interface

uses SysUtils, WinTypes, WinProcs, Messages, Classes, Graphics,
  Controls, Forms, Dialogs, StdCtrls, ExtCtrls, C_rcmemo;

type
  TForm1 = class(TForm)
    Panel1: TPanel;
    Button1: TButton;
    RCMemo1: TRCMemo;
    procedure Button1Click(Sender: TObject);
    procedure FormCreate(Sender: TObject);
  end;

var Form1: TForm1;

implementation

{$R *.DFM}

procedure TForm1.FormCreate(Sender: TObject);
CONST Animals: PChar = 'llama'#13'orangutan'#13'bear'#13'goat'#13+
  'rhino'#13'zebra'#13'jackal'#13'kudu'#13'quetzlcoatl'#13'dog'+
  #13'tiger'#13'eagle'#13'narwhal'#13'yak'#13'pika'#13'salamander'+
  #13'xylophone'#13'vulture'#13'alpaca'#13'hippo'#13'moose'#13+
  'fennec'#13'umbrella bird'#13'iguana'#13'cow'#13'wolverine';
begin

  RCMemo1.Lines.SetText(Animals);
end;

procedure TForm1.Button1Click(Sender: TObject);
VAR
  SL                       : TStringList;
  N, RowStart, RowEnd,
  WasSelStart, WasSelEnd : Integer;
begin
  SL := TStringList.Create;
  WITH SL DO
    try
      IF RCMemo1.SelLength = 0 THEN
        BEGIN
```

```
            Assign(RCMemo1.Lines);
            Sort;
            RCMemo1.Lines := SL;
         END
      ELSE
        WITH RCMemo1 DO
          BEGIN
            {Set WasSelStart to start of first row}
            RowStart := Row;
            WasSelEnd := SelStart + SelLength;
            Col := 0;
            WasSelStart := SelStart;
            {Set WasSelEnd just past end of last row}
            SelStart := WasSelEnd;
            IF Col > 0 THEN Row := Row+1;
            RowEnd   := Row;
            Col := 0;
            WasSelEnd := SelStart;
            FOR N := RowStart TO RowEnd-1 DO Add(Lines[N]);
            Sort;
            FOR N := 0 TO Count-1 DO
              Lines[N+RowStart] := Strings[N];
            SelStart   := WasSelStart;
            SelLength := WasSelEnd - WasSelStart;
          END;
    finally
      Free;
    end;
  end;

  end.
```

Sorting the entire contents of the memo box is quite simple. The Sort button's OnClick event handler assigns the memo's lines to a temporary TStringList, sorts the list, and assigns the sorted lines back into the memo. However, it's a little more work to sort just the selection.

First, it makes no sense to sort partial lines, so the program must determine the starting and ending rows of the selection. That's why we used the RCMemo component defined in the previous section—it gives easy access to the current row and column. After determining the range of rows to use, the OnClick handler adds the lines one-by-one to the temporary string list. It sorts the list and then assigns the sorted lines directly to the corresponding elements of the memo's Lines property, thus copying them over the previous lines in sorted order. Then it restores the selection, which has been extended to entirely select the first and last lines selected.

Right-aligning an edit box

16 32

An edit box for text entry is automatically left-aligned. If you want one that will take numeric data, for example, you might prefer to have it right-aligned.

It would be possible to create a TEdit descendant that's right-aligned. However, it's a Windows requirement that, in order to get the right-aligned style, you must also give it the multiline style. Once you do that, you've reinvented the TMemo! The program in Figure 6-4 demonstrates that a TMemo can serve as a right-aligned edit box.

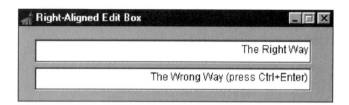

FIGURE 6-4: You can use a memo box as a right-aligned edit box, but restricting it to a single line is tough.

EDRITE

EDRITEU.DEX

```
object Form1: TForm1
  BorderIcons = [biSystemMenu, biMinimize]
  BorderStyle = bsSingle
  Caption = 'Right-Aligned Edit Box'
  KeyPreview = True
  Position = poDefault
  Scaled = False
  OnCreate = FormCreate
  object Memo1: TMemo
    Alignment = taRightJustify
    MaxLength = 50
    WantReturns = False
    WordWrap = False
    OnKeyDown = Memo1KeyDown
    OnKeyPress = Memo1KeyPress
  end
  object Memo2: TMemo
    Alignment = taRightJustify
    MaxLength = 50
    WantReturns = False
```

```
        WordWrap = False
    end
end
```

EDRITEU.PAS

```
unit Edriteu;

interface

uses SysUtils, WinTypes, WinProcs, Messages, Classes, Graphics,
  Controls, Forms, Dialogs, StdCtrls;

type
  TForm1 = class(TForm)
    Memo1: TMemo;
    Memo2: TMemo;
    procedure Memo1KeyPress(Sender: TObject; var Key: Char);
    procedure FormCreate(Sender: TObject);
    procedure Memo1KeyDown(Sender: TObject; var Key: Word;
      Shift: TShiftState);
  end;

var Form1: TForm1;

implementation

{$R *.DFM}

procedure TForm1.FormCreate(Sender: TObject);
begin
  Memo1.Text := 'The Right Way';
  Memo1.SelStart := Length(Memo1.Text);
  Memo2.Text := 'The Wrong Way (press Ctrl+Enter)';
  Memo2.SelStart := Length(Memo2.Text);
end;

procedure TForm1.Memo1KeyPress(Sender: TObject; var Key: Char);
begin
  IF Key = #10 THEN Key := #0;
end;

procedure TForm1.Memo1KeyDown(Sender: TObject; var Key: Word;
  Shift: TShiftState);
begin
  IF (Key = VK_TAB) AND (ssCtrl IN Shift) THEN Key := 0;
end;

end.
```

Getting right-alignment is a simple matter of setting the Alignment property to taRightJustify. It's also important to set the memo's WordWrap and WantReturns properties to False, and to limit the number of characters by setting MaxLength. Set ScrollBars to ssNone, and *don't* use the Lines property at design time or at runtime to set the text. When you add a single line to the Lines property, you effectively create a blank line following it. If the user presses down-arrow, that blank line will move into view and the user's text will disappear—frightening! Do place the cursor at the end of any text you add at runtime by setting the SelStart property to the length of the text.

There's one more thing you need to do to keep the user from accidentally "losing" the text in a right-aligned, single-line memo box. Even when WantReturns is False, the user can normally press Ctrl+Enter to force a new line. In the example program, the first memo box has an OnKeyPress event handler that suppresses the Ctrl+Enter keystroke (ASCII character 10) by setting the Key argument to #0. In the same way, Ctrl+Tab will insert a tab even when WantTabs is False—the OnKeyDown event handler suppresses those Ctrl+Tab keystrokes.

This is the best way to create a right-aligned edit box. If you try building it from TEdit by changing the style bits to include ES_MULTILINE, you'll have to take all the same precautions, but you won't be able to do so using the convenient properties of TMemo!

Be sure to give your single-line TMemo sufficient height to fit the text. A TEdit that is not high enough will clip its text; a TMemo that's not high enough will display nothing at all.

 ## *Adding a simple Undo command to memo*

Implementing a fancy, multilevel Undo feature requires quite a bit of programming and design. However, the basic Windows edit control and its variations (including TEdit and TMemo) all support a simple one-level Undo. How can you get access to it?

As with the row and the column positioning problem, Windows messages are the solution here.

MEMUNDO

MEMUNDOU.DEX

```
object Form1: TForm1
  Caption = 'Memo with simple Undo'
  Menu = MainMenu1
  Position = poDefault
  Scaled = False
  object Memo1: TMemo
    Align = alClient
  end
  object MainMenu1: TMainMenu
    object Edit1: TMenuItem
      Caption = '&Edit'
```

```
      OnClick = Edit1Click
      object Undo1: TMenuItem
        Caption = '&Undo'
        OnClick = Undo1Click
        ShortCutText = 'Ctrl+Z'
      end
      object Copy1: TMenuItem
        Caption = '&Copy'
        OnClick = Copy1Click
        ShortCutText = 'Ctrl+C'
      end
      object Cut1: TMenuItem
        Caption = 'Cu&t'
        OnClick = Cut1Click
        ShortCutText = 'Ctrl+X'
      end
      object Paste1: TMenuItem
        Caption = '&Paste'
        OnClick = Paste1Click
        ShortCutText = 'Ctrl+V'
      end
    end
  end
end
```

MEMUNDOU.PAS

```
unit Memundou;

interface

uses SysUtils, WinTypes, WinProcs, Messages, Classes, Graphics,
  Controls, Forms, Dialogs, StdCtrls, Menus;

type
  TForm1 = class(TForm)
    MainMenu1: TMainMenu;
    Edit1: TMenuItem;
    Undo1: TMenuItem;
    Copy1: TMenuItem;
    Cut1: TMenuItem;
    Paste1: TMenuItem;
    Memo1: TMemo;
    procedure Edit1Click(Sender: TObject);
    procedure Paste1Click(Sender: TObject);
    procedure Cut1Click(Sender: TObject);
    procedure Copy1Click(Sender: TObject);
    procedure Undo1Click(Sender: TObject);
  end;

var Form1: TForm1;

implementation
USES ClipBrd;
{$R *.DFM}
```

```
procedure TForm1.Edit1Click(Sender: TObject);
begin
  Undo1.Enabled  := Memo1.Perform(EM_CANUNDO, 0, 0) <> 0;
  Copy1.Enabled  := Memo1.SelLength > 0;
  Cut1.Enabled   := Copy1.Enabled;
  Paste1.Enabled := Clipboard.HasFormat(CF_TEXT);
end;

procedure TForm1.Paste1Click(Sender: TObject);
begin
  Memo1.PasteFromClipboard;
end;

procedure TForm1.Cut1Click(Sender: TObject);
begin
  Memo1.CutToClipboard;
end;

procedure TForm1.Copy1Click(Sender: TObject);
begin
  Memo1.CopyToClipboard;
end;

procedure TForm1.Undo1Click(Sender: TObject);
begin
  Memo1.Perform(EM_UNDO, 0, 0);
end;

end.
```

When the user clicks the Edit menu, its OnClick handler appropriately enables or disables the four menu items. To find out whether the memo is prepared to Undo, it sends EM_CANUNDO. To perform the Undo operation, it sends EM_UNDO. It's as simple as that! If you're using 32-bit Delphi, replace the memo box with a Rich Edit box named Memo1. The Undo feature will work just as it did with the simple memo box.

Inserting characters in the current edit control, no matter what kind it is

16 32

The ANSI character set is decidedly biased toward the English language. If your program needs to accept the accented characters defined by the upper half of the ANSI character set, you'll have to find a way to insert those characters wherever you need them.

The main problem here is making sure the special characters are available in any Edit box, Memo box, Rich Edit box, or editable string grid. The program in Figure 6-5 demonstrates one possible technique.

FIGURE 6-5: The twenty tiny speed buttons on this form are created at runtime; pressing one of them inserts its caption character in the active edit component.

MODEDIT

MODEDITU.DEX

```
object Form1: TForm1
  BorderIcons = [biSystemMenu]
  BorderStyle = bsSingle
  Caption = 'Character Insertion Demo'
  Position = poDefault
  Scaled = False
  OnCreate = FormCreate
  object Edit1: TEdit
  end
  object Edit2: TEdit
  end
  object StringGrid1: TStringGrid
    ColCount = 1
    DefaultColWidth = 128
    FixedCols = 0
    FixedRows = 0
    Options = [goFixedVertLine, goFixedHorzLine, goVertLine,
  goHorzLine, goRangeSelect, goEditing]
    RowCount = 8
    ScrollBars = ssNone
  end
  object Memo1: TMemo
  end
end
```

MODEDITU.PAS

```
unit Modeditu;

interface

uses SysUtils, WinTypes, WinProcs, Messages, Classes, Graphics,
  Controls, Forms, {$IFDEF Win32}ComCtrls, {$ENDIF} StdCtrls,
  Grids, Buttons;

type
  TForm1 = class(TForm)
    Edit1: TEdit;
    Edit2: TEdit;
    StringGrid1: TStringGrid;
    Memo1: TMemo;
    procedure SpeedButton1Click(Sender: TObject);
    procedure FormCreate(Sender: TObject);
  end;

var Form1: TForm1;

implementation

{$R *.DFM}

procedure TForm1.SpeedButton1Click(Sender: TObject);
begin
  IF ActiveControl IS TCustomEdit THEN
    WITH TCustomEdit(ActiveControl) DO
      SelText := (Sender AS TSpeedButton).Caption
  ELSE IF ActiveControl IS TCustomGrid THEN
    WITH TCustomGrid(ActiveControl) DO
      IF ControlCount > 0 THEN
        IF Controls[0] IS TCustomEdit THEN
          WITH TCustomEdit(Controls[0]) DO
            SelText := (Sender AS TSpeedButton).Caption;
end;

procedure TForm1.FormCreate(Sender: TObject);
CONST Chars: String = 'àèìòùáéíóúâêîôûäëïöü';
VAR Co, Ro : Integer;
begin
  FOR Ro := 0 TO 3 DO
    FOR Co := 0 TO 4 DO
      WITH TSpeedButton.Create(Self) DO
        BEGIN
          Parent := Self;
          Width := 17;
          Height := 17;
          Caption := Chars[Ro*5+Co+1];
          Left := 138+16*Co;
          Top := 4+16*Ro;
          OnClick := SpeedButton1Click;
        END;
```

```
WITH StringGrid1 DO
  BEGIN
    Cells[0,0] := 'Ole!';
    Cells[0,1] := 'deja vu';
    Cells[0,2] := 'voila';
    Cells[0,3] := 'Chichen Itza';
    Cells[0,4] := 'Uber Alles';
  END;
{$IFDEF Win32}
WITH TRichEdit.Create(Self) DO
  BEGIN
    Parent := Self;
    Name := 'RichEdit1';
    Memo1.Height := Memo1.Height DIV 2;
    BoundsRect := Memo1.BoundsRect;
    Top := Memo1.Top + Memo1.Height + 2;
  END;
{$ENDIF}
end;

end.
```

Rather than hand-design the twenty speed buttons that correspond to the five vowels with four diacritical marks added, the program builds them using the code in its OnCreate event handler. Also, if compiled under Delphi32, the program adds a TRichEdit that occupies half the space originally assigned to the TMemo.

All the speed buttons are hooked to the same OnClick event handler. If the active control is a TCustomEdit or any component type descended from a TCustomEdit, it sets the component's SelText to the selected character. That means the selected text is replaced by that character or, if no text is selected, the character is inserted at the current cursor location.

If the active control is a TCustomGrid or any descendant thereof, things are slightly different. Unless the grid's Options.AlwaysShowEditor property is True, an edit control for the current cell exists only while the cell is being edited. If that's the case, the 0th element of the grid's Controls array will be that editor, and Controls[0] will be a TCustomEdit. In that case, the event handler again sets the now-found edit component's SelText to the selected character.

You may find other uses for the code that locates a grid's current cell editor. And, of course, it's always handy to be able to identify whether the active component is some variety of edit control. You'll see this example later in the book, with support added for inserting text into *data-aware* components.

Cutting and copying from active edit or memo

|16| |32|

Earlier in this chapter, we built a program whose Edit menu had Cut, Copy, Paste, and Undo items tied to a particular memo or Rich Edit box. It's not so easy, though, when the form includes multiple components that could reasonably be affected by these menu items.

A technique used in the preceding example will serve here. We'll disable the Edit menu's items, if the active control is a button or other component without text-editing capabilities. If the active controls can edit text, we'll enable or disable the menu items based on the active control's status. As Figure 6-6 illustrates, this works with editable string grids, too.

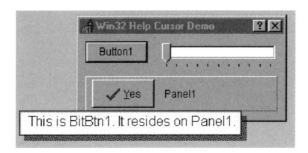

FIGURE 6-6: The Undo and Paste operations are available for the active control (the Rich Edit box), but, as no text is selected, Cut and Copy are grayed out.

CUTCOPY

CUTCOPYU.DEX

```
object Form1: TForm1
  BorderIcons = [biSystemMenu, biMinimize]
  BorderStyle = bsSingle
  Caption = 'Clipboard operations for multiple components'
  Menu = MainMenu1
  Position = poDefault
  Scaled = False
  OnCreate = FormCreate
  object Memo1: TMemo
```

```
      end
      object Edit2: TEdit
      end
      object StringGrid1: TStringGrid
        ColCount = 1
        DefaultColWidth = 128
        DefaultRowHeight = 28
        FixedCols = 0
        FixedRows = 0
        Options = [goFixedVertLine, goFixedHorzLine, goVertLine,
      goHorzLine, goRangeSelect, goEditing]
        ScrollBars = ssNone
      end
      object MainMenu1: TMainMenu
        object Edit1: TMenuItem
          Caption = '&Edit'
          OnClick = Edit1Click
          object Undo1: TMenuItem
            Caption = '&Undo'
            OnClick = Undo1Click
            ShortCutText = 'Ctrl+Z'
          end
          object Cut1: TMenuItem
            Caption = 'Cu&t'
            OnClick = Cut1Click
            ShortCutText = 'Ctrl+X'
          end
          object Copy1: TMenuItem
            Caption = '&Copy'
            OnClick = Copy1Click
            ShortCutText = 'Ctrl+C'
          end
          object Paste1: TMenuItem
            Caption = '&Paste'
            OnClick = Paste1Click
            ShortCutText = 'Ctrl+V'
          end
        end
      end
    end
end
```

CUTCOPYU.PAS

```
unit Cutcopyu;

interface

uses SysUtils, WinTypes, WinProcs, Messages, Classes, Graphics,
  Controls, Forms, Dialogs, {$IFDEF Win32} ComCtrls, {$ENDIF}
  StdCtrls, Menus, Grids;

type
  TForm1 = class(TForm)
    MainMenu1: TMainMenu;
```

```
      Edit1: TMenuItem;
      Cut1: TMenuItem;
      Copy1: TMenuItem;
      Paste1: TMenuItem;
      Memo1: TMemo;
      Edit2: TEdit;
      Undo1: TMenuItem;
      StringGrid1: TStringGrid;
      procedure Edit1Click(Sender: TObject);
      procedure Cut1Click(Sender: TObject);
      procedure Copy1Click(Sender: TObject);
      procedure Paste1Click(Sender: TObject);
      procedure Undo1Click(Sender: TObject);
      procedure FormCreate(Sender: TObject);
    private
      TheCE : TCustomEdit;
    end;

var Form1: TForm1;

implementation
USES ClipBrd;
{$R *.DFM}

procedure TForm1.FormCreate(Sender: TObject);
begin
  {$IFDEF Win32}
  Memo1.Height := Memo1.Height DIV 2;
  WITH TRichEdit.Create(Self) DO
    BEGIN
      Parent := Self;
      Name := 'RichEdit1';
      BoundsRect := Memo1.BoundsRect;
      Top := Memo1.Top + Memo1.Height + 8;
    END;
  {$ENDIF}
end;

procedure TForm1.Edit1Click(Sender: TObject);
begin
  TheCE := NIL;
  IF ActiveControl IS TCustomEdit THEN
    TheCE := TCustomEdit(ActiveControl)
  ELSE IF ActiveControl IS TStringGrid THEN
    WITH TStringGrid(ActiveControl) DO
      IF (ControlCount > 0) AND EditorMode THEN
        IF Controls[0] IS TInplaceEdit THEN
          TheCE := TInplaceEdit(Controls[0]);
  IF TheCE <> NIL THEN
    BEGIN
      Undo1.Enabled := TheCE.Perform(EM_CANUNDO, 0, 0) <> 0;
      Cut1.Enabled := TheCE.SelLength > 0;
      Copy1.Enabled := Cut1.Enabled;
      Paste1.Enabled := Clipboard.HasFormat(CF_TEXT);
    END
```

```
      ELSE
        BEGIN
          Undo1.Enabled  := False;
          Cut1.Enabled   := False;
          Copy1.Enabled  := False;
          Paste1.Enabled := False;
        END;
  end;

  procedure TForm1.Cut1Click(Sender: TObject);
  begin
    TheCE.CutToClipboard;
  end;

  procedure TForm1.Copy1Click(Sender: TObject);
  begin
    TheCE.CopyToClipboard;
  end;

  procedure TForm1.Paste1Click(Sender: TObject);
  begin
    TheCE.PasteFromClipboard;
  end;

  procedure TForm1.Undo1Click(Sender: TObject);
  begin
    TheCE.Perform(EM_UNDO,0,0);
  end;

  end.
```

As with several other projects in this chapter, if compiled under Delphi32, this program creates a Rich Edit component at runtime. The Edit1 top-level menu item's OnClick handler sets the private data field TheCE to the active TCustomEdit descendant, or to NIL, if the active control is not a TCustomEdit descendant. If TheCE is NIL, it disables its four submenu items; if not, it selectively enables them. Note that the processing of editable grid cells is more stringent than in the previous example. The grid must be a TStringGrid, the editable component must be a TInPlaceEdit, and the grid's EditorMode property must be True. This is necessary because the in-place edit component can exist without being active. That wasn't important in the previous example, but it *is* in the current one.

Event Handler Errors

It's always possible to make a mistake programming an event handler. However, it seems that there are a few especially popular pitfalls on the path to controlling edit and memo boxes.

Getting stack overflow in OnChange

16 32

It's easy to make this mistake. If you are running Windows 3.1 and you have turned on the Stack Checking option, it's not a major problem. The same error under Windows 95 can and will crash the whole system, though, so beware! The problem is not in Delphi; it's Windows 95. Windows NT survives stack faults with no problem.

The problem comes from failing to realize that a line like:

```
Edit1.Text := Edit1.Text + 'X';
```

will trigger an OnChange event. It's important to remember that Delphi component properties can have Read and Write methods associated with them. In truth, an edit box component doesn't store its text. When the program reads the value of the Text property, it's calling a method that gets the text from the underlying edit control and formats it as a Delphi string. When the program writes to the Text property, the method that's called uses a Windows message to change the text in the edit control. And one more thing . . . it triggers the OnChange event.

If an OnChange event handler changes the text of the edit component, that will trigger another OnChange event, and another, and another, until the system stack overflows. The only way you can safely change the edit box's text within an OnChange handler is if the change you make is not cumulative. For example, the line

```
Edit1.Text := UpperCase(Edit1.Text);
```

is safe. Delphi components are smart enough to signal a change only when the value really does change. This line converts the edit box's text to all uppercase, which triggers another OnChange event. The second time around, though, the text is already all uppercase, so no further change occurs.

Any time you get an unexpected stack overflow error in Windows 3.1 or in NT, or an unexplained system crash in Windows 95, consider the possibility that one of your event handlers is entering a tail-chasing, recursive loop. Note that 32-bit programs can take a while to die from infinite recursion, because the available stack space is so much greater.

Edit box's text coming out backward

16 32

How can this be a common error? What kind of peculiar event handler could cause it?

The core of this problem is the fact that setting a new value for the Text property of an edit component resets the SelStart property to zero. New characters are inserted at the location defined by SelStart. Thus, if an event handler such as OnKeyPress happens to set a new value for the edit box's text, the insertion point will return to the start of the text for each keystroke, and the inserted text will come out backward!

If your program's edit boxes behave weirdly in a way that seems related to the insertion point, look for event handlers that set the value of the edit box's text. If you find one, try saving and restoring the SelStart property; for example:

```
WITH Sender AS TEdit DO
  BEGIN
    Temp := SelStart;
    Text := UpperCase(Text);
    SelStart := Temp;
  END;
```

Chances are good that this will solve the problem.

Rich Edit Riches

There comes a time when the memo box just isn't enough. Its limitations are manifold—the worst among them being the 32K text limitation and the inability to set different fonts and styles for different parts of the text. Unfortunately, if you're using Windows 3.1 and 16-bit Delphi, your only real solution is to purchase a third-party, full-function editor component—this is almost invariably more cost-effective than trying to build one yourself. But, in Delphi32, the Rich Edit component comes to the rescue.

 Getting beyond the 32K limit

Even in 32-bit Delphi, the Windows 95 multiline edit control (which is the core of a TMemo) holds a limited amount of text. In the 32-bit version, it's possible to come closer to the theoretical maximum of 64K, but that is still the absolute limit. Just switching to 32-bit Delphi does not make TMemo hold more text. Windows NT's multiline edit control holds megabytes of text, but, in general, 32-bit programs need to support *both* Windows 95 and Windows NT.

The solution is to use a TRichEdit. You don't have to do anything special; the LoadFromFile method of the Rich Edit box's Lines property will load a hugely long file. The corresponding SaveToFile property will save it. If all you want is the ability to manage huge files, you can set the Rich Edit box's PlainText property to True. Read on for an example program using the Rich Edit box.

Using multiple fonts and styles

32

It may be mildly useful to set all the text in a memo box to the same new typeface or size, but, in most cases, what you really want is the ability to *change* text styles within the text. You want to underline some words, *italicize* others, and perhaps use a larger font for headings.

Where the memo box fails, the Rich Edit box brings hope. You can set the typeface, the font size, the font styles, and even the color for the selected text in a rich edit quite easily. The SelAttributes property represents the font information for the current selection, and has the same set of properties as a TFont object. In addition, the ConsistentAttributes property is a set that indicates which of the text styles is valid throughout the selected text. If all the text is Times New Roman, but some is 10 point and some is 12 point, ConsistentAttributes will contain caFace, but not caSize.

Using the Rich Edit component in an editor

32

A simple editor created to use the Rich Edit component can be quite powerful. As noted before, it holds virtually any size file of plain text or rich text. The component permits the setting of text styles for whatever text is selected, and indicates whether each style has a consistent value throughout the selected text. Paragraph styles, such as indentation, alignment, and bullets, can also be set. The example program shown in Figure 6-7 is a complete editor built around a Rich Edit box, implementing virtually all the features except paragraph formatting.

CPRICH

CPRICHU.DEX

```
object Form1: TForm1
  ActiveControl = RichEdit1
  Caption = 'Rich Editor - (untitled)'
  Menu = MainMenu1
  Position = poDefault
```

```
Scaled = False
OnCloseQuery = FormCloseQuery
OnCreate = FormCreate
OnResize = FormResize
object Panel1: TPanel
  Align = alTop
  BevelInner = bvLowered
  object BtnB: TSpeedButton
    AllowAllUp = True
    GroupIndex = 1
    Caption = 'B'
    Font.Height = -16
    Font.Style = [fsBold]
    ParentFont = False
    OnClick = BtnBClick
  end
  object BtnI: TSpeedButton
    Tag = 1
    AllowAllUp = True
    GroupIndex = 2
    Caption = 'I'
    Font.Height = -16
    Font.Name = 'MS Serif'
    Font.Style = [fsItalic]
    ParentFont = False
    OnClick = BtnBClick
  end
  object BtnU: TSpeedButton
    Tag = 2
    AllowAllUp = True
    GroupIndex = 3
    Caption = 'U'
    Font.Height = -16
    Font.Style = [fsUnderline]
    ParentFont = False
    OnClick = BtnBClick
  end
  object ComboBox1: TComboBox
    Style = csDropDownList
    Sorted = True
    OnChange = ComboBox1Change
  end
  object ComboBox2: TComboBox
    Items.Strings = (
      '8'
      '9'
      '10'
      '11'
      '12'
      '14'
      '16'
      '18'
      '20'
```

```
          '24'
          '36'
          '48'
          '72')
      OnChange = ComboBox2Change
    end
    object ComboBox3: TComboBox
      Style = csOwnerDrawFixed
      Items.Strings = (
        'clWindowText'
        'clBlack'
        'clMaroon'
        'clGreen'
        'clOlive'
        'clNavy'
        'clPurple'
        'clTeal'
        'clGray'
        'clSilver'
        'clRed'
        'clLime'
        'clYellow'
        'clBlue'
        'clFuchsia'
        'clAqua'
        'clWhite')
      OnChange = ComboBox3Change
      OnDrawItem = ComboBox3DrawItem
    end
  end
  object RichEdit1: TRichEdit
    Align = alClient
    HideSelection = False
    ScrollBars = ssVertical
    OnSelectionChange = RichEdit1SelectionChange
  end
  object StatusBar1: TStatusBar
    Panels = <
      item
        Width = 100
      end
      item
        Width = 100
      end
      item
        Width = 100
      end
      item
        Width = 50
      end>
    SimplePanel = False
  end
  object MainMenu1: TMainMenu
```

```
object File1: TMenuItem
  Caption = '&File'
  object New1: TMenuItem
    Caption = '&New'
    OnClick = New1Click
    ShortCutText = 'Ctrl+N'
  end
  object Open1: TMenuItem
    Caption = '&Open...'
    OnClick = Open1Click
    ShortCutText = 'Ctrl+O'
  end
  object Save1: TMenuItem
    Caption = '&Save'
    OnClick = Save1Click
    ShortCutText = 'Ctrl+S'
  end
  object SaveAs1: TMenuItem
    Caption = 'Save &As...'
    OnClick = SaveAs1Click
  end
  object N1: TMenuItem
    Caption = '-'
  end
  object PrintSetup1: TMenuItem
    Caption = 'P&rint Setup...'
    OnClick = PrintSetup1Click
  end
  object Print1: TMenuItem
    Caption = '&Print...'
    OnClick = Print1Click
    ShortCutText = 'Ctrl+P'
  end
  object N2: TMenuItem
    Caption = '-'
  end
  object Exit1: TMenuItem
    Caption = 'E&xit'
    OnClick = Exit1Click
  end
end
object Edit1: TMenuItem
  Caption = '&Edit'
  OnClick = Edit1Click
  object Undo1: TMenuItem
    Caption = '&Undo'
    OnClick = Undo1Click
    ShortCutText = 'Ctrl+Z'
  end
  object SelectAll1: TMenuItem
    Caption = 'Select &All'
    OnClick = SelectAll1Click
    ShortCutText = 'Ctrl+A'
```

```
          end
          object N3: TMenuItem
            Caption = '-'
          end
          object Cut1: TMenuItem
            Caption = 'Cu&t'
            OnClick = Cut1Click
            ShortCutText = 'Ctrl+X'
          end
          object Copy1: TMenuItem
            Caption = '&Copy'
            OnClick = Copy1Click
            ShortCutText = 'Ctrl+C'
          end
          object Paste1: TMenuItem
            Caption = '&Paste'
            OnClick = Paste1Click
            ShortCutText = 'Ctrl+V'
          end
          object N4: TMenuItem
            Caption = '-'
          end
          object Find1: TMenuItem
            Caption = '&Find...'
            OnClick = Find1Click
            ShortCutText = 'Ctrl+F'
          end
          object FindNext1: TMenuItem
            Caption = 'Find &Next'
            OnClick = FindDialog1Find
            ShortCutText = 'F3'
          end
          object Replace1: TMenuItem
            Caption = '&Replace...'
            OnClick = Replace1Click
            ShortCutText = 'Ctrl+R'
          end
        end
        object Invisible1: TMenuItem
          Caption = 'Invisible'
          Visible = False
          object Bold1: TMenuItem
            Caption = 'Bold'
            OnClick = Bold1Click
            ShortCutText = 'Ctrl+B'
          end
          object Italic1: TMenuItem
            Tag = 1
            Caption = 'Italic'
            OnClick = Bold1Click
            ShortCutText = 'Ctrl+I'
          end
          object Underline1: TMenuItem
            Tag = 2
            Caption = 'Underline'
            OnClick = Bold1Click
```

```
        ShortCutText = 'Ctrl+U'
      end
    end
  end
  object OpenDialog1: TOpenDialog
    DefaultExt = 'RTF'
    Filter = 'Rich Text Files|*.RTF|Text Files|*.TXT|All Files|*.*'
    Options = [ofHideReadOnly, ofFileMustExist, ofNoReadOnlyReturn]
    Title = 'Open RTF File'
  end
  object SaveDialog1: TSaveDialog
    Filter = 'Rich Text File|*.RTF|Text File|*.TXT'
    Options = [ofOverwritePrompt, ofHideReadOnly, ofPathMustExist]
    Title = 'Save RTF File'
  end
  object PrinterSetupDialog1: TPrinterSetupDialog
  end
  object PrintDialog1: TPrintDialog
    Options = [poDisablePrintToFile]
  end
  object FindDialog1: TFindDialog
    Options = [frDown, frHideUpDown, frDisableUpDown]
    OnFind = FindDialog1Find
  end
  object ReplaceDialog1: TReplaceDialog
    Options = [frDown, frHideUpDown, frDisableUpDown]
    OnFind = FindDialog1Find
    OnReplace = ReplaceDialog1Replace
  end
end
```

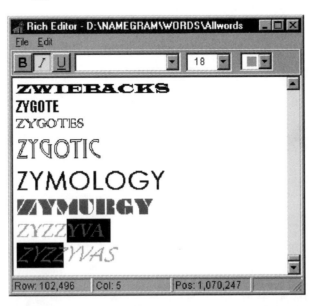

FIGURE 6-7: The Rich Edit component has no trouble loading and formatting this 1MB file with over 100,000 lines of text.

CPRICHU.PAS

```
unit cprichu;
{$IFNDEF Win32}
HALT! This program requires 32-bit Delphi
{$ENDIF}
interface

uses SysUtils, Windows, Messages, Classes, Graphics, Controls,
  Forms, Dialogs, Menus, StdCtrls, ComCtrls, RichEdit,
  Buttons, ExtCtrls;

type
  TForm1 = class(TForm)
    MainMenu1: TMainMenu;
    Edit1: TMenuItem;
    Undo1: TMenuItem;
    Cut1: TMenuItem;
    Copy1: TMenuItem;
    Paste1: TMenuItem;
    Invisible1: TMenuItem;
    Bold1: TMenuItem;
    Italic1: TMenuItem;
    Underline1: TMenuItem;
    Panel1: TPanel;
    BtnB: TSpeedButton;
    BtnI: TSpeedButton;
    BtnU: TSpeedButton;
    ComboBox1: TComboBox;
    ComboBox2: TComboBox;
    ComboBox3: TComboBox;
    File1: TMenuItem;
    Open1: TMenuItem;
    Save1: TMenuItem;
    SaveAs1: TMenuItem;
    N1: TMenuItem;
    Exit1: TMenuItem;
    OpenDialog1: TOpenDialog;
    SaveDialog1: TSaveDialog;
    New1: TMenuItem;
    Print1: TMenuItem;
    N2: TMenuItem;
    PrintSetup1: TMenuItem;
    PrinterSetupDialog1: TPrinterSetupDialog;
    PrintDialog1: TPrintDialog;
    RichEdit1: TRichEdit;
    StatusBar1: TStatusBar;
    N3: TMenuItem;
    N4: TMenuItem;
    Find1: TMenuItem;
    FindNext1: TMenuItem;
    Replace1: TMenuItem;
    FindDialog1: TFindDialog;
    ReplaceDialog1: TReplaceDialog;
```

```
      SelectAll1: TMenuItem;
      procedure Edit1Click(Sender: TObject);
      procedure FormCreate(Sender: TObject);
      procedure Undo1Click(Sender: TObject);
      procedure Cut1Click(Sender: TObject);
      procedure Copy1Click(Sender: TObject);
      procedure Paste1Click(Sender: TObject);
      procedure BtnBClick(Sender: TObject);
      procedure RichEdit1SelectionChange(Sender: TObject);
      procedure Bold1Click(Sender: TObject);
      procedure ComboBox1Change(Sender: TObject);
      procedure ComboBox2Change(Sender: TObject);
      procedure ComboBox3DrawItem(Control: TWinControl; Index:
        Integer; Rect: TRect; State: TOwnerDrawState);
      procedure ComboBox3Change(Sender: TObject);
      procedure Exit1Click(Sender: TObject);
      procedure Open1Click(Sender: TObject);
      procedure SaveAs1Click(Sender: TObject);
      procedure Save1Click(Sender: TObject);
      procedure New1Click(Sender: TObject);
      procedure FormCloseQuery(Sender: TObject; var CanClose:
        Boolean);
      procedure PrintSetup1Click(Sender: TObject);
      procedure Print1Click(Sender: TObject);
      procedure FormResize(Sender: TObject);
      procedure Find1Click(Sender: TObject);
      procedure FindDialog1Find(Sender: TObject);
      procedure Replace1Click(Sender: TObject);
      procedure ReplaceDialog1Replace(Sender: TObject);
      procedure SelectAll1Click(Sender: TObject);
    end;

var Form1: TForm1;

implementation
uses ClipBrd;
{$R *.DFM}

procedure TForm1.Edit1Click(Sender: TObject);
begin
  Paste1.Enabled := Clipboard.HasFormat(CF_TEXT);
  Undo1.Enabled := RichEdit1.Perform(EM_CANUNDO, 0, 0) <> 0;
  Cut1.Enabled := RichEdit1.SelLength > 0;
  Copy1.Enabled := RichEdit1.SelLength > 0;
  FindNext1.Enabled := FindDialog1.FindText <> '';
end;

procedure TForm1.FormCreate(Sender: TObject);
VAR N : Integer;
begin
  WITH ComboBox3 DO
    FOR N := 0 TO Items.Count-1 DO
      Items.Objects[N] := Pointer(StringToColor(Items[N]));
  Bold1.Tag := LongInt(BtnB);
  Italic1.Tag := LongInt(BtnI);
```

```
    Underline1.Tag := LongInt(BtnU);
    ComboBox1.Items := Screen.Fonts;
    RichEdit1SelectionChange(RichEdit1);
    RichEdit1.Modified := False;
end;

procedure TForm1.Undo1Click(Sender: TObject);
begin
  RichEdit1.Perform(EM_UNDO, 0, 0);
end;

procedure TForm1.Cut1Click(Sender: TObject);
begin
  RichEdit1.CutToClipboard;
end;

procedure TForm1.Copy1Click(Sender: TObject);
begin
  RichEdit1.CopyToClipboard;
end;

procedure TForm1.Paste1Click(Sender: TObject);
begin
  RichEdit1.PasteFromClipboard;
end;

procedure TForm1.BtnBClick(Sender: TObject);
begin
  WITH Sender AS TSpeedButton, RichEdit1.SelAttributes DO
    IF Down THEN Style := Style + [TFontStyle(Tag)]
    ELSE Style := Style - [TFontStyle(Tag)];
end;

procedure TForm1.RichEdit1SelectionChange(Sender: TObject);
VAR
  TCA : TConsistentAttributes;
  Ro, Co : Integer;
begin
  WITH RichEdit1.SelAttributes DO
    BEGIN
      TCA := ConsistentAttributes;
      BtnB.Down := (caBold IN TCA) AND (fsBold IN Style);
      BtnI.Down := (caItalic IN TCA) AND (fsItalic IN Style);
      BtnU.Down := (caUnderline IN TCA) AND (fsUnderline IN Style);
      IF NOT (caFace IN TCA) THEN ComboBox1.ItemIndex := -1
      ELSE ComboBox1.ItemIndex := ComboBox1.Items.IndexOf(Name);
      IF NOT (caSize IN TCA) THEN ComboBox2.Text := ''
      ELSE ComboBox2.Text := IntToStr(Size);
      IF NOT (caColor IN TCA) THEN ComboBox3.ItemIndex := -1
      ELSE ComboBox3.ItemIndex := ComboBox3.Items.IndexOfObject(
        TObject(Color))
    END;
  WITH Sender AS TCustomEdit DO
    BEGIN
      Ro := Perform(EM_LINEFROMCHAR, SelStart, 0);
      Co := SelStart - Perform(EM_LINEINDEX, Ro, 0);
```

```
        StatusBar1.Panels[0].Text := 'Row: ' +
          FormatFloat('0,', Ro+1);
        StatusBar1.Panels[1].Text := 'Col: ' +
          FormatFloat('0,', Co+1);
        StatusBar1.Panels[2].Text := 'Pos: ' +
          FormatFloat(',0', SelStart);
    END;
end;
procedure TForm1.Bold1Click(Sender: TObject);
begin
  Screen.Cursor := crHourglass;
  try
    WITH Sender AS TMenuItem DO
      BEGIN
        WITH TSpeedButton(Tag) DO Down := NOT Down;
        BtnBClick(TSpeedButton(Tag));
      END;
  finally
    Screen.Cursor := crDefault;
  end;
end;
procedure TForm1.ComboBox1Change(Sender: TObject);
begin
  Screen.Cursor := crHourglass;
  try
    WITH Sender AS TComboBox DO
      RichEdit1.SelAttributes.Name := Items[ItemIndex];
  finally
    Screen.Cursor := crDefault;
  end;
end;
procedure TForm1.ComboBox2Change(Sender: TObject);
begin
  Screen.Cursor := crHourglass;
  try
    WITH Sender AS TComboBox DO
      RichEdit1.SelAttributes.Size :=
        StrToIntDef(Items[ItemIndex], 10);
  finally
    Screen.Cursor := crDefault;
  end;
end;
procedure TForm1.ComboBox3DrawItem(Control: TWinControl; Index:
  Integer; Rect: TRect; State: TOwnerDrawState);
begin
  WITH Control AS TComboBox, Canvas DO
    BEGIN
      FillRect(Rect);
      InflateRect(Rect, -2, -2);
      Rect.Left := Rect.Left + 3;
      Brush.Color := LongInt(Items.Objects[Index]);
```

```
          FillRect(Rect);
      END;
end;
procedure TForm1.ComboBox3Change(Sender: TObject);
begin
  Screen.Cursor := crHourglass;
  try
    WITH Sender AS TComboBox DO
      BEGIN
        RichEdit1.SelAttributes.Color :=
          LongInt(Items.Objects[ItemIndex]);
      END;
  finally
    Screen.Cursor := crDefault;
  end;
end;

procedure TForm1.Exit1Click(Sender: TObject);
begin
  Close;
end;

procedure TForm1.Open1Click(Sender: TObject);
begin
  WITH OpenDialog1 DO
    IF Execute THEN
      BEGIN
        Self.Refresh;
        Screen.Cursor := crHourglass;
        try
          RichEdit1.Lines.LoadFromFile(Filename);
        finally
          Screen.Cursor := crDefault;
        end;
        RichEdit1.Modified := False;
        Caption := 'Rich Editor - ' + Filename;
        SaveDialog1.Filename := Filename;
        SaveDialog1.FilterIndex := FilterIndex;
        RichEdit1.PlainText := FilterIndex > 1;
        Filename := '';
      END;
end;

procedure TForm1.SaveAs1Click(Sender: TObject);
begin
  WITH SaveDialog1 DO
    IF Execute THEN
      BEGIN
        RichEdit1.PlainText := FilterIndex > 1;
        RichEdit1.Lines.SaveToFile(Filename);
        RichEdit1.Modified := False;
        Caption := 'Rich Editor - ' + Filename;
      END;
end;
```

```
procedure TForm1.Save1Click(Sender: TObject);
begin
  IF SaveDialog1.Filename = '' THEN
    SaveAs1Click(Sender)
  ELSE
    BEGIN
      RichEdit1.Lines.SaveToFile(SaveDialog1.Filename);
      RichEdit1.Modified := False;
    END;
end;

procedure TForm1.New1Click(Sender: TObject);
begin
  RichEdit1.Lines.Clear;
  Caption := 'Rich Editor - (untitled)';
  SaveDialog1.Filename := '';
  SaveDialog1.FilterIndex := 1;
  RichEdit1.PlainText := False;
  RichEdit1.Modified := False;
end;

procedure TForm1.FormCloseQuery(Sender: TObject;
  var CanClose: Boolean);
begin
  IF RichEdit1.Modified THEN
    CASE MessageDlg('File ' +
      ExtractFileName(SaveDialog1.Filename) +
      ' has changed. Save now?', mtConfirmation,
      mbYesNoCancel, 0) OF
      idYES  : Save1Click(Sender);
      idNO   : ;
      idCANCEL: CanClose := False;
    END;
end;

procedure TForm1.PrintSetup1Click(Sender: TObject);
begin
  WITH PrinterSetupDialog1 DO Execute;
end;

procedure TForm1.Print1Click(Sender: TObject);
begin
  WITH PrintDialog1 DO
    IF Execute THEN
      RichEdit1.Print(SaveDialog1.Filename);
end;

procedure TForm1.FormResize(Sender: TObject);
VAR R : TRect;
begin
  R := ClientRect;
  InflateRect(R, -4, -4);
  SendMessage(RichEdit1.Handle, EM_SETRECT, 0, LongInt(@R));
end;
```

```
procedure TForm1.Find1Click(Sender: TObject);
begin
  WITH RichEdit1 DO
    BEGIN
      IF (SelLength > 0) AND (SelLength < 30) THEN
        FindDialog1.FindText := SelText;
      FindDialog1.Execute;
    END;
end;

procedure TForm1.FindDialog1Find(Sender: TObject);
CONST STypes : ARRAY[Boolean, Boolean] OF TSearchTypes =
  (([],            [stMatchCase]            ),
   ([stWholeWord], [stWholeWord, stMatchCase]));
VAR Start, Len, Loc : Integer;
begin
  Start := RichEdit1.SelStart + RichEdit1.SelLength;
  Len := RichEdit1.GetTextLen - Start;
  WITH Sender AS TFindDialog DO
    Loc := RichEdit1.FindText(FindText, Start, Len,
      STypes[frWholeword IN Options, frMatchCase IN Options]);
  IF Loc = -1 THEN MessageBeep(MB_ICONSTOP)
  ELSE
    BEGIN
      RichEdit1.SelStart := Loc;
      RichEdit1.SelLength :=
        Length((Sender AS TFindDialog).FindText);
    END;
  FindDialog1.FindText := (Sender AS TFindDialog).FindText;
  ReplaceDialog1.FindText := FindDialog1.FindText;
  FindNext1.Enabled := FindDialog1.FindText <> '';
end;

procedure TForm1.Replace1Click(Sender: TObject);
begin
  WITH RichEdit1 DO
    BEGIN
      IF (SelLength > 0) AND (SelLength < 30) THEN
        ReplaceDialog1.FindText := SelText;
      ReplaceDialog1.Execute;
    END;
end;

procedure TForm1.ReplaceDialog1Replace(Sender: TObject);
begin
  Enabled := False;
  Screen.Cursor := crHourglass;
  RichEdit1.Perform(WM_SETREDRAW, 0, 0);
  try
    WITH Sender AS TReplaceDialog DO
      WHILE True DO
        BEGIN
          IF RichEdit1.SelText <> FindText THEN
```

```
                    FindDialog1Find(Sender);
            IF RichEdit1.SelLength = 0 THEN Break;
            RichEdit1.SelText := ReplaceText;
            IF NOT (frReplaceAll IN Options) THEN Break;
            Application.ProcessMessages;
            IF Application.Terminated THEN Break;
        END;
    finally
      Enabled := True;
      Screen.Cursor := crDefault;
       RichEdit1.Perform(WM_SETREDRAW, 1, 0);
      RichEdit1.Refresh;
    end;
  end;
procedure TForm1.SelectAll1Click(Sender: TObject);
begin
  RichEdit1.SelStart := 0;
  RichEdit1.SelLength := RichEdit1.GetTextLen;
end;

end.
```

The operations of loading, saving, and printing a file are all handled by the Rich Edit component. The Cut, Copy, Paste, and Undo menu items are implemented exactly as demonstrated earlier in this chapter. When the form is resized, the Rich Edit box resizes also; an EM_SETRECT message forces it to adjust its formatting rectangle to the new size. It's also possible to leave the formatting rectangle at the same size when the component's bounding rectangle changes; you see this behavior in Windows word processors, such as Word for Windows.

The three font-attribute combo boxes, the three font style buttons, and the three invisible menu items that supply hotkeys for the font style buttons all function in roughly the same way. They set the cursor to its hourglass shape, because formatting all the text in a long document can take a while. They change the Rich Edit box's SelAttributes property, which changes some aspect of the selected text. And, finally, they restore the default cursor.

The OnSelectionChange event for the Rich Edit box occurs when the user selects or enters text. Its event handler has two main functions. First, it sets the state of the font buttons and the combo boxes to match all attributes that are consistent within the selection. In Figure 6-7, the selected text is all 18 points, all gray, and all italic; however, there are two different typefaces within the selection, so the typeface combo box is blank. This event handler's second function is to display the current row, column, and absolute character position on the form's status bar.

Finding text in a Rich Edit box is easy because of the built-in FindText method. Pass this method a string, a starting location, and a length, and it will return the location of the first occurrence of that string within the specified range, or −1 if the string is not found. A fourth parameter controls whether the search is case sensitive, and whether only whole words will be found.

Replacing text in the OnReplace event handler is simply a matter of finding one string, selecting it, and setting the rich edit box's SelText property to the replacement string. If the user presses the Replace All button, this process continues until every instance has been replaced, or the user presses Cancel. This is anything but a speedy process, so the OnReplace event handler sets the cursor to an hourglass and disables the main program window while it's working.

You may have noticed that the Find dialog's OnFind event handler and the Select All menu item's OnClick event handler both call the RichEdit's GetTextLen method rather than passing RichEdit1.Text to the Length function. This is a very deliberate choice. Referencing the Text property requires copying its entire contents into another area of memory. Whenever a choice is available, avoid referencing a RichEdit's Text property.

This program is one of the longest in the book, but that's because it *does* a lot. You can use it as a substantial head start on creating an editor with all the features of Windows 95's WordPad application.

CHAPTER 7

List and Combo Boxes

*I*f you want the programs you develop to be popular, you must make them responsive to the user's needs. That means your applications have to find out what the user wants. If there are several specific mutually exclusive options, you can let the user choose from a set of radio buttons. However, too many radio buttons can overload a form, and sometimes you don't know all the options in advance. That's where a list box comes in handy, because you can display thousands of choices in a list box. If space is tight, you can accomplish the same thing using a drop-down combo box.

You can also use a list box to replace a group of check boxes—just make it a multiselect list box. This ability doesn't normally extend to combo boxes, but there are ways to work around that limitation.

In this chapter, we'll explore the quirks of the list box and, to a lesser degree, combo box components. We'll add some basic features that aren't exposed in the components, and go on to enhance these components with features you may never have considered. We'll also get into the details of using drag-and-drop with list boxes (a very nice user-interface enhancement).

Owner-Draw List Boxes

List boxes and combo boxes usually display text, but the owner-draw feature gives the form that owns them a chance to draw graphical data as well, or to modify their display of text. To make a list box owner-draw with fixed-height items, you set its Style property to lbOwnerDrawFixed and respond to the OnDrawItem event by drawing one item. If the items may vary in height, set the Style to lbOwnerDrawVariable and also respond to OnMeasureItem by specifying the height of the requested item. It's relatively simple, compared to doing the same thing without Delphi's help, but you'll find that questions do come up.

Varying text colors and styles

16 32

One reason to use an owner-draw list box is to display items using different text styles. You may even want to use different styles within a single item. You start by setting the list box's style to lbOwnerDrawFixed; then what?

If the items differ only in text style, you can use a fixed-height, owner-draw list box— just ensure ItemHeight is set large enough for the highest lines. Figure 7-1 shows two examples. In the left-hand list box, all vowels are displayed in bold, underlined, red text, while consonants show up in whatever color your system uses for standard window text. In the right-hand list box, every other line displays its text with a red background.

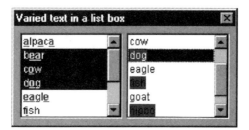

FIGURE 7-1: The right-hand list box uses a different style for every other item, whereas the one on the left varies text style within each item.

COLTEXT

COLTEXTU.DEX

```
object Form1: TForm1
  BorderIcons = [biSystemMenu]
  BorderStyle = bsDialog
  Caption = 'Varied text in a list box'
  Position = poDefault
  Scaled = False
  OnCreate = FormCreate
  object ListBox1: TListBox
    Items.Strings = (
      'alpaca'
      'bear'
      'cow'
      'dog'
      'eagle'
      'fish'
      'goat'
```

```
        'hippo')
      MultiSelect = True
      Style = lbOwnerDrawFixed
      OnDrawItem = ListBox1DrawItem
    end
    object ListBox2: TListBox
      MultiSelect = True
      Style = lbOwnerDrawFixed
      OnDrawItem = ListBox2DrawItem
    end
  end
```

COLTEXTU.PAS

```
unit Coltextu;

interface

uses SysUtils, WinTypes, WinProcs, Messages, Classes, Graphics,
  Controls, Forms, StdCtrls;

type
  TForm1 = class(TForm)
    ListBox1: TListBox;
    ListBox2: TListBox;
    procedure ListBox1DrawItem(Control: TWinControl;
      Index: Integer; Rect: TRect; State: TOwnerDrawState);
    procedure ListBox2DrawItem(Control: TWinControl;
      Index: Integer; Rect: TRect; State: TOwnerDrawState);
    procedure FormCreate(Sender: TObject);
  end;

var Form1: TForm1;

implementation

{$R *.DFM}

procedure TForm1.ListBox1DrawItem(Control: TWinControl;
  Index: Integer; Rect: TRect; State: TOwnerDrawState);
CONST
  VowelColor : ARRAY[Boolean] OF TColor = (clRed, clYellow);
  OtherColor : ARRAY[Boolean] OF TColor = (clWindowText,
    clHighlightText);
VAR
  S : String;
  N : Word;
begin
  WITH Control AS TListBox, Canvas DO
    BEGIN
      S := Items[Index];
      FillRect(Rect);
      MoveTo(Rect.Left+2, Rect.Top);
      SetTextAlign(Canvas.Handle, TA_UPDATECP);
      FOR N := 1 TO Length(S) DO
```

```
                    BEGIN
                      CASE UpCase(S[N]) OF
                        'A','E','I','O','U':
                          BEGIN
                            Font.Color := VowelColor[odSelected IN State];
                            Font.Style := [fsBold, fsUnderline];
                          END;
                        ELSE
                          BEGIN
                            Font.Color := OtherColor[odSelected IN State];
                            Font.Style := [];
                          END;
                      END;
                      WinProcs.TextOut(Canvas.Handle, 0, 0, @S[N], 1);
                    END;
                END;
            end;
            procedure TForm1.ListBox2DrawItem(Control: TWinControl;
              Index: Integer; Rect: TRect; State: TOwnerDrawState);
            begin
              WITH Control AS TListBox, Canvas DO
                BEGIN
                  FillRect(Rect);
                  IF Odd(Index) THEN Brush.Color := clRed;
                  TextOut(Rect.Left+2, Rect.Top, Items[Index]);
                END;
            end;
            procedure TForm1.FormCreate(Sender: TObject);
            begin
              ListBox2.Items := ListBox1.Items;
            end;
            end.
```

Note that both OnDrawItem event handlers call FillRect(Rect) before making any changes to the drawing objects used by the list box's canvas. This has the effect of correctly clearing the rectangle occupied by the item using the normal or highlighted colors. The right-hand list box's drawing is relatively simple. If the item index is odd, it sets the canvas's brush color to red before writing the text. As a result, odd-numbered items will have a red background behind the text. (Yes, you see the second, fourth, and other *even*-numbered items in red. But remember, internally the item numbering starts from 0, so those are items 1, 3, 5, and so on.)

The left-hand list box's OnDrawItem handler is decidedly more complicated because of the need to draw characters individually, with each character appearing just after the preceding one. The call to SetTextAlign sets the text alignment style TA_UPDATECP. This style changes the behavior of the Windows TextOut function; text is printed at the current position rather than at the specified X and Y coordinates, and the current position is updated to the end of the text. That's exactly what we want here. However, the Canvas object's TextOut method does not work correctly in this alignment mode. We need to call the underlying Windows API function, also named TextOut. Prefixing the function name with "WinProcs." distinguishes it from the same-named method.

Remember that SetTextAlign(TA_UPDATECP) does not work with Canvas.TextOut. It's easy enough to work around this by calling the API function TextOut, but, if you don't *know* the problem exists, you can waste time seeking an error in your own code. And, when you need to draw a line of text in varying text styles, use this program for reference.

 ## Varying fonts and font sizes

| 16 | 32 |

You'll also want an owner-draw list box if you need to present different items using different fonts. You could use a fixed-height, owner-draw list box and simply set the ItemHeight to whatever is necessary for the largest font you'll be using. But variable height can give a more attractive result, especially when you consider the fact that the height you request may not actually be available if the specified font isn't a TrueType font. Figure 7-2 shows a program that lists all available fonts, using the available size that's closest to 13-point.

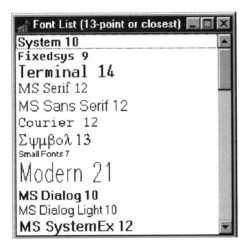

FIGURE 7-2: This program gets its list of fonts from the Screen object and displays each font name *using* the font itself.

FONTLIST

FONTLISU.DEX

```
object Form1: TForm1
  Caption = 'Font List (13-point or closest)'
  Position = poDefault
  Scaled = False
  OnCreate = FormCreate
  object ListBox1: TListBox
    Align = alClient
    Style = lbOwnerDrawVariable
    OnDrawItem = ListBox1DrawItem
    OnMeasureItem = ListBox1MeasureItem
  end
end
```

FONTLISU.PAS

```
unit Fontlisu;

interface

uses SysUtils, WinTypes, WinProcs, Messages, Classes, Graphics,
  Controls, Forms, Dialogs, StdCtrls;

type
  TForm1 = class(TForm)
    ListBox1: TListBox;
    procedure ListBox1MeasureItem(Control: TWinControl;
      Index: Integer; var Height: Integer);
    procedure ListBox1DrawItem(Control: TWinControl;
      Index: Integer; Rect: TRect; State: TOwnerDrawState);
    procedure FormCreate(Sender: TObject);
  end;

var Form1: TForm1;

implementation

{$R *.DFM}
VAR VRes: Integer;

function EnumFFProc(var LF: TLogFont; var TexMet: TTextMetric;
  FontType: Integer; FSize: PInteger): Integer; Export;
  {$IFDEF Win32}StdCall;{$ENDIF}
VAR CSize : Integer;
begin
  IF FontType AND TRUETYPE_FONTTYPE > 0 THEN
    BEGIN
      FSize^ := 13;
      Result := 0;
    END
  ELSE
    BEGIN
```

```
          WITH TexMet DO
            CSize := Round((tmHeight-tmInternalLeading)*72 / VRes);
          IF (FSize^=0) OR (Abs(CSize-13)<(Abs(FSize^-13))) THEN
            FSize^ := CSize;
          Result := 1;
      END;
end;

procedure TForm1.FormCreate(Sender: TObject);
VAR
  N, SizAvail : Integer;
  Buffer      : ARRAY[0..255] OF Char;
begin
  VRes := GetDeviceCaps(Canvas.Handle, LOGPIXELSY);
  ListBox1.Items := Screen.Fonts;
  WITH ListBox1 DO
    FOR N := 0 TO Items.Count-1 DO
      BEGIN
        Canvas.Font.Name := Items[N];
        StrPCopy(Buffer, Items[N]);
        SizAvail := 0;
        EnumFontFamilies(Canvas.Handle, Buffer, @EnumFFPRoc,
         {$IFDEF Win32}LongInt{$ELSE}PChar{$ENDIF}(@SizAvail));
        {Next line triggers OnMeasureItem for changed item}
        Items[N] := Format('%s %.2d', [Items[N], SizAvail]);
      END;
end;

procedure TForm1.ListBox1MeasureItem(Control: TWinControl;
  Index: Integer; var Height: Integer);
VAR S : String;
begin
  S := ListBox1.Items[Index];
  WITH ListBox1.Canvas DO
    BEGIN
      Font.Name := Copy(S, 1, Length(S)-3);
      Font.Size := StrToIntDef(Copy(S, Length(S)-1, 2), 13);
      Height := TextHeight(S);
    END;
end;

procedure TForm1.ListBox1DrawItem(Control: TWinControl;
  Index: Integer; Rect: TRect; State: TOwnerDrawState);
VAR S : String;
begin
  S := ListBox1.Items[Index];
  WITH ListBox1.Canvas DO
    BEGIN
      FillRect(Rect);
      Font.Name := Copy(S, 1, Length(S)-3);
      Font.Size := StrToIntDef(Copy(S, Length(S)-1, 2), 13);
      TextRect(Rect, Rect.Left+2, Rect.Top, S);
    END;
end;

end.
```

As you can see from the figure, many non-TrueType fonts are not available in the 13-point size. Windows will stretch or shrink the font as well as it can, but for the best display you should use a size that's officially available. To determine the closest possible match, the form's OnCreate event handler calls the API function EnumFontFamilies, which calls the function EnumFFProc for each variation on the named font. If it's a TrueType font, any size is available, so EnumFFProc sets the font size to 13 and sets its own Result to 0, ending the enumeration. Otherwise, EnumFFProc calculates the point size of the current variation and stores that size *if* it's closer to 13 than the previous choice.

If you need to display variable-height list box items using different fonts, either stick to TrueType fonts (which display in the point size you specify) or build on the technique shown here to determine a point size that's valid for the selected non-TrueType font.

Displaying bitmaps in a list box

16 32

The preceding examples used owner-draw list boxes, but they still displayed text. The *truly* impressive use of an owner-draw list box is to display graphics! Displaying a bitmap in the OnDrawItem event handler is as simple as calling the canvas's Draw or StretchDraw method and then optionally using TextOut to add text. Figure 7-3 shows a program that goes a bit beyond the basics—it displays Delphi glyph bitmaps on simulated speed buttons.

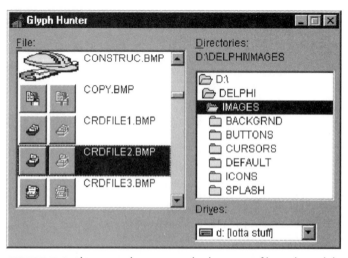

FIGURE 7-3: This example program displays .BMP files only; Delphi glyph bitmaps are displayed on speed buttons, while others are shoehorned into the available space.

LBBMP

LBBMPU.DEX

```
object Form1: TForm1
  BorderIcons = [biSystemMenu, biMinimize]
  BorderStyle = bsSingle
  Caption = 'Glyph Hunter'
  Position = poDefault
  Scaled = False
  object Label1: TLabel
  end
  object TLabel
    Caption = '&Directories:'
    FocusControl = DirectoryListBox1
  end
  object TLabel
    Caption = 'Dri&ves:'
    FocusControl = DriveComboBox1
  end
  object TLabel
    Caption = '&File:'
    FocusControl = ListBox1
  end
  object DriveComboBox1: TDriveComboBox
    DirList = DirectoryListBox1
  end
  object DirectoryListBox1: TDirectoryListBox
    DirLabel = Label1
    FileList = FileListBox1
  end
  object FileListBox1: TFileListBox
    Mask = '*.BMP'
    OnChange = FileListBox1Change
  end
  object ListBox1: TListBox
    IntegralHeight = True
    ItemHeight = 36
    Style = lbOwnerDrawFixed
    OnDrawItem = ListBox1DrawItem
  end
end
```

LBBMPU.PAS

```
unit lbbmpu;

interface

uses SysUtils, WinTypes, WinProcs, Messages, Classes, Graphics,
  Controls, Forms, StdCtrls, FileCtrl;

type
  TForm1 = class(TForm)
```

```
      DriveComboBox1: TDriveComboBox;
      DirectoryListBox1: TDirectoryListBox;
      Label1: TLabel;
      ListBox1: TListBox;
      FileListBox1: TFileListBox;
      procedure FileListBox1Change(Sender: TObject);
      procedure ListBox1DrawItem(Control: TWinControl;
        Index: Integer; Rect: TRect; State: TOwnerDrawState);
    end;

var Form1: TForm1;

implementation
uses Buttons; {for DrawButtonFace}
{$R *.DFM}

procedure TForm1.FileListBox1Change(Sender: TObject);
begin
  ListBox1.Items := FileListBox1.Items;
end;

procedure TForm1.ListBox1DrawItem(Control: TWinControl;
  Index: Integer; Rect: TRect; State: TOwnerDrawState);
VAR
  TB1, TB2    : TBitmap;
  TIL         : TImageList;
  W, H, RDelt : Integer;
  WasColor    : TColor;
  R           : TRect;
begin
  WITH Control AS TListBox, Canvas DO
    BEGIN
      FillRect(Rect);
      TB1 := TBitmap.Create;
      try try
        TB1.LoadFromFile(DirectoryListBox1.Directory + '\' +
          Items[Index]);
        W := TB1.Width; H := TB1.Height;
        IF (H<ItemHeight-8) AND (W MOD H = 0) AND (W DIV H <5) THEN
          BEGIN
            TIL := TImageList.CreateSize(H, H);
            WasColor := Brush.Color;
            try
              TB2 := TBitmap.Create;
              try
                TB2.Width := H;
                TB2.Height := H;
                TB2.Canvas.Draw(0,0,TB1);
                TIL.AddMasked(TB2, TB2.TransparentColor);
                R := Bounds(Rect.Left+2, Rect.Top+2, ItemHeight-3,
                  ItemHeight-3);
                RDelt := (ItemHeight - 3 - H) DIV 2;
                IF RDelt < 0 THEN RDelt := 0;
                {If there's a "disabled" version, create it
                 too and draw it first}
```

```
              IF W > H THEN
                BEGIN
                  TB2.Canvas.CopyRect(Classes.Rect(0, 0, H, H),
                    TB1.Canvas, Bounds(H, 0, H, H));
                  TIL.AddMasked(TB2, TB2.TransparentColor);
                  OffsetRect(R, ItemHeight, 0);
                  DrawButtonFace(Canvas, R, 1, bsNew, False,
                    False, False);
                  TIL.Draw(Canvas, R.Left+RDelt, R.Top+RDelt, 1);
                  OffsetRect(R, -ItemHeight, 0);
                END;
              DrawButtonFace(Canvas, R, 1, bsNew,
                False, False, False);
              TIL.Draw(Canvas, R.Left+RDelt, R.Top+RDelt, 0);
            finally
              TB2.Free;
            end;
          finally
            TIL.Free;
            Brush.Color := WasColor;
          end;
        END
      ELSE IF (H < ItemHeight-8) AND (W < 2*ItemHeight) THEN
        Draw(Rect.Left+2, Rect.Top, TB1)
      ELSE
        StretchDraw(Bounds(Rect.Left+2, Rect.Top,
          2*ItemHeight, ItemHeight-2), TB1);
    except
      ON Exception DO
        TextRect(Rect, Rect.Left+2, Rect.Left+2, 'INVALID');
    end;
    finally
      TB1.Free;
      Rect.Left := Rect.Left + 2*ItemHeight+6;
      TextRect(Rect, Rect.Left+2, Rect.Top, Items[Index]);
    end;
  END;
end;
end.
```

The LBBMP project uses the built-in Delphi file-management objects as much as possible—it links a DriveComboBox, a DirectoryListBox, and a FileListBox. However, the FileListBox is *hidden*, and its contents get copied to an owner-draw list box that displays the bitmaps.

The OnDrawItem event handler uses some functions and objects that you may not have run across before. The DrawButtonFace function is at least listed in Delphi's Help system; the TImageList object is only described in the help for Delphi 2.0. DrawButtonFace draws a blank button, while the TImageList object is used to hold the various representations of a glyph.

The OnDrawItem handler uses some arbitrary criteria to decide whether a particular bitmap is a glyph. The bitmap's height must be less than 26 pixels, and its width must be exactly 1, 2, 3, or 4 times its height. A bitmap that passes this test gets drawn as a speed button. The left-most square portion of the bitmap is copied into a TImageList using the AddMasked method, which lets the background show through any pixels that match the color of the bottom left pixel, effectively making them transparent. Then, if the bitmap is at least twice as wide as its height, the next square portion (which should be the disabled image) is added to the image list. For each image, the event handler draws a button, then draws the image on it.

If the bitmap doesn't pass the arbitrary test for glyph-hood, the event handler simply uses StretchDraw to display it in the available space. In Figure 7-3, CONSTRUC.BMP is drawn this way. Either way, after drawing the bitmap, the event handler displays the filename to its right.

Keep this example program in mind any time you need to draw a glyph-type bitmap. The TImageList object makes it relatively painless to perform the masking required to make one color appear transparent.

Owner-draw variable list box does not recognize changes in item height

16 32

At the time the item is added to the list box, Windows queries a variable-height, owner-draw list box about the height of an item exactly once. If your program makes changes that affect the calculations performed in your OnMeasureItem event handler, you don't see the result of those changes. The program shown in Figure 7-4 handles this problem by forcing the list box to recreate itself after each change that affects item height.

LBODVAR

LBODVARU.DEX

```
object Form1: TForm1
  BorderIcons = [biSystemMenu, biMinimize]
  BorderStyle = bsDialog
  Caption = 'OD List Height'
  Position = poDefault
  Scaled = False
  object ListBox1: TListBox
    Items.Strings = (
      'One'
      'Two'
```

```
        'Three'
        'Four'
        'Five'
        'Six'
        'Seven'
        'Eight')
      Style = lbOwnerDrawVariable
      OnDrawItem = ListBox1DrawItem
      OnMeasureItem = ListBox1MeasureItem
    end
    object Button1: TButton
      Caption = 'Change Item Height'
      OnClick = Button1Click
    end
  end
```

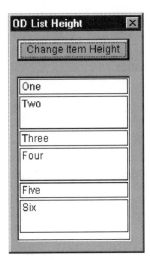

FIGURE 7-4: Initially, this program displays odd-numbered items in rectangles twice as high as even-numbered items; on each click of the button, the heights reverse.

LBODVARU.PAS

```
unit lbodvaru;

interface

uses SysUtils, WinTypes, WinProcs, Messages, Classes, Graphics,
  Controls, Forms, Dialogs, StdCtrls;

type
  TForm1 = class(TForm)
    ListBox1: TListBox;
    Button1: TButton;
```

```
      procedure ListBox1MeasureItem(Control: TWinControl;
        Index: Integer; var Height: Integer);
      procedure ListBox1DrawItem(Control: TWinControl;
        Index: Integer; Rect: TRect; State: TOwnerDrawState);
      procedure Button1Click(Sender: TObject);
    private
      Oddity : Boolean;
    end;

var Form1: TForm1;

implementation

{$R *.DFM}

procedure TForm1.ListBox1MeasureItem(Control: TWinControl;
    Index: Integer; var Height: Integer);
begin
    IF Odd(Index) = Oddity THEN Height := 40
    ELSE Height := 20;
end;

procedure TForm1.ListBox1DrawItem(Control: TWinControl;
    Index: Integer; Rect: TRect; State: TOwnerDrawState);
begin
    WITH Control AS TListBox, Canvas DO
      BEGIN
        FillRect(Rect);
        InflateRect(Rect, -1, -1);
        WITH Rect DO Rectangle(Left, Top, Right, Bottom);
        InflateRect(Rect, -1, -1);
        TextRect(Rect, Rect.Left+2, Rect.Top, Items[Index]);
      END;
end;

procedure TForm1.Button1Click(Sender: TObject);
begin
    Oddity := NOT Oddity;
    WITH ListBox1 DO
      BEGIN
        IntegralHeight := NOT IntegralHeight;
        IntegralHeight := NOT IntegralHeight;
      END;
end;

end.
```

The key here lies in changing the value of the list box's IntegralHeight property, and then changing it back. When IntegralHeight is False, the style bit LBS_NOINTEGRALHEIGHT is present, and vice versa. However, Windows does not permit changing this style after a list box has been created. Thus, when you change a Delphi list box object's IntegralHeight property, the object has to destroy the actual Windows list box and recreate it using the new style. As a convenient side effect, this causes all the items to be measured again.

This same behavior can cause trouble if you don't understand it. For example, if you store the window handle of a Delphi component in a variable and then make a property change that causes the component to be recreated, your stored window handle won't be valid any more.

Enhancing the List Box Object

Delphi does an excellent job of "wrapping" the standard Windows on-screen elements in components, and sometimes even adds brand-new functionality. However, occasionally the Delphi component will omit access to some features of the underlying Windows element. The list box component is a good example—it's missing the ability to scroll long items horizontally and to use tabs to line up columns.

 Items are wider than the list box

16 32

When the items in a list box are wider than the list box, your users expect to be able to scroll them horizontally. Unfortunately, Delphi list boxes do not do this automatically. You can send an LB_SETHORIZONTALEXTENT message to a list box component, but why not derive a new component that automates the process?

CREATING A NEW COMPONENT

To create a new component, select New Component from the File menu. Give the component a name, indicate its immediate ancestor, and tell Delphi which page of the component palette to place it on. Delphi will create an empty unit that defines the desired component. Add new properties and methods or override existing ones to add the desired functionality.

To add this component to the component palette, select Install Components from the Options menu. Click the Add button and Browse to locate the source file. After a few minutes of frantic disk access, your component palette will be updated with the new component.

COMPONENT TLISTBOXHORZ

C_LBHORZ.PAS

```pascal
unit c_lbhorz;

interface

uses SysUtils, WinTypes, WinProcs, Messages, Classes, Graphics,
  Controls, Forms, Dialogs, StdCtrls, p_about;

type
  TListBoxHorz = class(TListBox)
  private
    procedure CreateParams(VAR Params: TCreateParams);
      override;
    function GetScrollWidth : Integer;
    procedure SetScrollWidth(value : Integer);
    procedure LBAddString(VAR Msg: TMessage);
      message LB_ADDSTRING;
    procedure LBInsertString(VAR Msg: TMessage);
      message LB_INSERTSTRING;
    procedure LBDeleteString(VAR Msg: TMessage);
      message LB_DELETESTRING;
    procedure LBResetContent(VAR Msg: TMessage);
      message LB_RESETCONTENT;
    procedure CMFontChanged(VAR Msg: TMessage);
      message CM_FONTCHANGED;
  protected
    fAbout: TAbout;
    procedure AllWidths;
    procedure NewWidth(P : PChar);
    function WidthOfString(const S : String): Integer; virtual;
    function WidthOfPChar(P : PChar): Integer; virtual;
  published
    property ScrollWidth: Integer read GetScrollWidth write
      SetScrollWidth;
    property About: TAbout Read fAbout Write fAbout;
  end;

procedure Register;

implementation
{$IFDEF Win32}
{$R *.R32}
{$ELSE}
{$R *.R16}
{$ENDIF}

procedure TListBoxHorz.CreateParams(VAR Params: TCreateParams);
BEGIN
  Inherited CreateParams(Params);
  fAbout := 0.99;
END;

function TListBoxHorz.GetScrollWidth : Integer;
```

```
BEGIN
  Result := Perform(LB_GETHORIZONTALEXTENT, 0, 0);
END;

procedure TListBoxHorz.SetScrollWidth(value : Integer);
BEGIN
  Perform(LB_SETHORIZONTALEXTENT, value, 0);
END;

procedure TListBoxHorz.LBAddString(VAR Msg: TMessage);
BEGIN
  Inherited;
  NewWidth(PChar(Msg.lParam));
END;

procedure TListBoxHorz.LBInsertString(VAR Msg: TMessage);
BEGIN
  Inherited;
  NewWidth(PChar(Msg.lParam));
END;

procedure TListBoxHorz.LBDeleteString(VAR Msg: TMessage);
BEGIN
  Inherited;
  AllWidths;
END;

procedure TListBoxHorz.LBResetContent(VAR Msg: TMessage);
BEGIN
  Inherited;
  ScrollWidth := 0;
END;

procedure TListBoxHorz.CMFontChanged(VAR Msg: TMessage);
BEGIN
  Inherited;
  AllWidths;
END;

function TListBoxHorz.WidthOfString(const S : String): Integer;
begin
  Canvas.Font := Font;
  Result := Canvas.TextWidth(S+'X');
end;

function TListBoxHorz.WidthOfPChar(P : PChar): Integer;
begin
  Result := WidthOfString(StrPas(P));
end;

procedure TListBoxHorz.AllWidths;
VAR N, NewWid, Wid : Integer;
BEGIN
  NewWid := 0;
  FOR N := 0 TO Items.Count-1 DO
    BEGIN
      Wid := WidthOfString(Items[N]);
```

```
        IF Wid > NewWid THEN NewWid := Wid;
      END;
    ScrollWidth := NewWid;
  END;

  procedure TListBoxHorz.NewWidth(P : PChar);
  VAR Wid : Integer;
  BEGIN
    Canvas.Font := Font;
    Wid := WidthOfPChar(P);
    IF Wid > ScrollWidth THEN ScrollWidth := Wid;
  END;

  procedure Register;
  begin
    RegisterComponents('NJR', [TListBoxHorz]);
  end;

end.
```

The TListBoxHorz component publishes a property called ScrollWidth that reflects the current scrolling width of the list box. You can use this to get or to set the scrolling width, but, in general, you don't have to do a thing. Every time an event occurs that might change the width, the list box makes the necessary change. When you add or insert a string, it widens the scrolling width, as necessary. When you delete a string, it narrows the scrolling width, if possible. And, when you change the list box's font, it updates the scrolling width. The result is a list box that always scrolls horizontally exactly as much as is necessary.

This list box descendant also exposes a design-time property called About, of type TAbout. Properties of this type are handled by a special property editor that simply displays an About box. You'll find the definition of this special property editor in Chapter 6, "Edit Controls."

 ## *Using tabs in list box items*

16 32

A Windows list box control that's created with the style LBS_USETABSTOPS will automatically expand tab characters in item strings. It will also respond to the LB_SETTABSTOPS message, which specifies what tab stops should be used. Unfortunately, the list box component in 16-bit Delphi omits this style; a standard TListBox will not expand tabs at all.

Time for another new component! We'll make this one a descendant of the TListBoxHorz type defined in the preceding section.

COMPONENT TLISTBOXTABS

C_LBTAB.PAS

```
unit C_lbtab;

interface

uses SysUtils, WinTypes, WinProcs, Messages, Classes, Graphics,
  Controls, Forms, Dialogs, StdCtrls, c_lbhorz, p_about;

CONST MaxTabs = 40;
type
  TListBoxTabs = class(TListBoxHorz)
  private
    DlgBaseX : Integer;
    procedure CreateParams(VAR Params: TCreateParams);
      override;
  protected
    fDlgTabs, fPixTabs: ARRAY[0..MaxTabs] OF Integer;
    fHighTab: Integer;
    function WidthOfString(const S : String): Integer; override;
    function WidthOfPChar(P : PChar): Integer; override;
  published
    procedure SetTabsDlg(const Tabs: array OF Integer);
    procedure SetTabsPix(const Tabs: array OF Integer);
  end;

procedure Register;

implementation
{$IFDEF Win32}
{$R *.R32}
{$ELSE}
{$R *.R16}
{$ENDIF}

procedure TListBoxTabs.CreateParams(VAR Params: TCreateParams);
BEGIN
  Inherited CreateParams(Params);
  WITH Params DO Style := Style OR LBS_USETABSTOPS;
  fAbout := 0.99;
  DlgBaseX := LoWord(GetDialogBaseUnits);
END;

procedure TListBoxTabs.SetTabsDlg(const Tabs: ARRAY OF Integer);
VAR N : Integer;
begin
  fHighTab := High(Tabs);
  IF fHighTab > MaxTabs THEN fHighTab := MaxTabs;
  FOR N := 0 TO fHighTab DO
    BEGIN
      fDlgTabs[N] := Tabs[N];
      fPixTabs[N] := Round((Tabs[N] * DlgBaseX) / 4);
    END;
  Perform(LB_SETTABSTOPS, fHighTab+1, LongInt(@fDlgTabs));
```

```
     Refresh;
     AllWidths;
   end;
   procedure TListBoxTabs.SetTabsPix(const Tabs: ARRAY OF Integer);
   VAR N : WOrd;
   begin
     fHighTab := High(Tabs);
     IF fHighTab > MaxTabs THEN fHighTab := MaxTabs;
     FOR N := 0 TO fHighTab DO
       BEGIN
         fDlgTabs[N] := Round((Tabs[N]*4) / DlgBaseX);
         fPixTabs[N] := Tabs[N];
       END;
     Perform(LB_SETTABSTOPS, fHighTab+1, LongInt(@fDlgTabs));
     Refresh;
     AllWidths;
   end;
   function TListBoxTabs.WidthOfString(const S : String): Integer;
   VAR Buffer: ARRAY[0..255] OF Char;
   begin
     StrPCopy(Buffer, S);
     Result := WidthOfPChar(Buffer);
   end;
   function TListBoxTabs.WidthOfPChar(P : PChar): Integer;
   begin
     Canvas.Font := Font;
     Result := LoWord(GetTabbedTextExtent(Canvas.Handle, P, StrLen(P),
       fHighTab+1, fPixTabs)) + Canvas.TextWidth('X');
   end;
   procedure Register;
   begin
     RegisterComponents('NJR', [TListBoxTabs]);
   end;
   end.
```

This component's CreateParams method takes care of the essential LBS_USETABSTOPS style, and the methods SetTabsDlg and SetTabsPix uses dialog units or device units to set one or more tab stops. By default, device units are pixels; dialog units are relative to the size of the system font. Setting tabs with the LB_SETTABSTOPS message requires dialog units, while determining the width of a tabbed string requires device units, so the component stores tabs in both formats. As written, it stores a maximum of forty tabs, but you can change the MaxTabs constant and recompile, if necessary.

Getting the width of a string is important, because this component also adjusts its horizontal extent to match the widest string. The TListBoxHorz component from the previous section used the TextWidth method of the list box's canvas to determine string width. When the string contains tabs, though, this method won't serve. TListBoxTabs overrides the virtual methods WidthOfString and WidthOfPChar, and uses the Windows API function GetTabbedTextExtent to determine the width of a tabbed string.

Note that, in 32-bit Delphi, the TListBox component has a TabWidth property. If TabWidth is nonzero, it sets the spacing of all tab stops in dialog units. However, the TListBoxTabs component shown here still does a bit more; it handles nonequal tab stops. Figure 7-5 shows a simple example program.

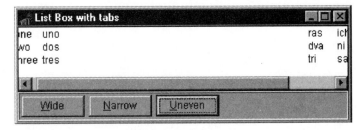

FIGURE 7-5: This list box has columns of text lined up by tab stops. It also sports a horizontal scroll bar because the tabbed text is wider than the list box.

LBTABS

LBTABSU.DEX

```
object Form1: TForm1
  Caption = 'List Box with tabs'
  Position = poDefault
  Scaled = False
  OnCreate = FormCreate
  object Panel1: TPanel
    Align = alBottom
    BevelInner = bvLowered
    object Button3: TButton
      Caption = '&Uneven'
      OnClick = Button3Click
    end
    object Button2: TButton
      Caption = '&Narrow'
      OnClick = Button2Click
    end
    object Button1: TButton
      Caption = '&Wide'
      OnClick = Button1Click
    end
  end
  object ListBoxTabs1: TListBoxTabs
```

```
      Align = alClient
      About = 0.99
    end
  end
```

LBTABSU.PAS

```pascal
unit lbtabsu;

interface

uses SysUtils, WinTypes, WinProcs, Messages, Classes, Graphics,
  Controls, Forms, Dialogs, StdCtrls, C_lbtab, ExtCtrls, c_lbhorz;

type
  TForm1 = class(TForm)
    Panel1: TPanel;
    Button3: TButton;
    Button2: TButton;
    Button1: TButton;
    ListBoxTabs1: TListBoxTabs;
    procedure Button1Click(Sender: TObject);
    procedure Button2Click(Sender: TObject);
    procedure Button3Click(Sender: TObject);
    procedure FormCreate(Sender: TObject);
  end;

var Form1: TForm1;

implementation

{$R *.DFM}

procedure TForm1.Button1Click(Sender: TObject);
begin
  ListBoxTabs1.SetTabsPix([160]);
end;

procedure TForm1.Button2Click(Sender: TObject);
begin
  ListBoxTabs1.SetTabsPix([40]);
end;

procedure TForm1.Button3Click(Sender: TObject);
begin
  ListBoxTabs1.SetTabsPix([40, 400, 440]);
end;

procedure TForm1.FormCreate(Sender: TObject);
begin
  ListBoxTabs1.Items.Add('one'#9'uno'#9'ras'#9'ichi');
  ListBoxTabs1.Items.Add('two'#9'dos'#9'dva'#9'ni');
  ListBoxTabs1.Items.Add('three'#9'tres'#9'tri'#9'san');
end;

end.
```

As you can see, passing a single value to SetTabsDlg or SetTabsPix produces repeating, equally spaced tab stops. Passing multiple values sets tab stops at each of those specific values. Note that the tab stops must be in strictly increasing order; that's what Windows wants to see!

Dragging and Lists

Delphi components include drag-and-drop as a built-in ability, but it may not be 100% clear just how to use this feature in a list box. You rarely want to drag a list box to a new location on the form, for example. More often, you'll be dragging an item or items from the list box to a new location.

Letting the user reorder items by dragging

16 32

If the order of items in a list box is important and if that order can be controlled by the user, drag-and-drop is an obvious choice for the implementation. But, what if you want to drag the first item to the last position in a list of 1,000 items? Simply reordering the list isn't enough; you need to arrange for it to *auto-scroll* during the drag process. Here's a simple example.

LBDRAG

LBDRAGU.DEX

```
object Form1: TForm1
  BorderIcons = [biSystemMenu]
  BorderStyle = bsDialog
  Caption = 'Draggable Items'
  Position = poDefault
  Scaled = False
  OnCreate = FormCreate
  object Label1: TLabel
  end
  object ListBox1: TListBox
    DragMode = dmAutomatic
    OnDragDrop = ListBox1DragDrop
    OnDragOver = ListBox1DragOver
    OnEndDrag = ListBox1EndDrag
  end
  object Timer1: TTimer
    Enabled = False
```

```
      Interval = 100
      OnTimer = Timer1Timer
    end
  end
end
```

LBDRAGU.PAS

```pascal
unit Lbdragu;

interface

uses SysUtils, WinTypes, WinProcs, Messages, Classes, Graphics,
  Controls, Forms, Dialogs, StdCtrls, ExtCtrls;

type
  TForm1 = class(TForm)
    ListBox1: TListBox;
    Label1: TLabel;
    Timer1: TTimer;
    procedure ListBox1DragOver(Sender, Source: TObject;
      X, Y: Integer; State: TDragState; var Accept: Boolean);
    procedure ListBox1DragDrop(Sender, Source: TObject;
      X, Y: Integer);
    procedure ListBox1EndDrag(Sender, Target: TObject;
       X, Y: Integer);
    procedure Timer1Timer(Sender: TObject);
    procedure FormCreate(Sender: TObject);
  private
    GoingUp : Boolean;
  end;

var Form1: TForm1;

implementation

{$R *.DFM}

procedure TForm1.FormCreate(Sender: TObject);
CONST Animals: PChar = 'alpaca'#13'bear'#13'cow'#13'dog'#13'eagle'+
  #13'fennec'#13'goat'#13'hippo'#13'iguana'#13'jackal'#13'kudu'#13+
  'llama'#13'moose'#13'narwhal'#13'orangutan'#13'pika'#13+
  'quetzlcoatl'#13'rhino'#13'salamander'#13'tiger'#13'umbrella '+
  'bird'#13'vulture'#13'wolverine'#13'xylophone'#13'yak'#13'zebra';
begin
  ListBox1.Items.SetText(Animals);
end;

procedure TForm1.ListBox1DragOver(Sender, Source: TObject;
  X, Y: Integer; State: TDragState; var Accept: Boolean);
begin
  Accept := (Sender = Source) AND
    (TListBox(Sender).ItemAtPos(Point(X,Y), False) >= 0);
  IF Accept THEN
    WITH Sender AS TListBox DO
      IF Y > Height - ItemHeight THEN
        BEGIN
```

```
            GoingUp := False;
            Timer1.Enabled := True;
          END
        ELSE IF Y < ItemHeight THEN
          BEGIN
            GoingUp := True;
            Timer1.Enabled := True;
          END
        ELSE Timer1.Enabled := False;
    end;
procedure TForm1.ListBox1DragDrop(Sender, Source: TObject;
   X, Y: Integer);
VAR NuPos: Integer;
begin
  WITH Sender AS TListBox DO
    BEGIN
      NuPos := ItemAtPos(Point(X,Y),False);
      IF NuPos >= Items.Count THEN Dec(NuPos);
      Label1.Caption := Format('Moved from %d to %d',
        [ItemIndex, NuPos]);
      Items.Move(ItemIndex, NuPos);
      ItemIndex := NuPos;
    END;
end;
procedure TForm1.Timer1Timer(Sender: TObject);
begin
  WITH ListBox1 DO
    IF GoingUp THEN
      IF TopIndex > 0 THEN TopIndex := TopIndex - 1
      ELSE Timer1.Enabled := False
    ELSE
      IF TopIndex < Items.Count - 1 THEN TopIndex := TopIndex + 1
      ELSE Timer1.Enabled := False;
end;
procedure TForm1.ListBox1EndDrag(Sender, Target: TObject;
   X, Y: Integer);
begin
  Timer1.Enabled := False;
end;
end.
```

The first statement in the OnDragOver event handler causes the list box to signal acceptance if the drag event originated with itself *and* if the cursor is over a list box item. The OnDragDrop event handler takes care of making the move, and sets the ItemIndex to the new position, so the just-moved item will be highlighted. The remainder of the OnDragOver handler is dedicated to auto-scrolling.

Auto-scrolling is handled with a timer. If the cursor is over the first or the last visible item, the OnDragOver handler sets the data field GoingUp to True or False, as appropriate, and enables the timer; if the cursor is anywhere else, it disables the timer. On each timer event, the list box scrolls up or down by one item. The list box's OnEndDrag event, which occurs whether or not a successful drag-and-drop operation had been completed, disables the timer.

Any time drag-and-drop is used to position text or graphical objects in an area that's not entirely visible, you'll need to implement auto-scrolling.

Dragging multiple items from a list box

16 32

List boxes allow the selection of multiple items at once, which is convenient. The user can gather all desired items and drag them to another component for action. Figure 7-6 shows a program that demonstrates one possible technique. The form contains two list boxes, and the user can drag items back and forth between them. Just to keep things interesting, one box is sorted, the other is not.

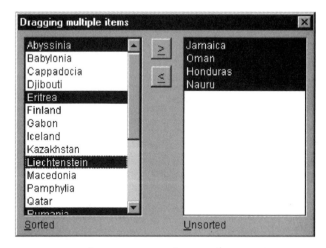

FIGURE 7-6: The user can transfer items between these two multiselect list boxes by dragging them or by using the buttons.

LDRAGMUL

LDRAGMUU.DEX

```
object Form1: TForm1
  BorderIcons = [biSystemMenu]
  BorderStyle = bsDialog
```

```
      Caption = 'Dragging multiple items'
      Position = poDefault
      Scaled = False
      OnCreate = FormCreate
      object Label1: TLabel
        Caption = '&Sorted'
        FocusControl = ListBox1
      end
      object Label2: TLabel
        Caption = '&Unsorted'
        FocusControl = ListBox2
      end
      object ListBox1: TListBox
        DragMode = dmAutomatic
        MultiSelect = True
        Sorted = True
        OnDragDrop = ListBox1DragDrop
        OnDragOver = ListBox1DragOver
      end
      object ListBox2: TListBox
        DragMode = dmAutomatic
        MultiSelect = True
        OnDragDrop = ListBox1DragDrop
        OnDragOver = ListBox1DragOver
      end
      object Button1: TButton
        Caption = '&>'
        Font.Height = -16
        ParentFont = False
        OnClick = Button1Click
      end
      object Button2: TButton
        Caption = '&<'
        Font.Height = -16
        ParentFont = False
        OnClick = Button2Click
      end
    end
```

LDRAGMUU.PAS

```
unit Ldragmuu;

interface

uses SysUtils, WinTypes, WinProcs, Messages, Classes, Graphics,
  Controls, Forms, Dialogs, StdCtrls, Buttons;

type
  TForm1 = class(TForm)
    ListBox1: TListBox;
    ListBox2: TListBox;
    Button1: TButton;
```

```
      Button2: TButton;
      Label1: TLabel;
      Label2: TLabel;
      procedure ListBox1DragOver(Sender, Source: TObject;
        X, Y: Integer; State: TDragState; var Accept: Boolean);
      procedure ListBox1DragDrop(Sender, Source: TObject;
        X, Y: Integer);
      procedure Button1Click(Sender: TObject);
      procedure Button2Click(Sender: TObject);
      procedure FormCreate(Sender: TObject);
    end;

var Form1: TForm1;

implementation
{$R *.DFM}

procedure TForm1.ListBox1DragOver(Sender, Source: TObject;
  X, Y: Integer; State: TDragState; var Accept: Boolean);
begin
  Accept := (Source IS TListBox) AND (Source <> Sender) AND
    (TListBox(Source).Items.Count>0);
end;

procedure TForm1.ListBox1DragDrop(Sender, Source: TObject;
  X, Y: Integer);
VAR N : Integer;
begin
  FOR N := 0 TO (Source AS TListBox).Items.Count-1 DO
    IF (Source AS TListBox).Selected[N] THEN
      WITH Sender AS TListBox DO
        Selected[Items.Add((Source AS TListBox).Items[N])] := True;
  WITH Source AS TListBox DO
    FOR N := Items.Count-1 DOWNTO 0 DO
      IF Selected[N] THEN
        Items.Delete(N);
end;

procedure TForm1.Button1Click(Sender: TObject);
begin
  ListBox1DragDrop(ListBox2, ListBox1,0,0);
end;

procedure TForm1.Button2Click(Sender: TObject);
begin
  ListBox1DragDrop(ListBox1, ListBox2,0,0);
end;

procedure TForm1.FormCreate(Sender: TObject);
CONST Countries = 'Abyssinia'#13'Babylonia'#13'Cappadocia'#13+
  'Djibouti'#13'Eritrea'#13'Finland'#13'Gabon'#13'Honduras'#13+
  'Iceland'#13'Jamaica'#13'Kazakhstan'#13'Liechtenstein'#13+
  'Macedonia'#13'Nauru'#13'Oman'#13'Pamphylia'#13'Qatar'#13+
  'Rumania'#13'Slovakia'#13'Tibet'#13'Uruguay'#13'Venezuela'#13+
  'Western Samoa'#13'Xerxesia'#13'Yemen'#13'Zimbabwe';
begin
  ListBox1.Items.SetText(Countries);
end;

end.
```

In this program, a list box using the OnDragOver event handler accepts drag-drop events from any non-empty list box that isn't itself. The OnDragDrop handler transfers the selected items in two passes. The first pass, performed in ascending order, copies the selected items from the source list box to the target and, at the same time, makes them selected in the target. The second pass, performed in descending order, actually deletes the items from the source list box.

As always, your program should accommodate the user who cannot or will not use drag and drop. This program uses two buttons labeled with the > and < symbols—the keys to activate these buttons are Alt+Shift+Comma and Alt+Shift+Period. The OnClick handlers for the two buttons couldn't be simpler; they just call the OnDragDrop handler, passing the dragged-to list box and the dragged-from list box as the Sender and Source parameters.

List Box Miscellany

People make lists of appointments, things to do, and groceries to buy. Programs make lists too, and then demand that their users make a choice, or several choices. The programmer is responsible for making the choosing process as straightforward as possible; just plopping a list in front of the user isn't always enough. Here are some more questions and answers about list boxes.

Sorting a list box my *way*

16 32

In the preceding two solutions, we derived new components from TListBox to gain access to standard list box functionality that's not exposed in the basic TListBox. But why stop there?

Your basic list box can be sorted or not; if you ask for the sorted type, the items will be sorted alphabetically according to their ANSI character values. The equivalent in Delphi terms is that they're sorted according to the results of the AnsiCompareStr function. But, what if you want to sort items in reverse order, or in numerical order (so 2 comes before 10 instead of after 19)? This component does the job.

TLISTBOXCOMP

C_LBSORT.PAS

```
unit C_lbcomp;

interface

uses SysUtils, WinTypes, WinProcs, Messages, Classes, Graphics,
  Controls, Forms, StdCtrls, Menus, p_about;

Type
  TCompareItemsEvent = procedure(Control: TWinControl;
    const S1, S2 : String; VAR leg: Integer) of object;

  TListBoxComp = class(TListBox)
  private
    fAbout: TAbout;
    fOnCompare: TCompareItemsEvent;
    function fCompareItems(const S1, S2 : String):Integer;
    procedure SetOnCompare(Value: TCompareItemsEvent);
    procedure CreateParams(VAR Params: TCreateParams);
      override;
  public
    Procedure SpecialSort;
  published
    property OnCompare: TCompareItemsEvent Read fOnCompare
      Write SetOnCompare;
    property About: TAbout read fAbout write fAbout;
  end;

procedure Register;

implementation
{$IFDEF Win32}
{$R *.R32}
{$ELSE}
{$R *.R16}
{$ENDIF}

procedure TListBoxComp.CreateParams(VAR Params: TCreateParams);
BEGIN
  Inherited CreateParams(Params);
  Params.Style := Params.Style OR LBS_USETABSTOPS;
  fAbout := 0.99;
END;

function TListBoxComp.fCompareItems(const S1, S2 : String):Integer;
BEGIN
  IF Assigned(fOnCompare) THEN
    fOnCompare(Self, S1, S2, Result)
  ELSE Result := AnsiCompareStr(S1,S2);
END;

procedure TListBoxComp.SpecialSort;
VAR
  TS : TStringList;
```

```
  N   : Integer;
  function FindPlace(const S: string): Integer;
  VAR vLo, vHi, vIdx: Integer;
  begin
    vLo := 0;
    vHi := TS.Count - 1;
    WHILE vLo <= vHi DO
      BEGIN
        vIdx := (vLo + vHi) shr 1;
        IF fCompareItems(TS[vIdx], S) < 0 THEN vLo := vIdx + 1
        ELSE vHi := vIdx - 1;
      END;
    Result := vLo;
  end;
begin
  Sorted := False;
  TS := TStringList.Create;
  try
    FOR N := 0 TO Items.Count-1 DO
      TS.InsertObject(FindPlace(Items[N]), Items[N],
        Items.Objects[N]);
    Items.Assign(TS);
  finally
    TS.Free;
  end;
end;
procedure TListBoxComp.SetOnCompare(Value: TCompareItemsEvent);
BEGIN
  fOnCompare := Value;
  SpecialSort;
END;
procedure Register;
begin
  RegisterComponents('NJR', [TListBoxComp]);
end;
end.
```

The Items property of a list box component is defined as being of type TStrings. However, internally its type is TListBoxStrings, a descendant of TStrings that uses the list box to store the items. Unfortunately, TListBoxStrings is entirely private, being defined only in the implementation section of STDCTRLS.PAS. If it were accessible, we could define a descendant that automatically handled inserting strings in the desired order.

Since deriving a TListBoxStrings descendent isn't an option, the TListBoxComp component defines an event property to handle comparisons, and a public method that sorts the list based on the current value of OnCompare. An OnCompare event handler takes two strings, S1 and S2, and sets the VAR parameter leg to negative, zero, or positive to indicate whether S1 is less than, equal to, or greater than S2.

To sort its strings according to the current OnCompare handler, this component inserts its strings one at a time to a temporary string list. The position for each string is determined by the binary search function FindPlace. Once the temporary string list is filled, its contents are assigned back to the list box's Items list. Figure 7-7 shows a program to demonstrate this handy new component.

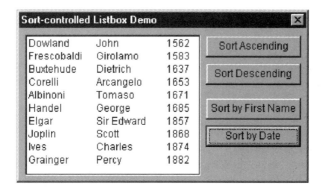

FIGURE 7-7: Using a TListBoxComp, your programs can sort list box items based on any criteria you can define.

LBCOMP

LBCOMPU.DEX

```
object Form1: TForm1
  BorderIcons = [biSystemMenu, biMinimize]
  BorderStyle = bsDialog
  Caption = 'Sort-controlled Listbox Demo'
  Position = poDefault
  Scaled = False
  OnCreate = FormCreate
  object ListBoxComp1: TListBoxComp
  end
  object Button4: TButton
    Caption = 'Sort by 2nd word'
    OnClick = Button4Click
  end
  object Button3: TButton
    Caption = 'Sort by Length'
    OnClick = Button3Click
  end
  object Button2: TButton
```

```
      Caption = 'Sort Descending'
      OnClick = Button2Click
    end
    object Button1: TButton
      Caption = 'Sort Ascending'
      OnClick = Button1Click
    end
  end
```

LBCOMPU.PAS

```
unit lbcompu;

interface

uses SysUtils, WinTypes, WinProcs, Messages, Classes, Graphics,
  Controls, Forms, c_lbcomp, StdCtrls;

type
  TForm1 = class(TForm)
    ListBoxComp1: TListBoxComp;
    Button4: TButton;
    Button3: TButton;
    Button2: TButton;
    Button1: TButton;
    procedure Button1Click(Sender: TObject);
    procedure Button2Click(Sender: TObject);
    procedure Button3Click(Sender: TObject);
    procedure Button4Click(Sender: TObject);
    procedure FormCreate(Sender: TObject);
  private
    procedure CompareDesc(Sender: TWinControl;
      const S1, S2 : String; VAR leg : Integer);
    procedure CompareFirst(Sender: TWinControl;
      const S1, S2 : String; VAR leg : Integer);
    procedure CompareDate(Sender: TWinControl;
      const S1, S2 : String; VAR leg : Integer);
  end;

var Form1: TForm1;

implementation

{$R *.DFM}

procedure TForm1.FormCreate(Sender: TObject);
CONST Composers : PChar = 'Albinoni'#9'Tomaso'#9'1671'#13+
  'Buxtehude'#9'Dietrich'#9'1637'#13+
  'Corelli'#9'Arcangelo'#9'1653'#13+
  'Dowland'#9'John'#9'1562'#13+
  'Elgar'#9'Sir Edward'#9'1857'#13+
  'Frescobaldi'#9'Girolamo'#9'1583'#13+
  'Grainger'#9'Percy'#9'1882'#13+
  'Handel'#9'George'#9'1685'#13+
  'Ives'#9'Charles'#9'1874'#13+
```

```
    'Joplin'#9'Scott'#9'1868'#13;
    Tab: Integer = 48;
begin
    ListBoxComp1.Items.SetText(Composers);
    ListBoxComp1.Perform(LB_SETTABSTOPS, 1, LongInt(@Tab));
end;
procedure TForm1.CompareDesc(Sender: TWinControl;
    const S1, S2 : String; VAR leg : Integer);
begin
    leg := AnsiCompareStr(S2, S1);
end;
procedure TForm1.CompareFirst(Sender: TWinControl;
    const S1, S2 : String; VAR leg : Integer);
VAR P1, P2 : Integer;
begin
    P1 := Pos(#9, S1)+1;
    P2 := Pos(#9, S2)+1;
    leg := AnsiCompareStr(Copy(S1,P1,length(S1)),
        Copy(S2,P2,Length(S2)));
end;
procedure TForm1.CompareDate(Sender: TWinControl;
    const S1, S2 : String; VAR leg : Integer);
VAR P1, P2 : Integer;
begin
    P1 := Pos(#9, S1)+1;
    P1 := Pos(#9, Copy(S1, P1, Length(S1))) + P1;
    P2 := Pos(#9, S2)+1;
    P2 := Pos(#9, Copy(S2, P2, Length(S2))) + P2;
    leg := AnsiCompareStr(Copy(S1,P1,length(S1)),
        Copy(S2,P2,Length(S2)));
end;
procedure TForm1.Button1Click(Sender: TObject);
begin
    ListBoxComp1.OnCompare := NIL;
end;
procedure TForm1.Button2Click(Sender: TObject);
begin
    ListBoxComp1.OnCompare := CompareDesc;
end;
procedure TForm1.Button3Click(Sender: TObject);
begin
    ListBoxComp1.OnCompare := CompareFirst;
end;
procedure TForm1.Button4Click(Sender: TObject);
begin
    ListBoxComp1.OnCompare := CompareDate;
end;

end.
```

This program fills a sort-controlled list box with the names and birth dates of ten composers, separating the elements of each line with tabs. The OnCompare event handler is initially NIL, so the items are sorted in ascending alphabetic order. The top button resets OnCompare to NIL; the other three set it to OnCompare handlers that produce different orderings of the elements. You're sure to find uses for this component!

Creating a multiselect combo box

16 32

The main feature present in a list box that's absent in a combo box is the ability to make multiple selections. That's not terribly surprising, as there's no way to *see* multiple selections in a combo box most of the time. However, it is possible to combine the convenience of a multiple selection list box with the small footprint of a combo box. Figure 7-8 shows one way to go about it.

FIGURE 7-8: This owner-draw combo box shows the selected status of each item using a simulated check box; pressing the space bar toggles the current item's check.

COMBOSEL

COMBSELU.DEX

```
object Form1: TForm1
  Caption = 'Checkable ComboBox'
  Position = poDefault
  Scaled = False
```

```
      object ComboBox1: TComboBox
        Style = csOwnerDrawFixed
        DropDownCount = 12
        ItemHeight = 24
        Items.Strings = (
          'Abstract'
          'Bauhaus'
          'Cubism'
          'Dada'
          'Expressionism'
          'Fauvism'
          'Greek Revival'
          'Hepplewhite'
          'Impressionism'
          'Minimalism'
          'Neoclassicism'
          'Op'
          'Photorealism'
          'Realism'
          'Surrealism'
          'Ukiyo-e'
          'Victorian')
        OnDrawItem = ComboBox1DrawItem
        OnKeyPress = ComboBox1KeyPress
      end
    end
```

COMBSELU.PAS

```
    unit Combselu;

    interface

    uses SysUtils, WinTypes, WinProcs, Messages, Classes, Graphics,
      Controls, Forms, Dialogs, StdCtrls;

    type
      TForm1 = class(TForm)
        ComboBox1: TComboBox;
        procedure ComboBox1DrawItem(Control: TWinControl;
          Index: Integer; Rect: TRect; State: TOwnerDrawState);
        procedure ComboBox1KeyPress(Sender: TObject; var Key: Char);
      end;

    var Form1: TForm1;

    implementation

    {$R *.DFM}

    procedure TForm1.ComboBox1DrawItem(Control: TWinControl;
      Index: Integer; Rect: TRect; State: TOwnerDrawState);
    begin
      WITH Control AS TComboBox, Canvas DO
        BEGIN
```

```
            FillRect(Rect);
            Canvas.Font.Name := 'WingDings';
            Canvas.Font.Size := 12;
            IF Items.Objects[Index] <> NIL THEN
              TextOut(Rect.Left, Rect.Top+2, #254)
            ELSE TextOut(Rect.Left, Rect.Top+2, #168);
            Canvas.Font.Name := Self.Font.Name;
            TextOut(Rect.Left+24,Rect.Top+1, Items[Index]);
        END;
  end;

  procedure TForm1.ComboBox1KeyPress(Sender: TObject; var Key: Char);
  VAR R : TRect;
  begin
    WITH Sender AS TComboBox, Items DO
      IF (Key = #32) AND (ItemIndex >= 0) THEN
        BEGIN
          IF Objects[ItemIndex] = NIL THEN
            Objects[ItemIndex] := Pointer(1)
          ELSE Objects[ItemIndex] := NIL;
          IF DroppedDown THEN
            BEGIN
              SendMessage(GetTopWindow(0), LB_GETITEMRECT,
                ItemIndex, Longint(@R));
              InvalidateRect(GetTopWindow(0), @R, False);
            END
          ELSE Refresh;
        END;
  end;
  end.
```

Rather than invent a separate property to hold the selection state of each item, this program uses the Objects property of the Items property. If the Nth element of Objects is NIL, as it is initially, the item is not selected; otherwise, it is selected. Internally, the Objects array is implemented by storing 4-byte object pointers in the ITEMDATA that Windows associates with every item in a list box.

The OnDrawItem handler sets the font to WingDings, a standard Windows font containing many symbols. If the current item is supposed to be checked, it draws character 254, a checked box; otherwise, it draws character 168, an empty box. That WingDings font is just full of useful symbols! Then it draws the actual item text.

The OnClick and OnChange events for a combo box occur while the user is simply scrolling through the list using the arrow keys. It would be a bit disconcerting to have the selection state of an item change on each click! Instead, the example program sets up an OnKeyPress handler for the combo box. If the space bar was pressed, it toggles the selection state of the current item.

The technique of storing nonpointer data in a TList like the Objects property is one that will prove useful again and again. It's a powerful technique, and a potentially dangerous one, since treating a simple number as a pointer or an object will almost certainly cause a General Protection Fault (GPF). As long as you never use the TList to refer to objects and to nonobjects at the same time, it should be safe.

Creating a list box with incremental search

16 32

When the number of items in a list box becomes large, finding a particular item can be tough. Windows provides a modicum of help—if the list box is sorted, the user can press a key repeatedly to cycle through the items that begin with that character. Repeatedly pressing B might go to Bill, then to Bob, then to Bubba, and then back to Bill. However, if there are hundreds of names beginning with a given letter, this isn't much help.

Figure 7-9 shows a program whose list box has an associated edit box for searching. As the user types, the highlight in the list box moves to the first item that begins with the letters typed thus far. If no word matches, the highlight disappears. For example, if the user typed *advent*, ADVENTITIOUSNESS would be highlighted; if the user then typed *u*, the highlight would disappear, as no item begins with ADVENTU.

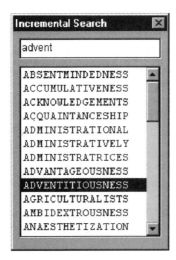

FIGURE 7-9: When implementing an incremental search, it's a good idea to display the searched-for text, as shown here.

INCSRCH

INCSRCHU.DEX

```
object Form1: TForm1
  BorderIcons = [biSystemMenu]
  BorderStyle = bsDialog
  Caption = 'Incremental Search'
  Position = poDefault
  Scaled = False
  object ListBox1: TListBox
    Font.Height = -13
    Font.Name = 'Courier New'
    Items.Strings = (
      'ABSENTMINDEDNESS'
      'CIRCUMNAVIGATION')
    ParentFont = False
    Sorted = True
    OnKeyPress = ListBox1KeyPress
  end
  object Edit1: TEdit
    OnChange = Edit1Change
  end
end
```

INCSRCHU.PAS

```
unit Incsrchu;

interface

uses SysUtils, WinTypes, WinProcs, Messages, Classes, Graphics,
  Controls, Forms, StdCtrls;

type
  TForm1 = class(TForm)
    ListBox1: TListBox;
    Edit1: TEdit;
    procedure Edit1Change(Sender: TObject);
    procedure ListBox1KeyPress(Sender: TObject; var Key: Char);
  end;

var Form1: TForm1;

implementation

{$R *.DFM}

procedure TForm1.Edit1Change(Sender: TObject);
VAR Buf : ARRAY[0..255] OF Char;
begin
  StrPCopy(Buf, Edit1.Text);
  WITH ListBox1 DO
    ItemIndex := Perform(LB_SELECTSTRING, 0, LongInt(@Buf));
end;
```

```
procedure TForm1.ListBox1KeyPress(Sender: TObject; var Key: Char);
begin
  IF Key < ' ' THEN Exit;
  Edit1.SetFocus;
  Edit1.Text := Key;
  Edit1.SelStart := 1;
end;

end.
```

If the user types a key when the list box has the focus, that character becomes the start of a new string in the edit box, which receives the focus. Each time the text of the edit box changes, the first item in the list box that begins with the edit box text gets highlighted. The list box's OnChange event handler uses the LB_SELECTSTRING message to request this behavior.

There are two other related messages that you may find useful. LB_FINDSTRING returns the index of the first string that begins with a specified string, or LB_ERR (-1) if there's no match. LB_FINDSTRINGEXACT does the same, but requires the entire item to match.

Taking control of list box scrolling

16 32

The Windows 3.1 list box component can display no more than 5,440 lines. With some effort, this limit can be raised to a bit over 8,000 lines. However, if the lines are at all lengthy, a second limit kicks in—the lines can occupy a maximum total of 32KB. It's not uncommon to run up against this limit. In Windows 95, 32-bit programs can have 32,768 items, and under Windows NT, there's no specific limit. However, you'll still find occasions to separate a list box's scrolling range from the actual number of items it contains.

Also, every list box sprouts a scroll bar when there are too many items to display at once. You can force the scroll bar to appear even when it's not needed, but not the reverse. Thus, the scroll bar will appear even when the list box's scrolling is controlled by some other means.

The program shown in Figure 7-10 contains what appears to be a list box of huge capacity, along with a pair of list boxes that share the same scroll bar. The two solutions *are* related, as you'll see.

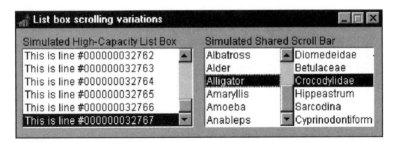

FIGURE 7-10: The list box on the left appears to have 32,767 lines; the two on the right appear linked to the same scroll bar.

SCROLL

SCROLLU.DEX

```
object Form1: TForm1
  BorderIcons = [biSystemMenu, biMinimize]
  BorderStyle = bsSingle
  Caption = 'List box scrolling variations'
  Position = poDefault
  Scaled = False
  OnCreate = FormCreate
  object Label1: TLabel
    Caption = 'Simulated High-Capacity List Box'
  end
  object Label2: TLabel
    Caption = 'Simulated Shared Scroll Bar'
  end
  object ListBox3: TListBox
    BorderStyle = bsNone
    Items.Strings = (
      'Orycteropus'
      'Fabaceae'
      'Viperidae'
      'Agavaceae'
      'Dasyproctidae'
      'Diomedeidae'
      'Betulaceae'
      'Crocodylidae'
      'Hippeastrum'
      'Sarcodina'
      'Cyprinodontiformes')
    Style = lbOwnerDrawFixed
    OnClick = ListBox3Click
    OnDrawItem = ListBox3DrawItem
  end
  object ScrollBar1: TScrollBar
    Kind = sbVertical
```

```
      LargeChange = 10
      Max = 32762
      OnChange = ScrollBar1Change
    end
    object ListBox1: TListBox
      Tag = -1
      BorderStyle = bsNone
      Items.Strings = (
        'x'
        'x'
        'x'
        'x'
        'x'
        'x')
      Style = lbOwnerDrawFixed
      OnClick = ListBox1Click
      OnDrawItem = ListBox1DrawItem
    end
    object ListBox2: TListBox
      BorderStyle = bsNone
      Items.Strings = (
        'Aardvark'
        'Acacia'
        'Adder'
        'Agave'
        'Agouti'
        'Albatross'
        'Alder'
        'Alligator'
        'Amaryllis'
        'Amoeba'
        'Anableps')
    end
  end
```

SCROLLU.PAS

```
unit Scrollu;

interface

uses SysUtils, WinTypes, WinProcs, Messages, Classes, Graphics,
  Controls, Forms, Dialogs, StdCtrls;

type
  TListBoxScr = class(TListBox)
  private
    fOnScroll: TScrollEvent;
    WasTopIndex: Integer;
    procedure WMVScroll(VAR Msg: TWMVScroll); message WM_VSCROLL;
  published
    property OnScroll: TScrollEvent read fOnScroll write fOnScroll;
  end;
```

```
  TForm1 = class(TForm)
    ListBox1: TListBox;
    ListBox2: TListBox;
    ListBox3: TListBox;
    ScrollBar1: TScrollBar;
    Label1: TLabel;
    Label2: TLabel;
    procedure ListBox3DrawItem(Control: TWinControl; Index:
      Integer; Rect: TRect; State: TOwnerDrawState);
    procedure ListBoxScr1Click(Sender: TObject);
    procedure ListBoxScr1Scroll(Sender: TObject; ScrollCode:
      TScrollCode; var ScrollPos: Integer);
    procedure ListBox3Click(Sender: TObject);
    procedure FormCreate(Sender: TObject);
    procedure ListBox1DrawItem(Control: TWinControl; Index:Integer;
      Rect: TRect; State: TOwnerDrawState);
    procedure ScrollBar1Change(Sender: TObject);
    procedure ListBox1Click(Sender: TObject);
  private
    SciNames: TStringList;
    ListBoxScr1: TListBoxScr;
  end;

var Form1: TForm1;

implementation

{$R *.DFM}
CONST
  cFore: ARRAY[Boolean] OF TColor = (clWindowText,clHighlightText);
  cBack: ARRAY[Boolean] OF TColor = (clWindow, clHighlight);

procedure TListBoxScr.WMVScroll(VAR Msg: TWMVScroll);
VAR vScrollPos: Integer;
begin
  Inherited;
  IF TopIndex <> WasTopIndex THEN
    IF Assigned(fOnScroll) THEN
      WITH Msg DO
        BEGIN
          vScrollPos := Pos; {necessary for 32-bit Delphi}
          fOnScroll(Self, TScrollCode(ScrollCode), vScrollPos);
        END;
  WasTopIndex := TopIndex;
end;

procedure TForm1.FormCreate(Sender: TObject);
VAR N : Integer;
begin
  ListBoxScr1 := TListBoxScr.Create(Self);
  WITH ListBoxScr1 DO
    BEGIN
      Parent      := Self;
      Tag         := -1;
      BoundsRect  := ListBox2.BoundsRect;
```

```
        Items       := ListBox2.Items;
        BorderStyle := bsNone;
        OnClick     := ListBoxScr1Click;
        OnScroll    := ListBoxScr1Scroll;
      END;
    ListBox2.Free;
    SciNames := TStringList.Create;
    SciNames.Assign(ListBox3.Items);
    ListBox3.Items.Clear;
    FOR N := 0 TO (ListBox3.Height DIV ListBox3.ItemHeight) - 1 DO
      ListBox3.Items.Add('x');
  end;
procedure TForm1.ListBox1DrawItem(Control: TWinControl; Index:
  Integer; Rect: TRect; State: TOwnerDrawState);
begin
  WITH Control AS TListBox, Canvas DO
    BEGIN
      Brush.Color := cBack[Tag = ScrollBar1.Position + Index];
      Font.Color  := cFore[Tag = ScrollBar1.Position + Index];
      FillRect(Rect);
      TextOut(Rect.Left+2, Rect.Top, Format('This is line #%.12d',
        [ScrollBar1.Position + Index]));
    END;
end;

procedure TForm1.ScrollBar1Change(Sender: TObject);
begin
  ListBox1.Refresh;
end;

procedure TForm1.ListBox1Click(Sender: TObject);
begin
  WITH Sender AS TListBox DO
    BEGIN
      Tag := ScrollBar1.Position + ItemIndex;
      Refresh;
    END;
end;

procedure TForm1.ListBox3DrawItem(Control: TWinControl; Index:
  Integer; Rect: TRect; State: TOwnerDrawState);
begin
  WITH Control AS TListBox, Canvas DO
    BEGIN
      Brush.Color := cBack[ListBoxScr1.Tag = Index];
      Font.Color := cFore[ListBoxScr1.Tag = Index];
      FillRect(Rect);
      WITH ListBoxScr1 DO
        TextOut(Rect.Left+2, Rect.Top, SciNames[TopIndex+Index]);
    END;
end;

procedure TForm1.ListBoxScr1Click(Sender: TObject);
begin
```

```
      WITH Sender AS TListBox DO Tag := ItemIndex - TopIndex;
      ListBox3.Refresh;
   end;
   procedure TForm1.ListBoxScr1Scroll(Sender: TObject; ScrollCode:
      TScrollCode; var ScrollPos: Integer);
   begin
      WITH Sender AS TListBox DO Tag := ItemIndex - TopIndex;
      ListBox3.Refresh;
   end;
   procedure TForm1.ListBox3Click(Sender: TObject);
   begin
      ListBoxScr1.ItemIndex := ListBoxScr1.TopIndex +
         (Sender AS TListBox).ItemIndex;
      ListBoxScr1.Tag := (Sender AS TListBox).ItemIndex;
      (Sender AS TListBox).Refresh;
   end;

   end.
```

The list box on the left acts as if it holds 32,767 lines, each of them using almost 30 bytes of memory—vastly more than a list box's normal capacity in 16-bit Windows. In truth, it has just six lines, exactly enough to fill its visible area without triggering the appearance of a scroll bar. What appears to be the list box's scroll bar is actually a separate scroll bar component. You can indeed scroll through 32,767 lines of text, but these lines are generated by the list box's OnDrawItem event handler. In a real program, the lines might be drawn from a database or a text file.

The far right-hand list box also has no scroll bar, and also draws its contents in response to the OnDrawItem event. In the form's OnCreate event handler, the list box's contents are stored in the string list variable SciNames. Then, the list box is cleared and enough blank lines added to fill it without requiring a scroll bar. This list box's OnDrawItem event handler gets its strings for display from the SciNames variable.

There's one catch involved in synchronizing the scrolling of two list boxes: the list box component does not generate an event when it scrolls. Getting notification of list box scrolling requires a descendant object. This time, though, the descendant is defined within the program, rather than as a separate component on the component palette. The form's OnCreate event handler creates an instance of this descendant type and copies certain properties from a placeholder list box, then destroys the placeholder.

Several small event handlers are devoted to keeping the two list boxes synchronized. When the middle list box is clicked or scrolled, it refreshes the right-hand list box, forcing it to redraw. When the right-hand list box is clicked, it adjusts the middle list box's ItemIndex to match.

The built-in Windows controls supply quite a bit of functionality, and the Delphi components that "wrap" them add even more. When you need to do something that a component *seems* to forbid, stop and consider whether you can get around the limitation. It's generally a lot easier than creating a new custom control from scratch!

MORE COMPONENTS

Delphi components range from the extremely simple, such as buttons and labels, to the extremely complex, such as grid and database components. Previous chapters have delved into menus, edit controls, and list boxes. Chapters in this part will cover grids, database components, buttons, and various other components.

Any time a Delphi component lacks a needed feature, chances are good you can add that feature in a descendant component. This section introduces four such components, including a label component that can display text at any angle and a button component whose caption can span multiple lines. A modified string grid component gains the ability to hold other components within its cells. And, with some effort, we manage to force a data-aware grid to display BLOB data, both memo fields and images.

Delphi's database support is worthy of a book all its own. This book doesn't attempt exhaustive coverage, but it will solve a number of common problems in the database realm. Please note, with the advent of Delphi 2.0, the built-in support for database programming is greatly enhanced.

8

Grid Components

*D*elphi's Grid components are similar to list boxes, but they arrange items in both rows *and columns. The draw grid can display billions of rows and columns; the string grid is "limited" to 32,767 of each. Their functionality begins with displaying data in tabular format, but it certainly doesn't end there!*

Cell Drawing and Alignment

A draw grid displays precisely what you tell it to, nothing more. It does handle such things as drawing fixed rows and columns in a different color, and displaying lines between the rows and columns, but if you want anything to *show* in the data cells, you have to write an OnDrawCell event handler. A string grid can store one string for each cell; its default drawing behavior is to display each stored string left-aligned in its cell, but here, too, you can take over drawing by writing an OnDrawCell handler.

BENEFITS OF BREAKING RULES

The general rule is that if Delphi created the code, Delphi is in charge of it and you must not touch it. Most of the programs in this chapter break that rule. The default method header Delphi creates for an OnDrawCell or an OnSelectCell event handler has parameters named Row and Col. These can easily be confused with the Row and Col fields of the grid. To avoid that problem, always change these parameter names to vRow and vCol, both in the form object definition and in the method implementation. The modified method is still acceptable to Delphi, and you won't get into trouble confusing the property named Row with the method parameter named Row.

Displaying a huge number of cells

16 32

A well-known media scientist is famous for his impassioned recitation of the phrase "billions and billions." As it happens, that's just what the draw grid can display—billions and billions of cells. Figure 8-1 shows the bottom right corner of a draw grid that contains one trillion cells.

Billions and Billions...		
999,992,999,998	999,992,999,999	999,993,000,000
999,993,999,998	999,993,999,999	999,994,000,000
999,994,999,998	999,994,999,999	999,995,000,000
999,995,999,998	999,995,999,999	999,996,000,000
999,996,999,998	999,996,999,999	999,997,000,000
999,997,999,998	999,997,999,999	999,998,000,000
999,998,999,998	999,998,999,999	999,999,000,000
999,999,999,998	999,999,999,999	1,000,000,000,000

FIGURE 8-1: Even without resorting to 32-bit programming, this draw grid displays one trillion cells.

BILLIONS

BILLIONU.DEX

```
object Form1: TForm1
  Caption = 'Billions and Billions...'
  Position = poDefault
  Scaled = False
  object DrawGrid1: TDrawGrid
    Align = alClient
    ColCount = 1000000
    DefaultColWidth = 120
    DefaultRowHeight = 20
    FixedCols = 0
    FixedRows = 0
```

```
      RowCount = 1000000
      OnDrawCell = DrawGrid1DrawCell
    end
  end
```

BILLIONU.PAS

```
unit Billionu;

interface

uses SysUtils, WinTypes, WinProcs, Messages, Classes, Graphics,
  Controls, Forms, Dialogs, Grids;

type
  TForm1 = class(TForm)
    DrawGrid1: TDrawGrid;
    procedure DrawGrid1DrawCell(Sender: TObject; vCol, vRow:
      Longint; Rect: TRect; State: TGridDrawState);
  end;

var Form1: TForm1;

implementation

{$R *.DFM}

procedure TForm1.DrawGrid1DrawCell(Sender: TObject; vCol,
  vRow: Longint; Rect: TRect; State: TGridDrawState);
begin
  WITH Sender AS TDrawGrid, Canvas DO
    TextRect(Rect, Rect.Left+2, Rect.Top+2,
      FormatFloat('0,', 1.0*vRow*ColCount+vCol+1));
end;

end.
```

The secret, of course, is that the draw grid's million rows and million columns have no permanent existence. They're not stored anywhere. The OnDrawCell event handler tells the draw grid how to draw any particular cell, but it never has to display more than a few dozen of the cells at a time. In this case, the OnDrawCell handler calculates the sequential number of the cell going left to right and top to bottom, and formats that number with thousand-separators every three digits using the FormatFloat function.

The draw grid is excellent when the data you want to display can be calculated from its row and column position. And it can be adapted to display more strings than a string grid can hold, simply by giving it an OnDrawCell handler that contains code to access the string corresponding to any particular location.

Right-justifying or centering text in a grid cell

16 32

By default, the values displayed in a string grid are left-aligned within their cells. Frequently it would be more logical to right-align the text, or to center it. However, there's no property that controls the formatting of individual cells.

As Figure 8-2 shows, when you take over the drawing of a grid's cells, you can format them any way you please. Left, right, and center alignment are easily obtained.

Right	Center	Left
1.0000	1.0000	1.0000
1,000	1,000	1,000
1.0	1.0	1.0
1	1	1
Oobleck	Oobleck	Oobleck

FIGURE 8-2: In this sample program, each grid column uses a different alignment style.

RITELEFT

RITELEFU.DEX

```
object Form1: TForm1
  BorderIcons = [biSystemMenu, biMinimize]
  BorderStyle = bsSingle
  Caption = 'Right, Left, and Center'
  Position = poDefault
  Scaled = False
  OnCreate = FormCreate
  object StringGrid1: TStringGrid
    Align = alClient
    ColCount = 3
    DefaultColWidth = 96
    FixedCols = 0
    RowCount = 6
    Options = [goFixedVertLine, goFixedHorzLine, goVertLine,
goHorzLine, goRangeSelect, goDrawFocusSelected, goColSizing,
goEditing]
    ScrollBars = ssNone
    OnDrawCell = StringGrid1DrawCell
  end
end
```

RITELEFU.PAS

```pascal
unit Ritelefu;

interface

uses SysUtils, WinTypes, WinProcs, Messages, Classes, Graphics,
  Controls, Forms, Dialogs, Grids;

type
  TForm1 = class(TForm)
    StringGrid1: TStringGrid;
    procedure FormCreate(Sender: TObject);
    procedure StringGrid1DrawCell(Sender: TObject; vCol,
      vRow: Longint; Rect: TRect; State: TGridDrawState);
  end;

var Form1: TForm1;

implementation

{$R *.DFM}

procedure TForm1.FormCreate(Sender: TObject);
VAR N : Integer;
begin
  FOR N := 0 TO 3 DO
    StringGrid1.Cols[N].SetText(' '#13'1.0000'#13'1,000'#13'1.0'+
      #13'1'#13'Oobleck');
  StringGrid1.Rows[0].SetText('Right'#13'Center'#13'Left');
end;

procedure TForm1.StringGrid1DrawCell(Sender: TObject; vCol,
  vRow: Longint; Rect: TRect; State: TGridDrawState);
VAR X : Integer;
begin
  WITH Sender AS TStringGrid DO
    BEGIN
      CASE vCol OF
        0 : BEGIN
              SetTextAlign(Canvas.Handle, TA_RIGHT);
              X := Rect.Right - 2;
            END;
        1 : BEGIN
              SetTextAlign(Canvas.Handle, TA_CENTER);
              X := (Rect.Left + Rect.Right) DIV 2;
            END;
        ELSE BEGIN
              SetTextAlign(Canvas.Handle, TA_LEFT);
              X := Rect.Left + 2;
            END;
      END;
      Canvas.TextRect(Rect, X, Rect.Top+2, Cells[vCol, vRow]);
    END;
end;

end.
```

The OnDrawCell handler calls the Windows API function SetTextAlign, passing the handle of the string grid's canvas, to set text alignment to right, to center, or to left. The X value passed to TextRect is different depending on the alignment. For left alignment, it's the beginning of the text, for right alignment it's the end, and for center alignment it's the middle.

Note also that SetTextAlign is called for *every* cell. When you change the text alignment for a canvas, you must either explicitly set it to the alignment you want before each call to TextOut or TextRect, or you must set it back to TA_LEFT after each change. Text alignment is not a property of the Canvas object, and the Canvas object can and does recreate its device context as needed. You can't assume that the text alignment will or will not retain the value you've set.

Decimal-aligning numbers in a grid

16 32

The previous example showed how to right-align strings, but when the strings are floating point numbers, you want to *decimal*-align them. That is, you want the decimal point in every cell in a column to be in exactly the same place.

The program in Figure 8-3 performs decimal alignment on numbers, and also displays negative numbers in red (too bad the figure isn't in color!). It adds a decimal point at the end of numbers that don't have one, and leaves non-numeric strings alone.

Numbers	Plus/Minus	With Text
1.	1.00	1.00
1.	-1.0	One
1.2	1.	-1.
1.23	-1.	1 oz.
1234567.00	12345678.00	123456789.987
1.234	-1.234	Too-too-long tex

StringGrid3 Row#5 = 123456789.987654321

FIGURE 8-3: Three string grids share the same OnDrawCell handler; it decimal-aligns numbers and displays negative numbers in red.

DECALIN

DECALINU.DEX

```
object Form1: TForm1
  BorderIcons = [biSystemMenu, biMinimize]
  BorderStyle = bsSingle
  Caption = 'Decimal Alignment Demo'
  Position = poDefault
  Scaled = False
  OnCreate = FormCreate
  object StringGrid1: TStringGrid
    ColCount = 1
    FixedCols = 0
    Options = [goFixedVertLine, goFixedHorzLine, goVertLine,
goHorzLine, goRangeSelect, goDrawFocusSelected, goEditing]
    RowCount = 7
    ScrollBars = ssNone
    OnClick = StringGrid1Click
    OnDrawCell = StringGrid1DrawCell
  end
  object StringGrid2: TStringGrid
    ColCount = 1
    FixedCols = 0
    Options = [goFixedVertLine, goFixedHorzLine, goVertLine,
goHorzLine, goRangeSelect, goDrawFocusSelected, goEditing]
    RowCount = 7
    ScrollBars = ssNone
    OnClick = StringGrid1Click
    OnDrawCell = StringGrid1DrawCell
  end
  object StringGrid3: TStringGrid
    ColCount = 1
    FixedCols = 0
    Options = [goFixedVertLine, goFixedHorzLine, goVertLine,
goHorzLine, goRangeSelect, goDrawFocusSelected, goEditing]
    RowCount = 7
    ScrollBars = ssNone
    OnClick = StringGrid1Click
    OnDrawCell = StringGrid1DrawCell
  end
  object Panel1: TPanel
    Align = alBottom
    BevelInner = bvLowered
  end
end
```

DECALINU.PAS

```
unit Decalinu;

interface

uses SysUtils, WinTypes, WinProcs, Messages, Classes, Graphics,
  Controls, Forms, Dialogs, Grids, StdCtrls, ExtCtrls;

type
  TForm1 = class(TForm)
    StringGrid1: TStringGrid;
    StringGrid2: TStringGrid;
    StringGrid3: TStringGrid;
    Panel1: TPanel;
    procedure FormCreate(Sender: TObject);
    procedure StringGrid1DrawCell(Sender: TObject;
      vCol, vRow: Longint; Rect: TRect; State: TGridDrawState);
    procedure StringGrid1Click(Sender: TObject);
  end;

var Form1: TForm1;

implementation

{$R *.DFM}

procedure TForm1.FormCreate(Sender: TObject);
begin
  StringGrid1.Cols[0].SetText('Numbers'#13'1'#13'1.'#13'1.2'#13+
    '1.23'#13'1234567.00'#13'1.234'#0);
  StringGrid2.Cols[0].SetText('Plus/Minus'#13'1.00'#13'-1.0'#13+
    '1.'#13'-1'#13'12345678.00'#13'-1.234'#0);
  StringGrid3.Cols[0].SetText('With Text'#13'1.00'#13'One'#13'-1.'+
    #13'1 oz.'#13'123456789.987654321'#13'Too-too-long text'#0);
end;

procedure TForm1.StringGrid1DrawCell(Sender: TObject;
  vCol, vRow: Longint; Rect: TRect; State: TGridDrawState);
VAR
  R          : TRect;
  S          : String;
  PtPos      : Integer;
begin
  WITH Sender AS TStringGrid, Canvas DO
    BEGIN
      {Leave fixed rows unchanged}
      IF vRow < FixedRows THEN Exit;
      S := Cells[vCol, vRow];
      try
        {red for negative numbers}
        IF StrToFloat(S) < 0 THEN Font.Color := clRed;
      except
        {Leave non-numeric rows unchanged}
        ON EConvertError DO Exit;
      end;
```

```
        IF Pos('.', S) = 0 THEN S := S + '.';
        PtPos := Pos('.', S);
        {right-align left-of-decimal portion}
        R := Rect;
        R.Right := R.Right - TextWidth('.00') - 4;
        SetTextAlign(Handle, TA_RIGHT);
        TextRect(R, R.Right, R.Top+2, Copy(S, 1, PtPos - 1));
        {left-align right-of-decimal portion}
        R.Left := R.Right;
        R.Right := Rect.Right;
        SetTextAlign(Handle, TA_LEFT);
        TextRect(R, R.Left, R.Top+2, Copy(S, PtPos, 255));
    END;
  end;
  procedure TForm1.StringGrid1Click(Sender: TObject);
  begin
    WITH Sender AS TStringGrid DO
      Panel1.Caption := Format('%s Row#%d = %s',
        [Name, Row, Cells[Col,Row]]);
  end;
  end.
```

Some of the numbers in the example are deliberately too large to fit. Overflow in the integer portion is cut off at the left, while surplus decimals are cut off at the right.

If the string in question represents a negative number, the OnDrawCell handler displays it in red. The test for a negative number occurs within a try . . . except . . . block that responds to the EConvertError exception resulting from a non-numeric string by exiting the method. A string that gets past this test will be decimal-aligned. As you can see, decimal alignment is just a matter of right-aligning the integer part of the number in one portion of the rectangle and left-aligning the fractional portion in the remainder.

Cell Selection

Several of the grid's numerous Options subproperties relate to cell selection. If goRangeSelect is True, the user can select a rectangular range of cells by dragging with the mouse. GoDrawFocusSelected causes the focused cell to be drawn using the selected color. And goRowSelect causes the grid to always select a whole row at a time. These are all handy modes, but there's room to improve on the default behavior.

Row select doesn't work right

16

Sometimes when you set the goRowSelect Options property to True in a Delphi 1.0 program, the grid doesn't seem to behave correctly. If you drag with the mouse, you get a rectangular range of cells that doesn't match the rows you dragged over. The solution here is simple; turn *off* goRangeSelect. These two options just don't mix under Delphi 1.0.

Disjointing selection of grid cells

16 32

Delphi's grid components can be programmed to accept three kinds of selection. If the goRangeSelect element of the Options property is True, the user can select a rectangular range of cells. If goRowSelect is True, the entire current row is always selected. If both are False, only the current cell is selected. There's no provision for generalized multiple selection.

The list box component has an array property called Selected that returns the selected state of each item. The program in Figure 8-4 uses a string grid's Objects array as a substitute for Selected. A cell is considered selected only if the corresponding Objects element is non-NIL.

Disjoint selection grid								
Selected: (3,1) (4,1) (5,1) (6,1) (7,1) (2,2) (8,2) (2,3) (4,3) (6,3) (8,3) (2,4) (8,4) (2,5) (4,5) (8,5) (2,6) (5,6) (6,6) (8,6) (2,7) (8,7) (3,8) (4,8) (5,8) (6,8) (7,8)								
(0,0)	(1,0)	(2,0)	(3,0)	(4,0)	(5,0)	(6,0)	(7,0)	(8,0)
(0,1)	(1,1)	(2,1)	(3,1)	(4,1)	(5,1)	(6,1)	(7,1)	(8,1)
(0,2)	(1,2)	(2,2)	(3,2)	(4,2)	(5,2)	(6,2)	(7,2)	(8,2)
(0,3)	(1,3)	(2,3)	(3,3)	(4,3)	(5,3)	(6,3)	(7,3)	(8,3)
(0,4)	(1,4)	(2,4)	(3,4)	(4,4)	(5,4)	(6,4)	(7,4)	(8,4)
(0,5)	(1,5)	(2,5)	(3,5)	(4,5)	(5,5)	(6,5)	(7,5)	(8,5)
(0,6)	(1,6)	(2,6)	(3,6)	(4,6)	(5,6)	(6,6)	(7,6)	(8,6)
(0,7)	(1,7)	(2,7)	(3,7)	(4,7)	(5,7)	(6,7)	(7,7)	(8,7)
(0,8)	(1,8)	(2,8)	(3,8)	(4,8)	(5,8)	(6,8)	(7,8)	(8,8)

FIGURE 8-4: This program demonstrates disjoint selection of grid items; clicking on an item or navigating to it and pressing the spacebar toggles its selected state.

SELGRID

SELGRIDU.DEX

```
object Form1: TForm1
  Caption = 'Disjoint selection grid'
  Position = poDefault
  Scaled = False
  OnCreate = FormCreate
  object StringGrid1: TStringGrid
    Align = alClient
    ColCount = 9
    RowCount = 9
    OnDrawCell = StringGrid1DrawCell
    OnKeyUp = StringGrid1KeyUp
    OnMouseUp = StringGrid1MouseUp
  end
  object Memo1: TMemo
    Align = alTop
    Lines.Strings = (
      'Selected:')
    ReadOnly = True
  end
end
```

SELGRIDU.PAS

```
unit Selgridu;

interface

uses SysUtils, WinTypes, WinProcs, Messages, Classes, Graphics,
  Controls, Forms, Dialogs, Grids, StdCtrls, ExtCtrls;

type
  TForm1 = class(TForm)
    StringGrid1: TStringGrid;
    Memo1: TMemo;
    procedure FormCreate(Sender: TObject);
    procedure StringGrid1DrawCell(Sender: TObject;
      vCol, vRow: Longint; Rect: TRect; State: TGridDrawState);
    procedure StringGrid1MouseUp(Sender: TObject; Button:
      TMouseButton; Shift: TShiftState; X, Y: Integer);
    procedure StringGrid1KeyUp(Sender: TObject; var Key: Word;
      Shift: TShiftState);
  private
    procedure ReportSelected;
  end;

var Form1: TForm1;

implementation

{$R *.DFM}

procedure TForm1.FormCreate(Sender: TObject);
```

```
    VAR ro,co : Word;
    begin
      FOR Ro := StringGrid1.FixedRows TO StringGrid1.RowCount-1 DO
        FOR co := StringGrid1.FixedCols TO StringGrid1.ColCount-1 DO
          StringGrid1.Cells[co,ro] := Format('(%d,%d)', [co, ro]);
    end;
    procedure TForm1.StringGrid1DrawCell(Sender: TObject;
      vCol, vRow: Longint; Rect: TRect; State: TGridDrawState);
    begin
      WITH Sender AS TStringGrid DO
        BEGIN
          IF (vCol < FixedCols) OR (vRow < FixedRows) THEN Exit;
          IF Objects[vCol,vRow] = NIL THEN
            BEGIN
              Canvas.Brush.Color := clWindow;
              Canvas.Font.Color  := clWindowText;
            END
          ELSE
            BEGIN
              Canvas.Brush.Color := clHighlight;
              Canvas.Font.Color  := clHighlightText;
            END;
          Canvas.TextRect(Rect, Rect.Left, Rect.Top, Cells[vCol, vRow]);
        END;
    end;

    procedure TForm1.ReportSelected;
    VAR ro, co, Last : Integer;
    begin
      Memo1.Lines.BeginUpdate;
      Memo1.Lines.Clear;
      Memo1.Lines.Add('Selected: ');
      FOR ro := StringGrid1.FixedRows TO StringGrid1.RowCount-1 DO
        FOR co := StringGrid1.FixedCols TO StringGrid1.ColCount-1 DO
          IF StringGrid1.Objects[co,ro] <> NIL THEN
            BEGIN
              Last := Memo1.Lines.Count-1;
              Memo1.Lines[Last] := Memo1.Lines[Last] + ' ' +
                StringGrid1.Cells[co,ro];
            END;
      Memo1.Lines.EndUpdate;
    end;

    procedure TForm1.StringGrid1MouseUp(Sender: TObject; Button:
      TMouseButton; Shift: TShiftState; X, Y: Integer);
    VAR vCol, vRow : LongInt;
    begin
      WITH Sender AS TStringGrid DO
        BEGIN
          MouseToCell(X, Y, vCol, vRow);
          IF (vCol < FixedCols) OR (vRow < FixedRows) THEN Exit;
          IF Objects[vCol, vRow] = NIL THEN
            Objects[vCol, vRow] := Pointer(1)
          ELSE Objects[vCol, vRow] := NIL;
        END;
```

```
      ReportSelected;
   end;
   procedure TForm1.StringGrid1KeyUp(Sender: TObject; var Key:
      Word; Shift: TShiftState);
   begin
      IF Key <> VK_SPACE THEN Exit;
      WITH Sender AS TStringGrid DO
         IF Objects[Col, Row] = NIL THEN
            Objects[Col, Row] := Pointer(1)
         ELSE Objects[Col, Row] := NIL;
      ReportSelected;
   end;

   end.
```

You might think of using the OnClick event to toggle the selected state of a cell when the user clicks with the mouse. However, OnClick is also triggered when the user navigates into a cell using the arrow keys, so cells would be flashing on and off as the user navigates. To avoid that problem, the grid responds to OnMouseUp and OnKeyUp. If the key was the spacebar, the OnKeyUp handler toggles the selection state of the current cell. That is, if the corresponding element of the Objects array was NIL, it gets set to a non-NIL value; otherwise, it gets set to NIL.

The OnMouseUp handler must first calculate the cell in which the mouse event occurred. If it was a fixed cell, nothing changes. Otherwise it toggles the selection state of the cell in the same way.

After either of these event handlers changes a cell's selection state, it calls the form's ReportSelected method. This method demonstrates how a program would determine just which cells in a grid are selected. It simply iterates through both dimensions of the Objects array and reports the Cell value corresponding to each non-NIL entry.

Finally, a special OnDrawCell handler is needed to *show* the selection state of each cell. If the corresponding object is non-NIL, the OnDrawCell handler uses the system highlight colors for background and text; otherwise it uses the normal window colors. Of course, this technique is only useful when your program is not already using the Objects array to store actual objects.

 ## Copying a selection to the clipboard

16 32

Many Delphi components have built-in methods to transfer their contents to and from the clipboard. The string grid does not, but the program in Figure 8-5 shows a

possible technique for copying a string grid's selection to the clipboard. It builds a
series of strings, one from each row in the selection, separating elements with a tab
character. Then it copies the result to the clipboard.

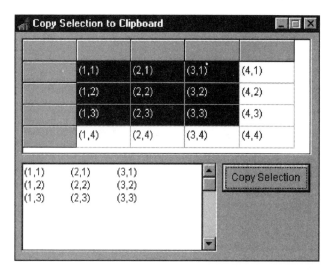

FIGURE 8-5: This example program demonstrates copying a grid's selection to the clipboard;
to show success, it immediately pastes the result into a memo box.

GRIDCLIP

GRIDCLIU.DEX

```
object Form1: TForm1
  BorderIcons = [biSystemMenu, biMinimize]
  BorderStyle = bsSingle
  Caption = 'Copy Selection to Clipboard'
  Position = poDefault
  Scaled = False
  OnCreate = FormCreate
  object StringGrid1: TStringGrid
    Options = [goFixedVertLine, goFixedHorzLine, goVertLine,
goHorzLine, goRangeSelect, goDrawFocusSelected]
  end
  object Memo1: TMemo
    ScrollBars = ssVertical
  end
  object Button1: TButton
    Caption = 'Copy Selection'
    Default = True
    OnClick = Button1Click
  end
end
```

GRIDCLIU.PAS

```
unit Gridcliu;

interface

uses SysUtils, WinTypes, WinProcs, Messages, Classes, Graphics,
  Controls, Forms, Dialogs, StdCtrls, Grids;

type
  TForm1 = class(TForm)
    StringGrid1: TStringGrid;
    Memo1: TMemo;
    Button1: TButton;
    procedure FormCreate(Sender: TObject);
    procedure Button1Click(Sender: TObject);
  end;

var Form1: TForm1;

implementation
USES ClipBrd;
{$R *.DFM}

procedure TForm1.FormCreate(Sender: TObject);
VAR co, ro : Word;
begin
  FOR co := 1 TO StringGrid1.ColCount-1 DO
    FOR ro := 1 TO StringGrid1.RowCount-1 DO
      StringGrid1.Cells[co,ro] := Format('(%d,%d)', [co,ro]);
end;

procedure TForm1.Button1Click(Sender: TObject);
VAR
  TS    : TStringList;
  co,ro : LongInt;
  S     : String;
begin
  TS := TStringList.Create;
  try
    WITH StringGrid1.Selection DO
      FOR ro := Top TO Bottom DO
        BEGIN
          S := '';
          FOR co := Left TO Right-1 DO
            S := S + StringGrid1.Cells[co,ro] + #9;
          S := S + StringGrid1.Cells[Right,ro];
          TS.Add(S);
        END;
    {$IFDEF Win32}
    ClipBoard.AsText := TS.Text;
    {$ELSE}
    Clipboard.SetTextBuf(TS.GetText);
    {$ENDIF}
    Memo1.PasteFromClipboard;
  finally
```

```
      TS.Free;
    end;
  end;
  end.
```

The string grid doesn't have a method for copying text to the clipboard, but a simple string list does. The button's OnClick handler creates a temporary string list and fills it by creating a line for each row in the selection. Then it copies the string list's text to the clipboard and, to show that it worked, pastes the result into a memo box. Finally, the temporary string list is freed.

It's possible that the total length of the strings in a row might exceed the 255-character limit for string length in 16-bit Delphi. In that case, you'll have to define a different format for passing the data, perhaps one cell per line with a blank line indicating the end of the row.

Responding when a new cell is selected

16 32

The OnClick event for a string grid occurs when the user selects a new cell, whether by mouse or by keyboard. However, this event does not provide any information about the *previously* selected cell. If you want to perform a calculation on a row each time a cell in that row changes, for example, OnClick will not help. We need an OnExitCell method!

There isn't such a method, though, and creating a string grid descendant would be more trouble than it's worth. Why? Because a combination of the OnSelectCell and OnExit events will do the job. The program shown in Figure 8-6 contains two rather different grids, both connected to the same OnSelectCell and OnExit handlers. When the user leaves a particular cell, the totals for that cell's row and column are updated.

CALC

CALCU.DEX

```
object Form1: TForm1
  BorderIcons = [biSystemMenu, biMinimize]
  BorderStyle = bsSingle
  Caption = 'Grid Calc Demo'
  Position = poDefault
  Scaled = False
  OnCreate = FormCreate
```

UNIVERSITY OF GLAMORGAN
PRIFYSGOL MORGANNWG
Learning Resources Centre

```
object StringGrid1: TStringGrid
  ColCount = 6
  FixedCols = 0
  FixedRows = 0
  Options = [goFixedVertLine, goFixedHorzLine, goVertLine,
goHorzLine, goEditing]
  RowCount = 6
  ScrollBars = ssNone
  OnDrawCell = StringGrid1DrawCell
  OnExit = StringGrid1Exit
  OnSelectCell = StringGrid1SelectCell
end
object StringGrid2: TStringGrid
  ColCount = 14
  Options = [goFixedVertLine, goFixedHorzLine, goVertLine,
goHorzLine, goEditing]
  OnDrawCell = StringGrid1DrawCell
  OnExit = StringGrid1Exit
  OnSelectCell = StringGrid1SelectCell
end
end
```

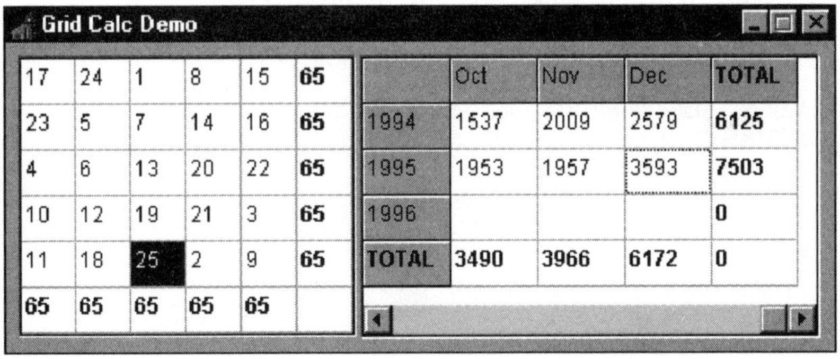

17	24	1	8	15	65		Oct	Nov	Dec	TOTAL
23	5	7	14	16	65	1994	1537	2009	2579	6125
4	6	13	20	22	65	1995	1953	1957	3593	7503
10	12	19	21	3	65	1996				0
11	18	25	2	9	65	TOTAL	3490	3966	6172	0
65	65	65	65	65						

FIGURE 8-6: To trigger an event any time the user moves away from the current grid cell, use a combination of OnSelectCell and OnExit.

CALCU.PAS

```
unit Calcu;

interface

uses SysUtils, WinTypes, WinProcs, Messages, Classes, Graphics,
  Controls, Forms, Dialogs, StdCtrls, Grids;

type
  TForm1 = class(TForm)
    StringGrid1: TStringGrid;
    StringGrid2: TStringGrid;
```

```
      procedure StringGrid1Exit(Sender: TObject);
      procedure FormCreate(Sender: TObject);
      procedure StringGrid1DrawCell(Sender: TObject; vCol,
        vRow: Longint; Rect: TRect; State: TGridDrawState);
      procedure StringGrid1SelectCell(Sender: TObject; vCol,
        vRow: Longint; var CanSelect: Boolean);
    private
      procedure SumRowCol(vBeg, vEnd : Integer; TS : TStrings);
      procedure SumAll(Gr: TStringGrid);
    end;

var Form1: TForm1;

implementation

{$R *.DFM}

procedure TForm1.FormCreate(Sender: TObject);
begin
  StringGrid2.Rows[0].SetText(' '#13'Jan'#13'Feb#13'Mar'#13'Apr'+
    #13'May'#13'Jun'#13'Jul'#13'Aug'#13'Sep'#13'Oct'#13'Nov'#13+
    'Dec'#13'TOTAL');
  StringGrid2.Cols[0].SetText(' '#13'1994'#13'1995'#13'1996'+
    #13'TOTAL');
  SumAll(StringGrid1);
  SumAll(StringGrid2);
end;

procedure TForm1.SumRowCol(vBeg, vEnd : Integer; TS: TStrings);
VAR N, Sum: LongInt;
BEGIN
  Sum := 0;
  FOR N := vBeg TO vEnd-1 DO Sum := Sum + StrToIntDef(TS[N], 0);
  TS[vEnd] := IntToStr(Sum);
END;

procedure TForm1.SumAll(Gr: TStringGrid);
VAR N : Integer;
BEGIN
  FOR N := Gr.FixedCols TO Gr.ColCount-2 DO
    SumRowCol(Gr.FixedRows, Gr.RowCount-1, Gr.Cols[N]);
  FOR N := Gr.FixedRows TO Gr.RowCount-2 DO
    SumRowCol(Gr.FixedCols, Gr.ColCount-1, Gr.Rows[N]);
END;

procedure TForm1.StringGrid1SelectCell(Sender: TObject;
  vCol, vRow: Longint; var CanSelect: Boolean);
begin
  StringGrid1Exit(Sender);
  WITH Sender AS TStringGrid DO
    IF (vRow=RowCount-1) OR (vCol=ColCount-1) THEN
      CanSelect := False;
end;

procedure TForm1.StringGrid1Exit(Sender: TObject);
begin
  WITH Sender AS TStringGrid DO
```

```
      BEGIN
        SumRowCol(FixedCols, ColCount-1, Rows[Row]);
        SumRowCol(FixedRows, RowCount-1, Cols[Col]);
      END;
  end;
  procedure TForm1.StringGrid1DrawCell(Sender: TObject;
    vCol, vRow: Longint; Rect: TRect; State: TGridDrawState);
  begin
    WITH Sender AS TStringGrid, Canvas DO
      BEGIN
        IF (vCol <> ColCount-1) AND (vRow <> RowCount-1) THEN Exit;
        Font.Style := [fsBold];
        TextRect(Rect, Rect.Left+2, Rect.Top+2, Cells[vCol, vRow]);
      END;
  end;

  end.
```

The OnExit event handler updates the totals for the current row and column when the user switches to another component. It calls the SumRowCol method to sum the cell values in the current row and column and assigns the result to the last item in the row or column.

The OnSelectCell event handler simply calls the OnExit handler to sum the previous row and column. When the OnSelectCell event occurs, the Row and Col properties hold the previous cell location—the new location is contained in the parameters vRow and vCol. If the user is attempting to select one of the total cells, the event handler sets CanSelect to False.

This program also sports an OnDrawCell event handler, though it's not strictly necessary. This event handler draws the cells containing totals in boldface, thus giving a visual indication that they're different from the rest.

The power of OnSelectCell to prevent selection of a particular cell can have interesting results. As you'll see later in this chapter, it can be used to control the user's ability to navigate in the grid.

Grid Colors

The draw grid insists that you take charge of drawing cells, and the string grid at least permits it. That's good, because there's a lot you can do by taking over, even if you don't want to display a different bitmap in each cell. There are also a couple of subtle problems that can trip you up when you start adding color to grids.

Grids show selection even when they don't have the focus

|16| |32|

The standard edit boxes and memo boxes have a property called HideSelection. When this property is True, as it is by default, the selected text is highlighted only when the component is active. Grids behave in nearly the opposite fashion, and do not offer an equivalent property to change this behavior. A grid's selection is always visible, so, if a form contains more than one grid, the user may be confused as to which is active.

The two grids on the left in Figure 8-7 show the default behavior—their selection is visible at all times. The two on the right use a modified OnDrawCell handler to ensure that the selection is visible only when the grid is selected.

FIGURE 8-7: A special OnDrawCell handler lets the two right-hand grids hide their selection when not active.

SGRIDNO

SGRIDNOU.DEX

```
object Form1: TForm1
  ActiveControl = StringGrid1
  BorderIcons = [biSystemMenu, biMinimize]
  BorderStyle = bsSingle
```

```
    Caption = 'Fix Grid Selection Display'
    Position = poDefault
    Scaled = False
    OnCreate = FormCreate
    object Label1: TLabel
      Caption = 'Fixed - Selection shows when active'
    end
    object Label2: TLabel
      Caption = 'Default  - Selection always shows'
    end
    object StringGrid3: TStringGrid
      Options = [goFixedVertLine, goFixedHorzLine, goVertLine,
  goHorzLine, goRangeSelect, goDrawFocusSelected]
      ScrollBars = ssNone
      OnDrawCell = StringGrid3DrawCell
      OnEnter = StringGrid1Enter
      OnExit = StringGrid1Exit
    end
    object StringGrid4: TStringGrid
      Options = [goFixedVertLine, goFixedHorzLine, goVertLine,
  goHorzLine, goRangeSelect, goDrawFocusSelected]
      ScrollBars = ssNone
      OnDrawCell = StringGrid3DrawCell
      OnEnter = StringGrid1Enter
      OnExit = StringGrid1Exit
    end
    object StringGrid1: TStringGrid
      Options = [goFixedVertLine, goFixedHorzLine, goVertLine,
  goHorzLine, goRangeSelect, goDrawFocusSelected]
      ScrollBars = ssNone
      OnEnter = StringGrid1Enter
      OnExit = StringGrid1Exit
    end
    object StringGrid2: TStringGrid
      Options = [goFixedVertLine, goFixedHorzLine, goVertLine,
  goHorzLine, goRangeSelect, goDrawFocusSelected]
      ScrollBars = ssNone
      OnEnter = StringGrid1Enter
      OnExit = StringGrid1Exit
    end
  end
```

SGRIDNOU.PAS

```
unit Sgridnou;

interface

uses SysUtils, WinTypes, WinProcs, Messages, Classes, Graphics,
  Controls, Forms, Dialogs, Grids, StdCtrls;

type
  TForm1 = class(TForm)
```

```
      StringGrid1: TStringGrid;
      StringGrid2: TStringGrid;
      StringGrid3: TStringGrid;
      StringGrid4: TStringGrid;
      Label1: TLabel;
      Label2: TLabel;
      procedure FormCreate(Sender: TObject);
      procedure StringGrid3DrawCell(Sender: TObject; vCol,
        vRow: Longint; Rect: TRect; State: TGridDrawState);
      procedure StringGrid1Enter(Sender: TObject);
      procedure StringGrid1Exit(Sender: TObject);
  end;

var Form1: TForm1;

implementation

{$R *.DFM}

procedure TForm1.FormCreate(Sender: TObject);
VAR ro,co : LongInt;
begin
  FOR ro := 1 TO StringGrid1.RowCount-1 DO
    FOR co := 1 TO StringGrid1.ColCount-1 DO
      BEGIN
        StringGrid1.Cells[co,ro] := Format('(%d,%d)', [co,ro]);
        StringGrid2.Cells[co,ro] := Format('(%d,%d)', [co,ro]);
        StringGrid3.Cells[co,ro] := Format('(%d,%d)', [co,ro]);
        StringGrid4.Cells[co,ro] := Format('(%d,%d)', [co,ro]);
      END;
end;

procedure TForm1.StringGrid3DrawCell(Sender: TObject; vCol,
  vRow: Longint; Rect: TRect; State: TGridDrawState);
begin
  IF Sender = ActiveControl THEN Exit;
  IF NOT (gdSelected IN State) THEN Exit;
  WITH Sender AS TStringGrid DO
    BEGIN
      Canvas.Brush.Color := Color;
      Canvas.Font := Font;
      Canvas.TextRect(Rect, Rect.Left+2, Rect.Top+2,
        Cells[vCol, vRow]);
    END;
end;
procedure TForm1.StringGrid1Enter(Sender: TObject);
begin
  WITH Sender AS TStringGrid DO Cells[0,0] := 'Active';
end;

procedure TForm1.StringGrid1Exit(Sender: TObject);
begin
  WITH Sender AS TStringGrid DO Cells[0,0] := '';
end;

end.
```

The special OnDrawCell handler does nothing if the grid is currently the form's active control. If the grid is not active, but the cell being drawn is not selected, again the event handler does nothing. Only if the grid is not active and the cell is selected does this event handler overwrite Delphi's default drawing. In this case, it simply draws the text using the colors appropriate to a nonselected cell.

To make the problem easier to see, all four grids are connected to OnEnter and OnExit event handlers. These handlers display the word "Active" in the top left corner of the active grid.

Fully controlling grid color

16 32

The grid components have a Color property which defines the background color of the cells . . . or does it? For a string grid, the background cell color is the nearest solid color to the specified value. In 256-color mode, the nearest color can be very different from the actual color. Figure 8-8 shows two grids whose background color is $00A0FFFF, a pale yellow whose "nearest" solid color is gray. The upper grid displays with a gray background, whereas the lower grid uses the specified color.

FIGURE 8-8: When a grid's Color property is a color that's very different from its nearest solid color, the results aren't pretty.

GCOLOR

GCOLORU.DEX

```
object Form1: TForm1
  Caption = 'Grid Background Color'
  Color = 10551295
  Position = poDefault
  Scaled = False
  OnCreate = FormCreate
  object StringGrid2: TStringGrid
    Options = [goFixedVertLine, goFixedHorzLine, goVertLine,
goHorzLine, goRangeSelect, goDrawFocusSelected, goEditing]
    ParentColor = True
    OnDrawCell = StringGrid2DrawCell
  end
  object StringGrid1: TStringGrid
    Options = [goFixedVertLine, goFixedHorzLine, goVertLine,
goHorzLine, goRangeSelect, goDrawFocusSelected, goEditing]
    ParentColor = True
  end
end
```

GCOLORU.PAS

```
unit Gcoloru;

interface

uses SysUtils, WinTypes, WinProcs, Messages, Classes, Graphics,
  Controls, Forms, Dialogs, StdCtrls, Grids;

type
  TForm1 = class(TForm)
    StringGrid2: TStringGrid;
    StringGrid1: TStringGrid;
    procedure FormCreate(Sender: TObject);
    procedure StringGrid2DrawCell(Sender: TObject; vCol,
      vRow: Longint; Rect: TRect; State: TGridDrawState);
  end;

var Form1: TForm1;

implementation

{$R *.DFM}

procedure TForm1.FormCreate(Sender: TObject);
VAR co,ro: Integer;
begin
  IF GetDeviceCaps(Canvas.Handle, BITSPIXEL) <> 8 THEN
    ShowMessage('This problem occurs only in 256 color modes');
  FOR ro := 1 TO StringGrid1.RowCount DO
    FOR co := 1 TO StringGrid1.ColCount DO
      BEGIN
```

```
            StringGrid1.Cells[co,ro] := Format('(%d,%d)',[co,ro]);
            StringGrid2.Cells[co,ro] := Format('(%d,%d)',[co,ro]);
         END;
     StringGrid1.Cells[0,0] := 'Bad';
     StringGrid2.Cells[0,0] := 'Good';
  end;
  procedure TForm1.StringGrid2DrawCell(Sender: TObject; vCol,
    vRow: Longint; Rect: TRect; State: TGridDrawState);
  begin
    WITH Sender AS TStringGrid, Canvas DO
      BEGIN
        IF (vRow < FixedRows) OR (vCol < FixedCols) THEN Exit;
        FillRect(Rect);
        SetBkMode(Handle, TRANSPARENT);
        TextOut(Rect.Left+2, Rect.Top+2, Cells[vCol, vRow]);
      END;
  end;

  end.
```

The essential line in the OnDrawCell handler is SetBkMode(Handle, TRANSPARENT). This Windows API function call sets the grid's canvas to have a transparent background. Without this call, the TextRect method call that follows would again draw the text and fill the background with the nearest solid color. However, you won't want to use this technique if the background color *is* a solid color, as it may cause a slight flicker in the grid's display.

Grid Miscellany

Delphi's grids are quite versatile, and we haven't come close to exhausting their abilities. Remaining examples will show a technique for inserting and deleting rows and allow you to fit other components into grid cells. You'll even create an on-screen analog of the ever-handy yellow notepad.

 ### *Deleting or inserting rows and columns*

16 32

The rows and columns in a string grid are represented by the Rows and Cols properties. These properties are nominally arrays of TStringLists, but they do not hold their values in the usual way. The Rows, Cols, and Cells properties all get their values from a special private sparse string list structure defined only in the implementation section of GRIDS.PAS.

As you can see from Figure 8-9, it *is* possible to insert and delete rows and columns. However, you have to manipulate the arrays "by hand."

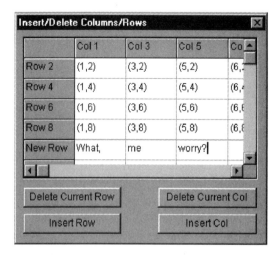

FIGURE 8-9: With a little work, you can insert and delete rows and columns in a grid.

DELGRID

DELGRIDU.DEX

```
object Form1: TForm1
  BorderStyle = bsDialog
  Caption = 'Insert/Delete Columns/Rows'
  Position = poDefault
  Scaled = False
  OnCreate = FormCreate
  object StringGrid1: TStringGrid
    ColCount = 10
    RowCount = 10
    Options = [goFixedVertLine, goFixedHorzLine, goVertLine,
goHorzLine, goDrawFocusSelected, goEditing]
  end
  object Button1: TButton
    Caption = 'Delete Current Row'
    OnClick = Button1Click
  end
  object Button2: TButton
    Caption = 'Delete Current Col'
    OnClick = Button2Click
  end
```

```
      object Button3: TButton
        Caption = 'Insert Row'
        OnClick = Button3Click
      end
      object Button4: TButton
        Caption = 'Insert Col'
        OnClick = Button4Click
      end
    end
```

DELGRIDU.PAS

```
    unit delgridu;

    interface

    uses SysUtils, WinTypes, WinProcs, Messages, Classes, Graphics,
      Controls, Forms, Dialogs, StdCtrls, Grids;

    type
      TForm1 = class(TForm)
        StringGrid1: TStringGrid;
        Button1: TButton;
        Button2: TButton;
        Button3: TButton;
        Button4: TButton;
        procedure FormCreate(Sender: TObject);
        procedure Button1Click(Sender: TObject);
        procedure Button2Click(Sender: TObject);
        procedure Button3Click(Sender: TObject);
        procedure Button4Click(Sender: TObject);
      end;

    var Form1: TForm1;

    implementation

    {$R *.DFM}

    procedure TForm1.FormCreate(Sender: TObject);
    var co, ro : Integer;
    begin
      FOR ro := 1 TO StringGrid1.RowCount-1 DO
        StringGrid1.Cells[0, ro] := Format('Row %d', [ro]);
      FOR co := 1 TO StringGrid1.ColCount-1 DO
        StringGrid1.Cells[co, 0] := Format('Col %d', [co]);
      FOR co := 1 TO StringGrid1.ColCount-1 DO
        FOR ro := 1 TO StringGrid1.RowCount-1 DO
          StringGrid1.Cells[co, ro] := Format('(%d,%d)', [co, ro]);
    end;

    procedure TForm1.Button1Click(Sender: TObject);
    VAR N : Word;
    begin
      WITH StringGrid1 DO
        BEGIN
          IF RowCount-1 = FixedRows THEN Exit;
```

```
          {move rows up}
          FOR N := Row TO RowCount-2 DO Rows[N] := Rows[N+1];
          RowCount := RowCount-1;
          Rows[RowCount].Clear;
        END;
  end;

  procedure TForm1.Button2Click(Sender: TObject);
  VAR N : Word;
  begin
    WITH StringGrid1 DO
      BEGIN
        IF ColCount-1 = FixedCols THEN Exit;
        {move cols left}
        FOR N := Col TO ColCount-2 DO Cols[N] := Cols[N+1];
        ColCount := ColCount-1;
        Cols[ColCount].Clear;
      END;
  end;

  procedure TForm1.Button3Click(Sender: TObject);
  VAR N : Integer;
  begin
    WITH StringGrid1 DO
      BEGIN
        RowCount := RowCount+1;
        {move rows down}
        FOR N := RowCount-1 DOWNTO Row+1 DO Rows[N] := Rows[N-1];
        Rows[Row].Clear;
        Cells[0,Row] := 'New Row';
      END;
  end;

  procedure TForm1.Button4Click(Sender: TObject);
  VAR N : Integer;
  begin
    WITH StringGrid1 DO
      BEGIN
        ColCount := ColCount+1;
        {move cols right}
        FOR N := ColCount-1 DOWNTO Col+1 DO Cols[N] := Cols[N-1];
        Cols[Col].Clear;
        Cells[Col,0] := 'New Col';
      END;
  end;

  end.
```

If you've done any old-fashioned array programming, you'll find this program's code
familiar. To delete a row, Button1's OnClick handler copies the contents of each
element of the Rows array into the preceding element, starting one row past the row
to be deleted and continuing to the end of the array. It then clears the last row and
reduces the grid's RowCount property.

To insert a row, Button3's OnClick handler first increases the grid's RowCount property. Then, starting with the next to last row and going down to the desired new row location, it copies the contents of each element of the Rows array to the next element. To finish, it clears the row at the new row location.

Most Delphi structures that need to support insertion and deletion of elements are based on the TList object, which has that support built in. The Rows and Cols properties are rare exceptions.

Controlling paging in a grid

16 32

The default behavior in a grid is to let the user scroll the rows and columns freely. In some cases, it would be much better to divide the grid into pages and only display a full page at a time. The program in Figure 8-10 shows a solution to this problem, but, as you can see, it goes further than that. It's a handy yellow notepad for your computer. Leave it running and jot those important notes!

Yellow Pad	
	Page 1
	Angelo's pizza 555-1234
	Call Uncle Vanya RE furniture
	bug report? check with
	Joe User
	1234 Potrzebie St.
	New York, NY 100??

FIGURE 8-10: The lines of this grid are divided into pages; to change pages, the user presses PgUp/PgDn, or clicks on the page-corner graphic.

YELPAD

YELPADU.DEX

```
object Form1: TForm1
  BorderIcons = [biSystemMenu, biMinimize]
  BorderStyle = bsSingle
  Caption = 'Yellow Pad'
  Position = poDefault
  Scaled = False
  OnCreate = FormCreate
  OnDestroy = FormDestroy
  object StringGrid1: TStringGrid
    Align = alClient
    BorderStyle = bsNone
    Color = 8454143
    ColCount = 2
    FixedColor = 8454143
    Options = [goFixedVertLine, goHorzLine, goEditing]
    ScrollBars = ssNone
    OnDrawCell = StringGrid1DrawCell
    OnKeyUp = StringGrid1KeyUp
    OnSelectCell = StringGrid1SelectCell
  end
  object Panel1: TPanel
    BevelOuter = bvNone
    Caption = 'Panel1'
    object PaintBox1: TPaintBox
      Align = alClient
      OnMouseUp = PaintBox1MouseUp
      OnPaint = PaintBox1Paint
    end
  end
end
```

YELPADU.PAS

```
unit Yelpadu;

interface

uses SysUtils, WinTypes, WinProcs, Messages, Classes, Graphics,
  Controls, Forms, Dialogs, Grids, StdCtrls, ExtCtrls;

type
  TForm1 = class(TForm)
    StringGrid1: TStringGrid;
    Panel1: TPanel;
    PaintBox1: TPaintBox;
    procedure StringGrid1DrawCell(Sender: TObject; vCol,
      vRow: Longint; Rect: TRect; State: TGridDrawState);
    procedure FormCreate(Sender: TObject);
    procedure StringGrid1KeyUp(Sender: TObject; var Key:
```

```
      Word; Shift: TShiftState);
    procedure StringGrid1SelectCell(Sender: TObject; vCol,
      vRow: Longint; var CanSelect: Boolean);
    procedure FormDestroy(Sender: TObject);
    procedure PaintBox1Paint(Sender: TObject);
    procedure PaintBox1MouseUp(Sender: TObject; Button:
      TMouseButton; Shift: TShiftState; X, Y: Integer);
  private
    EdRows: Integer; {# of editable rows on a page}
    NumPages: Integer; {total number of pages}
    DatName: String; {name for data file}
  end;

var Form1: TForm1;

implementation
{$R *.DFM}

procedure TForm1.FormCreate(Sender: TObject);
begin
  EdRows    := 14;
  NumPages := 20;
  DatName   := ChangeFileExt(Application.ExeName, '.DAT');
  WITH StringGrid1 DO
    BEGIN
      ColWidths[1] := ClientWidth - ColWidths[0]-1;
      RowHeights[0] := RowHeights[0] * 2;
      RowCount := (NumPages * Edrows) + 2;
      Self.ClientHeight := (EdRows+3)*(DefaultRowHeight+1)-2;
      try Cols[1].LoadFromFile(DatName);
      except ON EFOpenError DO;
      end;
      Cells[1,0] := 'Page 1';
      Tag := 1; {tag holds current page}
      Panel1.Left := Self.ClientWidth-DefaultRowHeight;
      Panel1.Top  := Self.ClientHeight-DefaultRowHeight;
    END
end;

procedure TForm1.StringGrid1SelectCell(Sender: TObject; vCol,
  vRow: Longint; var CanSelect: Boolean);
begin
  {can't click on or arrow to last visible row}
  IF vRow - (Sender AS TStringGrid).TopRow = EdRows THEN
    CanSelect := False;
  {can't arrow up past first visible row}
  IF vRow = (Sender AS TStringGrid).TopRow-1 THEN
    CanSelect := False;
end;

procedure TForm1.StringGrid1DrawCell(Sender: TObject; vCol,
  vRow: Longint; Rect: TRect; State: TGridDrawState);
begin
  WITH Sender AS TStringGrid DO
    BEGIN
```

```
        Canvas.FillRect(Rect);
        {don't write text in last visible row}
        IF vRow - TopRow = edRows THEN Exit;
        SetBkMode(Canvas.Handle, TRANSPARENT);
        Canvas.TextOut(Rect.Left+2, Rect.Top+2, Cells[vCol, vRow]);
      END;
end;

procedure TForm1.StringGrid1KeyUp(Sender: TObject; var Key: Word;
  Shift: TShiftState);
begin
  WITH Sender AS TStringGrid DO
    BEGIN
      {exit unless page changed}
      IF Tag = ((Row-1) DIV EdRows) + 1 THEN Exit;
      Tag := ((Row-1) DIV EdRows) + 1;
      Row := TopRow;
      Cells[1,0]:=Format('Page %d',[Tag]);
    END;
end;

procedure TForm1.FormDestroy(Sender: TObject);
VAR
  N         : Integer;
  SaveBlank : Boolean;
begin
  WITH StringGrid1 DO
    BEGIN
      {Only save blank lines if they precede non-blank lines}
      SaveBlank := False;
      FOR N := RowCount-1 DOWNTO 0 DO
        BEGIN
          IF Cells[1,N] <> '' THEN SaveBlank := True
          ELSE IF SaveBlank THEN Cells[1,N] := ' ';
        END;
      Cols[1].SaveToFile(DatName);
    END;
end;

procedure TForm1.PaintBox1Paint(Sender: TObject);
begin
  WITH Sender AS TPaintBox, Canvas DO
    BEGIN
      Brush.Color := StringGrid1.Color;
      FillRect(BoundsRect);
      Pen.Color   := clBlack;
      Brush.Color := clBlack;
      WITH BoundsRect DO Polygon([Point(Left, Bottom),
        Point(Right, Top), Point(Right, Bottom)]);
      Brush.Color := clYellow;
      WITH BoundsRect DO Polygon([Point(Left, Bottom),
        Point(Right, Top), Point(Left+4, Top+4)]);
    END;
end;
```

```
procedure TForm1.PaintBox1MouseUp(Sender: TObject; Button:
  TMouseButton; Shift: TShiftState; X, Y: Integer);
begin
  {if clicked on "back" triangle and not first pg}
  IF (X+Y < Panel1.Width) AND (StringGrid1.Tag > 1) THEN
    StringGrid1.TopRow := StringGrid1.TopRow - EdRows
  {if clicked on "forward" triangle and not last pg}
  ELSE IF (X+Y >= Panel1.Width) AND (StringGrid1.Tag<NumPages) THEN
    StringGrid1.TopRow := StringGrid1.TopRow + EdRows
  ELSE Exit;
  StringGrid1.Row := StringGrid1.TopRow;
  StringGrid1.Tag := ((StringGrid1.Row-1) DIV EdRows) + 1;
  StringGrid1.Cells[1,0]:=Format('Page %d',[StringGrid1.Tag]);
end;

end.
```

Obviously, this program goes a bit beyond simply answering the question. The process of forcing the grid lines to display one page at a time is handled completely within the OnSelectCell event handler. If the cell being selected is one row above the top visible row, the user is attempting to navigate past the top visible row; the event handler prevents this by setting CanSelect to False.

To prevent navigating past the bottom visible row, a slightly different technique is used. If the cell coordinates passed to OnSelectCell are in the last visible row, the event handler sets CanSelect to False. That means the user can neither navigate to the last visible row nor select it by clicking.

Of course, the grid has to be constrained in certain ways to make this technique work. It must not have a vertical scroll bar, and the rows must not be resizeable by the user. Since the number of visible rows is fixed, the grid must remain the same size.

The question remains, just how *does* the user get to the next page? PgUp, PgDn, and other navigation keys work just fine in the grid; all the program needs to do is make sure the page number is correctly displayed. The OnKeyUp event occurs *after* the grid has acted on a keystroke. Its handler calculates the page corresponding to the current row and compares it to the grid's Tag property. If they differ, it sets the Tag to the new page, selects the top visible row, and displays the new page number. Thus, no matter how the user navigates with the keyboard, if the page changes, it gets handled.

Of course, some users prefer the mouse. For their benefit, the program includes a graphical depiction of a turned-up corner at the bottom left of the grid. This is actually a paint box component whose OnPaint handler draws the turned-up corner. However, a paint box is a graphical component and will not display on top of a windowed component like a string grid. To solve this problem, the paint box is contained within a panel, which is a windowed component, and thus can be placed on top of the grid. When the paint box is clicked, the grid flips forward or backward by one page.

The grid's OnDrawCell handler skips drawing the last visible row; that's the row containing the turned-up corner graphic. For all the other rows, it sets the background to transparent before drawing the text, to retain the canary-yellow background.

When the program loads, it reads in the previous yellow pad contents from YELPAD.DAT. When it terminates, it writes the contents back again. It's quite a handy little utility, and a string grid does almost all the work.

Putting other components in cells

16 32

Delphi grids hold strings, or anything that can be drawn using Windows graphics. With a little help, a string grid can even hold other components. The basic string grid is not designed to be a container component, but a string grid descendant can take care of keeping its child components organized.

COMPONENT TSTRINGGRIDCONT

C_SGCONT.PAS

```
unit C_sgcont;

interface

uses SysUtils, WinTypes, WinProcs, Messages, Classes, Graphics,
  Controls, Forms, Dialogs, Grids;

type
  TStringGridCont = class(TStringGrid)
  protected
    procedure WMCommand(var Message: TWMCommand);
      message WM_COMMAND;
    procedure TopLeftChanged; override;
    procedure ColWidthsChanged; override;
    procedure RowHeightsChanged; override;
    procedure ColumnMoved(FromIndex, ToIndex: Longint); override;
    procedure RowMoved(FromIndex, ToIndex: Longint); override;
  public
    procedure PlaceControls;
  end;

procedure Register;

implementation
{$IFDEF Win32}
{$R *.R32}
```

```
{$ELSE}
{$R *.R16}
{$ENDIF}

procedure TStringGridCont.WMCommand(var Message: TWMCommand);
VAR Control : TWinControl;
begin
  Control := FindControl(Message.Ctl);
  IF Control = NIL THEN
    Inherited
  ELSE
    WITH TMessage(Message) DO
      Result := Control.Perform(Msg + CN_BASE, WParam, LParam);
end;

procedure TStringGridCont.TopLeftChanged;
begin
  Inherited TopLeftChanged;
  PlaceControls;
end;

procedure TStringGridCont.ColWidthsChanged;
begin
  Inherited ColWidthsChanged;
  PlaceControls;
end;

procedure TStringGridCont.RowHeightsChanged;
begin
  Inherited RowHeightsChanged;
  PlaceControls;
end;

procedure TStringGridCont.ColumnMoved(FromIndex, ToIndex: Longint);
begin
  Inherited ColumnMoved(FromIndex, ToIndex);
  PlaceControls;
end;

procedure TStringGridCont.RowMoved(FromIndex, ToIndex: Longint);
begin
  Inherited RowMoved(FromIndex, ToIndex);
  PlaceControls;
end;

procedure TStringGridCont.PlaceControls;
VAR
  Co, Ro : Integer;
  R      : TRect;
begin
  Perform(WM_SETREDRAW, 0, 0);
  FOR Co := FixedCols TO ColCount-1 DO
    FOR Ro := FixedRows TO RowCount-1 DO
      IF Objects[Co,Ro] IS TWinControl THEN
        WITH TWinControl(Objects[Co,Ro]) DO
          BEGIN
            R := CellRect(Co,Ro);
            IF (R.Right=R.Left) OR (R.Bottom=R.TOP) THEN
```

```
                    Visible := False
                ELSE
                  BEGIN
                    Visible := True;
                    Left := R.Left;
                    Top  := R.Top;
                    Width := ColWidths[Co];
                    Height := RowHeights[Ro];
                  END;
              END;
    Perform(WM_SETREDRAW, 1, 0);
    Refresh;
  end;

  procedure Register;
  begin
    RegisterComponents('NJR', [TStringGridCont]);
  end;

  end.
```

The TStringGridCont component handles the dispatching of notification messages to any components it contains in its WM_COMMAND message response method. This method is modeled after the one used by the TWinControl object. You might expect that the grid component, being descended from TWinControl, would simply inherit this behavior. However, the WM_COMMAND response method for TCustomGrid, the ancestor of all grid types, does not call the inherited handler.

The rest of this component's methods are devoted to adjusting the size and placement of components contained in its Objects array. The PlaceControls method flips through the entire array looking for elements that are TWinControl descendants. When one is found, this method sets its Left and Top properties to match the cell that contains it, and sets its Width and Height properties to match the current column width and row height. Any time a row or a column is resized or moved, this method gets called. A program using this component must call PlaceControls after all components have been added and before the grid is displayed.

Figure 8-11 shows an example grid containing 16 components. The components start out in the first four rows and columns, but they retain their integrity even when the rows and columns are moved and resized.

GRIDCONT

GRIDCONU.DEX

```
object Form1: TForm1
  Caption = 'Shoehorning components into a String Grid'
  Position = poScreenCenter
  Scaled = False
```

```
      OnCreate = FormCreate
      object StringGridCont1: TStringGridCont
        Align = alClient
        ColCount = 8
        Options = [goFixedVertLine, goFixedHorzLine, goVertLine,
    goHorzLine, goRangeSelect, goRowSizing, goColSizing, goRowMoving,
    goColMoving, goEditing]
        RowCount = 8
      end
    end
```

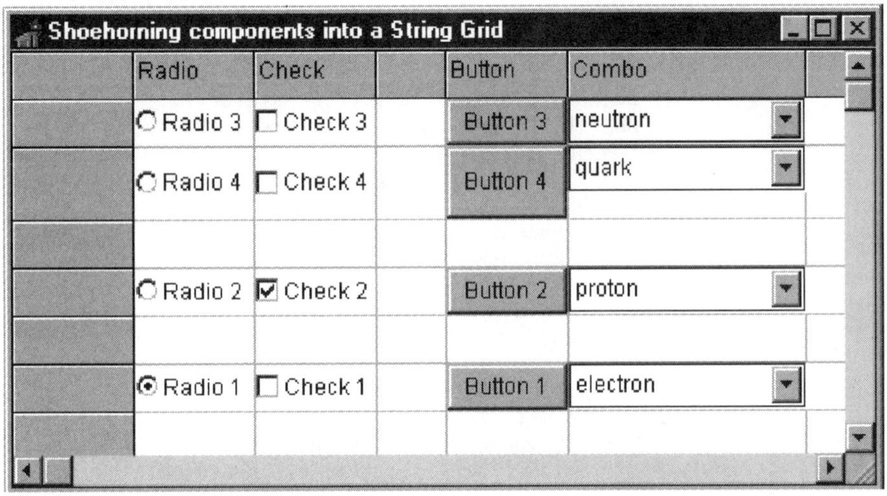

FIGURE 8-11: The components within this grid are associated with particular cells, and they move and scroll as the cells move.

GRIDCONU.PAS

```
    unit Gridconu;

    interface

    uses SysUtils, WinTypes, WinProcs, Messages, Classes, Graphics,
      Controls, Forms, Dialogs, Grids, C_sgcont;

    type
      TForm1 = class(TForm)
        StringGridCont1: TStringGridCont;
        procedure FormCreate(Sender: TObject);
      end;

    var Form1: TForm1;

    implementation
    USES StdCtrls;
    {$R *.DFM}
```

```
procedure TForm1.FormCreate(Sender: TObject);
VAR co, ro : Integer;
begin
  WITH StringGridCont1 DO
    BEGIN
      Rows[0].SetText(' '#13'Radio'#13'Check'#13'Button'#13+
        'Combo');
      ColWidths[4] := ColWidths[4] * 2;
      FOR Ro := 1 TO 4 DO
        BEGIN
          {Cell must be non-empty before creating object}
          FOR co := 1 TO 4 DO Cells[Co,Ro] := ' ';
          Objects[1,Ro] := TRadioButton.Create(Self);
          Objects[2,Ro] := TCheckBox.Create(Self);
          Objects[3,Ro] := TButton.Create(Self);
          Objects[4,Ro] := TComboBox.Create(Self);
          FOR Co := 1 TO 4 DO
            WITH TWinControl(Objects[Co,Ro]) DO
              BEGIN
                Parent :=StringGridCont1;
                BoundsRect := CellRect(Co,Ro);
                Width := ColWidths[Co];
                Height := RowHeights[Ro];
              END;
          FOR Co := 1 TO 3 DO
            TButton(Objects[Co,Ro]).Caption :=
              Format('%s %d', [Cells[Co,0], Ro]);
          WITH TComboBox(Objects[4,Ro]) DO
            Items.SetText('electron'#13'proton'#13'neutron'#13+
              'quark');
        END;
      PlaceControls;
    END;
end;
end.
```

The form's substantial OnCreate event handler creates and initializes four radio buttons, four check boxes, four regular buttons, and four combo boxes, assigning them to the first four rows and columns of the grid's Objects array. After completing the initialization, it calls PlaceControls, the special method defined in TStringGridCont. From that point on, the container string grid manages its contained controls.

There are a few minor limitations with this component. For example, all the radio buttons in the grid act as a single group. If you have three columns of radio buttons, only one of them can be selected at a time. And you wouldn't want to create hundreds of components, as the grid's display would slow down. But on the whole the container string grid works well.

9

Graphical Components

*D*elphi hides much of the tedium associated with the Windows Graphics Device Interface (GDI) in powerful graphical components. The image component displays any icon, bitmap, or metafile. The form's OnPaint event handler allows painting on the form. The paint box defines a rectangular area in which any kind of painting can take place. In this chapter, you'll learn how to create a metafile from scratch, how to drag a component as a rectangular outline, and how to animate a nonrectangular image against another image as background.

An Angle on Text

A Delphi form will usually include one or more labels and one or more buttons, all with their text reading left to right. Normally, that's what you want, but it's also possible to draw text bottom to top, top to bottom, or at any angle whatsoever!

 Drawing text at different angles

16 32

Windows TrueType fonts have a special built-in property not present in other fonts. Cryptically named lfEscapement, it controls the angle at which font text is drawn. Delphi's TFont component does not include an Angle property, so how can you take advantage of this feature?

If it's just a matter of drawing the text, you can copy and use the simple MyRotatePrint routine from the program in Figure 9-1. As you can see, this routine allows printing of text at any angle.

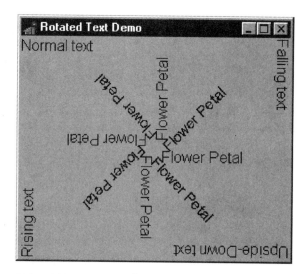

FIGURE 9-1: TrueType fonts can be rotated to any angle, though 90 degrees (straight up) and 270 degrees (straight down) will probably be the most useful.

TURNTX

TURNTXU.DEX

```
object Form1: TForm1
  Caption = 'Rotated Text Demo'
  Font.Color = clBlack
  Position = poDefault
  Scaled = False
  object PaintBox1: TPaintBox
    Align = alClient
    Font.Height = -16
    ParentFont = False
    OnPaint = PaintBox1Paint
  end
end
```

TURNTXU.PAS

```
unit Turntxu;

interface

uses SysUtils, WinTypes, WinProcs, Messages, Classes, Graphics,
  Controls, Forms, Dialogs, StdCtrls, Buttons, ExtCtrls;

type
  TForm1 = class(TForm)
    PaintBox1: TPaintBox;
```

```
      procedure PaintBox1Paint(Sender: TObject);
    end;
var Form1: TForm1;

implementation

{$R *.DFM}
procedure MyRotatePrint (CV: TCanvas; sText: String; X, Y, Angle:
    integer);
var LogFont : TLogFont;
begin
    GetObject(CV.Font.Handle, SizeOf(TLogFont), @LogFont);
    LogFont.lfEscapement := Angle*10;
    CV.Font.Handle := CreateFontIndirect(LogFont);
    CV.TextOut(X, Y, sText);
end;

procedure TForm1.PaintBox1Paint(Sender: TObject);
VAR X, Y, N : Integer;
begin
    WITH Sender AS TPaintBox DO
      BEGIN
        MyRotatePrint(Canvas,'Rising text', 0, Height, 90);
        MyRotatePrint(Canvas,'Normal text', 0, 0, 0);
        MyRotatePrint(Canvas,'Falling text', Width, 0, 270);
        MyRotatePrint(Canvas,'Upside-Down text', Width, Height, 180);
        X := Width DIV 2;
        Y := Height DIV 2;
        SetBkMode(Canvas.Handle, TRANSPARENT);
        FOR N := 0 TO 7 DO
          MyRotatePrint(Canvas, '  Flower Petal', X, Y, N*45);
      END;
end;

end.
```

The MyRotatePrint procedure draws on the Canvas object passed as its first parameter. It draws the specified text at the specified X,Y coordinates and angle. It's up to you to make sure that the font currently selected into the canvas is a TrueType font.

To change the angle of the canvas's font, MyRotatePrint calls the GetLogFont Windows API function to fill a TLogFont structure with details about the font. It sets the lfEscapement field of that structure to 10 times the requested angle, as this field is expressed in 1/10ths of a degree. Then, it creates a new font identical to the old except for the angle and assigns it to the canvas. To finish, it writes the text at the specified location using this font.

Use MyRotatePrint when you want to draw legends on graphs, for example, or create buttons with vertical captions.

Creating vertical and angled labels

16 32

Drawing angled text at runtime is a bit awkward, because you can't lay out the form visually unless you can see all the components. What we really need here is a label component whose caption can display at any angle. To make setting the angle property easy, we'll also define a special property editor for visually setting the Angle property (Figure 9-2).

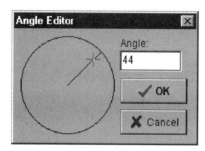

FIGURE 9-2: This specialized property editor lets you set the angle for an angled label visually by dragging with the mouse or entering the value in degrees.

TANGLELABEL

C_ANGLAB.PAS

```
unit C_anglab;

interface

uses
  SysUtils, WinTypes, WinProcs, Messages, Classes, Graphics,
  Controls, Forms, Dialogs, StdCtrls, Menus, p_angle;

type
  TAngleLabel = class(TCustomLabel)
  private
    fAngle : TAngle;
  protected
    procedure Paint; override;
    procedure SetAngle(Value: TAngle); virtual;
    procedure CMFontChanged(var Message: TMessage);
      message CM_FONTCHANGED;
  public
    constructor Create(AOwner: TComponent); override;
  published
    { properties published by TLabel but NOT by TAngleLabel:
```

```
      Alignment, AutoSize, ShowAccelChar, WordWrap }
      { Published properties declared in TCustomLabel}
      property Align;
      property Caption;
      property Color;
      property DragCursor;
      property DragMode;
      property Enabled;
      property FocusControl;
      property Font;
      property ParentColor;
      property ParentFont;
      property ParentShowHint;
      property PopupMenu;
      property ShowHint;
      property Transparent;
      property Visible;
      property OnClick;
      property OnDblClick;
      property OnDragDrop;
      property OnDragOver;
      property OnEndDrag;
      property OnMouseDown;
      property OnMouseMove;
      property OnMouseUp;
      {new properties}
      property Angle : TAngle read fAngle write SetAngle;
   end;

procedure Register;

implementation
{$IFDEF Win32}
{$R *.R32}
{$ELSE}
{$R *.R16}
{$ENDIF}

uses DsgnIntf;

procedure TAngleLabel.CMFontChanged(var Message: TMessage);
VAR TTM : TTextMetric;
begin
  Inherited;
  IF csLoading IN ComponentState THEN Exit;
  Canvas.Font := Font;
  GetTextMetrics(Canvas.Handle, TTM);
  IF TTM.tmPitchAndFamily AND TMPF_TRUETYPE = 0 THEN
    BEGIN
      Font.Name := 'Arial';
      MessageBeep(MB_ICONSTOP);
      ShowMessage('Only TrueType fonts permittted');
    END;
end;
```

```
procedure TAngleLabel.SetAngle(Value: TAngle);
begin
  IF Value <> fAngle THEN
    BEGIN
      fAngle := Value;
      Invalidate;
    END;
end;

constructor TAngleLabel.Create(AOwner: TComponent);
begin
  Inherited Create(AOwner);
  ControlStyle := ControlStyle + [csOpaque];
  Width        := 65;
  Height       := 65;
  AutoSize     := False;
  Transparent  := True;
end;

procedure TAngleLabel.Paint;
VAR
  TLF     : TLogFont;
  R       : TRect;
  X,Y     : Integer;
  TH, TW,             {text width and height}
  AW, AH : Integer; {width & height of rect enclosing angled label}
BEGIN
  R := ClientRect;
  GetObject(Font.Handle, SizeOf(TLF), @TLF);
  TLF.lfEscapement := (((Angle MOD 360) + 360) MOD 360) * 10;
  WITH Canvas DO
    BEGIN
      Font.Handle := CreateFontIndirect(TLF);
      WITH Brush DO
        IF NOT Transparent THEN
          BEGIN
            Style := bsSolid;
            Color := Self.Color;
          END
        ELSE Style := bsClear;
      TW := TextWidth(Caption);
      TH := TextHeight(Caption);
    END;
  AW := Round((TW * Cos(Angle*pi/180)) +
    (TH * Sin(Angle*pi/180)));
  AH := Round((TW * Cos((Angle+90)*pi/180)) +
    (TH * Sin((Angle+90)*pi/180)));
  X := (R.Right-AW) DIV 2;
  Y := (R.Bottom-AH) DIV 2;
  if not Enabled then Canvas.Font.Color := clGrayText;
  Canvas.TextOut(X, Y, Caption);
END;

procedure Register;
```

```
begin
  RegisterComponents('NJR', [TAngleLabel]);
  RegisterPropertyEditor(TypeInfo(TAngle), TAngleLabel,
    'Angle', TAngleProperty);
end;

end.
```

TANGLEPROPERTY

P_ANGLE.PAS

```
unit p_angle;

interface
USES SysUtils, WinTypes, WinProcs, Messages, Classes, Dialogs,
  DsgnIntF;
type
  TAngle = Integer;
  TAngleProperty = Class(TIntegerProperty)
    function GetAttributes: TPropertyAttributes; override;
    procedure Edit; override;
  end;

(*NO procedure Register; registered by c_anglab.pas*)

implementation
uses Forms, Controls, P_angleu;

function TAngleProperty.GetAttributes: TPropertyAttributes;
BEGIN
  Result := [paDialog, paMultiSelect];
END;

procedure TAngleProperty.Edit;
BEGIN
  WITH TAngleEditForm.Create(Application) DO
    try
      Angle := GetOrdValue;
      IF ShowModal = mrOK THEN
        SetOrdValue(Angle);
    finally
      Free;
    end;
END;

end.
```

P_ANGLEU.DEX

```
object AngleEditForm: TAngleEditForm
  BorderStyle = bsDialog
  Caption = 'Angle Editor'
```

```
object PaintBox1: TPaintBox
  DragCursor = crCross
  DragMode = dmAutomatic
  OnDragOver = PaintBox1DragOver
  OnPaint = PaintBox1Paint
end
object Label1: TLabel
  Caption = 'Angle:'
end
object Edit1: TEdit
  Text = '0'
  OnChange = Edit1Change
end
object BitBtn1: TBitBtn
  Kind = bkOK
end
object BitBtn2: TBitBtn
  Kind = bkCancel
end
end
```

P_ANGLEU.PAS

```
unit P_Angleu;

interface

uses SysUtils, WinTypes, WinProcs, Messages, Classes, Graphics,
  Controls, Forms, Dialogs, ExtCtrls, StdCtrls, Buttons;

type
  TAngleEditForm = class(TForm)
    PaintBox1: TPaintBox;
    Edit1: TEdit;
    Label1: TLabel;
    BitBtn1: TBitBtn;
    BitBtn2: TBitBtn;
    procedure PaintBox1Paint(Sender: TObject);
    procedure PaintBox1DragOver(Sender, Source: TObject;
      X, Y: Integer; State: TDragState; var Accept: Boolean);
    procedure Edit1Change(Sender: TObject);
  private
    fAngle: Integer;
    procedure SetAngle(Value: Integer);
  public
    property Angle: Integer read fAngle write SetAngle;
  end;

var AngleEditForm: TAngleEditForm;

implementation

{$R *.DFM}

procedure TAngleEditForm.SetAngle(Value: Integer);
```

```
begin
  Value := ((Value MOD 360) + 360) MOD 360;
  IF value = fAngle THEN Exit;
  fAngle := Value;
  PaintBox1.Refresh;
  Edit1.Text := IntToStr(fAngle);
end;

procedure TAngleEditForm.PaintBox1Paint(Sender: TObject);
begin
  WITH PaintBox1, Canvas DO
    BEGIN
      Brush.Style := bsClear;
      Pen.Color    := clWindowText;
      Ellipse(0, 0, Width, Height);
      MoveTo(Width DIV 2, Height DIV 2);
      LineTo(PenPos.X + Round(Width/2*Cos(fAngle*pi/180)),
        PenPos.Y - Round(Height/2*Sin(fAngle*pi/180)));
    END;
end;

procedure TAngleEditForm.PaintBox1DragOver(Sender, Source: TObject;
  X, Y: Integer; State: TDragState; var Accept: Boolean);
begin
  WITH Sender AS TPaintBox DO
    BEGIN
      IF X = Width DIV 2 THEN
        IF Y > Height DIV 2 THEN fAngle := 270
        ELSE fAngle := 90
      ELSE
        BEGIN
          fAngle := Round(ArcTan(((Height DIV 2)-Y)/
            (X-(Width DIV 2)))*180/pi);
          IF X < Width DIV 2 THEN
            fAngle := (fAngle + 540) MOD 360
          ELSE fAngle := (fAngle + 360) MOD 360;
        END;
      Refresh;
      Edit1.Text:= IntToStr(fAngle);
    END;
end;

procedure TAngleEditForm.Edit1Change(Sender: TObject);
begin
  {next line forces angle into range 0..359 and updates display}
  Angle := StrToIntDef(Edit1.Text, 0);
  Edit1.SelStart := Length(Edit1.Text);
end;

end.
```

The TAngleLabel is descended from TCustomLabel, not from TLabel. Remember, in Delphi, a descendant object can make a Protected property Public or Published, but not the reverse. A TAngleLabel component always centers itself in the bounding rectangle, so it shouldn't have Alignment and AutoSize properties. It always shows a single line without an underlined mnemonic character, so WordWrap and ShowAccelChar don't belong. Thus, TAngleLabel is defined as a descendant of TCustomLabel that publishes all the same properties as TLabel, *except* those four.

TAngleLabel paints itself using an enhanced version of the techniques from the preceding example. It sets the angle for its TrueType font by getting the logical font data into a TLogFont, changing the lfEscapement field, and creating a new font with the desired angle. Then, it uses trigonometry to calculate the correct X,Y coordinates to draw the label's text centered in its bounding rectangle.

Changes to the font are handled in the CMFontChanged method—if the specified font isn't a TrueType font, this method beeps, warns the user, and changes the font to Arial. Changing the Angle property calls the private SetAngle method. If the new angle is indeed different, this method invalidates the label, forcing a repaint.

The Register procedure in C_ANGLAB.PAS registers the TAngleLabel component and registers a property editor for the Angle property of TAngleLabel components only. The TAngleProperty's GetAttributes method tells Delphi that multiple angled labels can have their angles set at once (paMultiSelect), and that a dialog box is available for editing the property (paDialog). The Edit method calls on the dialog, which is contained in the P_Angleu unit.

The program in Figure 9-3 is a simple test engine for the angled label component. The angled label starts off at 90 degrees, but adjusts to whatever angle you set in the spin edit box.

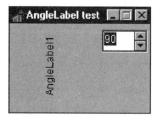

FIGURE 9-3: This program simply tests the angled label component and shows that it works.

ANGLTST

ANGLTSTU.DEX

```
object Form1: TForm1
  BorderIcons = [biSystemMenu, biMinimize]
  BorderStyle = bsSingle
```

```
        Caption = 'AngleLabel test'
        Position = poDefault
        Scaled = False
        object AngleLabel1: TAngleLabel
          Caption = 'AngleLabel1'
          ParentFont = False
          Transparent = True
          Angle = 90
        end
        object SpinEdit1: TSpinEdit
          Increment = 10
          MaxValue = 359
          MinValue = 0
          Value = 90
          OnChange = SpinEdit1Change
        end
      end
```

ANGLTSTU.PAS

```
unit Angltstu;

interface

uses SysUtils, WinTypes, WinProcs, Messages, Classes, Graphics,
  Controls, Forms, Dialogs, c_anglab, StdCtrls, Spin;

type
  TForm1 = class(TForm)
    SpinEdit1: TSpinEdit;
    AngleLabel1: TAngleLabel;
    procedure SpinEdit1Change(Sender: TObject);
  end;

var Form1: TForm1;

implementation

{$R *.DFM}

procedure TForm1.SpinEdit1Change(Sender: TObject);
begin
  WITH Sender AS TSpinEdit DO
    AngleLabel1.Angle := Value;
end;

end.
```

Because the angled label component does all the work internally, the test program is extremely simple. The OnChange handler for the spin edit box sets the label's angle to the spin edit box's value property.

Use the TAngleLabel component any time you need a label that runs top to bottom, bottom to top, or any angle you choose.

Dragging Graphics

Delphi components have the drag-and-drop capability built right into them. Set a component's DragMode to dmAutomatic, create OnDragOver and OnDragDrop handlers for the form, and you've got drag-and-drop working. Unless you write code to do otherwise, the dragged component is represented by a drag cursor. This section will demonstrate dragging with a full rectangular outline of the dragged component, and will explore other uses of drag-and-drop.

 Dragging and dropping components at runtime

16 32

When a Delphi component is being dragged, it appears as a drag cursor. It's possible to write OnDragOver event handlers for all the other components on the form that allow the dragged component to move with the cursor. However, this brings its problems. The component may flicker as it moves, and it may display _behind_ other components.

The simplest solution to this problem is to drag an outline of the component rather than the component itself. And, rather than try to draw on top of other components, we'll draw on a _picture_ of the actual form. Figure 9-4 shows the result.

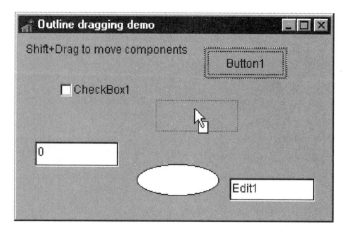

FIGURE 9-4: The components on this form have been moved around by dragging; at present, an outline of the pushbutton is being moved.

DRAGOUT

DRAGOUTU.DEX

```
object Form1: TForm1
  Caption = 'Outline dragging demo'
  Position = poDefault
  Scaled = False
  object Notebook1: TNotebook
    Align = alClient
    object TPage
      Caption = 'Default'
      object Label1: TLabel
        Caption = 'Shift+Drag to move components'
        OnEndDrag = Edit1EndDrag
        OnMouseDown = Button1MouseDown
      end
      object Shape1: TShape
        Shape = stEllipse
        OnEndDrag = Edit1EndDrag
        OnMouseDown = Button1MouseDown
      end
      object Button1: TButton
        Caption = 'Button1'
        OnEndDrag = Edit1EndDrag
        OnMouseDown = Button1MouseDown
      end
      object Edit1: TEdit
        Text = 'Edit1'
        OnEndDrag = Edit1EndDrag
        OnMouseDown = Button1MouseDown
      end
      object CheckBox1: TCheckBox
        Caption = 'CheckBox1'
        OnEndDrag = Edit1EndDrag
        OnMouseDown = Button1MouseDown
      end
      object SpinEdit1: TSpinEdit
        OnEndDrag = Edit1EndDrag
        OnMouseDown = Button1MouseDown
      end
    end
    object TPage
      Caption = 'Dragging'
      object PaintBox1: TPaintBox
        Align = alClient
        OnDragOver = PaintBox1DragOver
        OnPaint = PaintBox1Paint
      end
    end
  end
end
```

DRAGOUTU.PAS

```pascal
unit Dragoutu;

interface

uses SysUtils, WinTypes, WinProcs, Messages, Classes, Graphics,
  Controls, Forms, Dialogs, ExtCtrls, Spin, StdCtrls;

type
  TForm1 = class(TForm)
    Notebook1: TNotebook;
    Button1: TButton;
    PaintBox1: TPaintBox;
    Label1: TLabel;
    Edit1: TEdit;
    CheckBox1: TCheckBox;
    Shape1: TShape;
    SpinEdit1: TSpinEdit;
    procedure Button1MouseDown(Sender: TObject; Button:
      TMouseButton; Shift: TShiftState; X, Y: Integer);
    procedure PaintBox1Paint(Sender: TObject);
    procedure PaintBox1DragOver(Sender, Source: TObject;
      X, Y: Integer; State: TDragState; var Accept: Boolean);
    procedure Edit1EndDrag(Sender, Target: TObject;
      X, Y: Integer);
  private
    Img        : TBitmap;
    XOfs, YOfs : Integer;
    DragR      : TRect;
  end;

var Form1: TForm1;

implementation

{$R *.DFM}

procedure TForm1.Button1MouseDown(Sender: TObject; Button:
  TMouseButton; Shift: TShiftState; X, Y: Integer);
begin
  IF Shift * [ssShift, ssDouble] <> [ssShift] THEN Exit;
  Img := GetFormImage;
  Notebook1.PageIndex := 1;
  WITH Sender AS TControl DO
    BEGIN
      DragR := BoundsRect;
      OffsetRect(DragR, -X, -Y);
      XOfs := X;
      YOfs := Y;
      BeginDrag(True);
    END;
end;

procedure TForm1.PaintBox1Paint(Sender: TObject);
begin
  PaintBox1.Canvas.Draw(0,0,Img);
end;
```

```
procedure TForm1.PaintBox1DragOver(Sender, Source: TObject;
  X, Y: Integer; State: TDragState; var Accept: Boolean);
begin
  IF (X=DragR.Left+XOfs) AND (Y=DragR.Top+YOfs) THEN Exit;
  PaintBox1.Canvas.DrawFocusRect(DragR);
  OffsetRect(DragR, X-DragR.Left-XOfs, Y-DragR.Top-YOfs);
  PaintBox1.Canvas.DrawFocusRect(DragR);
end;

procedure TForm1.Edit1EndDrag(Sender, Target: TObject;
  X, Y: Integer);
begin
  IF Target = PaintBox1 THEN
    WITH Sender AS TControl DO
      BEGIN
        Left := DragR.Left;
        Top  := DragR.Top;
        BringToFront;
      END;
  Notebook1.PageIndex := 0;
  Img.Free;
end;

end.
```

The client area of the form is completely filled by a notebook component with two pages. The first page contains the form's components, all of which are attached to the same OnMouseDown and OnEndDrag event handlers. The second page is filled by a paint box.

If the user is holding down Shift and isn't double-clicking, the OnMouseDown handler prepares for outline dragging. It copies the form's image (returned by the FormImage method) to a private data field named Img and flips to the second page of the notebook. It records the bounding rectangle of the component that will be dragged into the data field DragR. And it stores the offset of the mouse cursor within that rectangle in the private data fields XOfs and YOfs. With preparations made, it calls the component's BeginDrag method, passing True to immediately start dragging.

As soon as the second page of the notebook is made visible, the paint box's OnPaint handler kicks in. This handler simply draws the form image that was saved. The paint box's OnDragOver handler moves a dotted rectangle as the mouse cursor moves. The dotted rectangle is drawn using the Windows API function DrawFocusRect. This function has a special virtue—if you call it twice with the same coordinates, the second rectangle wipes out the first.

When the user releases the mouse, it triggers an OnEndDrag event in the dragged component. If the mouse was over the paint box, the component is moved to its new location. Whether or not the drag process ended in a valid drop, the event handler flips back to the first page of the notebook and frees the stored image of the form.

Dragging components over other components on the form can get quite complicated. By dragging over a mere picture of the form, this program gains considerable freedom and simplicity.

"Rubber-band" drawing of a rectangle

16 32

The Windows paint accessory has a handy feature. It lets you draw a rectangle by dragging a "stretchy" outline, and then "snaps" the final rectangle into place. As Figure 9-5 shows, a Delphi program can get this same effect! This is a simple demonstration of technique, but you can apply it in many ways. You don't have to draw a rectangle; instead, you might copy the marked rectangle to a different bitmap. The details are up to you.

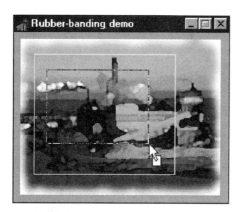

FIGURE 9-5: The large, yellow rectangle was already drawn; within it, another rectangle is being stretched into place.

RUBAND

RUBANDU.DEX

```
object Form1: TForm1
  BorderIcons = [biSystemMenu, biMinimize]
  BorderStyle = bsSingle
  Caption = 'Rubber-banding demo'
  Position = poDefault
  Scaled = False
  object Image1: TImage
    Stretch = True
    OnDragOver = Image1DragOver
```

```
      OnEndDrag = Image1EndDrag
      OnMouseDown = Image1MouseDown
    end
  end
```

RUBANDU.PAS

```
unit Rubandu;

interface

uses SysUtils, WinTypes, WinProcs, Messages, Classes, Graphics,
  Controls, Forms, Dialogs, ExtCtrls;

type
  TForm1 = class(TForm)
    Image1: TImage;
    procedure Image1MouseDown(Sender: TObject; Button:
      TMouseButton; Shift: TShiftState; X, Y: Integer);
    procedure Image1DragOver(Sender, Source: TObject;
      X, Y: Integer; State: TDragState; var Accept: Boolean);
    procedure Image1EndDrag(Sender, Target: TObject; X,Y: Integer);
  private
    TheRect : TRect;
  end;

var Form1: TForm1;

implementation

{$R *.DFM}

procedure TForm1.Image1MouseDown(Sender: TObject; Button:
  TMouseButton; Shift: TShiftState; X, Y: Integer);
begin
  TheRect := Bounds(X, Y, 0, 0);
  WITH Image1.Picture.Bitmap.Canvas DO
    BEGIN
      Brush.Style := bsClear;
      Pen.Color    := clWhite;
      Pen.Mode     := pmXor;
    END;
  Image1.BeginDrag(True);
end;

procedure TForm1.Image1DragOver(Sender, Source: TObject;
  X, Y: Integer; State: TDragState; var Accept: Boolean);
begin
  IF Source <> Sender THEN Accept := False
  ELSE WITH Image1.Picture.Bitmap.Canvas DO
    BEGIN
      WITH TheRect DO Rectangle(Left, Top, Right, Bottom);
      TheRect.BottomRight := Point(X,Y);
      WITH TheRect DO Rectangle(Left, Top, Right, Bottom);
    END;
end;
```

```
procedure TForm1.Image1EndDrag(Sender, Target: TObject;
  X, Y: Integer);
begin
  IF Target = Sender THEN {draw yellow rectangle}
    WITH Image1.Picture.Bitmap.Canvas DO
      BEGIN
        Pen.Color := clYellow;
        Pen.Mode  := pmCopy;
        Rectangle(TheRect.Left, TheRect.Top, X, Y);
      END
  ELSE  {erase "rubber band" rectangle}
    WITH Image1.Picture.Bitmap.Canvas DO
      WITH TheRect DO Rectangle(Left, Top, Right, Bottom);
end;

end.
```

Before attempting to run this program, load a bitmap into the image component. In the figure, FACTORY.BMP from the Delphi 1.0's image collection is displayed. The preceding example used the DrawFocusRect API function to draw and remove a rectangle. This program just uses the canvas's Rectangle method. The pen's mode property is set to pmXor and its color to clWhite. Lines drawn with this pen stand out even on a "busy" image, because every pixel along the line is inverted. Drawing another line in the same place inverts the pixels again, restoring them to their original colors.

The program uses a private data field called TheRect to track the position of the "rubber band" rectangle. Once the dragging process has started, each OnDragOver event wipes out the previous rectangle and draws the new rectangle. If dragging ends with a valid drag-drop on the image, the OnEndDrag handler draws a yellow rectangle at the stored location; otherwise, it simply erases the last "rubber band" rectangle.

 Creating a splitter bar

16 32

When a resizeable form has multiple panes, it's common to let the user resize the panes using a splitter bar. That's easy to do with drag-and-drop in Delphi, as long as you're willing to let the cursor represent the splitter bar during the process of resizing panes. However, the visual effect is much improved if the split is represented by a full vertical line, as shown in Figure 9-6. The vertical split line moves with the mouse cursor, and when the mouse is released, the panels that make up the left and right sides of the form resize to match the new split.

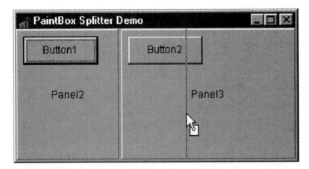

FIGURE 9-6: The split line tracks with the drag cursor; when the mouse is released, the panels resize.

SPLITP

FILE SPLITPU.DEX

```
object Form1: TForm1
  Caption = 'PaintBox Splitter Demo'
  Position = poDefault
  Scaled = False
  object Notebook1: TNotebook
    Align = alClient
    object TPage
      Caption = 'Regular'
      object Panel1: TPanel
        Cursor = crHSplit
        Align = alLeft
        BevelOuter = bvNone
        OnEndDrag = Panel1EndDrag
        OnMouseDown = Panel1MouseDown
      end
      object Panel2: TPanel
        Align = alLeft
        Caption = 'Panel2'
        object Button1: TButton
          Caption = 'Button1'
        end
      end
      object Panel3: TPanel
        Align = alClient
        Caption = 'Panel3'
        object Button2: TButton
          Caption = 'Button2'
        end
      end
    end
    object TPage
```

```
        Caption = 'Split'
        object PaintBox1: TPaintBox
          Align = alClient
          OnDragDrop = PaintBox1DragDrop
          OnDragOver = PaintBox1DragOver
          OnPaint = PaintBox1Paint
        end
      end
    end
end
```

SPLITPU.PAS

```
unit Splitpu;

interface

uses SysUtils, WinTypes, WinProcs, Messages, Classes, Graphics,
  Controls, Forms, Dialogs, ExtCtrls, StdCtrls;

type
  TForm1 = class(TForm)
    Notebook1: TNotebook;
    PaintBox1: TPaintBox;
    Panel1: TPanel;
    Panel2: TPanel;
    Panel3: TPanel;
    Button1: TButton;
    Button2: TButton;
    procedure Panel1MouseDown(Sender: TObject; Button:
      TMouseButton; Shift: TShiftState; X, Y: Integer);
    procedure Panel1EndDrag(Sender, Target: TObject; X,Y: Integer);
    procedure PaintBox1DragOver(Sender, Source: TObject;
      X, Y: Integer; State: TDragState; var Accept: Boolean);
    procedure PaintBox1Paint(Sender: TObject);
    procedure PaintBox1DragDrop(Sender, Source: TObject;
      X, Y: Integer);
  private
    Img  : TBitmap;
    WasX : Integer;
  end;

var Form1: TForm1;

implementation

{$R *.DFM}

procedure TForm1.Panel1MouseDown(Sender: TObject; Button:
  TMouseButton; Shift: TShiftState; X, Y: Integer);
begin
  Img  := GetFormImage;
  WasX := -(TControl(Sender).Left+X);
  Panel1.BeginDrag(True);
  Notebook1.PageIndex := 1;
end;
```

```
procedure TForm1.Panel1EndDrag(Sender, Target: TObject;
  X, Y: Integer);
begin
  Notebook1.PageIndex := 0;
  Img.Free;
end;

procedure TForm1.PaintBox1DragOver(Sender, Source: TObject;
  X, Y: Integer; State: TDragState; var Accept: Boolean);
begin
  Accept := Source=Panel1;
  IF Accept AND (WasX > 0) THEN
    WITH PaintBox1, Canvas DO
      BEGIN
        PolyLine([Point(WasX, 0), Point(WasX, Height)]);
        PolyLine([Point(X, 0),    Point(X, Height)]);
        WasX := X;
      END;
end;

procedure TForm1.PaintBox1Paint(Sender: TObject);
begin
  WITH Sender AS TPaintBox, Canvas DO
    BEGIN
      Draw(0,0,Img);
      IF WasX < 0 THEN {draw initial XOR-line}
        BEGIN
          WasX       := -WasX;
          Pen.Mode   := pmXor;
          Pen.Color  := clWhite;
          PolyLine([Point(WasX, 0), Point(WasX, Height)]);
        END;
    END;
end;

procedure TForm1.PaintBox1DragDrop(Sender, Source: TObject;
  X, Y: Integer);
begin
  Panel2.Width := TControl(Sender).Left + X;
end;

end.
```

You could draw a kind of splitter bar right on the form, but the line you draw will appear to be *behind* components on the form. The simplest way to ensure that the split line is drawn correctly is to draw on a *picture* of the form. This technique was used in the outline-dragging example earlier in this chapter.

The mechanics of the pane-resizing process are handled by three panels, two with the Align property set to alLeft and one with Align set to alClient. The middle panel is very narrow and represents the splitter bar. Pane-size adjustment is accomplished by resizing the left-hand panel, which forces the other two panels to accommodate. These three panels reside on the first page of a two-page notebook that fills the form. The other page is filled by a paint box.

The Cursor property of the splitter panel is set to crHSplit. This panel's OnMouseDown handler copies the form's image (returned by the GetFormImage method) to a private data field, records the current X-position of the mouse in another private data field, flips to the notebook's second page, and calls the panel's BeginDrag method.

The paint box immediately displays the stored image of the form and draws a line on it representing the splitter bar. The canvas's pen color is set to clWhite and its mode to pmXor, so each pixel along a line drawn with this pen has its color inverted. More important, redrawing in the same location will invert the pixels again, restoring them to their original color.

As the mouse moves, the paint box's OnDragOver event handler erases the previous split line and draws a new one at the new location. The OnDragDrop handler sets the width of the left-hand panel to the final split line location. Finally, whether or not a valid drop has occurred, the splitter panel's OnEndDrag event handler flips back to the notebook's first page and frees the stored form image.

There are a couple of nice things about this implementation of a splitter bar. First, it doesn't attempt to resize the panels while the mouse is being dragged, so it avoids any ugly flicker as components get redrawn. Second, there's no need for the rest of the components on the form to respond to the dragging process, because the dragging actually occurs over the paint box.

Bitmaps and Metafiles

Delphi's collection of graphic image objects includes the TImage component, and the TBitmap, TIcon, and TMetafile objects. These objects make short work of tasks like loading an image from a file—tasks that would have taken dozens of lines of code. But you can make them even more powerful by bringing in a few of the Windows API drawing functions.

Creating a metafile

Windows metafiles are a great way to store graphics, since they don't need to store all the pixels. A metafile is basically a set of instructions for recreating the graphic. Not only that, metafiles can be played back at different sizes; they stretch better than bitmaps. Delphi's TMetafile object can load and save metafiles, but how do you create something for it to save?

As is common, the answer involves a combination of Delphi objects and Windows API functions. Figure 9-7 shows a 1960s style image created as a metafile by the Delphi program that follows. Nearly anything that you draw using Windows line drawing functions, such as Ellipse, Rectangle, and LineTo, can be stored as a metafile and used in your programs or as clip art in your favorite word processor.

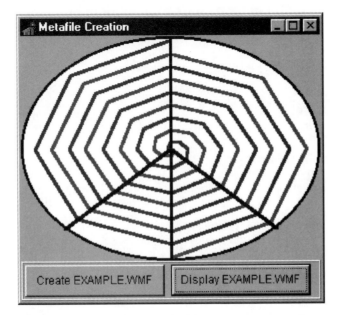

FIGURE 9-7: This pseudo-psychedelic image was created using Windows drawing functions and stored as a metafile.

CREMETA

CREMETAU.DEX

```
object Form1: TForm1
  Caption = 'Metafile Creation'
  Scaled = False
  object Image1: TImage
    Align = alClient
    Stretch = True
  end
  object Panel1: TPanel
    Align = alBottom
    BevelInner = bvLowered
    object Button1: TButton
```

```
        Caption = 'Create EXAMPLE.WMF'
        OnClick = Button1Click
      end
      object Button2: TButton
        Caption = 'Display EXAMPLE.WMF'
        OnClick = Button2Click
      end
    end
  end
end
```

CREMETAU.PAS

```
unit Cremetau;
{$IFDEF Win32}
HALT! Use CREM32.DPR instead
{$ENDIF}
interface

uses SysUtils, WinTypes, WinProcs, Messages, Classes, Graphics,
  Controls, Forms, Dialogs, StdCtrls, ExtCtrls;

type
  TForm1 = class(TForm)
    Image1: TImage;
    Panel1: TPanel;
    Button1: TButton;
    Button2: TButton;
    procedure Button1Click(Sender: TObject);
    procedure Button2Click(Sender: TObject);
  end;

var Form1: TForm1;

implementation

{$R *.DFM}
CONST W = 1000; H = 500; R2 = 353;

procedure TForm1.Button1Click(Sender: TObject);
VAR CDC : hDC;

  procedure spiral(CV: TCanvas; Colr: TColor; AngInc: Double;
    RInc: Integer; Sgn1, Sgn2: Integer);
  VAR Theta: Double;
  begin
    Sgn1 := Sgn1 DIV Abs(Sgn1);
    Sgn2 := Sgn2 DIV Abs(Sgn2);
    CV.pen.Color := Colr;
    Theta := 0;
    CV.MoveTo(H,H);
    WHILE Theta < pred(H DIV RInc) DO
      BEGIN
        Theta := Theta + AngInc;
        CV.LineTo(H+Sgn1*Round(RInc*Theta*Cos(Sgn2*Theta)),
                  H+Sgn1*Round(RInc*Theta*Sin(Sgn2*Theta)));
```

```
        END;
    end;
begin
  DeleteFile('EXAMPLE.WMF');
  WITH TBitmap.Create DO
    try
      CDC := CreateMetafile(NIL);
      Canvas.Handle := CDC;
      SetMapMode(Canvas.Handle, MM_ANISOTROPIC);
      SetWindowExt(Canvas.Handle, W, W);
      WITH Canvas DO
        BEGIN
          {==== replace with your own image-creation code ===}
          Brush.Color := clWhite;
          pen.Width := 10;
          pen.Style := psInsideFrame;
          pen.Color := clBlack;
          Ellipse(0,0,W,W);
          Spiral(Canvas, clRed, pi/4, 18, 1, 1);
          Spiral(Canvas, clBlue, pi/4, 18, -1, 1);
          Pen.Color := clBlack;
          PolyLine([Point(H,0), Point(H,H), Point(H-R2, H+R2),
            Point(H,H), Point(H,W), Point(H,H), Point(H+R2,H+R2)]);
          {====== end image-creation code =====}
        END;
      WITH TMetafile.Create DO
        try
          Handle := CloseMetafile(CDC);
          Inch   := W;
          Height := 128;
          Width  := 128;
          SaveToFile('EXAMPLE.WMF');
        finally
          Free;
        end;
    finally
      Free;
    end;
end;
procedure TForm1.Button2Click(Sender: TObject);
begin
  Image1.Picture.Metafile.LoadFromFile('EXAMPLE.WMF');
end;
end.
```

The first step toward creating a metafile in Delphi 1.0 is to create a bitmap and set its canvas's handle to the value returned by the CreateMetafile Windows function. The bitmap's canvas needs to have its mapping mode set to MM_ANISOTROPIC and its window extent to 1000 by 1000. After that, the program draws concentric blue and red spirals within an ellipse. (Technically, they are spirals of Archimedes, as the radius is directly proportional to the angle.) A single call to the PolyLine method draws a peace symbol within the ellipse. Naturally, you can modify these drawing functions to draw a different image!

When the drawing is finished, the program creates a metafile object and sets its handle to the metafile handle returned by the CloseMetafile function. The metafile's Inch property is set to match the window extent, and the Width and Height values will be used as defaults if, for example, you load the metafile into WinWord as clip art. The metafile's SaveToFile method saves the result. All that remains is to free the temporary metafile and bitmap objects. Just to prove it *did* something, the program's second button displays the created metafile by loading it into a TImage component.

Creating an enhanced metafile

32

The basic Windows metafile is fairly limited. You can do all the line drawing you want, but fonts don't scale with the rest of the image, and drawing bitmaps is chancy, as no palette information is saved. Calling a graphics function that isn't supported may have no effect, may return an error code, or may cause a GPF. That's why Borland didn't build support for metafile creation into the TMetafile object in Delphi 1.0. The enhanced metafile format, introduced with 32-bit Windows, supports all graphics functions, so Delphi 2.0's TMetafile object is substantially more powerful. Included in this power is built-in support for metafile creation, via the TMetafileCanvas object. Here is a version of the previous program, modified for use with Delphi 2.0.

CREM32

CREM32U.DEX

```
object Form1: TForm1
  Caption = 'Enhanced Metafile Creation'
  Scaled = False
  object Image1: TImage
    Align = alClient
    Stretch = True
  end
  object Panel1: TPanel
    Align = alBottom
    BevelInner = bvLowered
    object Button1: TButton
      Caption = 'Create EXAMPLE.EMF'
```

```
        OnClick = Button1Click
      end
      object Button2: TButton
        Caption = 'Display EXAMPLE.EMF'
        OnClick = Button2Click
      end
    end
  end
end
```

CREM32U.PAS

```
unit crem32u;
{$IFNDEF Win32}
HALT! Use CREMETA.DPR instead
{$ENDIF}
interface

uses SysUtils, Windows, Messages, Classes, Graphics, Controls,
  Forms, Dialogs, StdCtrls, ExtCtrls;

type
  TForm1 = class(TForm)
    Image1: TImage;
    Panel1: TPanel;
    Button1: TButton;
    Button2: TButton;
    procedure Button1Click(Sender: TObject);
    procedure Button2Click(Sender: TObject);
  end;

var Form1: TForm1;

implementation

{$R *.DFM}
CONST W = 1000; H = 500; R2 = 353;

procedure TForm1.Button1Click(Sender: TObject);
VAR
  TMF   : TMetaFile;
  TMFC  : TMetaFileCanvas;
  R     : TRect;
begin
  DeleteFile('EXAMPLE.EMF');
  TMF := TMetafile.Create;
  TMF.Width := W;
  TMF.Height := W;
  TMFC := TMetaFileCanvas.Create(TMF, 0);
  WITH TMFC DO
    try
      {==== replace with your own image-creation code ===}
      Brush.Color := clWhite;
      pen.Width := 10;
      pen.Style := psInsideFrame;
```

```
      pen.Color := clBlack;
      Ellipse(0,0, W, W);
      PolyLine([Point(H,0), Point(H,H), Point(H-R2, H+R2),
        Point(H,H), Point(H,W), Point(H,H), Point(H+R2,H+R2)]);
      SetBkMode(Handle, TRANSPARENT);
      Font.Color := clFuchsia;
      Font.Size := 720;
      Font.Name := 'WingDings';
      R := Rect(0, 0, 1000, 1000);
      DrawText(Handle, 'A', 1, R, DT_CENTER OR DT_SINGLELINE
        OR DT_VCENTER);
      {====== end image-creation code =====}
    finally
      Free;
    end;
    try
      TMF.SaveToFile('EXAMPLE.EMF');
    finally
      TMF.Free;
    end;
  end;
  procedure TForm1.Button2Click(Sender: TObject);
  begin
    Image1.Picture.Metafile.LoadFromFile('EXAMPLE.EMF');
  end;

  end.
```

Since fonts are supported and scaled properly in an enhanced metafile, this program replaces the spiral design with an oversized victory sign from the WingDings font. And, because scaling is automatic, you don't have to fool with the mapping mode or with setting the window or viewport extents. Instead, you simply set the Width and Height properties of the metafile object to dimensions that are convenient for the drawing you want to do.

The creation of an enhanced metafile in Delphi 2.0 is a four-step process:

1. Create a TMetafile object with the desired dimensions

2. Create a TMetafileCanvas object, passing it the TMetafile object

3. Call graphics functions to draw on the TMetafileCanvas

4. Destroy the TMetafileCanvas

Destroying a metafile to save it may sound incongruous, but it works. Internally, the TMetafileCanvas object's destructor passes its handle to the CloseEnhMetafile Windows API function, which returns a metafile handle corresponding to the drawing that was performed on the canvas. It assigns this handle to the Handle property of the TMetafile object that was originally passed to it.

Dragging a sprite

16 32

You can move a Delphi image component around on the screen, but it will always cover a rectangular area, even if the picture isn't rectangular. If you want to drag or animate a nonrectangular image, simply moving a TImage isn't sufficient.

One name for a nonrectangular movable image is *sprite*. Sprite programming is needed for animation and for drawing images with "transparent" areas that allow the underlying background to show through. Sprite programming in Delphi can be accomplished using nothing but Delphi graphics functions. Figure 9-8 shows a program that demonstrates how it's done, and provides a peek under the hood.

FIGURE 9-8: Normally, the three images at the right of the form would be hidden; they're shown in this program so you can see how sprite-drawing works.

MASKDEM

MASKDEMU.DEX

```
object Form1: TForm1
  BorderIcons = [biSystemMenu, biMinimize]
  BorderStyle = bsSingle
  Caption = 'Masked bitmap dragging demo'
  Position = poDefault
  Scaled = False
  OnCreate = FormCreate
  object Image1: TImage
    AutoSize = True
    DragCursor = crDefault
```

```
      OnDragOver = Image1DragOver
      OnEndDrag = Image1EndDrag
      OnMouseDown = Image1MouseDown
    end
    object TheSprite: TImage
    end
    object TheMask: TImage
    end
    object TheStorage: TImage
    end
    object Label1: TLabel
      Caption = 'Drag w/ mouse on bitmap'
    end
  end
end
```

MASKDEMU.PAS

```
unit Maskdemu;
interface

uses SysUtils, WinTypes, WinProcs, Messages, Classes, Graphics,
  Controls, Forms, Dialogs, StdCtrls, ExtCtrls;

type
  TForm1 = class(TForm)
    Image1: TImage;
    TheSprite: TImage;
    TheMask: TImage;
    TheStorage: TImage;
    Label1: TLabel;
    procedure Image1MouseDown(Sender: TObject; Button:
      TMouseButton; Shift: TShiftState; X, Y: Integer);
    procedure Image1DragOver(Sender, Source: TObject; X, Y:
      Integer; State: TDragState; var Accept: Boolean);
    procedure Image1EndDrag(Sender, Target: TObject; X, Y:
      Integer);
    procedure FormCreate(Sender: TObject);
  private
    WasX, WasY, BMW, BMH : Integer;
  end;

var Form1: TForm1;

implementation

{$R *.DFM}

procedure TForm1.Image1MouseDown(Sender: TObject; Button:
  TMouseButton; Shift: TShiftState; X, Y: Integer);
begin
  WasX := X; WasY := Y;
  TheStorage.Canvas.CopyRect(Rect(0, 0, BMW, BMH),
    Image1.Canvas, Bounds(X,Y, BMW, BMH));
  Image1.BeginDrag(True);
end;
```

```
procedure TForm1.Image1DragOver(Sender, Source: TObject; X, Y:
  Integer; State: TDragState; var Accept: Boolean);
VAR R1, R2 : TRect;
begin
  {draw stored section w/o sprite}
  R1 := Bounds(WasX, WasY, BMW, BMH);
  R2 := Rect(0, 0, BMW, BMH);
  Image1.Canvas.CopyRect(R1, TheStorage.Canvas, R2);
  WasX := X; WasY := Y;
  R1 := Bounds(X, Y, BMW, BMH);
  {store new section w/o sprite}
  TheStorage.Canvas.CopyRect(R2, Image1.Canvas, R1);
  Image1.Canvas.CopyMode := cmSrcInvert;
  {XOR sprite with image}
  Image1.Canvas.Draw(X, Y, TheSprite.Picture.Bitmap);
  Image1.Canvas.CopyMode := cmSrcAnd;
  {AND mask silhouette w/ image}
  Image1.Canvas.Draw(X, Y, TheMask.Picture.Bitmap);
  Image1.Canvas.CopyMode := cmSrcInvert;
  {XOR sprite with image again}
  Image1.Canvas.Draw(X, Y, TheSprite.Picture.Bitmap);
  Image1.Canvas.CopyMode := cmSrcCopy;
end;
procedure TForm1.Image1EndDrag(Sender, Target: TObject; X, Y:
  Integer);
begin
  Image1.Canvas.CopyRect(Bounds(WasX, WasY, BMW, BMH),
    TheStorage.Canvas, Rect(0, 0, BMW, BMH));
end;
procedure TForm1.FormCreate(Sender: TObject);
begin
  BMW := TheSprite.Width;
  BMH := TheSprite.Height;
  {Create mask w/ background color=white, image=black}
  WITH TheMask.Picture.Bitmap, Canvas DO
    BEGIN
      Width  := BMW;
      Height := BMH;
      Draw(0, 0, TheSprite.Picture.Bitmap);
      Brush.Color := TheSprite.Picture.Bitmap.TransparentColor;
      Monochrome := True;
    END;
end;
end.
```

The large bitmap here is an image control with CHEMICAL.BMP from Delphi's
IMAGES directory loaded. The top right bitmap is the sprite, a simple bitmap
consisting of two concentric circles. Note the olive background—this will become
the transparent part of the image.

The first step in animating the sprite bitmap is to create a corresponding mask bitmap. This is a monochrome bitmap the same size as the sprite, with black where the image should be opaque and white where the background should show through. Creating a mask bitmap is simple if you follow the strict sequence of events shown here. First, draw the sprite bitmap on the mask bitmap, set the brush for the mask bitmap's canvas to the color found in the sprite bitmap's top left pixel, and then set the mask's Monochrome property to True. This has the effect of turning all pixels matching the brush color to white, and all others to black.

In this example program, the sprite is not visible until the user presses the mouse button while over the background image. The image's OnMouseDown handler records the X,Y coordinates of the mouse event in private data fields, copies a rectangular chunk of the background to a storage bitmap the same size as the sprite, and starts the dragging process.

Each time the mouse moves, the OnDragOver handler goes through the same steps:

1. Copy the stored chunk of background back to its original location, wiping out the sprite.

2. Copy a chunk of background from the new location to storage.

3. Draw the sprite on the background using the SRCINVERT drawing mode, which XORs the image with the background.

4. Draw the mask on the background using the SRCAND mode, which blacks out the sprite area and leaves the background unchanged.

5. Draw the sprite on the background using SRCINVERT again. This restores the background to its original appearance, and draws the sprite image in the area blacked out in step 4.

All Windows programs that perform sprite animation have to go through a similar process. However, Delphi makes programming sprite animation substantially less complicated, because its canvas object handles many details that clutter a graphics program written strictly with Windows API functions.

Simulating VB PicClip control

Visual Basic's nifty PicClip control stores a multitude of small, same-sized bitmaps using just one bitmap handle. A Delphi program can do the same thing without resorting to loading PICCLIP.VBX.

It would be possible to create a component with the powers of the PicClip control, but it's so easy to do using a TImage that creating a component hardly seems worthwhile. The example program shown in Figure 9-9 extracts any one of the twelve small system bitmaps stored in the resource identified by the constant OBM_CHECKBOXES.

FIGURE 9-9: The drawing methods of the TImage component's canvas object make it simple to extract a particular rectangular area.

PICCLIP

PICCLIPU.DEX

```
object Form1: TForm1
  BorderIcons = [biSystemMenu, biMinimize]
  BorderStyle = bsSingle
  Caption = 'PicClip Equivalent'
  Font.Color = clBlack
  Position = poDefault
  Scaled = False
  OnCreate = FormCreate
  object Bevel1: TBevel
    Shape = bsFrame
  end
  object Image1: TImage
  end
  object Image2: TImage
  end
  object RadioGroup1: TRadioGroup
    Caption = 'Choose SubBitmap'
    Columns = 4
    OnClick = RadioGroup1Click
  end
end
```

PICCLIPU.PAS

```pascal
unit Picclipu;

interface

uses SysUtils, WinTypes, WinProcs, Messages, Classes, Graphics,
  Controls, Forms, Dialogs, ExtCtrls, StdCtrls;

type
  TForm1 = class(TForm)
    Image1: TImage;
    RadioGroup1: TRadioGroup;
    Image2: TImage;
    Bevel1: TBevel;
    procedure FormCreate(Sender: TObject);
    procedure RadioGroup1Click(Sender: TObject);
  private
    subW, subH : Word;
  end;

var Form1: TForm1;

implementation

{$R *.DFM}

procedure TForm1.FormCreate(Sender: TObject);
{$IFDEF Win32}
CONST OBM_CHECKBOXES = 32759;
{$ENDIF}
VAR Co, Ro: Integer;
begin
  Image1.Picture.Bitmap.Handle :=
    LoadBitmap(0, PChar(OBM_CHECKBOXES));
  subW := Image1.Picture.Bitmap.Width DIV 4;
  subH := Image1.Picture.Bitmap.Height DIV 3;
  FOR Co := 1 TO 4 DO
    FOR Ro := 1 TO 3 DO
      RadioGroup1.Items.Add(Format('R%d,C%d',[Ro, Co]));
  RadioGroup1.ItemIndex := 0;
  Image2.Canvas.CopyRect(Rect(0, 0, SubW, SubH), Image1.Canvas,
    Bounds(0, 0, SubW, SubH));
end;

procedure TForm1.RadioGroup1Click(Sender: TObject);
VAR Ro, Co : Word;
begin
  Ro := RadioGroup1.ItemIndex MOD 3;
  Co := RadioGroup1.ItemIndex DIV 3;
  Image2.Canvas.CopyRect(Rect(0, 0, SubW, SubH), Image1.Canvas,
    Bounds(Co*SubW, Ro*SubH, SubW, SubH));
end;

end.
```

As you can see, the OBM_CHECKBOXES bitmap resource loaded into Image1 contains a number of different views of the graphics used in radio buttons and check boxes—checked or unchecked, enabled or disabled, and so on. When you click on one of the radio buttons, the corresponding sub-bitmap gets copied to Image2. In a program that uses many small bitmaps, you could draw all of them as one large bitmap and use similar code to extract the small bitmaps when needed.

Creating a gradient fill background

`16` `32`

It seems that every set-up program in existence has a main window that shades from black at the top to dark blue at the bottom. How would a Delphi form get that effect?

You might think it would be enough to draw regions of different shades of blue in the form's WM_ERASEBKGND message response method. However, if you just do that, you'll get *dithered* shades of blue in 256-color mode. To get a true, smooth shading, like that in Figure 9-10, a program needs to check whether it's running in 256-color mode and adjust the palette accordingly.

FIGURE 9-10: Experiment with changing the number of blue levels in 256-color mode, up to a maximum of 234.

GRADBAK

GRADBAKU.DEX

```
object Form1: TForm1
  Position = poDefault
  Scaled = False
```

```
      OnCreate = FormCreate
      OnDestroy = FormDestroy
    object Label1: TLabel
      Caption = 'Big Label'
      Font.Color = clWhite
      Font.Height = -48
      Font.Name = 'Times New Roman'
      ParentFont = False
      Transparent = True
    end
  end
```

GRADBAKU.PAS

```pascal
unit Gradbaku;

interface

uses SysUtils, WinTypes, WinProcs, Messages, Classes, Graphics,
  Controls, Forms, Dialogs, StdCtrls, ExtCtrls;

type
  TForm1 = class(TForm)
    Label1: TLabel;
    procedure FormCreate(Sender: TObject);
    procedure FormDestroy(Sender: TObject);
  private
    BluePh   : hPalette;
    NumBlues, BlueLevel, BlueDelta : Integer;
    procedure CreateParams(VAR Params: TCreateParams);
      override;
    function GetPalette : hPalette; override;
    procedure WMEraseBkgnd(VAR Msg: TWmEraseBkgnd);
      message WM_ERASEBKGND;
  end;

var Form1: TForm1;

implementation
{$R *.DFM}

procedure TForm1.CreateParams(VAR Params: TCreateParams);
begin
  Inherited CreateParams(Params);
  WITH Params.WindowClass DO Style := Style OR CS_VREDRAW;
end;

procedure TForm1.FormCreate(Sender: TObject);
begin
  Caption := '%d blues gradient fill (%spalette)';
  IF GetDeviceCaps(Canvas.Handle, RASTERCAPS) AND RC_PALETTE=0 THEN
    BEGIN
      NumBlues := 256;
      Caption  := Format(Caption, [NumBlues, 'no ']);
    END
```

```
        ELSE
          BEGIN
            NumBlues := 64; {try 16, 32, 64, 128, or 234}
            Caption  := Format(Caption, [NumBlues, '']);
          END;
        BlueDelta := 256 DIV NumBlues;
        IF BlueDelta < 1 THEN BlueDelta := 1;
        GetPalette;
        Perform(WM_ERASEBKGND, Canvas.Handle, 0);
      end;
      procedure TForm1.FormDestroy(Sender: TObject);
      begin
        DeleteObject(BluePh);
      end;
      procedure TForm1.WMEraseBkgnd(VAR Msg: TWmEraseBkgnd);
      VAR
        OldPalette    : hPalette;
        Colr, OldColr : Integer;
        N             : LongInt;
        R             : TRect;
      begin
        Canvas.Handle := Msg.DC;
        IF BluePh = 0 THEN
          BlueLevel := 255 - (NumBlues-1)*BlueDelta
        ELSE
          BEGIN
            OldPalette := SelectPalette(Canvas.Handle,BluePh,False);
            RealizePalette(Canvas.Handle);
          END;
        R := Bounds(0, 0, ClientWidth, 0);
        OldColr := 0;
        FOR N := 0 TO ClientHeight DO
          BEGIN
            Colr := N*NumBlues DIV ClientHeight;
            IF Colr = NumBlues THEN Dec(Colr);
            IF (Colr <> OldColr) OR (N = ClientHeight) THEN
              BEGIN
                OldColr  := Colr;
                R.Top    := R.Bottom;
                R.Bottom := N;
                IF BluePh = 0 THEN
                  Canvas.Brush.Color := RGB(0, 0, BlueLevel)
                ELSE Canvas.Brush.Color := PaletteIndex(Colr+10);
                BlueLevel := BlueLevel + BlueDelta;
                Canvas.FillRect(R);
              END;
          END;
        IF BluePH <> 0 THEN
          SelectPalette(Canvas.Handle, OldPalette, False);
        Msg.Result := 1;
        Canvas.Handle := 0;
      end;
```

```
function TForm1.GetPalette: hPalette;
VAR
  N, PalSize : Integer;
  BluePal    : PLogPalette;
begin
  IF BluePH <> 0 THEN Result := BluePH
  ELSE IF GetDeviceCaps(Canvas.Handle, RASTERCAPS) AND
    RC_PALETTE=0 THEN Result := 0
  ELSE
    BEGIN
      PalSize := SizeOf(TLogPalette) +
        (10+NumBlues)*SizeOf(TPaletteEntry);
      GetMem(BluePal, PalSize);
      FillChar(BluePal^, PalSize, 0);
      BluePal^.palVersion    := $300;
      BluePal^.palNumEntries := 10+NumBlues;
      GetSystemPaletteEntries(Canvas.Handle, 0, 10,
        BluePal^.PalPalEntry);
      BlueLevel := 255 - (NumBlues-1)*BlueDelta;
      {$R-}
      FOR N := 0 TO NumBlues-1 DO
        WITH BluePal^.PalPalEntry[N+10] DO
          BEGIN
            peBlue     := BlueLevel;
            peFlags    := PC_NOCOLLAPSE;
            BlueLevel  := BlueLevel + BlueDelta;
          END;
      {$R+}
      BluePh := CreatePalette(BluePal^);
      FreeMem(BluePal, PalSize);
      Result := BluePh;
    END;
end;

end.
```

The form's OnCreate event handler checks whether the system is running in a palette-based video mode, and sets the caption to indicate the mode. In a 256-color mode, it uses 64 shades of blue; in nonpalette-based modes, it uses 256. A call to the overridden GetPalette method initializes a palette big enough for the ten system colors at the beginning, plus the 64 levels of blue; subsequent calls to GetPalette will return this palette. In a nonpalette-based mode, GetPalette simply returns zero.

The gradient fill background is drawn in response to the WM_ERASEBKGND message; the OnCreate event handler sends this message to force the initial display. The WM_ERASEBKGND message response method starts at the top of the form and paints successive rectangular portions of the client area with brighter and brighter shades of blue. If the video mode is palette-based, it selects the special, blue-only palette, and uses the Windows API function PaletteIndex to get the correct color for each rectangle. Otherwise, it simply calculates the color using the RGB function, passing 0 for red and green and a steadily increasing value for blue.

Note that the WM_ERASEBKGND response method starts by setting the form's Canvas.Handle to the device context passed with the message, and ends by setting Canvas.Handle to zero. You would think that the passed DC would be the same as the form's own DC (represented by Canvas.Handle), but, in fact, the passed DC contains clipping information that's necessary for correct painting. The next time Canvas.Handle is needed, the form will recreate it automatically.

On systems with nonpalette-based video, there's no problem using 256 shades of blue. However, in 256-color mode, you should restrict yourself to 32 or 64 levels of blue. As you assign more and more palette "slots" to levels of blue, you begin to make it hard for Windows to display, for example, a 256-color wallpaper. If you use all but the reserved twenty system palette entries in a blue-shade palette, then every nonblue pixel will be painted with the nearest system color. Don't even think about using the Windows API function SetSystemPaletteUse to permit changing all but two of the system colors. If you did that, everything on the screen would be black, white, or blue.

CHAPTER 10

Various Components

*T*his chapter collects solutions based on a variety of Delphi components not previously covered. The button family is represented, of course; other items deal with labels, panels, and common dialogs. You'll learn to build buttons with multiline text, to control the placement of common dialogs on the screen, and to use an icon as the glyph for a speed button or a bitmapped button.

Button Components

Buttons are ubiquitous in Windows programs. Users *understand* buttons; push them and something happens. A doorbell rings, a trapdoor opens, a dialog box goes away. Besides the basic button component, the one that wraps the standard Windows button control, Delphi has two others: the bitmap button and the speed button. Both of these can display a bitmap and a caption, though normally the speed button's caption is blank. The main distinction between the two is that the speed button has no window handle of its own, so pressing it does not change the focus away from the currently active control. And, of course, the absence of a window handle means that a speed button consumes fewer Windows resources.

 Using a bitmap resource as a button glyph

16 32

The glyph bitmaps used by bitmap buttons and speed buttons can contain up to four images, representing the button when it's enabled, disabled, pushed down, or latched down. The usual course of action is to load these buttons at design time. However, if several buttons use the same glyph, it's wasteful to load them all at design time. If the glyph were loaded directly from a resource at runtime, only one copy would be present in the .EXE file. Loading from a resource is definitely possible, but a multi-image glyph can come out looking terrible, like the right-hand column in Figure 10-1. One simple line of code fixes the glyphs, as shown in the left-hand column.

FIGURE 10-1: Loading a multi-image glyph bitmap directly from a resource yields the unfortunate results shown in the right-hand column of this program; one line of code corrects the problem.

GLYRES

GLYRESU.DEX

```
object Form1: TForm1
  BorderIcons = [biSystemMenu, biMinimize]
  BorderStyle = bsDialog
  Caption = 'Glyph from RES'
  Position = poDefault
  Scaled = False
  OnCreate = FormCreate
  object SpeedButton1: TSpeedButton
  end
  object SpeedButton2: TSpeedButton
  end
  object Label1: TLabel
    Caption = 'Right'
  end
  object Label2: TLabel
    Caption = 'Wrong'
  end
  object SpeedButton3: TSpeedButton
    Enabled = False
  end
  object SpeedButton4: TSpeedButton
    Enabled = False
  end
  object AngleLabel1: TAngleLabel
    Caption = 'Enabled'
```

```
      Transparent = True
      Angle = 90
    end
    object AngleLabel2: TAngleLabel
      Caption = 'Disabled'
      Transparent = True
      Angle = 90
    end
  end
end
```

GLYRESU.PAS

```
unit Glyresu;

interface

uses SysUtils, WinTypes, WinProcs, Messages, Classes, Graphics,
  Controls, Forms, Dialogs, Buttons, ExtCtrls, StdCtrls,
  C_anglab;

type
  TForm1 = class(TForm)
    SpeedButton1: TSpeedButton;
    SpeedButton2: TSpeedButton;
    Label1: TLabel;
    Label2: TLabel;
    SpeedButton3: TSpeedButton;
    SpeedButton4: TSpeedButton;
    AngleLabel1: TAngleLabel;
    AngleLabel2: TAngleLabel;
    procedure FormCreate(Sender: TObject);
  end;

var Form1: TForm1;

implementation

{$R *.DFM}
{$IFDEF Win32}
  {$R GLYRES32.RES}
{$ELSE}
  {$R GLYRES16.RES}
{$ENDIF}

procedure TForm1.FormCreate(Sender: TObject);
VAR bH : hBitmap;
begin
  SpeedButton1.Glyph.Handle := LoadBitmap(hInstance, 'FACE');
  SpeedButton2.Glyph.Handle := LoadBitmap(hInstance, 'FACE');
  SpeedButton3.Glyph.Handle := LoadBitmap(hInstance, 'FACE');
  SpeedButton4.Glyph.Handle := LoadBitmap(hInstance, 'FACE');
  SpeedButton1.Glyph := SpeedButton1.Glyph;
  SpeedButton3.Glyph := SpeedButton3.Glyph;
end;

end.
```

In most cases, assigning a valid Windows bitmap handle to the Handle property of a bitmap object is sufficient to get the bitmap displayed in the object. The problem is, the method that handles assigning a bitmap to the glyph property of a bitmap button or a speed button includes special processing to handle multiple images. This method checks whether the bitmap's width is precisely two, three, or four times its height. If so, it treats the bitmap as two, three, or four images representing different button states. When the glyph is loaded by setting its handle property to a bitmap handle returned by the API function LoadBitmap, this special processing is not invoked.

The solution? Assign the glyph bitmap to *itself* after loading it from the resource. That causes the multi-image processing to be invoked, and the glyph displays correctly.

Note that the program uses conditional compilation to load a 16-bit or a 32-bit resource, depending on whether 16-bit Delphi or Delphi32 is being used. Both of these resources contain the same .BMP file—in fact, they're compiled from the identical resource script. The script itself is a bizarre hybrid:

GLYRESMK.BAT

```
/*
@ECHO OFF
CLS
brcc -fo glyres16 -31 glyresmk.bat
brcc -fo glyres32 -w32 glyresmk.bat
GOTO End
*/
FACE BITMAP LOADONCALL MOVEABLE DISCARDABLE "funnyfac.bmp"
/*
:End */
```

When this file is executed as a batch file, the very first line causes a "Bad command or file name" message. However, the CLS in the third line clears the screen and hides the message. Two calls to BRCC.EXE, the Borland Resource Compiler, compile the batch file as a resource script, once in Windows 3.1 style and once in 32-bit style. A GOTO command jumps over the actual resource statements, and the string */ after the End label is ignored. When the file is processed as a resource script, everything between the /*...*/ delimiter pairs is treated as a comment, leaving just the resource statements to be processed. Thus, this file functions both as a resource script and as a batch file that compiles the resource script.

Using an icon as a button glyph

16 32

The Glyph property of speed buttons and bitmap buttons is defined as a TBitmap object. Icons are a convenient size for buttons, but you can't load them into the Glyph property because a TBitmap cannot load an icon. Even if you could, Delphi icon objects won't stretch or shrink, so you're limited to the standard 32×32 icon size.

Though you can't load an icon directly into a bitmap, you *can* draw an icon on the bitmap's canvas. As Figure 10-2 shows, this gives precisely the same effect as loading the icon directly. Strategic use of temporary bitmap objects makes it possible to stretch or to shrink the image.

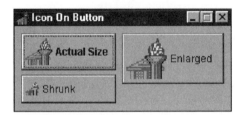

FIGURE 10-2: These three buttons use the standard Delphi icon as their glyph, in three sizes.

ICOBUTN

ICOBUTNU.DEX

```
object Form1: TForm1
  BorderIcons = [biSystemMenu, biMinimize]
  BorderStyle = bsSingle
  Caption = 'Icon On Button'
  Position = poDefault
  Scaled = False
  OnCreate = FormCreate
  object BitBtn1: TBitBtn
    Caption = 'Actual Size'
    Margin = 4
  end
  object BitBtn2: TBitBtn
    Caption = 'Shrunk'
    Margin = 4
  end
  object BitBtn3: TBitBtn
    Caption = 'Enlarged'
    Margin = 4
  end
end
```

ICOBUTNU.PAS

```pascal
unit Icobutnu;

interface

uses SysUtils, WinTypes, WinProcs, Messages, Classes, Graphics,
  Controls, Forms, Dialogs, Buttons, StdCtrls;

type
  TForm1 = class(TForm)
    BitBtn1: TBitBtn;
    BitBtn2: TBitBtn;
    BitBtn3: TBitBtn;
    procedure FormCreate(Sender: TObject);
  end;

var Form1: TForm1;

implementation

{$R *.DFM}

procedure TForm1.FormCreate(Sender: TObject);
VAR TB : TBitmap;
begin
  WITH BitBtn1.Glyph DO {actual size}
    BEGIN
      Width  := 32;
      Height := 32;
      Canvas.Draw(0, 0, Application.Icon);
    END;
  TB := TBitmap.Create;
  WITH TB DO
    try
      Width  := 32;
      Height := 32;
      Canvas.Draw(0, 0, Application.Icon);
      WITH BitBtn2.Glyph DO {Shrunk}
        BEGIN
          Width  := 16;
          Height := 16;
          Canvas.StretchDraw(Rect(0, 0, Width, Height), TB);
        END;
      WITH BitBtn3.Glyph DO {Enlarged}
        BEGIN
          Width  := 48;
          Height := 48;
          Canvas.StretchDraw(Rect(0, 0, Width, Height), TB);
        END;
    finally
      Free;
    end;
end;

end.
```

The form's OnCreate event handler loads the icon image onto all three buttons. Drawing the icon at its actual size is a snap—the event handler simply sets the button's Glyph property's width and height to the size of the icon, then uses the Draw method of its canvas to draw the icon. To create a different-sized glyph from the icon, this method first draws the icon on a temporary bitmap object and then uses the StretchDraw method of the destination glyph's canvas to draw the temporary bitmap at the desired size. An icon won't stretch or shrink, but a bitmap copy of the icon will.

We'll use this technique later in the chapter to write a simple conversion program that creates a bitmap file from any icon.

Building a button with a multiline caption

16 32

Standard Windows pushbuttons always show their captions in the color specified by the Windows system color for button text (clBtnText in Delphi), no matter what you've set their Font.Color to. And their captions must always fit on a single line. Bitmap buttons relieve the first limitation; their captions *do* display in the color defined by Font.Color. However, they're still limited to a single-line caption.

In a sense, a button just can't have a multiline caption. However, you can simulate a multiline caption so well that the difference doesn't matter. As Figure 10-3 shows, the wrapped-title button component displays correctly at design time as well as at runtime.

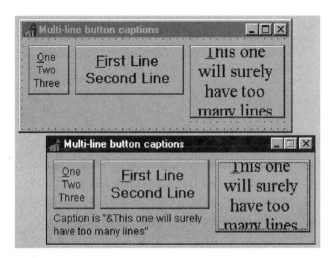

FIGURE 10-3: These appear to be buttons with word-wrapped titles; actually, they're displaying bitmap glyphs that simulate word-wrapped titles.

TWRAPBTN

C_WRAPB.PAS

```
unit C_wrapb;

interface

uses SysUtils, WinTypes, WinProcs, Messages, Classes, Graphics,
  Controls, Forms, Dialogs, StdCtrls, Buttons, p_about;

type
  TWrapBtn = class(TBitBtn)
  private
    fAbout : TAbout;
    function GetGlyph: TBitmap;
    procedure SetGlyph(value: TBitmap);
    function GetMargin: Integer;
    function GetSpacing: Integer;
    function GetKind: TBitBtnKind;
    function GetLayout: TButtonLayout;
    function GetNumGlyphs: TNumGlyphs;
    procedure CMTextChanged(var Message: TMessage);
      message CM_TEXTCHANGED;
    procedure CMFontChanged(var Message: TMessage);
      message CM_FONTCHANGED;
    procedure WMSize(var Msg: TWMSize);
      message WM_SIZE;
    procedure CaptionGlyph;
  protected
    procedure CreateParams(VAR Params: TCreateParams); override;
  published
    property About: TAbout Read fAbout Write fAbout;
    property Glyph: TBitmap Read GetGlyph Write SetGlyph;
    property Margin: Integer Read GetMargin;
    property Spacing: Integer Read GetSpacing;
    property Kind: TBitBtnKind Read GetKind;
    property Layout: TButtonLayout Read GetLayout;
    property NumGlyphs: TNumGlyphs Read GetNumGlyphs;
  end;

procedure Register;

implementation
{$IFDEF Win32}
{$R *.R32}
{$ELSE}
{$R *.R16}
{$ENDIF}

procedure TWrapBtn.CreateParams(VAR Params: TCreateParams);
begin
  Inherited CreateParams(Params);
  fAbout := 0.99;
end;
```

```
procedure TWrapBtn.CaptionGlyph;
{turn caption into a glyph}
VAR
  GP   : TBitmap;
  R    : TRect;
  Buff: ARRAY[0..255] OF Char;
begin
  GP := TBitmap.Create;
  try
    WITH GP DO
      BEGIN
        Canvas.Font := Self.Font;
        StrPCopy(Buff, Caption);
        Inherited Margin  := 0;
        Inherited Spacing := GetSpacing;
        Width  := Self.Width - GetSpacing;
        Height := Self.Height - GetSpacing;
        R := Bounds(0,0,Width,0);
        {Determine the necessary rectangle size}
        DrawText(Canvas.Handle, Buff, StrLen(Buff), R,
          DT_CENTER OR DT_WORDBREAK OR DT_CALCRECT);
        {Center the rectangle}
        OffsetRect(R, (Width-R.Right) DIV 2,
          (Height - R.Bottom) DIV 2);
        {DrawText handles underlining char after "&"}
        DrawText(Canvas.Handle, Buff, StrLen(Buff), R,
          DT_CENTER OR DT_VCENTER OR DT_WORDBREAK);
      END;
    Inherited Glyph := GP;
    Inherited NumGlyphs := 1;
  finally
    GP.Free;
  end;
end;

function TWrapBtn.GetGlyph: TBitmap;
BEGIN
  Result := NIL
END;

procedure TWrapBtn.SetGlyph(value: TBitmap);
begin
  ShowMessage('You cannot set the glyph property of a TWrapBtn '+
    'component');
end;

procedure TWrapBtn.CMTextChanged(var Message: TMessage);
begin
  Inherited;
  CaptionGlyph;
end;

procedure TWrapBtn.CMFontChanged(var Message: TMessage);
begin
  Inherited;
```

```
    CaptionGlyph;
end;
procedure TWrapBtn.WMSize(var Msg: TWMSize);
begin
  Inherited;
  CaptionGlyph;
end;
function TWrapBtn.GetMargin: Integer;
begin
  Result := 0;
end;
function TWrapBtn.GetSpacing: Integer;
begin
  {$IFDEF Win32}
  Result := 12;
  {$ELSE}
  Result := 6;
  {$ENDIF}
end;
function TWrapBtn.GetKind: TBitBtnKind;
BEGIN
  Result := bkCustom;
END;
function TWrapBtn.GetLayout: TButtonLayout;
begin
  Result := blGlyphLeft;
end;
function TWrapBtn.GetNumGlyphs: TNumGlyphs;
begin
  Result := 1;
end;
procedure Register;
begin
  RegisterComponents('NJR', [TWrapBtn]);
end;
end.
```

The private method CaptionGlyph is called when this component's size, caption, or font changes. CaptionGlyph uses the DrawText Windows API function to build a bitmap containing the button's caption word-wrapped, as necessary. A call to DrawText with the DT_CALCRECT and DT_WORDWRAP options doesn't draw any text; rather, it adjusts a TRect variable's height as high as necessary to word-wrap the specified text in the current width. CaptionGlyph then centers the rectangle and draws the text within it. Note that DrawText interprets the ampersand character as a command to underline the following character, just as in a regular button caption.

It's extremely important that the Margin property for this component be zero and that its Spacing property be set large enough that the actual caption won't show. To prevent the user from accidentally goofing up the display, TWrapBtn provides "decoy" read-only properties Margin and Spacing. Internally, the descendant component can set its inherited properties by preceding them with the keyword Inherited; for example, "Inherited Margin := 0;". Likewise the TWrapBtn suppresses the Glyph, NumGlyphs, Kind, and Layout properties.

The general rule is that descendant objects in Delphi can reveal methods and properties that were previously hidden (that is, move them from protected to public or published) but can't go the other way. This is completely true. The closest you can come to suppressing a public or a published property is to hide it behind a same-named, read-only property, as TWrapBtn does. A programmer intent on trouble could set the same-named properties inherited from TBitBtn simply by typecasting a TWrapBtn to TBitBtn. The Decoy properties don't entirely prevent access to the Inherited properties; they just make it difficult to access them accidentally.

Here is the code defining the simple program previously shown in Figure 10-3. It contains three wrapped-caption buttons, all attached to an OnClick handler that displays the caption of the pressed button on a label.

WRAPBTN

WRAPBTU.DEX

```
object Form1: TForm1
  BorderIcons = [biSystemMenu, biMinimize]
  BorderStyle = bsSingle
  Caption = 'Multi-line button captions'
  Position = poDefault
  Scaled = False
  object Label1: TLabel
    AutoSize = False
    ShowAccelChar = False
  end
  object WrapBtn1: TWrapBtn
    Caption = '&One Two Three'
    OnClick = WrapBtn1Click
    About = 0.99
  end
  object WrapBtn2: TWrapBtn
    Caption = '&First Line Second Line'
    Font.Height = -16
    Font.Name = 'MS Sans Serif'
    Font.Style = [fsBold]
    ParentFont = False
    OnClick = WrapBtn1Click
```

```
      About = 0.99
    end
    object WrapBtn3: TWrapBtn
      Caption = '&This one will surely have too many lines'
      Font.Height = -21
      Font.Name = 'Times New Roman'
      ParentFont = False
      OnClick = WrapBtn1Click
      About = 0.99
    end
  end
end
```

WRAPBTU.PAS

```
unit Wrapbtu;

interface

uses SysUtils, WinTypes, WinProcs, Messages, Classes, Graphics,
  Controls, Forms, Dialogs, StdCtrls, Buttons, C_wrapb;

type
  TForm1 = class(TForm)
    WrapBtn1: TWrapBtn;
    WrapBtn2: TWrapBtn;
    WrapBtn3: TWrapBtn;
    Label1: TLabel;
    procedure WrapBtn1Click(Sender: TObject);
  end;

var Form1: TForm1;

implementation

{$R *.DFM}

procedure TForm1.WrapBtn1Click(Sender: TObject);
begin
  Label1.Caption := Format('Caption is "%s"',
    [(Sender AS TWrapBtn).Caption]);
end;

end.
```

Making a button repeat when held down

16 32

After using the spin button and spin edit components, you may wonder what it would take to get a regular button to repeat in the same way. The default behavior for a button is to visibly depress on the mouse-down event and generate an OnClick event on mouse-up. How can you get a repeating effect like that of a spin button?

Naturally, accomplishing this task requires a timer. Rather than create a TButton descendant, we'll make use of a single timer component that's shared by any number of repeating buttons; the program in Figure 10-4 has six of them.

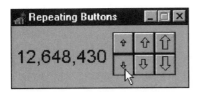

FIGURE 10-4: The small, medium, and large arrows on these buttons represent increments (up or down) of 1, 10, or 100.

HOLDBUTN

HOLDBUTU.DEX

```
object Form1: TForm1
  BorderIcons = [biSystemMenu, biMinimize]
  BorderStyle = bsSingle
  Caption = 'Repeating Buttons'
  Position = poDefault
  Scaled = False
  object SpeedButton1: TSpeedButton
    Tag = 1
    Caption = 'ñ'
    Font.Height = -11
    Font.Name = 'Wingdings'
    ParentFont = False
    OnClick = SpeedButton1Click
    OnMouseDown = SpeedButton1MouseDown
    OnMouseUp = SpeedButton1MouseUp
  end
  object SpeedButton3: TSpeedButton
    Tag = -1
    Caption = 'ò'
    Font.Height = -11
    Font.Name = 'WingDings'
    ParentFont = False
    OnClick = SpeedButton1Click
    OnMouseDown = SpeedButton1MouseDown
    OnMouseUp = SpeedButton1MouseUp
  end
  object Label1: TLabel
    Alignment = taRightJustify
    AutoSize = False
    Caption = '0'
    Font.Height = -21
    ParentFont = False
```

```
      end
      object SpeedButton2: TSpeedButton
        Tag = 10
        Caption = 'ñ'
        Font.Height = -16
        Font.Name = 'Wingdings'
        ParentFont = False
        OnClick = SpeedButton1Click
        OnMouseDown = SpeedButton1MouseDown
        OnMouseUp = SpeedButton1MouseUp
      end
      object SpeedButton6: TSpeedButton
        Tag = 100
        Caption = 'ñ'
        Font.Height = -24
        Font.Name = 'Wingdings'
        ParentFont = False
        OnClick = SpeedButton1Click
        OnMouseDown = SpeedButton1MouseDown
        OnMouseUp = SpeedButton1MouseUp
      end
      object SpeedButton4: TSpeedButton
        Tag = -10
        Caption = 'ò'
        Font.Height = -16
        Font.Name = 'Wingdings'
        ParentFont = False
        OnClick = SpeedButton1Click
        OnMouseDown = SpeedButton1MouseDown
        OnMouseUp = SpeedButton1MouseUp
      end
      object SpeedButton5: TSpeedButton
        Tag = -100
        Caption = 'ò'
        Font.Height = -24
        Font.Name = 'Wingdings'
        ParentFont = False
        OnClick = SpeedButton1Click
        OnMouseDown = SpeedButton1MouseDown
        OnMouseUp = SpeedButton1MouseUp
      end
      object Timer1: TTimer
        Enabled = False
        Interval = 500
        OnTimer = Timer1Timer
      end
    end
```

HOLDBUTU.PAS

```
    unit Holdbutu;
    interface
    uses SysUtils, WinTypes, WinProcs, Messages, Classes, Graphics,
```

```
      Controls, Forms, Dialogs, ExtCtrls, StdCtrls, Buttons;
type
  TForm1 = class(TForm)
    SpeedButton1: TSpeedButton;
    SpeedButton3: TSpeedButton;
    SpeedButton4: TSpeedButton;
    SpeedButton2: TSpeedButton;
    Label1: TLabel;
    Timer1: TTimer;
    SpeedButton5: TSpeedButton;
    SpeedButton6: TSpeedButton;
    procedure SpeedButton1MouseDown(Sender: TObject; Button:
      TMouseButton; Shift: TShiftState; X, Y: Integer);
    procedure Timer1Timer(Sender: TObject);
    procedure SpeedButton1MouseUp(Sender: TObject; Button:
      TMouseButton; Shift: TShiftState; X, Y: Integer);
    procedure SpeedButton1Click(Sender: TObject);
  private
    L : LongInt;
  end;

var Form1: TForm1;

implementation

{$R *.DFM}

procedure TForm1.SpeedButton1MouseDown(Sender: TObject;
  Button: TMouseButton; Shift: TShiftState; X, Y: Integer);
begin
  Timer1.Tag := (Sender AS TSpeedButton).Tag;
  Timer1.Interval := 500;
  Timer1.Enabled := True;
end;

procedure TForm1.Timer1Timer(Sender: TObject);
begin
  Timer1.Interval := 50;
  L := L + Timer1.Tag;
  Label1.Caption := FormatFloat('0,', L);
end;

procedure TForm1.SpeedButton1MouseUp(Sender: TObject; Button:
  TMouseButton; Shift: TShiftState; X, Y: Integer);
begin
  Timer1.Enabled := False;
end;

procedure TForm1.SpeedButton1Click(Sender: TObject);
begin
  L := L + (Sender AS TSpeedButton).Tag;
  Label1.Caption := FormatFloat('0,', L);
end;

end.
```

The six speed buttons have Tag property values of 1, 10, 100, −1, −10, and −100, and captions that represent up and down arrow characters in the WingDings font. They modify the value of the private data field L, a LongInt variable initially set to 0. In the OnMouseDown event handler shared by the six speed buttons, the timer's Tag property is set to match that of the button that was pressed, and its interval is set to ½ second. Then the timer is enabled.

Half a second later the timer's OnTimer event is triggered. The OnTimer event handler reduces the interval to 50, adds the amount stored in the timer's Tag property to the data field L, and displays L's value in a label. The OnMouseUp handler for the speed buttons disables the timer.

The reason for the two-tier timer interval, 500 milliseconds to start and 50 milliseconds thereafter, is to allow the user to make a single click. The repeating action doesn't begin until the button has been held down for half a second. Once begun, it repeats as quickly as possible (the smallest practical interval for a timer is about 55 milliseconds).

Deselecting all of a radio group or set of radio buttons

16 32

A radio group whose ItemIndex is −1 will initially display none of its buttons selected. The same is true of radio buttons in a group box, all of which initially have the Checked property set to False. However, once the user has clicked on any of the radio buttons, there's no obvious way to get back to that pristine state of nothing selected.

The Windows interface does not define a standard method for clearing all of a group of radio buttons. The program shown in Figure 10-5 implements a made-up standard in which clicking on the group box or the radio group outside any button clears all radio buttons. The keyboard equivalent is pressing Backspace.

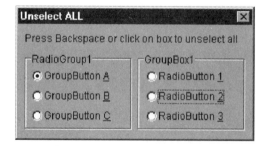

FIGURE 10-5: Clicking directly on the group box or the radio group in this example program will clear all radio buttons contained therein.

UNRADGP

UNRADGPU.DEX

```
object Form1: TForm1
  BorderIcons = [biSystemMenu, biMinimize]
  BorderStyle = bsDialog
  Caption = 'Unselect ALL'
  Position = poDefault
  Scaled = False
  OnCreate = FormCreate
  object Label1: TLabel
    Caption = 'Press Backspace or click on box to unselect all'
  end
  object RadioGroup1: TRadioGroup
    Caption = 'RadioGroup1'
    Items.Strings = (
      'GroupButton &A'
      'GroupButton &B'
      'GroupButton &C')
  end
  object GroupBox1: TGroupBox
    Caption = 'GroupBox1'
    OnClick = GroupBox1Click
    object RadioButton1: TRadioButton
      Caption = 'RadioButton &1'
      OnKeyPress = RadioButton1KeyPress
    end
    object RadioButton2: TRadioButton
      Caption = 'RadioButton &2'
      OnKeyPress = RadioButton1KeyPress
    end
    object RadioButton3: TRadioButton
      Caption = 'RadioButton &3'
      OnKeyPress = RadioButton1KeyPress
    end
  end
end
```

UNRADGPU.PAS

```
unit Unradgpu;

interface

uses SysUtils, WinTypes, WinProcs, Messages, Classes, Graphics,
  Controls, Forms, Dialogs, StdCtrls, ExtCtrls;

type
  TForm1 = class(TForm)
    RadioGroup1: TRadioGroup;
    GroupBox1: TGroupBox;
```

```
    RadioButton1: TRadioButton;
    RadioButton2: TRadioButton;
    RadioButton3: TRadioButton;
    Label1: TLabel;
    procedure GroupBox1Click(Sender: TObject);
    procedure FormCreate(Sender: TObject);
    procedure RadioButton1KeyPress(Sender: TObject;
      var Key: Char);
  private
    procedure RadioGroup1MouseUp(Sender: TObject; Button:
      TMouseButton; Shift: TShiftState; X, Y: Integer);
  end;

var Form1: TForm1;

implementation

{$R *.DFM}

procedure TForm1.FormCreate(Sender: TObject);
VAR N : Integer;
begin
    TGroupBox(RadioGroup1).OnMouseUp := RadioGroup1MouseUp;
  WITH RadioGroup1 DO
    FOR N := 0 TO ControlCount-1 DO
      IF Controls[N] IS TRadioButton THEN
        TRadioButton(Controls[N]).OnKeyPress :=
          RadioButton1KeyPress;
end;

procedure TForm1.GroupBox1Click(Sender: TObject);
VAR N : Integer;
begin
  WITH Sender AS TGroupBox DO
    FOR N := 0 TO ControlCount-1 DO
      IF Controls[N] IS TRadioButton THEN
        TRadioButton(Controls[N]).Checked := False;
end;

procedure TForm1.RadioGroup1MouseUp(Sender: TObject; Button:
  TMouseButton; Shift: TShiftState; X, Y: Integer);
begin
  IF (Button = mbLeft) AND (Shift = []) THEN
    WITH Sender AS TRadioGroup DO
      ItemIndex := -1;
end;

procedure TForm1.RadioButton1KeyPress(Sender: TObject;
  var Key: Char);
begin
  IF Key <> #8 THEN Exit;
  WITH Sender AS TRadioButton DO
  IF Parent IS TGroupBox THEN GroupBox1Click(Parent)
  ELSE IF Parent IS TRadioGroup THEN
```

```
        TRadioGroup(Parent).ItemIndex := -1;
    end;
  end.
```

Handling the group box is relatively simple. Its OnClick event handler flips through its Controls array and unchecks any radio buttons found. All radio buttons within the group box are connected to the same OnKeyPress event handler. If the Backspace key was pressed and the radio button's parent is a group box, this event handler calls on the same event handler that responds to a click on the group box. That's all it takes.

Responding to a Backspace keystroke in a radio group is almost as simple. All the radio buttons need to be connected at runtime to the same OnKeyPress event handler used by the loose radio buttons within the group box. If Backspace was pressed and the parent of the radio button in question is a radio group, the event handler sets the radio group's ItemIndex to −1, thus clearing the selection.

Getting the radio group to respond to a mouse click outside of its radio buttons is more of a challenge. The radio group has an OnClick handler, but it's only called when one of the radio buttons is clicked, and it doesn't even have an OnMouseUp property. Actually, the radio group component *does* have an OnMouseUp property, inherited from the generic TControl. It just happens that this property is protected and, hence, inaccessible. A little subterfuge will expose that property.

Normally, you only typecast an object to its actual type or to an ancestor of its actual type. That ensures that you won't attempt to access a property or a method that doesn't even exist in the actual object. However, you can usually get away with typecasting to a "cousin" rather than to an ancestor, as long as you only reference properties present in the common ancestor of the actual type and the cousin. In this case, the form's OnCreate event handler typecasts the radio group box to an ordinary group box and sets its OnMouseUp property to a handler that simply sets ItemIndex to −1.

Odds and Ends

The remainder of this chapter collects solutions involving a variety of components, from common dialogs to panels. It's a mixed bag of techniques, some to enhance the appearance and functionality of your programs, others to avoid mysterious and seemingly illogical problems.

Controlling common dialog position

16 32

Delphi's common dialogs always come up in the same position, roughly centered on the screen. That's not necessarily the right place—it may obscure some program element that should be visible to the user. Figure 10-6 shows the top left corner of the desktop. The Delphi program in the background has invoked the File Open dialog and forced it into a position corresponding to the selected cell in a 3×4 grid.

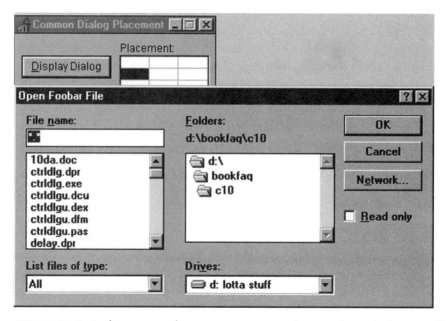

FIGURE 10-6: As this program demonstrates, you can take control over the location of the common dialog boxes.

CTRLDLG

CTRLDLGU.DEX

```
object Form1: TForm1
  BorderIcons = [biSystemMenu, biMinimize]
  BorderStyle = bsSingle
  Caption = 'Common Dialog Placement'
  Position = poDefault
  Scaled = False
  object Label1: TLabel
```

```
    Caption = 'Placement:'
  end
  object Button1: TButton
    Caption = '&Display Dialog'
    Default = True
    OnClick = Button1Click
  end
  object DrawGrid1: TDrawGrid
    ColCount = 3
    DefaultColWidth = 32
    DefaultRowHeight = 12
    FixedCols = 0
    FixedRows = 0
    Options = [goFixedVertLine, goFixedHorzLine, goVertLine,
goHorzLine, goDrawFocusSelected]
    RowCount = 4
    ScrollBars = ssNone
  end
  object Timer1: TTimer
    Enabled = False
    Interval = 50
    OnTimer = Timer1Timer
  end
  object OpenDialog1: TOpenDialog
    Filter = 'All|*.*'
    Title = 'Open Foobar File'
  end
end
```

CTRLDLGU.PAS

```
unit Ctrldlgu;

interface

uses SysUtils, WinTypes, WinProcs, Messages, Classes, Graphics,
  Controls, Forms, Dialogs, ExtCtrls, StdCtrls, Grids;

type
  TForm1 = class(TForm)
    Button1: TButton;
    Timer1: TTimer;
    OpenDialog1: TOpenDialog;
    DrawGrid1: TDrawGrid;
    Label1: TLabel;
    procedure Button1Click(Sender: TObject);
    procedure Timer1Timer(Sender: TObject);
  private
    TitleBuff: ARRAY[0..255] OF Char;
  end;

var Form1: TForm1;

implementation
```

```
{$R *.DFM}
procedure TForm1.Button1Click(Sender: TObject);
begin
  Timer1.Enabled := True;
  StrPCopy(TitleBuff, OpenDialog1.Title);
  OpenDialog1.Execute;
end;

procedure TForm1.Timer1Timer(Sender: TObject);
VAR
  H    : hWnd;
  R    : TRect;
  X, Y : Integer;
begin
  H := FindWindow('#32770', TitleBuff);
  IF H <> 0 THEN
    BEGIN
      GetWindowRect(H, R);
      WITH DrawGrid1 DO
        BEGIN
          CASE Selection.Left OF
            0 : X := 4;
            1 : X := (Screen.Width-R.Right+R.Left) DIV 2;
            2 : X := (Screen.Width-R.Right+R.Left) - 4
          END;
          CASE Selection.Top OF
            0 : Y := 4;
            1 : Y :=   (Screen.Height-R.Bottom+R.Top) DIV 3;
            2 : Y := 2*(Screen.Height-R.Bottom+R.Top) DIV 3;
            3 : Y :=   (Screen.Height-R.Bottom+R.Top) - 4;
          END;
        END;
      SetWindowPos(H, 0, X, Y, 0, 0, SWP_NOSIZE OR SWP_NOZORDER);
      Timer1.Enabled := False;
    END;
end;

end.
```

To control the location of a common dialog or of any window outside your Delphi program, you need its window handle. The example program activates a timer just before executing the common dialog. The timer uses the Windows API function FindWindow to locate a window whose class name is 32770 (the standard class name string for common dialogs) and whose title matches the title property of the common dialog component. Upon finding this window, the timer disables itself and positions the dialog at a screen location corresponding to the selected cell in the draw grid. On some systems, you will see a momentary flash as the common dialog appears in its default location and then moves to the location you've chosen for it.

Converting an .ICO file to .BMP

16 32

Icon files are necessary if an icon is what you want, but they have serious limitations. You can't stretch a TImage that contains an icon, for example, and you can't load an icon into the Windows paint accessory. Can Delphi assist in transforming an icon file into a bitmap file? Of course!

ICO2BMP

ICO2BMPU.DEX

```
object Form1: TForm1
  BorderIcons = [biSystemMenu, biMinimize]
  BorderStyle = bsDialog
  Caption = 'Icon to Bitmap'
  Position = poDefault
  Scaled = False
  object Image1: TImage
  end
  object Button1: TButton
    Caption = 'Select .ICO File'
    Default = True
    OnClick = Button1Click
  end
  object OpenDialog1: TOpenDialog
    DefaultExt = 'ICO'
    Filter = 'Icons|*.ICO'
    Options = [ofHideReadOnly, ofFileMustExist]
    Title = 'Open Icon File'
  end
end
```

ICO2BMPU.PAS

```
unit Ico2bmpu;

interface

uses SysUtils, WinTypes, WinProcs, Messages, Classes, Graphics,
  Controls, Forms, Dialogs, StdCtrls, ExtCtrls;

type
  TForm1 = class(TForm)
    OpenDialog1: TOpenDialog;
    Image1: TImage;
    Button1: TButton;
    procedure Button1Click(Sender: TObject);
  end;
```

```
var Form1: TForm1;

implementation

{$R *.DFM}

procedure TForm1.Button1Click(Sender: TObject);
VAR OutName : String;
begin
  WITH OpenDialog1 DO
    IF Execute THEN
      BEGIN
        OutName := ChangeFileExt(Filename, '.BMP')
        Image1.Picture.LoadFromFile(Filename);
        Filename := '';
        WITH TBitmap.Create DO
          try
            Height := Image1.Picture.Height;
            Width  := Image1.Picture.Width;
            Canvas.Draw(0,0,Image1.Picture.Icon);
            SaveToFile(OutName);
            ShowMessage(OutName + ' saved.');
          finally
            Free;
          end;
      END;
end;

end.
```

The conversion process is extremely simple. First, the selected icon file is loaded into an image component. A temporary TBitmap object is created and sized to match the icon-bearing image component. The next step is to draw the icon on the temporary bitmap, and to use the bitmap's SaveToFile method to save the result as a bitmap file. That's it! Take care when using this tiny example program, as it will overwrite an existing .BMP file with the same filename in the same directory as the .ICO file.

The process is simple enough that you may want to skip the step of creating a .BMP file and simply draw the desired icon on a temporary bitmap at runtime. Earlier in this chapter, the same technique was used to display icons on bitmap buttons.

Panels shift position at runtime!

16 32

By using the Align property and putting panels within panels, it's possible to make a high-class status bar or speed bar. However, when a number of aligned subpanels are stacked up, an amazing thing can happen. When the user shrinks the window and then expands it again, *sometimes* the order of the panels changes. You may suspect gremlins, since the problem occurs only sporadically. If you haven't experienced this problem, it's hard to believe; the program shown in Figure 10-7 demonstrates it.

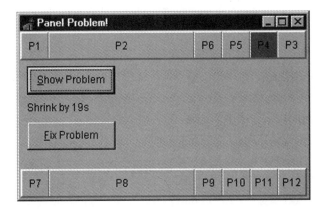

FIGURE 10-7: When several components are aligned against the same side of a container object, resizing the window can cause components to change their relative position.

PANPROB

PANPROBU.DEX

```
object Form1: TForm1
  Caption = 'Panel Problem!'
  Scaled = False
  OnCreate = FormCreate
  OnResize = FormResize
  object Label1: TLabel
  end
  object Button1: TButton
    Caption = '&Show Problem'
    OnClick = Button1Click
  end
  object Button2: TButton
    Caption = '&Fix Problem'
    OnClick = Button2Click
  end
  object Panel1: TPanel
    Align = alTop
    Caption = 'Panel1'
  end
  object Panel2: TPanel
    Align = alBottom
    Caption = 'Panel2'
  end
end
```

PANPROBU.PAS

```
unit panprobu;

interface

uses SysUtils, WinTypes, WinProcs, Messages, Classes, Graphics,
  Controls, Forms, Dialogs, ExtCtrls, StdCtrls, Grids;

type
  TForm1 = class(TForm)
    Button1: TButton;
    Button2: TButton;
    Label1: TLabel;
    Panel1: TPanel;
    Panel2: TPanel;
    procedure Button2Click(Sender: TObject);
    procedure FormCreate(Sender: TObject);
    procedure FormResize(Sender: TObject);
    procedure Button1Click(Sender: TObject);
  private
    Panels : ARRAY[0..11] OF TPanel;
    Busy   : Boolean;
  end;

var Form1: TForm1;

implementation

{$R *.DFM}

procedure TForm1.FormCreate(Sender: TObject);
VAR N : Integer;
begin
  Randomize;
  FOR N := 0 TO 11 DO
    BEGIN
      Panels[N] := TPanel.Create(Self);
      WITH Panels[N] DO
        BEGIN
          Caption := 'P' + IntToStr(N+1);
          IF N <= 5 THEN Parent := Panel1
          ELSE Parent := Panel2;
          Width := 33;
          CASE N OF
            0,6: Align := alLeft;
            1,7: Align := alClient;
            ELSE Align := alRight;
          END;
        END;
    END;
end;

procedure TForm1.Button1Click(Sender: TObject);
VAR WasWidth, BadPanel, N, Delta : Integer;
begin
  IF Busy THEN Exit;
```

```
      Busy     := True;
      WasWidth := Width;
      Delta    := 10 + Random(10);
      BadPanel := -1;
      REPEAT
        Label1.Caption := Format('Shrink by %ds', [Delta]);
        REPEAT
          Width := Width - Delta;
          Application.ProcessMessages;
          FOR N := 5 DOWNTO 1 DO
            IF Panels[N].Left < Panels[N-1].Left THEN BadPanel := N;
          IF BadPanel <> -1 THEN
            BEGIN
              Panels[BadPanel].Color := clRed;
              Width := WasWidth;
              Busy  := FALSE;
              Exit;
            END;
        UNTIL (Width <= HorzScrollBar.Range) OR Application.Terminated;
        Delta := Delta - 1;
        Width := WasWidth;
      UNTIL (Delta <= 0) OR Application.Terminated;
      Busy := False;
    end;
procedure TForm1.Button2Click(Sender: TObject);
VAR N : Integer;
begin
  IF Busy THEN Exit;
  FOR N := 0 TO 5 DO
    BEGIN
      IF N = 0 THEN Panels[1].Left := 0
      ELSE Panels[N].Left := Panels[N-1].Left + 1;
      Panels[N].Color := clBtnFace;
    END;
end;
procedure TForm1.FormResize(Sender: TObject);
VAR N : Integer;
begin
  {Keep lower set of panels in order}
  FOR N := 7 TO 11 DO
    IF Panels[N].Left < Panels[N-1].Left THEN
      Panels[N].Left := Panels[N-1].Left + 1;
end;
end.
```

Initially, the form holds two panels aligned at its top and its bottom. The OnCreate event handler puts six subpanels inside each of these: one aligned at the left, four aligned at the right, and one in the middle aligned to take the remaining client area.

The OnClick event for the Show Problem button shrinks the window in stages, ten to twenty pixels at a time. If it fails to produce a problem, it tries again with a different increment. In most cases, though, it won't take long before one of the panels pops up in the wrong place. The problem is substantially less common under Delphi 2.0, because *most* of the time the panels return to their correct order when the window goes back to its original width.

Fixing the problem is a simple matter of setting each panel's Left property to one greater than the Left property of the panel that *should* precede it. The Align property setting ensures that the panels don't actually stack up in the same place. Since the subpanels were created as elements of an array, it's easy to step through the array and fix each one.

Of course, in an actual program, you wouldn't want to let the problem occur and then fix it; rather, you'd want to prevent trouble. One possibility is to do as the example program does for its bottom panel. Each time the form is resized, the OnResize event handler flips through the subpanels on the bottom panel and sets each Left property one greater than that of the previous panel. It works!

Creating a simple splitter bar

16 32

The preceding chapter showed how to create a splitter bar using a two-page notebook and some fancy paint box drawing. If you can accept a slightly less elegant display, the panel component provides a much easier implementation. The program in Figure 10-8 demonstrates three possible techniques.

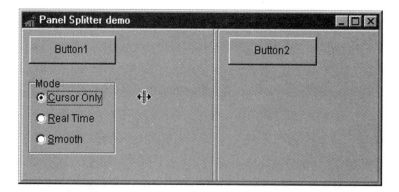

FIGURE 10-8: The easiest way to implement a splitter bar is to let the crHSplit cursor represent it; however, rearranging the form in real time gives a classier effect.

SPLITP

SPLITPU.DEX

```
object Form1: TForm1
  Caption = 'Panel Splitter demo'
  object Panel1: TPanel
    Cursor = crHSplit
    Align = alLeft
    DragCursor = crHSplit
    DragMode = dmAutomatic
    OnDragDrop = Panel2DragDrop
    OnDragOver = Panel2DragOverA
  end
  object Panel2: TPanel
    Align = alLeft
    OnDragDrop = Panel2DragDrop
    OnDragOver = Panel2DragOverA
    object Button1: TButton
      Caption = 'Button1'
      OnDragDrop = Panel2DragDrop
      OnDragOver = Panel2DragOverA
    end
    object RadioGroup1: TRadioGroup
      Caption = 'Mode'
      ItemIndex = 0
      Items.Strings = (
        '&Cursor Only'
        '&Real Time'
        '&Smooth')
      OnClick = RadioGroup1Click
      OnDragDrop = Panel2DragDrop
      OnDragOver = Panel2DragOverA
    end
  end
  object Panel3: TPanel
    Align = alClient
    OnDragDrop = Panel2DragDrop
    OnDragOver = Panel2DragOverA
    object Button2: TButton
      Caption = 'Button2'
      OnDragDrop = Panel2DragDrop
      OnDragOver = Panel2DragOverA
    end
  end
end
```

SPLITPU.PAS

```
unit Splitpu;

interface

uses SysUtils, WinTypes, WinProcs, Messages, Classes, Graphics,
```

```
      Controls, Forms, Dialogs, StdCtrls, ExtCtrls;
type
  TForm1 = class(TForm)
    Panel1: TPanel;
    Panel2: TPanel;
    Panel3: TPanel;
    Button1: TButton;
    Button2: TButton;
    RadioGroup1: TRadioGroup;
    procedure Panel2DragOverA(Sender, Source: TObject;
      X, Y: Integer; State: TDragState; var Accept: Boolean);
    procedure Panel2DragOverB(Sender, Source: TObject;
      X, Y: Integer; State: TDragState; var Accept: Boolean);
    procedure Panel2DragOverC(Sender, Source: TObject;
      X, Y: Integer; State: TDragState; var Accept: Boolean);
    procedure Panel2DragDrop(Sender, Source: TObject;
      X, Y: Integer);
    procedure RadioGroup1Click(Sender: TObject);
  end;

var Form1: TForm1;

implementation

{$R *.DFM}

procedure TForm1.Panel2DragOverA(Sender, Source: TObject;
  X, Y: Integer; State: TDragState; var Accept: Boolean);
begin
  Accept := Source=Panel1;
end;

procedure TForm1.Panel2DragOverB(Sender, Source: TObject;
  X, Y: Integer; State: TDragState; var Accept: Boolean);
begin
  Accept := Source=Panel1;
  Panel2.Width := ScreenToClient(
    TControl(Sender).ClientToScreen(Point(X,Y))).X;
end;

procedure TForm1.Panel2DragOverC(Sender, Source: TObject;
  X, Y: Integer; State: TDragState; var Accept: Boolean);
begin
  Accept := Source=Panel1;
  LockWindowUpdate(Handle);
  Panel2.Width := ScreenToClient(
    TControl(Sender).ClientToScreen(Point(X,Y))).X;
  LockWindowUpdate(0);
  Refresh;
end;

procedure TForm1.Panel2DragDrop(Sender, Source: TObject;
  X, Y: Integer);
begin
  Panel2.Width := ScreenToClient(
    TControl(Sender).ClientToScreen(Point(X,Y))).X;
end;
```

```
procedure TForm1.RadioGroup1Click(Sender: TObject);
VAR
  IsDO, WasDO : TDragOverEvent;
  N           : Integer;
begin
  WasDO := Panel2.OnDragOver;
  WITH Sender AS TRadioGroup DO
    CASE ItemIndex OF
      0 : Panel2.OnDragOver := Panel2DragOverA;
      1 : Panel2.OnDragOver := Panel2DragOverB;
      2 : Panel2.OnDragOver := Panel2DragOverC;
    END;
  FOR N := 0 TO ComponentCount-1 DO
    IF Components[N] IS TControl THEN
      {TControl has OnDragOver protected; typecast to
       TButton, which publishes it}
      WITH TButton(Components[N]) DO
        BEGIN
          IsDO := OnDragOver;
          IF @IsDO = @WasDO THEN OnDragOver := Panel2.OnDragOver;
        END;
  end;
  end.
```

The background of this form consists of three panels, one aligned alLeft, a very narrow one also aligned alLeft, and another aligned alClient. The narrow, middle panel functions as the splitter bar; its cursor property is set to crHSplit, so that the mouse cursor visibly suggests its function.

Initially, every component on the form has its OnDragOver event handler set to Panel2DragOverA. This event handler simply accepts any drag-over event that comes from Panel1, the splitter panel. Every component has its OnDragDrop event handler set to Panel2DragDrop. This handler sets the width of the left-hand panel to the location of the drop event. Because the X and Y values are relative to the top left corner of the dropped-on component, it's necessary to convert the drop location to screen coordinates, and then back to client coordinates of the form.

However, using the mouse cursor as a splitter bar is rather inelegant. It doesn't fill the form vertically, and it just doesn't look like it's doing anything. The Panel2DragOverB event handler actually resizes the left-hand panel on every drag-over event. This has the effect of rearranging the whole form in real time.

Unfortunately, the resizing and rearranging of components produces a really ugly flicker. Panel2DragOverC is an event handler that reduces that flicker by hiding most of it. The LockWindowUpdate Windows API function prevents redrawing of the window whose handle you pass it. This remains in effect until you call

LockWindowUpdate again, passing zero. Adding these two lines to the process comes as close as possible to a perfectly smooth splitter bar using panels.

The OnClick handler for the radio group is worth a bit of study. Its purpose is to switch the OnDragOver handler for all components between Panel2DragOverA, Panel2DragOverB, and Panel2DragOverC. If a component is currently attached to the same OnDragOver handler as the radio group, this event handler should switch it to the newly chosen OnDragOver handler. The process of comparing two event handler properties is surprisingly complicated. First, you define two variables of the proper event type and assign them to the two event handler properties. Then, compare the two variables, prefixing each with the @ symbol. Normally, the @ operator represents the address of the variable or expression that follows it. When the variables are a procedural type, @ tells the compiler you want to refer to the variable itself rather than call the procedure it represents.

If you don't like any of the options demonstrated by this program, you'll find a much more elegant (and more complicated) splitter bar example in the preceding chapter.

Alignment property for labels doesn't work!

16 32

Delphi's label component includes an Alignment property that can be set to left, to right, or to center. However, you may find it doesn't seem to do anything.

Here's the problem. The label component also has an AutoSize property, which causes the component to automatically size itself just large enough to hold its text. When the component is no bigger than the text, right and center alignment have no meaning! Right alignment means that the automatic sizing moves the left edge of the label rather than the right. If you want a label right- or center-aligned within a particular space, first set its AutoSize property to False. Adjust the label's width to the desired space, *then* set the Alignment property.

Need a Delay procedure!

16

Programmers who cut their teeth on DOS-based programs are accustomed to being able to pause the program's execution temporarily with a Delay procedure. For example, display a message, wait five seconds, and erase the message. Delphi 2.0 programs can pass the desired delay in milliseconds to the Windows API function Sleep. Where is Delphi 1.0's Delay procedure?

Of course, a Delay procedure that simply enters a tight loop for the desired amount of time would be a disaster in Windows, or any cooperative multitasking environment. A Windows-based Delay procedure will usually rely on a timer, as this example does.

DELAY

DELAYU.DEX

```
object Form1: TForm1
  BorderIcons = [biSystemMenu, biMinimize]
  BorderStyle = bsDialog
  Caption = 'Delay using Timer'
  Scaled = False
  object Label1: TLabel
    Caption = 'Visible for 1 second'
    Visible = False
  end
  object Label2: TLabel
    Caption = 'Visible for 5 seconds'
    Visible = False
  end
  object Button1: TButton
    Caption = 'Test Delay &1'
    OnClick = Button1Click
  end
  object Button2: TButton
    Caption = 'Test Delay &2'
    OnClick = Button2Click
  end
end
```

DELAYU.PAS

```
unit Delayu;

interface

uses SysUtils, WinTypes, WinProcs, Messages, Classes, Graphics,
  Controls, Forms, Dialogs, StdCtrls, ExtCtrls;

type
  TForm1 = class(TForm)
    Button1: TButton;
    Label1: TLabel;
    Button2: TButton;
    Label2: TLabel;
    procedure Button1Click(Sender: TObject);
    procedure Button2Click(Sender: TObject);
  private
    Delaying : Boolean;
    procedure Delay(ms : Integer);
    procedure DelayTimerTimer(Sender: TObject);
  end;
```

```
var Form1: TForm1;

implementation

{$R *.DFM}

procedure TForm1.Delay(ms : Integer);
BEGIN
  IF Delaying THEN Exit;
  WITH TTimer.Create(Self) DO
    try
      OnTimer  := DelayTimerTimer;
      Interval := ms;
      Enabled  := True;
      Delaying := True;
      WHILE Enabled AND (NOT Application.Terminated) DO
        Application.ProcessMessages;
    finally
      free;
      Delaying := False;
    end;
END;

procedure TForm1.DelayTimerTimer(Sender: TObject);
begin
  WITH Sender AS TTimer DO Enabled := False;
end;

procedure TForm1.Button1Click(Sender: TObject);
begin
  Label1.Visible := True;
  Delay(1000);
  Label1.Visible := False;
end;

procedure TForm1.Button2Click(Sender: TObject);
begin
  Label2.Visible := True;
  Delay(5000);
  Label2.Visible := False;
end;

end.
```

The Delay procedure creates a timer component, sets its interval to the desired number of milliseconds, and sets its OnTimer event handler to DelayTimerTimer. This event handler does nothing but set the timer's Enabled property to False. After starting the timer, the Delay procedure enters a loop that continues until the timer is disabled or the application terminates. Within the loop, it calls Application.ProcessMessages to allow Windows to continue processing messages. Of course, letting Windows continue processing messages means the user could start another delay process. To avoid potential problems, the Delay procedure exits immediately if a delay is already occurring.

CHAPTER

11

Database Programming

O ne of Delphi's claims to fame is that it encapsulates database programming in a set of easy-to-use, data-access components and data-aware user interface components. These components are relatively simple to use, yes, but there are still a lot of questions a Delphi programmer will run into in database programming. In this chapter, you'll learn how to update variable-length fields, how to highlight rows in a database based on the value of one field, and how to avoid a pitfall involving database units and DLLs. This chapter also introduces a component that gets past one of the major limitations of the data-aware grid—it displays memo and graphic fields within the grid.

Grid Appearance

The data-aware grid component in Delphi 2.0 gives the programmer fairly complete control over the look of individual columns, to the point of building in buttons whose function is defined by the programmer and drop-down lists for lookup fields. In Delphi 1.0, the DBGrid is nowhere near as obliging, but you can still enhance its appearance.

Centered fields look ugly!

16

Double-clicking on an open Delphi table component brings up the fields editor, which allows you to set properties for individual fields, including such things as the label that will be displayed and the alignment. If you choose taCenter for alignment, though, the field's display in a DBGrid in a 16-bit Delphi app looks awful in Windows 95.

The second column in Figure 11-1 shows the problem—the text is centered, indeed, but it's surrounded by black on both sides. The first column in the same figure shows that centered text *can* be displayed in an aesthetically pleasing fashion.

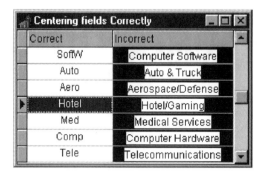

FIGURE 11-1: The second column in this grid shows the default display of a centered field; it's ugly! The first column is displayed nicely by using a few lines of code.

FLDCNTR

FLDCNTRU.DEX

```
object Form1: TForm1
  Caption = 'Centering fields Correctly'
  Position = poDefault
  Scaled = False
  OnCreate = FormCreate
  object DBGrid1: TDBGrid
    Align = alClient
    DataSource = DataSource1
    OnDrawDataCell = DBGrid1DrawDataCell
  end
  object Table1: TTable
    Active = True
    DatabaseName = 'DBDEMOS'
    TableName = 'INDUSTRY.DBF'
    object Table1IND_NAME: TStringField
      Alignment = taCenter
      DisplayLabel = 'Correct'
      DisplayWidth = 14
      FieldName = 'IND_NAME'
      Size = 5
    end
    object Table1LONG_NAME: TStringField
      Alignment = taCenter
      DisplayLabel = 'Incorrect'
      DisplayWidth = 20
      FieldName = 'LONG_NAME'
```

```
        end
      end
      object DataSource1: TDataSource
        DataSet = Table1
      end
    end
  end
```

FLDCNTRU.PAS

```pascal
unit Fldcntru;

interface

uses SysUtils, WinTypes, WinProcs, Messages, Classes, Graphics,
  Controls, Forms, Dialogs, DB, DBTables, Grids, DBGrids,
  DBCtrls, ExtCtrls;

type
  TForm1 = class(TForm)
    Table1: TTable;
    DataSource1: TDataSource;
    DBGrid1: TDBGrid;
    Table1IND_NAME: TStringField;
    Table1LONG_NAME: TStringField;
    procedure DBGrid1DrawDataCell(Sender: TObject; const Rect:
      TRect; Field: TField; State: TGridDrawState);
    procedure FormCreate(Sender: TObject);
  end;

var Form1: TForm1;

implementation

{$R *.DFM}

procedure TForm1.DBGrid1DrawDataCell(Sender: TObject; const Rect:
  TRect; Field: TField; State: TGridDrawState);
begin
  WITH Sender AS TDBGrid, Canvas DO
    IF (Field.Alignment = taCenter) AND (Field.FieldNo = 2) THEN
      BEGIN
        FillRect(Rect);
        SetTextAlign(Handle, TA_CENTER);
        TextRect(Rect, (Rect.Left+Rect.Right) DIV 2, Rect.Top,
          Field.DisplayText);
        SetTextAlign(Handle, TA_LEFT);
      END;
end;

procedure TForm1.FormCreate(Sender: TObject);
begin
  {$IFNDEF Win32}IF Swap(LoWord(GetVersion)) <> $35F THEN{$ENDIF}
    ShowMessage('This problem only appears in 16-bit '+
      'Delphi under Windows 95');
end;

end.
```

The OnDrawDataCell event handler for the grid lets Delphi's default drawing handle most cells. If the field's alignment is taCenter and the field number is 2, though, it takes over. Drawing the field text centered is a simple matter of using the SetTextAlign Windows API function to select centered text and then calling the canvas object's TextRect method to draw the text within the specified rectangle. Notice that, when the text is center-aligned, the X value passed to TextRect must be the horizontal center of the rectangle. Not only does this problem disappear in Delphi 2.0, the OnDrawDataCell event is superseded by the new OnDrawColumnCell event, which provides detailed formatting information, as defined by the grid column editor.

Using the grid column editor in Delphi 2.0

32

The data-aware grid is vastly more configurable in 32-bit Delphi. Double-click on a DBGrid and the column editor dialog lets you control the appearance of columns individually. You can also specify that values in certain columns must come from a list of predefined values, and even add a button that triggers an event that your program can respond to. Figure 11-2 shows a grid that has been thoroughly customized.

	Cust #	Company Name	Order #	Sale Date	Ship VIA
▶	CN 1351	Sight Diver	#1003	4/12/88	UPS
	CN 2156	Kauai Dive Shoppe	#1004	4/17/88	DHL
	CN 1356	Unisco / Sight Diver	#1005	4/20/88	UPS
	CN 1380	Cayman Divers World Unlimited	#1006	11/6/94	Emery
	CN 1384	Tom Sawyer Diving Centre	#1007	5/1/88	US Mail
	CN 1510	Blue Jack Aqua Center / VIP Divers Club	#1008	5/3/88	US Mail
	CN 1513	Fantastique Aquatica	#1009	5/11/88	US Mail
	CN 1551	Marmot Divers Club	#1010	5/11/88	DHL
	CN 1560	The Depth Charge	#1011	5/18/88	Emery / FedEx
	CN 1563	Blue Sports	#1012	5/19/88	UPS
	CN 1624	Makai SCUBA Club	#1013	5/25/88	US Mail / Emery

Using the DBGrid Columns Editor

FIGURE 11-2: This composite screen shot shows a lookup field in the Company Name column, an ellipsis button in the Sale Date column, and a pick list in the Ship VIA column, along with variations in column formatting

GRIDED

GRIDEDM.DEX

```
object DataModule1: TDataModule1
  object Table1: TTable
    Active = True
    DatabaseName = 'DBDEMOS'
    TableName = 'ORDERS.DB'
    object Table1OrderNo: TFloatField
      FieldName = 'OrderNo'
      DisplayFormat = #39'#'#39'0000'
    end
    object Table1CustNo: TFloatField
      Alignment = taLeftJustify
      FieldName = 'CustNo'
      DisplayFormat = 'CN 0000'
      MaxValue = 9999
      MinValue = 1000
    end
    object Table1SaleDate: TDateTimeField
      FieldName = 'SaleDate'
    end
    object Table1ShipVIA: TStringField
      FieldName = 'ShipVIA'
      Size = 7
    end
    object Table1CompanyName: TStringField
      DisplayWidth = 30
      FieldName = 'CompanyName'
      Lookup = True
      LookupDataSet = Table2
      LookupKeyFields = 'CustNo'
      LookupResultField = 'Company'
      KeyFields = 'CustNo'
      Size = 30
    end
  end
  object Table2: TTable
    Active = True
    DatabaseName = 'DBDEMOS'
    TableName = 'CUSTOMER.DB'
  end
  object DataSource1: TDataSource
    DataSet = Table1
  end
  object DataSource2: TDataSource
    DataSet = Table2
  end
end
```

GRIDEDM.PAS

```pascal
unit gridedm;

interface

uses Windows, Messages, SysUtils, Classes, Graphics, Controls, Forms,
  Dialogs, DBTables, DB;

type
  TDataModule1 = class(TDataModule)
    Table1: TTable;
    Table2: TTable;
    DataSource1: TDataSource;
    DataSource2: TDataSource;
    Table1OrderNo: TFloatField;
    Table1CustNo: TFloatField;
    Table1SaleDate: TDateTimeField;
    Table1ShipVIA: TStringField;
    Table1CompanyName: TStringField;
  end;

var DataModule1: TDataModule1;

implementation

{$R *.DFM}

end.
```

GRIDEDU.DEX

```
object Form1: TForm1
  Caption = 'Using the DBGrid Columns Editor'
  Position = poDefault
  Scaled = False
  object DBGrid1: TDBGrid
    Align = alClient
    Columns = <
      item
        Alignment = taRightJustify
        FieldName = 'CustNo'
        ReadOnly = True
        Title.Alignment = taRightJustify
        Title.Caption = 'Cust #'
      end
      item
        FieldName = 'CompanyName'
        Font.Height = -13
        Font.Style = [fsBold]
        Title.Caption = 'Company Name'
        Title.Font.Height = -13
        Title.Font.Style = [fsBold]
      end
      item
        FieldName = 'OrderNo'
        Font.Height = -13
```

```
              Font.Name = 'Century Gothic'
              Title.Alignment = taRightJustify
              Title.Caption = 'Order #'
              Title.Font.Height = -13
              Title.Font.Name = 'Century Gothic'
              Width = 56
            end
            item
              ButtonStyle = cbsEllipsis
              FieldName = 'SaleDate'
              Title.Caption = 'Sale Date'
            end
            item
              Alignment = taCenter
              Color = clYellow
              FieldName = 'ShipVIA'
              Font.Height = -13
              Font.Name = 'Arial MT Black'
              Font.Style = [fsBold]
              PickList.Strings = (
                'DHL'
                'Emery'
                'FedEx'
                'UPS'
                'US Mail')
              Title.Alignment = taCenter
              Title.Caption = 'Ship VIA'
              Title.Font.Height = -13
              Title.Font.Name = 'Arial MT Black'
              Title.Font.Style = [fsBold]
            end>
        DataSource = DataModule1.DataSource1
        TabOrder = 0
        OnEditButtonClick = DBGrid1EditButtonClick
      end
    end
```

GRIDEDU.PAS

```
unit gridedu;

interface

uses Windows, Messages, SysUtils, Classes, Graphics, Controls, Forms,
  Dialogs, Grids, DBGrids, ExtCtrls, DBCtrls;

type
  TForm1 = class(TForm)
    DBGrid1: TDBGrid;
    procedure DBGrid1EditButtonClick(Sender: TObject);
  end;

var Form1: TForm1;

implementation
```

```
uses gridedm;
{$R *.DFM}
procedure TForm1.DBGrid1EditButtonClick(Sender: TObject);
begin
  WITH Sender AS TDBGrid DO
    BEGIN
      DataSource.DataSet.Edit;
      SelectedField.AsDateTime := Date;
    END;
end;

end.
```

Several of the columns have had specialized formatting applied—the alignment, the font, and the background color can be controlled separately for the title and the data values in each column. The Cust # field is displayed in gray text, to indicate that it is marked as read only. Users enter a customer number by pulling down the lookup list in the Company Name column. The grid automatically supplies a lookup list when a field is defined as a lookup field; no code is required. And, when a company name is chosen, the Cust # field updates automatically.

The Ship VIA column also has a pull-down list, but this one is a simple pick list that allows the user to choose from a set of hard-coded values. Again, no code is required. The values for the pick list are entered in the Columns Editor.

Note the ellipsis button next to the active cell in the Sale Date column. Setting the ButtonStyle property to cbsEllipsis in the Columns Editor causes this button to appear. When the user presses the button, it generates an OnEditButtonClick event. Here, finally, the program uses a few lines of code to set the selected field to the current date. Of course, in reality the grid would not display all three of these features at once—the figure is a composite.

Delphi 1.0 permitted a certain level of control over column display through its DataSet Designer. However, changes made in the DataSet Designer affect *all* components connected to the table in question. Formatting choices made in the Columns Editor affect only the grid whose Columns property is being edited.

Highlighting a row based on field value

16 32

It's possible to control the way a data-aware grid cell is drawn based on the column it's in, as the preceding example showed, or on the contents of the cell. How, though, can you control the drawing of a cell based on the value of *another* field in the current row?

The example program in Figure 11-3 displays the Vendors example database in a grid. If the Preferred field is True, all the cells in the row are displayed with underlined red text.

FIGURE 11-3: All fields are displayed in underlined red text for preferred vendors in this example program; other formatting from the Delphi 2.0 Columns Editor is retained.

FLDRED

FLDREDU.DEX

```
object Form1: TForm1
  Caption = 'Preferred Vendors Emphasized'
  object DBGrid1: TDBGrid
    Align = alClient
    DataSource = DataSource1
    OnDrawDataCell = DBGrid1DrawDataCell
  end
  object Table1: TTable
    Active = True
    DatabaseName = 'DBDEMOS'
    TableName = 'VENDORS.DB'
  end
  object DataSource1: TDataSource
    DataSet = Table1
  end
end
```

FLDREDU.PAS

```
unit fldredu;

interface

uses WinTypes, WinProcs, Messages, SysUtils, Classes, Graphics,
  Controls, Forms, Dialogs, Grids, DBGrids, DB, DBTables;
```

```
type
  TForm1 = class(TForm)
    Table1: TTable;
    DataSource1: TDataSource;
    DBGrid1: TDBGrid;
    procedure DBGrid1DrawDataCell(Sender: TObject; const Rect:
      TRect; Field: TField; State: TGridDrawState);
    procedure FormCreate(Sender: TObject);
  private
    {$IFDEF Win32}
    procedure DBGrid1DrawColumnCell(Sender: TObject;
      const Rect: TRect; DataCol: Integer; Column: TColumn;
      State: TGridDrawState);
    {$ENDIF}
    procedure DrawField(const Value: String; const Rect: TRect;
      vCanvas: TCanvas; vFont: TFont; vAlignment: TAlignment);
  end;

var Form1: TForm1;

implementation

{$R *.DFM}

procedure TForm1.DrawField(const Value: String; const Rect: TRect;
  vCanvas: TCanvas; vFont: TFont; vAlignment: TAlignment);
VAR X : Integer;
BEGIN
  vCanvas.Font := vFont;
  vCanvas.Font.Color := clRed;
  vCanvas.Font.Style := vCanvas.Font.Style + [fsUnderline];
  CASE vAlignment OF
    taRightJustify : BEGIN
      SetTextAlign(vCanvas.Handle, TA_RIGHT);
      X := Rect.Right-2;
    END;
    taLeftJustify  : BEGIN
      SetTextAlign(vCanvas.Handle, TA_LEFT);
      X := Rect.Left+2;
    END;
    taCenter       : BEGIN
      SetTextAlign(vCanvas.Handle, TA_CENTER);
      X := (Rect.Right+Rect.Left) DIV 2;
    END;
  END;
  vCanvas.TextRect(Rect, X, Rect.Top+2, Value);
  SetTextAlign(vCanvas.Handle, TA_LEFT);
END;

procedure TForm1.DBGrid1DrawDataCell(Sender: TObject; const Rect:
  TRect; Field: TField; State: TGridDrawState);
begin
  WITH Sender AS TDBGrid, DataSource.DataSet DO
    BEGIN
      IF FieldByName('Preferred').AsString <> 'True' THEN Exit;
      DrawField(Field.DisplayText, Rect, Canvas, Canvas.Font,
```

```
        Field.Alignment);
    END;
  end;
  {$IFDEF Win32}
  procedure TForm1.DBGrid1DrawColumnCell(Sender: TObject;
    const Rect: TRect; DataCol: Integer; Column: TColumn;
    State: TGridDrawState);
  begin
    WITH Sender AS TDBGrid, DataSource.DataSet DO
      BEGIN
        IF FieldByName('Preferred').AsString <> 'True' THEN Exit;
        DrawField(Column.Field.DisplayText, Rect, Canvas,
          Column.Font, Column.Alignment);
      END;
  end;
  {$ENDIF}
  procedure TForm1.FormCreate(Sender: TObject);
  begin
    {$IFDEF Win32}
    DBGrid1.OnDrawDataCell := NIL;
    DBGrid1.OnDrawColumnCell := DBGrid1DrawColumnCell;
    {$ENDIF}
  end;

  end.
```

The important thing to realize here is that, although the Field parameter passed to the OnDrawDataCell handler defines the field for the specific cell being drawn, the Fields property of the grid contains all the field values for the current row. Thus, the event handler can check the value of the Preferred field and determine how to draw any cell in the row based on that field's value.

In Delphi 2.0, the OnDrawColumnCell event replaces OnDrawDataCell. To allow this program to compile with both versions of Delphi, the OnDrawColumnCell event handler is installed in the form's OnCreate event handler. It calls the same private DrawField method as the OnDrawDataCell handler did, but it uses the font, the alignment, and the field information from the TColumn object. Thus, any formatting applied in the Columns Editor will be retained.

Problems moving and resizing columns at design time

16 32

When a data-aware grid object's dgColumnResize option property is True, the user can move or resize the columns at runtime by dragging the column titles or the lines that separate them. The programmer can move and resize the columns at design time, too, but only sometimes. What makes the difference?

It turns out that you can't manipulate columns at design time unless you've added field components to your form by double-clicking the table to which the grid is connected and using the Fields editor or, in Delphi 2.0, using the Columns Editor to define persistent columns. There's no place to store the position and field display width information if you haven't created field components, so Delphi does not permit moving or resizing.

Updating Edit Controls

Most data entry in Delphi database programs will occur through a data-aware edit control of one kind or another. The data-aware versions of edit boxes, memo boxes, and grid-owned in-place editors work in almost the same way as their nonaware counterparts. However, getting past that "almost" can take a bit of work.

 Updating a memo field

16 32

It's easy for the user of a Delphi program to update a data-aware memo box by simply clicking on it and typing changes. However, when you attempt to change a memo field under program control, it doesn't always "take." The missing step is this: you must put the corresponding data set into edit mode first. The program shown in Figure 11-4 illustrates a technique for copying a data-aware memo component's contents to and from a plain memo box.

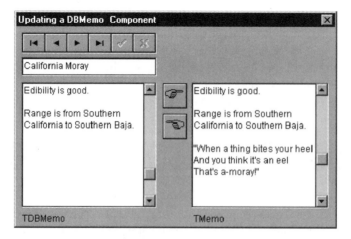

FIGURE 11-4: To change the contents of a data-aware memo box, you must put its data set into edit mode first.

UPDMEMF

UPDMEMFU.DEX

```
object Form1: TForm1
  BorderIcons = [biSystemMenu]
  BorderStyle = bsDialog
  Caption = 'Updating a DBMemo  Component'
  Position = poDefault
  Scaled = False
  object SpeedButton1: TSpeedButton
    Caption = 'F'
    Font.Height = -32
    Font.Name = 'WingDings'
    ParentFont = False
    OnClick = SpeedButton1Click
  end
  object SpeedButton2: TSpeedButton
    Caption = 'E'
    Font.Height = -32
    Font.Name = 'WingDings'
    ParentFont = False
    OnClick = SpeedButton2Click
  end
  object Label1: TLabel
    Caption = 'TDBMemo'
  end
  object Label2: TLabel
    Caption = 'TMemo'
  end
  object DBNavigator1: TDBNavigator
    DataSource = DataSource1
    VisibleButtons = [nbFirst, nbPrior, nbNext, nbLast, nbPost,
nbCancel]
  end
  object DBMemo1: TDBMemo
    DataField = 'Notes'
    DataSource = DataSource1
    ReadOnly = True
    ScrollBars = ssVertical
  end
  object Memo1: TMemo
    ScrollBars = ssVertical
  end
  object DBEdit1: TDBEdit
    DataField = 'Common_Name'
    DataSource = DataSource1
    MaxLength = 30
  end
  object Table1: TTable
    Active = True
    DatabaseName = 'DBDEMOS'
    TableName = 'BIOLIFE.DB'
```

```
      end
    object DataSource1: TDataSource
      DataSet = Table1
    end
  end
end
```

UPDMEMFU.PAS

```pascal
unit Updmemfu;

interface

uses SysUtils, WinTypes, WinProcs, Messages, Classes, Graphics,
  Controls, Forms, Dialogs, DB, DBTables, Mask, DBCtrls,
  StdCtrls, ExtCtrls, Buttons;

type
  TForm1 = class(TForm)
    Table1: TTable;
    DataSource1: TDataSource;
    DBNavigator1: TDBNavigator;
    DBMemo1: TDBMemo;
    Memo1: TMemo;
    DBEdit1: TDBEdit;
    SpeedButton1: TSpeedButton;
    SpeedButton2: TSpeedButton;
    Label1: TLabel;
    Label2: TLabel;
    procedure SpeedButton1Click(Sender: TObject);
    procedure SpeedButton2Click(Sender: TObject);
  end;

var Form1: TForm1;

implementation

{$R *.DFM}

procedure TForm1.SpeedButton1Click(Sender: TObject);
begin
  Memo1.Lines := DBMemo1.Lines;
end;

procedure TForm1.SpeedButton2Click(Sender: TObject);
begin
  Table1.Edit;
  DBMemo1.Lines := Memo1.Lines;
end;

end.
```

To copy the data-aware memo box's lines to the ordinary memo box, a simple assignment statement is sufficient. To go the other way, the program must put the table in edit mode first. Note that, after you move text into the memo box, the table is not immediately updated. You can accept the change by moving to another record or by pressing the post (check mark) button on the navigator. Or, you can reject it by pressing the cancel (X) button on the navigator.

The design of this program is fancier than the code, by far. You'll want to keep in mind the technique of creating speed button glyphs by using a caption consisting of one large character in the WingDings font. The CharMap accessory present in Windows 3.1, Windows 95, and Windows NT, provides an easy way to match symbols to their corresponding text character. For example, the left and right pointing hand symbols correspond to E and F.

Modifying data-aware edit text

16 32

Chapter 6, "Edit Controls," illustrated a technique for inserting text into edit controls of all sorts, including the in-place editor of a string grid. Extending this technique to data-aware edit components is a matter of putting the source data set in edit mode first. Incorporating the in-place editor for a data-aware grid also requires that the change be copied back to the data field that's being edited. Figure 11-5 is a demonstration program that shows how this might be done.

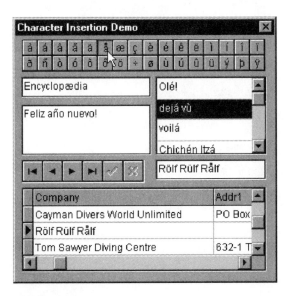

FIGURE 11-5: The 32 tiny speed buttons serve to insert foreign characters in any regular or data-aware edit control.

MODEDID

MODEDIDU.DEX

```
object Form1: TForm1
  BorderIcons = [biSystemMenu]
  BorderStyle = bsDialog
  Caption = 'Character Insertion Demo'
  Position = poDefault
  Scaled = False
  OnCreate = FormCreate
  object Edit1: TEdit
  end
  object StringGrid1: TStringGrid
    ColCount = 1
    FixedCols = 0
    FixedRows = 0
    Options = [goFixedVertLine, goFixedHorzLine, goVertLine,
goHorzLine, goRangeSelect, goEditing]
    RowCount = 4
    ScrollBars = ssVertical
  end
  object Memo1: TMemo
  end
  object DBGrid1: TDBGrid
    DataSource = DataSource1
  end
  object DBEdit1: TDBEdit
    DataField = 'Company'
    DataSource = DataSource1
    MaxLength = 30
  end
  object DBNavigator1: TDBNavigator
    DataSource = DataSource1
    VisibleButtons = [nbFirst, nbPrior, nbNext, nbLast, nbPost,
nbCancel]
  end
  object Table1: TTable
    Active = True
    DatabaseName = 'DBDEMOS'
    TableName = 'CUSTOMER.DB'
  end
  object DataSource1: TDataSource
    DataSet = Table1
  end
end
```

MODEDIDU.PAS

```
unit Modedidu;

interface

uses SysUtils, WinTypes, WinProcs, Messages, Classes, Graphics,
```

```
    Controls, Forms, Dialogs, Mask, DBCtrls, DBGrids, DB,
    DBTables, StdCtrls, Grids, Buttons, ExtCtrls;
type
  TForm1 = class(TForm)
    Edit1: TEdit;
    StringGrid1: TStringGrid;
    Memo1: TMemo;
    Table1: TTable;
    DataSource1: TDataSource;
    DBGrid1: TDBGrid;
    DBEdit1: TDBEdit;
    DBNavigator1: TDBNavigator;
    procedure SpeedButton1Click(Sender: TObject);
    procedure FormCreate(Sender: TObject);
  end;

var Form1: TForm1;

implementation

{$R *.DFM}
procedure TForm1.SpeedButton1Click(Sender: TObject);
begin
  IF ActiveControl IS TDBEdit THEN {*before* TCustomEdit}
    WITH TDBEdit(ActiveControl) DO
      BEGIN
        DataSource.Edit;
        SelText := (Sender AS TSpeedButton).Caption;
      END
  ELSE IF ActiveControl IS TCustomEdit THEN
    WITH TCustomEdit(ActiveControl) DO
      SelText := (Sender AS TSpeedButton).Caption
  ELSE IF ActiveControl IS TDBGrid THEN {*before* TCustomGrid}
    BEGIN
      WITH TDBGrid(ActiveControl) DO
        IF ControlCount > 0 THEN
          IF (Controls[0] IS TInPlaceEdit) AND EditorMode THEN
            BEGIN
              DataSource.Edit;
              TInPlaceEdit(Controls[0]).SelText :=
                (Sender AS TSpeedButton).Caption;
              SelectedField.AsString :=
                TInPlaceEdit(Controls[0]).Text;
            END;
    END
  ELSE IF ActiveControl IS TCustomGrid THEN
    WITH TCustomGrid(ActiveControl) DO
      IF ControlCount > 0 THEN
        IF Controls[0] IS TCustomEdit THEN
          WITH TCustomEdit(Controls[0]) DO
            SelText := (Sender AS TSpeedButton).Caption;
end;

procedure TForm1.FormCreate(Sender: TObject);
VAR Co, Ro : Integer;
begin
```

```
    FOR Ro := 0 TO 1 DO
      FOR Co := 0 TO 15 DO
        WITH TSpeedButton.Create(Self) DO
          BEGIN
            Parent  := Self;
            Width   := 19;
            Height  := 19;
            Caption := Char(224+Ro*16+co);
            Left    := 8+18*Co;
            Top     := 4+18*Ro;
            OnClick := SpeedButton1Click;
          END;
    StringGrid1.Cols[0].SetText ('Ole!'#13'deja vu'#13'voila'+
      #13'Chichen Itza');
  end;

end.
```

The 32 special-character speed buttons are created in the form's OnCreate event handler. It's important that speed buttons be used here. A regular or bitmapped button wouldn't work because clicking it would make it the active control. This would take the input focus away from the edit component, and the ActiveControl property would no longer identify the active edit component. Speed buttons are graphic controls, with no window handle of their own. They never become the active control.

Each of these speed buttons is connected to the same OnClick event handler. The OnClick event handler for these speed buttons inserts the specified character into the text of the active control. If a bitmapped or a regular button were used, the button itself would be the active control!

The handler is very similar to the one used in Chapter 6, "Edit Controls." Because the IS operator returns True if the actual object is any descendant of the requested type, it checks for TDBEdit before TCustomEdit, and for TDBGrid before TCustomGrid. Both of the data-aware components must have their source data set put into edit mode before the insertion. In addition, the text of the grid's in-place editor must be copied into the corresponding data field. It's a bit more complicated than the earlier example, but the same code will service any number of edit controls, data-aware and otherwise.

More Grid Goodies

The data-aware grid is incredibly versatile and simple to use. Connect a table, a data source, and a grid and you've got an instant database editor that doesn't need any advance information about the table it's processing. Or, connect a grid to a specific table and fine-tune its display characteristics. There's little you can't do with a grid, especially if you're willing to wade in and add a few enhancements.

Showing memo and graphic fields in a grid

16 32

The data-aware grid is an extremely handy component for getting a quick look at table contents. However, it looks really tacky to have memo fields simply display as "(Memo)" and graphic fields as "(BMP)". The component shown in Figure 11-6 displays both memo and graphic fields within its cells. Two clicks on a graphic brings up a full-size display window; two clicks on a memo brings up an editable window on the same field.

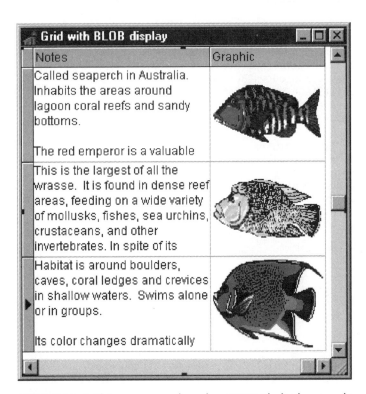

FIGURE 11-6: This component, based on TDBGrid, displays graphic and memo fields in the allotted space. Look closely; this screen shot was snapped at design time!

TDBGRIDBLOB

C_DGBLOB.PAS

```
unit C_dgblob;

interface

uses SysUtils, WinTypes, WinProcs, Messages, Classes, Graphics,
  Controls, Forms, Dialogs, Grids, DBGrids, DB, DBTables,
  DBCtrls, p_about;

type
  TDBGridBlob = class(TDBGrid)
  private
    fAbout : TAbout;
    fMyDefaultRowHeight : Integer;
    function GetDefaultRowHeight: Integer;
    procedure SetDefaultRowHeight(Value: Integer);
  protected
    procedure LayoutChanged; override;
    procedure RowHeightsChanged; override;
    procedure DrawCell(ACol, ARow: Longint; ARect: TRect;
      AState: TGridDrawState); override;
    procedure MouseDown(Button: TMouseButton; Shift:
      TShiftState; X, Y: Integer); override;
    procedure ColEnter; override;
    procedure ColExit; override;
  public
    property RowHeights;
    constructor Create(AOwner: TComponent); override;
  published
    property About: TAbout read fAbout write fAbout;
    property DefaultRowHeight:Integer Read GetDefaultRowHeight
      Write SetDefaultRowHeight;
  end;

procedure Register;

implementation
USES f_dbgmem, f_dbggra;
{$IFDEF Win32}
{$R *.R32}
{$ELSE}
{$R *.R16}
{$ENDIF}

constructor TDBGridBlob.Create(AOwner: TComponent);
begin
  Inherited Create(AOwner);
  fAbout := 0.99;
  WITH TStringGrid(Self) DO Options := Options + [goRowSizing];
end;

function TDBGridBlob.GetDefaultRowHeight: Integer;
```

```
begin
  Result := Inherited DefaultRowHeight;
end;
procedure TDBGridBlob.SetDefaultRowHeight(Value: Integer);
begin
  Inherited DefaultRowHeight := Value;
  fMyDefaultRowHeight := Value;
  IF dgTitles IN Options THEN
    BEGIN
      Canvas.Font := TitleFont;
      RowHeights[0] := Canvas.TextHeight('W') + 4;
    END;
end;
procedure TDBGridBlob.LayoutChanged;
begin
  Inherited LayoutChanged;
  SetDefaultRowHeight(fMyDefaultRowHeight);
end;
procedure TDBGridBlob.RowHeightsChanged;
VAR N, WhichOneChanged, Start : Integer;
BEGIN
  WhichOneChanged := -1;
  Start           := 0;
  IF dgTitles IN Options THEN Start := 1;
  FOR N := Start TO RowCount DO
    IF RowHeights[N] <> DefaultRowHeight THEN
      WhichOneChanged := N;
  IF WhichOneChanged <> -1 THEN
    SetDefaultRowHeight(RowHeights[WhichOneChanged]);
END;
procedure TDBGridBlob.DrawCell(ACol, ARow: Longint; ARect:
  TRect; AState: TGridDrawState);
VAR
  Field     : TField;
  TB        : TBitmap;
  R         : TRect;
  P         : PChar;
  OldActive : Integer;
begin
  Field := GetColField(ACol-Ord(dgIndicator in Options));
  IF (gdFixed IN AState) OR (NOT (Field IS TBlobField)) THEN
    BEGIN
      Inherited DrawCell(ACol, ARow, ARect, AState);
      Exit;
    END;
  Dec(ARow, Ord(dgTitles in Options));
  Dec(ACol, Ord(dgIndicator in Options));
  OldActive := DataLink.ActiveRecord;
  try
    DataLink.ActiveRecord := ARow;
```

```
      IF Field IS TMemoField THEN
        BEGIN
          IF HighlightCell(ACol, ARow, ' ', AState) THEN
            BEGIN
              Canvas.Brush.Color := clHighlight;
              Canvas.Font.Color := clHighlightText;
            END
          ELSE
            BEGIN
              Canvas.Brush.Color := Color;
              Canvas.Font.Color := Font.Color;
            END;
          Canvas.FillRect(ARect);
          R := ARect;
          {$IFDEF Win32}
          WITH TMemoField(Field) DO
            DrawText(Canvas.Handle, PChar(Value), Length(Value), R,
              DT_WORDBREAK OR DT_NOPREFIX);
          {$ELSE}
          WITH TStringList.Create DO
            try
              Assign(TMemoField(Field));
              P := GetText;
              DrawText(Canvas.Handle, P, StrLen(P), R,
                DT_WORDBREAK OR DT_NOPREFIX);
              StrDispose(P);
            finally
              Free;
            end;
          {$ENDIF}
          IF gdFocused in AState THEN Canvas.DrawFocusRect(ARect);
        END
      ELSE IF Field IS TGraphicField THEN
        BEGIN
          TB := TBitmap.Create;
          try
            TB.Assign(TGraphicField(Field));
            Canvas.StretchDraw(ARect, TB);
          finally
            TB.Free;
          end;
          IF gdFocused in AState THEN Canvas.DrawFocusRect(ARect);
        END;
    finally
      DataLink.ActiveRecord := OldActive;
    end;
end;

procedure TDBGridBlob.MouseDown(Button: TMouseButton; Shift:
  TShiftState; X, Y: Integer);
VAR
  IsBlobTwice : Boolean;
  Location    : TPoint;
```

```
BEGIN
  Location := ClientToScreen(Point(X,Y));
  IsBlobTwice := False;
  IF (NOT ((ssDouble in Shift) and (Button = mbLeft))) AND
    (NOT Sizing(X, Y)) THEN
    begin
      WITH MouseCoord(X, Y) DO
        IF (X = Col) AND (Y = Row) THEN
          IF SelectedField IS TBlobField THEN
            IsBlobTwice := True;
    end;
  IF IsBlobTwice THEN
    BEGIN
      IF SelectedField IS TMemoField THEN
        WITH TDBGridMemoForm.Create(Self) DO
          try
            Left := Location.X;
            Top := Location.Y;
            Caption := Format('Edit Memo Field "%s"',
              [SelectedField.FieldName]);
            Memo1.Lines.Assign(TMemoField(SelectedField));
            IF (ShowModal = mrOK) AND Memo1.Modified THEN
              BEGIN
                DataSource.DataSet.Edit;
                TMemoField(SelectedField).Assign(Memo1.Lines);
                DataSource.DataSet.Post;
              END;
          finally
            Free;
          end
      ELSE IF SelectedField IS TGraphicField THEN
        WITH TDBGridGrafForm.Create(Self) DO
          try
            Left := Location.X;
            Top := Location.Y;
            Caption := Format('View Graphic Field "%s"',
              [SelectedField.FieldName]);
            Image1.Picture.Bitmap.Assign(
              TGraphicField(SelectedField));
            ClientWidth := Image1.Width;
            ClientHeight := Image1.Height + Panel1.Height;
            ShowModal;
          finally
            free;
          end;
    END
  ELSE Inherited MouseDown(Button, Shift, X, Y)
END;

procedure TDBGridBlob.ColEnter;
begin
  IF SelectedField IS TBlobField THEN
```

```
      BEGIN
        Options := Options - [dgEditing];
        WITH TStringGrid(Self) DO
          Options := Options + [goRowSizing];
      END;
    Inherited ColEnter;
  end;

  procedure TDBGridBlob.ColExit;
  begin
    Options := Options + [dgEditing];
    WITH TStringGrid(Self) DO Options := Options + [goRowSizing];
    Inherited ColExit;
  end;

  procedure Register;
  begin
    RegisterComponents('NJR', [TDBGridBlob]);
  end;

  end.
```

F_DBGMEM.DEX

```
  object DBGridMemoForm: TDBGridMemoForm
    BorderIcons = [biSystemMenu]
    BorderStyle = bsDialog
    Caption = 'Edit Memo Field'
    Position = poDefault
    Scaled = False
    object Panel1: TPanel
      Align = alBottom
      BevelOuter = bvNone
      object BitBtn1: TBitBtn
        Kind = bkOK
      end
      object BitBtn2: TBitBtn
        Kind = bkCancel
      end
    end
    object Memo1: TMemo
      Align = alClient
      BorderStyle = bsNone
      ScrollBars = ssVertical
    end
  end
```

F_DBGGRA.DEX

```
  object DBGridGrafForm: TDBGridGrafForm
    BorderIcons = [biSystemMenu]
```

```
      BorderStyle = bsDialog
      Caption = 'DBGridGrafForm'
      object Image1: TImage
        AutoSize = True
      end
      object Panel1: TPanel
        Align = alBottom
        BevelOuter = bvNone
        object BitBtn1: TBitBtn
          Kind = bkOK
        end
      end
    end
```

It's surprisingly difficult to modify the behavior of the data-aware grid. The component's inner workings are so intricate that you almost have to rewrite it from scratch to add new behavior. Certainly, it would not have been possible without frequent reference to the VCL source code.

The core of this component is the DrawCell method. If the field to be drawn is a memo field, this method uses the powerful Windows API function DrawText to display as much of it as will fit in the cell, with word-wrapping. If it's a graphic field, the method assigns it to a temporary TBitmap object and stretches that object to display in the cell. Any other field type simply gets passed to the Default handler.

Most of the other methods in this component are defenses against TDBGrid's default behavior coming through. For example, it's necessary to prevent these fields from going into ordinary edit mode when the user clicks twice. Edit mode for blob fields is pointless in the first place, as any attempts to change the default strings are rejected. The TDBGridBlob component overrides the MouseDown method and watches for the situation that normally triggers the in-place editor—two clicks in the same cell. If this occurs and the column is a memo field, the MouseDown method displays the full text of the memo in a modal form. If the column is a graphic field, the method displays it at full size in a modal form.

Also, there's not much point in allowing the display of memo fields and graphics if they're going to be squeezed into a long, skinny rectangle. The TDBGridBlob component's constructor enables the goRowSizing option inherited from TCustomGrid. It overrides the LayoutChanged and RowHeightsChanged methods and the read/write methods of the DefaultRowHeight property to adjust the grid's row heights, so that all except the title row (if any) get changed when any one of them is changed. The result is that resizing one row by dragging the row separator line in the indicator column will resize them all.

Duplicating Paradox multirecord objects

32

In Delphi 1.0, a form for data entry takes one of two basic formats. It can contain an arrangement of individual data-aware components for the individual fields of a table, or it can use a single data-aware grid for editing the whole table, with each record stretched horizontally into one long row. With Delphi 2.0, there's a third option that falls between these two extremes. Paradox programmers are already familiar with this option—they call it a multirecord object. Delphi 2.0 implements it as the TDBCtrlGrid. This component is included in the Delphi Developer package and the Delphi Client/Server Suite, but not in the low-end Delphi Desktop package. Figure 11-7 shows the kind of form layout this component makes possible.

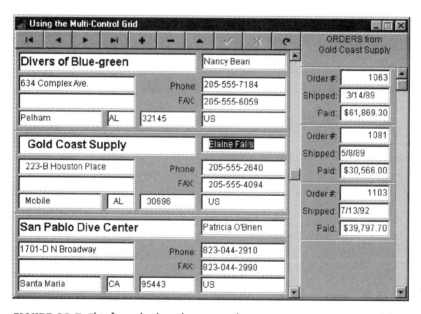

FIGURE 11-7: This form displays three records at a time in an easy-to-read format; order information for the selected record appears in a column at the right.

DBCTLGR

DBCTLGRU.DEX

```
object Form1: TForm1
  BorderIcons = [biSystemMenu, biMinimize]
  BorderStyle = bsSingle
  Caption = 'Using the Multi-Control Grid'
```

```
Position = poDefault
Scaled = False
object DBCtrlGrid1: TDBCtrlGrid
  DataSource = DataModule1.DataSource1
  RowCount = 3
  object TLabel
    Alignment = taRightJustify
    Caption = 'Phone:'
  end
  object TLabel
    Alignment = taRightJustify
    Caption = 'FAX:'
  end
  object DBEdit1: TDBEdit
    DataField = 'Company'
    DataSource = DataModule1.DataSource1
    Font.Height = -16
    Font.Style = [fsBold]
    MaxLength = 0
    ParentFont = False
  end
  object DBEdit2: TDBEdit
    DataField = 'Contact'
    DataSource = DataModule1.DataSource1
    MaxLength = 0
  end
  object DBEdit3: TDBEdit
    DataField = 'Addr1'
    DataSource = DataModule1.DataSource1
    MaxLength = 0
  end
  object DBEdit4: TDBEdit
    DataField = 'Addr2'
    DataSource = DataModule1.DataSource1
    MaxLength = 0
  end
  object DBEdit5: TDBEdit
    DataField = 'City'
    DataSource = DataModule1.DataSource1
    MaxLength = 0
  end
  object DBEdit6: TDBEdit
    DataField = 'State'
    DataSource = DataModule1.DataSource1
    MaxLength = 0
  end
  object DBEdit7: TDBEdit
    DataField = 'Zip'
    DataSource = DataModule1.DataSource1
    MaxLength = 0
  end
  object DBEdit8: TDBEdit
    DataField = 'Country'
```

```
      DataSource = DataModule1.DataSource1
      MaxLength = 0
    end
    object DBEdit9: TDBEdit
      DataField = 'Phone'
      DataSource = DataModule1.DataSource1
      MaxLength = 0
    end
    object DBEdit10: TDBEdit
      DataField = 'FAX'
      DataSource = DataModule1.DataSource1
      MaxLength = 0
    end
  end
  object DBNavigator1: TDBNavigator
    DataSource = DataModule1.DataSource1
  end
  object DBCtrlGrid2: TDBCtrlGrid
    DataSource = DataModule1.DataSource2
    RowCount = 4
    object TLabel
      Alignment = taRightJustify
      Caption = 'Order #:'
    end
    object TLabel
      Alignment = taRightJustify
      Caption = 'Shipped:'
    end
    object TLabel
      Alignment = taRightJustify
      Caption = 'Paid:'
    end
    object DBEdit12: TDBEdit
      DataField = 'ShipDate'
      DataSource = DataModule1.DataSource2
      MaxLength = 0
    end
    object DBEdit14: TDBEdit
      DataField = 'AmountPaid'
      DataSource = DataModule1.DataSource2
      MaxLength = 0
    end
    object DBEdit15: TDBEdit
      DataField = 'OrderNo'
      DataSource = DataModule1.DataSource2
      MaxLength = 0
    end
  end
  object Panel1: TPanel
    object DBText1: TDBText
      Align = alClient
      Alignment = taCenter
```

```
      DataField = 'Company'
      DataSource = DataModule1.DataSource1
      WordWrap = True
    end
    object Label1: TLabel
      Align = alTop
      Alignment = taCenter
      AutoSize = False
      Caption = 'ORDERS from'
    end
  end
end
```

DBCTLGRM.DEX

```
object DataModule1: TDataModule1
  object Table1: TTable
    Active = True
    DatabaseName = 'DBDEMOS'
    TableName = 'CUSTOMER.DB'
  end
  object DataSource1: TDataSource
    DataSet = Table1
  end
  object Table2: TTable
    Active = True
    DatabaseName = 'DBDEMOS'
    IndexName = 'CustNo'
    MasterFields = 'CustNo'
    MasterSource = DataSource1
    TableName = 'ORDERS.DB'
  end
  object DataSource2: TDataSource
    DataSet = Table2
  end
end
```

Because this program can only be compiled using Delphi 2.0, it's free to make use of the new data module concept as well. All the nonvisual database components are stored in a separate pseudo-form, created by selecting New Data Module . . . from the File menu. Once this unit is added to the main form's uses clause, the components it contains are available for use by data-aware components on the main form.

To lay out a DBCtrlGrid, you connect it to a data source and start placing data-aware components in its first cell. All these components will automatically use the same data source as the grid. You set the RowCount and ColCount properties to determine how many records will be visible at once in the grid. Components placed in the first cell will be replicated in each of the visible grid cells.

Note that not every component can be used within the DBCtrlGrid. Data-aware labels, edit boxes, and check boxes can be used, but not data-aware images or memo components, nor any of the data-aware list or combo boxes. Non-data-aware labels, group boxes, panels, shapes, images, and bevels can be inserted, but not every component is permitted.

This component exists as a happy medium between the grid, which displays many records at once but forces you to scroll horizontally to see a whole record, and the component-filled form which shows a whole record, but only one record. With a DBCtrlGrid, you can display several records at a time, much more readably than if they appeared in a grid.

Sharing Tables

When multiple forms in your application need to access the same database tables, you need to ensure they use the same table *objects*. Otherwise synchronization problems can arise. Delphi 2.0 makes this sharing simple, though it's certainly possible in Delphi 1.0.

 Two forms accessing the same table

16

It's not uncommon for a database program to use a secondary form for data entry. Perhaps the main form contains the most common data fields and the secondary form is used for fields that aren't always used. Naturally, you can put a table component on each form to give both of them access, but problems can arise if both tables are modifying the same record. The solution in 16-bit Delphi is to use a single table owned by the main form and connect the secondary form to it at runtime, as shown in this program:

SHARTBL

SHARTB1U.DEX

```
object Form1: TForm1
  Caption = 'Shared Table Demo'
  Position = poDefault
  Scaled = False
  object DBGrid1: TDBGrid
    Align = alClient
    DataSource = DataSource1
  end
```

```
object Panel1: TPanel
  Align = alTop
  BevelInner = bvLowered
  object Button1: TButton
    Caption = 'Edit Address'
    OnClick = Button1Click
  end
  object DBNavigator1: TDBNavigator
    DataSource = DataSource1
  end
end
object Table1: TTable
  Active = True
  DatabaseName = 'DBDEMOS'
  TableName = 'CUSTOMER.DB'
end
object DataSource1: TDataSource
  DataSet = Table1
end
end
```

SHARTB1U.PAS

```
unit Shartb1u;

interface

uses SysUtils, WinTypes, WinProcs, Messages, Classes, Graphics,
  Controls, Forms, Dialogs, DB, DBTables, DBCtrls, StdCtrls,
  ExtCtrls, Grids, DBGrids;

type
  TForm1 = class(TForm)
    Table1: TTable;
    DataSource1: TDataSource;
    DBGrid1: TDBGrid;
    Panel1: TPanel;
    Button1: TButton;
    DBNavigator1: TDBNavigator;
    procedure Button1Click(Sender: TObject);
  end;

var Form1: TForm1;

implementation
Uses shartb2u;
{$R *.DFM}

procedure TForm1.Button1Click(Sender: TObject);
begin
  WITH TForm2.Create(Application) DO
    try
      DataSource1.DataSet := Table1;
      IF ShowModal = mrOK THEN
        BEGIN
```

```
                IF Table1.Modified THEN Table1.Post;
              END
            ELSE Table1.Cancel;
        finally
          Free;
        end;
  end;

  end.
```

SHARTB2U.DEX

```
object Form2: TForm2
  BorderIcons = [biSystemMenu]
  BorderStyle = bsDialog
  Caption = 'Address Form'
  Position = poDefault
  Scaled = False
  object DBEdit1: TDBEdit
    DataField = 'Company'
    DataSource = DataSource1
    MaxLength = 0
  end
  object DBEdit2: TDBEdit
    DataField = 'Addr1'
    DataSource = DataSource1
    MaxLength = 0
  end
  object DBEdit3: TDBEdit
    DataField = 'Addr2'
    DataSource = DataSource1
    MaxLength = 0
  end
  object DBEdit4: TDBEdit
    DataField = 'City'
    DataSource = DataSource1
    MaxLength = 0
  end
  object DBEdit5: TDBEdit
    DataField = 'State'
    DataSource = DataSource1
    MaxLength = 0
  end
  object DBEdit6: TDBEdit
    DataField = 'Zip'
    DataSource = DataSource1
    MaxLength = 0
  end
  object BitBtn1: TBitBtn
    Kind = bkOK
  end
  object BitBtn2: TBitBtn
```

```
      Kind = bkCancel
    end
    object DataSource1: TDataSource
    end
  end
end
```

There's no need to show the code for SHARTB2U.PAS, as it consists of nothing but Delphi-created declarations. When the user presses the Edit Address button on the main form, it creates and displays a modal instance of the secondary form. However, before calling ShowModal, it connects the data source on the secondary form to the table on the main form. Changes made in the secondary form are reflected in the main form as soon as you press OK—the forms stay in synch.

When designing such a system, it's best to place a table component on the secondary form during the design process, so you'll have access to the field names. Simply delete it when you're done placing data-aware components.

Two forms accessing the same table

32

In Delphi 2.0, hooking two forms to the same table is utterly simple. Just put a table component and a data source into a data module, set the two forms to use the data module's unit, then connect all appropriate components in both forms to that data source. The program shown in Figure 11-8 takes further advantage of Delphi 2.0 by invoking the address dialog from an edit button in the Company column of the grid, rather than using an external button component.

SHAR32

SHAR321U.DEX

```
object Form1: TForm1
  Caption = 'Shared Table Demo (32-bit)'
  Position = poDefault
  Scaled = False
  object DBGrid1: TDBGrid
    Align = alClient
    Columns = <
      item
        FieldName = 'CustNo'
        Width = 55
      end
      item
        ButtonStyle = cbsEllipsis
```

```
            FieldName = 'Company'
        end
        item
            FieldName = 'Phone'
        end
        item
            FieldName = 'FAX'
        end
        item
            FieldName = 'TaxRate'
        end
        item
            FieldName = 'Contact'
        end
        item
            FieldName = 'LastInvoiceDate'
            Width = 103
        end>
      DataSource = DataModule1.DataSource1
      OnEditButtonClick = DBGrid1EditButtonClick
    end
    object DBNavigator1: TDBNavigator
      DataSource = DataModule1.DataSource1
      Align = alTop
    end
  end
end
```

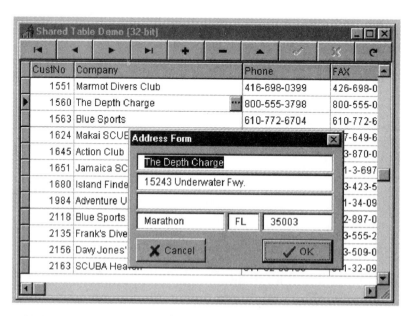

FIGURE 11-8: Components on the address form are connected to the same table as the grid on the main form.

SHAR321U.PAS

```
unit shar321u;

interface

uses
  Windows, Messages, SysUtils, Classes, Graphics, Controls, Forms,
  Dialogs, DB, DBTables, DBCtrls, StdCtrls, ExtCtrls, Grids,
  DBGrids;

type
  TForm1 = class(TForm)
    DBGrid1: TDBGrid;
    DBNavigator1: TDBNavigator;
    procedure DBGrid1EditButtonClick(Sender: TObject);
  end;

var Form1: TForm1;

implementation
Uses shar322u, shar32m;
{$R *.DFM}

procedure TForm1.DBGrid1EditButtonClick(Sender: TObject);
begin
  WITH TForm2.Create(Application) DO
    try
      IF ShowModal = mrOK THEN
        BEGIN
          IF DataModule1.Table1.Modified THEN
            DataModule1.Table1.Post;
        END
      ELSE DataModule1.Table1.Cancel;
    finally
      Free;
    end;
end;

end.
```

SHAR322U.DEX

```
object Form2: TForm2
  BorderIcons = [biSystemMenu]
  BorderStyle = bsDialog
  Caption = 'Address Form'
  Position = poDefault
  Scaled = False
  object DBEdit1: TDBEdit
    DataField = 'Company'
    DataSource = DataModule1.DataSource1
    MaxLength = 30
  end
  object DBEdit2: TDBEdit
```

```
        DataField = 'Addr1'
        DataSource = DataModule1.DataSource1
        MaxLength = 30
      end
      object DBEdit3: TDBEdit
        DataField = 'Addr2'
        DataSource = DataModule1.DataSource1
        MaxLength = 30
      end
      object DBEdit4: TDBEdit
        DataField = 'City'
        DataSource = DataModule1.DataSource1
        MaxLength = 15
      end
      object DBEdit5: TDBEdit
        DataField = 'State'
        DataSource = DataModule1.DataSource1
        MaxLength = 20
      end
      object DBEdit6: TDBEdit
        DataField = 'Zip'
        DataSource = DataModule1.DataSource1
        MaxLength = 10
      end
      object BitBtn1: TBitBtn
        Kind = bkOK
      end
      object BitBtn2: TBitBtn
        Kind = bkCancel
      end
    end
```

SHAR32M.DEX

```
    object DataModule1: TDataModule1
      object Table1: TTable
        Active = True
        DatabaseName = 'DBDEMOS'
        TableName = 'CUSTOMER.DB'
      end
      object DataSource1: TDataSource
        DataSet = Table1
      end
    end
```

As in the 16-bit example, there's no need to show the code unit for the secondary form, as it contains only Delphi-generated code. The same is true of the data module. Note that this is just one example of Delphi 2.0's form linking. In general, if form A uses form B's unit, component properties in form A can refer directly to components on form B.

INSIDE DELPHI

When you start writing the code that makes your program's components work together, you're using the Object Pascal programming language. Skill at selecting and manipulating components doesn't necessarily help you know the ins and outs of Object Pascal. Solutions in this section will cover special techniques for using arrays and dates, as well as a wide range of common problems.

The second chapter in this section will turn the spotlight on the normally reclusive Application object. You can write dozens of Delphi programs without ever thinking about the fact that each relies on an invisible Application object. However, certain program features can only be programmed by manipulating this object's properties or by calling its methods. Other features require you to modify the program's main .DPR file, which is normally maintained by Delphi alone.

CHAPTER 12

The Object Pascal Language

*D*elphi's programming language is the latest version of Borland's Object Pascal, which has features not present in earlier versions. Some tasks that were not possible in Borland Pascal are now simple, and other tasks are handled differently. This chapter will answer questions about using the Delphi language, including features specific to Delphi 2.0. Topics include writing functions that take a variable number and type of parameters, performing date and time math, and dealing with packed records in Delphi 2.0.

Variable Size Arrays

The Pascal language is rather strict when it comes to data types. In standard Pascal, if you want to use an array, you must hard-code the size of the array in advance. If you don't know how many elements will be needed, this can be wasteful of memory. Naturally, Delphi provides several ways to get around this problem.

 Arrays with fixed size determined at runtime

16 32

Start by declaring the largest possible array of the specified type. The type definition for the largest array of type T that's possible in 16-bit Delphi is:

```
TYPE ArrayOfT = ARRAY[0..High(Cardinal) DIV SizeOf(T)] OF T;
```

You can't actually declare a *variable* of this type in 16-bit Delphi, as it would overflow the data segment or the stack, but you can declare a *pointer* to such an array and allocate it dynamically on the heap. Even in Delphi 2.0, an array that large would normally be allocated on the heap. You save memory by using GetMem to allocate only as many elements as needed. For example, if you've declared the variable A as a pointer to ArrayOfT and you need N elements as shown here:

```
GetMem(A, N * SizeOf(T));
```

Don't forget to call FreeMem to free up that memory when you no longer need the array, and, if you're using Delphi 1.0, be sure to deallocate the same number of bytes you allocated. In Delphi 2.0, call FreeMem *without* a size parameter to automatically deallocate the correct number of bytes. If A is a local variable, you absolutely must free the allocated memory before exiting the routine in which A is declared.

Arrays whose size will vary at runtime

The preceding solution works for an array whose size is fixed once the program is running, but it doesn't help if the array size must change *during* the program's execution. If the values you need to store will fit in 4 bytes (a LongInt, a Single, or an array of four characters, for example), you can shoehorn them into a Delphi TList object. A TList grows and shrinks as needed, and can hold up to 16,384 items in Delphi 1.0 and over 500 million items in Delphi 2.0.

A TList is officially a variable-length list of objects, but the elements it stores are actually simple, untyped pointers. By typecasting a 4-byte variable to the Pointer type, you can add it directly to a TList, as the program shown in Figure 12-1 demonstrates. It uses TLists to store three different kinds of variable, each of which occupies precisely 4 bytes.

VSARRAY

VSARRAYU.DEX

```
object Form1: TForm1
  BorderIcons = [biSystemMenu, biMinimize]
  BorderStyle = bsSingle
  Caption = 'TList Array Demo'
  Position = poDefault
  Scaled = False
  OnCreate = FormCreate
  object RadioGroup1: TRadioGroup
    Caption = 'Select List'
```

```
      Items.Strings = (
        '&LongInts'
        '&Singles'
        '&4-Char Strings')
    OnClick = RadioGroup1Click
  end
  object ListBox1: TListBox
  end
end
```

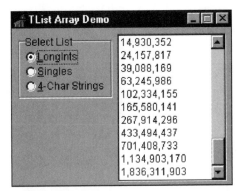

FIGURE 12-1: This program demonstrates the use of TList objects to hold data elements that fit precisely in 4 bytes.

VSARRAYU.PAS

```
unit Vsarrayu;

interface

uses SysUtils, WinTypes, WinProcs, Messages, Classes, Graphics,
  Controls, Forms, Dialogs, StdCtrls, Buttons, ExtCtrls;

type
  TForm1 = class(TForm)
    RadioGroup1: TRadioGroup;
    ListBox1: TListBox;
    procedure FormCreate(Sender: TObject);
    procedure RadioGroup1Click(Sender: TObject);
  private
    ListLong,
    ListSingle,
    List4Char : TList;
  end;

var Form1: TForm1;

implementation

{$R *.DFM}
CONST ListMax = 45;
```

```
procedure TForm1.FormCreate(Sender: TObject);
VAR
  N, M     : Integer;
  LongVar : LongInt;
  SingVar : Single;
  Charay4 : ARRAY[0..3] OF Char;
begin
  ListLong    := TList.Create;
  ListSingle := TList.Create;
  List4Char   := TList.Create;
  SingVar     := 0;
  LongVar     := 1;
  FOR N := 0 TO ListMax DO
    BEGIN
      IF N > 1 THEN
        LongVar := LongInt(ListLong[N-1]) + LongInt(ListLong[N-2]);
      ListLong.Add(Pointer(LongVar));
      SingVar := SingVar + pi / 4;
      ListSingle.Add(Pointer(SingVar));
      FOR M := 0 TO 3 DO
        Charay4[M] := Char(65 + (N MOD 23) + M);
      List4Char.Add(Pointer(Charay4));
    END;
end;

procedure TForm1.RadioGroup1Click(Sender: TObject);
VAR
  N       : Integer;
  SingVar : Single;
  Charay4 : ARRAY[0..3] OF Char;
begin
  ListBox1.Clear;
  WITH ListBox1.Items DO
    FOR N := 0 TO ListMax DO
      CASE (Sender AS TRadioGroup).ItemIndex OF
        0 : Add(FormatFloat(',0', LongInt(ListLong[N])));
        1 : BEGIN
          Pointer(SingVar) := ListSingle[N];
          Add(FloatToStrF(SingVar, ffFixed, 7, 5));
        END;
        2 : BEGIN
          Pointer(Charay4) := List4Char[N];
          Add(Copy(StrPas(Charay4), 1, 4));
        END;
      END;
end;

end.
```

The form's OnCreate event handler initializes three TList objects and fills them with 4-byte values. ListLong gets LongInts, each of which is the sum of the two preceding values. ListSingle holds single-precision, floating-point values that are multiples of pi / 4. And

List4Char holds arrays of four characters. Each value is added to its corresponding TList by typecasting it to a Pointer and passing it to the TList's Add method.

When you click one of the radio buttons, the list box is cleared and refilled to display the contents of the selected list. This time, there's a slight difference in technique. The LongInt elements of ListLong can be accessed simply by typecasting them to LongInt. However, for the single and 4-character array values, the assignment must be made with the typecast on the left:

```
Pointer(SingVar) := ListSingle[N];
```

You can use this technique to manage variable-size arrays of any 4-byte data type.

 ### Storing objects in a list

16 32

The preceding section demonstrated typecasting the elements of a TList to store 4-byte chunks of data. That can be handy, but the real purpose of a TList is storing *objects*. The objects in question don't have to be components; they don't have to be anything fancy at all. You can create a simple object type that's little more than a glorified record. Give it public data fields to hold the desired data and a constructor that initializes the data fields—that's all you need. The program in Figure 12-2 uses this technique to store detailed information about the files whose names are stored in its list box. As an added bonus, when compiled under Delphi 2.0, it uses long file names.

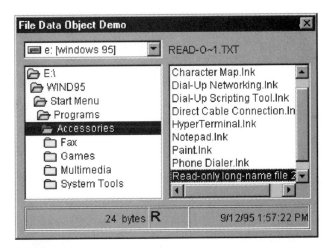

FIGURE 12-2: This program stores a file data object along with each filename in its list box.

TSOBJ

TSOBJU.DEX

```
object Form1: TForm1
  BorderIcons = [biSystemMenu, biMinimize]
  BorderStyle = bsDialog
  Caption = 'File Data Object Demo'
  Position = poDefault
  Scaled = False
  OnCreate = FormCreate
  object Label4: TLabel
  end
  object DirectoryListBox1: TDirectoryListBox
    OnChange = DirectoryListBox1Change
  end
  object Panel1: TPanel
    BevelInner = bvRaised
    BevelOuter = bvLowered
    object Panel2: TPanel
      Align = alLeft
      Alignment = taRightJustify
      BevelOuter = bvLowered
    end
    object Panel3: TPanel
      Align = alRight
      Alignment = taRightJustify
      BevelOuter = bvLowered
    end
    object Panel4: TPanel
      Align = alClient
      BevelInner = bvLowered
      BevelOuter = bvNone
      object Label1: TLabel
        Align = alLeft
        AutoSize = False
        Caption = 'R'
        Font.Color = clBtnFace
        Font.Height = -16
        Font.Style = [fsBold]
        ParentFont = False
      end
      object Label2: TLabel
        Align = alClient
        Alignment = taCenter
        AutoSize = False
        Caption = 'H'
        Font.Color = clBtnFace
        Font.Height = -16
        Font.Style = [fsBold]
        ParentFont = False
      end
```

```
        object Label3: TLabel
          Align = alRight
          AutoSize = False
          Caption = 'S'
          Font.Color = clBtnFace
          Font.Height = -16
          Font.Style = [fsBold]
          ParentFont = False
        end
      end
    end
  end
  object DriveComboBox1: TDriveComboBox
    DirList = DirectoryListBox1
  end
  object ListBoxHorz1: TListBoxHorz
    Sorted = True
    OnClick = ListBoxHorz1Click
  end
end
```

TSOBJU.PAS

```
unit Tsobju;

interface

uses SysUtils, WinTypes, WinProcs, Messages, Classes, Graphics,
  Controls, Forms, StdCtrls, FileCtrl, ExtCtrls, c_lbhorz;

type
  AltName = ARRAY[0..13] OF Char;

  TDataObj = Class(TObject)
    CONSTRUCTOR Create(vTime: LongInt; vSize: LongInt;
      vAttr: Integer; const vName: AltName);
  public
    tsT: LongInt;    {time/date}
    tsS: LongInt;    {size}
    tsA: Integer;    {attributes}
    tsN: AltName;    {8.3 name for long filenames}
  END;

  TForm1 = class(TForm)
    DirectoryListBox1: TDirectoryListBox;
    Panel1: TPanel;
    Panel2: TPanel;
    Panel3: TPanel;
    Panel4: TPanel;
    DriveComboBox1: TDriveComboBox;
    ListBoxHorz1: TListBoxHorz;
    Label1: TLabel;
    Label2: TLabel;
    Label3: TLabel;
    Label4: TLabel;
```

```
     procedure DirectoryListBox1Change(Sender: TObject);
     procedure ListBoxHorz1Click(Sender: TObject);
     procedure FormCreate(Sender: TObject);
   end;

var Form1: TForm1;

implementation

{$R *.DFM}

CONSTRUCTOR TDataObj.Create(vTime: LongInt; vSize: LongInt;
  vAttr: Integer; const vName: AltName);
BEGIN
  Inherited Create;
  tsT := vTime;
  tsS := vSize;
  tsA := vAttr;
  tsN := vName;
END;

procedure TForm1.FormCreate(Sender: TObject);
begin
  DirectoryListBox1Change(DirectoryListBox1);
end;

CONST Blank: AltName = '              ';

procedure TForm1.DirectoryListBox1Change(Sender: TObject);
VAR
  TS   : TSearchRec;
  Rslt : Integer;
  Mask : String;
begin
  {Remember to dispose of objects; Clear doesn't do it}
  FOR Rslt := 0 TO ListBoxHorz1.Items.Count-1 DO
    ListBoxHorz1.Items.Objects[Rslt].Free;
  ListBoxHorz1.Clear;
  Label4.Caption := '';
  WITH Sender AS TDirectoryListBox DO
    BEGIN
      IF Directory[length(Directory)]='\' THEN
        Mask := Directory + '*.*'
      ELSE Mask := Directory + '\*.*';
      Rslt := FindFirst(Mask, faReadOnly OR faHidden OR
        faSysfile, TS);
      WHILE Rslt = 0 DO
        BEGIN
          WITH TS DO ListBoxHorz1.Items.AddObject(Name,
            TDataObj.Create(Time, Size, Attr, {$IFDEF Win32}
              AltName(FindData.cAlternateFilename)
              {$ELSE}Blank{$ENDIF}));
          Rslt := FindNext(TS);
        END;
```

```
        FindClose({$IFDEF Win32}Rslt{$ELSE}TS{$ENDIF});
      END;
    IF ListBoxHorz1.Items.Count > 0 THEN
      BEGIN
        ListBoxHorz1.ItemIndex := 0;
        ListBoxHorz1Click(ListBoxHorz1);
      END;
  end;
  procedure TForm1.ListBoxHorz1Click(Sender: TObject);
  CONST
    AttribClr: ARRAY[Bool] OF TColorRef = (clBtnFace, clWindowText);
  begin
    WITH Sender AS TListBox DO
      WITH Items.Objects[ItemIndex] AS TDataObj DO
        BEGIN
          Panel2.Caption := FormatFloat('0, ', tsS)+ ' bytes ';
          Panel3.Caption := DateTimeToStr(FileDateToDateTime(tsT));
          Label1.Font.Color := AttribClr[tsA AND faReadOnly > 0];
          Label2.Font.Color := AttribClr[tsA AND faHidden > 0];
          Label3.Font.Color := AttribClr[tsA AND faSysfile > 0];
          Label4.Caption    := tsN;
        END;
  end;
  end.
```

TDataObj is a direct descendant of the ultimate ancestor TObject. It defines four data fields and a constructor that initializes them. The fields store the date/time, size, and attributes of a file, plus the DOS-style short file name for long file names. The fields of TDataObj are defined so as to hold the file data returned from either the 16-bit or the 32-bit file searching functions.

Each time the directory list box changes to a new directory, its OnChange event handler loads the list box with the names of the files in the new directory. Each name is added to the Items list, and a corresponding TDataObj is stored in the corresponding slot in the Items.Objects list. The list box's OnClick event handler displays the data for the selected file, extracting it from the corresponding TDataObj. Note that, as this component is actually a TListBoxHorz (a TListBox descendant previously defined in Chapter 7, "List and Combo Boxes"), it will automatically maintain a horizontal scroll bar to allow viewing long file names.

In general, storing data records in a TList is just this simple. You define a TObject descendant to hold the data, with a constructor that initializes the data fields. You create the object within the method call that adds it to the list. And you access the data fields by typecasting a particular element of the list to the desired object type.

Date and Time

Delphi's TDateTime data type encodes a date and time into a single floating-point number. Conversion functions pack year, month, day, hour, minute, and second information into a TDateTime, and extract them again. The data format of TDateTime makes date and time math surprisingly easy, once you understand it.

Understanding TDateTime

16 **32**

The TDateTime type is a double-precision, floating-point number in which the integer part represents the number of days since an arbitrary starting point. In Delphi 1.0, this starting point is just before January 1, 0001. For example, the date of the first manned moon landing is represented by the number 718,998. Delphi 2.0 changes the starting point to December 30, 1899, to bring Delphi's TDateTime type into line with the standard OLE variant date/time encoding. The fractional portion of a TDateTime is the time represented as a fraction of a 24-hour day.

Time calculations are fairly simple. Delphi defines a constant MSecsPerDay, which is the number of milliseconds in a day. From this, you can derive other constants that represent one hour, one minute, one second, or 100th of a second, thus:

```
CONST
  cHour   = 3600000 / MSecsPerDay;
  cMinute = 60000 / MSecsPerDay;
  cSecond = 1000 / MSecsPerDay;
  cSec100 = 10 / MSecsPerDay;
```

Another way to get these values is via the EncodeTime function. For example, the value of one hour is EncodeTime(1, 0, 0, 0). However, you can't call EncodeTime within a constant definition. The program in Figure 12-3 shows the constant and EncodeTime values side-by-side, and performs simple time math using the constants.

TIMMATH

TIMMATHU.DEX

```
object Form1: TForm1
  BorderIcons = [biSystemMenu]
  BorderStyle = bsDialog
  Caption = 'Time Math Demo'
```

```
      Position = poDefault
      Scaled = False
      OnCreate = FormCreate
      object Label1: TLabel
      end
      object StringGrid1: TStringGrid
        ColCount = 3
        Options = [goFixedVertLine, goFixedHorzLine, goVertLine,
goHorzLine]
        ScrollBars = ssNone
      end
      object MaskEdit1: TMaskEdit
        EditMask = '!90:00:00;1;_'
        MaxLength = 8
      end
      object RadioGroup1: TRadioGroup
        ItemIndex = 1
        Items.Strings = (
          'Hours'
          'Minutes'
          'Seconds')
        OnClick = RadioGroup1Click
      end
      object SpinEdit1: TSpinEdit
        MaxLength = 3
        MaxValue = 60
        MinValue = -60
        Value = 5
        OnChange = RadioGroup1Click
      end
    end
```

Time Math Demo		
	Const	EncodeTime
Hour	0.0416666666666667	0.0416666666666667
Minute	0.000694444444444444	0.000694444444444444
Second	1.15740740740741E-5	1.15740740740741E-5
Sec/100	1.15740740740741E-7	1.15740740740741E-7

```
10:00:00   -42      ○ Hours      9:18:00 AM
                    ◉ Minutes
                    ○ Seconds
```

FIGURE 12-3: You can calculate what fraction of a day corresponds to one hour, one minute, or one second, and use that information to perform time math.

TIMMATHU.PAS

```pascal
unit Timmathu;

interface

uses SysUtils, WinTypes, WinProcs, Messages, Classes, Graphics,
  Controls, Forms, StdCtrls, Spin, ExtCtrls, Mask, Grids;

type
  TForm1 = class(TForm)
    StringGrid1: TStringGrid;
    MaskEdit1: TMaskEdit;
    RadioGroup1: TRadioGroup;
    Label1: TLabel;
    SpinEdit1: TSpinEdit;
    procedure RadioGroup1Click(Sender: TObject);
    procedure FormCreate(Sender: TObject);
  end;

var Form1: TForm1;

implementation

{$R *.DFM}
CONST
  cHour   = 3600000 / MSecsPerDay;
  cMinute = 60000 / MSecsPerDay;
  cSecond = 1000 / MSecsPerDay;
  cSec100 = 10 / MSecsPerDay;

procedure TForm1.FormCreate(Sender: TObject);
begin
  MaskEdit1.Text := FormatDateTime('hh:mm:ss', Now);
  WITH StringGrid1 DO
    BEGIN
      Cols[0].SetText(' '#13'Hour'#13'Minute'#13'Second'#13+
        'Sec/100'#0);
      Rows[0].SetText(' '#13'Const'#13'EncodeTime'#0);
      Cells[1,1]  := FloatToStr(cHour);
      Cells[1,2]  := FloatToStr(cMinute);
      Cells[1,3]  := FloatToStr(cSecond);
      Cells[1,4]  := FloatToStr(cSec100);
      Cells[2,1]  := FloatToStr(EncodeTime(1,0,0,0));
      Cells[2,2]  := FloatToStr(EncodeTime(0,1,0,0));
      Cells[2,3]  := FloatToStr(EncodeTime(0,0,1,0));
      Cells[2,4]  := FloatToStr(EncodeTime(0,0,0,10));
    END;
end;

procedure TForm1.RadioGroup1Click(Sender: TObject);
VAR TD   : TDateTime;
begin
  CASE RadioGroup1.ItemIndex OF
    0 : TD := StrToTime(MaskEdit1.Text) + SpinEdit1.Value*cHour;
```

```
    1 : TD := StrToTime(MaskEdit1.Text) + SpinEdit1.Value*cMinute;
    2 : TD := StrToTime(MaskEdit1.Text) + SpinEdit1.Value*cSecond;
  END;
  WHILE TD < 0 DO TD := TD + 1.0;
  Label1.Caption := TimeToStr(TD);
end;

end.
```

The majority of the program's code is occupied with initializing the grid that displays what fraction of a day corresponds to each time interval. Once the program is running, you can set a starting time and calculate from −60 to 60 hours, minutes, or seconds from that starting time. It's surprisingly simple!

Formatting elapsed time

16 32

The TimeToStr function is useful for formatting a TDateTime that represents the time of day, as the preceding example shows. It produces output of the form "5:00:00 PM", assuming your language and locale preferences specify the standard United States format. However, if you use this function to format a TDateTime that represents an elapsed time, you won't like the results. "AM" and "PM" are irrelevant here, and you certainly don't want to display an elapsed time of zero as "12:00:00 AM".

For formatting elapsed time, use the FormatDateTime function instead, and pass a format string of 'hh:mm:ss'. This will yield a logical hours, minutes, seconds display, and an elapsed time of zero will correctly display as 00:00:00. (Actually, the colon separators in the format string are replaced by whatever time separator character is specified in your user preferences.)

Performing date math

16 32

As previously noted, variables of type TDateTime are actually double-precision, floating-point values. You can add days to a given date using simple addition, and calculate the number of days between two dates using simple subtraction. That's fine if your purpose is to calculate elapsed time in days and fractions of a day. If your real need is to calculate the number of times the date has *changed*, you'll want to perform the subtraction using the integer portion of each date.

What does that distinction mean? Suppose your two TDateTime variables represent one minute before midnight Saturday and one minute after midnight Sunday. If you simply subtract the first from the second, you'll get zero for the number of days—zero days, zero hours, and two minutes. If, on the other hand, you use the Int function to get the integer portion of each number and then subtract, the result will be one day, because the date changed at midnight. The simple program that follows calculates several future dates and displays a clock whose time represents the days, the hours, the minutes, and the seconds since your birth. You must adjust the FormCreate method to use your own birth date and time, of course. As written, the starting time is one minute after midnight on Blaise Pascal's birthday.

DATEDIF

DATEDIFU.DEX

```
object Form1: TForm1
  BorderIcons = [biSystemMenu, biMinimize]
  BorderStyle = bsSingle
  Caption = 'Date Math Demo'
  Position = poDefault
  Scaled = False
  OnCreate = FormCreate
  object Label1: TLabel
    Caption = 'Biological Clock'
  end
  object Label2: TLabel
    Caption = 'Today plus...'
  end
  object StringGrid2: TStringGrid
    ColCount = 4
    FixedCols = 0
    RowCount = 2
    Options = [goFixedVertLine, goFixedHorzLine, goVertLine,
goHorzLine, goDrawFocusSelected]
  end
  object StringGrid1: TStringGrid
    ColCount = 4
    FixedCols = 0
    RowCount = 2
    Options = [goFixedVertLine, goFixedHorzLine, goVertLine,
goHorzLine, goDrawFocusSelected]
  end
  object Timer1: TTimer
    OnTimer = Timer1Timer
  end
end
```

DATEDIFU.PAS

```pascal
unit Datedifu;

interface

uses SysUtils, WinTypes, WinProcs, Messages, Classes, Graphics,
  Controls, Forms, Dialogs, ExtCtrls, Grids, StdCtrls;

type
  TForm1 = class(TForm)
    StringGrid1: TStringGrid;
    StringGrid2: TStringGrid;
    Timer1: TTimer;
    Label1: TLabel;
    Label2: TLabel;
    procedure FormCreate(Sender: TObject);
    procedure Timer1Timer(Sender: TObject);
  private
    YourBirthday : TDateTime;
  end;

var Form1: TForm1;

implementation

{$R *.DFM}

procedure TForm1.FormCreate(Sender: TObject);
begin
  YourBirthday := StrToDateTime('06/19/1623 00:00:01');
  WITH StringGrid1 DO
    BEGIN
      Rows[0].SetText('30 days'#13'45 days'#13'60 days'#13+
        '90 days'#0);
      ShortDateFormat := 'ddd, mm/dd/yyyy';
      Cells[0,1] := DateToStr(Now+30);
      Cells[1,1] := DateToStr(Now+45);
      Cells[2,1] := DateToStr(Now+60);
      Cells[3,1] := DateToStr(Now+90);
      ShortDateFormat := 'mm/dd/yyyy';
    END;
  StringGrid2.Rows[0].SetText('Days'#13'Hours'#13'Minutes'#13+
    'Seconds'#0);
  Timer1Timer(Timer1);
end;

procedure TForm1.Timer1Timer(Sender: TObject);
VAR H, M, S, Sh : Word;
begin
  WITH StringGrid2 DO
    BEGIN
      DecodeTime(Now - YourBirthday, H, M, S, Sh);
      Cells[0,1] := FormatFloat(',#', Trunc(Now - YourBirthday));
```

```
        Cells[1,1] := IntToStr(H);
        Cells[2,1] := IntToStr(M);
        Cells[3,1] := IntToStr(S);
      END;
  end;

  end.
```

The form's OnCreate handler fills in the cells of the upper grid with the dates 30, 45, 60, and 90 days from today. It sets the variable YourBirthday to a specific date and time—replace this value with your *own* birthday. Finally, it calls the timer's OnTimer event handler, to avoid having the clock grid remain blank for the first second. The OnTimer handler fills in the clock grid with the number of days, hours, minutes, and seconds since you were born, so you can *see* your biological clock ticking away.

There are a few pitfalls to note in handling date and time data. Under Delphi 1.0, most of the time-related functions, such as DecodeTime and TimeToStr, expect a *positive* value; a negative value will cause an exception. Also, you must not use the date conversion or the formatting routines on a value that represents elapsed days. Why not? Because these routines treat the passed date value as a number of days counting from a specific starting date, with leap years accounted for. The result of subtracting two dates should be expressed in days, as the example program does.

Function Arguments

The Pascal language used in Delphi, and its predecessors Borland Pascal and Turbo Pascal, has always included built-in functions like Reset and Rewrite that take a variable number of parameters. Other built-in functions, like Write and WriteLn, handle arguments that vary both in number and in type. You can't write such functions yourself—they're given special handling by the compiler. However, using some new features present in Delphi's version of Pascal, you can do *almost* the same thing.

 ## *Using a variable number of parameters*

There are certain commonly useful functions that just cry out for variable-length parameter lists; for example, Min and Max functions that return the minimum or maximum value of the passed parameters. Because of a difference in the way function arguments are handled, programs written in C or C++ can have functions with variable numbers of parameters. Delphi's cdecl directive causes a function to be compiled in the style of the C language, but still does not permit a variable number of arguments.

The solution lies in another Delphi feature called *open array parameters.* An open array parameter is declared simply as an array of a particular type, without specified lower or upper bounds. Any array of any size can be passed as an open array parameter, as long as the elements match the declared type. Within the function, the first element is referenced using the index 0, and the last using the index returned by passing the array to the built-in High function. Here's an example Min function that returns the smallest LongInt in the passed array:

```
function Min(const A: ARRAY OF LongInt): LongInt;
VAR N : Integer;
begin
  Result := MaxLongInt;
  FOR N := Low(A) TO High(A) DO
    IF A[N] < Result THEN
      Result := A[N];
end;
```

Note that the array is passed as a const parameter. That means the compiler does not make a copy of the array, but it also does not permit any code that would modify the passed array.

Passing a partial array as an open array

16 32

You'll find that many calls to functions with open array parameters create the passed array on the fly; for example:

```
Canvas.Polygon([Point(0,0), Point(100,0), Point(0,100)]);
```

You can also pass any variable defined as an array of the specified type. However, the entire defined size of the array is always used. If your program only uses a portion of the array, you've got a problem.

Delphi 2.0 provides the built-in function Slice. Pass it an array and a number, and it effectively returns an array sliced down to the specified number of elements. As the program in Figure 12-4 shows, a little ASM code can simulate the Slice function, even in 16-bit Delphi.

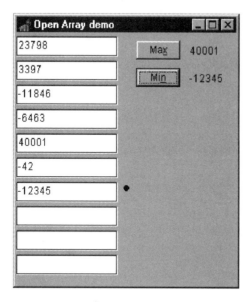

FIGURE 12-4: This program passes a "slice" of an array of LongInts to Min and Max functions.

OPENARR

OPENARRU.DEX

```
object Form1: TForm1
  Caption = 'Open Array demo'
  Position = poDefault
  Scaled = False
  object Label1: TLabel
    AutoSize = False
  end
  object Label2: TLabel
    AutoSize = False
  end
  object Edit1: TEdit
    MaxLength = 11
  end
  object Edit2: TEdit
    MaxLength = 11
  end
  object Edit3: TEdit
    MaxLength = 11
  end
  object Edit4: TEdit
    MaxLength = 11
  end
```

```
    object Edit5: TEdit
      MaxLength = 11
    end
    object Button1: TButton
      Caption = 'Ma&x'
      OnClick = Button1Click
    end
    object Button2: TButton
      Caption = 'Mi&n'
      OnClick = Button2Click
    end
  end
end
```

OPENARRU.PAS

```
unit Openarru;

interface

uses SysUtils, WinTypes, WinProcs, Messages, Classes, Graphics,
  Controls, Forms, Dialogs, StdCtrls;

type
  TForm1 = class(TForm)
    Button1: TButton;
    Button2: TButton;
    Label1: TLabel;
    Label2: TLabel;
    Label3: TLabel;
    procedure Button1Click(Sender: TObject);
    procedure Button2Click(Sender: TObject);
    procedure FormCreate(Sender: TObject);
  private
    Edits : ARRAY[0..9] OF TEdit;
  end;

var Form1: TForm1;

  implementation

{$R *.DFM}
function Max(const A: ARRAY OF LongInt): LongInt;
VAR N : Integer;
begin
  Result := $80000000;
  FOR N := Low(A) TO High(A) DO
    IF A[N] > Result THEN
      Result := A[N];
end;

function Min(const A: ARRAY OF LongInt): LongInt;
VAR N : Integer;
begin
  Result := MaxLongInt;
  FOR N := Low(A) TO High(A) DO
```

```
      IF A[N] < Result THEN
        Result := A[N];
end;

{$IFNDEF Win32}
TYPE
  ArrayFunc = function(const A : ARRAY OF LongInt): LongInt;

function Slice(Fn: ArrayFunc; const A : ARRAY OF LongInt;
  Last: Integer): LongInt; Assembler;
ASM
  les    di,A
  push   es
  push   di
  mov    ax, Last
  dec    ax
  push   ax
  call   Fn
END;
{$ENDIF}

procedure TForm1.Button1Click(Sender: TObject);
VAR
  A : ARRAY[0..9] OF LongInt;
  N : Integer;
begin
  N := 0;
  REPEAT
    try
      A[N] := StrToInt(Edits[N].Text);
    except
      ON EConvertError DO
        IF N = 0 THEN Exit
        ELSE Break;
    end;
    N := N + 1;
  UNTIL N > 9;
  Label3.Top := Edits[N-1].Top;
  {$IFDEF Win32}
  Label1.Caption := IntToStr(Max(Slice(A, N)));
  {$ELSE}
  Label1.Caption := IntToStr(Slice(Max, A, N));
  {$ENDIF}
end;

procedure TForm1.Button2Click(Sender: TObject);
VAR
  A : ARRAY[0..9] OF LongInt;
  N : Integer;
begin
  N := 0;
  REPEAT
    try
      A[N] := StrToInt(Edits[N].Text);
```

```
      except
        ON EConvertError DO
          IF N = 0 THEN Exit
          ELSE Break;
      end;
       N := N + 1;
    UNTIL N > 9;
    Label3.Top := Edits[N-1].Top;
    {$IFDEF Win32}
    Label2.Caption := IntToStr(Min(Slice(A, N)));
    {$ELSE}
    Label2.Caption := IntToStr(Slice(Min,A, N));
    {$ENDIF}
  end;
  procedure TForm1.FormCreate(Sender: TObject);
  VAR N : Integer;
  begin
    FOR N := 0 TO 9 DO
      BEGIN
        Edits[N] := TEdit.Create(Self);
        WITH Edits[N] DO
          BEGIN
            Parent := Self;
            Top    := 4 + 28*N;
          END;
      END;
    Randomize;
    FOR N := 0 TO 1 + Random(9) DO
      Edits[N].Text := IntToStr(Integer(Random(MaxInt)) -
      (MaxInt DIV 2));  ActiveControl := Edits[0];
  end;

  end.
```

The form's OnCreate event handler creates ten edit boxes and fills from two to ten of them with random LongInts. The event handler invoked by pressing the Max button fills an array of LongInts with the values contained in the edit boxes, stopping when it reaches an edit box that's empty or contains non-numeric data. Under Delphi 2.0, it uses the Slice function to pass the valid portion of the array to the Max function, which, as described in the preceding section, takes an open array parameter.

The line of code for 16-bit Delphi *looks* similar, but the Slice function it uses is not built in. This Slice function takes three parameters: a function of a specific type, an open array of LongInts, and the number of items to be used from the array. The ASM code it uses to call the specified function is *almost* identical to the code Delphi would generate. The only difference is, where Delphi's code would push the hard-coded, defined size of the array, the Slice function pushes the Last parameter. This technique is not as powerful as Delphi 2.0's built-in Slice function. You'd have to define a new assembler function for each type of array element and for each type of array-processing function. But it works!

The program shown in Figure 12-5 uses a similar technique to pass a variable-size array of points to the Polygon method of a TCanvas object. This time, though, the ASM code required in 16-bit Delphi isn't pulled out into a separate function.

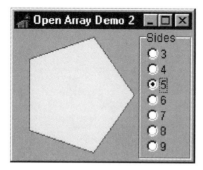

FIGURE 12-5: The Polygon method of the TCanvas object takes an open array of points as its parameter; this program passes just the in-use portion of such an array.

OPARR2

OPARR2U.DEX

```
object Form1: TForm1
  Caption = 'Open Array Demo 2'
  Position = poDefault
  Scaled = False
  object PaintBox1: TPaintBox
    Align = alClient
    OnPaint = PaintBox1Paint
  end
  object RadioGroup1: TRadioGroup
    Align = alRight
    Caption = 'Sides'
    ItemIndex = 0
    Items.Strings = (
      '3'
      '4'
      '5'
      '6'
      '7'
      '8'
      '9')
```

```
        OnClick = RadioGroup1Click
    end
end
```

OPARR2U.PAS

```pascal
unit oparr2u;

interface

uses SysUtils, WinTypes, WinProcs, Messages, Classes, Graphics,
  Controls, Forms, Dialogs, StdCtrls, ExtCtrls;

type
  TForm1 = class(TForm)
    PaintBox1: TPaintBox;
    RadioGroup1: TRadioGroup;
    procedure PaintBox1Paint(Sender: TObject);
    procedure RadioGroup1Click(Sender: TObject);
  private
    procedure SPolygon(A : ARRAY of TPoint);
  end;

var Form1: TForm1;

implementation

{$R *.DFM}

procedure TForm1.SPolygon(A : ARRAY OF TPoint);
BEGIN
  PaintBox1.Canvas.Polygon(A);
END;

procedure TForm1.PaintBox1Paint(Sender: TObject);
VAR
  Verts       : ARRAY[0..8] OF TPoint;
  N, LastPt,
  CtrX, CtrY : Integer;
  Radius      : Double;
begin
  LastPt := RadioGroup1.ItemIndex + 2;
  WITH Sender AS TPaintBox DO
    BEGIN
      CtrX := Width DIV 2;
      CtrY := Height DIV 2;
      IF CtrX < CtrY THEN Radius := CtrX - 4
      ELSE Radius := CtrY - 4;
      FOR N := 0 TO LastPt DO
        BEGIN
          Verts[N].X := Round(CtrX+ Radius*Cos(N*2*pi/(LastPt+1)));
          Verts[N].Y := Round(CtrY+ Radius*Sin(N*2*pi/(LastPt+1)));
        END;
      Canvas.Brush.Color := clYellow;
```

```
            Canvas.Pen.Color := clRed;
            {$IFDEF Win32}
            Canvas.Polygon(Slice(Verts, LastPt+1));
            {$ELSE}
            ASM
              lea    di, Verts
              push   ss
              push   di
              push   LastPt
              les    di, Self
              push   es
              push   di
              call   TFORM1.SPOLYGON
            END;
            {$ENDIF}
          END;
      end;

      procedure TForm1.RadioGroup1Click(Sender: TObject);
      begin
        PaintBox1.Refresh;
      end;

      end.
```

The radio group's OnClick method fills the array Verts with the vertices for a polygon with the specified number of sides. In Delphi 2.0, it uses the built-in Slice function to pass only the in-use portion of the array to the canvas's Polygon method. In 16-bit Delphi, ASM code serves the same purpose.

Note that the actual call to Canvas.Polygon occurs in a private method of the form object. This avoids the complex coding that would otherwise be required to get access to the Polygon method of the Canvas property of the form object. The only serious difference here is that the ASM code needs to push Self on the stack before making the method call. This code and the ASM code used in the previous example were both derived by using Turbo Debugger for Windows to examine the code Delphi generates for a call to a function with an open array parameter.

Using variable types of parameters

16 32

Every now and then, you'll come up with an idea for a function that needs to handle arguments of varying types. One solution would be to pass a variant record type containing all the necessary types. As the program in Figure 12-6 shows, Delphi already contains such a type, and you're free to use it as you please.

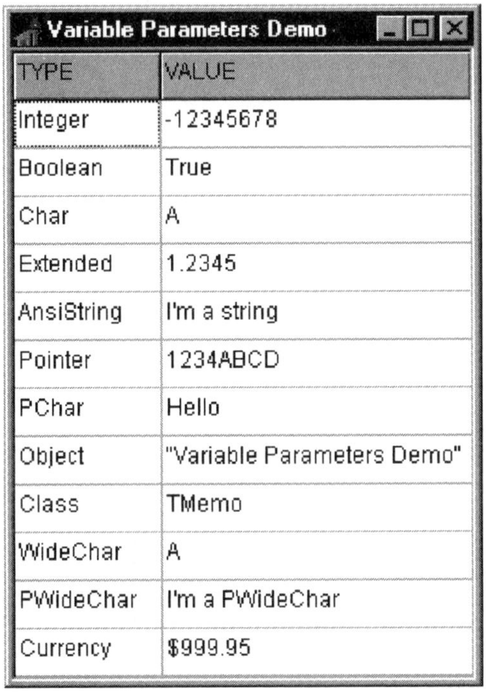

FIGURE 12-6: The twelve values displayed in the grid were passed as a single array parameter in which both the number and the type of elements can vary.

VARREC

VARRECU.DEX

```
object Form1: TForm1
  Caption = 'Variable Parameters Demo'
  Position = poDefault
  Scaled = False
  OnCreate = FormCreate
  object StringGrid1: TStringGrid
    Align = alClient
    ColCount = 2
    FixedCols = 0
    RowCount = 2
    Options = [goFixedVertLine, goFixedHorzLine, goVertLine,
goHorzLine, goRangeSelect, goColSizing]
    ScrollBars = ssVertical
  end
end
```

VARRECU.PAS

```pascal
unit Varrecu;

interface

uses SysUtils, WinTypes, WinProcs, Messages, Classes, Graphics,
  Controls, Forms, Dialogs, StdCtrls, Grids;

type
  TForm1 = class(TForm)
    StringGrid1: TStringGrid;
    procedure FormCreate(Sender: TObject);
  private
    procedure Display(const X: array of const);
  end;

var Form1: TForm1;

implementation

{$R *.DFM}
CONST
  vtLast = {$IFDEF Win32}vtVariant{$ELSE}vtClass{$ENDIF};
  vtNames : ARRAY[vtInteger..vtLast] OF String[11] = ('Integer',
    'Boolean', 'Char', 'Extended', 'String', 'Pointer', 'PChar',
    'Object', 'Class' {$IFDEF Win32}, 'WideChar', 'PWideChar',
    'AnsiString', 'Currency', 'Variant'{$ENDIF});

function StringOf(VR: TVarRec) : string;
CONST TF : ARRAY[Boolean] OF String[5] = ('False', 'True');
begin
  WITH VR DO
    CASE VType OF
      vtInteger : Result := IntToStr(VInteger);
      vtBoolean : Result := TF[VBoolean];
      vtChar    : Result := VChar;
      vtExtended: Result := FloatToStr(VExtended^);
      vtString  : Result := VString^;
      vtPointer : Result := Format('%p', [VPointer]);
      vtPChar   : Result := StrPas(VPChar);
      vtObject  : Result := '"' + (VObject AS TForm).Caption+'"';
      vtClass   : Result := VClass.ClassName;
      {$IFDEF Win32}
      vtWideChar   : Result := WideCharLenToString(@VWideChar, 1);
      vtPWideChar  : Result := WideCharToString(VPWideChar);
      vtAnsiString : Result := String(PChar(VAnsiString));
      vtCurrency   : Result := CurrToStrF(VCurrency^, ffCurrency,
        CurrencyDecimals);
      {$ENDIF}
    END;
end;

procedure TForm1.Display(const X: array of const);
VAR N : Word;
```

```pascal
begin
  WITH StringGrid1 DO
    BEGIN
      FOR N := 0 TO High(X) DO
        BEGIN
          Cells[0, RowCount-1] := vtNames[TVarRec(X[N]).VType];
          Cells[1, RowCount-1] := StringOf(TVarRec(X[N]));
          RowCount := RowCount + 1;
        END;
      RowCount := RowCount-1;
    END;
end;
procedure TForm1.FormCreate(Sender: TObject);
VAR
  StringVar : String;
  DoubleVar : Double;
  {$IFDEF Win32}
  CurrencyVar  : Currency;
  WideCharVar  : WideChar;
  PWideCharVar : PWideChar;
  {$ENDIF}
begin
  StringGrid1.Cells[0,0] := 'TYPE';
  StringGrid1.Cells[1,0] := 'VALUE';
  StringVar := 'I''m a string';
  DoubleVar := 1.2345;
  {$IFDEF Win32}
  CurrencyVar := 999.95;
  WideCharVar := WideChar(65);
  GetMem(PWideCharVar, 16*SizeOf(WideChar));
  StringToWideChar('I''m a PWideChar', PWideCharVar, 16);
  {$ENDIF}
  Display([
    -12345678,              {LongInt}
    True,                   {Boolean}
    'A',                    {Char}
    DoubleVar,              {Floating point}
    StringVar,              {String}
    Pointer($1234ABCD),     {Pointer}
    PChar('Hello'#0),       {PChar}
    Form1,                  {Object}
    TMemo                   {Class}
    {$IFDEF Win32}
    , WideCharVar,          {WideChar}
    PWideCharVar,           {PWideChar}
    CurrencyVar             {Currency}
    {$ENDIF}
  ]);
end;

end.
```

The Display method takes a single parameter X, defined as "ARRAY OF const"; this type of parameter is called a *type-safe open array parameter*. The data type for elements of such an array is TVarRec, which is defined in Delphi's system unit along with the constants vtInteger, vtBoolean, and so on. In fact, the X parameter could have been defined as "ARRAY OF TVarRec". Delphi generates code that automatically initializes a TVarRec for each array element. The Display method flips through the array X and adds the name of each element's data type to the first grid column and its value to the second. The function StringOf returns a string for each of the data types that can be contained in a TVarRec.

The type-safe open array parameter is a powerful feature that Delphi uses internally. For example, the Format function, which embeds data in a specially formatted string, accepts that data in the form of a type-safe open array parameter. You're sure to find your own uses for it.

Language Miscellany

Obviously, there's no way to cover every possible question about the Object Pascal language. The remainder of this chapter will cover a variety of questions that have perplexed particular Delphi users at one time or another.

"Call to RegisterClass is missing"

 16

The mysterious error message "Call to RegisterClass is missing or incorrect" may appear when you try to compile a Delphi 1.0 program after doing some editing. It's baffling, as the program never did call a routine named RegisterClass.

The real meaning of this message is that you have deleted, commented out, or otherwise disabled the final "end." line of the unit. Re-examine your most recent changes, match up begin . . . end pairs, and double-check that all comment delimiters are paired as well.

Can't create a Delphi object variable!

16 32

If your attempt to initialize a Delphi object fails with a GPF, you're almost certainly letting old Object Pascal habits trick you into errors in Delphi. Delphi object constructors are *class methods* that return an initialized object instance. For example, to initialize the TStrings variable T, you'd use:

```
T := TStrings.Create;
```

However, in pre-Delphi Object Pascal, a constructor was a method of the object itself, and calling the constructor served to initialize the object. Based on this old mind-set, you'd use:

```
T.Create;
```

This code successfully creates a TStrings object, but does not assign it to any variable. Specifically, the variable T is not initialized, so a GPF results when you attempt to use the uninitialized object. Always initialize a Delphi object variable by assigning it the result of a call to the class constructor. Delphi 2.0 will warn you when it detects that an object variable may not have been initialized, as long as you've enabled compiler warnings.

Raising numbers to a specified power

16 32

In Visual Basic, the ∧ character is the power operator. Many other languages include some kind of power operator, but not standard Pascal. So, how do you raise a number to a specified power?

Delphi 2.0 users who selected the Developer or Client/Server Suite version have an absolute wealth of math functions available in the Math unit (sorry, this unit is not present in the low-end Desktop version). The IntPower function raises a floating-point number to an integer power; the Power function does the same for noninteger powers. For 16-bit Delphi users, the following unit implements the two power functions. IntPower handles integer powers using a technique called halving and squaring, and Power calculates noninteger powers using logarithms.

POWERS UNIT

POWERS.PAS

```
unit powers;

interface
function IntPower(Base: Extended; Expon: LongInt): Extended;
function Power(Base, Expon : Extended): Extended;

implementation
const epsilon = 0.00000001;
```

```
function IntPower(Base: Extended; Expon: LongInt): Extended;
{get integer power by halving and squaring}
  function P(pE: LongInt): Extended;
  begin
    IF pE = 0 THEN Result := 1
    ELSE IF Odd(pE) THEN
      Result := Sqr(P(pE DIV 2))*Base
    ELSE Result := Sqr(P(pE DIV 2));
  end;
begin
  IF Base=0 THEN Result := 1
  ELSE IF Expon >= 0 THEN Result := P(Expon)
  ELSE Result := 1/P(-Expon);
end;

function Power(Base, Expon : Extended): Extended;
{non-integer power of negative number causes exception}
begin
  IF (Base < 0) AND (Frac(Expon) < epsilon) THEN
    Result := (1-2*Ord(Odd(Round(Expon))))*Exp(Ln(-Base)*Expon)
  ELSE Result := Exp(Ln(Base)*Expon);
end;

end.
```

The halving and squaring technique used in IntPower effectively breaks down the exponent into a sum of powers of two. That means the result will be obtained by repeatedly squaring the base, and multiplying the result by the values corresponding to powers of two that are present in the exponent. This intriguing technique works *only* for integer powers.

The Power function raises the base to the specified exponent using logarithmic functions. If the base is negative, only integer powers are defined. In that case, Power raises the absolute value of the base to the desired power and multiplies it by −1 if the power is odd, 1 if even. The same techniques are used in the Math unit's IntPower and Power functions, although the implementation differs slightly.

Getting a DOS environment variable

16

Long-time Object Pascal users will remember GetEnv and related environment functions. For example, to get the name of the command processor, you could use the expression "GetEnv('COMSPEC')". What a shock to find that Delphi's version of Object Pascal does not include GetEnv!

Fortunately, 16-bit Windows supports a function called GetDOSEnvironment, which returns a pointer to a DOS environment block. Using this function and some Delphi tricks, it's not hard to cobble up replacement functions, as the unit that follows shows.

GETENVIR UNIT

GETENVIR.PAS

```
unit Getenvir;
{$IFDEF Win32}
HALT: GetDOSEnvironment function not supported in Win32
{$ENDIF}

interface
USES Classes;

PROCEDURE GetEnvironmentStrings(TSEnv : TStrings);
FUNCTION GetEnv(const VarName : String) : String;

implementation
USES WinProcs, SysUtils;

PROCEDURE GetEnvironmentStrings(TSEnv : TStrings);
{TSEnv must already have been created by calling routine}
VAR P : PChar;
BEGIN
  P := GetDOSEnvironment;
  WITH TSEnv DO
    BEGIN
      Clear;
      WHILE P[0] <> #0 DO
        BEGIN
          Add(StrPas(P));
          P := StrEnd(P)+1;
        END;
    END;
END;

FUNCTION GetEnv(const VarName : String) : String;
VAR TS : TStringList;
BEGIN
  TS := TStringList.Create;
  WITH TS DO
    try
      Sorted := True;
      GetEnvironmentStrings(TS);
      Result := Values[VarName];
    finally
      Free;
    end;
END;

end.
```

In 16-bit Windows, the GetEnvironmentStrings function will fill a string list supplied by the calling program with the entire environment. To load the environment strings into a list box, for example, you'd do something like this:

```
GetEnvironmentStrings(ListBox1.Items);
```

The GetEnv function will return the value of a specified variable. Note that the DOS environment is considered irrelevant in 32-bit Windows—the necessary GetDOSEnvironment function does not exist.

Pixels change color unexpectedly

| 16 | 32 |

When you set a variable's value and then immediately read the variable, you expect to get back the value you put in. So, naturally, you'll be surprised to find that in certain video modes you can set pixels the standard clXxx color constants and find that the actual color doesn't match up.

The problem is most likely to surface in 15-bit and 16-bit color modes, commonly called high color, though you can run into it in other modes as well. It happens because the precise colors corresponding to the clXxx color constants don't exist. For example, clNavy has the value $80000; the closest available value may be $84000. Your program can set the pixel's color to clNavy, but, when it compares the color with clNavy, the two are different. Figure 12-7 shows the problem.

Color	Value	Pixel Value
clMaroon	000080	*000084*
clGreen	008000	*008200*
clOlive	008080	*008284*
clNavy	800000	*840000*

16 bits per pixel

FIGURE 12-7: This screen shot, snapped in high color mode under Windows NT, shows that pixels may not get set to the precise color you specify.

COMPCOLR

COMPCOLU.DEX

```
object Form1: TForm1
  BorderIcons = [biSystemMenu, biMinimize]
  BorderStyle = bsSingle
  Caption = 'Color Constants Problem'
  Position = poDefault
  Scaled = False
  OnCreate = FormCreate
  object Label1: TLabel
    Caption = 'Label1'
  end
  object StringGrid1: TStringGrid
    ColCount = 4
    FixedCols = 0
    RowCount = 18
    OnDrawCell = StringGrid1DrawCell
  end
end
```

COMPCOLU.PAS

```
unit Compcolu;

interface

uses SysUtils, WinTypes, WinProcs, Messages, Classes, Graphics,
  Controls, Forms, Dialogs, Grids, StdCtrls;

type
  TForm1 = class(TForm)
    Label1: TLabel;
    StringGrid1: TStringGrid;
    procedure StringGrid1DrawCell(Sender: TObject; vCol, vRow:
      Longint; Rect: TRect; State: TGridDrawState);
    procedure FormCreate(Sender: TObject);
  end;

var Form1: TForm1;

implementation

{$R *.DFM}

procedure TForm1.FormCreate(Sender: TObject);
VAR BitsPerPix : Word;
begin
  StringGrid1.Rows[0].SetText(' '#13'Color'#13'Value'#13+
```

```
                'Pixel Value');
        BitsPerPix := GetDeviceCaps(Canvas.Handle, BITSPIXEL) *
          GetDeviceCaps(Canvas.Handle, PLANES);
        Label1.Caption := Format('%d bits per pixel', [BitsPerPix]);
      end;
    procedure TForm1.StringGrid1DrawCell(Sender: TObject; vCol, vRow:
      Longint; Rect: TRect; State: TGridDrawState);
    CONST ColRefs : ARRAY[1..17] OF TColorRef= (clBlack, clMaroon,
      clGreen, clOlive, clNavy, clPurple, clTeal, clGray, clSilver,
      clRed, clLime, clYellow, clBlue, clFuchsia, clAqua, clDkGray,
      clWhite);
    CONST Actual : ARRAY[1..17] OF TColorRef = (-1, -1, -1, -1, -1, -1,
      -1, -1, -1, -1, -1, -1, -1, -1, -1, -1, -1);
    VAR vLeft, vTop : Integer;
    begin
      vLeft := Rect.Left+2; vTop := Rect.Top+1;
      WITH Sender AS TDrawGrid, Canvas DO
        IF vRow <> 0 THEN
          CASE vCol OF
            0 : BEGIN
                  Brush.Color := ColRefs[vRow];
                  FillRect(Rect);
                  IF Actual[vRow] = -1 THEN
                    Actual[vRow] := Pixels[Rect.Left+3, Rect.Top+3];
                END;
            1 : TextOut(vLeft, vTop, ColorToString(ColRefs[vRow]));
            2 : TextOut(vLeft, vTop, Format('%.6x', [ColRefs[vRow]]));
            3 : BEGIN
                  IF Actual[vRow] <> ColRefs[vRow] THEN
                    Font.Style := [fsBold, fsItalic];
                  TextOut(vLeft,vTop,Format('%.6x', [Actual[vRow]]));
                END;
          END;
    end;
    end.
```

Each grid row represents a color. The first column is filled with the color, the second names it, the third shows its numeric value. The fourth column is the numeric value of the color of a pixel from the first column, in bold italic if it doesn't match the specified value. As you can see, there are frequent differences.

In general, if a program needs to compare the color of a pixel with one or more predefined colors, it will need an initial calibration step. During this step, the program will attempt to set a pixel to each of the predefined colors, and record the color that actually appeared.

Padding or chopping a string to a given length

16 32

For display purposes, it's often necessary to cram a string into a particular length. If it's shorter, you want it padded with blanks. If it's longer, you need to chop it off. Old-fashioned solutions involved setting the string's length byte to chop it and using FillChar to add spaces. These solutions are no longer valid with Delphi 2.0's Huge strings.

The versatile Format command provides a solution that will work on both platforms. To convert a string S into a string of precisely 8 characters, padding at the end or chopping as necessary, use the expression:

```
Format('%-8.8s', [S]);
```

The initial minus sign chooses left alignment, and the first 8 specifies a field 8 characters wide. The second 8 tells Format to permit a maximum of 8 characters.

You'll find it worthwhile to study and experiment with Format. With it you can easily produce all sorts of formatting effects. For example, to right-align a string of no more than 8 characters in a 12-character field, you'd use the format string '%12.8s'.

Can't read files written by older programs

32

There are quite a few programs in this world that originated in early Turbo Pascal and have gained features and moved along into Borland Pascal and on to Delphi. File and record formats have kept pace so far, but, when you recompile for Delphi32, you may suddenly find that your files don't read correctly any more.

The original Turbo Pascal included a keyword "packed" that could be applied to arrays and records, but had no effect. Suddenly, though, in Delphi 2.0, the packed keyword is meaningful. A record defined without packed keywords will have fields larger than 2 bytes aligned on 4-byte boundaries. This speeds the program's execution, as the CPU takes up to four times longer to process variables whose addresses are not aligned on 4-byte boundaries. Add the packed keyword and the record's fields will be continuous in memory. If you try to read a file whose records are packed using a record type that's not packed, you'll be out of synch with the file, as the program in Figure 12-8 shows.

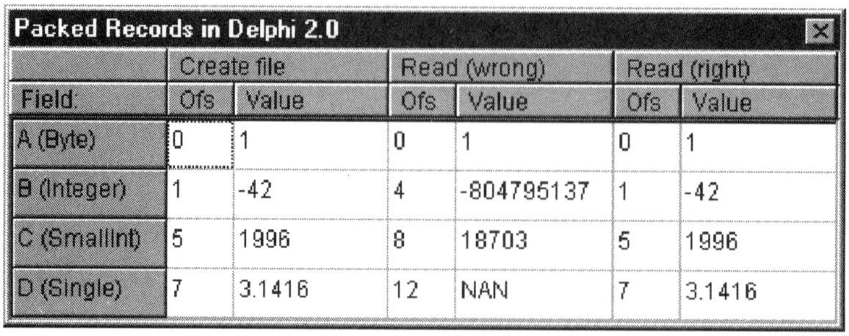

Packed Records in Delphi 2.0						⊠
	Create file		Read (wrong)		Read (right)	
Field:	Ofs	Value	Ofs	Value	Ofs	Value
A (Byte)	0	1	0	1	0	1
B (Integer)	1	-42	4	-804795137	1	-42
C (SmallInt)	5	1996	8	18703	5	1996
D (Single)	7	3.1416	12	NAN	7	3.1416

FIGURE 12-8: Trying to read a file of packed records using a record definition without the packed keyword is disastrous!

PACKDEMO

PACKDEMU.DEX

```
object Form1: TForm1
  BorderIcons = [biSystemMenu, biMinimize]
  BorderStyle = bsDialog
  Caption = 'Packed Records in Delphi 2.0'
  Position = poDefault
  Scaled = False
  OnCreate = FormCreate
  object StringGrid1: TStringGrid
    Align = alClient
    ColCount = 7
    RowCount = 4
    FixedRows = 0
    Options = [goFixedVertLine, goFixedHorzLine, goVertLine,
goHorzLine]
    ScrollBars = ssNone
  end
  object HeaderControl1: THeaderControl
    Enabled = False
    Sections = <
      item
        AllowClick = False
      end
      item
        AllowClick = False
        Text = 'Create file'
      end
      item
        AllowClick = False
        Text = 'Read (wrong)'
      end
      item
        AllowClick = False
```

```
              Text = 'Read (right)'
          end>
    end
    object HeaderControl2: THeaderControl
      Enabled = False
      Sections = <
        item
          AllowClick = False
          Text = 'Field:'
        end
        item
          AllowClick = False
          Text = 'Ofs'
        end
        item
          AllowClick = False
          Text = 'Value'
        end
        item
          AllowClick = False
          Text = 'Ofs'
        end
        item
          AllowClick = False
          Text = 'Value'
        end
        item
          AllowClick = False
          Text = 'Ofs'
        end
        item
          AllowClick = False
          Text = 'Value'
        end>
    end
end
```

PACKDEMU.PAS

```
unit packdemu;
  {$IFNDEF Win32}
  HALT: This program requires 32-bit Delphi
  {$ENDIF}
interface

uses Windows, SysUtils, Messages, Classes, Graphics, Controls, Forms,
  Dialogs, StdCtrls, Grids, ComCtrls;

type
  TForm1 = class(TForm)
    StringGrid1: TStringGrid;
    HeaderControl1: THeaderControl;
```

```
      HeaderControl2: THeaderControl;
      procedure FormCreate(Sender: TObject);
    end;
var Form1: TForm1;
implementation
{$R *.DFM}
TYPE
  RightRec = packed Record
    A : Byte;
    B : Integer;
    C : SmallInt;
    D : Single;
  END;
  WrongRec = Record
    A : Byte;
    B : Integer;
    C : SmallInt;
    D : Single;
  END;
procedure TForm1.FormCreate(Sender: TObject);
VAR
  RRec  : RightRec;
  RFile : File OF RightRec;
  WRec  : WrongRec;
  WFile : File OF WrongRec;
begin
  WITH StringGrid1 DO
    BEGIN
      ColWidths[1] := 34;
      ColWidths[3] := 34;
      ColWidths[5] := 34;
      Cols[0].Text := 'A (Byte)'#13'B (Integer)'#13'C (SmallInt)'+
        #13'D (Single)';
      AssignFile(RFile, 'TEMP.$$$');
      Rewrite(RFile);
      WITH RRec DO
        BEGIN A := 1; B := -42; C := 1996; D := 3.14159; END;
      Cells[1,0] := IntToStr(LongInt(@RRec.A)-LongInt(@RRec));
      Cells[1,1] := IntToStr(LongInt(@RRec.B)-LongInt(@RRec));
      Cells[1,2] := IntToStr(LongInt(@RRec.C)-LongInt(@RRec));
      Cells[1,3] := IntToStr(LongInt(@RRec.D)-LongInt(@RRec));
      Cells[2,0] := IntToStr(RRec.A);
      Cells[2,1] := IntToStr(RRec.B);
      Cells[2,2] := IntToStr(RRec.C);
      Cells[2,3] := FormatFloat('0.0000', RRec.D);
      Write(RFile, RRec);
      Write(RFile, RRec);
      CloseFile(RFile);
      AssignFile(WFile, 'TEMP.$$$');
      Reset(WFile);
      Read(WFile, WRec);
```

```
      CloseFile(WFile);
      Cells[3,0] := IntToStr(LongInt(@WRec.A)-LongInt(@WRec));
      Cells[3,1] := IntToStr(LongInt(@WRec.B)-LongInt(@WRec));
      Cells[3,2] := IntToStr(LongInt(@WRec.C)-LongInt(@WRec));
      Cells[3,3] := IntToStr(LongInt(@WRec.D)-LongInt(@WRec));
      Cells[4,0] := IntToStr(WRec.A);
      Cells[4,1] := IntToStr(WRec.B);
      Cells[4,2] := IntToStr(WRec.C);
      Cells[4,3] := FormatFloat('0.0000', WRec.D);
      AssignFile(RFile, 'TEMP.$$$');
      Reset(RFile);
      Read(RFile, RRec);
      CloseFile(RFile);
      Cells[5,0] := IntToStr(LongInt(@RRec.A)-LongInt(@RRec));
      Cells[5,1] := IntToStr(LongInt(@RRec.B)-LongInt(@RRec));
      Cells[5,2] := IntToStr(LongInt(@RRec.C)-LongInt(@RRec));
      Cells[5,3] := IntToStr(LongInt(@RRec.D)-LongInt(@RRec));
      Cells[6,0] := IntToStr(RRec.A);
      Cells[6,1] := IntToStr(RRec.B);
      Cells[6,2] := IntToStr(RRec.C);
      Cells[6,3] := FormatFloat('0.0000', RRec.D);
      DeleteFile('TEMP.$$$');
    END;
  end;

  end.
```

This program creates a temporary file using the record type RightRec. It then reads the file back using the record type WrongRec, and reads it again using RightRec. A grid displays the results. When you use the WrongRec type, all values beyond the first field are wrong—the single-precision field D is so wrong that it's not a number (NAN).

If your programs need to read and to write files created by programs compiled with 16-bit Delphi or older Pascal compilers, you must be sure to use the packed keyword in the record definitions. Packed is also important in records passed to DLL functions. Finally, even with programs that don't use old files, you may want to use packed records for files to save space. In the example program, the unpacked record was almost half again as large. Multiply that by 100,000 records and you've wasted a *lot* of space.

CHAPTER 13

The Application Object

*E*very visible form in a Delphi program is owned by the invisible Application object. This chapter covers questions that are answered by manipulating the Application object or by adding code to the project's .DPR file that gets executed before the Application object is initialized. Topics include handling drag and drop from the File Manager, displaying a "splash screen" while your program loads, and adding an always-on-top choice to your program's system menu.

Activity When Minimized

When you minimize an application, it shrinks down to an icon on the desktop in Windows 3.1 or in Windows NT. In Windows 95, the task-bar button provides access to minimized programs. A minimized program can still be working away, however. It's often convenient to use the program's icon to indicate just what the minimized program is doing.

Detecting Windows 95

`16` `32`

Many of the programs in this chapter operate one way under Windows 3.1 or Windows NT, another way under Windows 95. Rather than duplicate the code to test for Windows 95 again and again, I created the IsWin95 unit.

ISWIN95 UNIT

ISWIN95.PAS

```
unit IsWin95;
interface
uses WinTypes, WinProcs, SysUtils;
VAR Win95 : Boolean;

implementation

  {$IFDEF Win32}
VAR OSI : TOSVersionInfo;
Initialization
  OSI.dwOSVersionInfoSize := SizeOf(OSI);
  GetVersionEx(OSI);
  Win95 := OSI.dwPlatformID = VER_PLATFORM_WIN32_WINDOWS;
  {$ELSE}
initialization
  Win95 := Swap(LoWord(GetVersion)) >= $35F;
  {$ENDIF}
end.
```

The initialization code for this unit sets the variable Win95 to True, only if the operating system is Windows 95. When compiled under 16-bit Delphi, it checks for a Windows version of 3.95 or later. Under Delphi 2.0, it uses the more reliable GetVersionEx function. Any program that uses this unit can refer to the Win95 variable to determine whether Windows 95 is the operating system.

Keeping a program always iconic

16 32

This isn't as odd a request as it sounds. Some applications do all their work behind the scenes, leaving only an icon visible. It's not uncommon for such an application to add an item or two to the system menu; for example, to invoke a configuration dialog. Windows 95 does not support this kind of program, but it's simple enough to implement in Windows 3.1 or in Windows NT.

Start by setting the main form's WindowState property to wsMinimized. Now, add these two lines to the { Private declarations } section of the form object definition:

```
PROCEDURE WMQUERYOPEN(VAR Msg : TWMQueryOpen);
  message WM_QUERYOPEN;
```

In the implementation section of the unit, add this code:

```
PROCEDURE TForm1.WMQUERYOPEN(VAR Msg : TWMQueryOpen);
BEGIN
  Msg.Result := 0;
END;
```

When the user double-clicks the icon, Windows sends a WM_QUERYOPEN message to ask the application if it's willing to leave the iconic state. Setting the message result to zero responds with an emphatic "No."

 Changing an icon while running

If a program is meant to spend most of its time minimized, the icon can be used as a visual indicator of its state. However, changing the icon used by a Delphi program is complicated somewhat by the fact that the main form and the Application object each have an icon property. And, in Windows 95, it's not enough to change those properties. You must also send a message to the Application object and to the main form. The program shown in Figure 13-1 demonstrates this technique by switching among three possible icons once per second.

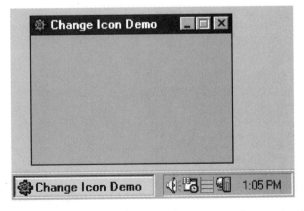

FIGURE 13-1: In Windows 95, this program changes its title-bar icon and the icon on its task-bar button once a second.

CHNGICON

CHNGICOU.DEX

```
object Form1: TForm1
  BorderIcons = [biSystemMenu, biMinimize]
  BorderStyle = bsSingle
  Caption = 'Change Icon Demo'
  Position = poDefault
  Scaled = False
  OnCreate = FormCreate
  object Image2: TImage
    Visible = False
  end
  object Image3: TImage
    Visible = False
  end
  object Image1: TImage
    Visible = False
  end
  object Timer1: TTimer
    OnTimer = Timer1Timer
  end
end
```

CHNGICOU.PAS

```
unit Chngicou;

interface

uses SysUtils, WinTypes, WinProcs, Messages, Classes, Graphics,
  Controls, Forms, Dialogs, StdCtrls, ExtCtrls;

type
  TForm1 = class(TForm)
    Image2: TImage;
    Image3: TImage;
    Image1: TImage;
    Timer1: TTimer;
    procedure FormCreate(Sender: TObject);
    procedure Timer1Timer(Sender: TObject);
  private
    Icons : ARRAY[0..2] OF TIcon;
  end;

var Form1: TForm1;

implementation
Uses IsWin95;
CONST WM_SETICON = 128; {not defined in 16-bit Delphi}
{$R *.DFM}

procedure TForm1.FormCreate(Sender: TObject);
```

```
begin
  Icons[0] := Image1.Picture.Icon;
  Icons[1] := Image2.Picture.Icon;
  Icons[2] := Image3.Picture.Icon;
  Icon := Icons[0];
  Application.Icon := Icon;
end;
procedure TForm1.Timer1Timer(Sender: TObject);
CONST Which: Integer = 1;
begin
  IF NOT (IsIconic(Application.Handle) OR Win95) THEN Exit;
  Icon := Icons[Which];
  Application.Icon := Icon;
  Which := Succ(Which) MOD 3;
  {Next two lines only required in Win95}
  Self.Perform(WM_SETICON, 1, Icon.Handle);
  SendMessage(Application.Handle, WM_SETICON, 1, Icon.Handle);
end;

end.
```

This program stores its three icons in three image components whose Visible property is set to False. In its OnCreate event handler, it initializes its private Icons array to point to the three icons, and sets the icon for both the main form and the application to the first of the three.

Once each second, the timer's OnTimer event handler gets triggered. If the application is not minimized and the operating system is not Windows 95, it does nothing. Otherwise, it selects the next icon into both the main form and the application. That's sufficient to change the icon in Windows 3.1 and in Windows NT. Windows 95 requires a little more effort—the program sends a WM_SETICON message to both the main form and the application to select the new icon.

Painting on an icon

16 32

The preceding section demonstrated how a program can change its icon. That's fine if all the program needs to do is signal an event, such as the appearance of new e-mail. It doesn't help when you need to display variable information on the icon, perhaps a graph of free system resources. The OnPaint event handler will not help, as this event doesn't occur when the project is minimized.

One solution is to paint the icon in response to WM_PAINT messages received by the minimized application object. This works in Windows 3.1 and in Windows NT.

However, in Windows 95, the only recourse is to build a new icon on the fly that displays the desired information. The program shown in Figure 13-2 implements both techniques.

FIGURE 13-2: In Windows 95, this program draws on its icon by literally building a new icon from scratch on demand.

DRAWICON

DRAWICOU.DEX

```
object Form1: TForm1
  Caption = 'Drawing On Icon'
  OnCreate = FormCreate
  object Timer1: TTimer
    Interval = 100
    OnTimer = Timer1Timer
  end
end
```

DRAWICOU.PAS

```
Unit Drawicou;

interface

uses SysUtils, WinTypes, WinProcs, Messages, Classes, Graphics,
  Controls, Forms, Dialogs, ExtCtrls, StdCtrls;

type
  TForm1 = class(TForm)
    Timer1: TTimer;
    procedure FormCreate(Sender: TObject);
    procedure Timer1Timer(Sender: TObject);
  private
    PictBmp, MaskBmp : TBitmap;
    vTB              : WinTypes.TBitmap;
    AndSize, XorSize : Integer;
    NewAnd, NewXor   : PByteArray;
    procedure AppOnMessage(var Msg: TMsg; var Handled: Boolean);
  end;
```

```
var Form1: TForm1;

implementation
USES IsWin95;
{$R *.DFM}

CONST WM_SETICON = 128; {not defined in 16-bit Delphi}

procedure TForm1.FormCreate(Sender: TObject);
begin
  PictBmp := TBitmap.Create;
  WITH PictBmp DO
    BEGIN
      Width  := GetSystemMetrics(SM_CXICON);
      Height := GetSystemMetrics(SM_CYICON);
      Canvas.Brush.Color := clBlack;
      Canvas.Pen.Color := clBlack;
      Canvas.FillRect(Rect(0, 0, Width, Height));
      GetObject(Handle, SizeOf(vTB), @vTB);
      AndSize := (LongInt(Height) * Width * vTB.bmBitsPixel *
        vTB.bmPlanes) DIV 8;
      XorSize := (Height * Width) DIV 8;
    END;
  GetMem(NewAnd, AndSize);
  GetMem(NewXor, XorSize);
  MaskBmp := TBitmap.Create;
  WITH MaskBmp DO
    BEGIN
      Width  := GetSystemMetrics(SM_CXICON);
      Height := GetSystemMetrics(SM_CYICON);
      Canvas.Brush.Color := clWhite;
      Canvas.FillRect(Rect(0, 0, Width, Height));
      Monochrome := True;
      Canvas.Brush.Color := clBlack;
    END;
  Application.Icon := NIL;
  Application.OnMessage := AppOnMessage;
end;

procedure TForm1.AppOnMessage(var Msg: TMsg; var Handled: Boolean);
VAR TP : TPaintStruct;
begin
  IF (Msg.Message=WM_PAINT) AND (Msg.hWnd=Application.Handle) AND
    IsIconic(Application.Handle) THEN
    BEGIN
      WITH TCanvas.Create DO
        try
          Handle := BeginPaint(Application.Handle, TP);
          {just paint the rectangle that NEEDS painting}
          CopyRect(TP.rcPaint, PictBmp.Canvas, TP.rcPaint);
          EndPaint(Application.Handle, TP);
        finally
          Free;
        end;
      Handled := True;
```

```
      END;
  end;
  procedure TForm1.Timer1Timer(Sender: TObject);
  VAR WasR : TRect;
  CONST
    R     : TRect = (Left:0; Top:0; Right:16; Bottom:16);
    Stage : Integer =0;
  begin
    IF NOT (IsIconic(Application.Handle) OR Win95) THEN Exit;
    WasR := R;
    {move rectangle to new position}
    CASE Stage DIV 4 OF
      0 : OffsetRect(R, PictBmp.Width DIV 8, 0);
      1 : OffsetRect(R, 0, PictBmp.Height DIV 8);
      2 : OffsetRect(R, -PictBmp.Width DIV 8, 0);
      3 : OffsetRect(R, 0, -PictBmp.Height DIV 8);
    END;
    UnionRect(WasR, WasR, R);
    Stage := Succ(Stage) MOD 16;
    {draw rectangle on picture bitmap}
    WITH PictBmp DO
      BEGIN
        Canvas.Brush.Color := clBlack;
        Canvas.FillRect(Rect(0, 0, Width, Height));
        Canvas.Brush.Color := clWhite;
        Canvas.Rectangle(R.Left, R.Top, R.Right, R.Bottom);
      END;
    {if not Windows 95, application will paint it}
    IF NOT Win95 THEN
      InvalidateRect(Application.Handle, @WasR, False)
    ELSE
    {if Win95, build and use a new icon}
      BEGIN
        WITH MaskBmp DO
          BEGIN
            Monochrome := False;
            Canvas.Brush.Color := clWhite;
            Canvas.FillRect(Rect(0, 0, Width, Height));
            Monochrome := True;
            Canvas.Brush.Color := clBlack;
            Canvas.FillRect(R);
          END;
        GetBitmapBits(PictBmp.Handle, AndSize, NewAnd);
        GetBitmapBits(MaskBmp.Handle, XorSize, NewXor);
        Icon.Handle := CreateIcon(hInstance,vTB.bmWidth,vTB.bmHeight,
          vTB.bmPlanes, vTB.bmBitsPixel, NewXor, NewAnd);
        Application.Icon := Icon;
        Perform(WM_SETICON, 1, Icon.Handle);
        SendMessage(Application.Handle, WM_SETICON, 1, Icon.Handle);
      END;
  end;

  end.
```

This program takes advantage of the fact that the bitmap data for an icon in memory is adjusted to the current video mode, as is the bitmap data for a TBitmap object. When the form is created, it initializes a color bitmap to match the icon's AND mask and a monochrome bitmap to match its XOR mask. It sets the application's Icon to NIL, which causes Windows 3.1 and Windows NT to send WM_PAINT messages to the application when minimized. And it sets the application's OnMessage property to the method AppOnMessage. This event handler will be called for each message received by the application.

The rest of the program's activity takes place in the OnTimer event handler. This routine keeps track of a rectangle approximately the size of the icon. It moves this rectangle around the perimeter of the icon, one move per timer tick, and draws it on the color bitmap. If Win95 is not the operating system, the OnTimer event handler simply invalidates an area that's the union of the old and the new rectangle positions. This triggers a WM_PAINT message, which is received by the AppOnMessage method. The AppOnMessage method simply copies the changed area from the color bitmap to the icon display area.

In Windows 95, the process is a bit more complex. The next step is to draw the same rectangle on the monochrome bitmap, black for the rectangle and white for the background. Two calls to the API function GetBitmapBits fill buffers with the AND and the XOR masks, and a call to CreateIcon builds a brand new icon from these masks.

If you write programs that cannot run under Windows 95 for some reason, you can paint on the icon using nothing but the WM_PAINT technique shown here. However, as most programs need to support Windows 95, the icon-building technique is the most widely applicable.

One warning is in order, though. Microsoft officially advises against using animated or dynamic icons. In fact, that's the reason WM_PAINTICON is no longer supported. Even if you choose to follow their recommendation and avoid painting on icons, the technique of building an icon at runtime is sure to be useful.

Drawing attention to an icon

16 32

The previous two items have covered different ways in which a program can change what's displayed on its icon. On a crowded desktop, though, the user may simply not notice the change. There are several possible techniques for drawing attention to the change. Figure 13-3 is a snapshot of a program that implements three such techniques.

FIGURE 13-3: This program is drawing attention to its icon by jiggling the icon title from side to side—notice that it's off to the left rather than centered as usual.

ICONTITL

ICONTTLU.DEX

```
object Form1: TForm1
  Caption = 'Icon Title Flasher'
  Position = poDefault
  Scaled = False
  OnCreate = FormCreate
  object RadioGroup1: TRadioGroup
    Caption = 'Icon Title Behavior'
    ItemIndex = 0
    Items.Strings = (
      '&Move'
      '&Flash'
      '&Blink')
  end
  object Timer1: TTimer
    Enabled = False
    Interval = 200
    OnTimer = Timer1Timer
  end
end
```

ICONTTLU.PAS

```
unit Iconttlu;

interface

uses SysUtils, WinTypes, WinProcs, Messages, Classes, Graphics,
  Controls, Forms, Dialogs, StdCtrls, ExtCtrls;

type
  PTitleData = ^TTitleData;
  TTitleData = RECORD
    AppHandle, TitleWin : HWnd;
  END;

  TForm1 = class(TForm)
    Timer1: TTimer;
    RadioGroup1: TRadioGroup;
    procedure FormCreate(Sender: TObject);
    procedure Timer1Timer(Sender: TObject);
```

```
  private
    TTD : TTitleData;
    procedure AppOnMinimize(Sender: TObject);
    procedure AppOnRestore(Sender: TObject);
  end;

var Form1: TForm1;

implementation
USES IsWin95;
{$R *.DFM}

procedure TForm1.FormCreate(Sender: TObject);
begin
  TTD.TitleWin := 0;
  Application.OnMinimize := AppOnMinimize;
  Application.OnRestore := AppOnRestore;
  IF Win95 THEN
    BEGIN
      RadioGroup1.Items.Delete(2);
      RadioGroup1.Items.Delete(1);
    END;
end;

function EnumWindowsProc(H: hWnd; P: PTitleData): boolean; Export;
  {$IFDEF Win32} stdcall; {$ENDIF}
VAR Buff : ARRAY[0..10] OF Char;
BEGIN
  Result := True;
  GetClassName(H, Buff, 10);
  IF (StrComp(Buff, '#32772') = 0) THEN
    IF (P^.AppHandle = GetParent(H)) THEN
      BEGIN
        P^.TitleWin := H;
        Result := False;
      END;
END;

procedure TForm1.AppOnRestore(Sender: TObject);
BEGIN
  Timer1.Enabled := False;
  TTD.TitleWin := 0;
END;

procedure TForm1.AppOnMinimize(Sender: TObject);
BEGIN
  TTD.AppHandle := Application.Handle;
  EnumWindows(@EnumWindowsProc, LongInt(@TTD));
  IF (TTD.TitleWin <> 0) OR Win95 THEN
    Timer1.Enabled := True;
END;

procedure TForm1.Timer1Timer(Sender: TObject);
CONST Delta : Integer = 16;
VAR R : TRect;
begin
```

```
      CASE RadioGroup1.ItemIndex OF
        0 : FlashWindow(Application.Handle, Delta > 0);
        1 : IF Delta > 0 THEN ShowWindow(TTD.TitleWin, SW_HIDE)
            ELSE ShowWindow(TTD.TitleWin, SW_SHOWNA);
        2 : BEGIN
              GetWindowRect(TTD.TitleWin, R);
              OffsetRect(R, Delta, 0);
              WITH R DO SetWindowPos(TTD.TitleWin, 0, Left, Top, 0, 0,
                SWP_NOSIZE OR SWP_NOACTIVATE OR SWP_NOZORDER);
            END;
      END;
      Delta := -Delta;
  end;
end.
```

The simplest technique calls the FlashWindow Windows API function to alternately invert the minimized window and restore it to normal on each timer tick. The other two methods involve getting the handle of the window that holds the minimized application's *title*. In Windows 95, the form's OnCreate event handler disables these two methods, as the icon title window is not accessible. The OnCreate handler also sets up OnMinimize and OnRestore event handlers for the application object.

When the application is minimized, the AppOnMinimize event handler uses the EnumWindows function to locate a window whose class name is "#32772" (code for an icon title window) and whose parent is the application. If such a window is found or if Windows 95 is running, the timer is enabled. The AppOnRestore event handler disables the timer.

The OnTimer event handler maintains a typed constant called Delta whose initial value is 16. On each tick, the sign of Delta is reversed. If the Flashing Title option was chosen, the event handler hides the icon title when Delta is greater than zero and shows it otherwise. If the Jiggling Title option was chosen, the event handler moves the icon title window by Delta pixels.

One or more of these techniques will serve to let your minimized program grab the user's attention.

Control Application Loading

In most Delphi programs, the essential .DPR file is never seen. It's generated and maintained by Delphi, and the programmer accesses it through the Forms and Application page of the Project Options dialog. There are occasions, though, when it's necessary to modify the .DPR file and take over the application loading process to get the desired result.

Displaying a "splash screen"

16 32

When a program's main form needs to do substantial processing before it shows, perhaps loading database information, the program can seem sluggish. It can take too long for that first form to appear on the screen. A splash screen comes up immediately and eliminates the impression of sluggishness.

The splash screen can also serve to hold a copyright notice, a company logo, or any information you want the user to see every time the program starts. In that case, it may be necessary to ensure that the splash screen stays visible for a certain minimum time, so the user can read it. Figure 13-4 is a simple splash screen with an imaginary company's logo.

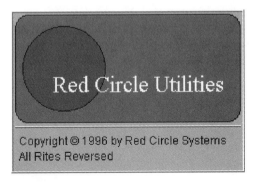

FIGURE 13-4: A splash screen such as this displays while the main form is loading and disappears for good afterward.

SPLASH

SPSPLSHU.DEX

```
object SplashForm: TSplashForm
  BorderStyle = bsNone
  Caption = 'SplashForm'
  Position = poScreenCenter
  Scaled = False
  object Panel1: TPanel
    Align = alClient
```

```
        BevelInner = bvLowered
        Caption = 'Panel1'
        object Shape2: TShape
          Brush.Color = clGray
          Shape = stRoundRect
        end
        object Shape1: TShape
          Brush.Color = clRed
          Shape = stCircle
        end
        object Label1: TLabel
          Caption = 'Red Circle Utilities'
          Font.Color = clWhite
          Font.Height = -24
          Font.Name = 'Times New Roman'
          ParentFont = False
          Transparent = True
        end
        object Bevel2: TBevel
          Shape = bsTopLine
          Style = bsRaised
        end
        object Label3: TLabel
          Caption = 'Copyright © 1996 by Red Circle Systems'
        end
        object Label4: TLabel
          Caption = 'All Rites Reversed'
        end
      end
    end
end
```

SPLASH.DPR

```
program Splash;
uses Forms,
{ WinProcs,                        {optional}
  Spmainu in 'SPMAINU.PAS' {Form1},
  Spsplshu in 'SPSPLSHU.PAS' {SplashForm};
{$R *.RES}
{VAR EndTick : LongInt;            {optional}
begin
{ EndTick := GetTickCount + 3000;  {optional}
  SplashForm := TSplashForm.Create(Application);
  SplashForm.Show;
  SplashForm.Update;
  Application.CreateForm(TForm1, Form1);
{ WHILE GetTickCount < EndTick DO; {optional}
  SplashForm.Hide;
  SplashForm.Free;
  Application.Run;
end.
```

Only the significant portions of the program are shown here, as you will design your own splash screen and find your own slow-loading forms. What's important is that you set the splash screen form's BorderStyle to bsNone and fill it with a client-aligned panel. In most cases, you'll also want to set its Position to poScreenCenter.

The .DPR file creates and displays the splash screen *before* the Delphi-supplied line of code that creates the main form. When the CreateForm call returns, meaning the main form is completely ready, the .DPR file hides and frees the splash screen *before* the Delphi-supplied line that starts the application running.

If the splash screen isn't staying visible long enough, you can remove the comment delimiter at the beginning of the four lines marked {optional}. This will force the splash screen to stay visible for at least three seconds.

Don't modify the .DPR file this way until you're finished adding new forms and deciding whether they'll be auto-created or just available. When you add forms or make changes in the Forms page of the Project Options dialog, Delphi adjusts the .DPR file, and this adjustment can be unhealthy for code you've written.

Loading only one instance

16 32

Although Windows will let you load multiple copies of a Delphi program, this doesn't always make sense. For example, you never need multiple copies of a free system resource monitor. If the user tries to load another copy, what you really want is for the previously loaded copy to leap forward and present itself. Achieving this effect requires modification of the program's .DPR file.

ONCE

ONCE.DPR

```
program Once;
uses WinTypes, WinProcs, SysUtils, Forms,
  Onceu in 'ONCEU.PAS' {OneInstanceForm1};
{$R *.RES}
{$IFDEF Win32}VAR Mutex: THandle; {$ENDIF}

PROCEDURE CheckPrevInst;
VAR PrevWnd: HWnd;
BEGIN
  {$IFDEF Win32}
  Mutex := CreateMutex(NIL, False, 'SingleInstanceProgramHMutex');
```

```
      {wait if other instance still initializing; quit if too long}
      IF WaitForSingleObject(Mutex, 10000) = WAIT_TIMEOUT THEN Halt;
      {$ELSE}
      IF HPrevInst = 0 THEN Exit;
      {$ENDIF}
      PrevWnd := FindWindow('TOneInstanceForm1', '1-Instance Program');
      IF PrevWnd <> 0 THEN
        PrevWnd := GetWindow(PrevWnd, GW_OWNER);
      IF PrevWnd <> 0 THEN
        BEGIN
          IF IsIconic(PrevWnd) THEN ShowWindow(PrevWnd,SW_SHOWNORMAL)
          ELSE
            {$IFDEF Win32}SetForegroundWindow(PrevWnd);{$ELSE}
            BringWindowToTop(PrevWnd);{$ENDIF}
          Halt;
        END;
  END;

begin
  try
    CheckPrevInst;
    Application.CreateForm(TOneInstanceForm1, OneInstanceForm1);
  finally
    {$IFDEF Win32}
    OneInstanceForm1.HandleNeeded;
    ReleaseMutex(Mutex);
    CloseHandle(Mutex);
    {$ENDIF}
  end;
  Application.Run;
end.
```

The CheckPrevInst function checks for a previous instance; if successful, it activates the previous instance and halts the program. A 16-bit Windows program gets some help here, as Windows sets the hPrevInst variable to the instance handle of any previous instance, or to zero if no previous instance exists. However, a 32-bit program runs in its own memory space and, thus, cannot "see" a previous instance.

The CheckPrevInst function uses the FindWindow API function to get the first window whose class name and caption match its two parameters. Clearly, it's important to have a unique combination of class name and caption for such a program. If a matching window is found, CheckPrevInst activates the window's owner (the application window) and halts.

If you run this program while it's loaded into Delphi, the FindWindow function call can find the form in the designer instead of the actual running form. To avoid this problem, you can leave the form caption set to its default and set the actual caption in the OnCreate event handler. On the other hand, if your main form's caption needs to change while the program is running, you will have to use NIL for the second parameter to FindWindow. In that case, you must simply make sure to avoid running the program from within the Delphi environment.

A second program comes up if a second instance of the program is launched before the main form of the first instance has been created. Under 32-bit Windows, this program uses a mutex (a Win32 synchronization object) to prevent this problem. The WaitForSingleObject API function will not return until the previous instance has created its main form and released the mutex. This situation is quite rare, but you can produce it by running the program twice in a row from a batch file in Windows 95 or in Windows NT.

To make any program into a single-instance program that will work under Delphi 1.0 or Delphi 2.0, you drop the CheckPrevInst procedure into the .DPR file, along with the declaration for the mutex variable. You add the needed units to the .DPR file's uses clause, and add the try..finally block shown in the example program immediately after the main "begin". It's important that the main form be created before the mutex is released, but other forms can be created after the try..finally block.

Choosing a main form at runtime

16 32

Most programs will always start with the same main form, invoking other forms as needed. Sometimes, though, an application needs to choose between multiple main forms at runtime. An accounting program might use a different main form on the last day of the month; an antivirus might load a special main form if a virus was detected in memory.

Unfortunately, Delphi does *not* approve of conditional loading of the main form. Here's some example code that randomly chooses to initialize Form1 or Form2:

```
Randomize;
IF Random < 0.5 THEN Application.CreateForm(TForm1, Form1)
ELSE Application.CreateForm(TForm2, Form2);
```

If you now try to open the Project Options dialog, Delphi will not let you. Instead, it will respond with the error message "Error in module <name>: Call to Application.CreateForm is missing or incorrect."

To get around this problem, precede the code that selects the main form with code based on the following:

```
IF FALSE THEN
  BEGIN
    Application.CreateForm(TForm1, Form1);
    Application.CreateForm(TForm2, Form2);
  END;
```

This code is never executed, but it satisfies the compiler. Do note that you shouldn't edit the .DPR file in this way until after you're finished adding forms and deciding which forms will be auto-created.

Application and Form as Partners

Most of the time, the active form in a program gets all the input. However, when the program is minimized, the application object takes charge. Frequently, you'll run across situations where the two must operate in parallel.

? Adding an always-on-top command to the system menu

16 32

There are really two problems here. First, how do you add a command to your program's system menu? Second, how do you change a program to and from the always-on-top state? Delphi's TForm object has a Style property in which one of the possible values is fsStayOnTop. However, this affects only the form itself; if the application is minimized, its icon will not be always on top. Also, changing a form's style from fsNormal to fsStayOnTop or vice versa causes the form to be destroyed and recreated, which nullifies any changes you've made to the system menu.

The crucial thing to remember here is that the simplest Delphi project has *two* important window handles. One is represented by the main form's Handle property and the other by the Application object's Handle property. When the project is minimized, the Application window is in charge. Thus, any item you want to add to the system menu must be added both to the main form's system menu and to the application's system menu. Figure 13-5 shows an example program that adds a stay-on-top command—when it's checked, the window is always on top.

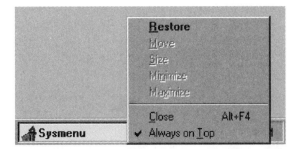

FIGURE 13-5: Though one Windows 95 task-bar button never overlaps another, the main form controlled by this button will float on top of all other windows.

SYSMENU

SYSMENUU.DEX

```
object Form1: TForm1
  Caption = 'System Menu Demo'
  Position = poDefault
  Scaled = False
  OnCreate = FormCreate
end
```

SYSMENUU.PAS

```
unit Sysmenuu;

interface

uses SysUtils, WinTypes, WinProcs, Messages, Classes, Graphics,
  Controls, Forms, Dialogs;

type
  TForm1 = class(TForm)
    procedure FormCreate(Sender: TObject);
  private
    procedure AppOnMessage(VAR Msg: TMsg; VAR Handled: Boolean);
  end;

var Form1: TForm1;

implementation

{$R *.DFM}
CONST SC_UDF = $EFF0;

procedure TForm1.FormCreate(Sender: TObject);
begin
```

```
    AppendMenu(GetSystemMenu(Handle, False),
      MF_STRING, SC_UDF, 'Always on &Top');
    AppendMenu(GetSystemMenu(Application.Handle, False),
      MF_STRING, SC_UDF, 'Always on &Top');
    Application.OnMessage := AppOnMessage;
  end;

  procedure TForm1.AppOnMessage(VAR Msg: TMsg; VAR Handled: BOolean);
  VAR
    Hf, Ha : hMenu;
    Checkd : Boolean;
  CONST
    NuFlag : ARRAY[Boolean] OF Word = (MF_CHECKED, MF_UNCHECKED);
    NuHWnd : ARRAY[Boolean] OF HWnd = (HWND_TOPMOST, HWND_NOTOPMOST);
  BEGIN
    IF Msg.Message <> WM_SYSCOMMAND THEN Exit;
    IF Msg.wParam AND $FFF0 <> SC_UDF THEN Exit;
    Hf := GetSystemMenu(Handle, False);
    Ha := GetSystemMenu(Application.Handle, False);
    Checkd := GetMenuState(Hf,SC_UDF,MF_BYCOMMAND) AND MF_CHECKED >0;
    CheckMenuItem(Hf, SC_UDF, NuFlag[Checkd]);
    CheckMenuItem(Ha, SC_UDF, NuFlag[Checkd]);
    SetWindowPos(Application.Handle, NuHWnd[Checkd], 0, 0, 0, 0,
      SWP_NOMOVE OR SWP_NOSIZE);
  END;

  end.
```

The regular system menu commands have ID values greater than or equal to $F000; Microsoft recommends using an ID less than $F000 for user-defined system menu items. Also, Windows makes special use of the lowest four bits of the ID in WM_SYSCOMMAND messages; therefore, a system command ID must have those bits set to zero. This program uses $EFF0 for its user-defined system command.

The form's OnCreate event handler adds the new menu item to the form's system menu and also to the Application window's system menu. It sets the Application's OnMessage handler to the method AppOnMessage. AppOnMessage gets a peek at *all* messages for a project, even those directed to the main form window, so it's not necessary to separately process WM_SYSCOMMAND in a message-handling method of the form.

When the AppOnMessage method receives a WM_SYSCOMMAND message from the new menu item, it starts by saving the checked state of that item in the local variable Checkd. If the item is currently checked, this method unchecks it in the system menu of the main form and the application, and uses the SetWindowPos API function to remove the program's always-on-top status. If the item wasn't checked, the method checks it in both system menus and makes the program always on top.

In general, if you want a *program* to stay on top, call SetWindowPos as shown here. Setting the main form's style to fsStayOnTop does not have the same effect.

Accepting files dragged from File Manager or Explorer

16 32

The drag/drop interface is an integral part of Windows 95, and it's fully functional in Windows 3.1 as well. Precisely how you'll implement it depends on whether your program needs to accept dropped files while minimized. In Windows 95, minimized programs can't accept dropped files, but in Windows 3.1 and Windows NT they can. The program in Figure 13-6 implements both possibilities.

```
Drag/Drop Acceptor                                      _□×
(037,048) E:\WIND95\Start Menu\Programs\Accessories\Dial-Up Scripting
(037,048) E:\WIND95\Start Menu\Programs\Accessories\Character Map.lnk
(037,048) E:\WIND95\Start Menu\Programs\Accessories\Dial-Up Networking
(037,048) E:\WIND95\Start Menu\Programs\Accessories\Calculator.lnk
(037,048) E:\WIND95\Start Menu\Programs\Accessories\Direct Cable Conne
(037,048) E:\WIND95\Start Menu\Programs\Accessories\HyperTerminal.lnk
(037,048) E:\WIND95\Start Menu\Programs\Accessories\Notepad.lnk
(037,048) E:\WIND95\Start Menu\Programs\Accessories\Paint.lnk
(037,048) E:\WIND95\Start Menu\Programs\Accessories\Phone Dialer.lnk
(037,048) E:\WIND95\Start Menu\Programs\Accessories\WordPad.lnk
```

FIGURE 13-6: This program reports the files dropped onto it along with the location at which they were dropped; note the automatic long filename support in Delphi 2.0.

FMDROP

FMDROPU.DEX

```
object Form1: TForm1
  Caption = 'Drag/Drop Acceptor'
  Position = poDefault
  Scaled = False
  OnCreate = FormCreate
  object Panel1: TPanel
    Align = alTop
    object CheckBox1: TCheckBox
      Caption = 'Accept when &Minimized'
      OnClick = CheckBox1Click
    end
  end
  object ListBox1: TListBoxHorz
    Align = alClient
    Font.Color = clBlack
    Font.Name = 'Terminal'
    ParentFont = False
  end
end
```

FMDROPU.PAS

```pascal
unit Fmdropu;

interface

uses SysUtils, WinTypes, WinProcs, Messages, Classes, Graphics,
  Controls, Forms, Dialogs, StdCtrls, ExtCtrls, c_lbhorz;

type
  TForm1 = class(TForm)
    Panel1: TPanel;
    CheckBox1: TCheckBox;
    ListBox1: TListBoxHorz;
    procedure FormCreate(Sender: TObject);
    procedure CheckBox1Click(Sender: TObject);
  private
    procedure RecordDragDrop(Drop: THandle; Min: Boolean);
    procedure WMDropFiles(VAR Msg: TWMDropFiles);
      message WM_DROPFILES;
    procedure AppOnMessage(VAR Msg: TMsg;
      VAR Handled : Boolean);
  end;

var Form1: TForm1;

implementation
USES ShellApi, IsWin95;
{$R *.DFM}

procedure TForm1.FormCreate(Sender: TObject);
begin
  DragAcceptFiles(Handle, True);
  IF Win95 THEN CheckBox1.Visible := False;
end;

procedure TForm1.CheckBox1Click(Sender: TObject);
begin
  DragAcceptFiles(Application.Handle, CheckBox1.Checked);
  IF CheckBox1.Checked THEN
    Application.OnMessage := AppOnMessage
  ELSE Application.OnMessage := NIL;
end;

procedure TForm1.RecordDragDrop(Drop: THandle; Min: Boolean);
VAR
  N      : Word;
  buffer : ARRAY[0..255] OF Char;
  TP     : TPoint;
BEGIN
  {"Cardinal(-1)" is $FFFF in 16-bit, $FFFFFFFF in 32-bit}
  FOR N := 0 TO DragQueryFile(Drop, Cardinal(-1), NIL, 255) - 1 DO
    BEGIN
      DragQueryFile(Drop, N, Buffer, 80);
      DragQueryPoint(Drop, TP);
```

```
        WITH ListBox1.Items DO
          IF Min THEN Add('minimized ' + StrPas(Buffer))
          ELSE Add(Format('(%.3d,%.3d) %s', [TP.X, TP.Y ,Buffer]));
      END;
    DragFinish(Drop);
END;

procedure TForm1.WMDropFiles(VAR Msg: TWMDropFiles);
{Called only if TApplication is NOT receiving drag/drop}
BEGIN
  RecordDragDrop(Msg.Drop, False);
  Msg.Result := 0;
END;

procedure TForm1.AppOnMessage(VAR Msg: TMsg; VAR Handled: Boolean);
{when active, receives ALL WM_DROPFILES messages}
BEGIN
  IF Msg.message = WM_DROPFILES THEN
    BEGIN
      RecordDragDrop(Msg.wParam, Msg.hWnd = Application.Handle);
      Handled := True;
    END;
END;

end.
```

The form is deliberately very simple. Files dropped on it are added to a list box, preceded by the pixel location within the form at which they were dropped. If the project was minimized at the time, the pixel location is replaced by the word Minimized. You don't always need to know exactly where on the form a drop occurred, but that information is available. Note that the list box is actually a TListBoxHorz, a TListBox descendant with automatic horizontal scrolling, defined in Chapter 7, "List and Combo Boxes."

This program uses a WM_DROPFILES response method for the main form object *and* an OnMessage handler for the Application. The check box determines which one catches the messages—when it's checked, the OnMessage handler gets all WM_DROPFILES messages, whether aimed at the Application's window or at the main form's window. When it's not checked, the application does not process WM_DROPFILES messages, and they go through to the Form's WmDropFiles method. In actual practice, you'd code one option or the other. Since Windows 95 does not permit dropping files on a minimized application, the form's OnCreate event handler hides the check box.

Any time you write a program that processes files the user selects from a File Open common dialog, consider including File Manager drag and drop capabilities as well. It's not at all difficult, and makes your program more flexible.

Application Miscellany

The Application object is not a visual object, so its properties and methods don't seem as immediate as those of the form object. However, there's great power built into this object. You can tap into the process that displays flyover help, for example, or allow a program to engage in a long calculation without stalling all of Windows.

 Tracking which component the mouse is over

Delphi's built-in flyover help tracks which component the mouse is over and, if the mouse remains there for a moment, displays the Hint property of that component in a hint box. A program can tap that useful information with an OnShowHint event handler. The OnShowHint event (not documented in Delphi 1.0's help system) comes with a THintInfo structure that points to the control for which a hint is desired. Your program can create or modify a hint string by changing the HintStr parameter, and can determine whether or not flyover help is activated by using the CanShow parameter. Figure 13-7 is an example program. Only the panel and check box at the top are represented in the code; you can drop any number of components of any type outside the panel, and their type and name will be correctly reported.

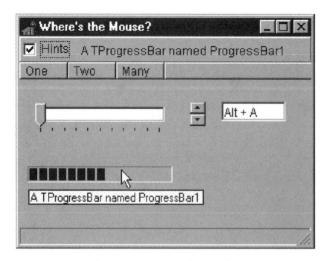

FIGURE 13-7: This program traps the OnShowHint event to get information about what component the mouse is over.

MUSOVER

MUSOVERU.DEX

```
object Form1: TForm1
  Caption = 'Where's the Mouse?'
  ShowHint = True
  OnCreate = FormCreate
  object Panel1: TPanel
    Align = alTop
    object Label1: TLabel
      Caption = 'Drop various components on the form and run.'
    end
    object CheckBox1: TCheckBox
      Caption = 'Hints'
    end
  end
end
```

MUSOVERU.PAS

```
unit Musoveru;

interface

uses SysUtils, WinTypes, WinProcs, Messages, Classes, Graphics,
  Controls, Forms, Dialogs, StdCtrls, ExtCtrls;

type
  TForm1 = class(TForm)
    Panel1: TPanel;
    CheckBox1: TCheckBox;
    Label1: TLabel;
    procedure FormCreate(Sender: TObject);
  private
    procedure AppOnShowHint(var HintStr: string; var CanShow:
      Boolean; var HintInfo: THintInfo);
  end;

var Form1: TForm1;

implementation

{$R *.DFM}

procedure TForm1.AppOnShowHint(var HintStr: string; var CanShow:
  Boolean; var HintInfo: THintInfo);
begin
  WITH HintInfo, HintControl DO
    IF Name <> '' THEN
      HintStr := Format('A %s named %s',[ClassName, Name])
    ELSE HintStr := Format('A %s', [ClassName]);
  Label1.Caption := HintStr;
  CanShow := CheckBox1.Checked;
end;
```

```
procedure TForm1.FormCreate(Sender: TObject);
begin
  Application.HintPause := 0;
  Application.OnShowHint := AppOnShowHint;
end;

end.
```

The form's OnCreate handler sets the application's HintPause property to zero, so the OnShowHint event will occur as soon as the mouse enters a component. And it sets the application's OnShowHint property to event handler AppOnShowHint.

If the component has a name, the OnShowHint event handler sets the HintStr string to the type and the name. If it has no name, the event handler builds the string using the type only. The handler displays the hint string in Label1's caption, and sets the CanShow parameter to the check box's Checked property. If CanShow is True, the program-built hint will appear in a hint box near each component.

One possible use for this technique is internationalization of hints. Instead of storing the hint text in each component, you'd store a numeric code, an index into a string list resource stored in a DLL. You'd load the DLL for the appropriate language, and in the OnShowHint handler you'd load the hint string.

 ## *"Run minimized" is ignored*

16 32

Windows 3.1 lets you specify that a program should run minimized. Windows 95 and Windows NT add the option to run *maximized*. And Delphi programs ignore all of them. The problem is, the data sent by Windows to tell the program how to display itself never reaches the main form. Here's a program that demonstrates a technique for responding to requests to run either minimized or maximized.

RUNMIN

RUNMINU.DEX

```
object Form1: TForm1
  Caption = 'MinMax Form'
  Position = poDefault
  Scaled = False
  OnActivate = FormActivate
  OnCreate = FormCreate
  object Label1: TLabel
  end
end
```

RUNMINU.PAS

```
unit Runminu;

interface

uses SysUtils, WinTypes, WinProcs, Messages, Classes, Graphics,
  Controls, Forms, Dialogs, StdCtrls;

type
  TForm1 = class(TForm)
    Label1: TLabel;
    procedure FormCreate(Sender: TObject);
    procedure FormActivate(Sender: TObject);
  private
    ShowHow : Word;
end;

var Form1: TForm1;

implementation

{$R *.DFM}

procedure TForm1.FormCreate(Sender: TObject);
CONST
{$IFNDEF Win32} SW_SHOWDEFAULT = 10; {$ENDIF}
  Names: ARRAY[SW_HIDE..SW_SHOWDEFAULT] OF PChar=('HIDE','NORMAL',
    'SHOWMINIMIZED','SHOWMAXIMIZED','SHOWNOACTIVATE','SHOW',
    'MINIMIZE','SHOWMINNOACTIVE','SHOWNA','RESTORE','SHOWDEFAULT');
{$IFDEF Win32}VAR SUI : TStartUpInfo;{$ENDIF}
begin
  Application.Title := Caption;
  {$IFDEF Win32}
  IF CmdShow = SW_SHOWDEFAULT THEN
    BEGIN
      GetStartupInfo(SUI);
      ShowHow := SUI.wShowWindow;
    END
  ELSE
  {$ENDIF}
    ShowHow := CmdShow;
  Label1.Caption := 'Show constant: SW_' + StrPas(Names[ShowHow]);
  IF ShowHow = SW_SHOWMAXIMIZED THEN WindowState := wsMaximized;
end;

procedure TForm1.FormActivate(Sender: TObject);
begin
  CASE ShowHow OF
    SW_SHOWMINIMIZED, SW_MINIMIZE, SW_SHOWMINNOACTIVE :
      Application.Minimize;
  END;
end;

end.
```

Windows provides 16-bit programs with a value called CmdShow, which specifies how the program should initially show itself. For 32-bit programs, this value is generally SW_SHOWDEFAULT, which means the program should get its initial display command by calling GetStartupInfo. Either way, this program displays the value that was passed to it, and then minimizes or maximizes as appropriate. Note that the form must wait for the OnActivate event before calling Application.Minimize.

Supplying context-sensitive help for text

16 32

Delphi automates the process of providing context-sensitive help for the active form or component. Just set the HelpContext property and assign the help file name to the Application's HelpFile property. When the user presses F1, the help for the active component's HelpContext appears automatically. But, what if you want the help that appears to reflect the *contents* of the active control as it does in Delphi's editor?

The solution lies in the Application object's OnHelp event. This event is triggered when the user presses F1, and its handler can control whether or not the built-in, context-sensitive help gets called. The program shown in Figure 13-8 uses Delphi's own help file and displays help based on the selected text in a memo box.

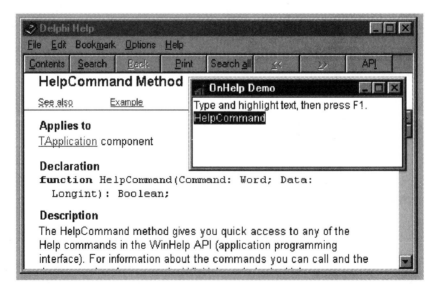

FIGURE 13-8: By trapping the application's OnHelp event, a program can provide context-sensitive help based on selected text.

CONHELP

CONHELPU.DEX

```
object Form1: TForm1
  ActiveControl = Memo1
  Caption = 'OnHelp Demo'
  Position = poDefault
  Scaled = False
  OnCreate = FormCreate
  object Memo1: TMemo
    HelpContext = 100
    Align = alClient
    HideSelection = False
    Lines.Strings = (
      'Type and highlight text, then press F1.')
  end
end
```

CONHELPU.PAS

```
unit Conhelpu;

interface

uses SysUtils, WinTypes, WinProcs, Messages, Classes, Graphics,
  Controls, Forms, Dialogs, StdCtrls, ExtCtrls;

type
  TForm1 = class(TForm)
    Memo1: TMemo;
    procedure FormCreate(Sender: TObject);
  private
    function AppOnHelp(Command:Word; Data: LongInt;
      VAR CallHelp: Boolean): Boolean;
  end;

var Form1: TForm1;

implementation

{$R *.DFM}
procedure TForm1.FormCreate(Sender: TObject);
begin
  {change next line to reflect location of Delphi on YOUR system}
  Application.HelpFile := 'D:\DELPHI\BIN\DELPHI.HLP';
  Application.OnHelp := AppOnHelp;
end;

function TForm1.AppOnHelp(Command:Word; Data: LongInt;
  VAR CallHelp: Boolean): Boolean;
VAR Buff : Array[0..255] OF Char;
BEGIN
  Result := False;
  IF Command = HELP_CONTEXT THEN
```

```
      IF Data = Memo1.HelpContext THEN
        BEGIN
          StrPCopy(Buff, Memo1.SelText);
          Result := Application.HelpCommand(HELP_PARTIALKEY,
            LongInt(@buff));
          CallHelp := False;
        END;
  END;
end.
```

The form's OnCreate event handler sets the application object's HelpFile to Delphi's own help—edit this line to reflect the location of Delphi on your particular system. It also sets the application's OnHelp handler to the method AppOnHelp.

AppOnHelp is called in response to the F1 key; its Command parameter is the help command being requested, and Data is the data that goes with that help command. If the command is HELP_CONTEXT, the data is the HelpContext property of the active control. When that value matches the memo box's help context, this method calls the application object's HelpCommand method, passing the HELP_PARTIALKEY constant, along with the address of a buffer containing the selected text. Besides bringing up WinHelp's search dialog, this triggers AppOnHelp again, but, since the command is not HELP_CONTEXT, there's no further action.

This example program uses Delphi's help file because it's available to every Delphi programmer. In your own programs, you can create finely tuned help files with specialized help for specific words and phrases.

Program is unresponsive when in a loop

| 16 | 32 |

The Pascal language includes several loop constructs. A FOR loop executes for a specified number of iterations, a WHILE loop repeats while a given condition is True, and a REPEAT loop executes *until* a specific condition is True. Under Windows 3.x, however, any of these constructs can cause your program to lock up.

The problem is that Windows 3.x is a non-preemptive, multitasking system. Every program needs to cooperate in the multitasking process, else the whole system comes to a halt. Windows messages don't get processed in this state; therefore, if a WHILE or REPEAT loop is waiting for a condition that occurs based on the processing of a Windows message, the loop will never terminate. This example program demonstrates the problem, along with two related difficulties.

LOOP

LOOPU.DEX

```
object Form1: TForm1
  BorderIcons = [biSystemMenu, biMinimize]
  BorderStyle = bsDialog
  Caption = 'Loop Trouble'
  Position = poDefault
  Scaled = False
  OnCreate = FormCreate
  object Gauge1: TGauge
    MaxValue = 1000
    Progress = 0
  end
  object Label1: TLabel
    AutoSize = False
    WordWrap = True
  end
  object Button1: TButton
    Tag = 1
    Caption = '&Nasty Loop'
    OnClick = Button1Click
  end
  object Button2: TButton
    Tag = 2
    Caption = '&Good Loop'
    OnClick = Button1Click
  end
  object Button3: TButton
    Tag = 3
    Caption = '&Best Loop'
    OnClick = Button1Click
  end
end
```

LOOPU.PAS

```
unit Loopu;

interface

uses SysUtils, WinTypes, WinProcs, Messages, Classes, Graphics,
  Controls, Forms, Dialogs, Gauges, StdCtrls;

type
  TForm1 = class(TForm)
    Button1: TButton;
    Gauge1: TGauge;
    Button2: TButton;
    Button3: TButton;
    Label1: TLabel;
    procedure Button1Click(Sender: TObject);
```

```
    procedure FormCreate(Sender: TObject);
  private
    Looping: Boolean;
    procedure Explain(which: Integer);
  end;

var Form1: TForm1;

implementation

{$R *.DFM}

procedure TForm1.Explain(which: Integer);
BEGIN
  CASE which OF
    0 : Label1.Caption := 'You cannot move, size, or close the '+
        'window, though in Win32 you CAN switch to another program.';
    1 : Label1.Caption := 'You cannot move, size, or close the '+
        'window, or switch to another program. Go ahead and try!';
    2 : Label1.Caption := 'You can move and size this window, or '+
        'switch to another app, but you cannot close this window';
    3 : Label1.Caption := 'You can move, size, or close the '+
        'window, or switch to another program.';
  END;
  Label1.Update;
END;

procedure TForm1.Button1Click(Sender: TObject);
VAR N : Integer;
begin
  IF Looping THEN Exit;
  Explain((Sender AS TButton).Tag);
  Looping := True;
  WITH Gauge1 DO
    FOR N := MinValue TO MaxValue DO
      BEGIN
        Progress := N;
        {IF "good" or "best" button...}
        IF (Sender AS TButton).Tag > 1 THEN
          Application.ProcessMessages;
        {IF "best" button}
        IF (Sender AS TButton).Tag > 2 THEN
          IF Application.Terminated THEN Break;
      END;
  Looping := False;
end;

procedure TForm1.FormCreate(Sender: TObject);
begin
  {$IFDEF Win32}
  Button1.Tag := 0;
  Gauge1.MaxValue := 10000;
  {$ENDIF}
end;

end.
```

Each of the three buttons triggers the same OnClick event handler. This event handler loops 1,000 times, updating a gauge component each time through the loop. The buttons have their Tag properties set to 1, 2, and 3 initially. Press the first button in a program compiled under 16-bit Delphi and your system will be completely unavailable until the gauge reaches 100%. If you compiled under Delphi 2.0, the program will be unresponsive, but you can use other programs while the loop is running.

Pressing the second button, the one labeled Good, adds a call to Application.ProcessMessages within the loop. This is the equivalent of DoEvents in Visual Basic. It allows Windows to continue processing messages. With this call in place, the program no longer interferes with multitasking. However, it still has a problem—you cannot terminate the program until the loop is complete.

When the OnClick handler is invoked by the third button, this final problem is laid to rest. Within the loop, it checks whether the Terminated property of the application object is True and, if so, breaks out of the loop.

Note also that the form defines a private Boolean data field called Looping. If this field is True, the OnClick handler exits immediately. Otherwise, Looping is set to True when the method starts, False when it finishes. This prevents the user from starting the method again before the previous invocation finishes. In general, you'll need to actively make sure this doesn't happen, either by using something like the Looping variable shown here or by disabling menu items or buttons that would start other processes.

PART V

WINDOWS PROGRAMMING

In the bad old days, Windows programmers didn't have the benefit of Delphi. To create a menu or a dialog box, they had to design and compile a Windows *resource*. The main body of each program was a gigantic CASE statement that included code to handle dozens of Windows *messages*. And the code for responding to those messages would normally involve calling numerous Windows API *functions*.

A Delphi program uses resources, responds to messages, and calls Windows API functions, but Delphi doesn't require the programmer to handle this tedium. The form information in a .DFM file is bound into the program as a resource; all the programmer sees is the Form Designer. Most common Windows messages are translated into events, and Delphi components define default behavior for many messages. And the code for Delphi's components naturally calls many Windows API functions.

Delphi handles the tedious aspects of these low-level elements of Windows programming, but a Delphi programmer is free to access them directly as well. Earlier chapters in this book have called on

Windows API functions or responded to Windows messages, as necessary. This part will concentrate on enhancing Delphi programs using low-level Windows elements. Its chapters will cover Windows API functions, sending and receiving messages, and binding user-defined resources into programs. The final chapter will discuss Dynamic Link Libraries (DLLs). A DLL written in Delphi can be called from any Windows programming language, so DLLs expand the range of tasks you can accomplish using Delphi.

Windows API Functions

*D*elphi's components and built-in functions handle the most common tasks and
behaviors needed in Windows programs, but they do not attempt to do everything.
*Since Delphi programs have full access to the hundreds of Windows API functions, any
Windows activity that isn't built into Delphi can easily be invoked by a program. The
WinProcs and WinTypes units, included automatically in every Delphi form's source code,
provide access to the standard API functions and their data structures. Delphi 2.0 combines
these two into the single Windows unit, but, thanks to the new unit aliasing feature,
programs can still refer to WinTypes and WinProcs.*

*These two units hold the declarations for Windows functions residing in the essential
KERNEL, GDI, and USER libraries. For access to other libraries, such as MMSYSTEM and
TOOLHELP, your program simply adds the corresponding Delphi unit to its uses clause.*

*Many of the earlier chapters in this book called on Windows API functions for specific
supporting tasks. In this chapter, API functions are the star attraction. The example
programs will demonstrate accessing forms within callback functions, launching and
controlling other applications, and playing sounds without using the media player
component, among other things.*

Callbacks

A huge number of Windows API functions return information about the system or
elements of the system. Most of them are simple, returning a number, a string, or a
simple data structure. Things get more complicated when the desired data is a list of
items, such as all active windows or all available fonts. Most Windows functions that
enumerate a varying number of elements use a *callback function* to do so. The callback
function is provided by the calling program; Windows calls it repeatedly until the list of

elements is exhausted or the callback function indicates that it doesn't need to see any more. Callback functions generally include as their final parameter a 32-bit quantity that's reserved for use by you, the programmer.

Listing windows and children

16 32

Windows and Windows utilities, such as WinSight and Spy, clearly have access to all windows on the screen. Your programs can get this same information using the EnumWindows and EnumChildWindows API functions. EnumWindows passes the window handle of each top-level window to its callback function; EnumChildWindows passes the handle of each child of the specified window. Both take the same type of callback function. In fact, the program in Figure 14-1 uses exactly the same function for both.

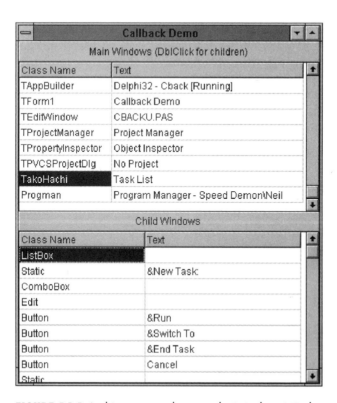

FIGURE 14-1: In this program shown under Windows NT, the upper grid lists all nonchildless, top-level windows, and double-clicking one lists its child windows in the lower grid.

CBACK

CBACKU.DEX

```
object Form1: TForm1
  Caption = 'Callback Demo'
  Position = poDefault
  Scaled = False
  OnCreate = FormCreate
  OnResize = FormResize
  object StringGrid1: TStringGrid
    Align = alTop
    ColCount = 2
    FixedCols = 0
    RowCount = 2
    Options = [goFixedVertLine, goFixedHorzLine, goVertLine,
goHorzLine, goDrawFocusSelected, goColSizing]
    OnDblClick = StringGrid1DblClick
  end
  object StringGrid2: TStringGrid
    Align = alClient
    ColCount = 2
    FixedCols = 0
    RowCount = 2
    Options = [goFixedVertLine, goFixedHorzLine, goVertLine,
goHorzLine, goDrawFocusSelected, goColSizing]
  end
  object Panel1: TPanel
    Align = alTop
    Caption = 'Main Windows (DblClick for children)'
  end
  object Panel2: TPanel
    Align = alTop
    Caption = 'Child Windows'
  end
end
```

CBACKU.PAS

```
unit Cbacku;

interface

uses SysUtils, WinTypes, WinProcs, Messages, Classes, Graphics,
  Controls, Forms, Dialogs, ExtCtrls, Grids;

type
  TForm1 = class(TForm)
    StringGrid1: TStringGrid;
    StringGrid2: TStringGrid;
    Panel1: TPanel;
    Panel2: TPanel;
    procedure FormCreate(Sender: TObject);
```

```
      procedure FormResize(Sender: TObject);
      procedure StringGrid1DblClick(Sender: TObject);
    private
      Grids : ARRAY[1..2] OF TStringGrid;
      WhichGrid: Integer;
    end;

var Form1: TForm1;

implementation
{$R *.DFM}

function MyEnumWindowsProc(H: HWnd; TF: TForm1): Boolean; Export;
  {$IFDEF Win32}StdCall;{$ENDIF}
VAR Buffer : ARRAY[0..255] OF Char;
BEGIN
  Result :=  True;
  IF (TF.WhichGrid = 1) AND (GetTopWindow(H)=0) THEN Exit;
  WITH TF.Grids[TF.WhichGrid] DO
    BEGIN
      RowCount := RowCount+1;
      GetClassName(H, Buffer, 255);
      Cells[0, RowCount-2] :=StrPas(Buffer);
      Objects[0, RowCount-2] := Pointer(H);
      GetWindowText(H, Buffer, 255);
      Cells[1, RowCount-2] := StrPas(Buffer);
    END;
END;

procedure TForm1.FormCreate(Sender: TObject);
begin
  StringGrid1.Cells[0,0] := 'Class Name';
  StringGrid1.Cells[1,0] := 'Text';
  StringGrid2.Rows[0] := StringGrid1.Rows[0];
  Grids[1] := StringGrid1;
  Grids[2] := StringGrid2;
  WhichGrid := 1;
  EnumWindows(@MyEnumWindowsProc, LongInt(Self));
  WITH StringGrid1 DO
    IF RowCount > 2 THEN RowCount := RowCount-1;
end;

procedure TForm1.FormResize(Sender: TObject);
begin
  StringGrid1.Height := (ClientHeight DIV 2) - Panel1.Height;
end;

procedure TForm1.StringGrid1DblClick(Sender: TObject);
VAR
  ro : Integer;
  H  : HWnd;
begin
  H := HWnd(StringGrid1.Objects[0, StringGrid1.Row]);
  FOR ro := StringGrid2.RowCount-1 DOWNTO 1 DO
    StringGrid2.Rows[ro].Clear;
  StringGrid2.RowCount := 2;
```

```
    WhichGrid := 2;
    EnumChildWindows(H, @MyEnumWindowsProc, LongInt(Self));
    WITH StringGrid2 DO
       IF RowCount > 2 THEN RowCount := RowCount-1;
  end;
end.
```

When the main form is created, it initializes the private array Grids to point to the two string grids and sets the private data field WhichGrid to 1 and calls EnumWindows, passing the procedure MyEnumWindowsProc as the first parameter and Self (typecast to a LongInt) as the second.

The callback function MyEnumWindowsProc sets its result to True, indicating that enumeration should continue. Each time it's called, it receives the handle of another top-level window. The TF parameter is a reference to the form, giving the callback function access to all components, data fields, and methods of the form. The function adds a new row to the grid indexed by WhichGrid and inserts the class name and window text of the passed window into the grid. It also stores the window handle in the Objects array element corresponding to the cell containing the class name.

When the user double-clicks on an item in the upper grid, the program sets WhichGrid to 2, then calls EnumChildWindows, passing the window handle for that item, the same callback function, and Self. This fills the lower list box with child windows of the selected item.

The EnumWindows callback lets your program do anything that requires access to the window handle of every top-level window. For example, the KnowExec program later in this chapter uses EnumWindows to find the top-level window belonging to a program that was just executed. Note that callback functions in Delphi 2.0 must be declared with the new StdCall directive, to force the necessary right to left parameter order and Pascal-style parameter cleanup.

Getting detailed font info

16   32

The Font common dialog is handy, but it interrupts the user's flow of work. Programs like WinWord provide toolbar-style instant access to typeface, point size, and special effects like bold, italic, and underline. Delphi programs can get a list of all available fonts simply by checking the Fonts property of the Screen object. However, getting the available sizes and identifying TrueType fonts requires a call to the EnumFontFamilies

API function. The program in Figure 14-2 shows an example status bar that lists available fonts and sizes, flags TrueType fonts, and sets the bold, italic, underline, and strikeout attributes using latchable speed buttons.

FIGURE 14-2: In this example program, the font status bar simply sets the font for a single label component; it could, of course, do much more.

FONTFAM

FONTFAMU.DEX

```
object Form1: TForm1
  BorderIcons = [biSystemMenu]
  BorderStyle = bsDialog
  Caption = 'Font Family Information'
  Font.Height = -16
  OnCreate = FormCreate
  object Panel1: TPanel
    Align = alTop
    BevelInner = bvLowered
    object PaintBox1: TPaintBox
      Font.Color = clBlack
      Font.Height = -24
      Font.Name = 'Times New Roman'
      Font.Style = [fsBold]
      ParentFont = False
      OnPaint = PaintBox1Paint
    end
    object SpeedButton1: TSpeedButton
      AllowAllUp = True
      GroupIndex = 1
      Caption = 'B'
      Font.Height = -16
      Font.Style = [fsBold]
```

```
        ParentFont = False
        OnClick = SpeedButton1Click
      end
      object SpeedButton2: TSpeedButton
        AllowAllUp = True
        GroupIndex = 2
        Caption = 'I'
        Font.Height = -16
        Font.Name = 'Courier'
        Font.Style = [fsItalic]
        ParentFont = False
        OnClick = SpeedButton1Click
      end
      object SpeedButton3: TSpeedButton
        AllowAllUp = True
        GroupIndex = 3
        Caption = 'U'
        Font.Height = -16
        Font.Style = [fsUnderline]
        ParentFont = False
        OnClick = SpeedButton1Click
      end
      object SpeedButton4: TSpeedButton
        AllowAllUp = True
        GroupIndex = 4
        Caption = 'S'
        Font.Height = -16
        Font.Style = [fsStrikeOut]
        ParentFont = False
        OnClick = SpeedButton1Click
      end
      object ComboBox1: TComboBox
        Style = csDropDownList
        Sorted = True
        OnClick = ComboBox1Click
      end
      object ComboBox2: TComboBox
        Style = csDropDownList
        Sorted = True
        OnClick = ComboBox2Click
      end
    end
    object ScrollBox1: TScrollBox
      Align = alClient
      BorderStyle = bsNone
      object Label1: TLabel
        Caption = 'AaBbCc '
      end
    end
  end
end
```

FONTFAMU.PAS

```pascal
unit Fontfamu;

interface

uses SysUtils, WinTypes, WinProcs, Messages, Classes, Graphics,
  Controls, Forms, Dialogs, StdCtrls, Buttons, ExtCtrls;

type
  TForm1 = class(TForm)
    Panel1: TPanel;
    ComboBox1: TComboBox;
    ComboBox2: TComboBox;
    PaintBox1: TPaintBox;
    SpeedButton1: TSpeedButton;
    SpeedButton2: TSpeedButton;
    SpeedButton3: TSpeedButton;
    SpeedButton4: TSpeedButton;
    ScrollBox1: TScrollBox;
    Label1: TLabel;
    procedure FormCreate(Sender: TObject);
    procedure ComboBox1Click(Sender: TObject);
    procedure ComboBox2Click(Sender: TObject);
    procedure PaintBox1Paint(Sender: TObject);
    procedure SpeedButton1Click(Sender: TObject);
  private
    VertResolu : Integer;
    IsTrueType : Boolean;
    procedure SetTrueType(Value: Boolean);
  end;

var Form1: TForm1;

implementation
{$R *.DFM}

procedure TForm1.FormCreate(Sender: TObject);
begin
  VertResolu := GetDeviceCaps(Canvas.Handle, LOGPIXELSY);
  WITH ComboBox1 DO
    BEGIN
      Items := Screen.Fonts;
      ItemIndex := Items.IndexOf(Label1.Font.Name);
      ComboBox1Click(ComboBox1);
    END;
end;

function EnumFontFamProc(var LogFont: TLogFont; var TextMetric:
  TTextMetric; FontType: Integer; TF: TForm1): Integer; Export;
{$IFDEF Win32}StdCall;{$ENDIF}
VAR S : String[5];
begin
  IF FontType AND TRUETYPE_FONTTYPE > 0 THEN
    Result := 0 {stop enumerating}
```

```
        ELSE
          BEGIN
            Result :=1;
            {calc points from TextMetric.tmHeight, per Microsoft}
            S := Format('%.2d', [Round((TextMetric.tmHeight -
              TextMetric.tmInternalLeading)*72 / TF.VertResolu)]);
            WITH TF.ComboBox2.Items DO
              IF IndexOf(S) = -1 THEN Add(S);
          END;
    end;
    procedure TForm1.SetTrueType(Value: Boolean);
    BEGIN
      IF Value <> IsTrueType THEN
        BEGIN
          IsTrueType := Value;
          PaintBox1.Refresh;
        END;
    END;
    procedure TForm1.ComboBox1Click(Sender: TObject);
    VAR
      Buffer : ARRAY[0..255] OF Char;
      Posn   : Integer;
    const
      TTSiz = '08'#13'09'#13'10'#13'11'#13'12'#13'14'#13'16'#13'18'#13+
        '20'#13'22'#13'24'#13'26'#13'28'#13'36'#13'48'#13'66'#13'72';
    begin
      WITH Sender AS TComboBox DO
        BEGIN
          IF ItemIndex < 0 THEN Exit;
          StrPCopy(Buffer, Items[ItemIndex]);
          Label1.Font.Name := Items[ItemIndex];
        END;
      ComboBox2.Clear;
      EnumFontFamilies(Canvas.Handle, Buffer, @EnumFontFamProc,
        {$IFDEF Win32}LongInt{$ELSE}PChar{$ENDIF}(Self));
      WITH ComboBox2 DO
        BEGIN
          IF Items.Count = 0 THEN {is TrueType}
            BEGIN
              Items.SetText(TTSiz);
              SetTrueType(True);
            END
          ELSE SetTrueType(False);
          {get closest item in list}
          Posn := Items.Add(Format('%.2d', [Label1.Font.Size]));
          Items.Delete(Posn);
          IF Posn > Items.Count-1 THEN Posn := Items.Count-1;
          ItemIndex := Posn;
          Label1.Font.Size := StrToInt(Items[ItemIndex]);
        END;
    end;
```

```
procedure TForm1.ComboBox2Click(Sender: TObject);
begin
  WITH Sender AS TComboBox DO
    Label1.Font.Size := StrToInt(Items[ItemIndex]);
end;

procedure TForm1.PaintBox1Paint(Sender: TObject);
begin
  WITH Sender AS TPaintBox DO
    BEGIN
      Canvas.Font := Font;
      SetBkMode(Canvas.Handle, TRANSPARENT);
      Canvas.Font.Color := clGray;   Canvas.TextOut(2,0,'T');
      Canvas.Font.Color := clBlack;  Canvas.TextOut(6,4,'T');
      IF NOT IsTrueType THEN
        BEGIN
          Canvas.Pen.Color := clRed;
          Canvas.Pen.Width := 2;
          Canvas.MoveTo(4,4); Canvas.LineTo(Width-4, Height-4);
          Canvas.MoveTo(Width-4,4); Canvas.LineTo(4, Height-4);
        END;
    END;
end;

procedure TForm1.SpeedButton1Click(Sender: TObject);
VAR BtnStyle : TFontStyle;
begin
  BtnStyle := TFontStyle((Sender AS TSpeedButton).GroupIndex-1);
  IF (Sender AS TSpeedButton).Down THEN
    Label1.Font.Style := Label1.Font.Style + [BtnStyle]
  ELSE Label1.Font.Style := Label1.Font.Style - [BtnStyle];
end;

end.
```

Getting a basic list of available fonts is as simple as setting the first combo box's items to Screen.Fonts in the form's OnCreate event handler. The event handler also sets the current item to the label's initial font, and triggers the combo box's OnClick event handler.

The OnClick handler sets the label's font to the selected item in the first list box, and also copies that font name to a PChar buffer. It clears the second combo box and calls EnumFontFamilies, passing the form's canvas's handle, the buffer containing the font name, and the EnumFontFamProc callback procedure. The final parameter to EnumFontFamProc is a user-defined 32-bit quantity; the most useful 32-bit value to pass is Self, a pointer to the calling form.

This EnumFontFamProc serves to collect a list of available font sizes. If the passed font is a TrueType font, it simply sets its result to False to stop further enumeration. For non-TrueType fonts, it uses a standard formula to convert the passed TextMetric information to a particular point size and adds that size to the second combo box, if not already present.

After the call to EnumFontFamilies, the second combo box will be empty, only if the selected font was a TrueType font. In that case, the OnClick handler fills the second combo box with an arbitrary list of standard TrueType font sizes. Either way, it calls the private SetTrue method to indicate whether the current selection is a TrueType font. SetTrue forces a repaint of the paint box, if necessary, to indicate the status of the current font. For TrueType fonts, it shows the usual double-T symbol; for other fonts, it draws an X through that symbol.

To finish, the OnClick handler sets the current selection in the second combo box to the available font size that's closest to the specified font size of Label1. The sorted list box and combo box components do not provide a means for determining where a particular item *would* go if it were present. Instead, the event handler simply inserts the item in the sorted combo box, notes where it wound up, and deletes it.

The rest of the program is relatively simple. Clicking an item in the second combo box changes the size of the label's text. Clicking one of the four latchable speed buttons turns the corresponding text effect on or off. Each of the speed buttons has a different GroupIndex, from 1 to 4. The corresponding font style constants have ordinal values from 0 to 3. Hence, a single OnClick handler manages all four buttons, simply by subtracting one from the GroupIndex, typecasting it to a TFontStyle, and adding or removing it from the font's Style property.

You can copy this font status bar and associated code into any program that needs to give the user quick and continuous font control.

 ## Using a method as a callback

Callback function types generally include a user-defined 32-bit quantity as their last parameter. Delphi methods all have an invisible 32-bit final parameter that's referenced within the method as Self. It's possible to take advantage of this similarity and use object methods as callback functions, but only in 16-bit Delphi. In 32-bit Delphi, the necessary Stdcall directive reverses the order of parameters on the stack, making the last parameter the first item on the stack. However, the implicit Self parameter is always last, even when Stdcall is used. Thus, the parameters don't match up in a 32-bit program. The program below lists all the brush and pen objects available to the form's canvas using this technique.

CBMETH

CBMETHU.DEX

```
object Form1: TForm1
  Caption = 'List GDI objects (method callback)'
  Position = poDefault
  Scaled = False
  OnCreate = FormCreate
  object ListBox1: TListBox
    Align = alClient
  end
end
```

CBMETHU.PAS

```
unit Cbmethu;
{$IFDEF Win32}
HALT: Method as callback does not work in 32-bit
{$ENDIF}
interface

uses SysUtils, WinTypes, WinProcs, Messages, Classes, Graphics,
  Controls, Forms, Dialogs, ExtCtrls, Grids, StdCtrls;

type
  TForm1 = class(TForm)
    ListBox1: TListBox;
    procedure FormCreate(Sender: TObject);
  private
    OType: Integer;
    function MyEnumObjProc(P : Pointer): Boolean; Export;
  end;

var Form1: TForm1;

implementation
{$R *.DFM}

function TForm1.MyEnumObjProc(P : Pointer): Boolean;
CONST PenStyleNames: ARRAY[PS_SOLID..PS_INSIDEFRAME] OF String[11]=
('Solid','Dash','Dot','DashDot','DashDotDot','Null','InsideFrame');
BEGIN
  Result := True;
  CASE OType OF
    OBJ_BRUSH:
      WITH PLogBrush(P)^ DO
        ListBox1.Items.Add('BRUSH: '+ ColorToString(lbColor));
    OBJ_PEN:
      WITH PLogPen(P)^ DO
```

```
        ListBox1.Items.Add(Format('PEN: %s, %s',
          [ColorToString(lopnColor), PenStyleNames[lopnStyle]]));
    END;
END;
procedure TForm1.FormCreate(Sender: TObject);
begin
  OType := OBJ_BRUSH;
  EnumObjects(Canvas.Handle, OType, @TForm1.MyEnumObjProc, (Self));
  OType := OBJ_PEN;
  EnumObjects(Canvas.Handle, OType, @TForm1.MyEnumObjProc, (Self));
end;

end.
```

As long as you stick to 16-bit Delphi, this technique is even simpler than passing Self to the callback function. The two points to remember are that the Export directive comes after the initial method declaration, and that the callback function name must be qualified with the object type when passed to the API function. For example, this program uses @TForm1.MyEnumObjProc, not just @MyEnumObjProc.

The EnumObjects API function is used much less frequently than EnumWindows and EnumFontFamilies. It appears in this example program simply for variety.

Playing Sounds

Modern computing is an audible experience. Windows 95 menus go "click," "splut," or even "woof!". Sounds alert the user to program problems, or add depth to stored data. Delphi's media player component is fine, if playing sound is your program's main emphasis. If sound is to be just a part of the experience, the media player is overkill.

Playing a .WAV file without the media player component

16 **32**

The media player can load and play any multimedia file the system supports, or activate non-file-based devices such as CD Audio. However, if all you need to do is play a .WAV file, the sndPlaySound API function is usually a better choice. Numerous flag values control precisely how the sound is played. You can run the program shown in Figure 14-3 to get a feel for what these flags do.

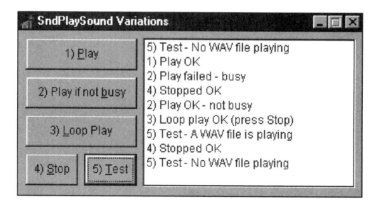

FIGURE 14-3: The API function sndPlaySound plays .WAV files; just how it plays them depends on a series of flags.

SNDPLAY

SNDPLAYU.DEX

```
object Form1: TForm1
  BorderIcons = [biSystemMenu, biMinimize]
  BorderStyle = bsSingle
  Caption = 'SndPlaySound Variations'
  Position = poDefault
  Scaled = False
  OnCreate = FormCreate
  OnDestroy = FormDestroy
  object Button1: TButton
    Caption = '1) &Play'
    OnClick = Button1Click
  end
  object Button2: TButton
    Caption = '2) Play if not &busy'
    OnClick = Button2Click
  end
  object Button4: TButton
    Caption = '4) &Stop'
    OnClick = Button4Click
  end
  object Button5: TButton
    Caption = '5) &Test'
    OnClick = Button5Click
  end
  object Button3: TButton
    Caption = '3) &Loop Play'
    OnClick = Button3Click
  end
  object ListBox1: TListBox
  end
end
```

SNDPLAYU.PAS

```pascal
unit Sndplayu;

interface

uses SysUtils, WinTypes, WinProcs, Messages, Classes, Graphics,
  Controls, Forms, Dialogs, StdCtrls, ExtCtrls;

type
  TForm1 = class(TForm)
    Button1: TButton;
    Button2: TButton;
    Button4: TButton;
    Button5: TButton;
    Button3: TButton;
    ListBox1: TListBox;
    procedure Button1Click(Sender: TObject);
    procedure Button2Click(Sender: TObject);
    procedure Button4Click(Sender: TObject);
    procedure Button5Click(Sender: TObject);
    procedure Button3Click(Sender: TObject);
    procedure FormCreate(Sender: TObject);
    procedure FormDestroy(Sender: TObject);
  end;

var Form1: TForm1;

implementation
USES MMSystem;
{$R *.DFM}
{Change next line to your choice of .WAV file}
CONST WavFile = 'THEMIC~1.WAV';
CONST SilentWav : ARRAY[0..59] OF Char = ('R','I','F','F',
  #$34, #$00, #$00, #$00, 'W','A','V','E','f','m','t',' ',
  #$12, #$00, #$00, #$00, #$01, #$00, #$01, #$00,
  #$22, #$56, #$00, #$00, #$22, #$56, #$00, #$00,
  #$01, #$00, #$08, #$00, #$28, #$00, 'f','a','c','t',
  #$04, #$00, #$00, #$00, #$01, #$00, #$00, #$00, 'd','a','t','a',
  #$01, #$00, #$0, #$00, #$80, #$00);

procedure TForm1.FormCreate(Sender: TObject);
begin
  IF WaveOutGetNumDevs = 0 THEN
    BEGIN
      Button1.Enabled := False;
      Button2.Enabled := False;
      Button3.Enabled := False;
      Button4.Enabled := False;
      Button5.Enabled := False;
      ListBox1.Items.Add('No .WAV file output device present');
    END;
end;
```

```
procedure TForm1.FormDestroy(Sender: TObject);
begin
  SndPlaySound(NIL, SND_ASYNC OR SND_NODEFAULT);
end;

procedure TForm1.Button1Click(Sender: TObject);
begin
  IF SndPlaySound(WavFile, SND_ASYNC) THEN
    ListBox1.Items.Add('1) Play OK')
  ELSE ListBox1.Items.Add('1) Play failed');
end;

procedure TForm1.Button2Click(Sender: TObject);
begin
  IF SndPlaySound(WavFile, SND_ASYNC OR SND_NOSTOP) THEN
    ListBox1.Items.Add('2) Play OK - not busy')
  ELSE ListBox1.Items.Add('2) Play failed - busy');
end;

procedure TForm1.Button3Click(Sender: TObject);
begin
  IF SndPlaySound(WavFile, SND_ASYNC OR SND_LOOP) THEN
    ListBox1.Items.Add('3) Loop play OK (press Stop)')
  ELSE ListBox1.Items.Add('3) Loop play failed');
end;

procedure TForm1.Button4Click(Sender: TObject);
begin
  IF SndPlaySound(NIL, SND_SYNC) THEN
    ListBox1.Items.Add('4) Stopped OK')
  ELSE ListBox1.Items.Add('4) Stop failed');
end;

procedure TForm1.Button5Click(Sender: TObject);
begin
  {Silent WAV rather than NIL in next line, for Win95 32-bit}
  IF SndPlaySound(SilentWav, SND_MEMORY OR SND_ASYNC OR
    SND_NOSTOP) THEN
    ListBox1.Items.Add('5) Test - No WAV file playing')
  ELSE ListBox1.Items.Add('5) Test - A WAV file is playing');
end;

end.
```

The media player component raises an exception if the requested multimedia driver isn't available. When you're using sndPlaySound, your program must handle checking for an available .WAV output device. That's what the form's OnCreate event handler does. If the WaveOutGetNumDevs function returns zero, there's no .WAV output device, and the buttons are disabled.

The most important flag passed to sndPlaySound is SND_ASYNC. Without this flag, the sndPlaySound function call will not return until the .WAV file finishes playing. With it, the function returns immediately and the sound keeps playing while your program continues to function. For those rare occasions when the sndPlaySound function *should* hold up your program's execution until it finishes, use SND_SYNC.

Normally, calling sndPlaySound will stop a sound that's in progress and start the new sound, but adding the SND_NOSTOP flag prevents this. Press the top button repeatedly and each attempt will start the sound anew. Press the second button repeatedly and the sound that's playing will not be interrupted.

Add the SND_LOOP flag and the sound will play again and again until it's stopped. Of course, you must always use SND_ASYNC in conjunction with SND_LOOP. To stop a looping sound, you pass NIL for the filename and use the SND_ASYNC flag. The buttons labeled Loop Play and Stop demonstrate these two techniques.

If the requested .WAV file isn't found, sndPlaySound plays the system-defined default sound, unless you've included the SND_NODEFAULT flag. Thus, you can test whether a sound is playing by using NIL for the filename and combining the SND_ASYNC, SND_NOSTOP, and SND_NODEFAULT flags. The function will return False if a sound is already playing, but won't make any noise if no other sound is playing.

The preceding paragraph is the standard wisdom on testing whether a sound is playing. However, in practice, this technique breaks down in 32-bit programs under Windows 95. Even using the correct combination of flags, passing a NIL value to sndPlaySound stops the current sound. To get around the problem, the Test button actually plays a silent .WAV file rather than passing NIL. In this case, the .WAV file's bytes are stored in memory as the array SilentWav, and the SND_MEMORY flag tells sndPlaySound that its first parameter points to data in memory rather than to a filename.

In 32-bit Windows, sndPlaySound is superseded by PlaySound, a functional superset. Perhaps its most substantial enhancement is the ability to automatically play a sound stored as a resource. However, sndPlaySound is sufficient for most programs, and works in both 16-bit and 32-bit programs. And, as you'll see in the next chapter, with a minimal amount of code, sndPlaySound can play sound resources too.

Playing sounds from memory

16 32

On a system with a slow disk, there can be a noticeable delay as sndPlaySound loads the .WAV file. If your program is going to play several .WAV files again and again, you can load them into memory once and play from memory. The SND_MEMORY flag tells sndPlaySound to treat its first parameter as a pointer to memory rather than a filename. And Delphi's stream support makes loading the file into memory incredibly simple.

MEMSND

MEMSNDU.DEX

```
object Form1: TForm1
  BorderIcons = [biSystemMenu, biMinimize]
  BorderStyle = bsDialog
  Caption = 'Play Sound from Memory'
  Position = poDefault
  Scaled = False
  OnCreate = FormCreate
  OnDestroy = FormDestroy
  object Label1: TLabel
    AutoSize = False
    Caption = 'Label1'
    WordWrap = True
  end
  object Button1: TButton
    Caption = 'Play'
    OnClick = Button1Click
  end
end
```

MEMSNDU.PAS

```
unit Memsndu;

interface

uses SysUtils, WinTypes, WinProcs, Messages, Classes, Graphics,
  Controls, Forms, Dialogs, StdCtrls, Buttons, C_wrapb;

type
  TForm1 = class(TForm)
    Button1: TButton;
    Label1: TLabel;
    procedure FormCreate(Sender: TObject);
    procedure Button1Click(Sender: TObject);
    procedure FormDestroy(Sender: TObject);
  private
    TMS : TMemoryStream;
  end;

var Form1: TForm1;

implementation
USES MMSystem;
{$R *.DFM}

procedure TForm1.FormCreate(Sender: TObject);
begin
  IF WaveOutGetNumDevs = 0 THEN
    BEGIN
      Button1.Enabled := False;
```

```
        Label1.Caption := 'No .WAV file output device present';
      END
    ELSE
      BEGIN
        TMS := TMemoryStream.Create;
        TMS.LoadFromFile('THEMIC~1.WAV');
        Label1.Caption := '.WAV file loaded into memory';
      END;
  end;

  procedure TForm1.Button1Click(Sender: TObject);
  begin
    SndPlaySound(TMS.Memory, SND_ASYNC OR SND_MEMORY);
  end;

  procedure TForm1.FormDestroy(Sender: TObject);
  begin
    SndPlaySound(NIL, SND_ASYNC OR SND_NODEFAULT);
    TMS.Free;
  end;

  end.
```

Don't blink; you'll miss the program! The form's OnCreate handler creates a memory stream object and loads it with the specified .WAV file. Pressing the button plays the file, passing the stream object's Memory property to sndPlaySound. And, when the program terminates, it makes sure the sound isn't still playing before destroying the memory stream.

Tasks

Windows is a multitasking system, so naturally the API includes functions for determining which tasks are currently active. One virtue of 32-bit Windows is better multitasking, and the related API functions provide substantially more information. Tracking tasks also becomes important when one program launches another and then needs to manipulate the program it launched.

 ## *Watching the clipboard's contents*

16 32

The clipboard is a Windows resource shared by all tasks. Any program can put data of any type into the clipboard (though text and bitmap data predominate). A Delphi program can check which clipboard formats are available by checking the Clipboard object's Formats property. However, it's often useful to get more involved in the process. By joining the *clipboard chain*, a program can arrange to be notified every time the clipboard's contents change. The program in Figure 14-4 watches for changes to the clipboard and displays text or bitmap contents.

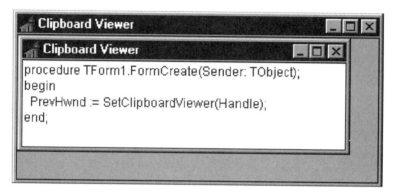

FIGURE 14-4: The clipboard viewer program initially displayed a snippet of code; pressing Alt+PrtSc put a copy of the viewer's own window into the clipboard.

CLIPVU

CLIPVUU.DEX

```
object Form1: TForm1
  Caption = 'Clipboard Viewer'
  Position = poDefault
  Scaled = False
  OnCreate = FormCreate
  OnDestroy = FormDestroy
  object Memo1: TMemo
    Align = alClient
    ReadOnly = True
  end
  object ScrollBox1: TScrollBox
    Align = alClient
    object Image1: TImage
      AutoSize = True
    end
  end
end
```

CLIPVUU.PAS

```
unit Clipvuu;

interface

uses SysUtils, WinTypes, WinProcs, Messages, Classes, Graphics,
  Controls, Forms, Dialogs, StdCtrls, ExtCtrls;

type
  TForm1 = class(TForm)
    Memo1: TMemo;
    ScrollBox1: TScrollBox;
    Image1: TImage;
    procedure FormCreate(Sender: TObject);
    procedure FormDestroy(Sender: TObject);
  private
    PrevHwnd : Hwnd;
    procedure WMChangeCBChain(VAR Msg: TWMChangeCBChain);
      message WM_CHANGECBCHAIN;
    procedure WMDrawClipboard(VAR Msg: TWMDrawClipboard);
      message WM_DRAWCLIPBOARD;
  end;

var Form1: TForm1;

implementation
uses ClipBrd;
{$R *.DFM}

procedure TForm1.FormCreate(Sender: TObject);
begin
  PrevHwnd := SetClipboardViewer(Handle);
end;

procedure TForm1.FormDestroy(Sender: TObject);
begin
  ChangeClipboardChain(Handle, PrevHwnd);
end;

procedure TForm1.WMChangeCBChain(VAR Msg: TWMChangeCBChain);
begin
  {If previous viewer is being removed, "patch" around it}
  IF PrevHWnd = Msg.Remove THEN PrevHWnd := Msg.Next;
  {If not SELF being removed, pass along the message}
  IF Msg.Remove <> Handle THEN
    SendMessage(PrevHWnd, WM_CHANGECBCHAIN, Msg.Remove, Msg.Next);
end;

procedure TForm1.WMDrawClipboard(VAR Msg: TWMDrawClipboard);
VAR H : THandle;
```

```
begin
  {pass along the message}
  WITH TMessage(Msg) DO
    SendMessage(PrevHWnd, WM_DRAWCLIPBOARD, wParam, lParam);
  IF Clipboard.HasFormat(CF_PICTURE) THEN
    BEGIN
      ScrollBox1.BringToFront;
      Image1.Picture.Assign(Clipboard);
    END
  ELSE IF Clipboard.HasFormat(CF_TEXT) THEN
    BEGIN
      Memo1.BringToFront;
      Memo1.Font.Color := clWindowText;
      {$IFDEF Win32}
      Memo1.Text := Clipboard.AsText;
      {$ELSE}
      H := Clipboard.GetAsHandle(CF_TEXT);
      Memo1.SetTextBuf(GlobalLock(H));
      GlobalUnlock(H);
      {$ENDIF}
    END
  ELSE
    BEGIN
      Memo1.BringToFront;
      Memo1.Font.Color := clGrayText;
      Memo1.Lines.Insert(0,'(no text or bitmap in clipboard)');
    END;
  Msg.Result := 0;
end;
end.
```

A call to SetClipboardViewer adds the main form's window handle to the clipboard viewer chain and returns the handle of the window that used to be at the end of the chain. When the form is destroyed, a call to ChangeClipboardChain removes the form from the chain. Since the clipboard viewer chain is dynamic, Windows sends a WM_CHANGECBCHAIN message to report changes. If the stored, previous window handle is being removed, the response method for that message records a new value for the previous window handle. Otherwise, if any window except the one belonging to this program is being removed, it passes the WM_CHANGECBCHAIN message to the next window in the chain.

When the contents of the clipboard change, Windows sends a WM_DRAWCLIPBOARD message to the first window in the chain. Each clipboard viewer is responsible for passing along that message to the next viewer in the chain; that's the first action taken in the example program's response method. Delphi defines this message as having no wParam or lParam, but that's not strictly correct. The information in wParam and lParam is not useful to the receiving program, but it must be passed along. To manage that, the example program typecasts the incoming message to TMessage.

Displaying the clipboard contents when a WM_DRAWCLIPBOARD message comes in is relatively simple. If the clipboard has a bitmap in it, the message response method brings the panel containing the image component to the front and assigns the clipboard bitmap to the image. The panel is required because TImage is a graphical component and cannot appear on top of the TMemo. If there's no bitmap in the clipboard, but there is text, the message handler brings the Memo box to the front and copies the clipboard's text into it.

Executing another program and waiting for it to end

16 32

In a single-tasking system like DOS, when one program launches another, the child program runs to completion before the parent program gets control again. That's useful if the child program is, for example, generating data to be used by the parent program. In Windows, though, the API functions that launch another program return immediately; the child and parent execute simultaneously.

In both versions of Delphi, it's possible to launch a child program and keep track of it, knowing when it has terminated, though the 16-bit and the 32-bit techniques are quite different. The example that follows illustrates both techniques, along with a method for *controlling* the child program.

Executing and controlling other programs

16 32

When one Windows program launches another, the two proceed simultaneously. After all, Windows is a multitasking system! However, the parent program can retain some special information about the child that will permit it to determine when the child program has finished. Under most circumstances, the parent can even take a fair amount of control over the child's execution. The program in Figure 14-5 uses conditional compilation to demonstrate techniques for doing this in both 16-bit Delphi and in Delphi 2.0.

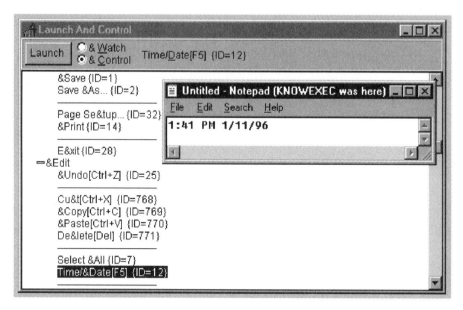

FIGURE 14-5: The KNOWEXEC program has launched the Notepad application and analyzed its menu; KNOWEXEC has sent Notepad the menu command to insert the current date and time.

KNOWEXEC

KNOWEXEU.DEX

```
object Form1: TForm1
  Caption = 'Launch And Control'
  Position = poDefault
  Scaled = False
  OnCreate = FormCreate
  object Panel1: TPanel
    Align = alTop
    BevelInner = bvLowered
    object Panel2: TPanel
      Align = alLeft
      BevelOuter = bvNone
      object Button1: TButton
        Caption = 'Launch '
        OnClick = Button1Click
      end
      object RadioButton1: TRadioButton
        Caption = '&& &Watch'
      end
      object RadioButton2: TRadioButton
        Caption = '&& &Control'
```

```
          Checked = True
          TabStop = True
        end
      end
      object Panel3: TPanel
        Align = alClient
        Alignment = taLeftJustify
        BevelOuter = bvNone
      end
    end
    object Outline1: TOutline
      OutlineStyle = osPlusMinusText
      Align = alClient
      OnDblClick = Outline1DblClick
      ItemSeparator = '\'
    end
    object OpenDialog1: TOpenDialog
      Filter = 'EXE files|*.EXE|All files|*.*'
      Options = [ofHideReadOnly, ofFileMustExist]
      Title = 'Exec what file?'
    end
  end
```

KNOWEXEU.PAS

```
unit Knowexeu;

interface

uses SysUtils, WinTypes, WinProcs, Messages, Classes, Graphics,
  Controls, Forms, Dialogs, Grids, Outline, StdCtrls,
  ExtCtrls;

type
  TForm1 = class(TForm)
    OpenDialog1: TOpenDialog;
    Panel1: TPanel;
    Outline1: TOutline;
    Panel2: TPanel;
    Button1: TButton;
    Panel3: TPanel;
    RadioButton1: TRadioButton;
    RadioButton2: TRadioButton;
    procedure Button1Click(Sender: TObject);
    procedure Outline1DblClick(Sender: TObject);
    procedure FormCreate(Sender: TObject);
  private
    Identifier : Integer; {instance handle or process ID}
    WndHandle : hWnd;
    Watching  : Boolean;
    FUNCTION WinExecAndGetHWnd(const fn: String) : Boolean;
    procedure WaitUntilGone;
  end;
```

```pascal
var Form1: TForm1;

implementation

{$R *.DFM}

procedure TForm1.FormCreate(Sender: TObject);
VAR Buff: ARRAY[0..255] OF Char;
begin
  GetWindowsDirectory(Buff, 255);
  OpenDialog1.Filename := StrPas(Buff) + '\NOTEPAD.EXE';
end;

{$IFDEF Win32}
function EnumFunc(H : HWnd; TF : TForm1) : Bool; StdCall; {32}
VAR TheID : LongInt;
BEGIN
  WITH TF DO
    BEGIN
      {Find the window matching the process ID}
      GetWindowThreadProcessID(H, @TheID);
      IF TheID = Identifier THEN
        BEGIN
          WndHandle := H;
          Result    := False;
        END
      ELSE Result := True;
    END;
END;

VAR TPI : TProcessInformation;
FUNCTION TForm1.WinExecAndGetHWnd(const fn: String) : Boolean; {32}
VAR TSI : TStartupInfo;
  FUNCTION IsWinNT : Boolean;
  VAR OSI : TOSVersionInfo;
  begin
    OSI.dwOSVersionInfoSize := SizeOf(OSI);
    GetVersionEx(OSI);
    Result := OSI.dwPlatformID = VER_PLATFORM_WIN32_NT;
  end;
begin
  WndHandle := 0;
  FillChar(TSI, SizeOf(TSI), 0);
  TSI.CB := SizeOf(TSI);
  IF CreateProcess(PChar(fn), NIL, NIL, NIL, False,
    DETACHED_PROCESS OR NORMAL_PRIORITY_CLASS, NIL, NIL,
    TSI, TPI) THEN
    BEGIN
      Identifier := TPI.dwProcessID;
      CloseHandle(TPI.hThread);
      WaitForInputIdle(TPI.hProcess, 10000); {let process start!}
      EnumWindows(@EnumFunc, LongInt(Self));
```

```
        IF (WndHandle = 0) AND IsWinNT THEN
          ShowMessage('Windows NT does not support this method for '+
            'getting the window handle of a 16-bit application. Try'+
            ' again with a 32-bit application');
      END;
    Result := WndHandle <> 0;
end;

procedure TForm1.WaitUntilGone; {32}
VAR ECP : Integer;
begin
  REPEAT
    Application.ProcessMessages;
    GetExitCodeProcess(TPI.hProcess, ECP);
  UNTIL (ECP <> STILL_ACTIVE) OR Application.Terminated;
  CloseHandle(TPI.hProcess);
end;

{$ELSE}
function EnumFunc(H : HWnd; TF : TForm1) : Bool; {16}
BEGIN
  WITH TF DO
    BEGIN
      {Find the window matching the instance handle}
      IF GetWindowWord(H, GWW_HINSTANCE) = Identifier THEN
        BEGIN
          WndHandle := H;
          Result    := False;
        END
      ELSE Result := True;
    END;
END;

FUNCTION TForm1.WinExecAndGetHWnd(const fn: String) : Boolean;{16}
VAR Cmd: ARRAY[0..255] OF Char;
begin
  WndHandle := 0;
  StrPCopy(Cmd, fn);
  Identifier := WinExec(Cmd, SW_SHOW);
  IF Identifier >= 32 THEN
    EnumWindows(@EnumFunc, LongInt(Self));
  Result := WndHandle <> 0;
end;

procedure TForm1.WaitUntilGone; {16}
begin
  REPEAT Application.ProcessMessages;
  UNTIL (GetModuleUsage(Identifier) = 0) OR
        Application.Terminated;
end;
{$ENDIF}
```

```
procedure TForm1.Button1Click(Sender: TObject);
VAR WCaption : ARRAY[0..255] OF Char;

  procedure AddChildMenus(Loc, Han : Integer);
  CONST Separator = #151#151#151#151#151#151#151#151#151#151;
  VAR
    MText : ARRAY[0..255] OF Char;
    N, M  : Integer;
    ID    : Integer;
    NuLoc : Integer;
  BEGIN
    FOR N := 0 TO GetMenuItemCount(Han)-1 DO
      BEGIN
        Id := Integer(GetMenuItemID(Han, N));
        GetMenuString(Han, N, MText, 255, MF_BYPOSITION);
        IF StrLen(MText) > 0 THEN
          FOR M := 0 TO StrLen(MText)-1 DO
            IF MText[M] = #9 THEN {put hotkey in [] brackets}
              BEGIN
                MText[M] := '[';
                StrLCat(MText, '] ', 255);
              END;
        IF ID = -1 THEN
          BEGIN
            NuLoc := Outline1.AddChild(Loc, StrPas(MText));
            AddChildMenus(NuLoc, GetSubMenu(Han, N));
          END
        ELSE IF StrLen(MText) > 0 THEN
          Outline1.AddChildObject(Loc, Format('%s {ID=%d}',
            [MText, Id]), Pointer(Id))
        ELSE Outline1.AddChild(Loc, Separator);
      END;
  END;

begin
  IF Watching THEN Exit;
  WITH OpenDialog1 DO
    IF Execute THEN
      IF WinExecAndGetHWnd(FileName) THEN
        BEGIN
          IF WndHandle = 0 THEN
            RadioButton1.Checked := True;
          Watching := True;
          Panel3.Caption := 'OK: ' + Filename;
          IF RadioButton2.Checked THEN
            BEGIN
              GetWindowText(WndHandle, WCaption, 255);
              StrLCat(WCaption, ' (KNOWEXEC was here)', 255);
              SetWindowText(WndHandle, WCaption);
              Outline1.Clear;
              IF GetMenu(WndHandle) <> 0 THEN
```

```
                BEGIN
                  Outline1.Add(0, 'Main Menu');
                  AddChildMenus(1, GetMenu(WndHandle));
                  Outline1.FullExpand;
                  Refresh;
                END;
            END;
          WaitUntilGone;
          Outline1.Clear;
          Panel3.Caption := 'Program has terminated';
          Watching := False;
        END;
end;

procedure TForm1.Outline1DblClick(Sender: TObject);
begin
  WITH Sender AS TOutline DO
    IF (Items[SelectedItem].Data <> NIL) THEN
      BEGIN
        Panel3.Caption := Items[SelectedItem].Text;
        BringWindowToTop(WndHandle);
        PostMessage(WndHandle, WM_COMMAND,
          Integer(Items[SelectedItem].Data), 0);
      END;
end;

end.
```

Press the Execute button and the program lets you choose an .EXE file to launch—it defaults to the Windows notepad. The method WinExecAndGetHWnd is implemented differently for 16-bit and for 32-bit Delphi. 16-bit Windows programs can launch other programs using the WinExec API function or the more modern ShellExecute. In a 32-bit program, those two functions rely on the 32-bit CreateProcess function; in general, 32-bit programs should call CreateProcess directly.

The 16-bit version uses WinExec to launch the selected program and stores the returned instance handle in the private data field Identifier. If this handle is not an error code, the program returns True and uses an EnumWindows callback to locate a top-level window whose instance handle matches the Identifier. If such a window is found, its handle is stored in the private data field WndHandle.

In Delphi32, the CreateProcess API function is used to launch the program, and the Identifier data field is set to the process ID of the launched program. A similar EnumWindows callback function searches for a top-level window whose process ID matches the stored Identifier. As before, if such a window is found, the window handle is stored in WndHandle.

If the Control radio button was checked and a Window handle obtained, the next block of code demonstrates control over the child process. Just to show it can be done, it adds "(KnowExec was here)" to the caption. Then, it uses a recursive function to store the launched program's menu structure in an outline component, stashing the ID of each menu item in the pointer associated with the outline node.

Whether or not the Control radio button was checked, the program next calls WaitUntilGone, another function that exists in separate 16-bit and 32-bit versions. Both versions repeatedly call Application.ProcessMessages until the launched program ends or KnowExec terminates. The 16-bit version waits for the usage count of the launched program's instance handle to drop to zero; the 32-bit version loops until GetExitCodeProcess no longer returns STILL_ACTIVE for the process handle of the launched program. When the launched program has terminated, KnowExec clears the outline.

Meanwhile, as long as the launched program is still running, double-clicking an element of the menu structure in KnowExec's outline will send the corresponding command to the child program. Most messages will have the desired effect even when they don't actually come from the child program's menu!

This program displays some extremely powerful techniques. It shows how to get a window handle to a program that your program has launched, and how to determine when that program has finished, both in 16-bit and in 32-bit Delphi. It also shows how to analyze a program's menu and send simulated menu commands.

 ## Getting a list of active tasks

16

The Windows 3.1 task list gives a quick look at all tasks that are running. Windows 95 does not make a similar list so easily available, but, if you press Ctrl+Alt+Del, it shows the list and asks which program you want to kill. Delphi programs can get access to this list using functions from TOOLHELP.DLL. These functions can step through the list of active tasks and get information about each, as the program in Figure 14-6 shows.

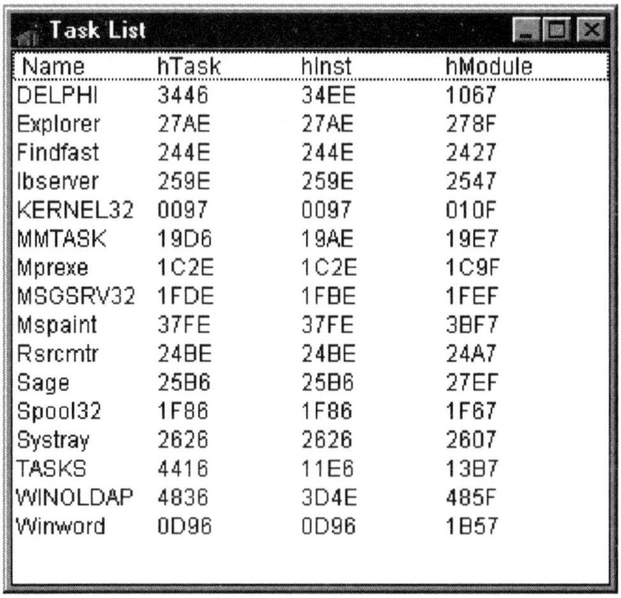

Name	hTask	hInst	hModule
DELPHI	3446	34EE	1067
Explorer	27AE	27AE	278F
Findfast	244E	244E	2427
lbserver	259E	259E	2547
KERNEL32	0097	0097	010F
MMTASK	19D6	19AE	19E7
Mprexe	1C2E	1C2E	1C9F
MSGSRV32	1FDE	1FBE	1FEF
Mspaint	37FE	37FE	3BF7
Rsrcmtr	24BE	24BE	24A7
Sage	25B6	25B6	27EF
Spool32	1F86	1F86	1F67
Systray	2626	2626	2607
TASKS	4416	11E6	13B7
WINOLDAP	4836	3D4E	485F
Winword	0D96	0D96	1B57

FIGURE 14-6: This program displays the name of each active task, along with its task handle, instance handle, and module handle.

TASKS

TASKSU.DEX

```
object Form1: TForm1
  Caption = 'Task List'
  Position = poDefault
  Scaled = False
  OnCreate = FormCreate
  object ListBoxTabs1: TListBoxTabs
    Align = alClient
    Sorted = True
  end
end
```

TASKSU.PAS

```
unit Tasksu;
{$IFDEF Win32}
HALT: Use TASKS32 project in 32-bit Delphi
{$ENDIF}
interface
```

```
uses SysUtils, WinTypes, WinProcs, Messages, Classes, Graphics,
  Controls, Forms, Dialogs, StdCtrls, C_lbtab, ExtCtrls, c_lbhorz;
type
  TForm1 = class(TForm)
    ListBoxTabs1: TListBoxTabs;
    procedure FormCreate(Sender: TObject);
  end;

var Form1: TForm1;

implementation
USES ToolHelp;
{$R *.DFM}

procedure TForm1.FormCreate(Sender: TObject);
VAR TE: TTaskEntry;
begin
  ListBoxTabs1.Items.Add(' Name'#9'hTask'#9'hInst'#9'hModule');
  TE.dwSize := SizeOf(TTaskEntry);
  IF TaskFirst(@TE) THEN
    REPEAT
      ListBoxTabs1.Items.AddObject(Format('%s'#9'%.4x'#9+
        '%.4x'#9'%.4x', [TE.szModule, TE.hTask, TE.hInst,
        TE.hModule]), Pointer(TE.hTask));
    UNTIL NOT TaskNext(@TE);
  ListBoxTabs1.SetTabsPix([88]);
end;

end.
```

Stepping through the task list is a lot like getting a list of files the old-fashioned way, using FindFirst and FindNext. In this case, the TaskFirst function fills a TTaskEntry data structure with information about the first task in the list, and the TaskNext function repeatedly fills the TTaskEntry with data about the next task. The example program displays the module name, task handle, instance, handle, and module handle for each task.

Getting a list of active processes

32

The 32-bit ToolHelp functions in Windows 95 expose a vast amount of information about processes. However, they do not work at all like their 16-bit counterparts, they're not 100% officially documented, and they do not exist in Windows NT. If these limitations don't bother you, the 32-bit ToolHelp functions can be quite useful, as the program in Figure 14-7 shows. The upper list view component lists all active processes; the lower lists all modules used by the selected process along with their sizes. Clicking on any of the column headers sorts the list by that column.

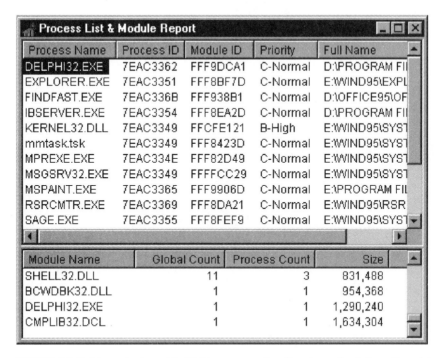

FIGURE 14-7: Not only does this 32-bit program list all active tasks, it lists all modules used by the selected task along with the amount of memory they occupy.

TASKS32

TASKS32U.DEX

```
object Form1: TForm1
  Caption = 'Process List & Module Report'
  Position = poDefault
  Scaled = False
  OnCreate = FormCreate
  object ListView1: TListView
    Align = alClient
    Columns = <
      item
        Caption = 'Process Name'
        Width = 120
      end
      item
        Caption = 'Process ID'
        Width = 80
      end
```

```
        item
          Caption = 'Module ID'
          Width = 80
        end
        item
          Caption = 'Priority'
          Width = 64
        end
        item
          Caption = 'Full Name'
          Width = 160
        end>
      ReadOnly = True
      HideSelection = False
      OnChange = ListView1Change
      OnColumnClick = ListView1ColumnClick
      ViewStyle = vsReport
    end
    object ListView2: TListView
      Align = alBottom
      Columns = <
        item
          Caption = 'Module Name'
          Width = 120
        end
        item
          Alignment = taRightJustify
          Caption = 'Global Count'
          Width = 96
        end
        item
          Alignment = taRightJustify
          Caption = 'Process Count'
          Width = 96
        end
        item
          Alignment = taRightJustify
          Caption = 'Size'
          Width = 80
        end>
      ReadOnly = True
      HideSelection = False
      OnColumnClick = ListView1ColumnClick
      ViewStyle = vsReport
    end
  end
end
```

TASKS32U.PAS

```
unit tasks32u;
{$IFNDEF Win32}
HALT: This version is only for 32-bit Delphi
{$ENDIF}
interface

uses SysUtils, Windows, Messages, Classes, Graphics, Controls,
  Forms, Dialogs, StdCtrls, C_lbtab, ExtCtrls, ComCtrls,
  CommCtrl;

type
  TForm1 = class(TForm)
    ListView1: TListView;
    ListView2: TListView;
    procedure FormCreate(Sender: TObject);
    procedure ListView1Change(Sender: TObject; vItem: TListItem;
      Change: TItemChange);
    procedure ListView1ColumnClick(Sender: TObject; vColumn:
      TListColumn);
  end;

var Form1: TForm1;

implementation
{$R *.DFM}
Const
  MAX_MODULE_NAME32 = 255;
  TH32CS_SNAPHEAPLIST = $00000001;
  TH32CS_SNAPPROCESS  = $00000002;
  TH32CS_SNAPTHREAD   = $00000004;
  TH32CS_SNAPMODULE   = $00000008;
  TH32CS_SNAPALL = (TH32CS_SNAPHEAPLIST OR TH32CS_SNAPPROCESS
    OR TH32CS_SNAPTHREAD OR TH32CS_SNAPMODULE);
  TH32CS_INHERIT      = $80000000;
TYPE
  TProcessEntry32 = record
    dwSize              : DWORD;
    cntUsage            : DWORD;
    th32ProcessID       : DWORD;
    th32DefaultHeapID   : DWORD;
    th32ModuleID        : DWORD;
    cntThreads          : DWORD;
    th32ParentProcessID : DWORD;
    pcPriClassBase      : LongInt;
    dwFlags             : DWORD;
    szExeFile           : Array[0..MAX_PATH-1] of Char;
  end; {TProcessEntry32}
  PPROCESSENTRY32 = ^TProcessEntry32;
```

```
    TMODULEENTRY32 = record
      dwSize        : DWORD;
      th32ModuleID  : DWORD;
      th32ProcessID : DWORD;
      GlblcntUsage  : DWORD;
      ProccntUsage  : DWORD;
      modBaseAddr   : PBYTE;
      modBaseSize   : DWORD;
      hModule       : HMODULE;
      szModule      : Array[0..MAX_MODULE_NAME32] of Char;
      szExePath     : Array[0..MAX_PATH-1] of Char;
    end;
    PMODULEENTRY32 = ^TMODULEENTRY32;

    TCreateToolhelp32Snapshot = function (dwFlags: DWORD;
      th32ProcessID: DWORD): THandle stdCall;
    TProcess32FirstNext = function (hSnapshot: THandle;
      VAR ppe: TPROCESSENTRY32): Bool stdCall;
    TModule32FirstNext = function (hSnapshot: THandle;
      VAR pme: TMODULEENTRY32): Bool stdcall;

VAR
  CreateToolHelp32Snapshot : TCreateToolhelp32Snapshot;
  Process32First           : TProcess32FirstNext;
  Process32Next            : TProcess32FirstNext;
  Module32First            : TModule32FirstNext;
  Module32Next             : TModule32FirstNext;

FUNCTION InitToolHelp32: Boolean;
VAR KH: hModule;
BEGIN
  Result := False;
  KH := GetModuleHandle('KERNEL32.DLL');
  IF KH = 0 THEN Exit;
  Process32First := GetProcAddress(KH, 'Process32First');
  Process32Next  := GetProcAddress(KH, 'Process32Next');
  Module32First  := GetProcAddress(KH, 'Module32First');
  Module32Next   := GetProcAddress(KH, 'Module32Next');
  CreateToolHelp32Snapshot := GetProcAddress(KH,
    'CreateToolhelp32Snapshot');
  IF @Process32First = NIL THEN Exit;
  IF @Process32Next  = NIL THEN Exit;
  IF @Module32First  = NIL THEN Exit;
  IF @Module32Next   = NIL THEN Exit;
  IF @CreateToolHelp32Snapshot = NIL THEN Exit;
  Result := True;
END;

procedure TForm1.FormCreate(Sender: TObject);
VAR
  hSnapshot : THandle;
  TPE       : TProcessEntry32;
```

```
      function PriName(PriValue: Integer): String;
      BEGIN
        CASE PriValue OF
          4  : Result := 'D-Idle';
          8  : Result := 'C-Normal';
          13 : Result := 'B-High';
          24 : Result := 'A-RealTime';
          ELSE Result := Format('?: %d', [PriValue]);
        END;
      END;
    begin
      IF NOT InitToolHelp32 THEN
        BEGIN
          ShowMessage('Unable to init TOOLHELP32 functions');
          Exit;
        END;
      hSnapshot := CreateToolhelp32Snapshot(TH32CS_SNAPPROCESS, 0);
      TPE.dwSize := SizeOf(TPE);
      IF Process32First(hSnapshot, TPE) THEN
        REPEAT
          WITH ListView1.Items.Add DO
            BEGIN
              Data := Pointer(TPE.th32ProcessId);
              Caption := ExtractFileName(TPE.szExeFile);
              SubItems.Add(Format('%.8x',[TPE.th32ModuleId]));
              SubItems.Add(Format('%.8x',[TPE.th32ProcessId]));
              SubItems.Add(PriName(TPE.pcPriClassBase));
              SubItems.Add(TPE.szExeFile);
            END;
        UNTIL NOT Process32Next(hSnapshot, TPE);
      CloseHandle(hSnapshot);
    end;

    procedure TForm1.ListView1Change(Sender: TObject; vItem: TListItem;
      Change: TItemChange);
    VAR
      PId       : DWORD;
      hSnapshot : THandle;
      TME       : TModuleEntry32;
    begin
      IF Change <> ctState THEN Exit;
      WITH Sender AS TListView DO
        BEGIN
          ListView2.Items.Clear;
          PId := DWORD(vItem.Data);
          hSnapshot := CreateToolhelp32Snapshot(TH32CS_SNAPMODULE,PId);
          TME.dwSize := SizeOf(TME);
          IF Module32First(hSnapshot, TME) THEN
            REPEAT
              WITH ListView2.Items.Add DO
```

```
                   BEGIN
                     Caption := TME.szModule;
                     SubItems.Add(IntToStr(TME.GlblCntUsage));
                     SubItems.Add(IntToStr(TME.ProcCntUsage));
                     SubItems.Add(FormatFloat('0,',TME.ModBaseSize));
                   END;
               UNTIL NOT Module32Next(hSnapshot, TME);
             CloseHandle(hSnapshot);
           END;
       end;
       function ListViewColSort(Item1, Item2: TListItem; lParam:
         Integer): Integer; stdcall;
       begin
         IF lParam = 0 THEN Result := lstrcmp(PChar(Item1.Caption),
           PChar(Item2.Caption))
         ELSE IF lParam > 0 THEN
           Result := lstrcmp(PChar(Item1.SubItems[lParam-1]),
             PChar(Item2.SubItems[lParam-1]))
         ELSE Result := lstrcmp(
           PChar(Format('%20s',[Item1.SubItems[-lParam-1]])),
           PChar(Format('%20s',[Item2.SubItems[-lParam-1]])));
       end;
       procedure TForm1.ListView1ColumnClick(Sender: TObject;
         vColumn: TListColumn);
       begin
         WITH Sender AS TListView DO
           IF vColumn.Alignment = taRightJustify THEN
             CustomSort(TLVCompare(@ListViewColSort), -vColumn.Index)
           ELSE CustomSort(TLVCompare(@ListViewColSort), vColumn.Index);
       end;
       end.
```

The complexity of this program is increased by the need to load the ToolHelp32 functions dynamically. These functions are present in Windows 95, but not in Windows NT. If they were compiled into the program implicitly, NT would refuse to load the program. The program's first action is to call its InitToolHelp32 function, which dynamically loads the five necessary functions.

If InitToolHelp32 succeeds, the program calls CreateToolHelp32Snapshot to get a static "snapshot" of the system status. This is necessary because, if a program attempted to step through the task list with other processes still running, the list could change. The rest of the processing relies on this snapshot.

The next step is similar to the 16-bit task list processing. After a call to Process32First to get the first process, repeated calls to Process32Next get the rest. For each process, the program records the name, the Module ID, the Process ID, the priority, and the full pathname. Once the list is complete, a call to CloseHandle disposes of the snapshot.

When the user clicks on a process in the main list view, a similar chunk of code fills the second list view with information about modules used by that process. Again, a call to CreateToolHelp32Snapshot starts the action, but the flags passed this time cause the snapshot to record all modules used by the selected process. Calls to Module32First and Module32Next iterate through the list. For each module, the program records the name, the global usage count, the process-specific usage count, and the size in bytes.

The OnColumnClick event handler for both list views sorts the view on the selected column. The sort routine ColumnListViewSort has to sort numeric columns differently from non-numeric. The OnColumnClick handler assumes that any right-justified field is numeric, and identifies it by passing the negative of the column number.

If the column number is zero, ColumnListViewSort simply compares the caption column, just like the default sort routine does. If the column number is greater than zero, it compares the contents of the appropriate column. And, if the column number is negative, it right-justifies the contents of the appropriate column before making its comparison.

Tasks32 is a more complex application than its 16-bit counterpart, but it *does* much more. It's actually quite useful to see all the modules any running program uses, with their sizes. If a module has a global usage count of 1, this particular process is the *only* one using it. And some of them are impressively large.

Windows Messages and Resources

*B*efore the age of visual programming, Windows programmers created menus, dialog boxes, and other user interface elements using a resource editor and compiler. Delphi's forms are actually stored in the .EXE as a private resource type, but you don't normally have to think about that. You can program in Delphi without ever accessing resources directly. In this chapter, you'll learn to use custom cursors, load bitmaps from a resource, and build string resources to make localization easier.

Along the same lines, old-style Windows programs centered around handling Windows messages, whereas Delphi translates the most common Windows messages into events. Responding to these messages involves writing an event handler, and Delphi even automates the creation of event handlers. Responding to a Windows message that's not translated into an event is hardly more difficult. Delphi even provides built-in data types for accessing the data supplied with all the documented Windows messages. These data types make message-handling code portable between 16-bit and 32-bit Windows, even for the messages whose data is packed differently. Many of the example programs thus far have relied on Windows messages for enhanced functionality; here we'll look into advanced topics involving messages.

Resource Basics

Even if you never actively add Windows resources to your program, you can run into resource trouble. When you do make your first forays into the resource realm, another common trap may trip you. We'll start by getting these troubles out of the way.

Understanding resource error message on program load

16

Sometimes upon loading a project into Delphi 1.0 you'll get a cryptic message like this:

```
Error creating form: Duplicate resource (Type: , Name: ).
```

This can occur regardless of whether you have added any resources to the program.

The problem here is that 16-bit and 32-bit Windows resources are not compatible with each other. Delphi creates a resource file to hold an application's icon, and the file is a 16-bit or a 32-bit resource, depending on the version of Delphi that created it. If you work on a project in Delphi32, a 32-bit resource will be created. When you try to load the project in 16-bit Delphi again, you get the cryptic error message shown above.

The easiest way to avoid this problem is to delete the application's .RES file any time you go to or from Delphi32. Delphi will recreate the .RES file as needed, using the default icon. Just before you create a final 16-bit or 32-bit .EXE for distribution, flip to the Application page of the Project Options dialog and select the actual icon for the application.

Avoiding resource disappearance

16 32

If the resources you create seem to disappear unpredictably, you're almost certainly trying to add or change resources in the .RES file that Delphi creates to go with your main project file. Never do that! Don't attempt to create an .RES file with the same name as your project, and don't edit the .RES file with the same name as your project. Always create a separate file for resources you add.

Here's a suggestion. The name for the default .RES file is the same as the name of the project. Since your additional resource file will probably need to exist in separate 16-bit and 32-bit versions, name these by clipping the project name to not more than six characters, then appending with 16 or 32. That's the convention used in this chapter's programs. For example, the default resource file for the BMPER program is BMPER.RES, and its additional resource files are named BMPER16.RES and BMPER32.RES.

Creating a resource file

16 32

Various utilities are available for creating and for editing resource files. Borland's Resource Workshop is one example, and the image editor that comes with Delphi is another. If all you need to do is compile existing bitmaps, cursors, or similar files into a resource, a command-line resource compiler is sufficient. By using a command-line compiler, you can automate the process of creating parallel 16-bit and 32-bit resource files.

You'll find the BRCC.EXE resource compiler in the same directory as DELPHI.EXE. It takes a number of command-line switches, but the most important ones are -31, -w32, and -fo. The -31 switch requests 16-bit output in Windows 3.1 format, whereas -w32 requests 32-bit output. The -fo precedes the desired output filename.

Rather than attempt to remember these switches, you may want to create resources using a batch file. In fact, all the example programs in this chapter use a hybrid file that functions both as a resource script and as a batch file that compiles the script. Here's an example:

BMPERMK.BAT

```
/*
@ECHO OFF
CLS
brcc -foBMPER16 -31 bmpermk.bat
brcc -foBMPER32 -w32 bmpermk.bat
GOTO End
*/
1 BITMAP LOADONCALL MOVEABLE DISCARDABLE "example1.bmp"
2 BITMAP LOADONCALL MOVEABLE DISCARDABLE "example2.bmp"
3 BITMAP LOADONCALL MOVEABLE DISCARDABLE "example3.bmp"
/*
:End */
```

In a resource script, /* and */ mark the start and end of a comment. Thus, when this file is viewed as a resource script, the only active lines are the three that define bitmap resources.

When this file runs as a batch file, its first line causes a "Bad command or file name" error, but the CLS command clears the screen and hides the error message. After creating 16-bit and 32-bit resources, the batch file jumps to the label :End, skipping over the resource script statements. Thus, the file compiles itself twice, producing 16-bit and 32-bit resource files.

Using Resources

Most of the things you can do with resources can also be done using Delphi components directly. However, there are often advantages to using resources, and some tasks, like adding a custom cursor, *require* them.

Storing bitmaps as resources

16 32

A Delphi component that has a bitmap assigned to it at design time stores that bitmap in the .DFM file, which is a specialized kind of resource. If several components use the same bitmap, it gets stored several times. This seems wasteful! Also, there are programs that need to use and reuse a bitmap, but don't actually require that it reside in a component.

Of course, one simple solution to the first problem would be to assign the bitmap to *one* component at design time, and copy it as needed at runtime. And the second could be solved by loading the .BMP file as needed. However, as the program in Figure 15-1 demonstrates, binding a bitmap resource into the program's .EXE file is a very clean and simple way to make it available.

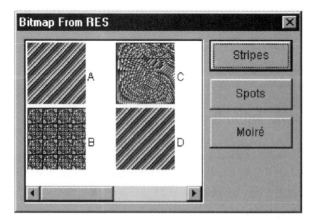

FIGURE 15-1: The three bitmaps displayed in the list box are stored as resources.

BMPER

BMPERMK.BAT

```
/*
@ECHO OFF
CLS
brcc -foBMPER16 -31 bmpermk.bat
brcc -foBMPER32 -w32 bmpermk.bat
GOTO End
*/
1 BITMAP LOADONCALL MOVEABLE DISCARDABLE "example1.bmp"
2 BITMAP LOADONCALL MOVEABLE DISCARDABLE "example2.bmp"
3 BITMAP LOADONCALL MOVEABLE DISCARDABLE "example3.bmp"
/*
:End */
```

BMPERU.DEX

```
object Form1: TForm1
  BorderIcons = [biSystemMenu, biMinimize]
  BorderStyle = bsDialog
  Caption = 'Bitmap From RES'
  Position = poDefault
  Scaled = False
  object ListBox1: TListBox
    Columns = 2
    ItemHeight = 68
    Style = lbOwnerDrawFixed
    OnDrawItem = ListBox1DrawItem
  end
  object Button1: TButton
    Tag = 1
    Caption = 'Stripes'
    OnClick = Button1Click
  end
  object Button2: TButton
    Tag = 2
    Caption = 'Spots'
    OnClick = Button1Click
  end
  object Button3: TButton
    Tag = 3
    Caption = 'Moiré'
    OnClick = Button1Click
  end
end
```

BMPERU.PAS

```
unit Bmperu;

interface

uses SysUtils, WinTypes, WinProcs, Messages, Classes, Graphics,
  Controls, Forms, Dialogs, StdCtrls, ExtCtrls, Buttons;

type
  TForm1 = class(TForm)
    ListBox1: TListBox;
    Button1: TButton;
    Button2: TButton;
    Button3: TButton;
    procedure ListBox1DrawItem(Control: TWinControl; Index:
      Integer; Rect: TRect; State: TOwnerDrawState);
    procedure Button1Click(Sender: TObject);
  end;

var Form1: TForm1;

implementation

{$R *.DFM}
{$IFDEF Win32}
{$R BMPER32.RES}
{$ELSE}
{$R BMPER16.RES}
{$ENDIF}

procedure TForm1.Button1Click(Sender: TObject);
begin
  WITH ListBox1.Items DO
    AddObject(Char(65+Count), Pointer((Sender AS TButton).Tag));
end;

procedure TForm1.ListBox1DrawItem(Control: TWinControl;
  Index: Integer; Rect: TRect; State: TOwnerDrawState);
VAR TB : TBitmap;
begin
  WITH Control AS TListbox, Canvas DO
    BEGIN
      FillRect(Rect);
      TB := TBitmap.Create;
      try
        {$IFDEF Win32}
        TB.LoadFromResourceID(hInstance,
          LongInt(Items.Objects[Index]));
        {$ELSE}
        TB.Handle := LoadBitmap(hInstance, MakeIntResource(
          LongInt(Items.Objects[Index])));
```

```
        {$ENDIF}
        Draw(Rect.Left+2, Rect.Top+2, TB);
      finally
        TB.free;
      end;
      TextOut(Rect.Left+68, Rect.Top+30, Items[Index]);
    END;
  end;

  end.
```

The 16-bit or the 32-bit resource file bound into the program contains three bitmaps, identified by the numbers 1, 2, and 3. The corresponding buttons have their Tag properties set to 1, 2, and 3. Pressing a button adds an item to the owner-draw list box, and stores the button's Tag in the corresponding slot in the Objects array. To draw an item, the list box creates a temporary TBitmap object and calls the API function LoadBitmap to get a bitmap handle for the resource having the specified number. It sets the bitmap object's handle to the value returned by LoadBitmap, draws the bitmap, and then frees it. In Delphi 2.0, the TBitmap object's LoadFromResourceID and LoadFromResourceName methods load the bitmap and also extract its palette. This program uses LoadFromResourceID when compiled under Delphi 2.0.

 Creating and using a special cursor

16 32

Delphi components have easy access to all the standard Windows cursors, plus a few more via their Cursor and DragCursor properties. Windows provides the LoadCursor API function that returns a handle to a cursor loaded from a resource. However, the obvious technique of setting the Cursor property to a cursor handle doesn't work.

Cursor and DragCursor are actually indices into the Cursors array, a property of the Screen object. To use a custom cursor, you must put its handle into the Cursors array, and reference it by its *index* within this array. All the standard cursors have indices less than or equal to zero, so a custom cursor should use a positive index. As the program in Figure 15-2 shows, implementing a custom cursor is quite simple.

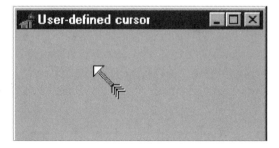

FIGURE 15-2: This custom cursor is larger than usual; the user will certainly see it without trouble.

CURSE

CURSEMK.BAT

```
/*
@ECHO OFF
CLS
brcc -foCURSE16 -31 cursemk.bat
brcc -foCURSE32 -w32 cursemk.bat
GOTO End
*/
MYARROW CURSOR "myarrow.cur"
/*
:End */
```

CURSEU.DEX

```
object Form1: TForm1
  Caption = 'User-defined cursor'
  Position = poDefault
  Scaled = False
  OnCreate = FormCreate
end
```

CURSEU.PAS

```
unit Curseu;

interface

uses SysUtils, WinTypes, WinProcs, Messages, Classes, Graphics,
  Controls, Forms, Dialogs;
```

```
type
  TForm1 = class(TForm)
    procedure FormCreate(Sender: TObject);
  end;

var Form1: TForm1;

implementation

{$R *.DFM}
{$IFDEF Win32}
{$R CURSE32.RES}
{$ELSE}
{$R CURSE16.RES}
{$ENDIF}

procedure TForm1.FormCreate(Sender: TObject);
begin
  Screen.Cursors[1] := LoadCursor(hInstance, 'MYARROW');
  Cursor := 1;
end;

end.
```

Remember, resources you create do *not* go in the application's own .RES file, the one whose filename is the same as the .DPR file's. In this case, the application's .RES file is CURSE.RES; the user-defined cursor is loaded from CURSE16.RES or CURSE32.RES, depending on which version of Delphi is used.

The LoadCursor API function returns the cursor handle, which is stored at index 1 in the Cursors array. Since the Screen object is specific to each Delphi application, you can always use 1 as the index for the first user-defined cursor. Once the cursor is loaded into the Cursors array, using it is as simple as setting the appropriate component's Cursor property to the index 1.

Supporting multiple languages

16 32

Localization is a hot topic these days. If you hard-code the captions of your Delphi components using the Form Designer, translating the user interface to Tagalog or Frisian will be tough. One way to prepare for globalization is to store captions and other text strings in a *string resource*. You can either recompile with a different .RES file to use a different language, or include multiple languages in one .RES file, as the program in Figure 15-3 does.

FIGURE 15-3: Press one of the four language buttons and the numeric labels all change to that language, along with the Yes and No buttons.

STRRES

STRRESMK.BAT

```
/*
@ECHO OFF
CLS
brcc -fostrres16 -31 strresmk.bat
brcc -fostrres32 -w32 strresmk.bat
GOTO End
*/
STRINGTABLE
{1, "One" 2, "Two" 3, "Three" 4, "Four" 5, "Five"
 6, "Six" 7, "Seven" 8, "Eight" 9, "Nine" 10, "Ten"
 11, "Yep" 12, "Nope"}
STRINGTABLE
{21, "Uno" 22, "Dos" 23, "Tres" 24, "Cuatro" 25, "Cinco"
 26, "Seis" 27, "Siete" 28, "Ocho" 29, "Nueve" 30, "Diez"
 31, "Si" 32, "No"}
STRINGTABLE
{41, "Ichi" 42, "Ni" 43, "San" 44, "Shi" 45, "Go"
 46, "Roku" 47, "Shichi" 48, "Hachi" 49, "Kyu" 50, "Ju"
 51, "Hai" 52, "Iie"}
STRINGTABLE
{61, "Odin" 62, "Dva" 63, "Tri" 64, "Chetirye" 65, "Pyats"
 66, "Shests" 67, "Syem" 68, "Vosyem" 69, "Dyevyats" 70, "Dyesyats"
 71, "Da" 72, "Nyet"}
/*
:End */
```

STRRESU.DEX

```
object Form1: TForm1
  BorderIcons = [biSystemMenu, biMinimize]
  BorderStyle = bsSingle
  Caption = 'String Resource Demo'
  Position = poDefault
  Scaled = False
  OnCreate = FormCreate
  object Label1: TLabel
  end
  object Label2: TLabel
  end
  object Label3: TLabel
  end
  object Label4: TLabel
  end
  object Label5: TLabel
  end
  object Label6: TLabel
  end
  object Label7: TLabel
  end
  object Label8: TLabel
  end
  object Label9: TLabel
  end
  object Label10: TLabel
  end
  object Button1: TButton
    Caption = '&English'
    OnClick = Button1Click
  end
  object Button2: TButton
    Tag = 20
    Caption = '&Spanish'
    OnClick = Button1Click
  end
  object Button3: TButton
    Tag = 40
    Caption = '&Japanese'
    OnClick = Button1Click
  end
  object Button4: TButton
    Tag = 60
    Caption = '&Russian'
    OnClick = Button1Click
  end
```

```
    object BitBtn1: TBitBtn
      Caption = '&Yes'
      Default = True
      ModalResult = 6
      Margin = 8
    end
    object BitBtn2: TBitBtn
      Cancel = True
      Caption = '&No'
      ModalResult = 7
      Margin = 8
    end
  end
end
```

STRRESU.PAS

```
unit Strresu;

interface

uses SysUtils, WinTypes, WinProcs, Messages, Classes, Graphics,
  Controls, Forms, Dialogs, StdCtrls, Buttons;

type
  TForm1 = class(TForm)
    Label1: TLabel;
    Label2: TLabel;
    Label3: TLabel;
    Label4: TLabel;
    Label5: TLabel;
    Label6: TLabel;
    Label7: TLabel;
    Label8: TLabel;
    Label9: TLabel;
    Button1: TButton;
    Button2: TButton;
    Button3: TButton;
    Label10: TLabel;
    Button4: TButton;
    BitBtn1: TBitBtn;
    BitBtn2: TBitBtn;
    procedure Button1Click(Sender: TObject);
    procedure FormCreate(Sender: TObject);
  end;

var Form1: TForm1;

implementation

{$R *.DFM}
{$IFDEF Win32}
{$R STRRES32.RES}
```

```
{$ELSE}
{$R STRRES16.RES}
{$ENDIF}

procedure TForm1.Button1Click(Sender: TObject);
VAR N, Off : Word;
begin
  Off := (Sender AS TButton).Tag;
  FOR N := 1 TO 10 DO
    WITH FindComponent('Label'+IntToStr(N)) AS TLabel DO
      Caption := LoadStr(N+Off);
  BitBtn1.Caption :=LoadStr(11+Off);
  BitBtn2.Caption :=LoadStr(12+Off);
end;

procedure TForm1.FormCreate(Sender: TObject);
begin
  Button1Click(Button1);
end;

end.
```

The LoadString Windows API function fills a PChar buffer with the string matching a particular ID number. Delphi's built-in LoadStr function uses LoadString internally, but returns a convenient Delphi string rather than a PChar. In the example program, each language button contains an offset (0, 20, 40, or 60) in its Tag field. A base string ID number from 1 to 12 is added to the offset to calculate the ID for the specified string in the selected language. Of course, in a full-scale program there might well be hundreds of strings, so you'd want to leave more room between the language base offsets.

This technique has its limitations. All the strings for all the languages take space in the .EXE program, and the only way to add another language is to recompile the program. In the next chapter, we'll use DLLs to get past these limitations.

Embedding .WAV files in a program

16 32

By default, a Delphi executable stands proudly alone, not relying on any external DLLs or support files. Even the small bitmaps that decorate such components as speed buttons are contained within the program. Adding sound support to such a program doesn't have to involve a clutter of loose .WAV files—you can include the .WAV files in a resource, as this program shows.

WAVRES

WAVRESMK.BAT

```
/*
@ECHO OFF
CLS
brcc -fowavres16 -31 wavresmk.bat
brcc -fowavres32 -w32 wavresmk.bat
GOTO End
*/
WAVE_1 WAVE LOADONCALL MOVEABLE DISCARDABLE "chimes.wav"
WAVE_2 WAVE LOADONCALL MOVEABLE DISCARDABLE "ding.wav"
WAVE_3 WAVE LOADONCALL MOVEABLE DISCARDABLE "chord.wav"
WAVE_4 WAVE LOADONCALL MOVEABLE DISCARDABLE "tada.wav"
/*
:End */
```

WAVRESU.DEX

```
object Form1: TForm1
  Caption = 'WAV file in a resource'
  Position = poDefault
  Scaled = False
  OnCreate = FormCreate
  OnDestroy = FormDestroy
  object Button1: TButton
    Caption = 'WAVE_1'
    OnClick = Button1Click
  end
  object Button2: TButton
    Caption = 'WAVE_2'
    OnClick = Button1Click
  end
  object Button3: TButton
    Caption = 'WAVE_3'
    OnClick = Button1Click
  end
  object Button4: TButton
    Caption = 'WAVE_4'
    OnClick = Button1Click
  end
end
```

WAVRESU.PAS

```
unit Wavresu;

interface
```

```
uses SysUtils, WinTypes, WinProcs, Messages, Classes, Graphics,
  Controls, Forms, Dialogs, StdCtrls;

type
  TForm1 = class(TForm)
    Button1: TButton;
    Button2: TButton;
    Button3: TButton;
    Button4: TButton;
    procedure Button1Click(Sender: TObject);
    procedure FormDestroy(Sender: TObject);
    procedure FormCreate(Sender: TObject);
  private
    ResH : THandle;
  end;

var Form1: TForm1;

implementation
USES MMSystem;
{$R *.DFM}
{$IFDEF Win32}
{$R WAVRES32.RES}
{$ELSE}
{$R WAVRES16.RES}
{$ENDIF}

procedure TForm1.FormCreate(Sender: TObject);
begin
  IF WaveOutGetNumDevs = 0 THEN
    BEGIN
      Button1.Enabled := False;
      Button2.Enabled := False;
      Button3.Enabled := False;
      Button4.Enabled := False;
      Caption := 'No .WAV out device';
    END;
end;

procedure TForm1.FormDestroy(Sender: TObject);
begin
  SndPlaySound(NIL, SND_ASYNC OR SND_NODEFAULT);
  IF ResH <> 0 THEN FreeResource(ResH);
end;

procedure TForm1.Button1Click(Sender: TObject);
VAR Buff : ARRAY[0..10] OF Char;
begin
{$IFDEF Win32}
  PlaySound(PChar((Sender AS TButton).Caption), hInstance,
    SND_RESOURCE OR SND_ASYNC);
{$ELSE}
  IF ResH <> 0 THEN FreeResource(ResH);
  ResH := FindResource(hInstance,
```

```
      StrPCopy(Buff, (Sender AS TButton).Caption), 'WAVE');
    ResH := LoadResource(hInstance, ResH);
    SndPlaySound(LockResource(ResH), SND_ASYNC OR SND_MEMORY);
  {$ENDIF}
  end;

  end.
```

The PlaySound function, a 32-bit successor to sndPlaySound, has the intrinsic ability to play a sound stored as a resource. Just pass the WAVE resource's name and the application's instance handle to PlaySound, making sure to add the SND_RESOURCE flag.

16-bit Windows has no built-in support for WAVE resources. Under 16-bit Delphi, the program uses FindResource and LoadResource to load the resource into memory and LockResource to get access to the resource. Because the sound is played using SND_ASYNC, the program does not free the resource until the program ends or a different resource is loaded.

The example program binds four standard Windows .WAV files into a resource and plays them when the same-named button is pressed. Your programs will store application-specific sounds in exactly the same way.

Using Windows Messages

More than half of the previous chapters include one or more programs that either send or receive Windows messages. It's really quite simple once you've seen an example or two, so we won't spend time on message basics. Most of the interesting problems that crop up will involve unusual situations, such as using messages that aren't documented, or messages that your program defines for itself.

 ### *Responding to an undocumented message*

Not all the functions in the Windows API are documented, and some of the undocumented ones can be useful. The same is true of Windows messages. If you scan a list of Windows message constants, you'll notice some gaps in the series of values. Some of these are simply unused; others represent undocumented Windows messages. However, frequently messages that were undocumented in Windows 3.1 become documented in Win32, and resources like Andrew Schulman's *Undocumented Windows*, list and explain numerous undocumented messages.

The only significant difference between responding to an undocumented message and a documented one is that Delphi has predefined message types for all the documented messages. As the program in Figure 15-4 shows, the absence of a predefined message is no obstacle to using these messages.

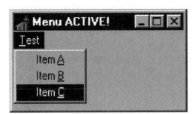

FIGURE 15-4: This program responds to two undocumented Windows messages; by doing so, it gets notified when the user enters and leaves the menu.

MENUACT

MENUACTU.DEX

```
object Form1: TForm1
  Caption = 'Menu not active'
  Menu = MainMenu1
  Position = poDefault
  Scaled = False
  object MainMenu1: TMainMenu
    object Test1: TMenuItem
      Caption = '&Test'
      object ItemA1: TMenuItem
        Caption = 'Item &A'
      end
      object ItemB1: TMenuItem
        Caption = 'Item &B'
      end
      object ItemC1: TMenuItem
        Caption = 'Item &C'
      end
    end
  end
end
```

MENUACTU.PAS

```
unit Menuactu;

interface

uses SysUtils, WinTypes, WinProcs, Messages, Classes, Graphics,
  Controls, Forms, Dialogs, Menus, StdCtrls;
const
  WM_EXITMENULOOP = $212;
type
  TForm1 = class(TForm)
    MainMenu1: TMainMenu;
    Test1: TMenuItem;
    ItemA1: TMenuItem;
    ItemB1: TMenuItem;
    ItemC1: TMenuItem;
  private
    procedure WMEnterMenuLoop(VAR Msg: TWMNoParams);
      message WM_ENTERMENULOOP;
    procedure WMExitMenuLoop(VAR Msg: TWMNoParams);
      message WM_EXITMENULOOP;
  end;

var Form1: TForm1;

implementation

{$R *.DFM}
procedure TForm1.WMEnterMenuLoop(VAR Msg: TWMNoParams);
BEGIN
  Inherited;
  Caption := 'Menu ACTIVE!';
END;

procedure TForm1.WMExitMenuLoop(VAR Msg: TWMNoParams);
BEGIN
  Inherited;
  Caption := 'Menu not active';
END;

end.
```

Delphi uses undocumented messages as needed—it defines the WM_ENTERMENULOOP constant in the Controls unit, and uses it in the Forms unit. The example program still needs to define WM_EXITMENULOOP, as will usually be necessary in a program using undocumented messages.

Both of the messages in question have no significant values passed in their wParam and lParam, so their message parameters are defined using the built-in TWMNoParams type. For a message in which the wParam and lParam are significant, use the TMessage type.

Sending an undocumented message

16 32

Sending an undocumented Windows message is as easy as sending a documented one. All you need to do is define the necessary WM_Xxx constant in your program and supply the correct parameters with it. The program shown in Figure 15-5 uses the WM_SETHOTKEY and WM_GETHOTKEY messages to maintain a system-wide hotkey for itself.

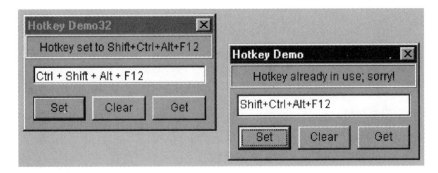

FIGURE 15-5: The 32-bit and the 16-bit versions of the HOTKEY program are shown here contending for the same key combination.

HOTKEY

HOTKEYU.DEX

```
object Form1: TForm1
  ActiveControl = Edit1
  BorderIcons = [biSystemMenu, biMinimize]
  BorderStyle = bsDialog
  Caption = 'Hotkey Demo'
  Position = poDefault
  Scaled = False
  OnCreate = FormCreate
  object Button1: TButton
    Caption = 'Set'
    OnClick = Button1Click
  end
  object Button2: TButton
    Caption = 'Clear'
    OnClick = Button2Click
  end
```

```
    object Button3: TButton
      Caption = 'Get'
      OnClick = Button3Click
    end
    object Panel1: TPanel
      Align = alTop
      BevelInner = bvLowered
    end
    object Edit1: TEdit
      Text = 'None'
      OnKeyDown = Edit1KeyDown
      OnKeyPress = Edit1KeyPress
      OnKeyUp = Edit1KeyUp
    end
  end
end
```

HOTKEYU.PAS

```
unit Hotkeyu;

interface

uses SysUtils, WinTypes, WinProcs, Messages, Classes, Graphics,
  Controls, Forms, Dialogs, ExtCtrls, StdCtrls, Mask, Menus
  {$IFDEF Win32}, ComCtrls{$ENDIF};

type
  TForm1 = class(TForm)
    Button1: TButton;
    Button2: TButton;
    Button3: TButton;
    Panel1: TPanel;
    Edit1: TEdit;
    procedure Button1Click(Sender: TObject);
    procedure Button2Click(Sender: TObject);
    procedure Button3Click(Sender: TObject);
    procedure Edit1KeyDown(Sender: TObject; var Key: Word;
      Shift: TShiftState);
    procedure Edit1KeyPress(Sender: TObject; var Key: Char);
    procedure Edit1KeyUp(Sender: TObject; var Key: Word;
      Shift: TShiftState);
    procedure FormCreate(Sender: TObject);
  private
    EHotKey : TShortCut;
    HKDone  : Boolean;
    {$IFDEF Win32}
    HotKey1 : THotKey;
    {$ENDIF}
  end;
```

```
var Form1: TForm1;

implementation

{$R *.DFM}
const
  WM_SETHOTKEY = $32;
  WM_GETHOTKEY = $33;

procedure TForm1.FormCreate(Sender: TObject);
begin
  {$IFDEF Win32}
  HotKey1 := THotKey.Create(Self);
  WITH HotKey1 DO
    BEGIN
      Parent := Self;
      Left   := Edit1.Left;
      Top    := Edit1.Top;
      Width  := Edit1.Width;
      InvalidKeys := [hcNone, hcShift, hcCtrl, hcShiftCtrl];
      HotKey := 0;
    END;
  ActiveControl := HotKey1;
  Edit1.Free;
  Caption := Caption + '32';
  {$ENDIF}
end;

procedure TForm1.Button1Click(Sender: TObject);
VAR Key: Word;
begin
  Panel1.Caption := 'No hotkey selected';
  Key := {$IFDEF Win32}HotKey1.HotKey{$ELSE}EHotKey{$ENDIF};
  IF Key = 0 THEN Exit;
  {Convert shortcut to WM_SETHOTKEY form}
  Key := (Key AND $FF00) SHR 5 + (Key AND $00FF);
  CASE SendMessage(Application.Handle, WM_SETHOTKEY, Key,0) OF
    2 : BEGIN
          Panel1.Caption := 'Hotkey already in use; sorry!';
          SendMessage(Application.Handle, WM_SETHOTKEY, 0, 0);
        END;
    1 : Panel1.Caption := 'Hotkey set to ' +
          ShortCutToText((Key AND $FF00) SHL 5 + (Key AND $00FF));
    0 : Panel1.Caption := 'Invalid window handle';
   -1 : Panel1.Caption := 'Invalid hotkey';
  END;
end;

procedure TForm1.Button2Click(Sender: TObject);
begin
```

```
      CASE SendMessage(Application.Handle, WM_SETHOTKEY, 0, 0) OF
        2, 1 : Panel1.Caption := 'Hotkey cleared';
        0    : Panel1.Caption := 'Invalid window handle';
        -1   : Panel1.Caption := 'Invalid hotkey';
      END;
  end;

  procedure TForm1.Button3Click(Sender: TObject);
  VAR Key : Word;
  begin
    Key := SendMessage(Application.Handle, WM_GETHOTKEY, 0, 0);
    IF Key = 0 THEN Panel1.Caption := 'No hotkey'
    ELSE Panel1.Caption := 'Hotkey is ' +
      ShortCutToText((Key AND $FF00) SHL 5 + (Key AND $00FF));
  end;

  procedure TForm1.Edit1KeyDown(Sender: TObject; var Key: Word;
    Shift: TShiftState);
  begin
    try
      EHotKey := 0;
      IF NOT (ssAlt IN Shift) THEN Exit;
      CASE Key OF
        VK_CONTROL, VK_SHIFT, VK_MENU : HKDone := False;
        Ord('A')..Ord('Z'),
        VK_F1..VK_F12,
        VK_INSERT, VK_DELETE, VK_BACK : HKDone := True;
        ELSE Exit;
      END;
      EHotKey := Key + $8000;
      Edit1.Text := 'Alt';
      IF ssCtrl IN Shift THEN
        BEGIN
          EHotKey := EHotKey + $4000;
          Edit1.Text := 'Ctrl + Alt';
        END;
      IF ssShift IN Shift THEN
        BEGIN
          EHotKey := EHotKey + $2000;
          Edit1.Text := 'Shift + ' + Edit1.Text;
        END;
    finally
      Key := 0;
      IF HKDone THEN Edit1.Text := ShortCutToText(EHotKey);
    end;
  end;

  procedure TForm1.Edit1KeyPress(Sender: TObject; var Key: Char);
  begin
    Key := #0;
    Edit1.Text := 'None';
  end;
```

```
procedure TForm1.Edit1KeyUp(Sender: TObject; var Key: Word;
  Shift: TShiftState);
begin
  IF NOT HKDone THEN
    BEGIN
      EHotKey := 0;
      Edit1.Text := 'None';
    END;
end;

end.
```

The WM_SETHOTKEY and WM_GETHOTKEY messages are documented in Win32, but not in Windows 3.1. The format for the hotkey code is very similar to that of the Delphi ShortCut data type. In both, the low byte is the key's scan code and the bits of the high byte indicate which shift keys are pressed. Converting a shortcut to a key code involves shifting the bits of the high byte right five places; converting a key code to a shortcut requires shifting them back again. This program benefits greatly from Delphi's ShortCutToText function, found in the Menus unit. Note that, since the form has no menu, you'll have to add menus to the uses clause by hand.

To set the hotkey, the OnClick handler for the Set button sends a WM_SETHOTKEY message to the *application* handle, passing the key code as the wParam and 0 as the lParam. A return value of 1 indicates success. To clear the hotkey, the program sends WM_SETHOTKEY with 0 as the wParam. Sending WM_GETHOTKEY with both wParam and lParam set to 0 returns the current hotkey.

In Delphi 2.0, the program uses a Windows 95 hotkey component. This component looks like an edit box, but does not accept typed text. Instead, it translates any key combination that's pressed while it has the focus into a text description. When compiled using Delphi 1.0, this program does its best to emulate the hotkey component using a plain edit box. It's surprising how close it comes to the hotkey component's behavior!

Communicating between programs

16 32

A program that needs private message-based communication with one or more other programs can simply define a new WM_Xxx constant and hope it doesn't conflict with any other program on the system. Of course, Murphy's Law requires that such a hard-coded message constant will *always* conflict. The Windows API function RegisterWindowsMessage returns a unique message number, thus avoiding conflict. Figure 15-6 shows three instances of a Delphi program that communicates with other programs.

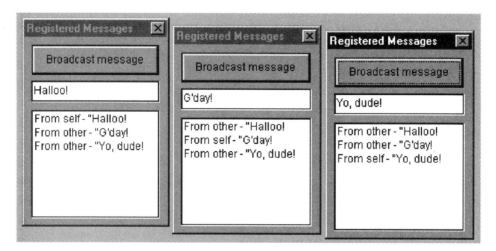

FIGURE 15-6: The private message defined in this program carries the sending program's window handle in its wParam and a text string in its lParam.

REGMSG

REGMSGU.DEX

```
object Form1: TForm1
  BorderIcons = [biSystemMenu]
  BorderStyle = bsDialog
  Caption = 'Registered Messages'
  Position = poDefault
  Scaled = False
  OnCreate = FormCreate
  object Button1: TButton
    Caption = 'Broadcast message'
    Default = True
    OnClick = Button1Click
  end
  object ListBox1: TListBox
  end
  object Edit1: TEdit
    MaxLength = 40
  end
end
```

REGMSGU.PAS

```
unit Regmsgu;

interface

uses SysUtils, WinTypes, WinProcs, Messages, Classes, Graphics,
  Controls, Forms, StdCtrls;

type
  TForm1 = class(TForm)
    Button1: TButton;
    ListBox1: TListBox;
    Edit1: TEdit;
    procedure Button1Click(Sender: TObject);
    procedure FormCreate(Sender: TObject);
  private
    WmX : Word;
    procedure DefaultHandler(VAR Message); override;
  end;

var Form1: TForm1;

implementation

{$R *.DFM}
procedure TForm1.DefaultHandler(VAR Message);
VAR Buffer : ARRAY[0..255] OF Char;
begin
  Inherited DefaultHandler(Message);
  WITH TMessage(Message) DO
    IF Msg = WmX THEN
      BEGIN
        IF GlobalGetAtomName(lParam, Buffer, 255) = 0 THEN
          StrCopy(Buffer, 'ERROR');
        IF wParam = Handle THEN
          ListBox1.Items.Add('From self - "' + StrPas(Buffer))
        ELSE ListBox1.Items.Add('From other - "' + StrPas(Buffer));
      END;
end;

procedure TForm1.Button1Click(Sender: TObject);
VAR
  Buffer : ARRAY[0..255] OF Char;
  Atom   : TAtom;
begin
  Atom := GlobalAddAtom(StrPCopy(Buffer, Edit1.Text));
  SendMessage(HWND_Broadcast, WmX, Handle, Atom);
  GlobalDeleteAtom(Atom);
end;

procedure TForm1.FormCreate(Sender: TObject);
begin
  WmX := RegisterWindowMessage('NJR message');
end;

end.
```

RegisterWindowsMessage takes a single PChar parameter. The first time a particular string of characters is passed during a given Windows session, it returns a message number that's guaranteed to be unique. Any further calls by *any* program using the same string of characters will get back the same message number.

Pressing the button causes the program to broadcast the registered message by using SendMessage to send it to the predefined handle HWND_BROADCAST. This causes Windows to send it to all top-level Windows, including the sending program. To distinguish messages coming from itself, the program passes its own window handle as the wParam for the message.

In a 16-bit world, the lParam could be a pointer to the desired character string. The receiving program would be able to access this string even though it resides in the sending program's memory space. 32-bit Windows puts an end to that kind of chicanery, so the program uses the global atom table to provide access to the string. The atom corresponding to the string is passed as the lParam. Since the SendMessage function doesn't return until the message has been processed, the program can safely delete the atom afterward.

Since the registered message is not available at compile time, it's not possible to create a standard Delphi response method for it. This kind of message must be handled by overriding the form's DefaultHandler method. When this method receives the special message, it compares the wParam with its window handle to see if the message came from itself. And it uses the GlobalGetAtomName API function to extract the string corresponding to the atom in the lParam.

Use this example as a starting point any time you need message-based communication between programs. Keep it in mind, too, when 32-bit programs need a simple method for sharing character strings—that global atom table can be handy.

Controlling the screen saver

Some programs shouldn't be interrupted by the Windows screen saver when they're active. Others may *want* to invoke it, as a password-protected screen saver can provide a modicum of security. Naturally, both suppressing the screen saver and activating it on demand involve Windows messages. This simple program demonstrates both techniques.

SCRNSV

SCRNSVU.DEX

```
object Form1: TForm1
  BorderIcons = [biSystemMenu, biMinimize]
  BorderStyle = bsDialog
  Caption = 'Control Screen Saver'
  Position = poDefault
  Scaled = False
  object Button1: TButton
    Caption = 'Activate &Now'
    Default = True
    OnClick = Button1Click
  end
  object CheckBox1: TCheckBox
    Alignment = taLeftJustify
    Caption = '&Prevent'
  end
  object ListBox1: TListBox
  end
end
```

SCRNSVU.PAS

```
unit Scrnsvu;

interface

uses SysUtils, WinTypes, WinProcs, Messages, Classes, Graphics,
  Controls, Forms, Dialogs, StdCtrls;

type
  TForm1 = class(TForm)
    Button1: TButton;
    CheckBox1: TCheckBox;
    ListBox1: TListBox;
    procedure Button1Click(Sender: TObject);
  private
    procedure WMSysCommand(VAR Msg: TWMSysCommand);
      message WM_SYSCOMMAND;
  end;

var Form1: TForm1;

implementation

{$R *.DFM}

procedure TForm1.Button1Click(Sender: TObject);
begin
  Perform(WM_SYSCOMMAND, SC_SCREENSAVE, 0);
end;
```

```
procedure TForm1.WMSysCommand(VAR Msg: TWMSysCommand);
BEGIN
  IF (Msg.CmdType AND $FFF0) = SC_SCREENSAVE THEN
    IF CheckBox1.Checked THEN
      BEGIN
        Msg.Result := 0;
        ListBox1.Items.Add(TimeToStr(Now) + ' Prevented');
        Exit;
      END
    ELSE ListBox1.Items.Add(TimeToStr(Now) + ' Allowed');
  Inherited;
END;
end.
```

As long as the system has a screen saver defined, a program can activate it by sending the WM_SYSCOMMAND message to its own top-level window, passing SC_SCREENSAVE as the wParam. That's what the OnClick method for the example program's button does.

To prevent the screen saver from kicking in, a program needs to respond to that same message by returning zero. The WMSysCommand message in the example program checks to see if the message's command type is SC_SCREENSAVE. Windows uses the lowest four bits of this value for internal purposes, so the program masks them off before making the comparison. If this is indeed an SC_SCREENSAVE message *and* the check box is checked, the method sets the message's result to zero; otherwise, it passes the message along to the inherited handler.

Just so you'll know it's actually doing something, the program displays the time of every attempted activation, and whether it was permitted. Only the foreground program can control activation of the screen saver in this way, of course. But that actually makes sense. Most users would object to a program that disabled their screen saver even when running in the background.

16

Dynamic Link Libraries

*D*ynamic Link Libraries are the heart of Windows, and all Windows programs rely on the essential DLLs USER, GDI, and KERNEL. You can enhance your programming by writing your own DLLs, and these DLLs can be called from programs written in any language, not just Delphi. In this chapter, you'll learn to write DLLs, call DLL functions from Delphi and other languages, and load DLLs dynamically at runtime.

DLL Basics

Every time you write a program that calls Windows API functions, you're calling on DLLs. Even when you don't explicitly call API functions, Delphi's components are making plenty of function calls below the surface. Learning to write DLLs yourself is a step toward complete mastery of Windows programming.

Writing and using a DLL

16	32

You've written many Delphi project and unit files; the former begin with the word Program and the latter with Unit. DLL files are a third type, and they begin with the word Library. Here's an example of a tiny DLL:

EXAMPLE

EXAMPLE.DPR

```
Library Example;
Uses SysUtils;
FUNCTION tDiskSize(Drive: Integer): LongInt; Export;
  {$IFDEF Win32}StdCall;{$ENDIF}
BEGIN
  Result := DiskSize(Drive);
END;
FUNCTION tDiskFree(Drive: Integer): LongInt; Export;
  {$IFDEF Win32}StdCall;{$ENDIF}
BEGIN
  Result := DiskFree(Drive);
END;
FUNCTION NowString(P : PChar; Len: Integer) : PChar; Export;
  {$IFDEF Win32}StdCall;{$ENDIF}
VAR S : String;
BEGIN
  S := DateTimeToStr(Now);
  S := Copy(S, 1, Len);
  StrPCopy(P, S);
  Result := P;
END;
exports
  tDiskSize INDEX 1,
  tDiskFree INDEX 2,
  NowString INDEX 3;
begin
end.
```

Note that all three functions have the export directive appended to their headers. When this file is compiled under Delphi 2.0, the StdCall directive is also added. Without the StdCall directive, the compiler optimization in Delphi 2.0 could compile the function to use code that's register-based and highly efficient—and totally unintelligible to programs that expect the Microsoft standard calling convention. To complete the process of exporting the DLL functions, the exports list, located just before the end of the module, lists all the exported functions and assigns an index to each.

Of course, a Delphi program doesn't need to call DLL functions to get the capacity and amount of free space on a disk. However, other languages, such as WordBasic and Visual Basic 3.0, do not include such functions, so this DLL can actually be useful.

The DLL ends with a main program block, even if it's just an empty begin . . . end pair. Any initialization that must occur the *first* time the DLL is loaded can be placed in this main program block.

DLL functions using integer parameters are quite simple and generally compatible with any calling program, as long as the language of the calling program includes an integer type to match the size of the Delphi parameter. For example, a Delphi LongInt matches a Visual Basic Long; both are 4 bytes. Some languages may not support 1-byte integer types, so it's safest to avoid using the Byte and ShortInt types as DLL function parameters.

Floating-point types can cause difficulty because of varying internal methods for returning floating-point values. Don't write a DLL function that returns Single, Double, Extended, or Comp. Instead, write a *procedure*, and return the floating-point value in a VAR parameter. Never use the Real data type in a DLL, as it is a proprietary data type used only in Delphi and Borland Pascal.

DLL functions that return string data should always require the calling program to provide a buffer to hold the string data, along with the size of the buffer. The NowString function in the example program does this, and it uses a PChar rather than a Delphi String. The PChar type can be handled by just about any language, while String is specific to Delphi.

The short program that follows calls the example DLL's functions.

EXTEST

EXTESTU.DEX

```
object Form1: TForm1
  BorderIcons = [biSystemMenu, biMinimize]
  BorderStyle = bsDialog
  Caption = 'Test Example DLL'
  Position = poDefault
  Scaled = False
  OnCreate = FormCreate
  object Label1: TLabel
  end
  object Label2: TLabel
    AutoSize = False
  end
end
```

EXTESTU.PAS

```
unit Extestu;

interface

uses SysUtils, WinTypes, WinProcs, Messages, Classes, Graphics,
  Controls, Forms, Dialogs, StdCtrls;

type
  TForm1 = class(TForm)
    Label1: TLabel;
    Label2: TLabel;
    procedure FormCreate(Sender: TObject);
  end;

var Form1: TForm1;

implementation
CONST
{Windows NT requires *presence* of .DLL extension for Externals,
 Windows 3.1 requires its *absence*. Win95 goes either way}
  Example = {$IFDEF Win32}'EXAMPLE.DLL'{$ELSE}'EXAMPLE'{$ENDIF};

function tDiskSize(Drive: Integer): LongInt; Far; {$IFDEF Win32}
  StdCall;{$ENDIF} External Example name 'tDiskSize';
function tDiskFree(Drive: Integer): LongInt; Far; {$IFDEF Win32}
  StdCall;{$ENDIF} External Example name 'tDiskFree';
function NowString(P: PChar; Len: Integer): PChar; Far;
  {$IFDEF Win32}StdCall;{$ENDIF} External Example index 3;
{$R *.DFM}

procedure TForm1.FormCreate(Sender: TObject);
VAR Buffer: ARRAY[0..255] OF Char;
begin
  Label1.Caption := StrPas(NowString(Buffer,255));
  Label2.Caption := 'Current drive has ' + FormatFloat('0.',
    tDiskFree(0)) + ' of ' + FormatFloat('0.', tDiskSize(0)) +
    ' bytes free.';
end;

end.
```

The declarations for the DLL functions look just like the headers in the DLL file, up to a point. The basic header is followed by the Far directive and, if compiled under Delphi 2.0, the StdCall directive. The declaration ends with the External directive, a string naming the DLL, and the name or the index of the function.

If you want to write code that will compile and run under all current versions of Windows, you must take care with the way you name the DLL. For DLL functions imported implicitly using the External directive, Windows NT requires that the .DLL extension be included in the filename. However, Windows 3.x requires that it *not* be included. Windows 95 will accept the filename either way, with extension or without.

Putting a form inside a DLL

16 32

DLLs that simply contain "calculation engine" functions can be useful. How much more useful, though, if the DLL can have a user interface. Figure 16-1 shows a Delphi program calling a form that's contained in a DLL. In order to make the DLL usable by other languages, its interface functions are defined in such a way that the calling program needs no internal knowledge of Delphi.

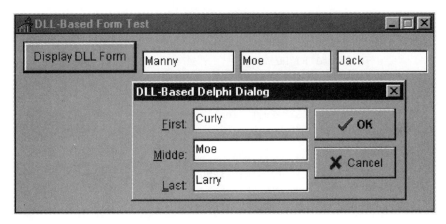

FIGURE 16-1: Although you can't tell by looking, the dialog box in this figure resides in a DLL, completely separate from the main program.

FORMDLL

FORMDLL.DPR

```
Library Formdll;

uses SysUtils, Forms,
  Formdllu in 'FORMDLLU.PAS' {Form1};

FUNCTION CreateTheForm: Pointer; Export;
  {$IFDEF Win32} StdCall; {$ENDIF}
BEGIN
  Result := TForm1.Create(NIL);
END;

PROCEDURE LoadTheForm(P: Pointer; S1, S2, S3: PChar); Export;
  {$IFDEF Win32} StdCall; {$ENDIF}
BEGIN
  WITH TForm1(P) DO
```

```
      BEGIN
        Edit1.Text := StrPas(S1);
        Edit2.Text := StrPas(S2);
        Edit3.Text := StrPas(S3);
      END;
END;

FUNCTION ShowTheForm(P: Pointer): Boolean; Export;
  {$IFDEF Win32} StdCall; {$ENDIF}
CONST mrOK = 1;
BEGIN
  Result := TForm1(P).ShowModal = mrOK;
END;

PROCEDURE ReadTheForm(P:Pointer; S1, S2, S3: PChar); Export;
  {$IFDEF Win32} StdCall; {$ENDIF}
BEGIN
  WITH TForm1(P) DO
    BEGIN
      StrPCopy(S1, Edit1.Text);
      StrPCopy(S2, Edit2.Text);
      StrPCopy(S3, Edit3.Text);
    END;
END;

PROCEDURE DestroyTheForm(P : Pointer); Export;
  {$IFDEF Win32} StdCall; {$ENDIF}
BEGIN
  TForm1(P).Free;
END;

Exports
  CreateTheForm     INDEX 1,
  LoadTheForm       INDEX 2,
  ReadTheForm       INDEX 3,
  ShowTheForm       INDEX 4,
  DestroyTheForm    INDEX 5;

begin
end.
```

FORMDLLU.DEX

```
object Form1: TForm1
  BorderIcons = [biSystemMenu, biMinimize]
  BorderStyle = bsDialog
  Caption = 'DLL-Based Delphi Dialog'
  object Label1: TLabel
    Alignment = taRightJustify
    AutoSize = False
    Caption = '&First:'
    FocusControl = Edit1
  end
```

```
      object Label2: TLabel
        Alignment = taRightJustify
        AutoSize = False
        Caption = '&Midde:'
        FocusControl = Edit2
      end
      object Label3: TLabel
        Alignment = taRightJustify
        AutoSize = False
        Caption = '&Last:'
        FocusControl = Edit3
      end
      object Edit1: TEdit
        MaxLength = 20
        Text = 'Edit1'
      end
      object Edit2: TEdit
        MaxLength = 20
        Text = 'Edit2'
      end
      object Edit3: TEdit
        MaxLength = 20
        Text = 'Edit3'
      end
      object BitBtn1: TBitBtn
        Kind = bkOK
      end
      object BitBtn2: TBitBtn
        Kind = bkCancel
      end
    end
end
```

FORMDLLU.PAS

```
unit Formdllu;

interface

uses SysUtils, WinTypes, WinProcs, Messages, Classes, Graphics,
  Controls, Forms, Dialogs, StdCtrls, Buttons;

type
  TForm1 = class(TForm)
    Edit1: TEdit;
    Edit2: TEdit;
    Edit3: TEdit;
    Label1: TLabel;
    Label2: TLabel;
    Label3: TLabel;
    BitBtn1: TBitBtn;
    BitBtn2: TBitBtn;
  end;
```

```
var Form1: TForm1;
implementation
{$R *.DFM}
end.
```

Each of the exported functions is followed by the Export keyword and listed in the Exports list. In Delphi 2.0, the StdCall keyword is added as well. The CreateTheForm function creates a Delphi form and returns a pointer to it. This pointer is held by the calling program and passed back for each of the other function calls. Besides obviating the need for the calling programs to "understand" Delphi forms, this makes it possible for multiple programs to use the 16-bit version of the DLL at once without confusion, as each program has its own instance of the DLL-based form.

Strings are passed as PChars, for compatibility with other languages. Procedure LoadTheForm loads the three edit boxes with strings passed by the calling program, function ShowTheForm displays it and returns True if OK was pressed, and ReadTheForm reads the contents of the edit boxes back into variables supplied by the calling program. In this case, it's assumed that the calling program has provided variables that will hold twenty characters. Finally, a call to DestroyTheForm frees the dialog form when the calling program is done with it. Here's a simple program to test this DLL.

FORMTEST

FORMTSTU.DEX

```
object Form1: TForm1
  BorderIcons = [biSystemMenu, biMinimize]
  BorderStyle = bsSingle
  Caption = 'DLL-Based Form Test'
  Position = poDefault
  Scaled = False
  object Button1: TButton
    Caption = 'Display DLL Form'
    OnClick = Button1Click
  end
  object Edit1: TEdit
    MaxLength = 20
    Text = 'Edit1'
  end
  object Edit2: TEdit
    MaxLength = 20
    Text = 'Edit2'
  end
```

```
    object Edit3: TEdit
      MaxLength = 20
      Text = 'Edit3'
    end
  end
end
```

FORMTSTU.PAS

```pascal
unit Formtstu;

interface

uses SysUtils, WinTypes, WinProcs, Messages, Classes, Graphics,
  Controls, Forms, Dialogs, StdCtrls;

type
  TForm1 = class(TForm)
    Button1: TButton;
    Edit1: TEdit;
    Edit2: TEdit;
    Edit3: TEdit;
    procedure Button1Click(Sender: TObject);
  private
    FormPtr : Pointer;
  end;

var Form1: TForm1;

implementation

{$R *.DFM}
CONST
  FormDLL = {$IFDEF Win32}'FORMDLL.DLL'{$ELSE}'FORMDLL'{$ENDIF};

FUNCTION CreateTheForm: Pointer; Far; {$IFDEF Win32}StdCall;
  {$ENDIF} External FormDLL name 'CreateTheForm';
PROCEDURE LoadTheForm(P: Pointer; S1, S2, S3: PChar); Far;
  {$IFDEF Win32}StdCall;{$ENDIF} External FormDLL index 2;
FUNCTION ShowTheForm(P: Pointer): Boolean; Far; {$IFDEF Win32}
  StdCall;{$ENDIF} External FormDLL name 'ShowTheForm';
PROCEDURE ReadTheForm(P:Pointer; S1, S2, S3: PChar); Far;
  {$IFDEF Win32}StdCall;{$ENDIF} External FormDLL index 3;
PROCEDURE DestroyTheForm(P : Pointer); Far; {$IFDEF Win32}StdCall;
  {$ENDIF} External FormDLL name 'DestroyTheForm';

procedure TForm1.Button1Click(Sender: TObject);
VAR B1, B2, B3 : ARRAY[0..20] OF Char;
begin
  FormPtr := CreateTheForm;
  StrPCopy(B1, Edit1.Text);
  StrPCopy(B2, Edit2.Text);
  StrPCopy(B3, Edit3.Text);
  LoadTheForm(FormPtr, B1, B2, B3);
  IF ShowTheForm(FormPtr) THEN
```

```
     BEGIN
       ReadTheForm(FormPtr, B1, B2, B3);
       Edit1.Text := StrPas(B1);
       Edit2.Text := StrPas(B2);
       Edit3.Text := StrPas(B3);
     END;
   DestroyTheForm(FormPtr);
 end;

 end.
```

In general, when you write DLL functions for 16-bit Windows, you must bear in mind that the DLL may be called by multiple programs, or multiple instances of the same program. It's best to avoid storing any data that belongs to the calling program. Rather, make the calling program hang onto it and supply it along with each function call.

DLL Calling Variations

Naturally, it's simple to call a Delphi DLL function from another Delphi program. By avoiding language-specific constructs, you can make it just as easy to call Delphi DLL functions from other languages.

 Calling DLLs from Visual Basic

16 32

Calling a properly written Delphi DLL from VB is simply a matter of working out the correct declaration for the functions in VB. Figure 16-2 shows a VB program that makes use of both the DLLs defined earlier in this chapter. The code is in VB3 format, but it can be loaded into VB4 with no trouble. Just make sure to use 16-bit versions of the DLLs with VB3 and 32-bit with VB4.

TESTDLLF

TESTDLLF.MAK

```
TESTDLLF.TXT
ProjWinSize=152,402,248,215
ProjWinShow=0
IconForm="Form1"
```

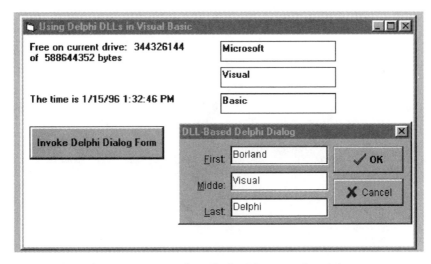

FIGURE 16-2: This VB program calls on both of the example Delphi DLLs.

TESTDLLF.TXT

```
VERSION 2.00
Begin Form Form1
   Caption          =   "Using Delphi DLLs in Visual Basic"
   ClientHeight     =   3900
   ClientLeft       =   2340
   ClientTop        =   2190
   ClientWidth      =   7365
   Height           =   4305
   Left             =   2280
   LinkTopic        =   "Form1"
   ScaleHeight      =   3900
   ScaleWidth       =   7365
   Top              =   1845
   Width            =   7485
   Begin TextBox Text3
      Height        =   375
      Left          =   3720
      TabIndex      =   0
      Text          =   "Text3"
      Top           =   1080
      Width         =   2175
   End
   Begin TextBox Text2
      Height        =   375
      Left          =   3720
      TabIndex      =   5
      Text          =   "Text2"
      Top           =   600
```

```
            Width          =    2175
      End
      Begin TextBox Text1
         Height          =    375
         Left            =    3720
         TabIndex        =    4
         Text            =    "Text1"
         Top             =    120
         Width           =    2175
      End
      Begin CommandButton Command1
         Caption         =    "Invoke Delphi Dialog Form"
         Height          =    615
         Left            =    120
         TabIndex        =    3
         Top             =    1680
         Width           =    2535
      End
      Begin Label Label2
         Caption         =    "Label2"
         Height          =    375
         Left            =    120
         TabIndex        =    2
         Top             =    1080
         Width           =    3255
      End
      Begin Label Label1
         Caption         =    "Label1"
         Height          =    615
         Left            =    120
         TabIndex        =    1
         Top             =    120
         Width           =    3135
      End
   End
End
Option Explicit
Declare Function tDiskSize& Lib "EXAMPLE.DLL" (ByVal Drive%)
Declare Function tDiskFree& Lib "EXAMPLE.DLL" (ByVal Drive%)
Declare Sub NowString Lib "EXAMPLE.DLL" (ByVal P$, ByVal L%)

Declare Function CreateTheForm& Lib "FORMDLL.DLL" ()
Declare Sub LoadTheForm Lib "FORMDLL.DLL" (ByVal F&, ByVal S1$,🖝
   ByVal S2$, ByVal S3$)
Declare Function ShowTheForm% Lib "FORMDLL.DLL" (ByVal F&)
Declare Sub ReadTheForm Lib "FORMDLL.DLL" (ByVal F&, ByVal S1$,🖝
   ByVal S2$, ByVal S3$)
Declare Sub DestroyTheForm Lib "FORMDLL.DLL" (ByVal F&)

Sub Command1_Click ()
Dim TheForm&, S1$, S2$, S3$
   TheForm = CreateTheForm()
   LoadTheForm TheForm, Text1.Text, Text2.Text, Text3.Text
   If ShowTheForm(TheForm) Then
      S1 = String$(20, 32)
```

```
         S2 = String$(20, 32)
         S3 = String$(20, 32)
         ReadTheForm TheForm, S1, S2, S3
         Text1.Text = S1
         Text2.Text = S2
         Text3.Text = S3
      End If
      DestroyTheForm TheForm
   End Sub

   Sub Form_Load ()
   Dim TimeStr$
      Label1.Caption = "Free on current drive: " + Str$(tDiskFree(0))
      Label1.Caption = Label1.Caption + " of " + Str$(tDiskSize(0))
      Label1.Caption = Label1.Caption + " bytes"
      TimeStr = String$(40, 32)
      NowString TimeStr, 40
      Label2.Caption = "The time is " + TimeStr
   End Sub
```

The declarations for imported DLL functions in VB are parallel to those in Delphi. The VB version always begins with Declare Function or Declare Sub followed by the name of the function or procedure. If it's a function, the name is followed by a type-declaration suffix indicating the return type. For example, the & in tDiskSize& indicates a 4-byte integer return value (a Long in VB), and the % in ShowTheForm% indicates a 2-byte Integer return value. VB doesn't have a pointer type as such, but its 4-byte Long type serves to store the 4-byte pointer returned by GetTheForm and passed to the other four FormDLL functions.

Next comes the word Lib followed by the DLL name in quotes. Finally, the parameters are listed, again with type-declaration suffixes to indicate their type. The ByVal keyword identifies parameters passed by value; this corresponds to Delphi function parameters that are declared *without* the VAR keyword preceding them. Omitting ByVal in a VB function declaration is the same as adding VAR in a Delphi function declaration.

This book is about Delphi, not VB, so we won't go into further detail about the VB program. The important point is, when you put functions into a DLL, they become available to virtually any language.

Calling DLLs from a macro language

16 32

Modern application programs supply macro languages that approach the power of stand-alone languages. Delphi DLLs can serve to supply any functions that are missing from such a language, assuming the macro language supports calling DLL functions. Figure 16-3 shows a WordBasic macro that calls functions from both of the DLLs defined earlier in this chapter. You will, of course, need to compile the DLLs under Delphi 2.0 for use with WinWord 7; under Delphi 1.0, for WinWord 6.

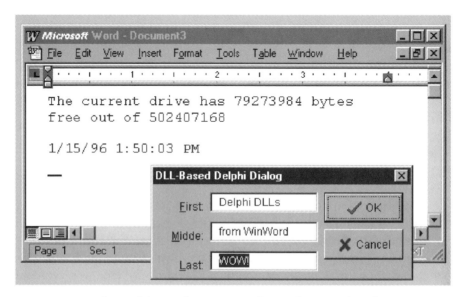

FIGURE 16-3: Calling Delphi DLLs from WinWord is nearly as simple as from VB.

MACRO DLLMAC.TXT

```
Declare Function tDiskSize Lib "EXAMPLE.DLL"(Drive As Integer) As Long
Declare Function tDiskFree Lib "EXAMPLE.DLL"(Drive As Integer) As Long
Declare Sub NowString Lib "EXAMPLE.DLL"(P$, L As Integer)

Declare Function CreateTheForm Lib "FORMDLL.DLL"() As Long
Declare Sub LoadTheForm Lib "FORMDLL.DLL"(F As Long, S1$, S2$, S3$)
Declare Function ShowTheForm Lib "FORMDLL.DLL"(F As Long) As Integer
Declare Sub ReadTheForm Lib "FORMDLL.DLL"(F As Long, S1$, S2$, S3$)
Declare Sub DestroyTheForm Lib "FORMDLL.DLL"(F As Long)
Sub main
  Insert "The current drive has" + Str$(tDiskFree(0))
  Insert " bytes free out of" + Str$(tDiskSize(0))
  InsertPara
  TimeStr$ = String$(40, 32)
  NowString TimeStr$, 40
  Insert TimeStr$
  TheForm = CreateTheForm
  LoadTheForm TheForm, "Delphi DLLs", "from WinWord", "WOW!"
  If ShowTheForm(TheForm) Then
```

```
    S1$ = String$(20, 32)
    S2$ = String$(20, 32)
    S3$ = String$(20, 32)
    ReadTheForm TheForm, S1$, S2$, S3$
    Insert S1$
    InsertPara
    Insert S2$
    InsertPara
    Insert S3$
    InsertPara
  EndIf
  DestroyTheForm TheForm
End Sub
```

In terms of DLL function declarations, the biggest difference between VB and WordBasic is that WordBasic supports fewer data types and has only one type-declaration suffix. A final dollar sign ($) indicates a string type variable or function. To represent the other data types, you add As Integer, As Long, or As Double. But as the figure shows, a WordBasic macro can call Delphi DLL functions, both those that simply perform calculations and those that display a form.

Loading a DLL at runtime

| 16 | 32 |

The Windows system DLLs are always present, but users can move, rename, or delete program-specific DLLs. If you use explicit external declarations for functions in a DLL, your program becomes totally dependent on that DLL. If a required DLL is missing, Windows will not load your program. Instead, it will display a message about how it can't find the program or one of its components, without specifying which component is missing. By switching to true dynamic loading of DLL functions at runtime, it's possible to write a program that will fail gracefully with an informative message for the user when a DLL goes missing.

Even though the very name specifies dynamic linking, loading DLLs via External declarations is a relatively static process. True dynamic linking involves opening the DLL and loading each desired function at runtime. If the DLL can't be found, the program can inform the user, or even permit the user to specify a location for the DLL. If a particular function can't be loaded, perhaps because the DLL exists as an older version, the program may be able to work around that function's absence. In fact, one technique for distinguishing Windows for Workgroups from ordinary Windows is to try loading a function that's present in the former, but not in the latter.

Another reason to load DLLs at runtime involves choosing between multiple DLLs with the same interface. The next example program uses this technique to load language-specific DLLs. Because the language information is stored externally, all that's required to add support for Finnish or Croatian is the creation of another DLL.

Creating a language-flexible program

16 32

An example in the preceding chapter demonstrated one way to internationalize a program. It used a string table resource with a set of strings for each language. The identifiers for the strings in each language started at a different numeric offset. However, this approach can be too limiting. Adding another language requires recompiling the program. And adding another string to the system requires precisely calculating the correct ID for each language. If the offsets were chosen too close together, adding another string can mean recalculating the ID for *every* existing string.

A better solution is to store the string resource in a DLL whose single exported function returns the desired string. Each language will have its own DLL, and a new language can be added without any change to the main program. Here's an example DLL, followed by resource files for four different languages.

LANGS

LANGS.DPR

```
library LangS;

USES WinTypes, WinProcs, SysUtils;
{$IFDEF Win32}
{$R LANGS32.RES}
{$ELSE}
{$R LANGS16.RES}
{$ENDIF}
function GetString(N: Integer; P: PChar; Len: Integer): PChar;
  Export; {$IFDEF Win32}StdCall;{$ENDIF}
begin
  LoadString(hInstance, N, P, Len);
  Result := P;
end;

exports
  GetString INDEX 1;
begin
end.
```

LANGS.RC

```
#include "intl.inc"
STRINGTABLE
BEGIN
  rLabel1, "Uno"
  rLabel2, "Dos"
  rLabel3, "Tres"
  rButton1, "Cuatro"
  rButton2, "Cinco"
  rListItem1, "Seis"
  rListItem2, "Siete"
  rListItem3, "Ocho"
  rListItem4, "Nueve"
  rListItem5, "Diez"
  rYes, "Si"
  rNo, "No"
END
```

LANGR.RC

```
#include "intl.inc"
STRINGTABLE
BEGIN
  rLabel1, "Odin"
  rLabel2, "Dva"
  rLabel3, "Tri"
  rButton1, "Chetirye"
  rButton2, "Pyats"
  rListItem1, "Shests"
  rListItem2, "Syem"
  rListItem3, "Vosyem"
  rListItem4, "Dyevyats"
  rListItem5, "Dyesyats"
  rYes, "Da"
  rNo, "Nyet"
END
```

LANGJ.RC

```
#include "intl.inc"
STRINGTABLE
BEGIN
  rLabel1, "Ichi"
  rLabel2, "Ni"
  rLabel3, "San"
  rButton1, "Shi"
  rButton2, "Go"
  rListItem1, "Roku"
  rListItem2, "Shichi"
```

```
  rListItem3, "Hachi"
  rListItem4, "Kyu"
  rListItem5, "Ju"
  rYes, "Hai"
  rNo, "Iie"
END
```

LANGE.RC

```
#include "intl.inc"
STRINGTABLE
BEGIN
  rLabel1, "One"
  rLabel2, "Two"
  rLabel3, "Three"
  rButton1, "Four"
  rButton2, "Five"
  rListItem1, "Six"
  rListItem2, "Seven"
  rListItem3, "Eight"
  rListItem4, "Nine"
  rListItem5, "Ten"
  rYes, "Yes"
  rNo, "No"
END
```

INTL.INC

```
const
  rLabel1      =      1;
  rLabel2      =      2;
  rLabel3      =      3;
  rButton1     =      4;
  rButton2     =      5;
  rListItem1   =      6;
  rListItem2   =      7;
  rListItem3   =      8;
  rListItem4   =      9;
  rListItem5   =     10;
  rYes         =     11;
  rNo          =     12;
```

Only the project file corresponding to the Spanish-language DLL is shown; the other three are identical except for the library name (LangR, LangJ, and LangE) and the corresponding difference in the 16-bit and the 32-bit .RES file names. Note that the include file INTL.INC defines named constants for each of the strings the calling program will need.

Even though these DLLs are intended for use only with other Delphi programs, the GetString function still returns its strings in a PChar supplied by the calling program. If the DLLs were meant only for 16-bit Delphi, the functions could return a Delphi string. However, in a 32-bit program, a string allocated by the DLL is not accessible to the calling program. Figure 16-4 shows an example program using the language DLLs.

FIGURE 16-4: This program uses the language DLL whose name is passed on its command line; if the DLL can't be found, it attempts to use the English-language version.

INTL

INTLU.DEX

```
object Form1: TForm1
  Caption = 'International'
  OnCreate = FormCreate
  OnDestroy = FormDestroy
  object Label1: TLabel
  end
  object Label2: TLabel
  end
  object Label3: TLabel
  end
  object Button1: TButton
  end
  object Button2: TButton
  end
  object ListBox1: TListBox
  end
  object BitBtn1: TBitBtn
```

```
    Kind = bkNo
    Margin = 4
  end
  object BitBtn2: TBitBtn
    Kind = bkYes
    Margin = 4
  end
end
```

INTLU.PAS

```pascal
unit Intlu;

interface

uses SysUtils, WinTypes, WinProcs, Messages, Classes, Graphics,
  Controls, Forms, Dialogs, StdCtrls, Buttons;

type
  GetStringType = function (N: Integer; P: PChar;
    Len: Integer): PChar {$IFDEF Win32}StdCall{$ENDIF};

  TForm1 = class(TForm)
    Label1: TLabel;
    Label2: TLabel;
    Label3: TLabel;
    Button1: TButton;
    Button2: TButton;
    ListBox1: TListBox;
    BitBtn1: TBitBtn;
    BitBtn2: TBitBtn;
    procedure FormCreate(Sender: TObject);
    procedure FormDestroy(Sender: TObject);
  private
    DllHan : THandle;
    GetString : GetStringType;
  end;

var Form1: TForm1;

implementation

{$R *.DFM}
{$I INTL.INC}
procedure TForm1.FormCreate(Sender: TObject);
VAR Buffer : ARRAY[0..255] OF Char;
begin
  IF ParamCount = 0 THEN StrCopy(Buffer, 'LANGE.DLL')
  ELSE StrPCopy(Buffer, ParamStr(1));
  DllHan := LoadLibrary(Buffer);
  IF DllHan < HINSTANCE_ERROR THEN
    BEGIN
      ShowMessage(StrPas(Buffer) + ' not found. '+
        'Attempting to load English language DLL');
```

```
            StrCopy(Buffer, 'LANGE.DLL');
            DllHan := LoadLibrary(Buffer);
        END;
    Caption := 'International - ' + ExtractFileName(StrPas(Buffer));
    IF DllHan < HINSTANCE_ERROR THEN
        BEGIN
            ShowMessage('Could not load language DLL');
            PostQuitMessage(1);
            Exit;
        END;
    @GetString := GetProcAddress(DllHan,'GetString');
    IF @GetString = NIL THEN
        BEGIN
            ShowMessage('Could not load GetString function');
            PostQuitMessage(2);                          -
            Exit;
        END;
    Label1.Caption := StrPas(GetString(rLabel1, Buffer, 255));
    Label2.Caption := StrPas(GetString(rLabel2, Buffer, 255));
    Label3.Caption := StrPas(GetString(rLabel3, Buffer, 255));
    Button1.Caption := StrPas(GetString(rButton1, Buffer, 255));
    Button2.Caption := StrPas(GetString(rButton2, Buffer, 255));
    ListBox1.Items.Add(StrPas(GetString(rListItem1, Buffer, 255)));
    ListBox1.Items.Add(StrPas(GetString(rListItem2, Buffer, 255)));
    ListBox1.Items.Add(StrPas(GetString(rListItem3, Buffer, 255)));
    ListBox1.Items.Add(StrPas(GetString(rListItem4, Buffer, 255)));
    ListBox1.Items.Add(StrPas(GetString(rListItem5, Buffer, 255)));
    BitBtn1.Caption := StrPas(GetString(rNo, Buffer, 255));
    BitBtn2.Caption := StrPas(GetString(rYes, Buffer, 255));
end;

procedure TForm1.FormDestroy(Sender: TObject);
begin
    IF DllHan >= HINSTANCE_ERROR THEN FreeLibrary(DllHan);
end;

end.
```

The run-time DLL loading occurs in the form's OnCreate event handler. A call to LoadLibrary loads the DLL, or returns an error value. (Note that the error value 21 means you've attempted to load a 32-bit DLL in a 16-bit program.) Assuming the DLL was loaded successfully, the next step is to set up access to the GetString function.

Loading a DLL function at runtime requires a procedural type variable whose declaration precisely matches the expected declaration for the function. In this case, the private data field GetString is defined as a function taking an integer parameter identifying the desired string, a PChar buffer, and the length of the buffer, just like the GetString function in the language DLLs. Note that, when defining this type in

Delphi 2.0, the StdCall directive is appended after the function return type with no intervening semicolon.

The GetProcAddress DLL function returns the address of the desired function within the DLL. To assign that address to the GetString variable, we must prefix GetString with the @ symbol. Normally, the @ operator returns the address of a variable, but, when applied to a procedural type variable, it indicates that the code is a reference to the value of the variable rather than a call to the procedure or the function. If the result of this assignment is non-NIL, we've succeeded, and the program calls GetString to get all the program's strings.

Once the last call to GetString has been made, it would be reasonable to free the DLL with a call to FreeLibrary. However, there's always a chance you might add a call to GetString elsewhere in the program. Just to be safe, the example program waits and calls FreeLibrary in the main form's OnDestroy event handler.

DLL Difficulties

Plenty of experienced Windows and Delphi programmers have never written a DLL. The first DLL you write is likely to be a traumatic experience. DLLs present different sorts of problems from ordinary programs, and a mistake can have spectacular consequences.

DLL changes don't take effect

Sometimes, when you're working on a 16-bit DLL, you may find that your changes don't seem to have any effect. You can fix a problem and recompile, but the calling program will still demonstrate the problem. You can add a function and recompile, but the calling program can't call the new function.

The problem here almost certainly involves an earlier program crash. When a program crashes badly, Windows cannot necessarily perform its usual cleanup activities. In particular, Windows may not decrement the reference count of DLLs used by that program. That means that, after a program crash, the DLL you're working on may still be in memory. Windows won't load the newly recompiled version when there's already a copy of the DLL in memory, so your changes seem to have no effect.

There are techniques for locating the "orphaned" DLL and getting it out of memory. However, it's both safer and more straightforward to just restart Windows.

Avoiding DLL trouble

16 32

A mistake in DLL programming is substantially more serious than a mistake within a simple executable program. If you call a simple function with the wrong parameters, the Delphi compiler will alert you immediately. Do the same with a DLL function declaration and the *best* you can hope for is that your program will crash sedately. It's quite possible to crash Windows 3.1 or Windows 95 with an error in a DLL. Thus, it's especially important to program defensively to avoid the opportunity for errors.

To assist in this, a number of the following safety tips were mentioned in context in this chapter.

◆ Don't use Delphi strings as parameters or function results. Other languages don't support them.

◆ Do make the calling program perform any necessary memory allocation and pass a buffer to be filled. A 16-bit DLL that allocates memory and passes it back to the calling program can cause serious problems.

◆ Do include a length parameter along with every PChar parameter, and use PChar functions that include a length restriction. A DLL function that writes outside the supplied buffer can cause serious problems.

◆ Don't write functions that return floating-point values; instead, use a procedure that returns its value through a floating-point VAR parameter. Borland and Microsoft languages use different conventions for DLL functions that return floating-point values.

◆ Do use the .DLL extension when importing DLL functions under Windows NT; otherwise, NT will not recognize the DLL.

◆ Don't use the .DLL extension when importing DLL functions under Windows 3.1; otherwise, Windows 3.1 will not recognize the DLL .

◆ Do use the simplest possible data types as parameters and function results (Integer, LongInt, Double, and PChar). These data types are available in virtually any language.

◆ Don't use global variables to share information between programs using a DLL. This may work in 16-bit programs, but 32-bit programs load DLLs in their own memory spaces, so no communication is possible.

◆ Don't use the Real data type, sets, enumerated types, strings, or file variables for DLL parameters or function results. These data types are proprietary and are supported only by Delphi and Borland Pascal.

◆ Don't use the Delphi-generated global form variable in a DLL that includes a Delphi form. Each program that calls on the DLL should have a new instance of the form type created for it.

◆ Do put multiple forms in a single DLL if multiple forms are required. Each DLL that contains a form will be at least 100KB in size because of the necessary component libraries, so giving each form its own DLL would waste memory.

◆ Do consider using run-time loading of DLL functions in professional applications. Your programs will be able to recover gracefully if the DLL is not found.

◆ Do use ByVal in front of Visual Basic function parameters corresponding to Delphi non-VAR parameters.

◆ Do omit ByVal in front of Visual Basic function parameters corresponding to Delphi VAR parameters.

IDG BOOKS WORLDWIDE, INC. END-USER LICENSE AGREEMENT

Read This. You should carefully read these terms and conditions before opening the software packet(s) included with this book ("Book"). This is a license agreement ("Agreement") between you and IDG Books Worldwide, Inc. ("IDGB"). By opening the accompanying software packet(s), you acknowledge that you have read and accept the following terms and conditions. If you do not agree and do not want to be bound by such terms and conditions, promptly return the Book and the unopened software packet(s) to the place you obtained them for a full refund.

1. **License Grant.** IDGB grants to you (either an individual or entity) a nonexclusive license to use one copy of the enclosed software program(s) (collectively, the "Software") solely for your own personal or business purposes on a single computer (whether a standard computer or a workstation component of a multi-user network). The Software is in use on a computer when it is loaded into temporary memory (i.e., RAM) or installed into permanent memory (e.g., hard disk, CD-ROM or other storage device). IDGB reserves all rights not expressly granted herein.

2. **Ownership.** IDGB is the owner of all right, title and interest, including copyright, in and to the compilation of the Software recorded on the disk(s)/CD-ROM. Copyright to the individual programs on the disk(s)/CD-ROM is owned by the

author or other authorized copyright owner of each program. Ownership of the Software and all proprietary rights relating thereto remain with IDGB and its licensors.

3. **Restrictions On Use and Transfer.**

   (a) You may only (i) make one copy of the Software for backup or archival purposes, or (ii) transfer the Software to a single hard disk, provided that you keep the original for backup or archival purposes. You may not (i) rent or lease the Software, (ii) copy or reproduce the Software through a LAN or other network system or through any computer subscriber system or bulletin-board system, or (iii) modify, adapt or create derivative works based on the Software.

   (b) You may not reverse engineer, decompile, or disassemble the Software. You may transfer the Software and user documentation on a permanent basis, provided that the transferee agrees to accept the terms and conditions of this Agreement and you retain no copies. If the Software is an update or has been updated, any transfer must include the most recent update and all prior versions.

4. **Restrictions on Use of Individual Programs.** You must follow the individual requirements and restrictions detailed for each individual program in this Book. These limitations are contained in the individual license agreements recorded on the disk(s)/CD-ROM. These restrictions include a requirement that after using the program for the period of time specified in its text, the user must pay a registration fee or discontinue use. By opening the Software packet(s), you will be agreeing to abide by the licenses and restrictions for these individual programs. None of the material on this disk(s) or listed in this Book may ever be distributed, in original or modified form, for commercial purposes.

5. **Limited Warranty.**

   (a) IDGB warrants that the Software and disk(s)/CD-ROM are free from defects in materials and workmanship under normal use for a period of sixty (60) days from the date of purchase of this Book. If IDGB receives notification within the warranty period of defects in materials or workmanship, IDGB will replace the defective disk(s)/CD-ROM.

   (b) IDGB AND THE AUTHOR OF THE BOOK DISCLAIM ALL OTHER WARRANTIES, EXPRESS OR IMPLIED, INCLUDING WITHOUT LIMITATION IMPLIED WARRANTIES OF MERCHANTABILITY AND FITNESS FOR A PARTICULAR PURPOSE, WITH RESPECT TO THE SOFTWARE, THE PROGRAMS, THE SOURCE CODE CONTAINED THEREIN, AND/OR THE TECHNIQUES DESCRIBED IN THIS BOOK. IDGB DOES NOT WARRANT THAT THE FUNCTIONS CONTAINED IN THE SOFTWARE WILL MEET

YOUR REQUIREMENTS OR THAT THE OPERATION OF THE SOFTWARE WILL BE ERROR FREE.

(c) This limited warranty gives you specific legal rights, and you may have other rights which vary from jurisdiction to jurisdiction.

6. **Remedies.**

(a) IDGB's entire liability and your exclusive remedy for defects in materials and workmanship shall be limited to replacement of the Software, which is returned to IDGB at the address set forth below with a copy of your receipt. This Limited Warranty is void if failure of the Software has resulted from accident, abuse, or misapplication. Any replacement Software will be warranted for the remainder of the original warranty period or thirty (30) days, whichever is longer.

(b) In no event shall IDGB or the author be liable for any damages whatsoever (including without limitation damages for loss of business profits, business interruption, loss of business information, or any other pecuniary loss) arising out of the use of or inability to use the Book or the Software, even if IDGB has been advised of the possibility of such damages.

(c) Because some jurisdictions do not allow the exclusion or limitation of liability for consequential or incidental damages, the above limitation or exclusion may not apply to you.

7. **U.S. Government Restricted Rights.** Use, duplication, or disclosure of the Software by the U.S. Government is subject to restrictions stated in paragraph (c) (1) (ii) of the Rights in Technical Data and Computer Software clause of DFARS 252.227-7013, and in subparagraphs (a) through (d) of the Commercial Computer—Restricted Rights clause at FAR 52.227-19, and in similar clauses in the NASA FAR supplement, when applicable.

8. **General.** This Agreement constitutes the entire understanding of the parties, and revokes and supersedes all prior agreements, oral or written, between them and may not be modified or amended except in a writing signed by both parties hereto which specifically refers to this Agreement. This Agreement shall take precedence over any other documents that may be in conflict herewith. If any one or more provisions contained in this Agreement are held by any court or tribunal to be invalid, illegal or otherwise unenforceable, each and every other provision shall remain in full force and effect.

Alternate Disk Format Available

The enclosed disk in 3 1/2" 1.44MB, high-density format. If you have a different size drive, or a low-density drive, and you cannot arrange to transfer the data to the disk size you need, you can obtain the programs by writing to the following address: Disk Fulfillment Department, Attn: *Delphi™ Programming Problem Solver*, IDG Books Worldwide, Inc., 7260 Shadeland Station, Indianapolis, IN 46256, or call 1-800-762-2974. Please specify the size of disk you need and allow 3 to 4 weeks for delivery.

INDEX

@ (at sign), 366, 572
[] (brackets), 166
$ (dollar sign), 565
< (left-arrow), 237
> (right-arrow), 237
| (vertical bar), 133–134
256-color mode, 329, 332, 333
32K limit, 193–194, 248

About box, 146
About property, 175
ACCEL, 140–141
ACCELERATOR resource, 139–142
ACCELU.DEX, 140
ACCELU.PAS, 140–141
Access, 87
active
    processes, lists of, 514–521
    tasks, lists of, 512–514
ActiveControl property, 386
ActiveMDIChild property, 88
Add method, 410
AddMasked method, 220
alClient setting, 17, 315, 365
alignment
    of cells, 257–265
    of edit boxes, 180–182
    of fields, 369–372

of numbers in grids, 262–265
of strings, 441
of text in list boxes, 212–213
Alignment property, 181, 304, 366
Align property, 315, 358–362
ALLEDIT, 122–125
ALLEDITU.DEX, 122–123
ALLEDITU.PAS, 123–125
alLeft setting, 315, 365
always-on-top command, 464–466
AND masks, 455
angle(s)
    drawing text at different, 295–297
    labels and, 298–305
Angle property, 304
ANGLTST, 304–305
ANGLTSTU.DEX, 304–305
ANGLTSTU.PAS, 305
animation, of sprite bitmaps, 326
anonymity, maintaining, 88
ANSI character set, 184, 237
AnsiCompareStr, 237
API (Application Programming Interface) 1,
        481–482. *See also* specific functions
    callback functions, 483–495
    overview of, 483–521
    undocumented functions, 538
Application.CreateForm, 463
Application.HelpFile, 144
Application.MainForm, 88, 102

Application.Minimize, 474
Application object, 405
    loading applications and, 458–464
    minimized activity and, 447–458
    overview of, 447–479
Application page, 524
Application.ProcessMessages, 368, 479, 512
AppOnHelp method, 476
AppOnHint method, 133
AppOnMessage method, 455, 466
AppOnMinimize event handler, 458
AppOnRestore event handler, 458
AppOnShowHint event handler, 472
Archimedes, 319
arguments, function, 422–434
array(s)
    components, creating, 115–121, 126–129
    fixed size, 407–408
    passing partial, as open arrays, 423–430
    variable size, 407–422
ArrayOfT, 408
ASCII code, 142, 182
at sign (@), 366, 572
audio files
    embedding, 535–538
    playing, from memory, 499–501
    playing, without the media player, 495–499
Auto-Create list, 40, 55
AutoMerge property, 88, 94
AutoPop property, 137
AutoPopup property, 139
auto-scrolling, 231
AutoSize property, 304, 366
Available list, 40

B

backgrounds
    dialog forms and, 65
    gradient fill, 329–333
    grids and, 279–281, 376
    list boxes and, 210
    MDI forms and, 103–107
    painting on, with patterns, 17–22
Backspace key, deselecting radio buttons with, 350, 353
base form types, creating, 47–48
Begin Drag method, 316
biHelp setting, 65

BILLIONS, 258–259
BILLIONU.DEX, 258–259
BILLIONU.PAS, 259
biMaximize setting, 65
biMinimize setting, 65
bitmap(s)
    backgrounds and, 103, 107
    component arrays and, 126
    displaying, in the Clipboard, 502, 505
    displaying, in list boxes, 216–220
    glyph-type, 216–220
    icons and, 357–358, 455
    menu items and, 147–150, 153
    painting on forms and, 17–18, 23
    resources, used as button glyphs, 335–338
    storing, in metafiles, 316–322
    storing, as resources, 526–529
    storing, without the VB PicClip control, 326–329
BITMENU, 148–150
BITMENUU.DEX, 148
BITMENUU.PAS, 149–150
BMPER, 524, 527–529
BMPER.RES, 524
BMPER16.RES, 524
BMPER32.RES, 524
BMPERMK.BAT, 525, 527
BMPERU.DEX, 527
BMPERU.PAS, 528–529
BorderIcons.biHelp property, 108, 111
borders, retaining, when eliminating captions, 9–12
BorderStyle property, 9–12, 35, 60, 65, 461
BRCC.EXE, 338, 525
brackets ([]), 166
Bring to Front command, 129
Brush property, 17
bsDialog setting, 10, 35
bsNone setting, 9, 461
bsSizable setting, 10
button(s)
    deselecting sets/radio groups of, 350–353
    glyphs, using bitmap resources as, 335–338
    glyphs, using icons as, 339–341
    with multiline captions, 341–346
    overview of, 335–353
    that repeat when held down, creating, 346–350
Button1Click method, 125
ButtonStyle property, 376
ByVal keyword, 563, 574

C

CALC, 272–273
CALCU.DEX, 272–273
calculation engine functions, 555
CALCU.PAS, 273–275
callback functions, 483–495
caMinimize setting, 35
C_ANGLAB.PAS, 209–301, 304
CanSelect, 289
CanShow parameter, 470, 472
Canvas object, 30, 262, 297
Canvas.Polygon, 430
Canvas property, 26, 430
Canvas.TextOut, 213
caption(s)
    drawing, 23–27
    eliminating, but leaving the border, 9–12
    fonts and, 383
    multiline, building buttons with, 341–346
CaptionGlyph method, 344
Caption property, 26, 136
CARRAY, 116–118
CARRAYU.DEX, 116–117
CARRAYU.PAS, 117–118
Cascade command, 94, 99–103
Cascade method, 88
CBACK, 485–487
CBACKU.DEX, 485
CBACKU.PAS, 485–486
CBMETH, 494
CBMETHU.DEX, 494
CBMETHU.PAS, 494–495
cbsEllipsis setting, 376
CD Audio, 495
cdecl directive, 423
C_DGBLOB.PAS, 388–392
cell(s)
    alignment of, 257–265
    centering text in, 260–262
    copying, 269–271
    displaying huge numbers of, 258–259
    drawing of, 257–265
    putting other components in, 290–294
    right-justifying text in, 260–262
    selecting, 265–275
Cells property, 281–282
ChangeCliboardChain, 504
CharMap, 383
CheckBox1Click method, 47

Checked property, 150–151, 154, 472
check marks, changing, 150–155
CheckMenuItem, 150, 154, 160
CheckPrevInst, 462
CHEMICAL.BMP, 325
CHILDCU.DEX, 34
CHILDCU.PAS, 34–35
CHILDMU.DEX, 33
CHILDMU.PAS, 33–34
children, listing, 484–487
CHILDWIN, 33–34
CHNGICON, 450–451
CHNGICOU.DEX, 450
CHNGICOU.PAS, 450–451
class methods, 435
C_LBHORZ.PAS, 224–226
C_LBSORT.PAS, 238–239
C_LBTAB.PAS, 227–228
Clear All button, 122
ClearContainer procedure, 125
ClientHandle property, 93, 106
Client/Server Suite, 394, 435
Clipboard
    chain, 502
    contents, watching, 501–505
    copying cell selections to, 269–271
CLIPVU, 502–505
CLIPVUU.DEX, 502
CLIPVUU.PAS, 503–504
CLIST, 127–129
CLISTU.DEX, 127
CLISTU.PAS, 127–128
Close command, 17
CloseEnhMetafile, 322
CloseHandle, 520
CloseMetafile, 320
CLS command, 525
clWhite setting, 312, 316
clXxx color constants, 438–440
CmdShow, 474
CMFontChanged method, 304
Code Editor, 3, 130
code listings, 2–4
    ACCEL, 140–141
    ACCELU.DEX, 140
    ACCELU.PAS, 140–141
    ALLEDIT, 122–125
    ALLEDITU.DEX, 122–123
    ALLEDITU.PAS, 123–125
    ANGLTST, 304–305

ANGLTSTU.DEX, 304–305
ANGLTSTU.PAS, 305
BILLIONS, 258–259
BILLIONU.DEX, 258–259
BILLIONU.PAS, 259
BITMENU, 148–150
BITMENUU.DEX, 148
BITMENUU.PAS, 149–150
BMPER, 524, 527–529
BMPER.RES, 524
BMPER16.RES, 524
BMPER32.RES, 524
BMPERMK.BAT, 525, 527
BMPERU.DEX, 527
BMPERU.PAS, 528–529
CALC, 272–273
CALCU.DEX, 272–273
CALCU.PAS, 273–275
C_ANGLAB.PAS, 209–301, 304
CARRAY, 116–118
CARRAYU.DEX, 116–117
CARRAYU.PAS, 117–118
CBACK, 485–487
CBACKU.DEX, 485
CBACKU.PAS, 485–486
CBMETH, 494
CBMETHU.DEX, 494
CBMETHU.PAS, 494–495
CHILDWIN, 33–34
CHNGICON, 450–451
CHNGICOU.DEX, 450
CHNGICOU.PAS, 450–451
C_LBHORZ.PAS, 224–226
C_LBSORT.PAS, 238–239
C_LBTAB.PAS, 227–228
CLIPVU, 502–505
CLIPVUU.DEX, 502
CLIPVUU.PAS, 503–504
CLIST, 127–129
CLISTU.DEX, 127
CLISTU.PAS, 127–128
COLTEXT, 210–213
COLTEXTU.DEX, 210–211
COLTEXTU.PAS, 211–212
COMBOSEL, 243–246
COMBSELU.DEX, 243–244
COMBSELU.PAS, 244–245
COMPARR, 119–121
COMPARRU.DEX, 119–120
COMPARRU.PAS, 120–121

COMPCOLR, 439–440
COMPCOLRU.DEX, 439
COMPCOLRU.PAS, 439–440
COMPONENT TRCMEMO, 172–174
CONHELP, 475–476
CONHELPU.DEX, 475
CONHELPU.PAS, 475–476
COORD95, 168–171
COORD95U.DEX, 168–169
COORD95U.PAS, 169–170
COORDS, 168, 170–171
COORDSU.DEX, 170
COORDSU.PAS, 170–171
CPRICH, 194–208
CPRICHU.DEX, 194–199
CPRICHU.PAS, 200–208
CREM32, 320–322
CREM32U.DEX, 320–321
CREM32U.PAS, 321–322
CREMETA, 317–318
CREMETAU.DEX, 317–318
CREMETAU.PAS, 318–319
CTRLDLG, 354–356
CTRLDLGU.DEX, 354–355
CTRLDLGU.PAS, 355–356
CURSE, 530–531
CURSE16.RES, 531
CURSE32.RES, 531
CURSEMK.BAT, 530
CURSE.RES, 531
CURSEU.DEX, 530
CURSEU.PAS, 530–531
CUTCOPY, 188–191
CUTCOPYU.DEX, 188–189
CUTCOPYU.PAS, 189–191
C_WRAPB.PAS, 342–344
DATEDIF, 420–422
DATEDIFU, 421–422
DATEDIFU.DEX, 420
DBCTLGR, 394–398
DBCTLGRU.DEX, 394–397
DBCTLGRU.PAS, 397
DECALIN, 263–265
DECALINU.DEX, 263
DECALINU.PAS, 264–265
DELAY, 367–368
DELAYU.DEX, 367
DELAYU.PAS, 367–368
DELGRID, 282–285
DELGRIDU.DEX, 282–283

DELGRIDU.PAS, 283–285
DLGMENU, 36–37
DLGMENUU.DEX, 36
DLGMENUU.PAS, 36–37
DRAGOUT, 307–310
DRAGOUTU.DEX, 307
DRAGOUTU.PAS, 308–309
DRAWICON, 5, 452–455
DRAWICOU.DEX, 452
DRAWICOU.PAS, 452–454
EDGE, 74–78
EDGEU.DEX, 74–75
EDGEU.PAS, 75–78
EDRITE, 180–182
EDRITEU.DEX, 180–181
EDRITEU.PAS, 181
EXEMPT, 99–103
EXEMPT1U.DEX, 99–100
EXEMPT1U.PAS, 100–101
EXEMPT2U.DEX, 101
EXEMPT2U.PAS, 101–102
EXEMPT3U.DEX, 102
EXEMPT3U.PAS, 102
EXTEST, 553–554
EXTESTU.DEX, 553
EXTESTU.PAS, 554
FLDCNTR, 370–371
FLDCNTRU.DEX, 370
FLDCNTRU.PAS, 370–371
FLDRED, 377–379
FLDREDU.DEX, 377
FLDREDU.PAS, 377–379
FMDROP, 467–469
FMDROPU.DEX, 467
FMDROPU.PAS, 468–469
FONTFAM, 488–493
FONTFAMU.DEX, 488–489
FONTFAMU.PAS, 490–492
FONTLIST, 214–215
FONTLISU.DEX, 214
FONTLISU.PAS, 214–215
FORMDLL, 555–558
FORMDLL.DPR, 555–556
FORMDLLU.DEX, 556–557
FORMDLLU.PAS, 557–558
FORMTEST, 558–560
FORMTSTU.DEX, 558–559
FORMTSTU.PAS, 559–560
GCOLOR, 280–281
GCOLORU.DEX, 280

GCOLORU.PAS, 280–281
GETENVIR.PAS, 437–438
GETENVIR UNIT, 437–438
GLYRES, 336–338
GLYRESMK.BAT, 338
GLYRESU.DEX, 336–337
GLYRESU.PAS, 337–338
GRADBAK, 329–333
GRADBAKU.DEX, 329–330
GRADBAKU.PAS, 330–332
GRIDCLIP, 270–271
GRIDCLIU.DEX, 270
GRIDCLIU.PAS, 271
GRIDCONT, 292–294
GRIDCONU.DEX, 292–293
GRIDCONU.PAS, 293–294
GRIDED, 373–376
GRIDEDM.DEX, 373
GRIDEDM.PAS, 374
GRIDEDU.DEX, 374–375
GRIDEDU.PAS, 375–376
GRIDS.PAS, 282
HELPBTN, 66–67
HELPBTNU.DEX, 66
HELPBTNU.PAS, 66–67
HEPCUR, 68–71
HEPCURU.DEX, 68
HEPCURU.PAS, 68–71
HINTS, 131–134
HINTSU.DEX, 131–132
HINTSU.PAS, 132–133
HOLDBUTN, 347–350
HOLDBUTU.DEX, 347–348
HOLDBUTU.PAS, 348–350
HOTKEY, 541–545
HOTKEY.DEX, 541–542
HOTKEYU.PAS, 542–545
ICO2BMP, 357–358
ICO2BMPU.DEX, 357
ICO2BMPU.PAS, 357–358
ICOBUTN, 339–341
ICOBUTNU.DEX, 339
ICOBUTNU.PAS, 340
ICONTITL, 456–458
ICONTITLU.DEX, 456
ICONTITLU.PAS, 456–458
INCRCH, 247–248
INCRCHU.DEX, 247
INCRCHU.PAS, 247–248
INTL, 569–571

INTL.INC, 568
INTLU.DEX, 569–570
INTLU.PAS, 570–571
ISTOPMN, 164–166
ISTOPMNU.DEX, 164
ISTOPMNU.PAS, 164–166
ISWIN95.PAS, 448
ISWIN95 UNIT, 447–448
KNOWEXEC, 487, 506–511, 512
KNOWEXECU.DEX, 506–507
KNOWEXECU.PAS, 507–511
LANGE.RC, 568
LANGJ.RC, 567–568
LANGR.RC, 567
LANGS, 566–569
LANGS.DPR, 566
LANGS.RC, 567
LBBMP, 217–220
LBBMPU.DEX, 217
LBBMPU.PAS, 217–219
LBCOMP, 240–242
LBCOMPU.DEX, 240–241
LBCOMPU.PAS, 241–242
LBDRAG, 231–234
LBDRAGU.DEX, 231–232
LBDRAGU.PAS, 232–233
LBODVAR, 220–223
LBODVARU.DEX, 220–221
LBODVARU.PAS, 221–222
LBTABS, 229–230
LBTABSU.DEX, 229–230
LBTABSU.PAS, 230
LDRAGMUL, 234–237
LDRAGMUU.DEX, 234–235
LDRAGMUU.PAS, 235–237
LONE, 90–93
LONE1U.DEX, 90
LONE1U.PAS, 90–91
LONE2U.DEX, 91
LONE2U.PAS, 91–92
LONE3U.DEX, 92
LONE3U.PAS, 92–93
LOOP, 477–479
LOOPU.DEX, 477
LOOPU.PAS, 477–479
MANAGE, 44–46
MANAGE1U.DEX, 44
MANAGE1U.PAS, 44–46
MANAGE2U.DEX, 46–47
MASKDEM, 323–326

MASKDEMU.DEX, 323–324
MASKDEMU.PAS, 324–325
MAXMDI, 82–83
MAXMDI1U.DEX, 82
MAXMDI1U.PAS, 82–83
MAXMDI2U.DEX, 83
MAXMDI2U.PAS 83
MDIHIDE, 84–87
MDIHIDU1.DEX, 84
MDIHIDU1.PAS, 85
MDIHIDU2.DEX, 86
MDIHIDU2.PAS, 86
MDIHLP, 108–112
MDIHLP1U.DEX, 108
MDIHLP1U.PAS, 108
MDIHLP2U.DEX, 109
MDIHLP2U.PAS, 110
MEMSND, 500–501
MEMSNDU.DEX, 500
MEMSNDU.PAS, 500–501
MEMUNDO, 182–184
MEMUNDOU.DEX, 182–183
MEMUNDOU.PAS, 183–184
MENUACT, 539–540
MENUACTU.DEX, 539–540
MENUACTU.PAS, 540
MERGE, 94–98
MERGE1U.DEX, 94–95
MERGE1U.PAS, 95–96
MERGE2U.DEX, 96
MERGE2U.PAS, 96–97
MODALD, 40–43
MODALD1U.DEX, 40
MODALD1U.PAS, 41
MODALD2U.DEX, 41–42
MODALD2U.PAS, 42–43
MODEDID, 384–386
MODEDIDU.DEX, 384
MODEDIDU.PAS, 384–386
MODEDIT, 185–187
MODEDITU.DEX, 185
MODEDITU.PAS, 186–187
MODMERGE, 160–163
MODMSGD, 61–65
MODMSGDU.DEX, 61–62
MODMSGDU.PAS, 62–64
MOUSEHOOK, 72–73
MOUSEHOOK.DPR, 72–73
MULFRM/, 50–51
MULFRM1U.DEX, 54

MULFRM1U.PAS, 54–55
MULFRM2U.DEX, 52
MULFRM2U.PAS, 52–53
MULFRM3U.DEX, 51
MULFRM3U.PAS, 51–52
MULFRM4U.DEX, 50
MULFRM4U.PAS, 50–51
MUSOVER, 471–472
MUSOVERU.DEX, 471
MUSOVERU.PAS, 471–472
MYTITLE, 24–26
MYTITLEU.DEX, 24
MYTITLEU.PAS, 24–26
NOPOP, 138–139
NOPOPU.DEX, 138
NOPOPU.PAS, 138–139
ODDFRAME, 30–32
ODDFRAMU.DEX, 30
ODDFRAMU.PAS, 31–32
ODMENU, 156–160
ODMENUU.DEX, 156–157
ODMENUU.PAS, 157–159
ONCE, 461–463
ONCE.DPR, 461–462
OPARR2, 428–430
OPARR2U.DEX, 428
OPARR2U.PAS, 429–430
OPENARR, 424–428
OPENARRU.DEX, 424–425
OPENARRU.PAS, 425–427
P_ABOUT.PAS, 175–176
PACKDEMO, 442–445
PACKDEMU.DEX, 442–443
PACKDEMU.PAS, 443–445
PANPROB, 359–361
PANPROBU.DEX, 359
PANPROBU.PAS, 360–361
PICCLIP, 327–329
PICCLIPU.DEX, 327
PICCLIPU.PAS, 328
POWERS.PAS, 435–436
POWERS UNIT, 435–436
RADMENU, 151–155
RADMENUU.DEX, 151
RADMENUU.PAS, 151–152
RADMN32, 154–155
RADMN32U.DEX, 154–155
RADMN32U.PAS, 155
RITEHELP, 143–144
RITEHLPU.DEX, 143

RITEHLPU.PAS, 143–144
RITELEFT, 260–262
RITELEFU.DEX, 260
RITELEFU.PAS, 261
RUBAND, 310–312
RUBANDU.DEX, 310–311
RUBANDU.PAS, 311–312
RUNMIN, 472–474
RUNMINU.DEX, 472
RUNMINU.PAS, 473
SCRNSV, 549–550
SCRNSVU.DEX, 549
SCRNSVU.PAS, 549–550
SCROLL, 249–253
SELGRID, 267–269
SELGRIDU.DEX, 267
SELGRIDU.PAS, 267–269
SGRIDNO, 276–279
SGRIDNOU.DEX, 276–277
SGRIDNOU.PAS, 277–278
SHAR32, 401–404
SHAR321U.DEX, 401–402
SHAR321U.PAS, 403
SHAR322U.DEX, 403–404
SHAR32M.DEX, 404
SHAREV, 135–136
SHAREVU.DEX, 135
SHAREVU.PAS, 135–136
SHARTBL, 398–401
SIZCTRL, 58–60
SIZCTRLU.DEX, 58
SIZCTRLU.PAS, 58–60
SIZFRAM, 10–11
SIZFRAMU.DEX, 10
SNDPLAY, 496–499
SORTMEM, 177–179
SORTMEMU.DEX, 177
SORTMEMU.PAS, 178–179
SPLASH, 459–461
SPLASH.DPR, 460
SPLITP, 313–315, 363–365
SPLITPU.DEX, 363
SPLITPU.PAS, 314–315, 363–365
STDHLP, 145–146
STDHLPU.DEX, 145
STDHLPU.PAS, 145–146
STRRES, 532–535
STRRESMK.BAT, 532
STRRESU.DEX, 533–534
STRRESU.PAS, 534–535

SYSMENU, 465–466
SYSMENUU.DEX, 465
SYSMENUU.PAS, 465–466
TANGLELABEL, 298–304, 305
TANGLEPROPERTY, 301–304
TASKS, 513–514
TASKS32, 515–521
TASKS32U.DEX, 515–516
TASKS32U.PAS, 517–520
TASKSU.DEX, 513
TASKSU.PAS, 513–514
TDBGRIDBLOB, 388–393
TESTDLLF, 560–563
TESTDLLF.MAK, 560
TESTDLLF.TXT, 561–563
TEXTUR1U.DEX, 18–19
TEXTUR1U.PAS, 19–20
TEXTUR2U.DEX, 21
TEXTUR2U.PAS, 21–22
TEXTURE, 18–23
TIMMATH, 416–418
TIMMATHU.DEX, 416–417
TIMMATHU.PAS, 418–419
TINYT, 12–17
TINYT95U.DEX, 13
TINYT95U.PAS, 14
TINYTMU.DEX, 12
TINYTMU.PAS, 13
TINYTTU.DEX, 14–15
TINYTTU.PAS, 15–16
TITLBTN, 27–30
TITLBTNU.DEX, 27–28
TITLBTNU.PAS, 28–29
TListBoxComp, 238–240
TListBoxHorz, 4, 224–226, 228, 415, 469
TListBoxTabs, 227–231
TSOBJ, 412–415
TSOBJU.DEX, 412–413
TSOBJU.PAS, 413–415
TStringGridCont, 290–292, 294
TURNTX, 296–297
TURNTX.DEX, 296
TURNTX.PAS, 296–297
TWRAPBTN, 342–346
UNRADGP, 351–353
UNRADGPU.DEX, 351
UNRADGPU.PAS, 351–353
UPDMEMF, 381–382
UPDMEMFU.DEX, 381
UPDMEMFU.PAS, 382

VARREC, 431–434
VARRECU.DEX, 431
VARRECU.PAS, 434–433
VSARRAY, 409–410
VSARRAYU.DEX, 409
VSARRAYU.PAS, 409–410
WALLP, 103–107
WAVRES, 536–538
WAVRESMK.BAT, 536
WAVRESU.DEX, 536
WAVRESU.PAS, 536–538
WRAPBTN, 345–346
WRAPBTNU.DEX, 345–346
WRAPBTNU.PAS, 346
YELPAD, 286–290
YELPAD.DAT, 290
YELPADU.DEX, 286
YELPADU.PAS, 286–289
ColCount property, 397
color(s)
    256-color mode, 329, 332, 333
    dithered, 329
    in gradient-fill backgrounds, 329–333
    grids and, 275–281, 376
    list boxes and, 210–213
    multiline captions and, 341
    pixels which unexpectedly change, 438–440
Color property, 279–281
Col property, 172
Cols property, 281–282
COLTEXT, 210–213
COLTEXTU.DEX, 210–211
COLTEXTU.PAS, 211–212
column(s)
    enhancing the appearance of, with the Columns
        Editor, 372–377
    moving, 379–380
    resizing, 292, 379–380
ColumnListViewSort, 521
Columns property, 376
combo boxes, creating multiselect, 243–246
COMBOSEL, 243–246
COMBSELU.DEX, 243–244
COMBSELU.PAS, 244–245
command-line switches, 525
common dialogs
    controlling the position of, 354–356
    File Open dialog, 354, 469
    Font dialog, 487–493
communicating between programs, 545–548

COMPARR, 119–121
COMPARRU.DEX, 119–120
COMPARRU.PAS, 120–121
COMPCOLR, 439–440
COMPCOLRU.DEX, 439
COMPCOLRU.PAS, 439–440
compilation, conditional, 4–5
component(s). *See also* specific components
    arrays, 115–121
    creating new, list boxes and, 223–224
    distinguishing types of, in shared event
        handlers, 134–136
    finding lost, 129–130
    lists, 121–129
    overview of, 115–136
    processing all, of one type, 121–126
ComponentCount property, 122, 126
Component menu, 4
COMPONENT TRCMEMO, 172–174
CompuServe, 5, 86
CONHELP, 475–476
CONHELPU.DEX, 475
CONHELPU.PAS, 475–476
ConsistentAttributes property, 194
CONSTRUC.BMP, 220
constructors, 435
CONTROL.INI, 22, 23
Control radio button, 512
ControlCount property, 122, 126
Controls property, 60
CONVERT, 3
converting
    DEX files into Delphi forms, 3
    ICO files to BMP files, 357–358
COORD95, 168–171
COORD95U.DEX, 168–169
COORD95U.PAS, 169–170
COORDS, 168, 170–171
COORDSU.DEX, 170
COORDSU.PAS, 170–171
copying
    cell selections, 269–271
    from edit controls/memos, 188–191
"cousin" classes, 136
CPRICH, 194–208
CPRICHU.DEX, 194–199
CPRICHU.PAS, 200–208
CPUs (central processing units), 125, 441
crashes, 192, 572, 573
C_RCMEMO.PAS, 172–174

CreateForm, 461
CreateMetafile, 319
CreateParams method, 10–11, 16, 33, 35, 50,
    80, 228
CreateProcess, 511
CreateTheForm, 558
CreateToolHelp32Snapshot, 520–521
CreateWindowHandle method, 112
CREM32, 320–322
CREM32U.DEX, 320–321
CREM32U.PAS, 321–322
CREMETA, 317–318
CREMETAU.DEX, 317–318
CREMETAU.PAS, 318–319
crHSplit, 316, 362, 365
C_SGCONT.PAS, 290–292
Ctrl+Alt+Del, 512
CTRLDLG, 354–356
CTRLDLGU.DEX, 354–355
CTRLDLGU.PAS, 355–356
CURSE, 530–531
CURSE16.RES, 531
CURSE32.RES, 531
CURSEMK.BAT, 530
CURSE.RES, 531
CURSEU.DEX, 530
CURSEU.PAS, 530–531
Cursor property, 316, 529
cursors, creating/using, 529–531
Cursors array, 529, 531
CUTCOPY, 188–191
CUTCOPYU.DEX, 188–189
CUTCOPYU.PAS, 189–191
C_WRAPB.PAS, 342–344

D

data-aware edit text, modifying, 187, 383–386
database programming
    displaying graphics/memo fields, 387–393
    enhancing the appearance of columns, 372–376
    highlighting rows based on field values, 376–379
    moving/resizing columns, 379–380
    overview of, 369–404
    sharing tables, 398–404
    updating edit controls, 380–386
    updating memo fields, 380–383
DataSet Designer, 376
DATEDIF, 420–422
DATEDIFU, 421–422

DATEDIFU.DEX, 420
date/time data types, 416–422
DBCTLGR, 394–398
DBCTLGRU.DEX, 394–397
DBCTLGRU.PAS, 397
DBCtrlGrid, 397–398
DBGrid, 369, 372–376
DECALIN, 263–265
DECALINU.DEX, 263
DECALINU.PAS, 264–265
decimal-alignment, of numbers in grids, 262–265
DecodeTime, 422
DefaultHandler method, 77–78, 548
DefaultRowHeight property, 393
DELAY, 367–368
Delay procedure, 366–368
DELAYU.DEX, 367
DELAYU.PAS, 367–368
deleting, rows and columns in grids, 281–285
DELGRID, 282–285
DELGRIDU.DEX, 282–283
DELGRIDU.PAS, 283–285
Delphi
    Component Writer's Guide, 174
    CompuServe forum (GO DELPHI), 5, 86
    Developer Package, 394, 435
    versions of, 4–5
DELPHI.EXE, 525
Delta constant, 458
DestroyTheForm, 558
DestroyWindowHandle method, 111
Developer Package, 394, 435
DEX files, 3
dgColumnResize property, 379
dialog boxes. *See also* common dialogs
    adding menus to, 35–36
    controlling the position of, 354–356
    creating modal, as needed, 39–43
DIALOGS.PAS, 65
directories, storing source code files/EXE
    files in, 4
DirectoryListBox, 219
dithered color, 329
DLGMENU, 36–37
DLGMENUU.DEX, 36
DLGMENUU.PAS, 36–37
DLLs (Dynamic Link Libraries), 369, 482
    basics, 551–554

calling variations, 560–572
changes that don't take effect, 572–573
difficulties with, 572–574
hidden forms and, 72–74, 78
hints and, 472
language-flexible programs and, 566–572
language-specific, 566
loading, 565–566, 571–572, 574
overview of, 551–574
the packed keyword and, 445
putting a form inside, 555–560
task lists and, 512
writing and using, 551–554
DLLSHARE.INC, 73–74
dmAutomatic setting, 306
DoEvents, 479
dollar sign ($), 565
DOS (Disk Operating System)
    Delay procedures and, 366
    environment variables, 436–438
    filenames, 415
    as a single-tasking system, 505
DragCursor property, 529
dragging and dropping
    components at runtime, 306–310
    creating "rubber-band" drawings of rectangles
        and, 310–312
    creating splitter bars and, 312–315
    files from the File Manager or Explorer, 467–469
    sprites, 323–326
DragMode, 306
DRAGOUT, 307–310
DRAGOUTU.DEX, 307
DRAGOUTU.PAS, 308–309
DrawButtonFace, 29–30, 219
DrawCell method, 393
DrawFocusRect, 309, 312
DRAWICON, 5, 452–455
DRAWICOU.DEX, 452
DRAWICOU.PAS, 452–454
Draw method, 216, 341
DrawNewButton method, 29–30
DrawText, 65, 153, 344, 393
DrawTitle method, 26
DriveComboBox, 219
DT_CALCRECT, 65, 344
DT_WORDBREAK, 65
DT_WORDWRAP, 344

E

EConvertError exception, 265
EDGE, 74–78
EdgeMessage, 77–78
EDGEU.DEX, 74–75
EDGEU.PAS, 75–78
edit controls
    basic description of, 167–208
    cutting and copying from, 188–191
    event handler errors and, 191–193
    inserting characters in, 184–187
    right-aligning, 180–182
    setting up, with full row/column support,
        172–176
    updating, 380–386
Edit menu, 129, 184
EditorMode property, 191
EDRITE, 180–182
EDRITEU.DEX, 180–181
EDRITEU.PAS, 181
Ellipse function, 317
e-mail address, for Neil Rubenking, 5
embedding WAV files, 535–538
EM_CANUNDO, 184
EM_LINEFROMCHAR, 171
EM_LINEINDEX, 171
EM_SETRECT, 207
EM_UNDO, 184
Enabled property, 368
EnableMenuItem, 160
EncodeTime, 416
EnumChildWindows, 484, 487
EnumFFProc, 216
EnumFontFamilies, 216, 487–488, 492, 493, 495
EnumFontFamProc callback procedure, 492
EnumObjects, 495
EnumWindows, 458, 484, 487, 495, 511
environment variables, 436–438
errors, 320, 573. *See also* GPFs (General
        Protection Faults)
    "Bad command or file name," 525
    "Call to RegisterClass is missing or
        incorrect," 434
    "Error creating form: Duplicate resource
        (Type:, Name:), 524
    "Error in module <name>:Call to
        Application.CreateForm is missing or
        incorrect," 463
    "Unknown identifier" compiler, 87

ES_MULTILINE, 182
event handler(s). *See also* event handlers
        (listed by name)
    errors, 191–193
    shared, 134–136, 163–166
event handlers (listed by name). *See also* event
        handlers
    AppOnMinimize, 458
    AppOnRestore, 458
    AppOnShowHint, 472
    OnChange, 192, 245, 248, 305, 415
    OnClick, 4, 60, 93, 98, 116, 118, 134, 136, 163,
        166, 179, 191, 237, 245, 269, 272, 284–285,
        345–346, 353, 362, 366, 386, 479, 492–493,
        545, 550
    OnClose, 35, 43
    OnColumnClick, 521
    OnCompare, 239–240, 243
    OnCreate, 17, 23, 47, 56, 60, 77, 80, 128, 133,
        150, 159, 166, 187, 216, 253, 294, 332, 341,
        353, 361, 386, 410, 422, 427, 451, 458, 463,
        466, 469, 472, 476, 492, 498, 501, 571
    OnDblClick, 116
    OnDestroy, 572
    OnDragDrop, 233, 237, 306
    OnDragOver, 233, 237, 306, 312, 316, 326,
        365–366
    OnDrawCell, 257, 259, 262, 265, 269, 275–276,
        279, 281, 290
    OnDrawColumnCell, 372, 379
    OnDrawDataCell, 372, 379
    OnDrawItem, 209, 212, 216, 219, 220, 253
    OnEndDrag, 234, 309, 312, 316
    OnExit, 272, 275, 279
    OnFind, 208
    OnKeyDown, 182
    OnKeyPress, 182, 193, 245, 353
    OnKeyUp, 269, 289
    OnMeasureItem, 209, 220
    OnMinimize, 458
    OnMouseDown, 309, 316, 326, 350
    OnMouseUp, 71, 269, 350, 353
    OnPaint, 17, 289, 451
    OnPopup, 139
    OnReplace, 208
    OnResize, 47, 362
    OnRestore, 458
    OnSelectCell, 257, 272, 275, 289
    OnTimer, 61, 65, 350, 368, 422, 451, 455, 458
    RichEdit1SelectionChange, 171
EXAMPLE.DPR, 552

EXE files
    launching, 511
    resources and, 523, 526, 535
    storage of, in directories, 4
Execute button, 511
executing programs. *See also* loading applications
    and controlling other programs, 505–512
    and waiting for them to end, 505
EXEMPT, 99–103
EXEMPT1U.DEX, 99–100
EXEMPT1U.PAS, 100–101
EXEMPT2U.DEX, 101
EXEMPT2U.PAS, 101–102
EXEMPT3U.DEX, 102
EXEMPT3U.PAS, 102
Explorer, accepting files dragged from, 467–469
Export keyword, 558
EXTEST, 553–554
EXTESTU.DEX, 553
EXTESTU.PAS, 554

F

F1 key, 476
F_DBGGRA.DEX, 392–393
F_DBGMEM.DEX, 392
FACTORY.BMP, 312
field(s)
    centered, 369–372
    displaying, 387–393
    graphics, 387–393
    memo, 380–383, 387–393
    updating, 380–383
    value, highlighting rows based on, 376–379
Fields editor, 380
file(s). *See also* file extensions
    dragging and dropping, from the File
Manager/Explorer, 467–469
    metafiles, 316–333
    -names, DOS, 415
    written by older files, problems reading, 441–445
file extensions
    .DCR, 174
    .DFM, 3
    .DLL, 554, 573
    .DPR, 2
    .PAS, 2
    .R16, 4, 174
    .R32, 4, 174
FileListBox, 219

File Manager, accepting files dragged from,
    467–469
File menu, 90, 223, 397
File Open dialog box, 354, 469
FilePlace, 240
FILE SPLITU.DEX, 313–314
FILE UNIT1.PAS, 3
FillChar, 441
fills, gradient, 329–333
FindComponent, 118
FindDragTarget, 71
FindFirst, 514
FindNext, 514
FindResource, 538
FindText method, 208
FindWindow, 356, 462–463
Flashing Title option, 458
FlashWindow, 458
FLDCNTR, 370–371
FLDCNTRU.DEX, 370
FLDCNTRU.PAS, 370–371
FLDRED, 377–379
FLDREDU.DEX, 377
FLDREDU.PAS, 377–379
floating-point numbers, 416–422, 553, 573
FMDROP, 467–469
FMDROPU.DEX, 467
FMDROPU.PAS, 468–469
focus, displaying selections which lack, 276–279
Foley, Brian, 108
font(s). *See also* styles
    buttons and, 350
    captions and, 23–24, 383
    combo boxes and, 245
    component arrays and, 118, 121
    dialog forms and, 65
    drawing angles and, 295–297
    edit controls and, 194, 207
    information, getting detailed, 487–493
    list boxes and, 213–216, 228
    menu items and, 153, 159
    rotating, 295–297
    sizes, 213–216
    TrueType fonts, 295–297, 487–488, 492–493, 304
    using multiple, 194
    WingDings font, 11, 153, 350
FontColor, 341
Font common dialog, 487–493
FONTFAM, 488–493
FONTFAMU.DEX, 488–489
FONTFAMU.PAS, 490–492

FONTLIST, 214–215
FONTLISU.DEX, 214
FONTLISU.PAS, 214–215
Fonts property, 159
FOR loops, 476
form(s). *See also* MDI (Multiple Document
    Interface) forms
  basics, 9–37
  choosing main, at runtime, 463–464
  hidden, 71–78, 84–87
  inside DLLs, 555–560
  managing, 39–56
  modal, creating, 39–43
  multiple, 39–78
  sizing of, controlling, 57–60
  transforming, 32–37
  used as components of other forms, 33–34
Format command, 441
FormatDateTime, 419
Formats property, 502
FormCreate method, 146, 420
Form Designer, 5, 481, 531
FORMDLL, 555–558
FORMDLL.DPR, 555–556
FORMDLLU.DEX, 556–557
FORMDLLU.PAS, 557–558
Forms and Application page, 458
FormStyle, 43
FORMTEST, 558–560
FORMTSTU.DEX, 558–559
FORMTSTU.PAS, 559–560
frames, drawing, 30–32
FreeLibrary, 572
FreeMem, 408
Frisian, 531
fsMDIForm, 43
fsStayOnTop, 464, 466
function arguments, 422–434

G

GCOLOR, 280–281
GCOLORU.DEX, 280
GCOLORU.PAS, 280–281
GDI (Graphics Device Interface). *See also*
    graphics
  libraries, 483, 551
  overview of, 295–333
GetAttributes method, 176, 304
GetBitmapsBits, 455

GetDOSEnvironment, 437–438
GetEnv, 436, 438
GETENVIR.PAS, 437–438
GETENVIR UNIT, 437–438
GetEnvironmentStrings, 438
GetExitCodeProcess, 512
GetLogFont, 297
GetLoner method, 93
GetMem, 408
GetMenuCheckMarkDimensions, 153
GetPalette method, 332
GetProcAddress, 572
GetStartupInfo, 474
GetString, 569, 571, 572
GetSystemMetrics, 26
GetTabbedTextExtent, 229
GetTextBuf method, 55
GetTextLen method, 55, 208
GetTheForm, 563
GetValue method, 176
GetVersion, 144
GetVersionEx, 112, 448
GetWindowDC, 26
GlobalGetAtomName, 548
global variables, 573
Glyph property, 339, 341, 345
GLYRES, 336–338
GLYRESMK.BAT, 338
GLYRESU.DEX, 336–337
GLYRESU.PAS, 337–338
GO DELPHI forum (CompuServe), 5, 86
GoDrawFocusSelected, 265
goRangeSelect, 266
goRowSelectOptions property, 266
goRowSizing option, 393
GOTO command, 338
GPFs (General Protection Faults), 246, 320,
    434–435. *See also* errors
GRADBAK, 329–333
GRADBAKU.DEX, 329–330
GRADBAKU.PAS, 330–332
graphics
  backgrounds, 17–22, 65, 103–107, 210,
    279–281, 376, 329–333
  displaying, in the Clipboard, 502, 505
  dragging, 306–316
  fields, displaying, 387–393
  gradient fills, 329–333
  icons and, 357–358, 455

patterns, 17–22
storing, in metafiles, 316–322
storing, as resources, 526–529
storing, without the VB PicClip control, 326–329
grid(s)
    cell alignment and, 257–265
    cell selection and, 265–275
    colors, 275–281
    Column Editor, using, 372–376
    controlling paging in, 285–290
    database programming and, 369–379, 386–398
    deleting rows and columns in, 281–285
    displaying memo and graphic fields in, 387–393
    drawing cells with, 257–265
    edit controls and, 187, 191
    enhancing the appearance of, 369–379
    inserting rows and columns in, 281–285
    overview of, 257–294
GRIDCLIP, 270–271
GRIDCLIU.DEX, 270
GRIDCLIU.PAS, 271
GRIDCONT, 292–294
GRIDCONU.DEX, 292–293
GRIDCONU.PAS, 293–294
GRIDED, 373–376
GRIDEDM.DEX, 373
GRIDEDM.PAS, 374
GRIDEDU.DEX, 374–375
GRIDEDU.PAS, 375–376
GRIDS.PAS, 282
GroupIndex property, 88, 94, 97, 154, 493

H

Handle property, 26, 338, 464
Height property, 292
help
    buttons, adding, to MDI forms, 108–112
    context-sensitive, for text, 474–476
    Delphi, 219
    flyover, supplying, 130–134
    icon, question-mark, 65–71
    menus, 142–146
HELPBTN, 66–67
HELPBTNU.DEX, 66
HELPBTNU.PAS, 66–67
HelpCommand method, 146
HELP_CONTEXT, 476
HelpContext property, 71, 130, 144, 474
HelpFile property, 474, 476

HELP_PARTIALKEY constant, 476
HELP_WM_HELP, 111
HEPCUR, 68–71
HEPCURU.DEX, 68
HEPCURU.PAS, 68–71
hidden forms, 71–78, 84–87
HideSelection, 276
hinting, 130–134, 470–472
HintPause property, 472
Hint property, 133
HINTS, 131–134
HintStr string, 472
HITNSU.DEX, 131–132
HITNSU.PAS, 132–133
HOLDBUTN, 347–350
HOLDBUTU.DEX, 347–348
HOLDBUTU.PAS, 348–350
HookMouse, 77
HOTKEY, 541–545
HOTKEY.DEX, 541–542
hotkeys, defining accelerator resources for, 139–142
HOTKEYU.PAS, 542–545
hPrevInst variable, 462
HTCAPTION, 17
HTSYSMENU, 17
HWND_BROADCAST, 548

I

ICO2BMP, 357–358
ICO2BMPU.DEX, 357
ICO2BMPU.PAS, 357–358
ICOBUTN, 339–341
ICOBUTNU.DEX, 339
ICOBUTNU.PAS, 340
icon(s)
    changing, while running, 449–451
    drawing attention to, 455–458
    files, converting, to .BMP files, 357–358
    help, question-mark, 65–71
    painting on, 451–455
    setting iconic states, 448–449
    used as button glyphs, 339–341
ICONTITL, 456–458
ICONTITLU.DEX, 456
ICONTITLU.PAS, 456–458
IfEscapement property, 295–297, 304
IMAGES directory, 325
Inch property, 320
INCRCH, 247–248

INCRCHU.DEX, 247
INCRCHU.PAS, 247–248
INI files, 81
INIFORM.PAS, 80–81
INITSIZ.DPR, 81
InitToolHelp32, 520
Install... command, 4
IntegralHeight property, 222
internal names, of objects, 4
internationalization, 566–572
INTL, 569–571
INTL.INC, 568
INTLU.DEX, 569–570
INTLU.PAS, 570–571
IntPower, 435–436
IS operator, 386
ISTOPMN, 164–166
ISTOPMNU.DEX, 164
ISTOPMNU.PAS, 164–166
IsTrueTypeText, 159
ISWIN95.PAS, 448
ISWIN95 UNIT, 447–448
ITEMDATA, 245
ItemHeight setting, 210
Items property, 245

Jazdzewski, Chuck, 84

KERNEL libraries, 483, 551
keyboard
    Backspace key, 350, 353
    Ctrl+Alt+Del keystroke combination, 512
    F1 key, 476
KeyUp method, 174
Kind property, 345
KNOWEXEC, 487, 506–511, 512
KNOWEXECU.DEX, 506–507
KNOWEXECU.PAS, 507–511

labels
    the Alignment property and, 366
    creating vertical/angled, 298–305
LANGE.RC, 568

LANGJ.RC, 567–568
LANGR.RC, 567
LANGS, 566–569
LANGS.DPR, 566
LANGS.RC, 567
language-flexible programs, 566–572
launching. *See also* loading applications
    and controlling other programs, 505–512
    programs, and waiting for them to end, 505
LayoutChanged method, 393
Layout property, 345
LBBMP, 217–220
LBBMPU.DEX, 217
LBBMPU.PAS, 217–219
LBCOMP, 240–242
LBCOMPU.DEX, 240–241
LBCOMPU.PAS, 241–242
LBDRAG, 231–234
LBDRAGU.DEX, 231–232
LBDRAGU.PAS, 232–233
LB_FINDSTRING, 248
LB_FINDSTRINGEXACT, 248
LBODVAR, 220–223
LBODVARU.DEX, 220–221
LBODVARU.PAS, 221–222
lbOwnerDrawFixed setting, 209, 210
LB_SELECTSTRING, 248
LB_SETHORIZONALEXTENT, 223
LB_SETTABSTOPS, 226
LBS_NOINTEGRALHEIGHT, 222
LBS_USETABSTOPS, 226, 228
LBTABS, 229–230
LBTABSU.DEX, 229–230
LBTABSU.PAS, 230
LDRAGMUL, 234–237
LDRAGMUU.DEX, 234–235
LDRAGMUU.PAS, 235–237
left-arrow (<), 237
Left property, 129, 362
Length function, 208
Lines property, 179, 193
LineTo, 317
list(s). *See also* list boxes
    of active processes, 514–521
    of active tasks, 512–514
    storing objects in, 411–415
list box(es)
    changes in item height in, 220–223
    creating, with incremental searches, 246–248
    displaying bitmaps in, 217–220

dragging items in, 231–237
handling items wider than, 223–226
objects, enhancing, 223–231
scrolling in, 226, 248–254
scrolling width of, 226
sorting, 237–243
using tabs in, 226–231
ListLong, 410, 411
ListSingle, 410
LoadBitmap, 338, 529
LoadCursor, 529, 531
LoadData method, 55, 56
LoadFromFile method, 193–194
LoadFromResourceID method, 529
LoadFromResourceName method, 529
loading applications
displaying splash screens while, 459–461
loading DLLs, 565–566, 571–572, 574
loading sample programs, 4
overview of, 458–464
resource error messages when, 524
LoadLibrary, 571
LoadResource, 538
LoadStr, 535
LoadString, 535
LoadTheForm, 558
localization, 531
LockWindowUpdate, 81–83, 102, 365–366
LONE, 90–93
LONE1U.DEX, 90
LONE1U.PAS, 90–91
LONE2U.DEX, 91
LONE2U.PAS, 91–92
LONE3U.DEX, 92
LONE3U.PAS, 92–93
LongInt, 410, 423, 427, 553
LOOP, 477–479
Looping data field, 479
loops, unresponsive programs in, 476–479
LOOPU.DEX, 477
LOOPU.PAS, 477–479
lParam, 93, 505, 540, 548

◆ M

Macintosh, 143
MACRO DLLMAC.TXT, 564–565
macro languages, calling DLLs from, 563–565
MANAGE, 44–46
MANAGE1U.DEX, 44

MANAGE1U.PAS, 44–46
MANAGE2U.DEX, 46–47
Margin property, 345
MASKDEM, 323–326
MASKDEMU.DEX, 323–324
MASKDEMU.PAS, 324–325
Max, 422, 427
maximized activity
maximized MDI forms, 81–82, 87
requests to run applications as maximized, 472–474
MaxLength setting, 181
MAXMDI, 82–83
MAXMDI1U.DEX, 82
MAXMDI1U.PAS, 82–83
MAXMDI2U.DEX, 83
MAXMDI2U.PAS, 83
MaxPt field, 60
MaxTabs constant, 228
MB_MENUBARBREAK, 159
MDIChildCount property, 43, 88
MDI (Multiple Document Interface) forms, 33–34
adding background wallpaper to, 103–107
adding Windows 95 help buttons to, 108–112
hiding/showing, 84–87
managing multiple form instances without, 43–47
maximized, 81–82, 87
merged menus and, 160–163
overview of, 79–112
permitting just one type of, 89–93
placing, 79–81
referencing, 87–89
sizing, 79–81
MDIHIDE, 84–87
MDIHIDU1.DEX, 84
MDIHIDU1.PAS, 85
MDIHIDU2.DEX, 86
MDIHIDU2.PAS, 86
MDIHLP, 108–112
MDIHLP1U.DEX, 108
MDIHLP1U.PAS, 108
MDIHLP2U.DEX, 109
MDIHLP2U.PAS, 110
media player, playing WAV files without, 495–499
memo(s)
adding Undo commands to, 182–184
cutting and copying from, 188–191
event handler errors and, 191–193
fields, displaying, 387–393

with full row/column support, 172–176
sorting lines in, 177–179
memory. *See also* memory-mapped files
32K limit, 193–194, 248
DLLs and, 572, 573, 574
the packed keyword and, 441
playing sounds from, 499–501
Memory property, 501
memory-mapped files
definition of, 73
hidden forms and, 73, 77
MEMSND, 500–501
MEMSNDU.DEX, 500
MEMSNDU.PAS, 500–501
MEMUNDO, 182–184
MEMUNDOU.DEX, 182–183
MEMUNDOU.PAS, 183–184
menu(s)
adding, to dialog forms, 35–36
appearance of, 147–160
check marks, changing, 150–155
creating, for MDI forms, 94–98
creating structures for, at runtime, 163
help, 142–146
items, owner-draw, 156–160
MDI forms and, 94–98, 160–163
merged, changing properties of, 160–163
"nuts and bolts," 160–166
pop-up, 137–142
rows and columns, reporting, 167–171
shared event handlers and, 163–166
top-level items on, 163–166
MENUACT, 539–540
MENUACTU.DEX, 539–540
MENUACTU.PAS, 540
Menu Designer, 141, 144, 163
Menus.ShortCut, 142
MERGE, 94–98
MERGE1U.DEX, 94–95
MERGE1U.PAS, 95–96
MERGE2U.DEX, 96
MERGE2U.PAS, 96–97
Merge method, 163
MessageBeep, 4
MessageDlg, 61–65, 146
messages. *See also* specific messages
controlling screen savers with, 548–550
responding to undocumented, 538–540

sending undocumented, 541–545
using, overview of, 538–550
metafiles, 316–333
methods (listed by name)
Add, 410
AddMasked, 220
AppOnHelp, 476
AppOnHint, 133
AppOnMessage, 455, 466
Begin Drag, 316
Button1Click, 125
CaptionGlyph, 344
Cascade, 88
CheckBox1Click, 47
classs, 435
CMFontChanged, 304
CreateParams, 10–11, 16, 33, 35, 50, 80, 228
CreateWindowHandle, 112
DefaultHandler, 77–78, 548
DestroyWindowHandle, 111
DrawCell, 393
Draw, 216, 341
DrawNewButton, 29–30
DrawTitle, 26
FindText, 208
FormCreate, 146, 420
GetAttributes, 176, 304
GetLoner, 93
GetPalette, 332
GetTextBuf, 55
GetTextLen, 55, 208
GetValue, 176
HelpCommand, 146
KeyUp, 174
LayoutChanged, 393
LoadData, 55, 56
LoadFromFile, 193–194
LoadFromResourceID, 529
LoadFromResourceName, 529
Merge, 163
MouseDown, 393
MouseUp, 174
OnClick, 430
OnExitCell, 272
PaintUnderIcon, 107
Polygon, 30, 428, 430
PolyLine, 320
ReadSection, 22

RowHeightsChanged, 393
SaveToFile, 320, 358
Self, 493, 495
SetAngle, 304
SetTexture, 23
SetTrue, 493
SetWindowPos, 86–87, 102
ShowModal, 43, 401
StoreData, 55, 56
StretchDraw, 216, 220, 341
TextOut, 213, 262
TextRect, 26, 262, 281, 372
TextWidth, 228
Tile, 88
UnMerge, 163
WidthOfChar, 229
WidthOfString, 229
WmDropFiles, 469
WM_NCACTIVATE, 17, 23, 27, 29, 30
WM_NCHITTEST, 17, 30, 71
microprocessors. *See* CPUs (central processing
    units) minimized activity
  changing icons, 449–451
  drawing attention to icons, 455–458
  overview of, 447–458
  painting on icons, 451–455
  requests to run applications as minimized,
    472–474
  setting iconic states, 448–449
MODALD, 40–43
MODALD1U.DEX, 40
MODALD1U.PAS, 41
MODALD2U.DEX, 41–42
MODALD2U.PAS, 42–43
MODEDID, 384–386
MODEDIDU.DEX, 384
MODEDIDU.PAS, 384–386
MODEDIT, 185–187
MODEDITU.DEX, 185
MODEDITU.PAS, 186–187
ModifyMenu, 147, 159
MODMER1U.DEX, 160
MODMER1U.PAS, 161
MODMER2U.DEX, 161
MODMER2U.PAS, 162
MODMERGE, 160–163
MODMSGD, 61–65
MODMSGDU.DEX, 61–62
MODMSGDU.PAS, 62–64
Module32First, 521
Module32Next, 521

mouse. *See* dragging and dropping; hinting
MouseDown method, 393
MOUSEHOOK, 72–73
MOUSEHOOK.DPR, 72–73
MouseUp method, 174
Move command, 17
MSecsPerDay, 416
MULFRM/, 50–51
MULFRM1U.DEX, 54
MULFRM1U.PAS, 54–55
MULFRM2U.DEX, 52
MULFRM2U.PAS, 52–53
MULFRM3U.DEX, 51
MULFRM3U.PAS, 51–52
MULFRM4U.DEX, 50
MULFRM4U.PAS, 50–51
multipage forms, reducing resource consumption
  by, 48–56
multitasking, 476, 501–521
Murphy's Law, 545
MUSOVER, 471–472
MUSOVERU.DEX, 471
MUSOVERU.PAS, 471–472
MyEnumWindowsProc, 487
MyRotatePrint, 295–297
MYTITLE, 24–26
MYTITLEU.DEX, 24
MYTITLEU.PAS, 24–26

NewMenu, 142
NewPopupMenu, 142
NewSubMenu, 142, 166
NOPOP, 138–139
NOPOPU.DEX, 138
NOPOPU.PAS, 138–139
NowString, 553
numbers
  alignment of, in grids, 262–265
  floating-point, 416–422, 553, 573
  raising, to a specified power, 435–436
NumGlyphs, 345

Object Inspector, 116, 129, 176
Object Pascal, 2, 405, 407–445
Objects property, 245, 246
object variables, problems creating, 434–435

OBM_CHECKBOXES, 327, 329
ODDFRAME, 30–32
ODDFRAMU.DEX, 30
ODDFRAMU.PAS, 31–32
ODMENU, 156–160
ODMENUU.DEX, 156–157
ODMENUU.PAS, 157–159
OnActivate event, 474
ONCE, 461–463
ONCE.DPR, 461–462
OnChange event handler, 192, 245, 248, 305, 415
OnClick event handler, 4, 60, 93, 98, 116,
        118, 134, 136, 163, 166, 179, 191, 237, 245,
        269, 272, 284–285, 345–346, 353, 362, 366,
        386, 479, 492–493, 545, 550
OnClick method, 430
OnClick property, 140, 154
OnClose event handler, 35, 43
OnColumnClick event handler, 521
OnCompare event handler, 239–240, 243
OnCreate event handler, 17, 23, 47, 56, 60, 77, 80,
        128, 133, 150, 159, 166, 187, 216, 253, 294,
        332, 341, 353, 361, 386, 410, 422, 427, 451,
        458, 463, 466, 469, 472, 476, 492, 498, 501,
        571
OnDblClick event handler, 116
OnDestroy event handler, 572
OnDragDrop event handler, 233, 237, 306
OnDragOver event handler, 233, 237, 306, 312,
        316, 326, 365–366
OnDrawCell event handler, 257, 259, 262, 265,
        269, 275–276, 279, 281, 290
OnDrawColumnCell event handler, 372, 379
OnDrawDataCell event handler, 372, 379
OnDrawItem event handler, 209, 212, 216, 219,
        220, 253
OnEditButtonClick event, 376
OnEndDrag event handler, 234, 309, 312, 316
OnExitCell method, 272
OnExit event handler, 272, 275, 279
OnFind event handler, 208
OnKeyDown event handler, 182
OnKeyPress event handler, 182, 193, 245, 353
OnKeyUp event handler, 269, 289
OnKeyUp property, 174
OnMeasureItem event handler, 209, 220
OnMinimize event handler, 458
OnMouseDown event handler, 309, 316, 326, 350
OnMouseUp event handler, 71, 269, 350, 353

OnMouseUp property, 174
OnPaint event handler, 17, 289, 451
OnPopup event handler, 139
OnPosChanged event, 172, 174
OnReplace event handler, 208
OnResize event handler, 47, 362
OnRestore event handler, 458
OnSelectCell event handler, 257, 272, 275, 289
OnSelectionChange event, 168, 207
OnShowHint property, 472
OnTimer event handler, 61, 65, 350, 368, 422,
        451, 455, 458
OOP (Object Oriented Programming), 47–48, 72
OPARR2, 428–430
OPARR2U.DEX, 428
OPARR2U.PAS, 429–430
open arrays, passing partial arrays as 423–430
OPENARR, 424–428
OPENARRU.DEX, 424–425
OPENARRU.PAS, 425–427
Options.AlwaysShowEditor property, 187
Options menu, 4
Options property, 266
owner-draw
    combo boxes, 243–246
    list boxes, 209–223
    menu items, 156–160

P

P_ABOUT.PAS, 175–176
PACKDEMO, 442–445
PACKDEMU.DEX, 442–443
PACKDEMU.PAS, 443–445
packed keyword, 441–442
paDialog setting, 304
PageControl, 126
paging, in grids, 285–290
painting, on forms, 17–32
PaintUnderIcon method, 107
PaletteIndex, 332–333
paMultiSelect setting, 304
Panel2DragOverA setting, 365–366
Panel2DragOverB setting, 365–366
Panel2DragOverC setting, 365–366
P_ANGLE.PAS, 301
P_ANGLEU.DEX, 301–302
P_ANGLEU.PAS, 302–303
PANPROB, 359–361

PANPROBU.DEX, 359
PANPROBU.PAS, 360–361
Paradox, multirecord objects, duplicating, 394–398
parameters
    DLLs and, 573, 574
    open array, 423, 434
    type-safe open array, 434
    using variable numbers of, 422–423
    using variable types of, 430–434
ParentFont property, 65
partial arrays, passing, as open arrays, 423–430
PAS program listings, 2–4
Pascal, 47, 166
password-protected screen savers, 548
patterns, 17–22
PChar, 492, 535, 548, 553, 558, 569, 571, 573
PgForm, 55
PGFORM.PAS, 49–50
PICCLIP, 327–329
PICCLIPU.DEX, 327
PICCLIPU.PAS, 328
pixel(s)
    location, dragging files and, 469
    which unexpectedly change color, 438–440
PlaceControls, 292, 294
PlainText property, 194
Planets array, 47
PlaySound, 499, 538
pmXor setting, 312
poDefault setting, 3
poDesigned setting, 79
Polygon method, 30, 428, 430
PolyLine method, 320
PopupComponent property, 138
PopupMenu property, 137–138, 139
poScreenCenter, 461
Position property, 3, 79
Posn property, 172
POWERS.PAS, 435–436
POWERS UNIT, 435–436
Process32First, 520
Process32Next, 520
processors. See CPUs (central processing units)
program listings. See code listings
programs, communicating between, 545–548
Project Options dialog box, 40, 55, 144, 458, 461, 463, 524
PROPERTY EDITOR TABOUTBOXPROPERTY, 175–176
Protected property, 303

PtMinTrackSize field, 60
Public property, 303
Published property, 303

R

radio buttons, deselecting, 350–353
RadioItem property, 154
RADMENU, 151–155
RADMENUU.DEX, 151
RADMENUU.PAS, 151–152
RADMN32, 154–155
RADMN32U.DEX, 154–155
RADMN32U.PAS, 155
RCMemo, 174–176, 179
reading files, written by older files, 441–445
ReadSection method, 22
ReadTheForm, 558
Real data type, 574
rectangle(s)
    function, storing graphics created with, 317
    "rubber-band" drawings of, 310–312
RegisterClass, 434
Register procedure, 176
RegisterPropertyEditor, 176
RegisterWindowsMessage, 77, 546, 548
REGMSG, 546–548
REGMSGU.DEX, 546
REGMSGU.PAS, 547–548
REPEAT loops, 476
Reset, 422
resource(s)
    basics, 523–538
    disappearance, avoiding, 524
    error messages, 524
    files, creating, 525
    files, including multiple languages in, 531–535
    storing bitmaps as, 526–529
Resource Workshop, 525
Rewrite, 422
RGB function, 333
RichEdit, 193–208
RichEdit1SelectionChange event handler, 171
right-arrow (>), 237
RightRec, 445
RITEHELP, 143–144
RITEHLPU.DEX, 143
RITEHLPU.PAS, 143–144
RITELEFT, 260–262
RITELEFU.DEX, 260

RITELEFU.PAS, 261
row(s)
    based on field values, 376–379
    deleting, 281–285
    highlighting, 376–379
    reporting, 167–171
    resizing, 292
RowCount property, 397
RowHeightsChanged method, 393
Row property, 172
Rows property, 281–282
RUBAND, 310–312
RUBANDU.DEX, 310–311
RUBANDU.PAS, 311–312
rules, the benefits of breaking, 257
RUNMIN, 472–474
RUNMINU.DEX, 472
RUNMINU.PAS, 473
runtime
    arrays whose sizes vary at, 408–411
    arrays with fixed sizes determined at, 407–408
    choosing a main form at, 463–464
    creating component arrays at, 119–121
    creating submenu resources at, 142
    loading DLLs at, 565–566
    panel shifts at, 358–362

S

SaveToFile method, 320, 358
SaveToFile property, 194
Schulman, Andrew, 539
SciNames variable, 253
Screen.FormCount, 43
Screen.Forms, 47, 65
Screen object, 159, 531
screen savers, controlling, 548–550
SCRNSV, 549–550
SCRNSVU.DEX, 549
SCRNSVU.PAS, 549–550
SCROLL, 249–253
ScrollBar, 181
scrolling, in list boxes, 226, 248–254
SCROLLU.DEX, 249–250
SCROLLU.PAS, 250–253
ScrollWidth, 226
searches, incremental, 246–248
SelAttributes property, 194
Self method, 493, 495

SELGRID, 267–269
SELGRIDU.DEX, 267
SELGRIDU.PAS, 267–269
SelStart property, 167, 171, 182, 193
SelText, 187, 208
SEM_FAILCRITICALERRORS, 128
Sender parameter, 134
SendMessage, 548
SetAngle method, 304
SetBkMode, 281
Set button, 545
SetCapture, 71
SetClipboardViewer, 504
SetErrorMode, 128
SetFocus, 87, 102
SetMenuItemBitmaps, 153
SetSystemPaletteUse, 333
SetTabsDlg, 228, 231
SetTabsPix, 228, 231
SetTextAlign, 212, 213, 262, 372
SetTexture method, 23
SetTrue method, 493
SetWindowPos function, 466
SetWindowPos method, 86–87, 102
SGRIDNO, 276–279
SGRIDNOU.DEX, 276–277
SGRIDNOU.PAS, 277–278
SHAR32, 401–404
SHAR321U.DEX, 401–402
SHAR321U.PAS, 403
SHAR322U.DEX, 403–404
SHAR32M.DEX, 404
SHAREV, 135–136
SHAREVU.DEX, 135
SHAREVU.PAS, 135–136
sharing tables, 398–404
SHARTB1U.DEX, 398–399
SHARTB1U.PAS, 399–400
SHARTB2U.DEX, 400–401
SHARTB2U.PAS, 401
SHARTBL, 398–401
ShellExecute, 511
ShortCut data type, 545
ShortCut function, 141, 142
Shortcut property, 141
ShortCutToText, 545
ShowAccelChar, 304
ShowHint property, 133
ShowModal method, 43, 401
Show Problem button, 362

ShowTheForm, 558
ShowWindow, 86
SIFRAMMU.PAS, 10
SilentWav, 499
SIZCTRL, 58–60
SIZCTRLU.DEX, 58
SIZCTRLU.PAS, 58–60
SIZFRAM, 10–11
SIZFRAMU.DEX, 10
Sleep, 366
Slice, 423–430
snapshots, of system status, 520
SND_ASYNC, 498–499, 538
SND_LOOP, 499
SND_MEMORY, 499
SND_NODEFAULT, 499
SND_NOSTOP, 499
SNDPLAY, 496–499
sndPlaySound, 495–496, 498–499, 501, 538
SNDPLAYU.DEX, 496
SNDPLAYU.PAS, 497–498
SND_RESOURCE, 538
SND_SYNC, 499
sorting
    lines in memo boxes, 177–179
    list boxes, 237–243
SORTMEM, 177–179
SORTMEMU.DEX, 177
SORTMEMU.PAS, 178–179
sound files
    embedding, 535–538
    playing, from memory, 499–501
    playing, without the media player, 495–499
SPLASH, 459–461
SPLASH.DPR, 460
splash screens, displaying, 459–461
SPLITP, 313–315, 363–365
SPLITPU.DEX, 363
SPLITPU.PAS, 314–315, 363–365
splitter bars, creating, 312–315, 362–366
sprites
    definition of, 333
    dragging, 323–326
SPSPLSHU.DEX, 459–460
Spy, 484
SRCAND mode, 326
SRCINVERT mode, 326
ssNone setting, 181
Stack Checking option, 192

status-bar hints, supplying, 130–134
StdCall, 107, 493, 552, 554, 558, 572
STDCTRLS.PAS, 239
STDHLP, 145–146
STDHLPU.DEX, 145
STDHLPU.PAS, 145–146
STILL_ACTIVE, 512
StoreData method, 55, 56
StretchDraw method, 216, 220, 341
StringOf, 434
strings, padding/chopping, to a given length, 441
STRRES, 532–535
STRRESMK.BAT, 532
STRRESU.DEX, 533–534
STRRESU.PAS, 534–535
Style property, 209, 464, 493
styles. *See also* fonts
    in list boxes/combo boxes, 210–213
    using multiple, 194
    window, unusual, 9–17
SW_HIDE, 86
SW_SHOWDEFAULT, 474
symbols
    @ (at sign), 366, 572
    [] (brackets), 166
    $ (dollar sign), 565
    < (left-arrow), 237
    > (right-arrow), 237
    | (vertical bar), 133–134
SYSMENU, 465–466
SYSMENUU.DEX, 465
SYSMENUU.PAS, 465–466
system menu, adding an always-on-top command
    to, 464–466
system status, snapshots of, 520

T

tables, sharing, 398–404
TAbout, 176
TAboutBoxProperty, 4
tabs, used in list boxes, 226–231
TabSheet, 126
Tab Width property, 229
taCenter setting, 369, 372
Tagalog, 531
Tag property, 350, 479
TA_LEFT, 262
TANGLELABEL, 298–304, 305

TANGLEPROPERTY, 301–304
TaskFirst, 514
TASKS, 513–514
TASKS32, 515–521
TASKS32U.DEX, 515–516
TASKS32U.PAS, 517–520
TASKSU.DEX, 513
TASKSU.PAS, 513–514
TA_UPDATECP, 212–213
TBEdit, 386
TBitBtn, 345
TBitmap, 316, 339, 393, 455, 529
TButtonControl, 136
TCanvas, 26, 428
TCheckBox, 136
TColumn, 379
TComponent, 118, 121
TControl, 134, 353
TCustomEdit, 136, 171, 187, 191, 386
TCustomGrid, 187, 292, 386, 393
TCustomLabel, 303
TDataObj, 415
TDateTime, 416–422
TDBCtrlGrid, 394
TDBGrid, 386, 387, 393
TDBGRIDBLOB, 388–393
TEdit, 122, 125, 180, 182
TESTDLLF, 560–563
TESTDLLF.MAK, 560
TESTDLLF.TXT, 561–563
text. *See also* fonts; labels
    the 32K limit and, 193–194, 248
    centering, 260–262
    drawing, at different angles, 295–297
    edit boxes, which comes out backwards,
        192–193
    justifying, 260–262
    manipulating, overview of, 176–191
    sorting lines of, 177–179
    supplying context-sensitive help for, 474–476
    word-wrapped, 65, 181, 304, 341–344
TextMetric, 492–493
TextOut, 212, 213
TextOut method, 213, 262
Text property, 136, 193, 208
TextRect method, 26, 262, 281, 372
TEXTUR1U.DEX, 18–19
TEXTUR1U.PAS, 19–20
TEXTUR2U.DEX, 21
TEXTUR2U.PAS, 21–22

TEXTURE, 18–23
TextWidth method, 228
TFont, 295
TFontStyle, 493
TForm, 7, 10, 47–48, 50, 55–56, 65, 79, 81, 88, 93,
    98, 464
TForm2, 47, 87, 90, 163
TForm3, 90
TF parameter, 487
TGroupBox, 126
TIcon, 316
Tile command, 94, 99–103
Tile method, 88
TImage, 17, 219, 316, 327, 357, 505
TImageList, 220
time/date data types, 416–422
TimeToStr, 419, 422
TIMMATH, 416–418
TIMMATHU.DEX, 416–417
TIMMATHU.PAS, 418–419
TINYT, 12–17
TINYT95U.DEX, 13
TINYT95U.PAS, 14
TINYTMU.DEX, 12
TINYTMU.PAS, 13
TINYTTU.DEX, 14–15
TINYTTU.PAS, 15–16
TITLBTN, 27–30
TITLBTNU.DEX, 27–28
TITLBTNU.PAS, 28–29
title bars
    adding buttons to, 27–30
    "tiny title bar" effect for, 12–17
TLabel, 11, 136, 303
TList, 121–122, 126, 246, 408, 410, 411–415
TListBox, 226
TListBoxComp, 238–240
TListBoxHorz, 4, 224–226, 228, 415, 469
TListBoxStrings, 239
TListBoxTabs, 227–231
TMemo, 5, 125, 167, 174, 180, 182, 187, 505
TMenuItem, 134, 141, 150, 154
TMessage, 540
TMetafile, 316–317, 320, 322
TMetafileCanvas, 320, 322
TNotebook, 48
TObject, 415
Toolbox window, 12
ToolHelp, 514
ToolHelp32, 520

TOOLHELP.DLL, 512
Top property, 129
TPageControl, 48
TPageForm, 55
TPanel, 126
TParser object, 23
TPopupMenu, 141
TRadioButton, 136
TRichEdit, 5, 167–168, 187, 193–194
TrueType fonts, 295–297, 487–488, 492–493, 304
TSOBJ, 412–415
TSOBJU.DEX, 412–413
TSOBJU.PAS, 413–415
TString, 435
TStringGrid, 191
TStringGridCont, 290–292, 294
TStringList, 179, 281
TTabbedNotebook, 48
TTaskEntry, 514
Turbo Debugger for Windows, 430
TurboPower Software, 108
TurboVision, 166
TURNTX, 296–297
TURNTX.DEX, 296
TURNTX.PAS, 296–297
TVarRec, 434
TWinControl, 125, 292
TWMNoParams, 540
TWRAPBTN, 342–346

Undo actions, 182–184, 188, 207
undocumented messages, 539, 541–545
UnHookMouse, 77
UNIT1.DEX, 3
UnMerge method, 163
UNRADGP, 351–353
UNRADGPU.DEX, 351
UNRADGPU.PAS, 351–353
unresponsive programs, 476–479
UPDMEMF, 381–382
UPDMEMFU.DEX, 381
UPDMEMFU.PAS, 382
USER libraries, 483, 551

VAR keyword, 563
VAR parameter, 240, 553

VARREC, 431–434
VARRECU.DEX, 431
VARRECU.PAS, 434–433
VCL code, 93
vCol parameter, 257, 275
VER_PLATFORM_WIN32_WINDOWS, 112
vertical bar (|), 133–134
Visible property, 77, 79, 140, 451
Visual Basic (VB), 12, 115, 479
    DLLs and, 552, 553, 560–563, 565, 574
    PicClip control, simulating, 326–329
vRow parameter, 257, 275
VSARRAY, 409–410
VSARRAYU.DEX, 409
VSARRAYU.PAS, 409–410

WaitForSingleObject, 463
WALLP, 103–107
wallpaper
    256-color mode and, 333
    in MDI forms, 103–107
WALLPCU.DEX, 106
WALLPCU.PAS, 106
WALLPMU.DEX, 103–104
WALLPMU.PAS, 104–105
WantReturns property, 181–182
WAV files
    embedding, 535–538
    playing, from memory, 499–501
    playing, without the media player, 495–499
WaveOutGetNumDevs, 498
WAVRES, 536–538
WAVRESMK.BAT, 536
WAVRESU.DEX, 536
WAVRESU.PAS, 536–538
WH_MOUSE, 72
WhichGrid, 487
WHILE loops, 476
WidthOfChar method, 229
WidthOfString method, 229
Width property, 292
window(s)
    lists, 89, 93, 484–487
    sizing, 57–60, 79–81
    styles, unusual, 9–17
WindowMenu property, 93
Windows 3.x, 4–5, 573
    the Application object and, 447, 451, 455, 467–469

captions and, 26–27
CharMap, 383
dialog forms and, 36–37
edit controls and, 192, 193
File Manager, accepting files dragged from, 467–469
help button icons and, 67–71
help menus and, 142–144
list boxes and, 248
resources and, 525
task lists and, 512
title bars, 16
undocumented features, 539, 545
Windows 95, 5, 9, 573
  adding buttons in, 27
  the Application object and, 447–449, 451, 452, 455, 458, 463, 465–469, 472
  captions and, 26–27
  CharMap, 383
  component lists and, 126
  database programming and, 369, 383
  detecting, 447–448
  dialog forms and, 37
  edit controls, 192–194, 208
  event handler errors and, 192
  Explorer, accepting files dragged from, 467–469
  file extensions and, 554
  help, 65–67, 71, 108–112, 142–144, 154, 159
  hotkeys and, 545
  list boxes and, 248
  MDI forms and, 81
  menus and, 142–144, 154, 159
  question-mark help icon, 65–67
  run maximized requests, 472
  sounds, 495
  task lists and, 512
  title bars in, 12
  Toolhelp functions and, 514, 520
  WordPad, 208
Windows for Workgroups, 5, 565
Windows NT, 5, 16, 484
  the Application object and, 447, 451, 455, 463, 467, 472
  captions and, 26–27
  CharMap, 383
  dialog forms and, 37
  DLLs and, 554
  edit controls and, 193–194
  event handler errors and, 192
  help, 65–67, 71, 112, 142–144

list boxes and, 248
  menus and, 142–144, 154
  Toolhelp functions and, 514, 520
WindowState property, 81, 448
WindowState setting, 79
WinExec, 511
WinExecAndGetHWnd, 511
WingDings font, 11, 153, 350
Winsight, 484
WinWord (Word for Windows), 487, 564
WM_CHANGECBCHAIN, 504
WM_COMMAND, 139, 292
WM_DRAWCLIPBOARD, 504, 505
WM_DRAWITEM, 156, 159
WM_DROPFILES, 469
WmDropFiles method, 469
WM_ENTERMENULOOP, 540
WM_ERASEBKGND, 106–107, 329, 332–333
WM_EX_CONTEXTHELP, 111
WM_EXITMENULOOP, 540
WM_GETHOTKEY, 541, 545
WM_GETMINMAXINFO, 57, 60
WM_HELP, 111
WM_ICONERASEBKGND, 107
WM_MDICREATE, 111
WM_MEASUREITEM, 156, 159
WM_MOVE, 47
WM_NCACTIVATE method, 17, 23, 27, 29, 30
WM_NCHITTEST method, 17, 30, 71
WM_NCLBUTTONDOWN, 30
WM_NCPAINT, 23, 26, 27, 29
WM_NHITTEST, 11
WM_PAINT, 5, 451, 455
WM_PAINTICON, 455
WM_SETHOTKEY, 541, 545
WM_SETICON, 451
WM_SETMDIMENU, 93, 98
WM_SETTEXT, 17, 27, 29
WM_SYSCOMMAND, 466, 550
WndHandle, 511
WordBasic, 552, 564, 565
Word for Windows (WinWord), 487, 564
WordPad, 208
word-wrapped text, 65, 181, 304, 341–344
WordWrap property, 181
wParam, 78, 93, 504–505, 540, 545, 548, 550
WRAPBTN, 345–346
WRAPBTNU.DEX, 345–346
WRAPBTNU.PAS, 346
Write, 422

WriteLn, 422
WrongRec, 445
WS_CHILD, 9
WS_DLGFRAME, 10, 11–12
WS_EX_MDICHILD, 111
WS_EX_TOOLWINDOW, 16
WS_POPUP, 9, 10, 11–12
wsMaximized setting, 79, 81
wsMinimized setting, 448

X-Y coordinates, 297, 304, 326
XORs, 326, 455

YELPAD, 286–290
YELPAD.DAT, 290
YELPADU.DEX, 286
YELPADU.PAS, 286–289

Zindler, Uli, 87

Introducing the Foundations™ Series
For Working Programmers...

IDG BOOKS WORLDWIDE

Books in the *Foundations* series are designed to complement the way professional programmers work. Written only by seasoned software developers and trainers who understand programming, *Foundations* books help lighten workloads and provide solutions to development problems.

Foundations™ of Visual C++ Programming for Windows 95

by Paul Yao & Joseph Yao

Here is the organized guide for working programmers who want to master Visual C++. Includes tips on tools, internals, design issues, avoiding common mistakes, testing problems, and working sample code from the book. Bonus includes a hypertext version of the book, plus all the source code.

EXPERT AUTHOR PROFILE

Paul Yao (Bellevue, WA) is president of The Paul Yao Company. He is a contributing editor to *Microsoft Systems Journal* and has been a regular instructor of Windows programming since 1986. Joseph Yao (Fairfax, VA) is a principal software engineer at Hadron, Inc., and a C++ expert.

ISBN: 1-56884-321-6
$39.99 USA/$54.99 Canada
includes one CD-ROM

Foundations™ of Visual Basic "X" Programming

by Doug Hergert

This book lays the foundations of Visual Basic programming for working programmers. Comprehensive stand-alone tutorial chapters make programming a snap. Includes working sample code from the book and Visual Basic shareware.

EXPERT AUTHOR PROFILE

Doug Hergert (San Francisco, CA) has been writing about computers since 1981 and two of his past books have been bestsellers. He is also the author of IDG's *QBasic Programming For Dummies*.®

ISBN: 1-56884-320-8
$39.99 USA/$54.99 Canada
includes one CD-ROM

Foundations™ of Delphi Programming

by Tom Swan

Now working programmers can find a complete guide to Delphi. This book shows programmers how to produce programs as powerful and efficient as ones written in C and C++, and offers a comprehensive overview of Delphi and rapid application development. Bonus CD includes a handy, hypertext version of the book!

EXPERT AUTHOR PROFILE

Tom Swan (Key West, FL) is an internationally acclaimed author. He has written more than 30 computer books including IDG's bestselling *Type & Learn*™ *C*. Swan is also a former columnist for *PC Techniques* and has written for *Dr. Dobb's Journal* and *PC World*.

ISBN: 1-56884-347-X
$39.99 USA/$54.99 Canada
includes one CD-ROM

Foundations™ of World Wide Web Programming with HTML and CGI

by Ed Tittel, Mark Gaither, Sebastian Hassinger, & Mike Erwin

This book guides working programmers to create cutting-edge World Wide Web documents using Hypertext Markup Language (HTML) and advanced scripting techniques. Knowing how to produce and post Web pages is one of the most marketable skills around and the *Foundations*™ series will give programmers an extra advantage! Extra CD includes valuable Net programming tools.

EXPERT AUTHOR PROFILE

Ed Tittel (Austin, TX) is the author of ten computer books, including IDG's *HTML For Dummies*®. Mark Gaither (Cedar Park, TX) is a software engineer at HaL Software Systems. Sebastian Hassinger (Austin, TX) is an Internet consultant and an expert in CGI programming. Mike Erwin (Austin, TX) is an expert on Internet connectivity.

ISBN: 1-56884-703-3
$39.99 US/$54.99 Canada
includes one CD-ROM

FOR MORE INFORMATION OR TO PLACE AN ORDER CALL 1.800.762.2974

For volume discounts & special orders please call Tony Real, Special Sales, at 415.655.3048

ORDER FORM

Order Center: **(800) 762-2974** *(8 a.m.–6 p.m., EST, weekdays)*

5/8/95

Quantity	ISBN	Title	Price	Total

Shipping & Handling Charges

	Description	First book	Each additional book	Total
Domestic	Normal	$4.50	$1.50	$
	Two Day Air	$8.50	$2.50	$
	Overnight	$18.00	$3.00	$
International	Surface	$8.00	$8.00	$
	Airmail	$16.00	$16.00	$
	DHL Air	$17.00	$17.00	$

*For large quantities call for shipping & handling charges.
**Prices are subject to change without notice.

Ship to:

Name _____

Company _____

Address _____

City/State/Zip _____

Daytime Phone _____

Payment: ☐ Check to IDG Books (US Funds Only)

☐ VISA ☐ MasterCard ☐ American Express

Card # _____ Expires _____

Signature _____

Subtotal _____

CA residents add
applicable sales tax _____

IN, MA, and MD
residents add
5% sales tax _____

IL residents add
6.25% sales tax _____

RI residents add
7% sales tax _____

TX residents add
8.25% sales tax _____

Shipping _____

Total _____

Please send this order form to:

IDG Books Worldwide
7260 Shadeland Station, Suite 100
Indianapolis, IN 46256

*Allow up to 3 weeks for delivery.
Thank you!*

IDG BOOKS WORLDWIDE REGISTRATION CARD

RETURN THIS REGISTRATION CARD FOR FREE CATALOG

Title of this book: Delphi™ Programming Problem Solver™

My overall rating of this book: ☐ Very good [1] ☐ Good [2] ☐ Satisfactory [3] ☐ Fair [4] ☐ Poor [5]

How I first heard about this book:

☐ Found in bookstore; name: [6] ☐ Book review: [7]

☐ Advertisement: [8] ☐ Catalog: [9]

☐ Word of mouth; heard about book from friend, co-worker, etc.: [10] ☐ Other: [11]

What I liked most about this book:

What I would change, add, delete, etc., in future editions of this book:

Other comments:

Number of computer books I purchase in a year: ☐ 1 [12] ☐ 2-5 [13] ☐ 6-10 [14] ☐ More than 10 [15]

I would characterize my computer skills as: ☐ Beginner [16] ☐ Intermediate [17] ☐ Advanced [18] ☐ Professional [19]

I use ☐ DOS [20] ☐ Windows [21] ☐ OS/2 [22] ☐ Unix [23] ☐ Macintosh [24] ☐ Other: [25]_____
(please specify)

I would be interested in new books on the following subjects:
(please check all that apply, and use the spaces provided to identify specific software)

☐ Word processing: [26] ☐ Spreadsheets: [27]

☐ Data bases: [28] ☐ Desktop publishing: [29]

☐ File Utilities: [30] ☐ Money management: [31]

☐ Networking: [32] ☐ Programming languages: [33]

☐ Other: [34]

I use a PC at (please check all that apply): ☐ home [35] ☐ work [36] ☐ school [37] ☐ other: [38]_____

The disks I prefer to use are ☐ 5.25 [39] ☐ 3.5 [40] ☐ other: [41]_____

I have a CD ROM: ☐ yes [42] ☐ no [43]

I plan to buy or upgrade computer hardware this year: ☐ yes [44] ☐ no [45]

I plan to buy or upgrade computer software this year: ☐ yes [46] ☐ no [47]

Name: _____ Business title: [48] _____ Type of Business: [49]

Address (☐ home [50] ☐ work [51]/Company name: _____)

Street/Suite#

City [52]/State [53]/Zipcode [54]: _____ Country [55]

☐ **I liked this book!** You may quote me by name in future
IDG Books Worldwide promotional materials.

My daytime phone number is _____

IDG BOOKS

THE WORLD OF
COMPUTER
KNOWLEDGE

❏ YES!

Please keep me informed about IDG's World of Computer Knowledge.
Send me the latest IDG Books catalog.

NO POSTAGE
NECESSARY
IF MAILED
IN THE
UNITED STATES

BUSINESS REPLY MAIL
FIRST CLASS MAIL   PERMIT NO. 2605   FOSTER CITY, CALIFORNIA

IDG Books Worldwide
919 E Hillsdale Blvd, STE 400
Foster City, CA 94404-9691

University of Glamorgan
Prifysgol Morgannwg
Learning Resources
Centre